GOING TO THE SOURCE

A GUIDE
TO CRITICAL READING
AND WRITING

GOING TO THE SOURCE

A GUIDE TO CRITICAL READING AND WRITING

RICHARD STEIGER

ROY A. HELTON, JR.

Murray State University

Wadsworth Publishing Company
Belmont, California
A Division of Wadsworth, Inc.

Production Editor	Leland Moss
Designer	James Chadwick
Print Buyer	Barbara Britton
Copy Editor	Noel Deeley
Compositor	Thompson Type
Cover Design	James Chadwick
Cover and Text Illustrations	Masami Daijogo
Signing Representative	Mark Francisco

© 1989 by Wadsworth, Inc. All rights reserved. No part of this book may be reproduced, stored in a retrieval system, or transcribed, in any form or by any means, electronic, mechanical, photocopying, recording, or otherwise, without the prior written permission of the publisher, Wadsworth Publishing Company, Belmont, California 94002, a division of Wadsworth, Inc.

Printed in the United States of America

2 3 4 5 6 7 8 9 10—93 92 91

```
Library of Congress Cataloging in Publication Data
Steiger, Richard
   Going to the source: a guide to critical reading and
writing/Richard Steiger, Roy A. Helton, Jr.
      p.   cm.
   Includes index.
   ISBN 0-534-08934-8
   1. English language—Rhetoric.   2. College readers.
3. Report writing.   I. Helton, Roy A.   II. Title.
PE1478.S74  1989                              88-14431
808'.042—dc19                                      CIP
```

CONTENTS

PART ONE
WRITING PROJECTS

SUMMARIZING A SOURCE   3

The ability to read a source and restate its contents in your own words is the basis of all work with written source material. Because you cannot summarize a source without first understanding it on its own terms, this project stresses a careful reading of the text as the key to summarizing. (*Suggested anthology:* "Women in the Working World")

OVERVIEW   6

PREWRITING   7
  Discovering the Thesis   7
    Using Background Information   7
    Finding an Explicit Thesis   8
    Finding an Implicit Thesis   10
  Government in the Lead: Michael H. Moskow   11
  Finding the Key Ideas   15
    Subheads vs. Key Ideas   16
    The Key Ideas of a Source   17
    The One-Paragraph Summary   17
  Marking Significant Details   18
  Taking Notes   23
DRAFTING   25
  Organizing a Summary   26
  Characteristics of a Good Summary   29
REVISING   31

WRITING A SIMPLE SYNTHESIS   35

A simple synthesis consists of two summaries related by a simple connection. The addition of a second source involves two new considerations. The first is the formulation of an original thesis relating your sources to one another. The second is the technique of attribution, the means by which you separate sources from one another and from your own comments. (*Suggested anthology:* "Images of Early Human Life")

OVERVIEW   38

PREWRITING   39
   Discovering the Thesis   39
   Man as Predator: Raymond Dart   39
   Finding the Key Ideas   43
   Marking the Source   43
   Taking Notes   44
   Formulating a Thesis   45
      The Thesis of a Simple Synthesis   45

DRAFTING   46
   Drafting the Summaries   46
      Direct Quotation   47
      Avoiding Plagiarism   47
   Drafting the Simple Synthesis   49
      Attribution   50

REVISING   50

■

WRITING A CRITIQUE   53

In this project and the next one you will go beyond restating and combining sources. In these projects sources will serve as the subject matter of your own essay. This project will describe a number of ways to write about a source but will stress the process of evaluation. You will learn to read a source critically and present your evaluation of its effectiveness. (*Suggested anthology:* "Animal Rights")

OVERVIEW   55

PREWRITING   56
   Finding the Thesis and Key Ideas   56
   All Animals Are Equal: Peter Singer   56
   Asking Appropriate Questions   62
      The Nature of Evaluation   62
      Questions for Evaluation   63
   Reading for Evaluation   64
   Devising a Thesis   66
   Generating a Structure   67
   Returning to the Source   68

DRAFTING   69
   Summarizing Your Source   69
   Other Critique Projects   72

REVISING   73

COMPARING SOURCES   75

In this project you will apply one of the most common and fruitful learning techniques—comparison—to written sources. The project emphasizes comparison as a means of learning something new about a subject and communicating that knowledge to a reader. (*Suggested anthology:* "The Younger Generation")

OVERVIEW   78

PREWRITING   79
   Reading for Understanding   79
   The Younger Generation: The Editors of *Time*   79
   Finding Similarities and Differences   90
      What Can Be Compared?   91
      What's Worth Comparing?   93
      Drawing a Conclusion from Your Comparison   93

DRAFTING   94
   Choosing an Effective Structure   94
   A Functional Opening   98
   The Sense of an Ending   99

REVISING   100

BUILDING ON A SOURCE   103

In this and the next project you will use sources in a more indirect manner than in the previous projects. Rather than restating the contents of sources or writing about them, these projects stress using sources to develop your own argument on a subject. In this project an essay you read will serve as a point of departure for your own thinking. (*Suggested anthology:* "The Impact of Advertising")

OVERVIEW   104

PREWRITING   105
   Reading for Understanding   105
   Boob Rubes: The New Ruralism in TV Advertising: Jeff Greenfield   105
   Devising a Thesis   108
      Disagreeing   108
      Extending an Idea   110
      Exemplifying an Idea   112

DRAFTING   115

Unified Paragraphs   116
Coherent Paragraphs   117
Adequately Developed Paragraphs   119
REVISING   120

■

USING SOURCES AS EVIDENCE   123

In this project, your sources will serve as the evidence for your view on the subject of early reactions to rock 'n' roll. You will read a variety of items in the anthology included in the project, devise your own thesis on the subject, and use your sources to back up that thesis.

OVERVIEW   125

PREWRITING   126
  Surveying the Field   126
  Devising a Thesis   128
  Generating a Structure   129
  Taking Notes   130
DRAFTING   130
REVISING   134
Primary Sources: Early Reactions to Rock 'n' Roll (A collection of 28 magazine articles, newspaper articles, letters, and editorials)   136

PART TWO
READINGS

■

WOMEN IN THE WORKING WORLD 169

What's Holding Women Back? Robin L. Bartlett, Charles Poulton-Callahan, and Patricia Somers 170
Women and Men Working Together: Toward Androgyny, Alice G. Sargent 175
The Case for Comparable Worth, Michael Evan Gold 180
Comparable Worth: Unfair to Men and Women, Phyllis Schlafly 183
A Bright Woman Is Caught in a Double Bind, Matina Horner 187
The New Corporate Feminism, Suzanne Gordon 193
Additional Writing Assignments 198

■

THE NATURE OF EARLY HUMAN LIFE 201

Cain's Children, Robert Ardrey 202
The Naked Ape, Desmond Morris 205
The New Litany of "Innate Depravity," M.F. Ashley Montague 211
Is It Our Culture, Not Our Genes, That Makes Us Killers? Richard E. Leakey and Roger Lewin 214
On Becoming Human, Nancy Tanner 221
The Food Sharing Behavior of Protohuman Hominids, Glynn Isaac 223
Additional Writing Assignments 229

■

ANIMAL RIGHTS 231

The Logic of the Larder, Henry S. Salt 232
Of the So-Called Rights of Animals, Joseph Rickaby 236
Do Animals Have a Right to Life? James Rachels 237
Animals Do Not Have Moral Rights, Michael Fox 241
The Clouded Mirror: Animal Stereotypes and Human Cruelty, Thomas L. Benson 244
The Use of Animals in Educational Settings, Tom Regan 255
Animal Rights Evaluated, Michael E. Levin 259
Additional Writing Assignments 263

■

THE YOUNGER GENERATION 265

Change and Stability: Youth in the 1920's, Paula S. Fass 266
What They Really Think and Why, Irwin Ross 273
American Youth Today: A Bigger Cast, A Wider Screen,
 Reuel N. Denney 278
Youth in America, Tad Szulc 286
College Youth Attitudes Today, Rolf A. Weil 289
Now, the Self-Centered Generation, The Editors of *Time* 293
Who Are We? A Self-Portrait of College Students Today, David Wank 296
Additional Writing Assignments 303

THE IMPACT OF ADVERTISING 305

Weasel Words, Paul Stevens 306
It's Natural! It's Organic! Or Is It? The Editors of *Consumer Reports* 315
When TV Ads Become Most Disreputable, Maurine Christopher 320
Ads & Addictions: Booze on the Tube, Frank McConnell 323
Psychographics: Advertising Discovers the World According to VALS,
 William Meyers 327
Advertising Says "Let Us Feel Good About Ourselves,"
 Michael Schudson 333
Additional Writing Assignments 335

A CASEBOOK ON WILLIAM FAULKNER'S "A ROSE FOR EMILY" 337

A Rose for Emily, William Faulkner 338
An Interpretation of "A Rose for Emily," Cleanth Brooks and
 Robert Penn Warren 345
Atmosphere and Theme in Faulkner's "A Rose for Emily,"
 Ray B. West, Jr. 349
History in "A Rose for Emily," William Van O'Conner 354
*Emily Grierson's Oedipus Complex: Motif, Motive, and Meaning in Faulkner's
 "A Rose for Emily,"* Jack Scherting 355
A Rose for "A Rose for Emily," Judith Fetterley 362
Tobe's Significance in "A Rose for Emily," T. J. Stafford 369
*Emily's Rose of Love: Thematic Implications of Point of View in Faulkner's
 "A Rose for Emily,"* Helen E. Nebeker 371
How Readers Make Meaning, Robert Crosman 381
Writing Projects 389

Part Three
Writing the Research Paper: A Manual

FINDING A TOPIC 392

NARROWING THE TOPIC 393
   Developing Investigative Questions 395

GATHERING A WORKING BIBLIOGRAPHY 396
   Making a List of Subject Headings 397
   Using Indexes and Bibliographies 397
      The Card Catalog 399
      Periodical Indexes 401
      Other Types of Indexes 406
   Preparing Bibliography Cards 407
   Bibliographical Forms 409
      Forms for Books 409
      Forms for Periodicals 413
      Other Sources 415
      Bibliographical Forms in APA Format 416

TAKING NOTES FROM SOURCES 417
   Trial Thesis and Outline 418
   Note Card Format 419
   Writing the Notes 421
      Paraphrased Notes 423
      Quoted Notes 425

DEVISING A THESIS 428

GENERATING A STRUCTURE 429

DRAFTING THE RESEARCH PAPER 432
   Integrating Sources in Your Text 432
   Attributing Ideas to Sources 433
   Integrating Direct Quotations 435

DOCUMENTING SOURCES 438
   What to Document 439

Using Parenthetical Citations   439
  Parenthetical Citation in APA Style   442
Using Footnotes or Endnotes   443
  Forms for Books   444
  Forms for Periodicals   446
  Forms for Other Sources   447
  Subsequent References to the Same Source   447

PREPARING THE FINISHED COPY   448
The Sections of the Paper   448

A SAMPLE RESEARCH PAPER   455

ACKNOWLEDGMENTS   470

INDEX   474

Preface

Going to the Source: A Guide to Critical Reading and Writing is the result of our experience teaching Freshman Composition. It reflects our preference for composition texts that emphasize the student's own writing process. Such texts were readily available for the first semester of our course, where the subject matter for student essays generally comes from personal experience and observation. But we were never able to find a satisfactory text for our second-semester Freshman Composition course, which stresses the use of written source material. We have found over the years that our students are relatively familiar with writing essays based on personal experience, but they are often mystified by assignments requiring the integration of reading and writing skills, assignments that will be the models for most of their college writing experiences. We wanted a text explaining the entire process of working with written source materials—from reading a book or an article to revising an essay. Such a text, we believed, would help students realize how the books and essays they read can stimulate their own thinking and writing.

To answer this need, we decided to provide students with a series of writing projects, each representing one use of written source material. In "Summarizing a Source," for example, students are taught to summarize an essay. In "Using Sources as Evidence" they learn to use a variety of sources to prove an original thesis. To these projects, we added a readings section—a series of thematic anthologies designed for use with individual projects—and a research paper manual. The sequence of projects is designed to move students progressively through each skill to the integration of skills required in a research paper. If the instructor chooses to assign all six projects and the research paper manual in sequence, *Going to the Source* will provide a complete guide to working with sources, from summarizing an essay to writing a formal research paper.

We recognized from the start, however, that not every instructor would wish to follow the entire sequence of projects. For that reason we have made certain that each project can stand on its own. *Going to the Source* is designed to allow instructors to assign any of its individual projects with confidence.

Each writing project is keyed to a particular anthology in the readings. The illustrations used in our explanation of the process of summarizing, for example, are taken from the anthology entitled "Women in the Working World." The readings in that anthology have been chosen for use with the first writing assignment. But the pairing of a project and an anthology is merely a suggestion; instructors will find no difficulty in choosing as source material essays on any topic in the readings. The single exception is the final project, in which students are asked to write a paper based on the primary sources appended to the project. The readings conclude with an anthology that is not paired with any of the projects: a casebook on William Faulkner's "A Rose for Emily," consisting of Faulkner's story and a selection of literary criticism. The casebook is designed for instructors who wish to use literature and literary criticism as subject matter for writing assignments.

Overall Structure of the Text

The first section of *Going to the Source* is organized to provide detailed instruction in a series of increasingly complex skills: (1) summarizing sources, (2) writing about sources, and (3) working sources into an argument. Each skill is covered in two projects, the first employing one source, the second multiple sources. In carrying out the six projects, students will learn and practice the skills necessary for working with source material.

The examples used in discussing each project are keyed to one of the thematic anthologies in the second section of *Going to the Source*. Each anthology begins with a preface introducing students to the central issues of the readings. Each selection is preceded by a biographical and/or contextual introduction and followed by a set of study questions designed to aid comprehension and stimulate thought. Each anthology concludes with suggestions for additional writing assignments. The readings section concludes with the casebook on William Faulkner's "A Rose for Emily."

The third section of *Going to the Source*, a research paper manual, teaches students to apply the skills they have developed to the production of a formal library paper. It includes a sample student research paper.

Structure of the Projects

Each project consists of the following:

- An introduction to the project, including the usual information a writer needs before getting started (purpose, audience, length).
- A fully developed sequence of prewriting steps, tailored to the project and designed to help students formulate a thesis and collect the information necessary to support it.
- A section on drafting, which discusses the matters writers consider as they draft a piece of writing (outlining and paragraphing, for example).
- A section on revising, which consists of a series of activities designed to help students, working individually or in peer groups, evaluate the strengths and weaknesses of their drafts and begin the process of revision.

Acknowledgments

We would like to thank the many people who have helped us during the time we were writing *Going to the Source*. John Adams, Ron Cella, Mike Cohen, David Earnest, Ken Harrell, Bill Lalicker, Anita Lawson, Gordy Loberger, Deb and Edith Wylder, Murray State University; Charlie Duke, Utah State University; Richard Larschan, Southeast Massachusetts University; and Martha Satz, Southern Methodist University, provided support, friendship, and advice. Robin Adams, Linda Bartnik, Mike Clark, Susan Dunman, John Griffin, Jamie Helton, Betty Hornsby, Marcie Johnson, Melva Loveridge, Teresa Loveridge, and Rita McNabb contributed to the preparation of the manuscript. Professors Amy Doerr, State University of New York-Buffalo; Gretchen Flesher, Gustavus Adolphus College; Judith Gardner, University of Texas, San Antonio; Jim Hanlon, Shippensburg University; S. L. Jansen Jaech, Pacific Lutheran University; Kate Kiefer, Colorado State University; James Kinney, Virginia Commonwealth University; Barry Kroll, Indiana University; Susan Peck MacDonald, UC San Diego-Third College; Mary Francis Minton, Virginia Commonwealth University; Patricia Murray, DePaul University; Sara Murray, University of Texas, San Antonio; and Elisa Sparks, Clemson University, all read and commented on the manuscript, providing valuable insights. To those at Wadsworth who provided assistance, we are particularly grateful: Holly Allen, Mark Francisco, Steve Rutter, and John Strohmeier.

For my mother, Mae, and in memory of my father, Morris
R. S.

For Jamie and for Emily and Nicholas
R. H.

PART ONE

WRITING PROJECTS

SUMMARIZING A SOURCE

WRITING A SIMPLE SYNTHESIS

WRITING A CRITIQUE

COMPARING SOURCES

BUILDING ON A SOURCE

USING SOURCES AS EVIDENCE

Summarizing a Source

WRITING IS BASICALLY A MATTER OF TAKING SOME part of the world—a subject—and commenting on it to a reader. Once you have decided (or perhaps been assigned) to write on a certain subject—scuba diving, let's say—you need to find some material to comment upon. You can go to two places for material about scuba diving, two *sources* of information.

The first and most basic source of information about a subject is the writer's own memory. To use this source when writing about scuba diving, you need only consider what you already know about the subject. If you have dived yourself or seen other people diving, you have a natural place from which to begin making your own comments. If you have given the subject some thought in the past, you might find that you have some ideas and feelings about diving that you would like to communicate. Your memory has most likely been the primary source for most of the writing you have done so far—the letters, stories, and essays you have written in school and for your own pleasure.

The second source of information derives from other people's experiences, observations, ideas, and feelings. If, for example, you have no diving memories to draw upon, or if you wish to supplement your limited knowledge, you might turn to the vast amount of material about scuba diving that is outside your own experience—the books, articles, newspaper accounts, television shows, movies, recordings, and other people's personal reminiscences on the subject. You would be certain to find in these sources the information you need to begin thinking about the subject.

In this book we are going to stress these *external writing sources*. We'll concentrate on the kind of written source most often used by college students—*expository prose*, writing designed to communicate facts, opinions, and ideas. This project emphasizes the most basic skill required to use an external source effectively—writing a *summary*, a condensed version in your own words of the line of thought of a source.

Though we normally think of summarizing as a formal writing activity, we actually compose a mental summary whenever we read anything carefully. Consider, for example, the complicated process you carried out the last time you read a short story or a novel. A story itself does not consist of a series of isolated occurrences but of a coherent progression of events, a plot. To follow that plot you had to reconstruct that progression by relating each individual event to the events that preceded it and by forming expectations about future events. In other words, as you read the story you constructed a running plot summary in your mind. If a friend had asked you what happened in the story, you wouldn't have had much difficulty summarizing its plot; you wouldn't have needed to start from scratch by recalling the events of the story and then laboriously reconstructing their connections. Without giving the complexity of the process a second thought, you would have recalled your mental plot summary and communicated it to your friend.

The process of summarizing a source is essentially the same as that of summarizing a story line. Instead of a plot, an essay has an *argument*, a logically developed sequence of ideas. If you are reading an essay carefully, you are constantly relating a given idea to the ideas you have already read and anticipating the ideas that might follow. In short, you are summarizing the argument of the essay to yourself as you read. What is left in the summarizing process is to put that mental summary into written form.

If we could read expository prose with as much ease and pleasure as we generally read stories, summarizing essays would be as simple as retelling a story to a friend. Unfortunately, however, the relationship between ideas in an argument is often more difficult to figure out than the connection between events in a story. Furthermore, with our minds on other things, we often casually skim material we are supposed to be studying. At those times we neglect making the mental summary, read the essay as a series of vaguely related remarks, and end up with only a foggy notion of what has just passed under our eyes.

Of course, it is impossible to read that way and still produce a competently written summary. And that is one value of learning to produce a formal summary: the process encourages us to read more carefully by forcing us to become aware of our good and bad reading habits. Writing a formal summary forces us to concentrate on what we are reading, to seek out and write down its main point, to connect the ideas in the essay to one another, and to communicate what we have read to others.

Needless to say, improved reading awareness is not the only reason to learn to write a summary. The ability to put the basic point and key ideas of a source into your own words is also a skill you can put to practical use in college and on the job. In your college career you may summarize scholarly and technical articles in your papers and class reports. On examinations your teacher may ask you to summarize an argument to show that you understand the material in the course. In business you will often have to summarize reports and memos. And, in business as in college, written reports and oral presentations rely on evidence summarized from sources.

Whenever we think about the purpose of a piece of writing, we immediately begin thinking about its *audience*, the reader for whom it is intended. The audience for your summary might be the instructor in a course or the students in a classroom; it might be your supervisor on a job, your own assistants, the employees in another department, or the general public. Thinking about your audience—about what it knows and what it wants to know—can help you make important decisions: what ideas will be most effective, what order the ideas ought to be in, what words will best express those ideas, how long the piece of writing should be, to name a few.

In this project you'll be writing a summary of a single source. The purpose of your summary is to replace the original text, to provide your readers with the thesis and all the supporting ideas necessary to understand the argument of your source. The examples in this project are taken from the first anthology, "Women in the Working World," in the readings section of this book, although the techniques we discuss are applicable to any source you might summarize.

Suggested Assignment

You are in a management class in which each student has been asked to write a 500- to 700-word summary of a source on the topic of women in the working world. Copies of all the summaries will be distributed for class use in discussing this subject and preparing group reports.

Assume that your readers are roughly your own age and know roughly what you do about the topic. They have not, however, read the particular source you are summarizing and are depending on you to provide them with a clear and accurate picture of what your source says. You may find it best to think of your summary as one of a number of summaries to be used in a class project—not a masterpiece of ingenuity, just a practical summary of a source you've read.

Overview

This project stresses the skills necessary for writing a summary. The process of summarizing consists of two broad operations: understanding the text to be summarized and communicating that understanding to readers. Because the single most important requirement in summarizing is to understand the source, the prewriting section of this project focuses on a careful reading of the text, which includes finding the thesis and key ideas of the text, marking the text for later reference, and taking notes on significant facts and ideas. Such a reading has two purposes: assuring the summary writer of his or her own understanding of the text and generating the material used in drafting the summary. The section on drafting covers two kinds of communication skills: those applicable to writing in general and those related to the specific requirements of a summary. The final section of the project covers revision, the process of analyzing and improving a draft.

The Process of Summarizing

1. Discover the thesis of the source you are summarizing.
2. Find the key ideas that develop that thesis.
3. Write a one-paragraph summary of the source.
4. Mark the text of the source for the significant details you are likely to use in your complete summary.
5. Take notes on the source.
6. Develop a logical structure for your summary.
7. Draft your summary, paying particular attention to accuracy, completeness, and appropriate length.
8. Revise your summary, using the activities that are described in the project.

Prewriting

Many people find getting started the hardest part of the writing process—and for good reason. Once people have actually begun writing, once they have a general idea of what they are going to say and have put a few things down on paper, they usually find that one idea leads to another. But at the very beginning of the process, you have no momentum to build on, just a subject and a blank sheet of paper. What to do?

Although there is no magic recipe for getting into a writing project, a number of prewriting activities can help a writer ease into it. Many writers, for example, like to begin as we have by getting their bearings: considering the purpose, audience, and intended length of the project. Rather than plunging right in at that point, writers usually find it helpful to collect information on their subject, think about the point they want to make, perhaps get a few ideas down on paper, and consider how they will organize their comments. Each project in this book begins with a series of activities designed to help you build some momentum. In working with sources the first prewriting activity is always the same.

Discovering the Thesis

A famous recipe for rabbit stew begins, "First catch the rabbit." In working with sources the equivalent of catching the rabbit is understanding the thesis and structure of your source. You can't cook the stew without the rabbit, and you can't make any effective use of a source without understanding it on its own terms.

You begin by asking the most basic question any reader can pose: What is the point of what I am reading? Different readers have different ways of answering the question. Some people prefer to read straight through to the end without stopping, whereas others choose to move more slowly, pausing along the way to skip back to earlier pages. Some cannot imagine reading anything the first time without a pencil in hand to highlight ideas or eye-catching facts; others never mark anything on a first reading. These differences don't really matter; the only thing that counts is whether or not you are seeking to answer that question as you read.

Using Background Information Before you begin reading, it helps to take a few minutes to find out what you can about your source. Although you can discover the thesis of an essay only by carefully reading it, knowing some basic facts about the author and the text can point you in the right direction. Information about an author's background, for example, can alert you to his or her qualifications for writing on the subject and to any possible biases. Knowing when an essay was written often can help you understand it. Take advantage of the obvious: the title of a work, the first piece of information an author provides, often serves as a clear guide to the focus of an essay.

Take, for example, the essay by Michael H. Moskow (page 11). It is one of a number of essays on women in the working world, the focus of the readings in the first anthology section. As are all the readings in this book, this essay is preceded by an introduction providing basic information about the author and the text. Moskow's essay originally appeared in 1973 in a book entitled *Corporate Lib: Women's Challenge to Management*. Moskow has had a distinguished career in education, business, and government. At the time the essay was published, he was an assistant secretary in the Department of Labor, involved with policy matters. You can reasonably expect, then, to read a serious discussion of the topic by an inside, official, government voice. The title, "Government in the Lead," would lead you to suspect that Moskow's essay will focus on the ways in which the government is, or should be, a leader on the issue of women in the workplace.

Finding an Explicit Thesis Once you actually start reading a source, you'll find that an author develops a *thesis*, the main point of an argument, in one of two ways: either by stating the main point explicitly or by implying it. In the first case the author provides a *thesis statement*. In the latter case the author, relying on the logical presentation of information, leaves it to the reader to figure out the thesis. These are, in fact, the two ways we all have of getting our point across. Imagine, for example, a mother trying to get her child to clean up his or her room. Some mothers take the direct approach, providing an explicit thesis statement: "Clean up this place now. It's filthy." Others, however, prefer a more subtle strategy, providing such a graphically detailed description of the room ("This place looks like a cyclone hit it. Your clothes are scattered all over the room, the carpet hasn't been vacuumed in two months, and I think there's something growing on the food in your wastepaper basket.") that the child has no choice but to reply, "OK, OK, you don't have to say it—I get the message. I'll clean it up."

As you attempt to discover the thesis of a source, watch out for a generalization, a commitment to prove a point, a claim, an insight into the subject, or a conclusion the author has reached. Sometimes the thesis statement is obvious. Consider, for example, Matina Horner's article "A Bright Woman Is Caught in a Double Bind" (page 187). Here are the first nine paragraphs of the essay:

Consider Phil, a bright young college sophomore. He has always done well in school, he is in the honors program, he has wanted to be a doctor as long as he can remember. We ask him to tell us a story based on one clue: *After first-term finals, John finds himself at the top of his medical-school class*. Phil writes:

John is a conscientious young man who worked hard. He is pleased with himself. John has always wanted to go into medicine and is very dedicated. . . . John continues working hard and eventually graduates at the top of his class.

Now consider Monica, another honors student. She too has always done well and she too has visions of a flourishing career. We give her the same clue, but with "Anne" as the successful student—*after first-term finals, Anne finds herself at the top of her medical-school class.* Instead of identifying with Anne's triumph, Monica tells a bizarre tale:

> Anne starts proclaiming her surprise and joy. Her fellow classmates are so disgusted with her behavior that they jump on her in a body and beat her. She is maimed for life.

Next we ask Monica and Phil to work on a series of achievement tests by themselves. Monica scores higher than Phil. Finally we get them together, competing against each other on the same kind of tests. Phil performs magnificently, but Monica dissolves into a bundle of nerves.

The glaring contrast between the two stories and the dramatic changes in performance in competitive situations illustrate important differences between men and women in reacting to achievement.

In 1953, David McClelland, John Atkinson and colleagues published the first major work on the "achievement motive." Through the use of the Thematic Apperception Test (TAT), they were able to isolate the psychological characteristic of a *need to achieve*. This seemed to be an internalized standard of excellence, motivating the individual to do well in any achievement-oriented situation involving intelligence and leadership ability. Subsequent investigators studied innumerable facets of achievement motivation: How it is instilled in children, how it is expressed, how it relates to social class, even how it is connected to the rise and fall of civilizations. The result of all this research is an impressive and a theoretically consistent body of data about the achievement motive—in men.

Women, however, are conspicuously absent from almost all of the studies. In the few cases where the ladies were included, the results were contradictory or confusing. So women were eventually left out altogether. The predominantly male researchers apparently decided, as Freud had before them, that the only way to understand woman was to turn to the poets. Atkinson's 1958 book, *Motives in Fantasy, Action and Society*, is an 800-page compilation of all of the theories and facts on achievement motivation in men. Women got a footnote, reflecting the state of the science.

To help remedy this lopsided state of affairs, I undertook to explore the basis for sex differences in achievement motivation. But where to begin?

My first clue came from the one consistent finding on the women: they get higher test-anxiety scores than do the men. Eleanor Maccoby has suggested that the girl who is motivated to achieve is defying conventions of what girls "should" do. As a result, the intellectual woman pays a price in anxiety. Margaret Mead concurs, noting that intense intellectual striving can be viewed as "competitively aggressive behavior." And of course Freud thought that the whole essence of femininity lay in repressing aggressiveness (and hence intellectuality).

Thus consciously or unconsciously the girl equates intellectual achievement with loss of femininity. A bright woman is caught in a double bind. In testing and other achievement-oriented situations she worries not only about failure, but also about success. If she fails, she is not living up to her own standards of performance; if she succeeds she is not living up to societal expectations about the female role. Men in our society do not experience this kind of ambivalence, because they are not only permitted but actively encouraged to do well.

Horner opens her article in paragraphs 1–3 with a pair of examples illustrating the radical differences between the ways male and female college students view academic success, and in paragraphs 5–6 she describes the absence of research on women and achievement. In paragraph 7 she announces the subject of her research ("sex differences in achievement motivation") and in paragraph 8 mentions the first clue she discovered (women's test anxiety is higher than men's). Horner states her thesis explicitly in paragraph 9: "A bright woman is caught in a double bind. In testing and other achievement-oriented situations she worries not only about failure, but also about success."

Identifying a thesis statement is a beginning, but the only way you can be certain that you understand a thesis is to write it out in your own words. Remember that your summary is eventually going to replace an original source with a shorter version written in your own words. It will thus have to make sense on its own, apart from the original text, and you can communicate an idea only if you understand it. We might rephrase Horner's thesis statement as follows: *In competitive situations bright women fear both failure and success.*

Finding an Implicit Thesis Reading an essay with an implied thesis statement usually requires more work from readers. Sometimes, however, the difference is slight. If you can follow the argument of an essay easily, you often can find its thesis simply by asking yourself, "What was the point of all that?" You may very well be able to answer that question immediately.

But if the point of an essay is not clear after the first reading, don't panic: you are probably reading a complex essay that will take some extra work. Finding an implied thesis often requires you to read the essay a second time, skimming for main points, slowing down to examine specific details, and working back and forth between paragraphs, paying particular attention to how ideas relate to one another. This is nothing more than the normal procedure for reading a complex essay.

We will illustrate this procedure with Moskow's "Government in the Lead." This essay, written in 1973, provides us with background information for the more recent pieces in the anthology. It does not have an explicit thesis statement, but Moskow does have a specific point to make. Read the essay for its thesis and then compare your reading with the analysis that follows.

GOVERNMENT IN THE LEAD
Michael H. Moskow

Michael H. Moskow (b. 1938) was educated at Lafayette College and at the University of Pennsylvania, where he earned a Ph.D. His career has spanned teaching, government service, and private business. Besides being on the economics faculty at Temple University, he has held important government posts, including director of the Council on Wage and Price Stability and undersecretary of labor. The author of numerous books and articles on collective bargaining and employment relations, he is now a corporate executive.

Discrimination in employment by federal government contractors and subcontractors because of race, color, sex, or national origin was prohibited by Executive Order 11246, as amended by Executive Order 11375. Under this order, the Office of Federal Contract Compliance was established within the Department of Labor to administer its provisions and to coordinate the activities of all federal contracting agencies. My discussion will cover the activities of the Office of Federal Contract Compliance, and I will generalize a bit about some of the parallels and contrasts between problems of minorities and problems of women.

The compliance program is very important because it gives the federal government immediate and powerful leverage to discourage discrimination in employment. There are certain procedures that have been established to use this leverage—such as conciliation, show-cause hearings, and consultations—but ultimately the federal government has the power to refuse to do business with someone. It can cancel, terminate, or suspend existing contracts, or it can bar a contractor from receiving future government contracts. These are very powerful economic weapons to discourage employers from discrimination and to encourage them to take affirmative action to employ minorities and women.

Order Number 4 was issued by the Department of Labor to delineate the criteria to be used by federal contractors in developing plans of affirmative action to increase employment opportunities for minorities. Affirmative action requires the government contractor to go beyond refraining from employment discrimination. The contractor is required, as part of the contracting process, to analyze his* work force and to determine whether there are deficiencies in the utilization of minorities. If there are deficiencies, the contractor then must formulate written corrective measures, including goals, timetables, and a plan of action for their elimination. These written corrective measures are required to be established for each job classification. Together, they comprise the contractor's affirmative action plan.

A revised version of Order Number 4 was issued in December 1971, presenting criteria for the utilization of female workers, since the original order had

---

* *Editor's note:* In spite of this essay's use of only the masculine pronoun, we assume that the federal contractors mentioned here could very well be females.

applied only to minorities. In effect, the revision extended the mandate for affirmative action to women. This revision was developed after consultation with employers, women's groups, compliance agencies, minority groups, etc., and it tailored the principles and procedures dealing with the underutilization of minorities to the problems of the underutilization of women.

Contractors are required to revise any existing written affirmative action programs to include changes embodied in the order. They are also required to communicate to employees and to prospective employees the existence of their affirmative action programs and to make available the essential elements of their programs to allow the employees and prospective employees to avail themselves of the benefits.

When a contractor undertakes an analysis of his work force, Order Number 4 requires that he take the following criteria into consideration in determining female utilization.

First, he must consider the size of the female unemployment force in the labor area surrounding the facility. Second, he must look at the percentage of the female work force as compared to the total work force in the immediate labor market area. Third, he must consider the general availability of women having requisite skills in the immediate labor area. Fourth, he must ascertain the availability of women having requisite skills in an area in which the contractor could reasonably recruit, outside of his immediate labor market area.

Next, he should inquire into the availability of women seeking employment in his labor or recruitment area. He must also note the availability of promotable *and* transferable female employees within his own organization. He should have some idea of the anticipated expansion, contraction, and turnover of the work force—its growth or lack of growth. Finally, the existence of training institutions capable of training persons to develop the requisite skills and the degree of training which the contractor is reasonably able to undertake as a means of making all job classes available to women are important considerations. The contractor then must arrive at goals and timetables for the employment of women, based on these criteria.

The criteria for women are similar to those for minorities, modified to meet the particular problems attendant to sex discrimination. Where deficiencies are found, the contractor is required to establish separate goals and timetables for women and separate goals and timetables for minorities. The order provides that if it comes to the attention of the director of the Office of Federal Contract Compliance, or the compliance agencies, that there is a substantial disparity in the participation of different minority groups, then separate goals and timetables can be required for each of those minority groups, such as for Spanish Americans, for Indians, or for Orientals. If substantial disparities are found in the employment of men and women of a particular minority group, separate goals and timetables can be required for males and females of those groups. We plan to monitor these figures for minority and sex subgroups very closely to insure that problem subgroups are separately treated.

In terms of implementation, a search for evidence of sex discrimination is included as part of the general compliance review that is made of a contractor.

The person making the review looks at the distribution of the work force by sex as well as by race, religion, and national origin.

The general compliance review is automatically conducted for any supply contractor with a contract of more than a million dollars before the contract is awarded. Other contractors are chosen for a general compliance review based on apparent underutilization of minorities or women revealed in part by the Equal Employment Opportunity Commission annual compliance reports. Specific individual complaints are referred to the EEOC for investigation.

My own view is that Revised Order Number 4 represents a very significant change in public policy. No longer are we simply going on record against sex discrimination, although that was certainly a necessary preliminary step. Now we are requiring tangible evidence that meaningful steps are being taken to improve the employment prospects of women. This order goes beyond merely prohibiting discrimination against women to stimulating the recruitment of women. The great strength of the order is in the use of the federal government's compliance apparatus to put some teeth into the effort.

It will no longer be sufficient for a government contractor merely to refrain from overt acts of discrimination against women. Instead, he must present evidence that he has made a viable plan for finding and employing women who are potentially qualified for his work force.

There are parallels and contrasts between public policy regarding discrimination against minorities and against women. Let us look at some of the parallels. First, the obvious similarity is that the provisions of the Executive Order and of Order Number 4 now apply both to minorities and to females. Another parallel is that mere enforcement of equal pay for equal work will not suffice to bring about equality of opportunity for either group. Women, like blacks and other minorities, suffer not only from low wage rates relative to others in the same job but also from being denied entry into prestigious, well-paid, and challenging occupations. Both groups suffer from unequal opportunities for advancement and promotion, which means that an activist policy requiring affirmative action is a necessity.

Let me mention two contrasts between the situations of women and minorities. In the past, the status and income available to a married woman have depended primarily on the success of her husband, and she has found it in her interest to support his cause, although this may conflict with her own career interests. I do not think that minorities find it in their interest to support the interests of whites in that way.

The primacy of the husband's career interests operates as a constraint on the equal opportunity movement, as many married women are content either to play the traditional role of the housewife or to engage in labor market activity from a disadvantaged position. However, both male and female attitudes toward the appropriate role of married women are changing rapidly; over time this voluntary barrier to equal opportunity may be lifted.

Another difference between women and minorities is that there is really no approximation among the latter of the particular situation resulting from childbearing. Clearly, here is another area where attitudes are changing on the part of both men and women. Nevertheless, childbearing often continues to involve a long interruption in the work experience of women. By long interruption, I do not mean a month or two month's leave, but five years or more, until the children are in school.

When the female is off the job for five years, her male counterpart is on the job. He is learning and building up human capital, as the economists would say. When she returns after a five-year break in her employment, the woman will clearly be at a disadvantage. She is not going to have the same skills or the capital that he will have built up in that five-year period.

This has an important policy implication. If that type of break in the career of a female is to be eliminated or greatly reduced, is the development of improved day care facilities on a massive scale a prerequisite? We have already seen some steps in this direction. An attempt was made in the last session of Congress to pass a child development bill which would subsidize the child care expenses of poor and near-poor women. Another start in this direction is the proposed Family Assistance Plan. Here, child care would be provided specifically to facilitate the employment of welfare mothers in an attempt to help them leave the welfare rolls. It is a job-oriented type of child care service.

Both the extent and the type of child care to be provided for poor women are still under debate at this time. I mention it because I think it is one policy that attempts to ease the entry of women into the work force on a large scale.

Hopefully, the emphasis on affirmative action will facilitate the achievement of equal employment opportunity for women. In the battle against job discrimination, the compliance program of the federal government should be an effective complement to existing legislation. The compliance weapon enables us to reach about one-third of the U.S. labor force. Although it cannot have an immediate impact on the entire labor force, we believe that this effort will have a substantial impact and will significantly advance the equal opportunity movement.

■

Moskow's first two sentences indicate that in very general terms his subject matter is going to be federal efforts to combat discrimination by government contractors. His third sentence narrows the subject considerably: he's going to discuss the OFCC and compare the problems of women and minorities. But bear in mind that this sentence simply identifies the author's subject matter; it announces what he is going to discuss. The thesis will be the point Moskow makes *about* his subject. In this case the thesis will be Moskow's point about the OFCC and the relationship between the problems of women and the problems of minorities.

Moskow then establishes two basic facts needed to understand the rest of his discussion. In paragraph 2 he explains that the government's economic leverage gives it the power to discourage discrimination by contractors. Then in paragraph 3 he explains that the Department of Labor's Order Number 4 sets the standards for affirmative action plans—that is, for active attempts to utilize minorities in the workplace.

In paragraph 4 Moskow introduces *Revised* Order Number 4, which was specifically designed to include women in the framework of affirmative action. The next seven paragraphs form a block, providing a detailed description of how affirmative action works as applied to women, presenting the criteria contractors must use in analyzing their work force, and explaining how the plans are implemented and reviewed for compliance. In paragraphs 12 and 13 Moskow points out the significance of Revised Order Number 4 for women. He claims that it "put some teeth" into the government's efforts not only to end discrimination against women but to require contractors actively to recruit them for jobs. When we finish reading this section, we know that Moskow sees landmark significance in the revised order, a point which will certainly be part of his thesis.

With paragraph 14 Moskow turns from his first topic, the activities of the OFCC, to his second, the relationship between the problems faced by minorities and those faced by women. Paragraph 14 presents the similarities, concluding that both groups need affirmative action efforts to fight unequal opportunities for job advancement. Paragraphs 15–20 contrast the problems faced by the two groups. First, in paragraphs 15 and 16 Moskow points out that for women, unlike minority workers, careers are frequently tied to and limited by a husband's career interests. In paragraphs 17–20 he takes up a second contrast. Moskow argues that childbearing and the resulting extended period away from work can cost women job experience and skills. Childbearing itself is thus the source of a kind of discrimination against women.

Moskow has now finished discussing his two main topics, and it is time for us to stop and ask ourselves what his main point is. Two topics have stood out: Revised Order Number 4 and women's unique discrimination problems. We need to ask ourselves two questions: What point is Moskow making about each topic? What point is he making about their relationship? In the first part of the essay Moskow explains the importance of the revised order. In the second part he explains the uniqueness of some of the problems confronting women in the workplace. We might put his key ideas together in this thesis: *Revised Order Number 4 in 1971 significantly improved efforts to treat discrimination problems faced by women, problems that in some ways are more complex than those faced by minorities.*

You can use the procedure we have outlined for any source you summarize. Use the background material and the title to learn whatever you can and plunge right in. If you discover the thesis the first time through, make sure you understand it by writing it down in your own words. If you need to go back to the text for a second reading, work carefully through the source again, picking up ideas and relating them to one another until the main point becomes clear.

Finding the Key Ideas

If we were asked to briefly summarize Moskow's essay, we could do so with just our formulation of his thesis. But a thesis statement is no more adequate a summary of an essay than a final score is an adequate account of a baseball game. Although "Mariners win 6–5" tells a fan how the game came out, it provides no information about the events of the game itself. Similarly, a thesis alone conveys the author's main point but does not give any indication of the evidence on which that point is based. For readers to get a real sense of what "happens" in an essay, they must understand its most significant "events," the key ideas that develop the thesis. Once you have written down the thesis and the key ideas that support it, you have produced the essential information necessary to summarize anything from a brief essay to a full-length book.

Subheads vs. Key Ideas Some generous authors seem willing to help readers discover their most important ideas. They divide their articles or chapters with easy-to-spot boldfaced headlines or subheads. A number of the articles in this book are subdivided in this manner, and these subheads often help you separate the strands of the argument. But subheads can also be deceptive: they can give you an illusion of understanding the development of the argument without the reality. Before assuming that such headlines embody the main ideas of the source, we need to look a bit deeper. Sections or parts are not necessarily the same as ideas, and it is ideas you will need, not subject headings, to write your summary.

In fact, a source might very well have ten or twelve subdivisions but only two or three key ideas supporting its thesis. Let's take an example close to home. Suppose you announce to your parents that you would like to go to Tahiti for the spring break. Let's imagine that the response you get from your parents is a kind of spoken "article," in which you immediately detect the following boldfaced heads:

1. Cost of attending college
2. Cost of travel to the South Pacific
3. Your on-campus salary
4. The value of money, past and present
5. Vacation spots within ten miles of home
6. Vacations your parents never took
7. Your cousin Allan's catastrophe at Ft. Lauderdale
8. Complexity of world now vs. thirty years ago
9. The cause of your suspended driver's license
10. Parents' inability to help at range of 6,000 miles

There they are, ten distinct section headings, each one developed, no doubt, in excruciating detail. Since you will have to report a shorter version of this dismal lecture to your friends, you begin the mental "prewriting" of your summary. First, what's the implied thesis? That part is easy: Don't plan on going to Tahiti. But your friends will want some sort of explanation for this decision. Should you run through all ten points of your itemized list? If you look closely at the ten points, you'll soon discover that there are only two main ideas: A trip to Tahiti costs too much money (sections 1–6), and you are too immature to go there anyway (sections 7–10).

In short, what counts in an argument is ideas, not topics. When you summarize, you must distinguish sections from ideas. A straight outline of our Tahiti source might indeed have ten sections, but such an outline would not communicate the main point of the conversation or the development of its argument. With the thesis and the two key ideas, however, you would have the ingredients for a brief, but painfully complete, summary. If, for some reason, you wanted to provide a longer summary, you could go on to supply the specific details—the ten-item list—your parents used to back up their two key ideas.

The Key Ideas of a Source As our Tahiti example indicates, once you have clearly understood the thesis of a source, it is usually not very difficult to find its key ideas. Discovering the point of what you're reading, after all, is essentially a matter of finding the most important ideas and relating them to one another. To find the key ideas of a source, you retrace your steps by going back to the thesis and focusing on the main ideas that developed it.

The implied thesis of our sample essay, Michael Moskow's "Government in the Lead," was *Revised Order Number 4 significantly improved efforts to treat discrimination problems faced by women, problems that in some ways are more complex than those faced by minorities*. These are the ideas that led us to this conclusion:

1. In contract compliance the federal government has a very powerful weapon for restraining discrimination and promoting affirmative action.
2. Because Revised Order Number 4, unlike previous orders, isn't merely antidiscriminatory but actually promotes the recruitment of women for jobs, its implementation is an important policy change for women.
3. In some ways discrimination against women is similar to discrimination against minorities, yet marriage and childbearing can be sources of uniquely difficult problems for women.

Notice that we have expressed our key ideas as complete sentences, not as fragments. We have not, for example, written "Revised Order Number 4" as our second point because such an expression (which might appear as a subhead in an article) would be of no help in writing our summary. We must answer the question "What *about* Revised Order Number 4?" if we are to show how this topic fits into Moskow's argument. We need to put the author's point into a complete sentence because only a sentence can express ideas and relationships. Because a sentence has both a subject (what you are writing about) and a predicate (a comment about the subject), it is the shortest means by which an idea can be communicated. Thus, writing sentences is a kind of guarantee that we have gone beyond merely labeling topics to truly understanding the ideas in a source.

The One-Paragraph Summary If we were assigned to write a one-paragraph summary of "Government in the Lead," all we would have to do is combine our thesis statement and key ideas. Notice, however, that in the following summary we have made a number of adjustments in wording to turn our finished summary into a clear and coherent, a comprehensible, piece of writing. As we shall discuss later, comprehensibility is the first requirement for any summary. We have, for example, explained the meaning of the phrase "contract compliance."

> The Department of Labor's Revised Order Number 4 in 1971 significantly improved efforts to treat job discrimination problems faced by women, problems that are in some ways more complex than those faced by minorities. Because businesses with federal contracts must comply with federal regulations, contract compliance is a powerful weapon in the government's efforts to restrain discrimination in general and to promote affirmative action. Revised Order Number 4, unlike previous guidelines, is not merely antidiscriminatory but actually promotes the recruitment of women for jobs; thus, its implementation is an important policy change for women. Although in some ways discrimination against women and discrimination against minorities are similar, specific policies are needed for women because marriage and childbearing are the sources of uniquely difficult problems.

Placing the thesis statement at the beginning of the paragraph and making the alterations necessary to turn the key ideas into a coherent paragraph is an excellent way to check your grasp of the argument of the source you are summarizing. If you have trouble following the logic of the paragraph you have written, you should go back over the thesis and key ideas, making sure they are clear to you.

Marking Significant Details

The combination of thesis and key ideas that we have just drafted would provide a brief summary of Moskow's essay, an adequate summary if our purpose were simply to provide the thesis and key ideas of the essay. But our assignment, a 500- to 700-word summary to be used as part of a class project, requires more than the bare-bones minimum we have produced so far. In this case we want to give our readers a sense of the supporting evidence the author uses to back up the key ideas. We will take notes on this evidence before drafting our paper.

But before we take notes, it is a good idea to mark the text for the supporting details and important pieces of information the author has used to develop the key ideas. Although we are discussing marking the text at this point, there is no single stage in the summarizing process for this procedure. If you are one of those readers who like to mark significant details as soon as they start reading, you undoubtedly began marking your text some time ago. In any event, marking the text before you take notes will help you clarify the structure of your source's argument and decide which details belong in your summary.

No two readers mark texts precisely the same way, and there is no single correct technique for this procedure. For one thing, the way a text is marked depends on how the reader plans to use the text. People reading for pleasure, for example, might underline a few passages to remember later. Students might underline passages they expect to be questioned about on an exam. Book reviewers might write their critical responses in the margin. Even readers with the same purpose in mind will annotate their texts differently. There is a strong element of individuality in such matters. Some people tend to highlight facts, others ideas. One reader will insist that a particular piece of evidence is compelling and important; another reader might be less impressed by the same point. You are the one who will have to use these details in your summary, so you are the best judge of what is or is not significant.

Various techniques for identifying important details have proved helpful, and you can adapt them for your own purposes. Take advantage of the obvious in marking your text. As you begin to underline and make marginal notes, remember that the topic sentences of paragraphs usually contain important information. Labels such as *first, next, another,* and *finally* are all structural signals that can help you determine what to mark. In fact, it's not a bad idea to give such words special markings, perhaps circling them to make the placement of details stand out, as we have done in the following example.

Continuing with "Government in the Lead" as our chief example, we have provided a sample marking. We begin by reminding ourselves that paragraphs 1–3 contain the first key idea and include general material on the OFCC and affirmative action. If we haven't already marked the last sentence of paragraph 1, which announces the subject of the article, we should do so now. The first sentence in paragraph 2 contains the key terms "compliance program" and "discourage discrimination," in addition to which, flashing like a neon sign, are the words "very important." If Moskow thinks these terms are very important, who are we to disagree? As you can see, we continue underlining passages that we will most likely use in our summary.

You may find it helps to write marginal annotations—usually no more than short descriptive phrases or key words—to highlight details or provide a running outline of the author's train of thought.

■

GOVERNMENT IN THE LEAD

Michael H. Moskow

Discrimination in employment by federal government contractors and subcontractors because of race, color, sex, or national origin was prohibited by Executive Order 11246, as amended by Executive Order 11375. Under this order, the Office of Federal Contract Compliance was established within the Department of Labor to administer its provisions and to coordinate the activities of all federal contracting agencies. My discussion will cover the activities of the Office of Federal Contract Compliance, and I will generalize a bit about some of the parallels and contrasts between problems of minorities and problems of women.

The compliance program is very important because it gives the federal government immediate and powerful leverage to discourage discrimination in employment. There are certain procedures that have been established to use this leverage—such as conciliation, show-cause hearings, and consultations—but ultimately the federal government has the power to refuse to do business with someone. It can cancel, terminate, or suspend existing contracts, or it can bar a contractor from receiving future government contracts. These are very powerful economic weapons to discourage employers from discrimination and to encourage them to take affirmative action to employ minorities and women.

Order Number 4 was issued by the Department of Labor to delineate the criteria to be used by federal contractors in developing plans of affirmative action to increase employment opportunities for minorities. Affirmative action requires the government contractor to go beyond refraining from employment discrimination. The contractor is required, as part of the contracting process, to analyze his work force and to determine whether there are deficiencies in the utilization of minorities. If there are deficiencies, the contractor then must formulate written corrective measures, including goals, timetables, and a plan of action for their elimination. These written corrective measures are required to be established for each job classification. Together, they comprise the contractor's affirmative action plan.

A revised version of Order Number 4 was issued in December 1971, presenting criteria for the utilization of female workers, since the original order had applied only to minorities. In effect, the revision extended the mandate for affirmative action to women. This revision was developed after consultation with employers, women's groups, compliance agencies, minority groups, etc., and it tailored the principles and procedures dealing with the underutilization of minorities to the problems of the underutilization of women.

Contractors are required to revise any existing written affirmative action programs to include changes embodied in the order. They are also required to communicate to employees and to prospective employees the existence of their affirmative action programs and to make available the essential elements of their programs to allow the employees and prospective employees to avail themselves of the benefits.

When a contractor undertakes an analysis of his work force, Order Number 4 requires that he take the following criteria into consideration in determining female utilization.

First, he must consider the size of the female unemployment force in the labor area surrounding the facility. Second, he must look at the percentage of the female work force as compared to the total work force in the immediate labor market area. Third, he must consider the general availability of women having requisite skills in the immediate labor area. Fourth, he must ascertain the availability of women having requisite skills in an area in which the contractor could reasonably recruit, outside of his immediate labor market area.

(Next) he should inquire into the availability of women seeking employment in his labor or recruitment area. He must also note the availability of promotable *and* transferable female employees within his own organization. He should have some idea of the anticipated expansion, contraction, and turnover of the work force—its growth or lack of growth. (Finally,) the existence of training institutions capable of training persons to develop the requisite skills and the degree of training which the contractor is reasonably able to undertake as a means of making all job classes available to women are important considerations. The contractor then must arrive at goals and timetables for the employment of women, based on these criteria.

The criteria for women are similar to those for minorities, modified to meet the particular problems attendant to sex discrimination. Where deficiencies are found, the contractor is required to establish separate goals and timetables for women and separate goals and timetables for minorities. The order provides that if it comes to the attention of the director of the Office of Federal Contract Compliance, or the compliance agencies, that there is a substantial disparity in the participation of different minority groups, then separate goals and timetables can be required for each of those minority groups, such as for Spanish Americans, for Indians, or for Orientals. If substantial disparities are found in the employment of men and women of a particular minority group, separate goals and timetables can be required for males and females of those groups. We plan to monitor these figures for minority and sex subgroups very closely to insure that problem subgroups are separately treated.

In terms of implementation, a search for evidence of sex discrimination is included as part of the general compliance review that is made of a contractor. The person making the review looks at the distribution of the work force by sex as well as by race, religion, and national origin.

The general compliance review is automatically conducted for any supply contractor with a contract of more than a million dollars before the contract is awarded. Other contractors are chosen for a general compliance review based on apparent underutilization of minorities or women revealed in part by the Equal Employment Opportunity Commission annual compliance reports. Specific individual complaints are referred to the EEOC for investigation.

My own view is that Revised Order Number 4 represents a very significant change in public policy. No longer are we simply going on record against sex discrimination, although that was certainly a necessary preliminary step. Now we are requiring tangible evidence that meaningful steps are being taken to improve the employment prospects of women. This order goes beyond merely prohibiting discrimination against women to stimulating the recruitment of women. The great strength of the order is in the use of the federal government's compliance apparatus to put some teeth into the effort.

It will no longer be sufficient for a government contractor merely to refrain from overt acts of discrimination against women. Instead, he must present evidence that he has made a viable plan for finding and employing women who are potentially qualified for his work force.

There are parallels and contrasts between public policy regarding discrimination against minorities and against women. Let us look at some of the parallels.

First, the obvious similarity is that the provisions of the Executive Order and of Order Number 4 now apply both to minorities and to females. Another parallel is that mere enforcement of equal pay for equal work will not suffice to bring about equality of opportunity for either group. Women, like blacks and other minorities, suffer not only from low wage rates relative to others in the same job but also from being denied entry into prestigious, well-paid, and challenging occupations. Both groups suffer from unequal opportunities for advancement and promotion, which means that an activist policy requiring affirmative action is a necessity.

Let me mention two contrasts between the situations of women and minorities. In the past, the status and income available to a married woman have depended primarily on the success of her husband, and she has found it in her interest to support his cause, although this may conflict with her own career interests. I do not think that minorities find it in their interest to support the interests of whites in that way.

The primacy of the husband's career interests operates as a constraint on the equal opportunity movement, as many married women are content either to play the traditional role of the housewife or to engage in labor market activity from a disadvantaged position. However, both male and female attitudes toward the appropriate role of married women are changing rapidly; over time this voluntary barrier to equal opportunity may be lifted.

Another difference between women and minorities is that there is really no approximation among the latter of the particular situation resulting from childbearing. Clearly, here is another area where attitudes are changing on the part of both men and women. Nevertheless, childbearing often continues to involve a long interruption in the work experience of women. By long interruption, I do not mean a month or two month's leave, but five years or more, until the children are in school.

When the female is off the job for five years, her male counterpart is on the job. He is learning and building up human capital, as the economists would say. When she returns after a five-year break in her employment, the woman will clearly be at a disadvantage. She is not going to have the same skills or the capital that he will have built up in that five-year period.

This has an important policy implication. If that type of break in the career of a female is to be eliminated or greatly reduced, is the development of improved day care facilities on a massive scale a prerequisite? We have already seen some steps in this direction. An attempt was made in the last session of Congress to pass a child development bill which would subsidize the child care expenses of poor and near-poor women. Another start in this direction is the proposed Family Assistance Plan. Here, child care would be provided specifically to facilitate the employment of welfare mothers in an attempt to help them leave the welfare rolls. It is a job-oriented type of child care service.

Both the extent and the type of child care to be provided for poor women are still under debate at this time. I mention it because I think it is one policy that attempts to ease the entry of women into the work force on a large scale.

Hopefully, the emphasis on affirmative action will facilitate the achievement of equal employment opportunity for women. In the battle against job discrimination, the compliance program of the federal government should be an effective complement to existing legislation. The compliance weapon enables us to reach about one-third of the U.S. labor force. Although it cannot have an immediate impact on the entire labor force, we believe that this effort will have a substantial impact and will significantly advance the equal opportunity movement.

compliance program = impt. long-range impact

■

However you go about highlighting the significant details of the source you are going to summarize, keep in mind the general principle we have used in our example: the purpose of marking a text is to solidify your understanding of the relationship between the key ideas and the details that support them and to make it easier for you to take the notes from which you will actually draft your summary.

Taking Notes

We usually think of taking notes as part of the process of writing a research paper, for which we have to put together many sources. Because it is not convenient to keep returning to the original sources, our notes become a storehouse of the information we have collected. When it comes time to draft the paper, we unlock the storehouse and take out what we need.

But taking notes on a single source may seem unnecessary. Why not find the easily identifiable important ideas and details and begin drafting a summary? The answer is that note taking has a number of purposes, only one of which is to substitute for memory. For one thing, note taking contributes to your understanding of an essay. You will be writing your notes in your own words, and there is no better way to understand what someone else has written than to convert it into your own words. This is, of course, a familiar technique. You used it to ensure that you understood the thesis and key ideas of the essay; now you can do the same for the supporting details.

Another reason to draft your summary from your notes rather than from your source is that this technique makes plagiarism far less likely. We will discuss the matter of plagiarism fully in the Drafting section of "Writing a Simple Synthesis," but a few words might be helpful now. Unless you are quoting directly, the text of your finished summary must be in your own words. If instead it turns out to be a slightly rearranged copy of the original author's words, it can be considered plagiarized material. The tricky thing about plagiarism is that when you begin to draft a summary directly from a source, you immediately increase the chances of copying only slightly altered versions of the author's sentences. In fact, it is difficult for any of us to avoid copying when we are staring down at the source as we write. Taking notes in the manner described here should help you avoid unintentional plagiarizing.

Note taking is a relatively informal procedure. Its purpose is to get down in your own words the information you will need later. In taking notes, you can afford to work quickly without worrying about how specific details will eventually fit in. When you begin to draft your summary, you will have the time to make choices about how, or whether, to use any particular detail from your notes. You'll undoubtedly omit some notes and find yourself returning to the source to add more notes or clarify some you have already taken.

As we begin taking our notes, two obvious questions face us: Which details do we need to write down, and just how many will be enough? The answer, probably not much of a surprise, is that such decisions are educated guesses based on our purpose, our audience, the nature of our source, and the proposed length of our summary. In some sources, for example, statistical evidence—figures and percentages—may all be absolutely essential for a reader to comprehend an author's basic point. In other sources such evidence might be relevant but hardly crucial for a basic understanding. The sheer number of details appropriate for a 250-word summary will certainly be fewer than for a 1,000-word summary.

---

1. In contract compliance the federal government has a very powerful weapon for restraining discrimination and promoting affirmative action.
   —Office of Federal Contract Compliance established
   —Order Number 4: contractor standards for affirmative action plans
   —Required written plan for using minority workers
2. Because Revised Order Number 4, unlike previous orders, isn't merely antidiscriminatory, but actually promotes the recruitment of women for jobs, its implementation is an important policy change for women.
   —Adapted principles already used for minorities to needs of women
   —Contractors required to make appropriate revisions in existing affirmative action plans
   —Criteria for determining use of women in work force:
     a. Number of unemployed women
     b. Percentage of women in work force
     c. Availability of women with needed skills
     d. Availability of women with needed skills outside local area
     e. Availability of women looking for jobs or available within the company
     f. Availability of training to qualify women for available jobs
   —May have to formulate different goals, timetables for women and minorities to compensate for degrees of underutilization

An example of the notes we might take on Moskow's essay is boxed below. We have provided some overall order for our notes by keying them to Moskow's three main ideas.

Drafting

To most people "writing a paper" brings to mind the act of filling blank pages with sentences and paragraphs, what we are calling the *drafting* phase of the process. So far, however, most of your time has been spent learning the meaning of the source you are going to summarize. In the drafting phase of composing a summary, the focus shifts from understanding the ideas of your source to communicating those ideas to others. Although much of the drafting phase involves copying the material you have already accumulated, a summary is not a series of transcribed notes but a composition that must stand on its own. Its minimum requirement is the same as that of any piece of writing: Readers must be able to understand it. When you think about the structure of your summary, for

---

   —Implementation of affirmative action plans:
      a. Contractors reviewed for compliance
      b. $1 million and up contracts require prior compliance review
   —Significance of Revised Order Number 4: Used contract leverage to strengthen attempts both to end discrimination and to encourage active hiring of women
3. In some ways discrimination against women and discrimination against minorities are similar, yet marriage and childbearing can be sources of uniquely difficult problems for women.
   —Parallels:
      a. Women and minorities equally covered
      b. Chances for advancement not equal with rest of work force—action needed
   —Contrast—marriage:
      a. Married women's status and income tied to husbands'
      b. Women's chances and interests often limited by husbands' career needs
   —Contrast—childbearing:
      a. No minority equivalent
      b. Women away from work several years at disadvantage
      c. Loses out on building skills, human capital
      d. Implication: necessity of widespread day care opportunities

example, your primary concern will be to arrange the material so that your reader can understand the line of thought of the source.

Organizing a Summary

The *structure*—the order of the ideas—of a summary usually follows the structure of the source. In the following summary of Moskow's essay, for instance, we use the three main ideas in the order they appeared in the original. We had no difficulty following the structure of Moskow's argument, so it makes sense for us to use that same structure when we communicate the argument to others. But the structure of an essay does not always work in the context of a summary. The source we are summarizing may have been illogically structured, and the argument difficult to understand as a result. In such cases we should remember that what a summary replaces is not a series of isolated points but an argument, and our primary responsibility is to make sure that the argument is clear to our reader.

One way to communicate the point of the summary is by the careful placement of the thesis statement. The thesis statement (in a summary, the main point of the original source) is usually placed at the beginning of a summary to focus the reader's attention on the main point. In our single-paragraph summary, for example, we opened with the thesis statement before proceeding to the key ideas. In a multiparagraph summary you would ordinarily open the first paragraph with the thesis, followed immediately by the first key idea and its supporting details. You would then take up the remaining key ideas in the order you have decided upon.

Let's turn to our summary of Moskow's article, highlighted to show the thesis and key ideas. As you read the summary, notice the various adjustments we make of our one-paragraph version and our notes when we draft our paper. We'll discuss some of these adjustments at the conclusion of the summary.

A Summary of
Michael H. Moskow's
"Government in the Lead"

In its efforts to treat the problems of discrimination faced by women, problems that are in some ways more complex than those faced by minorities, the federal government took a highly significant step in 1971 when the Department of Labor issued Revised Order Number 4. Prior to 1971 the government had already begun to use contract compliance (withholding contracts from companies that don't follow regulations) as a very powerful weapon in its attempts to restrain discrimination in general and to promote affirmative action and had established the Office of Federal Contract Compliance to coordinate government efforts. The Department of Labor issued its original Order Number 4 to establish the standards contractors must follow in preparing their affirmative action plans. These standards required detailed written plans to show what was being done to employ underutilized minority workers.

Order Number 4 was revised in 1971 by the Department of Labor. Because Revised Order Number 4, unlike the previous order, isn't merely antidiscriminatory but actually promotes the recruitment of women for jobs, its implementation is an important policy change for women. Basically this revision adapted to the needs of women the principles already being used to fight minority discrimination and required contractors to make appropriate revisions in their present affirmative action plans.

First of all, Revised Order Number 4 spelled out the detailed criteria a contractor must use in analyzing the affected work force. The contractor must (1) determine the number of unemployed women in the local area; (2) determine the percentage of women in the work force in the same area; (3) ascertain the availability of women having the needed skills both within the local area and in surrounding areas; (4) discover the availability of women who are actually looking for jobs or who are available for promotion or transfer within the company; and (5) take into consideration the availability of training to qualify women for these jobs. The standards in the order also require that contractors be prepared to formulate goals and timetables for women separate from those for minorities to compensate for measurably different degrees of underutilization.

The order establishing these criteria also provides for their implementation. It requires that contractors be reviewed for compliance with their affirmative action plans, and it requires an automatic compliance review prior to the government's issuing any contract of $1 million or more.

The significance of Revised Order Number 4 is that it bolsters affirmative action efforts by making the most of the federal government's power to grant or withhold contracts. It insists on concrete proof from contractors not only that they do not discriminate against women but also that they have developed workable plans to seek out and hire qualified women.

Although in some ways conditions for women and minorities are similar, the specific policies of Revised Order Number 4 are needed because marriage and

<pre>
childbearing can be sources of uniquely difficult
problems for women. The situations of women and minorities
are parallel in two ways: First, both groups are now
equally covered by affirmative action regulations.
Second, because the chances of members of each group for
job advancement are not equal to those of the rest of the
work force, corrective action is still needed.

      But a woman's marital status can be the source of   7
problems quite unlike those confronting minorities. A
married woman's social status and income have
traditionally been tied to her husband's job and success.
As a result, a woman's job chances and interests are often
limited (with or without her consent) by her husband's
career needs. Childbearing also presents women with
unique problems. There is no minority equivalent for the
effects of childbearing, which may take women away from
work for several years while their co-workers continue to
build skills on the job. An important implication of this
disadvantage is the need for widespread day care
facilities.
</pre>

Our summary opens with Moskow's implied thesis. Although the actual content of the thesis has not changed, we have reworded it somewhat to bring out the sense of movement Moskow sees in the government's efforts on behalf of women. Specifically, Moskow notes that in combating discrimination, the government has moved away from an exclusive interest in the problems of minorities and toward an interest in the particular problems of women. Furthermore, the government is not only fighting overt acts of discrimination, but insisting on affirmative action in hiring. By opening with the words "In its efforts to treat the problems of discrimination faced by women," we can set up that sense of movement for the reader. We then need to do some more rewording from the notes in order to get from the thesis to the first key idea: "Prior to 1971 the government had already begun. . . ." The wording both picks up the idea of movement by the government and smooths the transition into the first key idea.

We now have a natural way to lead to the second key idea. The words "Order Number 4 was revised in 1971" complete the transition to the new idea. We present the third key idea in paragraphs 6–7 of our summary. We mark this major transition with the words "the specific policies of Revised Order Number 4 are needed because" and include in the same paragraph the two parallels between the situations of women and minorities.

One last point: Somehow you need to make your readers aware that they are in fact reading a summary. *When readers see your name at the top of an essay, they will assume that you are the source of all the material in the essay unless they are informed otherwise.* If you turn back to our summary of Moskow's article, you can easily see the problem that can arise.

We clarified the perspective in our summary by our title ("A Summary of Michael H. Moskow's 'Government in the Lead'"). But imagine this same essay with your name at the top under the title "A Turning Point for Women." Readers would have no way to know that the information and ideas expressed in the essay are Moskow's.

Thus, in summary assignments like this project, you can use a title to make the perspective and purpose clear, proceeding in the essay itself without any further references to the author of the original text. But in future assignments, where a summary is only one part of a paper and not its entire purpose, you cannot rely on a title to do the job. You will have to use references within your text to give credit to your sources. The following is a sample of how this technique works. Notice that we have inserted references to Moskow a number of times in our summary to remind our readers of the source of the information. We have also made a few adjustments for the sake of smoothness. In your own summary you can inform readers that they are reading a summary by the use of a title or by internal references. You may select (or your teacher may specify) either method, but it is a good idea to get used to introducing sources within your text.

```
                A Turning Point for Women
      In his 1973 article "Government in the Lead," Michael
H. Moskow asserts that in its efforts to treat the
problems of discrimination faced by women, problems that
are in some ways more complex than those faced by
minorities, the federal government took a highly
significant step in 1971 when the Department of Labor
issued Revised Order Number 4. Moskow begins by noting
that prior to 1971 the government had already begun to use
contract compliance. . . .
      Moskow points out that Order Number 4 was revised in
1971 by the Department of Labor. . . .
      In explaining how Revised Order Number 4 works for
the benefit of women, Moskow lists the detailed criteria
that spell out what a contractor must use in analyzing the
affected work force. . . .
```

Characteristics of a Good Summary

So far we have treated our summary as we would any piece of writing. We have discussed its thesis, its structure, and the techniques we use to make that structure clear to readers. It is appropriate to begin discussing the composition of a summary in these terms because *the first requirement of a summary is that it be comprehensible in and of itself.* A summary, however, is not an entirely original composition but a restatement of somebody else's ideas; thus, another set of criteria is applicable as well. Aside from the standards of good writing in general, a good summary has three specific characteristics:

1. Accuracy
2. Completeness
3. Appropriate length

The first standard—accuracy—is clear-cut and absolute. Because a summary is a substitute for the original source, we cannot put any ideas of our own into a summary or change any of our source's ideas. If, for example, our summary states or implies that Moskow believes the needs of women are basically opposed to those of minorities, we will be distorting his argument. If we were to confuse Order Number 4 and Revised Order Number 4, much of our summary would be incomprehensible.

The standard of accuracy includes other matters as well. If you summarize an article that reports information from a variety of other sources, your summary must make the source of each item of information clear. Matina Horner, for example, includes opinions from several authorities in "A Bright Woman Is in a Double Bind." In paragraph 8 Horner refers to the views of Eleanor Maccoby and Margaret Mead. If you choose to include this information in your summary, you need to clarify the source of each idea (by using the phrase "according to Margaret Mead," for example). We will cover this matter, which is called *attribution*, in detail in the synthesis project.

The second standard for a good summary—completeness—is also absolute. Completeness simply means that no facts or ideas that the reader needs in order to understand the author's argument are left out. Whether or not a summary is complete has little to do with its length: a one-paragraph summary, as we have seen, can provide all the key ideas of the original text, whereas a lengthy summary can omit crucial information. Our summary of the Moskow article, for example, would have been seriously deficient, perhaps even incomprehensible, if we had omitted one of the three key ideas.

We call the third standard for a good summary *appropriate length*, although it is often referred to as *brevity*. Of course, a summary, to deserve its name, must be considerably shorter than the original text, but it is not very useful to think of this standard in these terms. After all, what's brief? It's possible to summarize anything, from a paragraph to a book, in a sentence. For example, we could summarize Edward Gibbon's six-volume *The Decline and Fall of the Roman Empire* in one sentence: "Rome declined and fell." Or we could summarize it in fifty pages, which, given the monumental length of Gibbon's work, would still qualify as a brief summary.

It makes more sense to say that the length of a good summary is appropriate for its purpose and audience. In later projects, when your summaries are not ends in themselves, the use to which you put the source will largely determine the length of your summary. If, for example, you are merely going to refer to an essay in passing in a discussion of another work by the same author, your summary might be only a sentence or two. But if you are going to analyze the essay in depth, you will need to ensure that your reader is familiar with all the important ideas it contains.

Of course, often in college writing assignments the appropriate length of a summary is quite simply the length the teacher assigns. If your teacher requires a summary of five hundred words, then the appropriate length of your summary is five hundred words. In this project we are assuming a length appropriate for our class project (500–700 words), but your instructor might assign a different length. Keeping that length in mind as you draft will help you determine how much detail you need in your summary.

Accuracy, completeness, and appropriate length, then, are the specific criteria for a successful summary. But it is worth repeating that the first requirement of a summary is the first standard of all writing: *Whatever you write must make sense in and of itself.* As you draft your summary, keep in mind this basic principle: A successful summary is first and foremost a successful piece of writing.

By now you have collected most if not all the material you will need for your summary. You have a thesis and an outline of the key ideas you will use to back up the thesis. You have detailed notes from which to select the supporting evidence for your paragraphs. Now write up that material in a way that will accurately communicate the argument of the original source to your readers.

Revising

Revising, the phase of the writing process you are about to begin, includes all the activities writers perform after they have a draft down on paper: adding and deleting passages, shifting words and sentences around, correcting mistakes, and generally polishing things up. When they revise, writers take what they have written and get it ready for a public appearance.

Many people seem to find the idea of revising somewhat unsavory. They feel that once they have produced a draft, they have done their work and, in all fairness, ought to be left alone. This feeling is part of a tendency to overrate the relative importance of the drafting phase at the expense of the other phases of the writing process. The equation of drafting and writing leads people to believe that any writing activity is significant in direct proportion to the number of words it produces—and that once the words have been produced, the process is complete.

But writing is a flexible process, and writers can always go back over what they have done. If writing were like basketball, then revising would be like an offensive rebound: it gives you another shot at the basket. If you happen to be standing under the basket, all you need do is dunk the ball for an easy two-pointer. But if you get the ball somewhere near midcourt, you will have to work to set up your next shot. Similarly, the amount of revising you do depends on how close you are to fulfilling the purpose of the project.

You have certainly noticed that you started making changes almost as soon as you put pen to paper or finger to keyboard. As you began drafting your summary, you may have found that by the end of the first paragraph you had glanced back at something, marked it out, and replaced it with some other wording. Writers second-guess themselves throughout the writing process.

The activities described here can be called systematic second-guessing. They include two distinct activities, *revising* and *editing*, which for convenience we have placed under the general heading "Revising." When you revise a text, you go through it to see if any significant changes must be made. You may find you have to add paragraphs or rearrange their order, switch sentences around, and make major alterations of what you have written. Editing, on the other hand, is a matter of making certain cosmetic changes—in particular, catching the misspellings, grammatical foul-ups, and punctuation errors that were overlooked during drafting.

Writers usually begin revising by focusing on the large-scale concerns in a draft. For any piece of writing, that means first looking at the thesis to see if its point is clearly and fully stated. Then you can make sure that your key ideas and details are clearly related to your thesis. You should also check for coherent transitions. When you are satisfied with the content, organization, and clarity of the essay, you can turn your attention to the smaller-scale details such as spelling, punctuation, and other mechanical errors. A good way to begin is to read through your draft, asking yourself the following questions and making whatever adjustments are necessary:

1. Is the thesis statement identifiable, clear, and accurate?
2. Are there clear transitions to each key idea?
3. Is there sufficient detail for each key idea?
4. Is there a clear transition at the beginning of each paragraph?
5. Are there any sentences that sound awkward as you read them?
6. Are there any mechanical or typographical errors?

These questions are a practical way to discover the areas of your summary that might profit from revision or editing. At the same time, these questions are of limited usefulness because someone who has just finished writing an essay is not in the best position to answer them. It is very difficult for writers to criticize essays they have just drafted; they are too close to the drafting process. Writers tend to feel that if the meaning is perfectly clear to *them*, it ought to be clear to their readers. Unfortunately, this is not necessarily the case because readers start with a disadvantage: they have no idea what the writer *intended* to say.

For this reason the most fruitful comments are generally those made by a real, live reader. After you have made your preliminary revisions, you will find it most helpful to get someone else to read your draft and make suggestions for revision. You may be in a writing class in which your teacher uses a system to provide readers through organized peer response groups. If so, you may find yourself in a group of three or four classmates, passing your drafts around to one another and commenting on them. By the end of such a session each writer has a set of reader responses to use in making revisions and improvements. It is up to you whether or not to use these suggestions, but you certainly don't want to ignore this source of potential help in revising.

Ideally, the readers should help you revise according to the two kinds of standards discussed earlier: general writing standards and standards particularly relevant to summaries. The type of reader best qualified to check for the general qualities of successful writing is someone who has not read the original source and consequently does not begin already knowing the thesis and key ideas. Such a reader is primarily concerned with understanding what you have written and is in a better position to tell you whether or not your summary makes sense on its own.

On the other hand, the reader who comments about standards relevant to a summary must have knowledge of the original text. It is not possible to judge a summary *as a summary* without having read the original text. Only by comparing the two, the original text and the summarized version, can one tell whether a summary meets the standards of accuracy, completeness, and appropriate length.

The following are two series of activities designed to elicit helpful comments from readers. The first series checks general writing standards; the second checks standards appropriate to summaries.

GENERAL WRITING STANDARDS

Directions: Read the summary carefully and comment as indicated below. If you find any of these operations difficult or impossible to perform, indicate that fact to the writer and, if possible, try to explain the source of the difficulty.

1. Identify the thesis statement.
2. Rewrite the thesis in your own words.
3. List each of the key ideas that develop the thesis.
4. Point out any places where supporting detail is needed.
5. Point out any details without a clear purpose.
6. Indicate any places where the opening of a paragraph does not follow clearly from the conclusion of the previous one.
7. Indicate any sentences that are confusing.

STANDARDS FOR SUMMARIES

Directions: Read the summary carefully and, on the basis of your reading of the original source, comment as indicated below.

1. Point out any factual errors: incorrect names, dates, places, statistics, or statements.

2. Point out any places in which the writer of the summary has put in ideas or opinions not found in the original source.
3. Point out any crucial information in the source that is missing from the summary.

Revising is an important part of the writing process, a specific time for concentrating on the quality of your writing. To benefit from revision, however, you need to be somewhat hard-nosed about your work. We all form a deep attachment to what we write: it becomes a symbol of our own intellectual worth, and few of us derive pleasure from criticism, even "constructive" criticism. The trick is to accept criticism as a legitimate part of the writing process, not as a definitive statement about the quality of your mind. Then you can use self-criticism and criticism from others as means to an end, the production of an essay you can be proud of.

Writing a Simple Synthesis

IN THIS PROJECT YOU WILL BE WORKING WITH more than one source for the first time. Basically, what you are going to do is put two summaries together in a simple, efficient manner. One of the purposes of this project, then, is to provide further practice in summarizing. In addition, however, the project will focus on the specific problems writers face when they work with more than one source.

A paper that uses more than one source is known as a *synthesis*. This term takes in a lot of territory, and indeed two other projects in this book—the comparison and the "mini-research paper"—are also types of syntheses. This project is a *simple synthesis*, essentially two (or more) summaries related by a simple connection.

But adding a second source involves a number of extra considerations. We will illustrate some of these by returning to the example we used in the summary project, the plot summary narrated to a friend. In this case we'll let an old fairy tale illustrate an important writing principle:

> A family of bears (Papa, Mama, and Baby) leave their home to take a walk while their porridge cools. While they are out, a little girl named Goldilocks, inexplicably wandering about the forest, comes upon their house and, finding the door open, enters it. When she tries to sit down, she finds one chair (Papa Bear's) too high, one chair (Mama Bear's) too low, and one chair (Baby Bear's) "just right." She promptly sits in and breaks Baby Bear's chair. Similarly, when she tests the porridge, she finds Papa's portion too hot, Mama's too cold, and Baby's just right. Still making herself right at home, she enters the bedroom for a nap. There she finds one bed too hard, another too soft, and the third, Baby Bear's, just right. Goldilocks promptly falls

asleep in Baby Bear's bed. While she is sleeping, the Bears return and discover the unmistakable signs (chair broken, porridge consumed) of an intruder. In the bedroom the adult bears notice their beds have been tried out, and Baby Bear discovers Goldilocks herself, still sleeping. Goldilocks awakens, startled to find three bears gaping at her. She jumps out the window and trots home.

What we have just exemplified is, of course, the process of summarizing. If we wish to produce a synthesis, all we need do is follow our summary of Goldilocks with another summary, of Little Red Riding Hood, let's say.

But something vital is missing from that description of a synthesis. What we have described is a pointless combination of plot summaries, as if a synthesis consisted merely of slapping two summaries together without rhyme or reason. In the description above, for example, it would make no difference if we followed the summary of Goldilocks with a summary of Conan the Barbarian. If a synthesis were merely a mechanical combination of summaries, it would make no difference which sources we synthesized.

But we chose Little Red Riding Hood, and that choice is the key to understanding the purpose of a synthesis. We did not choose that story arbitrarily; rather, we chose to synthesize these two fairy tales because we recognized certain connections between them that make their coupling seem quite natural. That we had some connection in mind when we made our selection is illustrated by the fact that Little Red Riding Hood seems such a natural companion to Goldilocks, whereas Conan the Barbarian seems, at least at first, a strange bedfellow indeed. Our recognition of some relationship between the stories must have motivated us to synthesize the stories in the first place. This connection, the thesis of our synthesis, provides the overall purpose for our writing the synthesis. A simple synthesis is motivated by the discovery of a broad connection between sources.

We produce a simple synthesis, then, when we wish to communicate some relationship we have noticed between our sources. There are a number of possible relationships between Goldilocks and Little Red Riding Hood. We can choose for purposes of illustration one that is appropriate for this particular project. Too obvious a connection (for example, animals talk in both stories) would hardly require even a plot summary. Too subtle a connection (both stories embody deep-seated childhood fears) would require a more elaborate structure than that provided by a simple synthesis. Let's consider a relationship that will unify our summaries but will not necessitate an involved argument—in short, a thesis that is just right: "Goldilocks and Little Red Riding Hood are essentially fairy tales about little girls who get into trouble, but escape unharmed." It may not be a masterpiece of ingenuity, but this thesis does point out an essential relationship between the plots of the two stories.

We can now place this thesis at the beginning of our synthesis and summarize the two stories. But we must be careful to separate the stories from one another and from any comments we wish to make. This involves, first of all, keeping the two stories straight—not putting Little Red Riding Hood in Baby Bear's chair or Goldilocks in Grandma's bed. Second, when we switch from one story to the other, we must indicate what we are doing. We must introduce the second source so that our friend (or, in a formal writing situation, our reader) will not think we are telling one confusing story. The technique by which we separate sources from one another and from our own comments is known as *attribution*, and it will concern us in all projects using multiple sources.

An outline of our simple synthesis might run as follows:

1. Thesis: "*Goldilocks* and *Little Red Riding Hood* are essentially fairy tales about little girls who get into trouble, but escape unharmed."
2. Introduction of first source: "In *Goldilocks* . . ."
3. Summary of *Goldilocks*
4. Transition to second source: "In *Little Red Riding Hood* . . ."
5. Summary of *Little Red Riding Hood*

Suggested Assignment

You have been studying different images of early human life, derived from scholarly sources and sources of a more popular nature. Your assignment is a 500- to 700-word paper explaining the essential relationship between two of the sources you have read. Your purpose is to describe the image of early human life depicted in each of your sources and suggest a relationship between the images.

Overview

In this project, a simple synthesis, you will combine two summaries and relate them by a relatively simple connection. In a sense, then, the simple synthesis is halfway between a summary and an original composition. The prewriting section of this project will review—in abbreviated form—the process of summarizing. The section on drafting considers two additional matters related to summarizing—the use of direct quotation and the avoidance of plagiarism.

The purpose of a simple synthesis, however, is not merely to summarize two sources but to point out some connection between them. This connection, your perception of the relationship between the sources, is your *thesis*, the point you are making in your synthesis. This important subject—the writer's original thesis—is discussed in the prewriting section of this project.

Because the simple synthesis is a combination of two summaries, this project introduces the techniques necessary when you use more than one source in a paper. The drafting section discusses the technique of attribution, the means by which you separate sources from one another and from your own comments.

The Process of Writing a Simple Synthesis

1. Discover the thesis and key ideas of the sources you are considering for your synthesis.
2. Mark the texts of your sources for the significant details you are likely to use in your synthesis.
3. Take notes on your sources.
4. Formulate a thesis for your simple synthesis.
5. Draft the individual summaries that will make up the body of your synthesis.
6. Combine your summaries in a form appropriate to a simple synthesis, paying particular attention to separating your sources from one another and from your own comments.
7. Revise your simple synthesis, using the activities described in the project.

Prewriting

Discovering the Thesis

The prewriting activities for a simple synthesis do not differ very much from those for a summary, so much of what follows will be a review of the process of composing a summary. Obviously, the main difference in this project is that we are working with two sources instead of one. The prewriting consists of preparing to write two summaries and finding a connection tying them together.

We will exemplify the process of writing a simple synthesis with the essays "Images of Early Human Life" in the readings. Because the essays are all concerned with the same basic question—what was the human race like in its earliest days?—it will not be difficult to find at least one connection between any two of the essays—a connection that can be used as a thesis for a simple synthesis.

We will base our discussion of the prewriting steps in composing a simple synthesis on the following essay by Raymond Dart and its relationship to the other essays on the same topic in the anthology. There is a good reason for giving Dart's essay this pivotal position. For one thing, it is the earliest of the essays (1953), and, for another, you can be sure that Dart's description of the life of early humans is well known to every other author in the collection. Several of them refer to Dart's essay in their articles, and two even quote from it (the same passage, in fact). Dart's essay has been the subject of controversy since its publication. It describes early human life in powerful, almost lurid, terms. The other essays tend to either support or undercut Dart's position.

■

MAN AS PREDATOR

Raymond Dart

Raymond Dart (b. 1893), born and educated in Australia, was a professor of anatomy at the University of the Witwatersrand, Johannesburg, South Africa. In 1924 he discovered the first australopithecine (see the introductory comments in the anthology) at Taungs, South Africa, and from 1945 to 1955 developed the Makapansgat site mentioned in this excerpt, which first appeared in 1953 in the *International Anthropological and Linguistic Review*.

The australopithecine deposits of Taungs, Sterkfontein and Makapansgat tell us in this way a consistent, coherent story not of fruit-eating, forest-loving apes, but of the sanguinary pursuits and carnivorous habits of proto-men. They were human not merely in having the facial form and dental apparatus of humanity; they were also human in their cave life, in their love of flesh, in hunting wild game to secure meat and in employing implements, whether wielded and propelled to kill during hunting or systematically applied to the cracking of bones and the scraping of meat from them for food. Either these Procrustean proto-human folk tore the battered bodies of their quarries apart limb from limb and slaked their thirst with blood, consuming the flesh raw like every other carnivorous beast; or, like early man, some of them understood the advantages of fire as well as the use of missiles and clubs. At any rate there are no known features on the cultural side, other than the deliberate manufacture of tools and the systematic employment of fire, which separate these proto-men at the present time from early man.

A direct relationship exists between the carnivorous habit and acquiring an upright posture. The cerebral powers of these creatures were necessarily enhanced to carry out those striking, hurling and thrusting manual feats that are utterly beyond the skill of living apes; but it is absurd to imagine now that a large brain is essential to perform such berserk deeds.

Nobody knows what constitutes a human brain from the point of view of absolute size and weight. Individuals of apparently normal intelligence today need not have brains weighing more than 788 grams (i.e. the equivalent of a cranial volume of 830 cc. or only 175 cc. more than the greatest cranial capacity reported in a living ape). But human beings of subnormal intelligence can live long and fairly serviceable lives with a brain of anthropoidal dimensions. A microcephalic mental equipment was demonstrably more than adequate for the crude, carnivorous, cannibalistic, bone-club wielding, jawbone-cleaving Samsonian phase of human emergence.

Wherever found, all prehistoric and the most primitive living human types are hunters, i.e. flesh-eaters. Human carnivorous habits have an omnivorous range extending from grubs and insects on the one side to the most formidable of big game on the other. Secondly, man's taste for flesh is so great that human beings, whether in prehistoric (*Pithecanthropus–Sinanthropus*) or recent times and whether driven by need or not, have practiced either real or ritualistic cannibalism.

Through Herodotus, Strabo and other writers, the Greeks and Romans were familiar with contemporary peoples who, like the Scythian Massagetae north-east of the Caspian Sea, regularly killed old people and ate them. Marco Polo and other travellers informed Europeans of cannibalistic practices amongst the wild tribes of China, Tibet and elsewhere. Human flesh was habitually exposed for sale in the market place in West Africa; some tribes sold the corpses of dead relatives for consumption as food. Cannibalism prevailed until recently over a great part of West and Central Africa, New Guinea, Melanesia (especially Fiji), Australia, New Zealand, the Polynesian islands, Sumatra and other East Indian islands, in South America and formerly in North America. Cannibalism from necessity is found not only among Fuegians or Red Indian tribes, but also among civilized races, as the records of sieges and shipwrecks show (see "Cannibalism," *Encyclopaedia Britannica*, 14th ed.).

The loathsome cruelty of mankind to man forms one of his inescapable, characteristic and differentiative features; and it is explicable only in terms of his carnivorous and cannibalistic origin. As Robert Hartman (1885) said: "It is well-known that both rude and civilized peoples are capable of showing unspeakable, and, as it is erroneously called, inhuman cruelty towards each other. These acts of cruelty, murder and rapine are often the result of the inexorable logic of national characteristics, and, unhappily, are truly human, since nothing like them can be traced in the animal world. It would, for instance, be a grave mistake to compare a tiger with a blood-thirsty executioner of the Reign of Terror, since the former only satisfies his natural appetite in preying upon other animals. The atrocities of the trials for witchcraft, the indiscriminate slaughter committed by the Khonds, the dismemberment of living men by the Battas, finds no parallel in the habits of animals in savage state. And such a comparison, is above all, impossible in the case of the anthropoids, which display no hostility towards men or other animals unless they are first attacked. In this respect the anthropoid ape stands upon a higher plane than many men."

The blood-bespattered, slaughter-gutted archives of human history from the earliest Egyptian and Sumerian records to the most recent atrocities of the Second World War accord with early universal cannibalism, with animal and human sacrificial practices or their substitutes in formalized religions and with the world-wide scalping, headhunting, body-mutilating and necrophilic practices of mankind in proclaiming this common bloodlust differentiator, this predaceous habit, this mark of Cain that separates man dietetically from his anthropoidal relatives and allies him rather with the deadliest of Carnivora. 7

The predaceous habit is "living by preying," i.e. hunting down and killing animals for food. On this thesis man's predecessors differed from living apes in being confirmed killers: carnivorous creatures, that seized living quarries by violence, battered them to death, tore apart their broken bodies, dismembered them limb from limb, slaking their ravenous thirst with the hot blood of victims and greedily devouring livid writhing flesh. Further, man's erect posture is the concrete expression of signal success in this type of life. It emerged through and was consolidated by the defensive and offensive stone-throwing and club-swinging technique necessitated by attacking and killing prey from the standing position. 8

■

Dart introduces his basic idea about the nature of mankind early and considers its implications in the rest of the essay. He begins by describing the life of the "proto-men" from which the human race evolved. Recent findings show their culture to be indistinguishable from the culture of early humans (except for their failure to make tools and use fire systematically). The cultural characteristics Dart stresses in the first paragraph are all associated with protohuman carnivorousness, the implications of which Dart draws out in paragraph 2. After commenting on the close relationship between carnivorousness and the acquiring of an upright position, Dart goes on to point out that the activities associated with carnivorousness—"striking, hurling, and thrusting manual feats"—are by no means dependent upon a large brain. In paragraph 3 Dart notes that a small brain ("microcephalic mental equipment") is sufficient for the activities necessitated by the protohuman's bloodlust.

Let's stop right here and take stock. What has Dart accomplished in these paragraphs? He has been *defining* the nature of the protohuman's way of life. The dominant motif has been the carnivorousness upon which the bloodthirsty culture of the "man-apes" was based. If we peek at the beginning of paragraph 4, we will find that Dart is about to connect protohuman and human carnivorousness. In paragraph 3 he is anticipating an objection readers might have: The smaller brain of protohumans invalidates any comparison to humans. Dart argues that the difference in brain size between the two is insignificant compared to the similarities resulting from their carnivorousness.

In paragraph 4 Dart makes the connection clear by turning to early humans, focusing on two dominant characteristics: carnivorousness and cannibalism. In paragraph 5 he finds evidence of this cannibalism in history and in studies of contemporary primitive peoples. In the next paragraph Dart claims that carnivorousness and cannibalism account for human cruelty, which is found nowhere else in nature. In paragraph 7 Dart finds evidence for this cruelty throughout recorded history and attributes it to "this common bloodlust," which differentiates man from the anthropoids and "allies him rather with the deadliest of Carnivora."

We can begin our analysis by noting that Dart's primary purpose is to define human nature by finding a set of characteristics that are consistently present in early humans and in human behavior ever since. This purpose accounts for Dart's insistence on the connection between protohumans and early human beings; for a definition to be consistent it must be applicable at *all* times, from the very beginning to the present. We can see even from these few paragraphs why this essay provoked so much controversy and why the question of how early people lived has always been of enormous interest (even before anything substantial was known about prehistoric humans): the question of the nature of our early ancestors is inseparable from the question of human nature itself. In Dart's view the fundamental difference between a human being and an ape is the former's bloodthirstiness, which extends even to cannibalism and results in the "loathsome cruelty" that is one of humankind's "inescapable, characteristic and differentiative features."

We've read through the essay, focusing on the development of its ideas. It is now time to identify Dart's thesis. We need a single sentence to focus the diverse material Dart covers in his essay. Dart's purpose is to define human nature and show how his definition is applicable throughout history and prehistory—whenever human beings or their ancestors have been around, in fact. We can frame this purpose in our thesis: *Human nature, from the time of protohumans through recorded history, must be understood in terms of the carnivorousness that defines it.*

This is the time to read through the essays you are considering for this assignment. As you read a group of essays on the same subject, you will find it helpful to determine what basic question the writers attempt to answer in their essays. In the case of the anthology "Images of Early

Human Life," for example, the central question seems to be "What was the human race like in its earliest days?" You can probably find an equally significant question for each set of readings. Answering the question will help you discover the thesis of each essay, and it will start you thinking about the overall connection between your sources.

Finding the Key Ideas

When we read an essay carefully for its thesis, we are reading analytically. Once that thesis is clear, we can retrace our steps and find the key supporting ideas. When reading Raymond Dart's essay for its thesis, for example, we found that it was essentially divided into three parts: a descriptive definition of protohuman life, a discussion of the relative insignificance of brain size, and a broadening of the definition to include early humanity (with a few hints about later human life as well). The main ideas supporting Dart's thesis (*human nature, from the time of protohumans through recorded history, must be understood in terms of the carnivorousness that defines it*) are these:

1. Protohuman culture, dominated by bloodthirstiness, is virtually indistinguishable from early human culture.
2. The fact that human beings have larger brains than protohumans is insignificant compared to their cultural similarities.
3. The two dominant characteristics of early humans, carnivorousness and cannibalism, account for the unique cruelty that has always characterized our species.

If your instructor has given you the option of choosing the sources you will synthesize and you have not yet decided which essays to use, this would be a good time for a decision—after you have read and understood a variety of essays and before you start to reread and mark down specific details. One way to make your selection is to ask two questions: Which essays do I feel most comfortable with? Which essays are most clearly related to one another? This relationship will become the basis for your own thesis, so it makes sense to keep it in mind when you choose the essays you are going to synthesize. We will discuss the actual thesis of the synthesis later, but you should begin thinking of how you are eventually going to use your sources.

Marking the Sources

If you have the theses and main ideas of your sources down pat, it is time to go back to the texts and mark the significant details you may wish to use in your summaries. We will not repeat the entire process at this point but merely remind you of the basic technique. Here, for example, is one way we might mark the text of the opening paragraphs of Dart's essay to outline its main points and note its significant details:

Proto-humans — The australopithecine deposits of Taungs, Sterkfontein and Makapansgat tell us in this way a consistent, coherent story not of fruit-eating, forest-loving apes, but of the sanguinary pursuits and carnivorous habits of proto-men. They were human not merely in having the facial form and dental apparatus of humanity; they were also human in their cave life, in their love of flesh, in hunting wild game to secure meat and in employing implements, whether wielded and propelled to kill during hunting or systematically applied to the cracking of bones and the scraping of meat from them for food. Either these Procrustean proto-human folk tore the battered bodies of their quarries apart limb from limb and slaked their thirst with blood, consuming the flesh raw like every other carnivorous beast; or, like early man, some of them understood the advantages of fire as well as the use of missiles and clubs. At any rate there are no known features on the cultural side, other than the deliberate manufacture of tools and the systematic employment of fire, which separate these proto-men at the present time from early man.

large brain — insignificant — A direct relationship exists between the carnivorous habit and acquiring an upright posture. The cerebral powers of these creatures were necessarily enhanced to carry out these striking, hurling and thrusting manual feats that are utterly beyond the skill of living apes; but it is absurd to imagine now that a large brain is essential to perform such berserk deeds.

Taking Notes

Because you will draft your summary from your notes, it is particularly important to write them in your own words. Your primary purpose is to get the information you will need in your summary down on paper. This is not the time to worry about structure; you will almost certainly have to reorder

---

3. The two dominant characteristics of early human beings, carnivorousness and cannibalism, account for the unique cruelty that has always characterized humankind.
   — all early humans were carnivorous hunters
   — "taste for flesh" has always led to cannibalism, real or ritualized
   — cannibalism recognized by such writers as Herodotus and Marco Polo
   — cannibalism observable until recently among primitive tribes
   — humanity's "loathsome cruelty" the result of carnivorousness and cannibalism
   — cruelty is human; not found in animal world
   — cannibalism, human and animal sacrifices, scalping, body mutilation, and necrophilia characteristic of early humans all seen later in the "blood-bespattered, slaughter-gutted archives of human history"

your information when you actually draft the paper. As long as you grasp the main ideas and their relationship to one another and to the details in your notes, you will have little trouble converting somewhat fragmentary and disorganized notes into paragraph form.

We will use the concluding paragraphs of Dart's essay as an example. Our notes for the third main idea of the essay might look like those pictured in the box.

Notice that we have quoted a few passages. Not surprisingly, the passages we quote in our notes often turn out to be the very ones we previously underlined for their memorable phrasing. Phrases like "loathsome cruelty" and "taste for flesh" (not to mention those "blood-bespattered archives") give a feel for the style of Dart's argument that no paraphrase could. (We will discuss the reasons for quoting in the section on drafting the paper.)

Formulating a Thesis

The word *thesis* refers to the main point of any piece of writing, one we read or one we write ourselves. Up to now we have applied the term primarily to reading material. But just as we must find another writer's thesis when we read, so we must formulate our own thesis when we write.

This distinction was not necessary in the summarizing project, a "pure" summary, a restatement of the author's argument. In that case the thesis of the original text was the thesis of your summary. But in the remaining projects in this book, your purpose is no longer to summarize but to make a point of your own, in this case a point about the relationship between your sources.

Your thesis is the idea that unifies and focuses your essay. It is what you wish to communicate to your reader about the subject at hand. The sources you use are ultimately *evidence* for this thesis. To put it another way, the purpose of writing a paper with sources is not to use sources but to use sources to make a point.

The Thesis of a Simple Synthesis The thesis of a simple synthesis is a broad relationship between two essays. The most convenient general relationship between any two essays is the relationship between their theses, and that is how we are going to approach the thesis of our simple synthesis. Using Dart's essay as our central example, we can examine the relationship between his main point (that human nature, from the time of protohumans through recorded history, must be understood in terms of the carnivorousness that defines it) and the main points of the other essays on the same topic.

All the other essays in "Images of Early Human Life" tend either to support or undermine Dart's essay. We can break these essays down into three categories: those supporting Dart (Ardrey, Morris), those directly contradicting him (Leakey and Lewin, Montague), and those not directly contradicting Dart but offering models of early human life that clearly undermine his position (Isaac, Tanner).

If we chose to synthesize Dart's essay and either Ardrey's or Morris's, we would point out their similarity and offer our sources as authors who agree on a certain basic characteristic of human nature. Our essay would define this area of agreement as precisely as possible. If we used Isaac or Tanner, our thesis would make the opposite point: that the authors involved present contrasting views of the nature of early human life. If we used Leakey and Lewin or Montague, we would point out that one essay presents a view that the other directly repudiates.

You can follow the same procedure with any topic you are using as the subject of a synthesis. Take any essay that makes a strong impression on you and relate it to each of the other essays on the same topic. Examine the theses of the two essays and formulate their precise relationship. You can begin by asking whether the two writers basically agree or disagree. If they disagree, the specific nature of the disagreement should provide a thesis for your synthesis. If they generally agree, you will probably find that the essays emphasize different aspects of the topic. In this case, your own thesis could point out the basic agreement between the two writers and then isolate the particular aspect of the subject that concerns each writer. If you follow this procedure with several pairs of sources, you should come up with a number of possible theses for your simple synthesis.

DRAFTING

Drafting a simple synthesis consists of two basic operations: writing out the summaries of the two essays you have chosen and combining them into one paper controlled by your thesis.

Drafting the Summaries

Let's now return to the notes we took on the concluding section of Dart's essay and see what our summary of them might look like:

```
According to Raymond Dart, the nature and evolution
of early human beings must be understood in terms of their
carnivorous and cannibalistic origins. Recent findings
indicate that protohumans were not peaceful apes but
ferocious carnivores who loved every aspect of killing.
All early humans were carnivorous hunters. Their "taste
for flesh" led to real or ritualized cannibalism, which
was observable until recently among primitive tribes.
Humanity's "loathsome cruelty," which is not to be found
in the animal world, is the result of carnivorousness and
```

```
cannibalism. The cannibalism, human and animal
sacrifices, scalping, body mutilation, and necrophilia
characteristic of early human beings are all seen later in
the "blood-bespattered, slaughter-gutted archives of
human history."
```

In this summary we have retained the phrases we quoted in our notes, phrases we considered necessary to capture the style of Dart's argument. Let's consider this matter more closely.

Direct Quotation Your summary is a restatement in your own words of someone else's argument. Thus, it follows that a summary should be cast in your own style, should sound like an example of your writing. *Paraphrasing*, putting someone else's ideas into your own words, is the proper method for summarizing. *You should quote the source's words directly only when you have a good reason to do so.* Otherwise, you should paraphrase.

One good reason to quote directly motivated our quotations from Raymond Dart. An argument's *tone*, the attitude an author takes toward the material he or she is presenting, is often as important as its content, and this is certainly the case with Dart's essay. Dart's attitude, his obvious revulsion at the spectacle of human nature, can best be captured with a few of his own choice phrases. Furthermore, whenever you find a particularly well-phrased or succinct passage, one that seems to put the matter in a nutshell, you can consider quoting it.

How much direct quotation should your summary have? Unfortunately, there is no neat statistical answer to this question, and the best we can offer may seem hopelessly vague: A summary should have as much quotation as necessary. In later projects, in which you will be asked to use sources for more complex purposes, you will probably need to use more direct quotation than you do in a summary or simple synthesis. In this project there is little reason to quote, except in the cases mentioned, where quotation is necessary for the reader to appreciate the author's tone. Use that as your standard, remembering that paraphrase is the normal technique to use when summarizing a source.

When you choose to quote, whatever appears between the quotation marks must duplicate the original source *exactly*. That means you must preserve the language, typography, and spelling of the original text. If, for example, your source italicizes a word, you must italicize or underline that word. If your source spells a word in the British manner (*gaol* for *jail*, for example), you must transcribe the British spelling.

Avoiding Plagiarism One aspect of using sources is crucial for any work you do involving the words and ideas of others. This is the matter of plagiarism and how to avoid it. Because there is confusion about what precisely constitutes plagiarism, it is worth spending time clearing it up.

There are essentially two types of plagiarism. The first occurs when a writer uses the ideas or opinions of someone else and passes them off as his or her own. To avoid this kind of plagiarism, you must inform your reader whenever you are using someone else's ideas. We'll discuss this technique, known as *attribution*, in the next section.

The second type of plagiarism is concerned not with ideas, opinions, or facts—what we call the *content* of what we read—but with the language and sentence structure of the original text. At any point in your summary you are doing one of two things: paraphrasing or quoting directly. Your name at the top of an essay assures your reader that the language in the text is entirely your own, except where you have indicated otherwise by the use of quotation marks. Plagiarism occurs when you present as a paraphrase a passage that is too close to the original to be considered your own language.

Simply copying sentences from a source without indicating that they are quotations is an obvious violation of the reader's trust. But most examples of plagiarism are far more subtle than that; in fact, many unintentional plagiarisms result from the belief that only blatant copying constitutes plagiarism. To understand plagiarism, you should not think of it as a product, but as a process. In other words, don't think of it as a phrase or sentence copied from the original text without quotation marks. Instead think of it as a faulty technique, a process in which someone paraphrasing fails to turn the original source into his or her own words. What inevitably results is plagiarism.

Take, for example, the opening of Dart's essay:

> The australopithecine deposits of Taungs, Sterkfontein and Makapansgat tell us in this way a consistent, coherent story not of fruit-eating, forest-loving apes, but of the sanguinary pursuits and carnivorous habits of proto-men. They were human not merely in having the facial form and dental apparatus of humanity; they were also human in their cave life, in their love of flesh, in hunting wild game to secure meat and in employing implements, whether wielded and propelled to kill during hunting or systematically applied to the cracking of bones and the scraping of meat from them for food.

Suppose we come upon this paraphrase of it:

> The deposits left by australopithecines tell a story not about fruit-eating apes, but about the bloody activities and carnivorous habits of proto-men. They were not only human in appearance; they were also human in that they lived in caves, loved to eat flesh, hunted wild animals to get meat, and used implements to kill during the hunt and to scrape meat from bones.

This is a typical example of the most common type of plagiarism, and the interesting thing about it is how easily recognizable it is. Although changes have indeed been made in wording and syntax, it is perfectly obvious that the language and particularly the sentence structure are much too close to Dart's text to pass as a paraphrase. The writer should have either quoted the passage as it appeared in the original text, using quotation marks, or written the passage entirely in his or her own language. The problem is not only that a certain number of consecutive words appear in both source and summary without quotation marks. And it's not just the use of the isolated phrase "carnivorous habits." It's the writer's whole approach to the job of summarizing that is at fault here. In other words, instead of trying to avoid a certain result, writers should avoid the technique that produced the result. Let's ask ourselves what faulty technique produced the plagiarism.

We can all visualize our plagiarist seizing upon this passage and deciding to transfer it from Dart's page to his own without bothering to understand it. (Remember, it is only by understanding an argument that you can summarize it accurately.) So what does he do instead? Eyes glued to Dart's text, writing hand poised above notebook, he "translates" the original by making minor alterations in Dart's language and sentence structure. There you have it: "Portrait of a Plagiarist."

Let's contrast that to an honest paraphraser, one who has followed the prewriting process discussed in this book. This writer read the essay, made sure she understood it, and then marked significant passages. She made a point of *not* looking at the text while actually writing the notes. Furthermore, she wrote those notes in fragmentary form, making duplications of sentence structure nearly impossible. Then she drafted her paraphrase from her notes, not from the text, and used only that portion of the passage appropriate for the summary. She produced the following: "Recent findings indicate that protohumans were not peaceful apes but ferocious carnivores who loved every aspect of killing." She did not have to worry about counting "borrowed" words; her technique prevented plagiarism. The moral of our little story is clear: It's very easy to avoid committing plagiarism; just don't do what plagiarists do.

Drafting the Simple Synthesis

Early in this project we developed a five-part structure for the simple synthesis (using *Goldilocks* and *Little Red Riding Hood* as example sources):

1. Thesis statement
2. Transition to first source
3. Summary of first source
4. Transition to second source
5. Summary of second source

With some possible modifications, this is the form you are most likely to follow in your own synthesis. You will probably begin with your thesis, a statement of the connection you have found between your sources. You may need to make adjustments in the wording or emphasis of the thesis to make it compatible with the completed summaries. Once you have made your basic connection, you are ready to provide the evidence to back it up, the summaries you have already written.

Attribution When you go from your thesis statement to your first summary, you need to inform your reader of what you are doing. For example, suppose we were drafting a synthesis of the Tanner and Dart essays, and we moved from part 1 to part 3 of our skeletal outline without stopping off at part 2. Here is our opening:

>   Raymond Dart and Nancy Tanner present contrasting
>   views of the nature of early human beings. Protohuman
>   culture, dominated by bloodthirstiness, is virtually
>   indistinguishable from early human culture.

This is, to put it mildly, confusing. It is time to take a look at parts 2 and 4 of the outline and discuss attribution.

Attribution is the means by which you separate your sources from one another and from any comments of your own to make sure that the reader knows precisely who is responsible for what information in the synthesis. The primary responsibility for the whole paper is yours. Your name at the top of the paper implies that whatever follows represents your own ideas, opinions, and attitudes, and readers will assume that to be the case until informed otherwise. Whenever you make use of a source, therefore, you must inform readers that the material that follows is not your own invention.

Usually it is a simple matter to separate your source's ideas from your own comments. In the preceding example, the first sentence is our own thesis. The second sentence represents Dart's opinion, and we must make that clear. Notice how the confusion entirely disappears from that opening when we insert the phrase "according to Dart" at the beginning of the second sentence. We have now simply and effectively separated our own ideas from the views of our source.

By the same token, when we move from Dart's ideas to Tanner's, we must indicate to readers what we are doing in order to avoid confusion and assign responsibility for each of the ideas we are using. At the very least, the introduction of the second source would need a reference to Tanner. But another purpose can be served by these crucial transitions: the introduction of a source is often the place to inform or remind readers of the purpose served by that source in your paper. In this case, for example, a simple "Tanner, on the other hand, believes that" would not only separate Dart's views from Tanner's but would also reinforce the contrast underlying our own thesis.

Revising

The revising activities for all the projects in this book follow the same basic pattern. The first step is to reread your paper and, using the following list of questions, see if there are any problems that you yourself can spot and correct. This is the time for that thorough rereading you would give any of your work before showing it to someone else.

The two lists that follow are groups of writing activities designed to elicit helpful comments from a reader. The first group of activities deals with general writing matters, issues applicable to all essays. In this project, as in the summary project, these comments are best made by someone unfamiliar with the original essays. Notice that the first activity deals with the thesis of your draft. In the case of the summary project, that thesis was the same as the thesis of the source you were summarizing. But in this and all subsequent projects the thesis referred to in this activity is the original thesis you have constructed. In this case it is the connection you have found between the sources you have synthesized.

The second group of activities is specifically related to the simple synthesis project you have just drafted. It is designed to draw comment on the basic skills stressed in this project: summarizing, quoting, and clarifying the sources of information. This list is designed to elicit comments from readers familiar with your sources.

QUESTIONS FOR YOURSELF

1. Is the thesis statement identifiable, clear, and accurate?
2. Are there clear transitions to each key idea?
3. Is there sufficient detail for each key idea?
4. Is there a clear transition at the beginning of each paragraph?
5. Are there any sentences that sound awkward as you read them?
6. Are there any mechanical or typographical errors?

GENERAL WRITING STANDARDS

Directions: Read the summary carefully and comment as indicated below. If you find any of these operations difficult or impossible to perform, indicate that fact to the writer and, if possible, try to explain the source of the difficulty.

1. Identify the thesis statement of the essay and rewrite it in your own words.
2. List each of the key ideas that develop the thesis.
3. Point out any places where supporting detail is needed.
4. Point out any details without a clear purpose.
5. Indicate any places where the opening of a paragraph does not follow clearly from the conclusion of the previous one.
6. Indicate any sentences that are confusing.

STANDARDS FOR A SIMPLE SYNTHESIS

Directions: Read the simple synthesis carefully and, on the basis of your reading of the original sources, comment as indicated below.

1. Point out any factual errors: incorrect names, dates, places, statistics, or statements.

2. Indicate any quotation that is not exactly as it appears in the original source.
3. Write down the transitions the writer has used at the beginning of each summary.
4. Reread the thesis of the paper and ask yourself the following question: Do the two summaries clearly back up the thesis statement? If they don't, indicate what you think the problem is (for example, certain crucial information left out).

Writing a Critique

(EVALUATION)

When we are reading, we are aware of several things. Our primary concern usually is to grasp the author's point. But our attention is not focused entirely on the source; we also become aware of our own responses—whether we approve or disapprove, for example. Moreover, while we read, we constantly compare the information and ideas we encounter to our own experiences and observations. Thus, reading draws our attention to the world outside the text and stimulates our own thinking.

Although these reading activities cannot be completely separated, we usually stress one of them. If, for example, we are having difficulty understanding a source, or if our purpose is to summarize, we will naturally concentrate on understanding the point of what we are reading. As we read, however, we invariably react to the observations and ideas we encounter. We may find ourselves nodding in agreement or shaking our heads in disagreement, considering how the author's views relate to something else we've read recently, or considering what would happen if an author's proposal were put into action. In these cases our source has become the subject of our own thinking.

Written comments about a source are known as a *critique*, a critical commentary on a source. Since there are any number of possible responses to a source, the word is very broad in meaning. For example, a critique may evaluate a source, discuss its implications, analyze its assumptions, or exemplify its ideas. For our examples we are going to concentrate on the most common kind of critique, the evaluation, but the process is basically the same for all critique projects. In a critique, a source is the subject of your own essay. You treat that source as you would any subject you are planning to write about—consider your reactions, come up with a thesis that expresses them, and communicate your ideas to a reader. At the end of the discussion of evaluation, we will describe other possibilities for a critique.

Suggested Assignment

Your local humane society is putting together a set of critical reviews on the subject of animal rights. The society wishes to present a variety of perspectives on this controversial topic. The audience for these reviews consists of friends of the humane society, a mixed group sympathetic to animals but not always sure of precisely how they stand on such questions as animal experimentation and vegetarianism. Your purpose is to present them with a summary and evaluation of one prominent position on the subject.

Overview

■

Whereas the simple synthesis combines elements of both a summary and an original composition, this project, like all the remaining projects in this book, is an entirely original composition. In this project, writing a critique, a source will serve as the subject matter of your own essay. A number of critique projects are described at the end of the project, but we will stress the most common type of critique, the evaluation.

Because a critique is the first entirely original composition described in this book, the project focuses on the movement from reading to writing, from taking in somebody else's views to formulating an original idea. You will find that the prewriting section is divided into three general areas: (1) reading a source critically, paying particular attention to your own responses as you read; (2) devising a thesis for your evaluation; and (3) writing an outline from your thesis and notes. The drafting section explains how to turn that outline into an original essay and considers the question of the use of summary in an original essay.

The Process of Writing an Evaluation

1. Discover the thesis and key ideas of the source you are evaluating.
2. Reread your source critically, stopping at intervals to write down your responses to the text.
3. Devise a thesis for your evaluation.
4. Generate a sequence of ideas to support your thesis.
5. Return to the source for a final check.
6. Following your outline, draft your evaluation.
7. Revise your evaluation, using the activities that are described in the project.

■

Prewriting

Finding the Thesis and Key Ideas

It's useful to break the prewriting process for a critique into two readings, one to get the thesis and key ideas and the other to examine the source as a subject for writing. In this project we key our discussion to the "Animal Rights" essays in the readings section. We will use the following essay as the chief example.

■

ALL ANIMALS ARE EQUAL[1]
Peter Singer

> Peter Singer (b. 1946) is a professor of philosophy at Monash University in Australia. He is perhaps the most influential modern writer on the subject of animal rights. His many journal articles and his book *Animal Liberation* (1975) helped to revitalize interest in the subject. The following essay is excerpted from an article published in *Philosophic Exchange* in 1974.

When we say that all human beings, whatever their race, creed or sex, are equal, what is it that we are asserting? Those who wish to defend a hierarchical, inegalitarian society have often pointed out that by whatever test we choose, it simply is not true that all humans are equal. Like it or not, we must face the fact that humans come in different shapes and sizes; they come with differing moral capacities, differing intellectual abilities, differing amounts of benevolent feeling and sensitivity to the needs of others, differing abilities to communicate effectively, and differing capacities to experience pleasure and pain. In short, if the demand for equality were based on the actual equality of all human beings, we would have to stop demanding equality. It would be an unjustifiable demand.

Still, one might cling to the view that the demand for equality among human beings is based on the actual equality of the different races and sexes. Although humans differ as individuals in various ways, there are no differences between the races and sexes *as such*. From the mere fact that a person is black, or a woman, we cannot infer anything else about that person. This, it may be said, is what is wrong with racism and sexism. The white racist claims that whites are superior to blacks, but this is false—although there are differences between individuals, some blacks are superior to some whites in all of the capacities and abilities that could conceivably be relevant. The opponent of sexism would say the same: a person's sex is no guide to his or her abilities, and this is why it is unjustifiable to discriminate on the basis of sex.

This is a possible line of objection to racial and sexual discrimination. It is not, however, the way that someone really concerned about equality would choose, because taking this line could, in some circumstances, force one to accept a most inegalitarian society. The fact that humans differ as individuals, rather than as races or sexes, is a valid reply to someone who defends a hierarchical society like, say, South Africa, in which all whites are superior in status to all blacks. The existence of individual variations that cut across the lines of race or sex, however, provides us with no defence at all against a more sophisticated opponent of equality, one who proposes that, say, the interests of those with IQ scores below 100 be given less consideration than the interests of those with ratings above 100. Would a hierarchical society of this sort really be so much better than one based on race or sex? I think not. But if we tie the moral principle of equality to the factual equality of the different races or sexes, taken as a whole, our opposition to racism and sexism does not provide us with any basis for objecting to this kind of inegalitarianism.

There is a second important reason why we ought not to base our opposition to racism and sexism on any kind of factual equality, even the limited kind that asserts that variations in capacities and abilities are spread evenly between the different races and sexes: we can have no absolute guarantee that these abilities and capacities really are distributed evenly, without regard to race or sex, among human beings. So far as actual abilities are concerned, there do seem to be certain measurable differences between both races and sexes. These differences do not, of course, appear in each case, but only when averages are taken. More important still, we do not yet know how much of these differences is really due to the different genetic endowments of the various races and sexes, and how much is due to environmental differences that are the result of past and continuing discrimination. Perhaps all of the important differences will eventually prove to be environmental rather than genetic. Anyone opposed to racism and sexism will certainly hope that this will be so, for it will make the task of ending discrimination a lot easier; nevertheless it would be dangerous to rest the case against racism and sexism on the belief that all significant differences are environmental in origin. The opponent of, say, racism who takes this line will be unable to avoid conceding that if differences in ability did after all prove to have some genetic connection with race, racism would in some way be defensible.

It would be folly for the opponent of racism to stake his whole case on a dogmatic commitment to one particular outcome of a difficult scientific issue which is still a long way from being settled. While attempts to prove that differences in certain selected abilities between races and sexes are primarily genetic in origin have certainly not been conclusive, the same must be said of attempts to prove that these differences are largely the result of environment. At this stage of the investigation we cannot be certain which view is correct, however much we may hope it is the latter.

Fortunately, there is no need to pin the case for equality to one particular outcome of this scientific investigation. The appropriate response to those who claim to have found evidence of genetically-based differences in ability between the races or sexes is not to stick to the belief that the genetic explanation must be wrong, whatever evidence to the contrary may turn up: instead we should make it quite clear that the claim to equality does not depend on intelligence, moral capacity, physical strength, or similar matters of fact. Equality is a moral ideal, not a simple assertion of fact. There is no logically compelling reason for assuming that a factual difference in ability between two people justifies any difference in the amount of consideration we give to satisfying their needs and interests. The principle of the quality of human beings is not a description of an alleged actual equality among humans: it is a prescription of how we should treat humans.

Jeremy Bentham incorporated the essential basis of moral equality into his utilitarian system of ethics in the formula: "Each to count for one and none for more than one." In other words, the interests of every being affected by an action are to be taken into account and given the same weight as the like interests of any other being. A later utilitarian, Henry Sidgwick, put the point in this way: "The good of any one individual is of no more importance, from the point of view (if I may say so) of the Universe, than the good of any other."[2] More recently, the leading figures in contemporary moral philosophy have shown a great deal of agreement in specifying as a fundamental presupposition of their moral theories some similar requirement which operates so as to give everyone's interests equal consideration—although they cannot agree on how this requirement is best formulated.[3]

It is an implication of this principle of equality that our concern for others ought not to depend on what they are like, or what abilities they possess—although precisely what this concern requires us to do may vary according to the characteristics of those affected by what we do. It is on this basis that the case against racism and the case against sexism must both ultimately rest; and it is in accordance with this principle that speciesism is also to be condemned. If possessing a higher degree of intelligence does not entitle one human to use another for his own ends, how can it entitle humans to exploit non-humans?

Many philosophers have proposed the principle of equal consideration of interests, in some form or other, as a basic moral principle; but, as we shall see in more detail shortly, not many of them have recognised that this principle applies to members of other species as well as to our own. Bentham was one of the few who did realize this. In a forward-looking passage, written at a time when black slaves in the British dominions were still being treated much as we now treat non-human animals, Bentham wrote:

> The day *may* come when the rest of the animal creation may acquire those rights which never could have been witholden from them but by the hand of tyranny. The French have already discovered that the blackness of the skin is no reason why a human being should be abandoned without redress to the caprice of a tormentor. It may one day come to be recognised that the number of the legs, the villosity of the skin, or the termination of the *os sacrum*, are reasons equally insufficient for abandoning a sensitive being to the same fate. What else is it that should trace the insuperable line? Is it the faculty of reason, or perhaps the faculty of discourse? But a full-grown horse or dog is beyond comparison a more rational, as well as a more conversable animal, than an infant of a day, or a week, or even a month, old. But suppose they were otherwise, what would it avail? The question is not, *Can they reason?* nor *Can they talk?* but, *Can they suffer?*[4]

In this passage Bentham points to the capacity for suffering as the vital characteristic that gives a being the right to equal consideration. The capacity for suffering—or more strictly, for suffering and/or enjoyment or happiness—is not just another characteristic like the capacity for language, or for higher mathematics. Bentham is not saying that those who try to mark "the insuperable line" that determines whether the interests of a being should be considered happen to have selected the wrong characteristic. The capacity for suffering and enjoying things is a pre-requisite for having interests at all, a condition that must be satisfied before we can speak of interests in any meaningful way. It would be nonsense to say that it was not in the interests of a stone to be kicked along the road by a schoolboy. A stone does not have interests because it cannot suffer. Nothing that we can do to it could possibly make any difference to its welfare. A mouse, on the other hand, does have an interest in not being tormented, because it will suffer if it is.

If a being suffers, there can be no moral justification for refusing to take that suffering into consideration. No matter what the nature of the being, the principle of equality requires that its suffering be counted equally with the like suffering—in so far as rough comparisons can be made—of any other being. If a being is not capable of suffering, or of experiencing enjoyment or happiness, there is nothing to be taken into account. This is why the limit of sentience (using the term as a convenient, if not strictly accurate, shorthand for the capacity to suffer or experience enjoyment or happiness) is the only defensible boundary of concern for the interests of others. To mark this boundary by some characteristic like intelligence or rationality would be to mark it in an arbitrary way. Why not choose some other characteristic, like skin color?

The racist violates the principle of equality by giving greater weight to the interests of members of his own race, when there is a clash between their interests and the interests of those of another race. Similarly the speciesist allows the interests of his own species to override the greater interests of members of other species.[5] The pattern is the same in each case. Most human beings are speciesists. I shall now very briefly describe some of the practices that show this.

For the great majority of human beings, especially in urban, industrialized societies, the most direct form of contact with members of other species is at meal-times: we eat them. In doing so we treat them purely as means to our ends. We regard their life and well-being as subordinate to our taste for a particular kind of dish. I say "taste" deliberately—this is purely a matter of pleasing our palate. There can be no defence of eating flesh in terms of satisfying nutritional needs, since it has been established beyond doubt that we could satisfy our need for protein and other essential nutrients far more efficiently with a diet that replaced animal flesh by soy beans, or products derived from soy beans, and other high-protein vegetable products.[6]

It is not merely the act of killing that indicates what we are ready to do to other species in order to gratify our tastes. The suffering we inflict on the animals while they are alive is perhaps an even clearer indication of our speciesism than the fact that we are prepared to kill them.[7] In order to have meat on the table at a price that people can afford, our society tolerates methods of meat production that confine sentient animals in cramped, unsuitable conditions for the entire durations of their lives. Animals are treated like machines that convert fodder into flesh, and any innovation that results in a higher "conversion ratio" is liable to be adopted. As one authority on the subject has said, "cruelty is acknowledged only when profitability ceases."[8] So hens are crowded four or five to a cage with a floor area of twenty inches by eighteen inches, or around the size of a single page of the *New York Times*. The cages have wire floors, since this reduces cleaning costs, though wire is unsuitable for the hens' feet; the floors slope, since this makes the eggs roll down for easy collection, although this makes it difficult for the hens to rest comfortably. In these conditions all the birds' natural instincts are thwarted: they cannot stretch their wings fully, walk freely, dust-bathe, scratch the ground, or build a nest. Although they have never known other conditions, observers have noticed that the birds vainly try to perform these actions. Frustrated at their inability to do so, they often develop what farmers call "vices," and peck each other to death. To prevent this, the beaks of young birds are often cut off.

15 The same form of discrimination may be observed in the widespread practice of experimenting on other species in order to see if certain substances are safe for human beings, or to test some psychological theory about the effect of severe punishment on learning, or to try out various new compounds just in case something turns up. People sometimes think that all this experimentation is for vital medical purposes, and so will reduce suffering overall. This comfortable belief is very wide of the mark. Drug companies test new shampoos and cosmetics that they are intending to put on the market by dropping them into the eyes of rabbits, held open by metal clips, in order to observe what damage results. Food additives, like artificial colorings and preservatives, are tested by what is known as the "LD_{50}"—a test designed to find the level of consumption at which 50% of a group of animals will die. In the process, nearly all of the animals are made very sick before some finally die, and others pull through. If the substance is relatively harmless, as it often is, huge doses have to be force-fed to the animals, until in some cases sheer volume or concentration of the substance causes death.

16 Much of this pointless cruelty goes on in the universities. In many areas of science, non-human animals are regarded as an item of laboratory equipment, to be used and expended as desired. In psychology laboratories experimenters devise endless variations and repetitions of experiments that were of little value in the first place. To quote just one example, from the experimenter's own account in a psychology journal: at the University of Pennsylvania, Perrin S. Cohen hung six dogs in hammocks with electrodes taped to their hind feet. Electric shock of varying intensity was then administered through the electrodes. If the dog learnt to press its head against a panel on the left, the shock was turned off, but otherwise it remained on indefinitely. Three of the dogs, however, were required to wait periods varying from 2 to 7 seconds while being shocked before making the response that turned off the current. If they failed to wait, they received further shocks. Each dog was given from 26 to 46 "sessions" in the hammock, each session consisting of 80 "trials" or shocks, administered at intervals of one minute. The experimenter reported that the dogs, who were unable to move in the

hammock, barked or bobbed their heads when the current was applied. The reported findings of the experiment were that there was a delay in the dogs' responses that increased proportionately to the time the dogs were required to endure the shock, but a gradual increase in the intensity of the shock had no systematic effect in the timing of the response. The experiment was funded by the National Institutes of Health and the United States Public Health Service.[9]

In this example, and countless cases like it, the possible benefits to mankind are either non-existent or fantastically remote; while the certain losses to members of other species are very real. This is, again, a clear indication of speciesism.

Notes

[1] Passages of this article appeared in a review of *Animals, Men and Morals*, edited by S. and R. Godlovitch and J. Harris (Gollancz and Taplinger, London 1972) in *The New York Review of Books*, April 5, 1973. The whole direction of my thinking on this subject I owe to talks with a number of friends in Oxford in 1970–71, especially Richard Keshen, Stanley Godlovitch, and, above all, Roslind Godlovitch.

[2] *The Methods of Ethics* (7th Ed.) p. 382.

[3] For example, R. M. Hare, *Freedom and Reason* (Oxford, 1963) and J. Rawls, *A Theory of Justice* (Harvard, 1972); for a brief account of the essential agreement on this issue between these and other positions, see R. M. Hare, "Rules of War and Moral Reasoning," *Philosophy and Public Affairs*, vol. I, no. 2 (1972).

[4] *Introduction to the Principles of Morals and Legislation*, ch. XVII.

[5] I owe the term "speciesism" to Dr. Richard Ryder.

[6] In order to produce 1 lb. of protein in the form of beef or veal, we must feed 21 lbs. of protein to the animal. Other forms of livestock are slightly less inefficient, but the average ratio in the U.S. is still 1:8. It has been estimated that the amount of protein lost to humans in this way is equivalent to 90% of the annual world protein deficit. For a brief account, see Frances Moore Lappe, *Diet for a Small Planet* (Friends of The Earth/Ballantine, New York 1971) pp. 4–11.

[7] Although one might think that killing a being is obviously the ultimate wrong one can do to it, I think that the infliction of suffering is a clearer indication of speciesism because it might be argued that at least part of what is wrong with killing a human is that most humans are conscious of their existence over time, and have desires and purposes that extend into the future—see, for instance, M. Tooley, "Abortion and Infanticide," *Philosophy and Public Affairs*, vol. 2, no. 1 (1972). Of course, if one took this view one would have to hold—as Tooley does—that killing a human infant or mental defective is not in itself wrong, and is less serious than killing certain higher mammals that probably do have a sense of their own existence over time.

[8] Ruth Harrison, *Animal Machines* (Stuart, London, 1964). This book provides an eye-opening account of intensive farming methods for those unfamiliar with the subject.

[9] *Journal of the Experimental Analysis of Behavior*, vol. 13, no. 1 (1970). Any recent volume of this journal, or of other journals in the field, like the *Journal of Comparative and Physiological Psychology*, will contain reports of equally cruel and trivial experiments. For a fuller account, see Richard Ryder, "Experiments on Animals" in *Animals, Men and Morals*.

■

We may think at first that Singer's thesis is clearly stated in the title, but the title actually tells us very little. For one thing, much of Singer's effort in the essay goes into defining the concept of equality, and his thesis includes his definition. Furthermore, by "animal" Singer means human beings as well as dogs and cats. The "equality" Singer defines includes both humans and nonhumans (which we will continue to refer to as "animals"). Readers familiar with George Orwell's novel *Animal Farm* will also notice that Singer is equating the book's famous slogan ("All animals are equal. But some animals are more equal than others.") with discrimination against animals. In fact, it is probably part of Singer's strategy to confuse us at first, to get us to think he is about to explain that pigs are as good as dogs, in order to break through our complaisant attitudes.

In the first eight paragraphs of his essay Singer is concerned with defining the nature of equality. In paragraphs 1–5 he explains what equality is *not*. His point is made most clearly in the last sentence of paragraph 6: Equality is a moral prescription, not a fact of life. When we talk of "the principle of equality," according to Singer, we are referring to the way we *ought* to treat others, not to any alleged equality of ability among them. Once he has defined the principle, Singer moves on to the question of its applicability in paragraphs 9–12. The first sentence of paragraph 11 states the applicability of the principle of equality clearly: All beings capable of suffering (and/or enjoyment or happiness) deserve to be treated equally. In the final paragraphs of the essay, as the last sentence of paragraph 12 indicates, Singer describes practices that violate this principle: meat eating and animal experimentation.

If we have read this essay carefully, we now have its thesis and key ideas. Singer's main point is that *the principle of equality, which refers to the equal treatment of all creatures capable of suffering, is violated by meat eating and animal experimentation*. We can easily reconstruct the key ideas if we keep in mind the three sections of the essay: (1) the definition of the principle of equality, (2) the applicability of the principle, and (3) the violations of the principle. By turning Singer's main point about each of these topics into sentences, we will have the key ideas of his essay.

Asking Appropriate Questions

The Nature of Evaluation   For many people the idea of evaluation implies a thumbs up/thumbs down procedure similar to the verdict one might deliver on a new flavor of ice cream. Such an evaluation requires little more than an expression of our feelings, though we may try to explain why we feel as we do about it ("It's too sweet." "Its texture lacks consistency." "It doesn't really taste like strawberries."). When we give our opinion on a matter like this, we are expressing a subjective preference. Of course, there are some accepted standards for ice cream, but it seems unlikely that anyone could convince us by a logical argument that a flavor we didn't like was really good.

Few people feel nervous about evaluating a flavor of ice cream, but many people hesitate when it comes to expressing their opinions about ideas, particularly if those ideas appear in print. After all, they feel, anything in print must have been written by an expert, one who has studied a subject closely and reasoned carefully. As you begin your evaluation, remember that when you come right down to it, a printed source is just somebody else's ideas written down—nothing more, nothing less. You evaluate it by asking the same familiar questions you ask about any other idea:

- Is it logical?
- How strong is the evidence for the idea?
- Are there any important considerations left out?

The process of evaluating a printed source consists of asking these commonsense questions as you read through a source. Answering them will clarify and explain your response to a source.

Questions for Evaluation Before rereading a source for evaluation, you should consider your questions in more detail. These are the basic questions we ask when we consider the validity of any idea, so most of them will be quite familiar.

1. *Is the argument logical?* This is probably the first question we ask about any argument: Does its conclusion follow logically from the evidence? We ask this question all the time, whenever, for example, we decide whether or not to go along with a proposal. We consider all the evidence presented and then decide whether or not the proposal ought to be adopted. When you evaluate a written source, you can ask the same question, letting your common sense guide you to a response. If the conclusion of the source does not seem to follow logically from the evidence, try to put your finger on the reason the argument doesn't convince you.

2. *Is there enough evidence to back up the author's assertions?* Another question comes immediately to mind: How much evidence is "enough"? These are not easy questions to answer, but if you write down all the evidence an author is using to back up a conclusion, you can see at a glance just how much evidence there actually is. You may find the accumulated evidence impressive, or you may be surprised at how scanty it is.

3. *Has the author made any unwarranted assumptions?* An essay's assumptions are the ideas and alleged facts that the author does not attempt to prove and that are necessary for the logical development of the argument. Because assumptions usually are not directly stated, their significance is often neglected. It is important to uncover these assumptions and consider their validity.

One way to uncover an author's assumptions is to consider the subject the author is writing about. Anyone writing about animal rights, for example, will have to consider a number of issues: the nature of animals, the relationship between human beings and animals, the nature of right and wrong, to name the most obvious. If we framed these issues as questions, we might come up with the following:

- What is the author's conception of animal nature? What kind of creatures are animals?
- How does the author conceive of the relationship between human beings and animals? Is there a qualitative difference between them? Or are they merely different kinds of animals?
- What is the author's conception of the nature of good and evil?
- What does the author believe to be the source of morality? Does the author, for example, believe morality to be based on religious authority or on general principles?

Whatever the topic of the source you are evaluating, you will find it helpful to begin by making a list of the specific issues raised by the subject matter. Determining the stand an author has taken will help you uncover the assumptions behind his or her argument.

4. Is there anything important left out of the argument? Is there anything the author hasn't considered that might affect the conclusion?

5. How accurate is the information? This question generally concerns the factual content of a source. On one level you might be able to spot factual errors—incorrect names, dates, or statistics. But there is another level to this question. Remember that an author has to get factual information from somewhere. The information with which an author backs up a thesis might be outdated, unreliable, or biased. Thus, as part of the evaluating process, you should consider the sources of information in an essay.

Reading for Evaluation

Once you have a general sense of direction, you can return to your source for a *critical reading*. One way to define a critical reading is to distinguish it from a casual reading. When you read casually, your primary purpose is to understand the writer's argument—to grasp the thesis and key ideas. When you read critically, you actively involve yourself in the argument: weighing the validity and accuracy of the ideas, considering their implications, uncovering the assumptions behind them. You do not accept what the author says at face value; you analyze what you are being told.

There is no single method for this "close reading." A good method is to reread your source, keeping in mind the questions you have framed, making a note of your own responses as you read. You don't want to stop after every sentence or paragraph because you would quickly lose the thread of your source's argument that way. But you do want to make sure that you are gaining something from your rereading and not just repeating your first reading. The best general procedure is a compromise: stop at certain predesignated points (perhaps after each key idea) and consider what you have read so far. Give yourself ten minutes to write down your responses. If nothing comes immediately, you might return to the basic questions for evaluation and apply them to what you've just read. Follow this procedure at each stopping point in the text. Don't worry about how or if you'll be able to use your comments; all you are doing at this stage is stimulating your thinking about the source and keeping a running commentary of the results.

In our sample essay by Peter Singer, each key idea provides a convenient stopping place. Here are a few comments a reader might make after reading the first eight paragraphs of the essay:

- Singer believes that the principle of equality refers to the way people ought to be treated, not to equality of ability. So the idea that all people are equal doesn't mean that all people have equal ability, but that they deserve equal treatment. He believes that people of different races and sexes should be treated equally in accordance with this principle, not because they have equal abilities. This is an important distinction, but is it an adequate defense against racism and sexism? Racists and sexists have always based their arguments on the alleged inferiority of others, and here's Peter Singer claiming that we should simply ignore that idea and base our objections to racism and sexism on some unsupported moral position about how people ought to be treated. It's just too easy to argue that if certain people are "inferior," they ought to be treated in an inferior way.
- The last sentence of paragraph 8 makes a very significant assumption: the only difference between people and animals that Singer refers to is our "higher degree of intelligence." Singer doesn't consider other possible differences—such as the belief that human beings have souls and animals do not or the idea that human beings are morally responsible for their actions and animals are not. Shouldn't he at least consider these possibilities?

Much of our speculation turns on Singer's second key idea. Let's stop after paragraph 12 and consider some responses we might have to his explanation of the "principle of suffering" as the applicable criterion for equal treatment.

- Is Singer's argument really logical at this point? What proof does he offer for the idea that the capacity to suffer makes a being worthy of equal treatment? In paragraph 10 he says that the capacity to suffer is a prerequisite for equal treatment, that only beings capable of suffering (a mouse, but not a stone) qualify. It would be hard to disagree with that idea, but so what? Does that idea justify his comment in paragraph 11 that any being capable of suffering deserves equal treatment? What do we mean when we say a certain characteristic is a "prerequisite" for something? Does it mean that any being that has that characteristic automatically qualifies? For example, being at least thirty-five years old is a prerequisite for serving as president of the United States. Does that mean that any thirty-five-year-old in the world is eligible to be president? Of course not; there are other prerequisites for the job—American citizenship for one. The fact that having the capacity to suffer is a prerequisite for having moral rights doesn't mean that every being that suffers has moral rights. And Singer doesn't seem to offer any other proof.

Finally, let's consider some responses we might have after reading the entire essay.

- Has Singer taken other perspectives into consideration? The idea of animal inferiority has many traditional sanctions. The Judeo-Christian tradition, in particular, has always placed great emphasis on the subordinate status of animals. Should the biblical tradition of animal subordination be considered?
- Is "speciesism" a realistic conception? Aren't there natural reasons for preferring the interests of one's own species? For example, it would be hard to square this idea of equality among species with the theory of evolution, which implies competition among species for limited resources.

This demonstrates the range of comments you might find yourself making when you read your source critically. Your comments are bound to be a mixed bag: some usable remarks, some areas to be explored later, some ideas that never pan out. But you may also find that when you focus your own thoughts by making specific written comments, you begin to see the basic point you want to make about your source. That point will become the thesis of your evaluation.

Devising a Thesis

There is a tendency to think of the thesis of an essay as a kind of service a writer performs for a reader, as if writers were doing their readers a big favor by coming to some conclusion. But a thesis is as valuable to the writer as it is to the reader. Consider that what we have at this stage of our sample evaluation of Singer's essay is a lot of material and nothing in particular to do with it. We know we're going to evaluate the essay, but how should we start? Until we know what point we wish to make in our essay, we don't have a clue. That's why devising a thesis is so important. When we have formulated our thesis, when we know precisely what we want to say, we can think about communicating that point.

The thesis of an evaluation is the writer's assessment of the source evaluated. A good way to focus your general impression of the quality of an essay is to ask two questions:

1. Was the source worth reading?
2. What were its major strengths and weaknesses?

Answering these questions will help you clarify your response to the source and focus on the reasons behind it. First you need a balanced view of your response. Such assignments, after all, tend to focus attention on your reservations. Our commentary on Singer's essay, for example, emphasized certain questions we had about specific points. Those reservations did not, however, imply a negative evaluation of the whole argument. In fact, when we look back over our response to the *whole* essay, we might conclude that Singer made us think about the issue of animal rights from a new perspective: our belief in the principle of equality. We may not agree with every point he makes, but we'll certainly never think of animal rights in the same way again.

Our major objection was that Singer didn't prove one of his key ideas (that any being capable of suffering is worthy of equal treatment). We also notice that our reservations are closely related to another observation we made, Singer's equation of speciesism with racism. We believe that Singer is trying to convert his readers' antipathy toward racism to a similar response to speciesism, which is valid if the relationship between races can really be compared to the relationship between species. The only point of comparison Singer finds is that both humans and animals are capable of suffering and enjoying. But there are many things all humans and no animals are capable of. Why doesn't the capacity for moral responsibility or the possession of a soul, for example, determine whether a being is worthy of equal treatment? What's so special about the capacity to suffer?

If we put our entire reaction into a sentence, it might look like this: *Singer's essay is an original and stimulating contribution to the debate over animal rights, but it is flawed by his failure to prove the idea that all beings capable of suffering deserve equal treatment.* This thesis emphasizes our major criticism about Singer's second key idea and allows us to consider the problem with Singer's conception of speciesism. It also fulfills the overall purpose of a thesis by providing a clear evaluation of Singer's essay and an indication of the specific grounds of our criticism.

As you devise the thesis of your evaluation, concentrate on these two efforts: clarifying your response and putting your finger on the reasons behind it. Ask yourself the following questions:

1. What have I learned from the essay and how is it likely to affect my thinking?
2. What are my significant objections, the ones that affect the thesis of the essay?
3. Is there any general idea that connects all my individual comments?

Generating a Structure

Devising a thesis and developing a structure—a sequence of ideas—to communicate it are not really separate activities. In composing a thesis, we look over our different ideas and discover a single comment that unifies them. When generating a structure to communicate that thesis, we work backwards, beginning with the thesis and asking two basic questions:

1. What ideas must I develop to prove my thesis?
2. What is the most effective order for those ideas?

We generate a structure by analyzing a thesis, breaking it down into its component parts. Take for example the thesis we devised for an evaluation of Peter Singer's essay:

> Singer's essay is an original and stimulating contribution to the debate over animal rights, but it is flawed by his failure to prove the idea that all beings capable of suffering deserve equal treatment.

What are the main points we will have to make to back up this thesis? We want to indicate our generally favorable response to the essay early on, we want to make sure that the nature of our reservation is clear, and we want to explain why our reservation is significant. This thesis would seem to commit us to the following points:

1. Singer's essay is original and stimulating.
2. Singer fails to prove that the capacity for suffering is the criterion for the equal treatment of all creatures.
3. This failure flaws Singer's argument.

Your analysis of the thesis you have formulated should provide a broad outline for your evaluation. You can return to the notes you took during your close reading to fill in the key ideas to support your thesis. Remember, however, that because you are writing your evaluation for a reader who has not read your source, you'll have to begin your evaluation with a brief summary of your source.

A full outline of an evaluation of Peter Singer's essay might look like this:

> I. Summary of "All Animals Are Equal"
> II. Singer's essay is original and stimulating.
>   A. Singer views the subject from a fresh perspective.
>   B. Singer's argument shows an awareness of the complexity of the subject matter.
>   C. No reader is likely to view the subject the same way after reading the essay.
> III. Singer does not prove that the capacity for suffering is the criterion for the equal treatment of all creatures. Singer argues that because the capacity to suffer is a prerequisite for equal treatment, any creature that suffers ought to be treated equally.
> IV. This failure flaws Singer's argument.
>   A. The establishment of the criterion of the capacity to suffer is the pivotal step in Singer's argument.
>   B. Without this proof Singer's equation of speciesism with racism and sexism is open to serious question.

Returning to the Source

Taking one last look at a source just before you begin drafting is advisable. If you know you have all the material you need for the projected length of your evaluation, you need make only a brief run-through, perhaps adding a few comments to the notes you have taken. If, however, you have insufficient detail for your paper, you should reread the essay, perhaps making notes in the text and underlining significant information. Here are a few things to consider at this point:

- *Checking your thesis by rereading the source.* The only way to check the validity of your thesis is to read the source again and see if your reaction is consistent with your thesis. You probably won't find a radical difference, but you may find that you have overemphasized some part of your reaction. You may wish to strengthen or tone down your thesis.
- *Checking your sentence outline against the source.* It is possible that in trying to find something to say about the source, you have unintentionally confused a few points, overestimated the significance of part of the argument, or committed a factual error or two.
- *Finding additional material for your paper.* Each successive reading of the source will be more focused than the previous one. A third reading may very well reveal details that seemed irrelevant previously but now fit into your thesis.
- *Rereading the sections in the source most significant for your evaluation.* You may not need to reread the whole source, but you might wish to look over those passages on which your evaluation rests.
- *Checking quotations.* Check your quotations against the source, both at the prewriting and drafting stages of the process.

Drafting

A few drafting considerations are particularly relevant to this project. Let's begin at the beginning—with your summary. Remember that readers must be able to distinguish between your source's ideas and your own. This is an important consideration in a paper that alternates, as this one will, between the two. You are the author of the paper, so your readers will assume that you are responsible for any comments appearing in the paper, *unless they are informed otherwise*. You inform them otherwise by attributing your source. Begin your summary, for example, by mentioning the author and the title of the essay you are writing about.

What about the length of your summary? You can determine the appropriate length of your summary by considering its purpose. You need to summarize because your readers are unfamiliar with the original text (and even if they were familiar, it would be a good idea to remind them of the thesis). But your purpose is to evaluate, not to summarize. If your summary is too long, the purpose of the paper will become confusing; if it is too short, it won't serve its purpose at all. Your summary should be just long enough to enable the reader to follow the rest of the argument.

Logically, in a 500- to 700-word evaluation the summary should take a single paragraph. In most cases, this will mean you can use the source's thesis and key ideas, suitably drafted to make a coherent paragraph. Because readers need a basic knowledge of the source in order to appreciate an evaluation, you ought not to omit any of the key ideas. One way to proceed is to ask yourself: *What do my readers have to know before they can understand the rest of my paper?* The answer will suggest what you need to tell your readers immediately. In future papers you will often find that asking this question can help generate material for the part of the paper writers have the most trouble drafting, the opening paragraph.

Your first paragraph, then, will certainly include the introduction of the source and a summary. Many writers find it helpful to focus an evaluation by stating their thesis at the end of the summary. You might, however, find that you can explain your main point only after you have explained your specific criticisms. In the following evaluation of "All Animals Are Equal" we have included a thesis statement at the end of the first paragraph.

Your summary and thesis statement will prepare the ground for your evaluation. In the rest of the drafting process you can follow your outline, filling in the details from the notes you've taken. As in any writing assignment, keep your thesis clearly in mind as you draft and make sure every detail contributes to it. Let's take a look at a complete evaluation of Peter Singer's essay:

   An Evaluation of Peter Singer's "All Animals Are Equal"

      In his essay "All Animals Are Equal" Peter Singer
   asserts that the principle of equality refers to the equal
   treatment of any creature capable of suffering, a
   principle violated by meat eating and animal
   experimentation. Singer defines the principle of equality
   as a moral ideal underlying the way we should treat
   others, not as a description of actual equality of
   ability. The principle applies to all creatures capable
   of suffering (and/or enjoyment or happiness); therefore,
   all such creatures, humans and nonhumans alike, ought to
   be treated equally. We should strive to eliminate the two
   human practices that violate this principle: meat eating
   and animal experimentation. Singer's essay is an original
   and stimulating contribution to the debate over animal
   rights, but it is flawed by his failure to prove the idea
   that all beings capable of suffering deserve equal
   treatment.

      Singer's argument is both complex and original. He is
   aware that before we can discuss the relationship between
   humans and animals we must clarify our understanding of
   the basic principle of equality that most of us believe
   in. We would hardly expect that principle to be applicable
   to animals, but Singer's definition of equality as a moral

ideal and not a fact makes us consider the whole question from a fresh perspective. It is safe to say that no reader is ever likely to think of the relationship between humans and animals without considering Singer's essay.

But there is a flaw in Singer's argument, and that is his failure to prove that the capacity for suffering is the criterion for the equal treatment of all creatures. Singer is undoubtedly right when he asserts that "the capacity for suffering and enjoying things is a pre-requisite for having [moral] interests at all." But all this means is that any creature who has moral interests must be capable of suffering; it does not mean that any creature capable of suffering necessarily has moral interests. Nevertheless, this is the only proof Singer offers that all suffering should be counted equally.

The failure to prove that the capacity for suffering is the sole criterion for equal treatment is a serious flaw because it is the pivotal idea in Singer's argument. We may agree with his definition of the principle of equality, but if he does not prove its applicability to animals, his criticism of meat eating and animal experimentation lacks theoretical support. Furthermore, the failure to prove this point undermines Singer's equation of speciesism and racism. If the capacity for suffering, which humans and animals share, is not the basis for equal treatment, then discriminatory treatment against animals cannot be equated with racial discrimination.

The fact that Singer does not prove one of his key ideas does not, however, invalidate his argument. There may yet be some basis for believing that humans and animals should be treated equally. Singer's essay might inspire readers who agree with him to consider why they believe animals are entitled to equal treatment. This thought-provoking article is bound to make its readers reconsider their basic views about the relationship between humans and animals.

A few final comments about this evaluation might prove useful in general:

- Although Singer uses the word *animal* to refer to both humans and nonhumans, we have not followed this usage in our own comments because we are not fond of such expressions as *nonhuman animals*. Remember that you are writing *your* evaluation in your own style.
- In paragraph 3 we have added a word ("moral") to one of Singer's quotations in order to clarify his meaning. It is permissible to add your own words to a

quotation *if you put your own words in brackets*, thereby indicating material not found in the original quotation. You should always read over the quotations in your paper from the point of view of a reader unfamiliar with the source; sometimes a quotation taken out of its context can be confusing. A bracketed intrusion within a quotation is rarely necessary, but when it is, you should provide the most succinct clarification, as we have in this case.

Other Critique Projects

The general purpose of a critique is to clarify a source by commenting upon it. Although evaluation may be the most common way of discussing a source, it is by no means the only one. Any aspect of a source that you find interesting can serve as the basis for a critique. Here are some other critiques you can write about a source:

1. Analyze the assumptions in an argument. We have discussed the significance of uncovering assumptions in evaluating an essay. But uncovering an author's assumptions, particularly if they are not readily apparent, is itself a way of clarifying an argument. Your purpose in this case is not to evaluate those assumptions, but to uncover them and explain their significance in the essay.

One way to discover assumptions is by contrast. Although you will be writing about only one essay in this project, you can use a pair of contrasting essays to clarify their authors' assumptions. Take, for example, the essays by Henry Salt and Joseph Rickaby in the anthology on animal rights. Two authors, writing at roughly the same time, arrive at entirely different conclusions about our duties to animals. How do you account for this difference? What are the authors' different assumptions that explain, at least in part, their different conclusions? You might focus your analysis on the following comment: To Salt "the joyfulness of life" is a relevant issue in discussing the treatment of animals; to Rickaby it is not. What is the relevant issue to Rickaby? What does this distinction tell you about their assumptions about the source of morality, the nature of animals, and the relationship between human beings and animals?

You may also wish to compare the assumptions that Peter Singer and Michael Levin make in their essays. Both authors connect speciesism to racism and sexism, but for very different purposes. Focus on this distinction as a means of uncovering the political assumptions behind each essay. Then concentrate on explaining the assumptions underlying one of the essays.

You can use this method with contrasting essays on any subject. Put the sources side by side and try to isolate the fundamental reasons for the disagreement, the different assumptions the authors make in their arguments.

2. Clarify a complex idea in an essay. If you come across an important or complex idea the author does not fully explain (a fairly common experience in reading), you may wish to stop and think about it until it is clear to you. If you wrote up the results of your thinking, the purpose of your critique would be to help your readers understand the issue.

To prewrite such a critique, examine the central concepts an author uses in developing the argument. If a concept is not entirely clear on a first reading, it might make a good subject for a critique. You could, for example, explain what Michael Fox means by the concept of "autonomy" or by a "moral community." Other possibilities might include James Rachels's distinction between "being alive" and "having a life" and Michael Levin's use of the concept "legal ascriptivism." Taken out of context, these concepts might seem formidable. But you may find that reading them in context, thinking about them, and discussing them will enable you to enlighten your readers about an important idea in the essay.

3. *Exemplify the ideas in an essay.* In this case your purpose is to show how the ideas in an essay relate to your own and your readers' experience. You are clarifying an essay by fleshing out its ideas and explaining their relevance. Any descriptive essay is a particularly good subject for such a critique. Read, for example, Thomas Benson's descriptions of the various stereotypes humans inflict on animals and see if you can find examples familiar to your readers. Several essays in the other anthologies (for example, "Psychographics: Advertising Discovers the World According to VALS") are basically descriptive and would be suitable for this kind of critique.

4. *Explain the practical implications of an essay.* This critique answers this question: What would happen if the author's ideas were put into practice? Any essay whose author proposes a course of action would be suitable for such a critique. Tom Regan, for example, concludes by making specific proposals. Your critique could examine the practical consequences of these proposals.

Follow the same procedure in writing one of these critiques that you would in writing an evaluation. Read the source closely, taking notes on the ideas you find interesting. Devise a specific thesis and a clear structure to communicate the point you wish to make in your critique. Finally, go back to your source for any additional material you might need.

REVISING

As in other projects, the following list includes basic questions you can ask as soon as you have finished drafting, and the next list provides activities designed to elicit helpful comments from a reader, preferably a reader unfamiliar with the essay you are writing about.

The final group of activities is specifically related to this project. These activities are designed to draw comment on the requirements of a critique. Your reader will check to make sure that you have integrated your source successfully into your own argument and that the point of your critique is clear. These standards do not emphasize the summarizing process as strongly as the standards for writing summaries and simple syntheses do. Although it is preferable that these comments come from readers familiar with your sources, it is possible for someone who has not read the original source to provide helpful commentary.

QUESTIONS FOR YOURSELF

1. Is the thesis statement identifiable, clear, and accurate?
2. Are there clear transitions to each key idea?
3. Is there sufficient detail for each key idea?
4. Is there a clear transition at the beginning of each paragraph?
5. Are there any sentences that sound awkward as you read them?
6. Are there any mechanical or typographical errors?

GENERAL WRITING STANDARDS

Directions: Read the summary carefully and comment as indicated below. If you find any of these operations difficult or impossible to perform, indicate that fact to the writer and, if possible, try to explain the source of the difficulty.

1. Identify the thesis statement of the essay and rewrite it in your own words.
2. List each of the key ideas that develop the thesis.
3. Point out any places where supporting detail is needed.
4. Point out any details without a clear purpose.
5. Indicate any places where the opening of a paragraph does not follow clearly from the conclusion of the previous one.
6. Indicate any sentences that are confusing.

STANDARDS FOR A CRITIQUE

Directions: Read the summary carefully and comment as indicated below.

1. Indicate any places in the essay where more information from the original source would be helpful.
2. Reread all the sections in which the writer deals with specific material from the source. Indicate any places where there is confusion about the responsibility for a certain idea or fact.
3. If the essay is an evaluation, indicate which specific criteria for evaluation the writer is using (see the list of questions on page 63).
4. If the essay is an evaluation, list the specific strengths and weaknesses the writer finds in the original source.
5. If the essay is not an evaluation, indicate the overall purpose of the critique (see the list of critique projects on page 72).
6. If the essay is not an evaluation, indicate the specific point the writer is making about the original source.

COMPARING SOURCES

IN THIS PROJECT YOU WILL BE ENGAGING IN A familiar activity: comparison. Without thinking about it we constantly make informal comparisons: we compare movies, friends, courses, teachers, vacation spots, goals, cars, clothes, and political candidates. Every day we read and hear comparisons: articles and reports comparing diets, interior decorating plans, educational activities for children, varieties of Chinese cooking, or quarterbacking styles. Comparisons also underlie the daily planning and decision making of scientists, social planners, architects, corporate managers, and even judges, who compare cases to find legal precedents.

We can get a good idea of how useful comparison is by looking at some of the purposes it serves. Often we make comparisons purely for the inherent satisfaction of recognizing interesting similarities and differences. People have always delighted, for example, in comparisons from history, particularly involving events in the lives of famous people. After President Kennedy's assassination one writer caught the public's attention with a comparison of Presidents Lincoln and Kennedy: Lincoln had a secretary named Kennedy; Kennedy had a secretary named Lincoln. Both Lincoln and Kennedy were succeeded by Southerners named Johnson. Lincoln was shot in the head from behind in a theater by a man who was later himself killed in a warehouse; Kennedy was shot in the head from behind by a man in a warehouse, a man who was later captured in a theater. Although the list went on at some length, the comparisons didn't support any significant thesis; they merely appealed to the basic human interest in discovering such surprising similarities.

In another context we are called upon to use comparisons to prove that we understand a subject. This is, of course, the purpose of the "compare and contrast" examination question. Often teachers want to know if their students can do more than parrot information memorized from class notes and textbooks, if they really understand the knowledge they have acquired. One way to find out is to ask students to analyze two ideas and point out their similarities and differences.

Comparisons are an inevitable part of decision making. We may compare new car models, colleges, or career goals to decide what car to buy, what college to attend, or what career to pursue. Decision making in business and government is always based on a comparison of alternatives. A corporation, for example, will compare proposed sites before deciding where to locate a new plant.

If we stop and look back at what we have said about comparison so far, two things become apparent. One is that comparison is a *rhetorical mode*—a method of arranging material for an audience: Kennedy did this; Lincoln did that. Comparison is, in this sense, a means of communication, a way of making a thesis and its supporting evidence easy for a reader to follow. But, perhaps more important, comparison is also a *learning technique*. Whenever we compare two things (in this project, sources), we create the possibility of learning something new, of gaining an insight into a subject as a result of our thinking about the similarities and differences we have found and what they tell us. Naturally, if all we do is list points of comparison as an exercise in ingenuity, we are not likely to learn anything significant. But if we go beyond listing, if we ask ourselves what our comparison proves, we often discover something new about the subject.

This project stresses that aspect of comparison. Your purpose in the project is to compare two sources on the subject of the younger generation as depicted at different time periods. You may select both of these sources from the readings in the anthology, seeing what you can learn from a comparison of, say, the "Flaming Youth" of the Roaring Twenties and the "Silent Generation" of the 1950s. You have another option: You are (or have been) a member of a younger generation; you may compare your own generation to one of the younger generations you will read about. In that case, the source of information about your own generation will be your experiences, observations, and judgments. One of the anthology readings will furnish the information needed for the other half of the comparison.

Suggested Assignment

For this project assume that you are in a college course in which you've been discussing the distinctive personality each new generation seems to develop for itself. You have talked about Baby Boomers, the Swing Generation, the Beat Generation, and the Silent Generation, among others. During the discussion you've been asked to consider how different you might have been if you had grown up in another era. In other words, your instructor is trying to demonstrate that each generation reflects its own time period. To help you understand this point, your instructor has asked you to compare two generations of young people, noting the dominant characteristics of each and drawing some conclusion from the similarities and differences you observe. You may, if you wish, use your own generation in the comparison.

Overview

■

In this project your sources will serve as the subject of an original composition in which you use one of the most common and fruitful learning techniques—comparison. After reading two essays on the same subject, you will compare them to make a point (a thesis) of your own. Alternatively, you may use your own experience as one source, comparing it with a published essay. A comparison of sources is similar to a simple synthesis, but while the latter is halfway between a summary and an original composition, the comparison is entirely original. The point you make about the two sources you compare is the central concern, and the purpose of any summarizing you do is to help your reader grasp that point.

This project is set up to emphasize comparison as a means of learning something new about a subject and communicating that knowledge to a reader. The first part of the prewriting section stresses the ways of discovering specific points of similarity and difference between your sources. In the rest of the prewriting section you will learn to use those points in an original essay. The drafting section describes the two patterns writers most often use in organizing comparisons: the whole-to-whole and part-to-part patterns. The drafting section also includes some effective ways to open and close an essay.

The Process of Writing a Comparison

1. Read the sources you are considering carefully, noting the dominant impression and specific characteristics of each source.
2. Write down the specific similarities and differences between your sources.
3. Devise a thesis for your comparison.
4. Return to your sources for a final check.
5. Draft the body of your comparison, using the whole-to-whole or part-to-part pattern.
6. Draft the opening and closing paragraphs of your comparison.
7. Revise your summary, using the activities that are described in the project.

■

Prewriting

Reading for Understanding

The subject of the suggested readings in this project is the younger generation of Americans at various times in the twentieth century. Every age, of course, has something called a younger generation, and the older generation of the day is always busy trying to characterize it. Popular magazines, scholarly journals, books, and newspapers have always been filled with descriptions of the young and with speculations about why the older generation should or should not worry about them and their future. Sometimes these efforts result in colorful labels (the Swing Generation, the Silent Generation, Hippies, Yuppies) intended to capture the essential nature of the whole group or some highly visible segments of it.

The essays suggested for this project differ from previous essays in one major respect: they are descriptive rather than argumentative. Instead of proving a specific point, these essays describe the younger generation of the day. A description, however, is not a random collection of details. A well-focused description has a thesis, although it is not usually as formal as the thesis of an argumentative essay. *The thesis of a descriptive essay is the dominant impression the description conveys to the reader about its subject.* Each author in the anthology points out some common characteristics that create an overall impression about the younger generation. This overall impression, the generalization that unifies the description, is the thesis of each essay. And, like the thesis of an argumentative essay, that generalization may be stated directly or implied. As you read each essay, look for the author's overall impression of the younger generation (the thesis of the essay) and for the specific characteristics with which the author backs up that impression.

Let's focus on the 1951 *Time* magazine article "The Younger Generation," which is rich in information about what has been called the Silent Generation. In fact, this article exemplifies many of the attitudes of the '50s, including the sexist stereotyping typical of the period. It will help us illustrate how to read a rather long descriptive essay for its thesis and key ideas.

■

THE YOUNGER GENERATION

The Editors of Time

Is it possible to paint a portrait of an entire generation? Each generation has a million faces and a million voices. What the voices say is not necessarily what the generation believes, and what it believes is not necessarily what it will act on. Its motives and desires are often hidden. It is a medley of good and evil, promise and threat, hope and despair. Like a straggling army, it has no clear beginning or end. And yet each generation has some features that are more significant than others; each has a quality as distinctive as a man's accent, each makes a statement to the future, each leaves behind a picture of itself.

What of today's youth? Some are smoking marijuana; some are dying in Korea. Some are going to college with their wives; some are making $400 a week in television. Some are sure they will be blown to bits by the atom bomb. Some pray. Some are raising the highest towers and running the fastest machines in the world. Some wear blue jeans; some wear Dior gowns. Some want to vote the straight Republican ticket. Some want to fly to the moon.

Time's correspondents across the U.S. have tried to find out about this younger generation by talking to young people, and to their teachers and guardians. What do the young think, believe, and read? Who are their heroes? What are their ambitions? How do they see themselves and their time? These are some of the questions *Time*'s correspondents asked; the masses of answers—plus the correspondents' interpretation—contain many clashing shades of opinion, but nevertheless reveal a remarkably clear area of agreement on the state of the nation's youth.

Youth today is waiting for the hand of fate to fall on its shoulders, meanwhile working fairly hard and saying almost nothing. The most startling fact about the younger generation is its silence. With some rare exceptions, youth is nowhere near the rostrum. By comparison with the Flaming Youth of their fathers and mothers, today's younger generation is a still, small flame. It does not issue manifestoes, make speeches or carry posters. It has been called the "Silent Generation." But what does the silence mean? What, if anything, does it hide? Or are youth's elders merely hard of hearing?

They Are Grave and Fatalistic

Listen to their voices, in a college bull session:

"I think the draft has all the fellows upset. . . . They can't start figuring in high school or even in college what they want to do. . . . First thing you know, Uncle Sam has tagged them off base."

"The boys are upset about the Korean business because they can't tell from one day to the next what they are going to be doing, going into the Army or what."

"Sure, the boys say, 'What's the use? I'd just get started and whammo, I'm gone.'"

"It's hard to get married when you don't know what the deal is. Maybe your husband is off to Korea or somewhere, and there you are."

"With maybe a baby on the way."

"It's better to get a job and wait."

"That's the worst part."

The "Korean business"—and a lot of other business that may follow—is the dominant fact in the life of today's youth. "I observe that you share the prevailing mood of the hour," Yale's President A. Whitney Griswold told his graduating class last June, "which in your case consists of bargains privately struck with fate—on fate's terms." The hand of fate has been on the U.S. with special gravity since World War I; it has disturbed the lives of America's youth since the '30s, through depression and war. The fear of depression has receded; the fear of war remains. Those who have been to war and face recall, and those who face the draft at the end of their schooling, know that they may have to fight before they are much older.

But youth is taking its upsetting uncertainties with extraordinary calm. When the U.S. began to realize how deeply it had committed itself in Korea, youngsters of draft age had a bad case of jitters; but all reports agree that they have since settled down to studying or working for as long as they can. The majority seem to think that war with Russia is inevitable sooner or later, but they feel that they will survive it. Reports *Time*'s Los Angeles Bureau: "Today's youth does have some fear of the atomic age. But he does not feel as though he is living on the brink of disaster, nor does he flick on the radio (as was done in the '40s) and expect his life to be changed drastically by the news of the moment. There is a feeling that the world is in a ten-round bout, and that there will be no quick or easy knock-out."

Hardly anyone wants to go into the Army; there is little enthusiasm for the military life, no enthusiasm for war. Youngsters do not talk like heroes; they admit freely that they will try to stay out of the draft as long as they can. But there is none of the systematized and sentimentalized antiwar feeling of the '20s. Pacifism has been almost nonexistent since World War II; so are Oxford Oaths. Some observers regard this as a sign of youth's passivity. But, as a student at Harvard puts it: "When a fellow gets his draft notice in February and keeps on working and planning till June, instead of boozing up every night and having a succession of farewell parties, he has made a very difficult, positive decision. Most make that decision today."

They Are Conventional and Gregarious

On a sunny Sunday not long ago, Sociology Professor Carr B. Lavell of George Washington University took one of his students on a fishing trip. He is a brilliant student, president of his class, a big man on campus, evidently with a bright future in his chosen field, medicine. In the bracing air, professor and student had a quiet talk. Why had he gone into medicine? asked the professor. Answer: medicine looked lucrative. What did he want to do as a doctor? Get into the specialty that offered biggest fees. Did he think that a doctor owed some special service to the community? Probably not. "I am just like anyone else," said the student. "I just want to prepare myself so that I can get the most out of it for me. I hope to make a lot of money in a hurry. I'd like to retire in about ten years and do the things I really want to do." And what are those? "Oh," said the brilliant student, "fishing, traveling, taking it easy."

Then they stopped talking, because the student had a nibble.

Perhaps more than any of its predecessors, this generation wants a good, secure job. This does not mean that it specifically fears a depression, as some aging New Dealers claim. The feeling is widespread that anyone who wants to work can find a decent job; the facts confirm that feeling (and the starting pay is better than ever). But youth's ambitions have shrunk. Few youngsters today want to mine diamonds in South Africa, ranch in Paraguay, climb Mount Everest, find a cure for cancer, sail around the world, or build an industrial empire. Some would like to own a small, independent business, but most want a good job with a big firm, and with it, a kind of suburban idyll.

An official of the placement bureau at Stanford University finds college graduates mostly interested in big companies—and choosy about which ones they will work for. "Half the time a guy will turn down a good job because he has to work in the city [meaning San Francisco.] They all figure there's no future in being holed up in a little apartment in town for ten years or getting up at 6 in the morning to commute to work and then not getting home until after dark. So they all want to work down on the peninsula where they can have a little house in the country and play golf or tennis and live the good life."

Says one youthful observer who still likes his dreams bigger: "This generation suffers from lack of worlds to conquer. Its fathers, in a sense, did too well. Sure, there are slums left—but another Federal housing project can clean up the worst. Most of the fights in labor have simmered down to arguments around the bargaining table. Would-be heroes find themselves padded from harm—and hope—like lunatics in a cell. In business, the tax structure, social security and pension plans promise to soften the blow of depression or personal misfortune—and forbid the building of new empires. In science there is the great corporation (or the Government) glad to furnish the expensive machinery now necessary for the smallest advance—and to give its name, or that of its group research boss, to the new process, while plowing back the profits. A man goes bounding, with no visible bruises, among the pads of an overorganized society."

The facts are that the U.S. is a highly organized society, must be, and will get more rather than less organized; that the big corporation is here to stay (and is a progressive instrument of U.S. capitalism). What is discouraging to some observers is not so much that youth has accepted life within the well-padded structure of organized society and big corporations, but that it seems to have relatively little ambition to do any of society's organizing. What is even more disturbing is youth's certainty that Government will take care of it—a feeling which continues despite a good deal of political distrust of Government. Reports *Time*'s Seattle Bureau: "The Pacific Northwest is only yesterday removed from the frontier, but the 'root, hog, or die' spirit has almost disappeared. Into its place has moved a curious dependence on the biggest new employer—Government. A 28-year-old aerodynamics specialist at Boeing says: 'I hope to work toward an income of $500 or $600 a month, after taxes. You know, only on a sliding scale for inflation. I'd just like to net $600, and then my family would always be O.K. You start earning more than that, and it's taxed away from you, so what the hell.'"

Says a 26-year-old promotion manager in Dallas: "Sure, I'd like to do something on my own, but I want to get well fixed first—make plenty of money and then maybe start some innovations."

This cautious desire to be "well fixed" and a little more has many causes: the war; the lingering shock of the Big Depression (which this younger generation felt or heard about in its childhood); and the hard-to-kill belief (still expounded in some college economics courses) that the frontiers of the U.S. economy have been reached.

There is also the feeling that it is neither desirable nor practical to do things that are different from what the next fellow is doing. Said a girl in Minneapolis: "The individual is almost dead today, but the young people are unaware of it. They think of themselves as individuals, but really they are not. They are parts of groups. They are unhappy outside of a group. When they are alone, they are bored with themselves. There is a tendency now to date in foursomes, or sixsomes. Very few dates are just a boy and girl together. They have to be with a crowd. These kids in my group think of themselves as individuals, but actually it is as if you took a tube of toothpaste and squeezed out a number of little distinct blobs on a piece of paper. Each blob would be distinct—separated in space—but each blob would be the same."

The Girls Want a Career—and Marriage

At the corner of Manhattan's Lexington Avenue and 63rd Street stands a 23-story building populated entirely by women, in which men are not permitted above the first floor. This does not mean that its inhabitants are not interested in men. The Barbizon hotel for women is considered a good, respectable address for out-of-town girls who have come to make a name for themselves in New York. In the small green lobby, through which moves a constant stream of eager young women carrying an air of determination, one aspiring young actress from Providence, R.I. said: "The men in New York are all the same. They're out for what they can get. I have a boy friend from home who comes to see me about every three weeks. He's a real hometown boy, all-American, clean-cut. He wouldn't speak the same language as these New York men. They're all trying to be big shots. I go out with them when he isn't here, but since I've been in New York I haven't met one man I can call a friend. . . . I won't marry until I've convinced myself that I've gotten everything I can out of acting. Back home, everybody's a home-body, wants to raise big families. I'm not ready for that yet. If I married this fellow from home, I know I'd have to quit acting right away. He just wouldn't stand for it. I don't think I could do both, anyway."

American young women are, in many ways, the generation's most serious problem: they are emotional D.P.s [displaced persons]. The granddaughters of the suffragettes, the daughters of the cigarette-and-short-skirt crusaders, they were raised to believe in woman's emancipation and equality with man. Large numbers of them feel that a home and children alone would be a fate worse than death, and they invade the big cities in search of a career. They ride crowded subways on which men, enjoying equality, do not offer them seats. They compete with men in industry and the arts; and keep up with them, Martini for Martini, at the cocktail parties.

There is every evidence that women have not been made happy by their ascent to power. They are dressed to kill in femininity. The bosom is back; hair is longer again; office telephones echo with more cooing voices than St. Mark's Square at pigeon-feeding time. The career girl is not ready to admit that all she wants is to get married; but she has generally retreated from the brassy advance post of complete flat-chested emancipation, to the position that she would like, if possible, to have marriage and a career, both. In the cities, she usually lives with a roommate (for respectability and lower rent) in a small apartment, fitted with chintz slipcovers, middlebrow poetry and a well-equipped kitchenette. Rare and fortunate is the bachelor who has not been invited to a "real, home-cooked dinner," to be eaten off a shaky bridge table, by a young woman who during the daytime is a space buyer or a dentist's assistant.

Says a Minneapolis priest: "The young American male is increasingly bewildered and confused by the aggressive, coarse, dominant attitudes and behavior of his women. I believe it is one of the most serious social traits of our time—and one that is certain to have most serious social consequences."

Their Morals Are Confused

The shrieking blonde ripped the big tackle's shirt from his shoulder and Charlestoned off through the crowded room, fan-dancing with a ragged sleeve. In her wake, shirts fell in shreds on the floor, until half the male guests roared around bare to the waist. Shouts and laughs rose above the full-volume records from *Gentlemen Prefer Blondes*. The party, celebrating the departure of a University of Texas coed who had flunked out, had begun in midafternoon some three hours earlier. In one corner, four tipsily serious coeds tried to revive a passed-out couple with more salty dog (a mixture of gin, grapefruit juice and salt). About 10 p.m., a brunette bounded on to the coffee table, in a limited striptease. At 2 a.m., when the party broke up, one carload of youngsters decided to take off on a two-day drive into Mexico (they got there all right, and sent back picture postcards to the folks).

The younger generation can still raise hell. The significant thing is not that it does, but how it goes about doing it. Most of today's youngsters never seem to lose their heads; even when they let themselves go, an alarm clock seems to be ticking away at the back of their minds; it goes off sooner or later, and sends them back to school, to work, or to war. They are almost discreet about their indiscretions, largely because (unlike their parents) they no longer want or need to shock their elders. The generation has "won its latchkey." It sees no point or fun in yelling for freedom to do as it pleases, because generally no one keeps it from doing as it pleases. It is not rebellious—either against convention or instruction, the state or fate, Pop or Mom. Toward its parents, it exhibits an indulgent tolerance. As one young New Yorker put it with a shrug: "Why insult the folks?"

The younger generation seems to drink less. "There is nothing glorious or inglorious any more about getting stewed," says one college professor. Whether youth is more or less promiscuous than it used to be is a matter of disagreement. Fact is that it is less showy about sex. Whatever its immoralities, it commits them on the whole because it enjoys them, and not because it wants to demonstrate against Victorian conventions or shock Babbitt. In that sense, it is far less childish than its parents were. As a whole, it is more sober and conservative, but in individual cases, *e.g.*, the recent dope scandals, it makes Flaming Youth look like amateurs.

24 The younger generation is tolerant of almost anything, shocked by little. Young men who may personally think sex experience before marriage wrong are perfectly tolerant toward anyone who disagrees. Gay blades report that young women, when they turn down what is still known as a "pass," do so apologetically, as if they were exhibiting a social shortcoming like an inability to mambo. The girl's usual excuse: "I am *so* sorry, it's just the way I was brought up."

25 A paratrooper at Fort Bragg told a *Time* correspondent that he had nothing against pre-marital sex: "Before the property is yours, I don't see why anybody can't use it." But a buddy added: "After marriage, some guy taking my wife would be like taking my car and putting on a few extra miles. It might improve through use, but I like to drive my own." A student editor at Emory University states a widespread phenomenon among American women: "There are few who have any strong moral feelings against having affairs. They may be afraid. But if they kid themselves into falling madly in love, then it's all right."

26 Considering that its parents gave the younger generation few standards, few ideals, and an education increasingly specialized, *i.e.*, without cultural breadth, youth's morals have turned out far better than anyone had a right to hope. Almost of itself, it has picked up the right instincts from an American tradition older than its parents: it wants to marry, have children, found homes, and if necessary, defend them.

They Expect Disappointment

27 Intellectually, today's young people already seem a bit stodgy. Their adventures of the mind are apt to be mild and safe, and their literature too often runs to querulous and self-protective introspection, or voices a pale, orthodox liberalism that seems more second-hand than second nature. On the whole, the young writer today is a better craftsman than the beginner of the '20s. Novelists like Truman Capote, William Styron and Frederick Buechner are precocious technicians, but their books have the air of suspecting that life is long on treachery, short on rewards. What some critics took for healthy revolt in James Jones's *From Here to Eternity* was really a massively reiterated gripe against life. But Jones is not the only young writer to wallow in a world of seemingly private resentments. Most of his fellow writers suffer from what has become their occupational disease: belief that disappointment is life's only certainty. The young writers of the '20s were at least original enough to create personal styles. Today the young writer's flair sometimes turns out to be nothing more than a byproduct of his neuroses.

28 Educators across the U.S. complain that young people seem to have no militant beliefs. They do not speak out for anything. Professors who used to enjoy

baiting students by outrageously praising child labor or damning Shelley now find that they cannot get a rise out of the docile note-takers in their classes. The only two issues about which the younger generation seem to get worked up are race relations and world government; but neither of these issues rouses anything approaching an absorbing faith.

Many students and teachers blame this lack of conviction on fear—the fear of being tagged "subversive." Today's generation, either through fear, passivity or conviction, is ready to conform.

Marxism seems dead among the U.S. young; belief in democracy is strong but inarticulate. The one new movement that has begun in the younger generation is what Poet-Professor Peter Viereck calls the revolt against revolt—an attempt to give youth a conservative credo to stand up against the bankrupt but lingering political radicalism of the '20s and '30s.

One of the most significant facts about the younger generation is that increasingly larger numbers of it are seeking their faith not in secular panaceas but in God.

They Want a Faith

Near the Mount Zion Methodist Church just outside Atlanta, on Highway 41, a onetime barbecue pit has been turned into a Bible classroom. One evening recently, eleven disciples watched Robert L. West go over and flip off the light switch. "It's kinda dark in here without the lights," apologized West, as he walked behind the crepe-wrapped white cross now lighted up by two candles, "but I would ask you to look upon this symbol—perhaps the greatest in the world."

West, an 18-year-old son of a paper-plant foreman, who quit Georgia Tech because he found nothing but "hard, cold facts of engineering," looked like a churchly Frank Sinatra, in his Paisley bow tie and purple jacket, his big ears enlarged in shadows on the blackboard behind him. He read his long text (*Luke 9:20-27:* ". . . *And be rejected of the elders* . . ."), and in a businesslike manner proceeded to expound it—the job of youth today. "Unless we, the young people of today, go to work, we're going to lose in the end. This symbol has stood for thousands of years. To us today it stands for sacrifice, the greatest sacrifice that He made for us. . . . And it stands for a call, a call to work. . . . But we're afraid to take on something if we have to call on God to do it. We're ready to do anything if we can handle it with our own two hands. But we're afraid to try something too big, a job that takes God's help. . . . This place should be filled. . . . As we stand in front of this cross, lift up our shamed hearts to the work that is ours. . . ."

The younger generation is looking for a faith. The fact that it has not found one—that it isn't even sure where to look—is less significant than the fact that it feels the need to believe.

The generation of the '20s was devoutly iconoclastic. It put on (in the words of T.S. Eliot) "the black cap of *je m'en foutisme*"—of I-don't-give-a-damn-ism. It discovered with a mixture of horror and delight that it was living in a brand-new age, the 20th Century, and it decided to burn all the old cultural furniture. This huge fire, while it caused incalculable damage, cast a sharp, new light across U.S. civilization—and encouraged the younger generation of that day to do a whooping war dance around it. Gertrude Stein christened it the "lost generation," but she may have spoken too soon.

To some, it seems that today's youth is really the lost generation. It does not believe that the wrecking of the '20s made sense, and even if it did, the '20s did not leave many values to wreck. Present-day youth has no living heroes and few villains. Said a professor of sociology: "We spend all our time debunking. We have no heroes, so how can you expect the young people to have any? We destroy them all. We've even done it in the sports world. Kids today feel they have to go all the way back to Babe Ruth to find a hero. Today the only heroes are the ones whom they can't destroy. And who are those? The heroes of the comic strips."

There is no formal religious revival among the young. God, for most young Americans, is still a vaguely comforting thought, theology a waste of time, and denominations beside the point. To large numbers of them, religion is still merely an ethical code. But God (whoever or whatever they understand by that word) has once more become a factor in the younger generation's thoughts. The old argument of religion *v.* science is subsiding; a system which does not make room for both makes little sense to today's younger generation. It is no longer shockingly unfashionable to discuss God.

Church attendance among the young has increased, partly because churches have made strong efforts to win new followers through social and sport activities. But there is an unquestioned spiritual need at work, too. Says Dean Robert Strozier of the University of Chicago: "They all have a conscience." Says Historian Viereck: "They believe they believe; they do not necessarily believe. Not many of today's young people say they have seen God, but they think everybody needs to see God."

They Will Serve

Beside a Quonset hut at Kimpo Airport, more than 100 tired, unshaven infantrymen lolled in the dust, waiting patiently for planes that would take them to Tokyo. For some, Tokyo meant the first leg of the trip home. For others it meant only a temporary break in the dirty business of war. They had no yarns to swap, no desire to learn any more than they already knew about war. From a few groups came the click of dice, and the only voices audible over the distant roar of engines were the urgent pleas of crapshooters. At one group, a Red Cross worker paused to chat with a sergeant who had spent 13 months in Korea. Said the sergeant: "For 15 months the guys have been running up and down these mountains getting their fannies full of lead. And what have we proved? I got news for you, Mister: the next time this boy fights to defend anybody's country, it'll damn well be his own." But an officer said: "You seen Seoul? Well, I'd hate for that to be Decatur, Illinois."

The soldier in the combat zone is too preoccupied to do much thinking about the underlying reasons for his presence in Korea. He is concerned almost exclusively with personal problems, and the personal problem that overshadows all others is the problem of getting home. To justify his personal yearning to go home, he often subscribes to the thesis that Korea was a mistake (once back in the States, he will probably change his mind). In Korea, he does his job—because of his sense of duty to his country and his buddies, and because of his pride in his country and himself.

G.I. Joe's younger brother is better informed and educated, much better trained, and less sorry for himself. Mauldin[1] cartoons today would not find the popularity they did in World War II. The AWOL rate is down, even the use of profanity has fallen off (at least in Stateside camps). "Little Joe" gripes about his officers, distrusts politics and government (it is universally believed that "Harry Vaughan[2] can transfer any man"). He does not go in for heroics, or believe in them. He is short on ideals, lacks self-reliance, is for personal security at any price. He singularly lacks flame. In spite of this, he makes a good, efficient soldier—relying on superior firepower.

The best thing that can be said for American youth, in or out of uniform, is that it has learned that it must try to make the best of a bad and difficult job, whether that job is life, war, or both. The generation which has been called the oldest young generation in the world has achieved a certain maturity.

Young people do not feel cheated. And they do not blame anyone. Before this generation, "they" were always to blame. It was a standard prewar feeling that "they" had let them down. But this generation puts the blame on life as a whole, not on parents, politicians, cartels, etc. The fact of this world is war, uncertainty, the need for work, courage, sacrifice. Nobody likes that fact. But youth does not blame that fact on its parents dropping the ball. In real life, youth seems to know, people always drop the ball. Youth today has little cynicism, because it never hoped for much.

Says a *Time* correspondent in Boston: "Young people most bitterly know the frightful cost of living to keep peace in the world, and they willingly submit to the cost, not from want of spirit, but from a knowledge that it is the best thing to do. You cannot say of them, 'Youth Will Be Served,' because the phrase suggests a voracious striking out from security, wealth and stability. The best you can say for this younger generation is, 'Youth Will Serve.'"

■

We learn from the introductory paragraphs that *Time*'s correspondents found "many clashing shades of opinion" but nevertheless decided there was "a remarkably clear area of agreement on the state of the nation's youth." The paragraphs that follow are grouped into seven sections, each headed with a statement characterizing the younger generation of 1951:

---

[1] *Editor's note:* Bill Mauldin's cartoons during World War II popularized "G.I. Joe."
[2] *Editor's note:* An advisor and political friend of President Harry S. Truman, whose administration was often accused of political cronyism.

1. They are grave and fatalistic.
2. They are conventional and gregarious.
3. The girls want a career—and marriage.
4. Their morals are confused.
5. They expect disappointment.
6. They want a faith.
7. They will serve.

It is clear from the fourth paragraph of the introduction, however, that the writers intend to do more than present a random catalog of characteristics of the young. They open the paragraph with a general impression of the younger generation: It awaits its destiny, working hard and keeping its mouth shut. Then they focus on "the most startling fact about the younger generation"—its silence—and conclude the paragraph by asking what this silence means. In the final section of the essay the writers explain this silence as the stoic maturity of a generation that "has learned that it must try to make the best of a bad and difficult job, whether that job is life, war, or both." We might now restate this overall impression in our own words: *The younger generation has developed a stoic maturity as its response to the harsh realities of life and war.*

When we read the rest of the essay with this thesis in mind, we discover that each of the seven sections proves or explains the silent endurance of the younger generation. Rather than simply copying out *Time*'s brief descriptions, we rewrite them as follows, making sure the relationship between each characteristic and the overall impression conveyed by the description is clear:

1. Young people calmly, fatalistically wait either to be drafted for the Korean War or to witness the beginning of war with the Soviet Union.
2. Young people don't seek ambitious challenges in jobs but want to be like others, taking comfort in the security of big corporations and big government.
3. Young women are not happy with their new status in the business world, and young men are confused by women's behavior.
4. Young people are relaxed, uncertain, and broadly tolerant in their moral behavior, feeling no need for rebellion.
5. Young people expect disappointment from the world and seek conformity rather than great militant causes aimed at changing the world.
6. Young people lack strong religious beliefs and are a "lost generation," without heroes, finding little value in orthodox religion.
7. Young people do their job in the Korean War out of duty and pride, without ideals and heroism, and without blaming anyone.

Reading a description for its thesis and structure, then, is essentially a matter of identifying the overall impression left by the description and analyzing the specific characteristics on which that impression is based.

At this point, if you are using your own generation in your comparison, you will need to "read" your experience as you did your written source. If you don't have a single impression of your own generation, you might begin by listing some of its characteristics, trying to be as inclusive as possible. What are the career interests of your contemporaries? What moral values do they profess? How do those values relate to their actual behavior? How do they feel about religion? Politics? What are their favorite forms of entertainment? Who are their heroes? Do they seem idealistic or materialistic to you? How do they feel about school? What do they think about the future?

When you are through, review your list to see what dominant impression stands out. In other words, what do you think is most important for someone to realize about your generation? If you were writing a magazine article about your own generation, what would it be called? What would its thesis be? Answering that last question should help you focus on your dominant impression of your own generation.

Finding Similarities and Differences

Once you've grasped the thesis and key ideas of each of your sources (written or otherwise), you can begin to compare them. The first step is to clarify the relationship between your sources by placing them side by side and noting precisely how they agree and how they disagree. The following methods should prove helpful.

- If you already have a strong perception of the relationship between the two descriptions, you can begin with that perception and work back to specifics. In fact, that is the way we normally make comparisons: rather than itemizing similarities and differences, we form a general impression of the relationship between the items we are comparing. Begin by writing down your impression of the relationship between the two generations and then try to identify their specific similarities and differences.
- Any discussion of the younger generation invariably includes several topics in common. Writers seldom miss an opportunity, for example, to describe the social—and particularly the moral—values of the young. In fact, the areas of discussion are fairly predictable: the career interests of young people, their school life, religious and political attitudes, forms of entertainment, and attitudes toward the future.

  That being the case, one way to begin is to write down the broad areas of interest you've noticed and go back to the sources to take notes on specific comments. You can place your notes side by side on a page by dividing a sheet of paper into two columns, one for each generation. Then list the characteristics of each generation in parallel columns, grouping them under broad headings like "Moral Values" and "Entertainment." You will then have an index to the two generations, which will enable you to see their similarities and differences at a glance.
- You may wish to begin by listing the dominant impression and specific characteristics of the younger generation described in one essay. Then you

can go through a second essay or the list you generated for your own generation, keeping the first list in mind and noting any similarities or differences you come across.

The method you use for establishing specific points of comparison is not important. What counts is that you move beyond understanding each source in isolation and establish the connections between them.

Listing points of comparison enables you to grasp the specific similarities and differences between your sources. Now is the time to consider the point of the comparison—the thesis of your paper.

What Can Be Compared? Before discussing the thesis, we should consider an important question: What can be reasonably compared in a paper? Some subjects for comparison are fairly obvious—say, two presidents of the United States or two regions of the country. With greater effort we could even compare very dissimilar things—portable radios and marsupials, for example. After all, both emit sounds, can be a source of amusement, are smaller than railroad boxcars, and are frequently found in pouches. If you stop and think about it, any two things in the world are similar in some ways, different in others, and hence comparable.

It is not the nature of a subject, then, that determines whether or not it is comparable to another subject; there is no truth to the old cliché that you can't compare apples and oranges. You *can* compare an apple and an orange as long as you limit yourself to *comparable aspects* of the fruits. You could easily compare the color of an apple and the color of an orange or the taste of an apple and the taste of an orange. What you can't compare is the color of an apple and the taste of an orange. Those are simply not comparable aspects of the objects.

In comparing descriptions, this distinction is less obvious but equally important. The essays in the suggested readings are all descriptions of the younger generation written by members of the older generation. You might assume that any comparison of these essays would be drawn between two younger generations—their behavior, values, hopes, and so on. But as you read the essays, you will see that they also provide another kind of evidence, evidence about the attitude of the older generation toward the younger generation. In fact, any description can be taken in two ways: as a description of the subject itself or as a description of the attitude the person doing the describing has toward the subject. There are, then, at least two different aspects of descriptive writing, and confusing them could be as illogical as comparing the color of an apple and the taste of an orange.

You can clarify this distinction by asking one question about each of your sources: Is this description evidence about the *nature* of the younger generation or about the *attitude* of the older generation? Let's examine two selections, taken from sources similar to the ones you will be using in this project, and see how we would go about answering that question. The first consists of two passages from a 1984 article entitled "Are Today's Young a Disillusioned Generation?":

> Many of the nation's young people are convinced that, despite the economy's steady climb out of recession, they will get only a tiny share of the spreading prosperity—or nothing at all. . . .
>
> Large numbers of them, even with college degrees, are hard pressed to find jobs of any kind, let alone good jobs. Median income for their age group has plunged from that of just a decade ago. To them, housing prices seem outlandish, and new cars are out of sight for all but the affluent.

What does this description best lend itself to—drawing a conclusion about the younger generation or about the attitudes of the older generation? The kind of material we have here—description of the feelings of the young, of their hopes and prospects—would best serve as evidence about the younger generation itself. If that is not clear, compare that selection to the following passages from a 1976 article, "Silence on Campus," written by a college professor:

> A lot of Americans—most of them I suspect—are relieved at the quiet that has fallen over our college campuses after the chaos of the Vietnam war years. I am not. . . .
>
> Last year, a high-school civics teacher wrote to a Los Angeles newspaper: "The majority of young people with whom I come in contact was never enthralled by politics. Now, they seem to be sinking even deeper into an apolitical torpor. Watergate taught them not to care. I see the silent majority growing in my classroom every school day. It is a frightening development." . . .
>
> [Speaking in a school a little more than a decade after the assassination of President Kennedy] it came as a shock to me that many in my audience were no more inspired by John Kennedy than by Grover Cleveland or Millard Fillmore. A few minutes into my talk, and I realized that we weren't even on the same planet.

In this passage the emphasis is less on the students themselves than on the author's dislike for their silence, as seen in the author's own comments and the comments of the quoted teacher. In the previous passage the emphasis was on the nature of the younger generation itself, with little editorial commentary from the writer. Although the two passages are descriptions of the younger generation, they are not really comparable because one is evidence about the younger generation itself and the other is evidence about the attitude of the writer.

As you look at your own sources, decide what the material in each could best be used to explain. In most sources you will undoubtedly find material about both the younger generation and the attitudes of the older generation, but you will probably also find that one kind of evidence dominates. Before you work on devising a thesis, decide which aspect of the subject you wish to comment about, to ensure that you consistently match your thesis and your evidence.

What's Worth Comparing? So far we have considered the question What *can* be compared? Now we turn to a related question: What's *worth* comparing?

Consider the following as a thesis for your paper: *There are a number of distinct similarities and differences between these two generations.* This statement meets all the technical requirements of a thesis: it is a complete sentence making a coherent comment that unifies various aspects of a subject. But is it a worthwhile observation? As we have said, there are similarities and differences between any two things in the universe. But you want to point out something significant to your readers. If the "somewhat alike/somewhat different" formula comes to mind, you'll know it's time to look for ways to focus your observation. A worthwhile thesis is more than a statement of the existence of similarities and differences—it is your insight about the *significance* of those similarities and differences. For example, you may have discovered that a generation of the past shares many of the hopes and anxieties of your own generation, even though the two generations live in vastly different worlds. Your thesis is what you have learned from your comparison.

Drawing a Conclusion from Your Comparison You already may have come up with a thesis about the two generations you are comparing, but if you haven't, here are a few ways to proceed:

- Examine the dominant impression you have of each generation. A clear difference or similarity between them could serve as a thesis for your comparison. Your thesis would be a generalization about the overall relationship between the two generations. You might point out, for example, that *as a whole, younger generation A was content with the status quo, whereas younger generation B often seemed to rebel against authority.*

    Notice that this thesis works because there is a coherent relationship between these two generations. The thesis of each description points to the relationship between the younger generation and authority, and hence the two are comparable. But that may not be the case with the sources you are comparing. Consider, for example, the following relationship: *Younger generation A was concerned about the future, but younger generation B often seemed to rebel against authority.* What exactly is the relationship between these two generations? Are they essentially similar or different? Since concern for the future is not comparable to attitudes toward authority, there is no way to answer the question.
- If you do not find a coherent generalization by examining the dominant impression left by each generation, you may find it helpful to compare specific characteristics. Remember that your sources are bound to have

discussed a number of common areas (moral values, political attitudes, education). If you examine these areas, you may find that the two generations are similar in most ways but different in one crucial respect. In this case your thesis would point out the characteristic that distinguishes the two generations. The opposite pattern, that the two generations are different in most ways but similar in one respect, is also workable. Then your thesis would point out a surprising similarity between two very different generations. For example, you might point out that *although younger generation A and younger generation B differed greatly in their attitudes toward authority, they shared an optimistic attitude about the future.*

These are merely two of the patterns you may find when you review your material. The important thing is to ask yourself what you have *learned* from comparing your sources.

Before drafting your comparison, however, you should return to your sources. Rereading them with your thesis in mind will give you the opportunity to check the accuracy of your information and add material you overlooked the first time through.

Drafting

Choosing an Effective Structure

Two structures, or organizational patterns, are suitable for comparisons, each with its particular strengths. In the *whole-to-whole pattern* you focus your reader's attention on one whole side of the comparison, and after finishing that side, turn to the other, developing it completely. For example, you would begin with a complete description of generation A, make all of your comments about it, and then move on to a complete description of generation B.

Using the other structure, called the *part-to-part pattern*, you take up each individual point of comparison and present both sides before moving on to the next point. In a paper on the younger generation, you might begin with a discussion of the moral values of younger generation A and then compare them to the moral values of younger generation B. You would then move on to some other point of comparison (forms of entertainment, for example). In this pattern the large comparison is built up from a number of smaller comparisons.

We can use the Lincoln/Kennedy comparison we mentioned earlier to demonstrate the uses of these two structures. Let's assume that the thesis we want to prove about the rather odd list of Lincoln/Kennedy similarities is something like this: *It is amazing how much alike the Lincoln and Kennedy assassinations were.* What happens if we try the whole-to-whole approach—all the details about Lincoln first, followed by all the details about Kennedy? We would record for our readers that Lincoln had a secretary named Kennedy, that Lincoln was shot in the head from behind, that he was shot in a theater, that his assassin was killed in a warehouse, that he was succeeded by a Southerner named Johnson, and so on through our list. Then we would start all over with the Kennedy side of the story: Kennedy had a secretary named Lincoln; Kennedy was shot in the head from behind; his assassin was located in a warehouse; his assassin was captured in a theater, and so on. Would such a structure make our point effectively? Hardly, because by the time readers got to the Kennedy side of the "amazing similarities," they would have forgotten the Lincoln side. Our thesis in this case depends upon the reader's recognition of a series of individual comparisons. If, however, we place the similarities side by side in a part-to-part arrangement, readers will readily grasp that thesis: Lincoln had a secretary named Kennedy; Kennedy had a secretary named Lincoln, and so on. Each individual coincidence will contribute to the development of the thesis.

But let's examine another Lincoln/Kennedy example, this time assuming we have read biographical sketches that include these two descriptions:

LINCOLN
The face of Abraham Lincoln, for all its familiarity, is one of the more unusual faces in American history books. Every part of it seems to be doing something different. The eyebrows bush out in one direction, the hair pops up in another. The prominent nose is red-tipped and lopsided. The ears project whimsically. The bottom lip droops at one corner. From a deep, leathery crease in the right cheek, a mole unexpectedly blossoms. He always seemed to be moving. Even when sitting, he shifted constantly in his chair—first slouching with one leg hung over an arm of the chair, then sitting upright with his long legs jackknifing at sharp angles. The President had a large reserve of anecdotes and jokes, including some "risqué" ones, which he enjoyed telling. Occasionally, however, his humor seemed inopportune, grating those who were attempting to discuss serious matters.

KENNEDY
An observer once remarked rather drily that Kennedy supporters seemed more often to ask for the man's autograph than for his credo. Indeed, with his youthful good looks, his model wife, and the backing of the powerful Kennedy clan, John Kennedy managed to dazzle much of the nation. His style continued to be a national obsession. A Kennedy cult, which had grown during his campaign to enormous proportions, revolved around the President's personal traits and preferences. Everyone seemed to have the Kennedy bug; White House staffers even found themselves unconsciously imitating the President's gestures, pushing (sometimes nonexistent) locks of hair from their foreheads or chopping the air with their hands to emphasize a point.

From this and other readings on the subject, we might conclude that *Lincoln was the type of man whose appearance and manner were often unappealing, whereas Kennedy was the type whose appearance and manner usually attracted people.* Which structure would be appropriate for an essay with this thesis? If we tried a part-to-part structure, we would produce a very fragmented picture: Abraham Lincoln's face was rather odd; John Kennedy's was handsome, vital, and young. Lincoln's humor at times seemed inappropriate and grating; Kennedy's was sophisticated and restrained. Lincoln's body was awkward and gangling; Kennedy's was well-proportioned and athletic. A series of isolated comparisons of presidential noses, ears, smiles, and accents is not the most appropriate way to make our point to readers. Since it is the overall contrast between Lincoln and Kennedy that counts in this case, we will best prove our thesis by describing all the details that contribute to our dominant impression of Lincoln and then, in the same manner, detailing our dominant impression of Kennedy. Whole-to-whole is clearly the more appropriate structure for this thesis.

Although your own paper is on a different subject, your choice of structure raises similar questions, which can be answered only by a careful examination of your thesis. Let us say, for example, that your thesis is a generalization derived from your comparison: *Younger generation A seemed content with the status quo, whereas younger generation B seemed deeply concerned about the state of the world.* Since the basis of this thesis is a broad overall relationship between generations, it is best suited to the broadbrush effect of the whole-to-whole approach. Let's take a look at this pattern:

Whole-to-Whole Pattern

Thesis: *Younger generation A seemed content with the status quo, whereas younger generation B seemed deeply concerned about the state of the world.*
   (A) Younger generation A
      1. Young people favor escapist entertainment.
      2. Young people are relatively unconcerned about politics.
      3. Young people share their parents' moral values.
   (B) Younger generation B
      1. Young people worry about the state of the economy.
      2. Young people are deeply involved in political reform.
      3. Many young people reassess their moral values.

The whole-to-whole pattern enables you to present two strong, contrasting descriptions, the most effective way to communicate this thesis. If you find the whole-to-whole pattern appropriate for your own thesis, here are some points to consider:

- In this pattern you are comparing two large-scale descriptions. Nevertheless, the two descriptions will have a number of points of comparison in

common. In the outline above, for example, both descriptions cover attitudes toward politics and attitudes toward morality. You can help maintain clarity in your essay by keeping these points of comparison in the same order in both halves.
- The whole-to-whole pattern needs a major transition between its two parts. You can help your readers by including a sentence or two making clear that you have completed the discussion of your first source and are taking up your second source. Such a transition can also help clarify the relationship between the two descriptions. For example, we might begin our description of younger generation B, "The generally passive and carefree attitude of younger generation A contrasts sharply with the attitude of younger generation B."
- In the second half of your comparison, it is helpful to remind readers of the relationship between the characteristics of the two generations. A transitional sentence will do the trick: "Unlike younger generation A, younger generation B was deeply involved in politics."

Suppose, however, that your research had led to the following thesis: *Although younger generation A and younger generation B differed greatly in their attitudes toward authority, they shared an optimistic attitude toward the future.* The basis of this thesis is the contrast between a number of specific differences and one surprising similarity. Such a thesis is far better suited to the part-to-part pattern. Let's see how we would use such a structure to develop this thesis.

Part-to-Part Pattern

Thesis: *Although younger generation A and younger generation B differed greatly in their attitudes toward authority, they shared an optimistic attitude toward the future.*

A. Different attitudes toward the older generation
   1. Younger generation A tended to accept adult authority.
   2. Younger generation B was often rebellious.
B. Different degrees of political involvement
   1. Younger generation A was relatively unconcerned with politics.
   2. Younger generation B was actively involved in politics.
C. Different attitudes toward moral values
   1. Younger generation A accepted traditional moral values.
   2. Younger generation B experimented with alternative value systems.
D. Similar attitude toward the future
   1. Younger generation A expected good times to continue.
   2. Younger generation B believed it could make the world a better place.

If individual points of comparison are what count in your thesis, then the part-to-part pattern, which highlights specific similarities and differences, will be appropriate. In using this pattern, keep the following considerations in mind:

- In switching back and forth between your sources, you must be particularly careful about perspective, informing your readers whenever you switch from one source to another.
- The thesis of a comparison essay can easily get lost in the intricacies of the part-to-part structure. Readers must understand that the purpose of your essay is to make a point, not merely to itemize similarities and differences. The best way to make sure that readers don't miss the forest for the trees is to use transitions to inform them of the direction your argument is taking. You might, for example, begin your draft of section D in this example as follows: "Although the two generations expressed different attitudes about the existing state of the world, they shared a similar optimism about the future."

A Functional Opening

One of the most common observations about the writing process is that the opening is the most difficult part of an essay to write. It is relatively easy to draft the body of a paper, the section that develops the thesis, because the thesis provides guidance at every step. The thesis helps determine the content and placement of each paragraph in the paper. Of course, the writer must make many decisions at each point (a thesis does not *predetermine* the structure and content of an essay), but the decisions are made within the context of one basic question: What will best communicate the thesis? That question helps the writer decide what to say and when to say it.

In this project, for example, the whole-to-whole or part-to-part pattern will form the body of your comparison paper. But opening your paper with your first key idea might be abrupt and confusing; it is usually necessary to orient readers to a subject before formally developing an argument. The "opening" of an essay is by definition the material that precedes the formal development of the argument. Therefore, the thesis does not yet provide any guidance. As a result, at the beginning of an essay, many writers feel that they must invent something out of thin air, and they often settle for some well-worn, rather uninteresting opening devices: the generalization, the dictionary definition, the reference to the beginning of time, and others.

The way to avoid wheel spinning at the beginning of a paper is to consider the *function* of the opening paragraph. To emphasize that point in this book, we generally avoid the word *introduction*, which seems to imply a detachable section unrelated to the rest of the paper. In fact, the question "How can I introduce my subject?" provides very little guidance for writers. Instead, try asking, "What do my readers have to know to follow my argument?" The answer will provide a *functional opening*, one that serves a purpose in the overall structure of your paper.

Before looking at ways to open your comparison essay, we can make a few general comments about the kinds of information you can use at the start of any paper. The opening usually identifies the subject under discussion. The amount of information needed to identify the subject depends on the probable familiarity of your readers with the subject. If the subject is well known to your readers, a brief identification, perhaps merely a name (say, Elvis Presley—everyone knows him), is sufficient. But if the subject is likely to be unfamiliar to your readers, you may need a longer description. The description should be functional—just enough to give readers the information they need to understand the rest of the paper. Once you've identified the subject, you will probably wish to make clear how you are going to treat it—describing, attacking, defending, analyzing, comparing, or evaluating it.

The opening of an essay is often the place for a thesis statement. Placing such a statement at the beginning of a paper gives readers a clear sense of the direction your paper will take. But don't automatically assume that your opening paragraph must have a thesis statement. You may decide, for example, that you want to lead your readers through your evidence first, allowing them to see precisely how you reached your conclusion. If that is the case, opening with a simple statement of the questions you are trying to answer will provide a sense of direction. For an example, see the opening paragraph of "College Youth Attitudes Today" (p. 290).

Let's look specifically at some possibilities for the opening paragraph of your paper comparing younger generations:

- *Clarify the subject matter for your readers.* Identify the two generations you are comparing. Let readers know whether you are comparing the characteristics of two younger generations or the attitudes of two older generations.
- *Identify your sources.* When you first refer to a generation, also refer briefly to the source of your information. If you are using your own generation, tell your readers that you are basing your description on your own experiences and observations.
- *Include your thesis statement* if you have chosen to make it part of the opening paragraph. If you have decided to place it elsewhere, you might want to end your first paragraph by stating your purpose (to compare the two generations).

The Sense of an Ending

For reasons very similar to those discussed in connection with openings, most writers find the ending the second most difficult part of a paper to draft. At the end of an essay, writers wish to give their readers the sense of an ending and leave them with something to think about. At times the conclusion of a paper almost writes itself; the final key idea or the thesis statement often forms an effective conclusion. Sometimes an ingenious ending comes easily, but more often writers have to sit back and think about how to end their essays.

The first possibility that comes to mind is often a summary, and in a long article or a book a summary may be valuable to readers. But a summarizing paragraph at the end of a 500- to 700-word essay is unnecessary. On the other hand, the final paragraph is not the place to introduce new information; it is the conclusion of one essay, not the beginning of another. The most effective conclusion is often one that places the argument of the essay in a broader perspective by putting a somewhat different slant on the subject. Notice, for example, how Rolf A. Weil uses his final paragraph to speculate about the future (p. 292). Here are some other possibilities for this project:

- If you have compared two past generations, you can bring your subject up to date by briefly comparing the two generations of the past with your own generation. Do young people today seem similar to the youth of one of the earlier generations? Different from either? A combination of the two? Of course, you will be able to do little more than suggest the relationship. After all, the purpose of a conclusion is not to develop an argument but to leave readers with something to think about.
- Most of your paper will deal with *how* the two generations differ or *how* they are similar. If you have formed an opinion about *why* this is so, you can explain it in your conclusion. A conclusion is often the place to reexamine the information and ideas in the body of a paper and speculate about their significance.

Revising

The revising activities in this project begin with a group of questions designed to help you review your work before you pass it along to others for their responses. The two groups of activities that follow are intended to generate responses on general writing standards and on the standards particularly relevant to a comparison.

QUESTIONS FOR YOURSELF

1. Is the thesis statement identifiable and clear?
2. Are there clear transitions to each key idea?
3. Is each key idea developed in sufficient detail?
4. Is there a clear transition at the beginning of each paragraph?
5. Are there any sentences that sound awkward as you read them?
6. Are there any mechanical or typographical errors?

GENERAL WRITING STANDARDS

Directions: Read the draft carefully and comment as indicated. If you find any of these operations difficult or impossible to perform, indicate that fact to the writer and, if possible, try to explain the source of the difficulty.

1. Identify the thesis statement of the essay and rewrite it in your own words.
2. List each of the key ideas that develop the thesis.
3. Point out any places where supporting detail is needed.
4. Point out any details without a clear purpose.
5. Indicate any places where the opening of a paragraph does not clearly follow from the conclusion of the previous one.
6. Indicate any sentences that are confusing.

STANDARDS FOR A COMPARISON

Directions: Read the comparison carefully and comment as indicated.

1. Write down the thesis of the comparison.
2. Write down the individual points of comparison.
3. Check each specific point of comparison and indicate any place the writer does not clearly show what the point has to do with proving the thesis.
4. Explain why the structure (whole-to-whole or part-to-part) is or is not appropriate for proving the thesis.

Building on a Source

When we read actively, our attention is divided between the ideas in our source and our own reactions to what we are reading; we carry on a kind of conversation with the author of a book or essay. If we think of the writing assignments in this book as a series of conversations with sources, then this project is the most complex conversation thus far. Although you have hardly been passive in your responses to texts up to now, this assignment requires you to take a more active role, to go beyond the text itself and explore the relationship between your reading and your own thinking on a subject. Consequently, in this project we are going to suggest a few strategies that might help you relate the essays in the anthology to your own ideas.

Suggested Assignment

For this project assume that you've been considering writing an essay for a column called "Your Turn" in your school newspaper. In this column each week the paper runs an essay of about 700 words on a topic of general interest to readers. You've been reading a number of essays about advertising, and they've stimulated your thinking. You'd like to build on your reading by presenting your original ideas on that topic in a way that will entertain and enlighten readers. Keep in mind that your audience is almost exclusively the college students, faculty, and staff who are likely to read the paper. You want to catch their attention with an interesting angle on the subject and keep them reading with a clearly developed argument.

Overview

■

Two projects in this book stress the skill of summarizing—a single source (the summary) and multiple sources (the simple synthesis). In two other projects the emphasis shifts to the use of sources—singular (the critique) and multiple (the comparison)—as a subject for writing. In the remaining projects we turn to a third use of sources: as a means of stimulating original thinking about a subject. We will consider the use of both single and multiple sources. This project explains the use of a source as a point of departure for original thinking, while "Using Sources as Evidence" explains how to use a variety of primary sources to devise and communicate a thesis.

The primary concern of this project is the movement from reading to thinking and writing, from taking in somebody else's views to formulating an original idea. The prewriting section suggests a number of strategies designed to help you relate the essays you read to your own ideas. These strategies include disagreeing with an idea, extending an idea, and exemplifying an idea. The drafting section focuses on the way writers use paragraphs to clarify the structure of an argument.

The Process of Building on a Source

1. Discover the thesis and key ideas of your source.
2. Using one of the strategies described in the prewriting section of the project, take notes on your responses to stimulating ideas in the source.
3. Devise a thesis and generate a structure for your original essay.
4. Draft your essay, paying particular attention to the unity, coherence, and development of your paragraphs.
5. Revise your original essay, using the activities described in the project.

■

Prewriting

Reading for Understanding

The subject of the suggested essays for this project is the impact of advertising, a topic on which we are all, in a sense, authorities. The essays in the anthology address a broad range of issues, including, for example, political advertising, the advertising of potentially harmful products, and the means advertisers use to identify and influence consumers. The prewriting technique in this project is similar to that in the critique project: you will carefully read a source and then consider your own responses to the ideas you have encountered.

The following essay, "Boob Rubes: The New Ruralism in TV Advertising," by Jeff Greenfield is our example in this project. Greenfield discusses the trend (in 1975) toward idealizing the rural way of life in television commercials. As you read the essay, you might consider its relevance to the present day.

■

BOOB RUBES: THE NEW RURALISM IN TV ADVERTISING

Jeff Greenfield

Jeff Greenfield (b. 1943), educated at the University of Wisconsin and Yale University, has written extensively on politics and the media.

The city has been a repellent attraction throughout America's history; and the more we have become urbanized, the more our culture has reflected a longing for our abandoned rural past. Jefferson said of Americans that "when they get piled upon one another, in large cities, as in Europe, they will become corrupt as in Europe"; Benjamin Rush described cities as "pestilential to the morals, the health, and the liberties of man."

In the popular culture of our century, Norman Rockwell has given us visions of corner drugstores, village doctors, old swimming holes, and lazy summer evenings on the front porch. Hollywood gave us Indiana moonlit nights and heroes abandoning the wicked city for the farm, in dreams shaped by expatriate New Yorkers whose view of rural America was fashioned through the bar car window of the Super Chief. And today, *nostalgie pour le boue* [nostalgia for the soil] is alive and flourishing, in the hands of the advertising community.

To watch television commercials over the last year or so is to find a yearning for the countryside that rivals that of the new Cambodian government. Home, hearth, fresh air are now as pervasive a cliché of the advertising community as were rock music and freeze frames a few years ago.

A country singer warbles that she "was raised on country sunshine" as a fetching young woman returns to her dusty farm home, to be refreshed by family, boyfriend, and Coca-Cola. Not to be outdone, RC Cola presents a young farm woman, barefoot and blue-jean clad, singing that her new country life "is the way to put down roots." Euell Gibbons touts Post's Grape-Nuts at family reunions, which feature breakfasts set out on huge tables in the yard of a country home. A folksinger on behalf of Country Morning (a new breakfast cereal) urges us to "let Country Morning take you back again," as a wholesome-looking family devours the stuff along a huge table in the yard of a country home. Come dinner time, and another apple-cheeked family is seen wolfing down Kentucky Fried Chicken at a huge table in the yard of a country home. Families snap Polaroid pictures of each other while gamboling in the yard of a country home. And Chevrolet helps bring ma and pa out to the country, where their children have set up housekeeping, finding once again the joys of gathering around the huge table in the yard of. . . . I assume you are getting the gist of the idea.

These advertisements represent a significant shift in Madison Avenue's judgment of what our yearnings are. In the postwar years, and all through the 1950s, the suburban home was the (assumed) centerpiece of our national longing. Whether it was an Oldsmobile ad with a family cruising along a Sylvan Acres development, or an ad in *The Saturday Evening Post* featuring a new ultramodern kitchen in the ranch house, the suburban sensibility was the critical frame of reference in our advertising. To a generation crowded into barracks, apartments, and war plants, the dream of a private house and a plot of land was dominant.

In the 1960s, much of the advertising message attempted to cash in on the new political sensibility. A feminine napkin advertisement promised "Freedom Now," a straight-faced echo of the civil-rights movement. A Jergens lotion ad flashed the peace sign. And the sensual explosion of rock music, bright lights, quick cuts, and cross-dissolves crowded into the world of television commercials.

Now, however, there is a new mood in the land—at least if we measure the national mood by the calculations wedged beneath the sell-lines of advertising. What these ads tell us is that the yearning for simplicity, for quiet, for roots, for a "real home" has once again surfaced, and with a vengeance. Few Americans are actually willing to throw over the traces of their lives and go back to the hamlets and villages their fathers and grandfathers deserted, but—if the massive research studies are to be believed—the disaffection with the living patterns of an overcrowded city or atomized suburb has made America's old way of living once again a compelling frame of reference for selling a product.

The evocation of this regional, isolated, slow-paced America on prime-time commercial television is awesome in its level of irony. (One of the gratifying things about the mass media is that there is no need to root out the ironies; they run up to you and slam you in the face.) It probably goes without saying, in the first place, that any product with enough resources to use prime-time network television is an unambiguous product of homogenized America. Kentucky Fried Chicken is not dispensed by some white-suited colonel with a skillet; it is a nationwide operation which—according to Colonel Sanders—has moved substantially away from the quality controls he instituted (enough so that Sanders, who sold his interest some time ago, is now contemplating the opening of a rival chain). Country Morning may come in an old-fashioned-looking cereal box with old-fashioned graphics, but the product is made in a plant, not in a shed out behind the mill.

What is more ironic is that mass packaging and promotion itself helped to uproot so much of the stable, tranquil America in the first place. It was the power first of nationally circulated magazines, then of network radio, that made nationally distributed products feasible, and which, among other pressures, wiped out small, regional producers of everything from cigarettes to beer. It is the nationally franchised fast food chains—McDonald's, Kentucky Fried Chicken, Hardee's—that are replacing the individually owned food shops all over the country. It was the reach of new fashions, new clothes, new ideas into the most remote hamlets of the country that helped trigger the wave of migration from rural to urban America in the first place, and the incredible power of television which continues today to eat away at the barriers of distance that once kept our humor, our politics, our customs distinctly regional.

The uprooting of Americans—either from their homelands or their homes within our heartland—is the central story of the twentieth century. And, almost as if in expiation, those institutions which helped in that uprooting seem most determined to celebrate what they destroyed. Just before the start of the Indianapolis 500 auto race, for example, a celebrity is introduced to the crowd of 300,000 people to sing "Back Home Again, in Indiana." Yet this race is essentially a celebration of the machine that gave hundreds of thousands of Americans the freedom to leave their homes in Indiana (or Kansas, or Dakota). This is what is happening on our television screens as night after night the products of an urbanized, industrialized, homogenized land are sold with the visual symbols of what that society has helped eradicate.

Perhaps the ultimate irony is to be found in the audience intended to be reached by these paeans to the Older, Better, Country Way of Life. I recently completed a major study of the National Broadcasting Company's new television season. With unanimity, the network executives emphasized the demographic influence on their programming. Advertisers, they said, do not want just numbers; they want "the demographics"—the economically desirable audiences, who are young-to-middle-aged, relatively well educated, and urbanized. The older, rural audiences are considered so undesirable that television shows—like *Lawrence Welk* and *Gunsmoke*—are canceled *despite* their ratings, because they do not deliver the right audience to the advertiser.

Thus we face the ultimate joke—the advertising community is busily engaged in appealing to a big city-suburban cosmopolitan audience by evoking for them a way of life whose current adherents are considered undesirable. They are selling products which have contributed mightily to the collapse of that way of life; and they are using a medium which, more than any other force, put the last coffin nails in that way of life.

See you at the corn-husking.

■

As you've probably noticed, Greenfield's thesis is conveniently summarized at the end of the essay (paragraph 12). We might summarize the argument briefly as follows: *It is ironic that television advertisements featuring idealized rural images glorify the way of life they helped to destroy.* Since the concept of irony is crucial to Greenfield's essay, we ought to make sure we understand precisely what it is.

Irony comes into existence when we perceive a jarring discrepancy in a remark or situation. For a situation to be ironic, we must understand it on two levels that we perceive as directly contradictory to one another. In the case of television advertising, the same phenomenon—rural images used to sell products—implies two contradictory facts, namely the *glorification* of "country values" (in the content of the commercials) and the *destruction* of those very values (by the mass production of the products being sold in the commercials). Greenfield's essay centers on his perception of this ironic situation, which suggests a topic for a writing project— the ironies of modern life. Can we find any similarly ironic situations in American life? Are there any other instances of a phenomenon that we glorify with our words and reject with our actions? Try substituting other values for the rural values Greenfield discusses and see if they fit the pattern.

Although Greenfield's essay is primarily concerned with pointing out these ironies, his argument includes the historical context of the phenomenon he is discussing. Hence, he begins with an overview of the glorification of the rural image in American culture and places television advertising in that context. The following are the key ideas of the essay:

1. The country has had a wholesome image in American culture since the eighteenth century.
2. In the 1950s and 1960s, suburbia and "the new political sensibility" (that is, the radical counterculture of the late 1960s) dominated advertising, but yearning for the country has resurfaced in recent advertisements, largely as a result of widespread dissatisfaction with urban and suburban life.
3. This glorification of rural life is ironic in three ways: (A) Although country images are glorified, those who live in rural areas are generally disdained. (B) The products advertised helped destroy the very way of life they celebrate. (C) The advertising medium—television—"put the last coffin nails in that way of life."

Devising a Thesis

Sometimes your immediate response to an essay will provide a thesis for your paper. More often, however, it takes some time and effort to come up with a workable idea for a writing project. If an idea for a paper doesn't come to you while reading, you'll want to think systematically about your reactions to what you have read. In the following pages you'll find three strategies that should help stimulate your thought on the relationship between the sources you have read and your own ideas and experiences.

Disagreeing We don't usually think of a negative response to an idea as a stimulus to thought. On the contrary, disagreement is most often presented to us as unthinking rejection of the other person's opinion. The classic example, the prototype, is the commercial in which two opposing parties attempt to shout each other down on the question of a beer's primary virtue ("Less filling!" "Tastes great!"). Occasionally we are all tempted to respond similarly to reading matter we disagree with, perhaps slamming a book down in disgust and muttering about its author's incompetence.

But disagreement can also be a stimulus to thought. In the conversation we carry on with a source we are reading, our disagreement may induce us to explain *why* we hold a different opinion. The need to explain our position forces us to reconsider our own ideas, to test their validity, and to communicate them to another person in what is often called a "position paper." Your reading of an essay may have already suggested such a project. If you disagree with the essay's thesis or one of its key ideas, you have a ready-made purpose for writing. Disagreement is most likely in the case of controversial essays (such as "Ads and Addictions: Booze on the Tube" in the advertising anthology). Descriptive essays (such as "Psychographics," which describes the way advertisers classify and appeal to different audiences) are less likely to provoke disagreement and might be more useful for another purpose.

If a position paper does not suggest itself after you have read an essay, do not give up on the possibility. So far, after all, you have been concentrating on understanding the thesis and key ideas of the essay. Your primary focus has been on the essay itself. A second reading, in which you consciously compare the author's assertions to your own views, might very well yield different results. It is not necessary to disagree with the thesis of the essay or even with one of its key assertions. You may find a point you would like to refute in an essay you generally agree with. When you find such a point, your attempt to correct the idea, to state the case accurately, will motivate you to reconsider and communicate your own views on the subject.

Let's return to Greenfield's essay and assume that we agree with its thesis, that we find it a fresh and convincing discussion of a phenomenon even more common now than it was when the essay was first published in 1975. Suppose that as we reread the essay we stop after the first sentence:

> The city has been a repellent attraction throughout America's history; and the more we have become urbanized, the more our culture has reflected a longing for our abandoned rural past.

Having read the entire essay, we are aware that these assertions provide the context of Greenfield's argument. Greenfield believes that in American culture the city represents corruption, whereas the country tends to stand for home, hearth, and fresh air. We might ask ourselves the following question: Do the author's assertions correspond to our own experiences? If we answer this question in the negative, we have a possible subject and a way to approach that subject—a writing strategy.

The next step is to identify the precise nature of our disagreement by asking how our views differ from Greenfield's. Here is one response to that question:

> Jeff Greenfield seems to believe that American culture always stereotypes the city as "wicked" and the country as "pure." But the opposite is just as often the case: the city is often seen as an exciting place full of dynamic people on the way up, and the country as a cultural desert full of ignorant hayseeds.

Identifying the precise nature of our disagreement with Greenfield will provide a thesis:

Thesis 1: Our culture tends to stereotype the city as an exciting place full of dynamic people and the country as a cultural desert full of ignorant hayseeds.

Or we could expand the thesis to include Greenfield's perspective:

Thesis 2: American culture has contradictory feelings about the city, depicting it at different times [at the same time?] as a den of iniquity and as an exciting place full of dynamic people on the way up.

Thesis 3: American culture has contradictory feelings about the country, depicting it at different times [at the same time?] as a clean and wholesome environment and as a cultural desert full of ignorant hayseeds.

We would now be ready to generate a series of ideas to communicate the thesis. We would probably develop thesis 1 as a series of examples drawn from different areas of American culture. (Even though Greenfield has confined himself to television, there is no reason for us to limit ourselves in this way. Greenfield's perception was merely the starting point of our paper, which has now taken on a life of its own.) Theses 2 and 3 would be based on a comparison, either in whole-to-whole or part-to-part form.

Notice one other service a source can provide for a writer. Since Greenfield's essay inspired our own thoughts, it can be mentioned in the opening of our draft. We can get over the first-paragraph hurdle by citing Greenfield's opinion and then expressing our modification of it in the form of a thesis statement:

> In his essay "Boob Rubes: The New Ruralism in TV Advertising," Jeff Greenfield contrasts the image of the city and the country in American culture. Greenfield notes that since the eighteenth century the city has been depicted as a den of iniquity and the country as a wholesome environment. Although it is impossible to deny that these stereotypes have a powerful hold on the American mind, it is also true that the opposite images are equally common. In our culture the city is often depicted as an exciting place full of dynamic people on the way up, and the country as a cultural wasteland full of ignorant hayseeds.

Extending an Idea Agreeing with an idea may not produce the immediate stimulation that disagreeing does, but it is by no means a dead end. You can find a way to extend your source's comment and make it the point of departure for your own comments. One technique for generating your own ideas is to let your mind play freely with the source's ideas. Using the following list of relationships between ideas might be helpful. We've put each relationship in the form of a transitional phrase.

- We can provide a causal explanation for the observation our source has made: *The reason for this [fact, situation] is* . . .
- We can explain the implications of the comment: *As a result of this [fact, situation]* . . .
- We can make a collateral observation of our own: *But it is also true that* . . .
- We can turn in a somewhat different direction: *But* . . . ("But" is the first transition to try because it forces us to consider the other sides of a question.)
- We can point to a phenomenon similar to the one the author is writing about: *Similarly* . . .

These are merely a few of the transitional phrases that signal connections between ideas. We mentioned, however, that the first transition to try is the word *but*. Here are a few implications of the word:

- This does not mean that . . .
- We should not forget that . . .
- It is equally true that . . .

You can use these lists to generate ideas. First, write down the transitional phrases (adding to them any others you find helpful). Next, write down one of the interesting ideas from the essay. Then read the author's idea, followed by the first transitional phrase. Write down whatever comes immediately into your head. Keep writing as long as ideas suggest themselves, and when you feel you've gone as far as you can, turn to the second transitional phrase and begin again. If the key idea and transitional phrase do not suggest anything immediately, rack your brain for a few minutes; if nothing comes to mind, go on to the next phrase. Do this for about fifteen minutes, and then read over what you have written.

What are you likely to find? You will probably discover that most of your remarks lead up blind alleys, but this should not discourage you. For it is also likely that this exercise will suggest some interesting possibilities, avenues of exploration you were not aware of before you gave your mind free rein.

Let's use as an example Jeff Greenfield's first key idea, simplifying it slightly for convenience (in this exercise Greenfield's reference to the eighteenth century is likely to clutter our minds):

The country has long had a wholesome image in American culture.

By applying some transitional phrases to this idea, we produce the following possibilities:

The country has long had a wholesome image in American culture. The reason behind this image is that the country represents certain

> values that are always appealing. In my paper I would like to describe some of these values, citing examples from television, books, and movies.
>
> The country has long had a wholesome image in American culture. But the reality of country life is far different from the stereotype. In my paper I would like to contrast the image of country life and its reality.

In these examples we have carried the process one step further and formulated a statement of purpose for our paper. It is unlikely, however, that you will be able to travel from your source's idea to a statement of purpose within three sentences. It is far more likely that you will have to ride your train of thought through several stations before you are ready to disembark. The following example might be more typical:

> The country has long had a wholesome image in American culture. But it is also true that Americans have increasingly opted to live in urban areas. People tend to move from the country to the city, and not the other way around. You rarely hear about anybody leaving Chicago in order to "make it" on the farm. If the country is so wonderful, why are people so anxious to get away from it? But if people find urban life preferable, why do they continue to respond positively to the image of country life? In my paper, I would like to suggest some reasons for this discrepancy.

If you employ a technique like the one described here, which provides a disciplined framework for the free play of your thinking, you may be surprised at the results. You will discover that it is not really the author's idea that counts in this project, but your own active participation in the reading process. Because they misunderstand this point, some people get hung up worrying about zeroing in on the right source idea, the one that will prove most fruitful. Although you will begin your thinking with an interesting idea from the source, your own thought process will eventually produce the results. An idea in a book or magazine just sits there until a reader comes along, reads it, and integrates it into his or her own thinking. This is one of the most complex and rewarding uses you can make of a source.

Exemplifying an Idea Sometimes an essay makes a point that strikes a responsive chord. For example, an author may surprise us by remarking upon something we hadn't noticed previously. At first we might be skeptical, but when we think about it for a few moments, we may find that the observation matches our own experience. If we haven't thought about the idea before, we may be tempted to provide some examples from that experience.

That is the impulse we exploit in this section, in which we consider exemplifying an idea in a source. Your purpose in this case is to find an idea you agree with and back it up with specific examples of your own. This strategy is particularly appropriate for descriptive essays ("Psychographics" and "Weasel Words" in the advertising anthology, for example). Exemplifying a source idea is somewhat less ambitious than disputing or extending an idea, but it is a valid and often imaginative way of using a source.

Because Jeff Greenfield's essay is both descriptive and argumentative, we can use it to exemplify all the writing strategies we are discussing. In this case we need to find an idea in Greenfield's essay that conforms to our own observations. Since his subject is advertising, we have a broad and familiar range of materials to work with. Assuming we have already marked Greenfield's essay, we can start our search for ideas with the comments we found worthy of underlining when we first read the text. A likely candidate, for example, would be the following:

> To watch television commercials over the last year or so is to find a yearning for the countryside. . . .

If we choose to exemplify this idea, we can use one of two general strategies:

1. Exemplify the specific observation of the source. We can directly exemplify Greenfield's point by describing television commercials that reflect a yearning for the countryside. This shouldn't be very difficult; many advertisers seem determined to associate their products with images suggesting the fresh, pure, and natural.

2. Show how the source's idea is applicable to another area. We can extend Greenfield's point into some other area. We can find examples of the yearning for the countryside in printed advertisements. Or we can abandon advertising entirely and show that Greenfield's general comment is equally applicable to other areas of American culture—movies, books, music, even the television shows presented between commercials.

You can get a feel for the availability of material for your essay by listing. Choose one of the two strategies just described. Write down the idea you are considering for exemplification, and then simply list any examples that come into your head. Do not worry about the order of the examples or whether some items duplicate others; just jot down whatever comes to mind for about fifteen minutes. Then take a look at what you have written. Since the purpose of your essay will not be to list as many examples as possible, the *number* of examples you have listed is not terribly important. Two or three solid examples should be enough for a 500- to 700-word essay. Consider these questions in selecting examples for your paper:

- *Can I describe these examples in detail?* Because you don't want your essay to be a list of brief examples, look for material you can write about in detail.

- *Are these examples fresh and original?* You should be on the lookout for examples that might not immediately suggest themselves to your reader. These are usually the examples that come later in your listing, when you have noted all the obvious examples and find yourself having to work hard to find some more. The examples that don't come immediately to mind are often the most interesting ones. That is why you should spend at least fifteen minutes listing, even if you immediately come up with many items.

Once you have decided on the examples you will use, you can easily construct a thesis for your paper. Here are two examples based on Greenfield's essay:

Thesis 1: Popular television commercials often reflect what Jeff Greenfield calls "a yearning for the countryside."

Thesis 2: The same "yearning for the countryside" that Jeff Greenfield finds in television commercials can also be found in print advertising.

The structure of the paper would be a series of descriptions exemplifying our thesis. We would begin by crediting Greenfield and going on to a statement of our own purpose. In the case of thesis 1 we would point out that what Greenfield wrote in 1975 is still applicable today:

> In his essay "Boob Rubes: The New Ruralism in TV Advertising," Jeff Greenfield notes that many television commercials reflect a "yearning for the countryside." Greenfield illustrates his point with several commercials, including Euell Gibbons touting Grape-Nuts. Greenfield published his essay in 1975, and since then the trend he pointed to has continued. I would like to discuss how television commercials of the eighties use rural images to sell products that have nothing to do with the country.

If we are using thesis 2, we will certainly wish to alert our readers to the fact that we are extending Greenfield's remarks to another area:

> In his essay, "Boob Rubes: The New Ruralism in TV Advertising," Jeff Greenfield notes that many television commercials reflect a "yearning for the countryside." Greenfield illustrates his point with several commercials, including Euell Gibbons touting Grape-Nuts. This yearning is not, however, confined to television commercials: we can find the same country images used to sell products in the print media as well. I would like to discuss the way print advertisers use rural images to sell their products.

If you have not yet decided on a strategy for building on a source, consider your reaction to an essay you have read. Go back over the essay and skim its important points. What stands out in your mind? Was it an idea with which you disagreed? If so, you will probably wish to draft an essay expressing your own point of view. If, on the other hand, your dominant reaction is agreement, consider another way to proceed. Can you carry the argument one step further, or would you prefer to exemplify it with information based on your own experiences and observations? If you're not sure, try the prewriting exercises given in this project—using transitional phrases to stimulate ideas and listing examples of an idea in the source—and see which proves most fruitful.

Remember, however, that the three writing strategies described in this section are merely three ways to work the ideas of a source into your own argument. By no means do these techniques exhaust the possibilities. What really counts in this project is your own active participation in the reading process. The strategies and exercises we have described are designed to encourage that active participation and stimulate your thinking. If your reading inspires a workable idea for a paper, by all means pursue your own line of thinking.

Drafting

In other projects in this book we have discussed the process of structuring an essay as the writer of the essay views that process. The writer begins with a thesis in mind and then generates a logical structure, a series of assertions, that will communicate that idea. But if we think of structure from the reader's point of view, we have to invert our priorities. To a reader an essay is a series of assertions leading to a conclusion (the thesis). This is true even if the writer presents a thesis statement at the beginning of the essay. After all, readers cannot deduce the key ideas merely by reading a thesis statement; they have to follow the sequence of ideas underlying that thesis. While writers develop their arguments from the major point to the key ideas and supporting evidence, readers view the argument from the other end of the telescope, working from the smallest unit, a single piece of evidence, up to the largest, the thesis of the essay.

Thus, one of the most important tasks of a writer is to make certain this progressive buildup of ideas is clear. To help readers follow their arguments, writers break down their key ideas into more manageable units—paragraphs. The end of a paragraph is like a public rest area on a highway: readers stop there for a moment and get their bearings before moving on. Careful readers, in fact, use the little pause between paragraphs to mentally summarize what they have just read, to clarify how the main point of the paragraph relates to what they read earlier, and to anticipate ideas that might follow in the next paragraph. If they do not understand the point of the paragraph, they go back over the material before proceeding. (Rereading paragraphs is, in fact, very common.)

Because readers rely so heavily on paragraphs for their understanding of an essay's overall structure, writers need to pay particular attention to the clarity of their individual paragraphs. A good paragraph has three basic qualities:

1. Unity
2. Coherence
3. Adequate development

Let's take a look at each quality from the point of view of a writer drafting an essay.

Unified Paragraphs

A paragraph is *unified* if it conveys a single point to the reader. That point, or *controlling idea*, is made up of a number of subsidiary ideas (the individual sentences). A paragraph may or may not have a *topic sentence*, a direct statement of the controlling idea. If we look back at Greenfield's essay, we find that paragraph 9 opens with a topic sentence, which the rest of the paragraph backs up:

> What is more ironic is that mass packaging and promotion itself helped to uproot so much of the stable, tranquil America in the first place. It was the power first of nationally circulated magazines, then of network radio, that made nationally distributed products feasible, and which, among other pressures, wiped out small, regional producers of everything from cigarettes to beer. It is the nationally franchised fast food chains—McDonald's, Kentucky Fried Chicken, Hardee's—that are replacing the individually owned food shops all over the country. It was the reach of new fashions, new clothes, new ideas into the most remote hamlets of the country that helped trigger the wave of migration from rural to urban America in the first place, and the incredible power of television which continues today to eat away at the barriers of distance that once kept our humor, our politics, our customs distinctly regional.

Paragraph 4, on the other hand, has no explicit topic sentence:

> A country singer warbles that she "was raised on country sunshine" as a fetching young woman returns to her dusty farm home, to be refreshed by family, boyfriend, and Coca-Cola. Not to be outdone, RC Cola presents a young farm woman, barefoot and blue-jean clad, singing that her new country life "is the way to put down roots." Euell Gibbons touts Post's Grape-Nuts at family reunions, which feature breakfasts set out on huge tables in the yard of a country home. A folksinger on behalf of Country Morning (a new breakfast cereal) urges us to "let Country Morning take you back again," as a wholesome-looking family devours the stuff along a huge table in the yard of a country home. Come dinner time, and another apple-cheeked family is seen wolfing down Kentucky Fried Chicken at a huge table

> in the yard of a country home. Families snap Polaroid pictures of each other while gamboling in the yard of a country home. And Chevrolet helps bring ma and pa out to the country, where their children have set up housekeeping, finding once again the joys of gathering around the huge table in the yard of. . . . I assume you are getting the gist of the idea.

Greenfield's examples in paragraph 4 clearly illustrate the point made in paragraph 3 (that television commercials express a yearning for the countryside); therefore, he need not state the controlling idea directly.

Nevertheless, every paragraph must convey a controlling idea to its reader. A topic sentence alone cannot confer unity on a paragraph. Suppose, for example, we take that ninth paragraph, retaining its clear topic sentence but altering the rest of the paragraph:

> What is more ironic is that mass packaging and promotion itself helped to uproot so much of the stable, tranquil America in the first place. America was once a basically rural country, but most people now live in urban areas. This has resulted in huge demographic changes over the years, and it is time we revised our shopworn stereotypes about the city and the country. It was the power first of nationally circulated magazines, then of network radio, that made nationally distributed products feasible, and which, among other pressures, wiped out small, regional producers of everything from cigarettes to beer. The decline of these regional industries was an economic tragedy from which rural areas have yet to recover.

It should be obvious that our topic sentence is no help at all in creating unity out of the unrelated ideas that follow. How would a reader even know that the first sentence is intended as a topic sentence? Only the fourth sentence bears any relation to the "mass packaging and promotion" mentioned in the first sentence. It is not, then, the existence of a topic sentence that unifies a paragraph. A paragraph is *unified* if every sentence in it clearly helps to support its main (stated or unstated) point. You can help ensure unity if you write down the controlling idea of a paragraph before you draft it. Then consider the logic of your paragraph, the way the individual ideas relate to one another and to the controlling idea. When you have clarified the progression of ideas, begin writing the individual sentences, keeping the controlling idea in mind as you write. When you have finished writing, read over the paragraph in the manner described in the revising section.

Coherent Paragraphs

The second quality, coherence, is, in a sense, the servant of unity. A paragraph is *coherent* if its structure, its organization, is clear to the reader. *Unity* refers to the logical content of a paragraph; *coherence*, to the clarity with which that content is presented. Writers can make sure relationships between ideas are clear by providing signals—transitional words and phrases that guide the reader's understanding.

Take, for example, paragraph 10 of Greenfield's essay. The transitional words and phrases are italicized:

> The uprooting of Americans—either from their homelands or their homes within our heartland—is the central story of the twentieth century. *And*, almost as if in expiation, those institutions which helped in that uprooting seem most determined to celebrate what they destroyed. Just before the start of the Indianapolis 500 auto race, *for example*, a celebrity is introduced to the crowd of 300,000 people to sing "Back Home Again, in Indiana." *Yet* this race is essentially a celebration of the machine that gave hundreds of thousands of Americans the freedom to leave their homes in Indiana (or Kansas, or Dakota). *This* is what is happening on our television screens as night after night the products of an urbanized, industrialized, homogenized land are sold with the visual symbols of what that society has helped eradicate.

Greenfield opens his second sentence with a very simple transition ("and") to indicate the addition of a second observation about the behavior of those institutions that helped uproot rural Americans. He clarifies the purpose of his third sentence with the phrase "for example." He points out the disparity between the ceremonial glorification of rural values (the song "Back Home Again, in Indiana") and the glorification of the machine that helped destroy those values (the automobile) by the little transitional word "yet." These transitions have two purposes in Greenfield's essay: they point out the logical relationships between his sentences, and they enable the paragraph to flow more smoothly.

Notice, however, how lightly Greenfield has used his transitions, placing one only when he feels that his reader needs a logical signal. Sometimes the relationship between sentences is obvious, and transitions are unnecessary. At other times, when the relationship between the sentences is not immediately obvious, the strategic use of transitional phrases is extremely important. It is up to the writer to determine when the reader needs help in grasping the relationship between sentences.

As you begin working on the coherence of your own paragraphs, you need to understand the limitations of transitions. A transition can help clarify the relationship between sentences in a logically organized paragraph. But a transition cannot *create* logic in a disunified paragraph. If, for example, we tried to clarify the relationships between sentences in our disunified paragraph, we might come up with the following:

> What is more ironic is that mass packaging and promotion itself helped to uproot so much of the stable, tranquil America in the first

place. *Furthermore*, America was once a basically rural country, but most people now live in urban areas. *However*, this has resulted in huge demographic changes over the years, and it is time we revised our shopworn stereotypes about the city and the country. *For example*, it was the power first of nationally circulated magazines, then of network radio, that made nationally distributed products feasible, and which, among other pressures, wiped out small, regional producers of everything from cigarettes to beer. *Therefore*, the decline of these regional industries was an economic tragedy from which rural areas have yet to recover.

No better, is it? In fact, it's worse. The point is clear: If a paragraph is unified and logically organized, providing transitions to clarify the relationships between ideas is easy. If a paragraph is not unified, transitions are of no help whatsoever.

As you write your paragraphs, consider how your sentences are related to one another. Is one sentence an example of a general point made in the previous sentence? Does it provide additional information, or does it indicate a movement in a different direction? Once you are sure of these relationships, you can consult the following list to see if any of these transitions will help clarify the relationships for your reader:

- *Transitions indicating addition:* and, also, besides, first, furthermore, in addition, moreover, second, still
- *Transitions indicating comparison or contrast:* but, however, in contrast, likewise, nevertheless, on the contrary, on the other hand, similarly, still, yet, whereas
- *Transitions introducing examples:* for example, for instance, such as
- *Transitions indicating temporal relationships:* afterward, at last, at that time, before, earlier, formerly, in the meantime, later, meanwhile, now, soon, subsequently, then, while, since
- *Transitions showing cause or effect:* accordingly, as a result, consequently, then, therefore, thus, because
- *Transitions repeating, summarizing, or concluding:* in brief, in conclusion, in other words, in short, in summary, that is, therefore, to summarize

Adequately Developed Paragraphs

The third characteristic of a good paragraph has to do with the evidence used to back up the controlling idea. A paragraph is *adequately developed* if it has sufficient detail to convince the reader of its main point. But what constitutes sufficient detail? As is usually the case with the writing process, there is no neat formula: only the experience we gain as writers and readers enables us to determine whether or not a paragraph is adequately developed. We often have a tendency in drafting to hurry through our paragraphs, to get on to the next point as soon as possible. This is perfectly reasonable as long as we do not communicate that impatience to our reader. To avoid giving the impression of haste, it helps to go back to individual paragraphs and make sure they are adequately developed.

The first point to check is also the most obvious: the length of your paragraphs. The appropriate length of a paragraph depends on a number of factors (its purpose, importance, complexity, and others), but if your paper consists of a series of two- to four-sentence paragraphs, it will create the impression of skimpiness. You might adopt a rule for yourself—say, at least five sentences per paragraph. This is a rather mechanical rule, but following it for a while will help you learn to develop your paragraphs adequately.

Answering the following question should help you fill in some skimpy paragraphs: *Are there any generalizations in my paragraph that need to be backed up?* One of the causes of inadequate paragraph development is the unsupported generalization. Look over your paragraphs and consider whether you have backed up your general statements with appropriate examples. If you find any unsupported generalizations, ask yourself how *you* know the statement is true. Your answer should generate the examples you need.

REVISING

The revising activities for this project consist of a set of questions to help you review your own work and two groups of activities designed to elicit responses from a reader. The second group of activities stresses the subject of the drafting section of this project: paragraphs.

QUESTIONS FOR YOURSELF

1. Is the thesis statement identifiable and clear?
2. Are there clear transitions to each key idea?
3. Is each key idea developed in sufficient detail?
4. Is there a clear transition at the beginning of each paragraph?
5. Are there any sentences that sound awkward as you read them?
6. Are there any mechanical or typographical errors?

GENERAL WRITING STANDARDS

Directions: Read the draft carefully and comment as indicated. If you find any of these operations difficult or impossible to perform, indicate that fact to the writer and, if possible, try to explain the source of the difficulty.

1. Identify the thesis statement of the essay and rewrite it in your own words.
2. List each of the key ideas that develop the thesis.
3. Point out any places where supporting detail is needed.

4. Point out any details without a clear purpose.
5. Indicate any places where the opening of a paragraph does not clearly follow from the conclusion of the previous one.
6. Indicate any sentences that are confusing.

STANDARDS FOR PARAGRAPHS

Directions: Read the entire essay. Then reread *each* paragraph and comment about it as indicated.

1. Indicate whether or not the paragraph has an explicit thesis statement.
2. Write down the controlling idea of the paragraph in your own words.
3. Note down any sentences that do not clearly help to develop the controlling idea of the paragraph.
4. Write down the transitions the writer uses to help clarify the relationships between sentences. Indicate any places where a sentence does not follow clearly from the previous sentence.
5. Indicate whether the controlling idea is developed in sufficient detail. If the paragraph seems skimpy, explain which ideas in the paragraph could use further development.

Using Sources as Evidence

THE PROJECTS IN THIS BOOK ARE DIVIDED INTO three phases: prewriting, drafting, and revising. But we could also refer to prewriting as the *learning phase* (in which the writer's main concern is to come up with something to say) and to drafting and revising as the *communicating phase* (in which the writer must find an effective way to communicate the thesis). Although these phases are not entirely separate, at some point in the process, writers become reasonably confident in the point they wish to make and turn to the matter of communicating that point.

In this project we focus on the learning phase of the writing process. The suggested anthology for the project is "Early Reactions to Rock 'n' Roll" (covering the period from 1954 to 1960), and the material in the anthology consists entirely of primary sources. (The anthology is included at the end of the project.) Your purpose will be to learn about the subject by reading through the primary sources, devise an original thesis based on your reading, and communicate what you have learned to your reader.

Suggested Assignment

Most of the papers you write as a college student will not be directed to audiences outside your school or even to your classmates. They will be class papers, reports, and research papers handed in to your instructor for a grade. This is the case with this project, a multiple-source paper on early reactions to rock 'n' roll, which will be read by your instructor and evaluated as any other class writing assignment would be. The paper should be about 1000 words long, although your instructor may specify a different length.

To help you focus on your audience, you should consider precisely what teachers hope to accomplish with papers of this sort. Teachers use the research paper to determine whether you have understood the material you have read. At the same time, they are checking your ability to formulate and express your own insight into the subject covered in the sources. Instructors want to see if you can read a variety of sources, come up with an original thesis, and marshall your evidence in a clear and logical fashion to support the thesis. Your instructor may ask you to write this project as a formal research paper documented as described in the research paper manual. Or your instructor may ask you to attribute sources as you have in previous projects.

Overview

■

In this project you will read a variety of primary sources on the subject "Early Reactions to Rock 'n' Roll," develop an original thesis from your reading, and communicate your thesis to readers. The project has two broad phases: a learning phase (in which your main concern is to come up with something to say) and a communicating phase (in which you find an effective way to communicate the thesis). In the learning phase you will read through all the sources, noting relationships between them and looking for areas of exploration. This reading will help prepare for the major step in the learning phase: devising an original thesis. In the communicating phase, you will invert the procedure, beginning with your thesis and working backwards to your key ideas and the evidence supporting it. Because your paper will include information from a variety of sources, the drafting section of this project discusses the integration of sources and original text in detail.

The Process of Writing a Multiple-Source Paper

1. Read through your sources noting relationships between them and looking for areas of exploration.
2. Devise an original thesis based on your sources.
3. Analyze your thesis and work out the key ideas that develop it.
4. Take notes on the specific information you will need to back up your key ideas.
5. Draft your paper. Be sure that your reader is aware of the source of each item of information in your text.
6. Revise your multiple-source paper, using the activities described in the project.

■

Prewriting

Surveying the Field

You will focus in this project on the most crucial part of the process of writing a research paper: reading source material and coming up with an idea you wish to communicate. The sources collected in the anthology have a number of points in common. They are all on the subject of the early responses to rock 'n' roll. Their publication dates range from 1955 to 1960, the period of Bill Haley and the Comets, Elvis Presley, riots at rock 'n' roll shows, and widespread concern by members of the older generation about the deep significance of the emergence of rock 'n' roll for the future of civilization. Furthermore, each item in the anthology is a *primary source*, a direct reaction to rock 'n' roll dating from the period in question. Thus, the sources are direct evidence of the early reaction to rock 'n' roll, not somebody's later opinion *about* that reaction. (To your reader, of course, your paper will be just such a *secondary source* on the subject.)

In most other ways, however, the anthology is a mixed bag, opening up a large number of possibilities for exploration. It includes newspaper accounts of particular incidents, trade paper descriptions of various trends, compilations of reactions from the "person in the street," personal opinion essays—precisely the kind of variety you would find in researching any topic. It is not necessary for you to use all of this material in your paper. Your job, after all, is to go through this material to find some unifying idea, and that process includes discovering the material that is *not* relevant to your purpose. But before you can begin to make such decisions, you need to have some idea of the range of possibilities, and the first step is to survey the available material, looking for a connection between the sources, a strategy for investigation. We will discuss formulating a thesis later, but a writer can come up with a thesis at any stage of a writing project. If you think of an idea that seems promising as you read through the source material, write it down and keep it in mind as you continue reading.

The first step in all the projects has been to read for thesis and structure, and that is certainly the case here. But the primary sources you will use in this project consist for the most part of articles in newspapers and popular magazines. Such sources are not usually formal arguments, as your previous sources have been, but reports of events and comments upon them. Because the thesis of a newspaper or popular magazine article is almost always announced in its headline or title, a formal "thesis search" is usually not necessary in these cases. You can survey the entire field as represented by the material in the anthology, speculate on some of the possible avenues of exploration, and return to the sources later to determine what specific point to make and to find the evidence with which to back it up.

There is, of course, no specific technique for reading through sources and considering their implications. The point you eventually make in your paper will depend upon the connections you make between your sources and the ideas you develop from those connections—in other words, from what you learn. Here are a few techniques that may help you focus your attention while reading:

1. Classify your material. As you are reading, compose a subject catalog of your resources. "Negative reactions of parents," for example, can serve as a heading for material drawn from a number of items. One item, moreover, can be classified under a number of different headings. You cannot know in advance the specific headings you will use (though you can probably guess at several), and you may find that your first headings are too broad, too narrow, or perhaps imprecise. But if you keep refining your headings as you go along—crossing out some, adding others, reclassifying items—eventually you will have a very convenient system for finding all the information on a particular aspect of the topic.

There is a second advantage to classifying material as you read through it for the first time: classifying forces you to break down your material, to analyze its component parts. Devising a thesis is essentially a learning experience, a process in which you learn something about the subject you are investigating. Classifying items of information will help focus your thoughts. You may not devise a thesis at this point, but classifying the material you have to work with will help you do so later.

Take, for example, "Why They Rock 'n' Roll—And Should They?" by Gertrude Samuels (p. 151), an account of the rock 'n' roll phenomenon, which appeared in the *New York Times Magazine* on January 12, 1958. The article provides a broad range of reactions to rock 'n' roll, including comments from young people, from Frank Sinatra, from the manager of the Paramount theater (scene of the Alan Freed rock 'n' roll show Samuels attended), and from a psychiatrist. The author's descriptions of what she sees are also of interest. You cannot know precisely how you are going to use this article the first time you read it, but you can begin thinking about it by classifying the information it contains. Noticing that Samuels defines *rock 'n' roll* in paragraph 6, you might write down a phrase like "Definition of rock 'n' roll" with Samuels' name under it. If any other essay defines rock 'n' roll, you can place it under the same heading. You also might use the headings "Reactions of young people" and "Reactions of adults" to classify the material you find. Later you can narrow and subdivide your classifications as you learn more about the nature of the available material. In some cases you may wish to broaden your headings. For example, you might come up with the heading "Reaction of Frank Sinatra" when you read the Samuels article; if you later discover reactions from other musicians, you can broaden the heading to "Reactions of non–rock 'n' roll musicians."

The important thing is not that you find the "right" classifications. In fact, the fluidity of the headings is the greatest asset of this technique. As you refine your categories, you are making connections between separate items. That mental work, which helps you formulate your overall point, is more significant than the headings themselves, useful as they are for helping you find information later.

2. Note similarities and differences. As you classify your material, you will see the broad similarities and differences between items. Taking notes on similar or opposing facts, ideas, and opinions is another helpful reading technique. We have stressed that writing a paper, particularly one based on source material, is a learning process. A key to the process of learning through research is to relate each item of information to everything else you have read. As you read, be on the lookout for any information that "clicks," that relates to a point you have read previously. You might notice, for example, that predictions about the future of rock 'n' roll are scattered throughout your sources. One of them, "Rock 'N' Roll's Global Wane," describes a trend toward "a more standard brand of music." Another, "R & R Still Beams Plenty of Life," published the same year, begins by commenting that "Rock and roll's demise, like that of Mark Twain's, has been greatly exaggerated." It is certainly worth noting this difference of opinion and finding out whether any other sources have anything to say on this controversy. Comparing specific ideas, opinions, and facts is a major part of the process of discovering an overall point.

3. Summarize each source. It is a good idea to write a précis, a summary of perhaps a sentence or two, after you read a source. A collection of such brief summaries can serve as a kind of table of contents for your source material. Even more important, these summaries will help you to take stock of where you are in your reading. Stopping after you write each précis and looking over those you have already written will give you an overview of your sources.

4. Ask questions. Along with the brief summaries and comments on the relationships between sources, you should jot down any questions you wish to explore as you continue reading. For example, "Why They Rock 'n' Roll—And Should They?" might stimulate the following questions: What about teenagers who didn't attend rock 'n' roll shows? Was there any controversy among teenagers themselves? Did any non–rock 'n' roll musicians stand up for rock 'n' roll?

As you read through the sources, remember that you have two basic purposes in mind. For one thing, you wish to find out what information is available and where it is, so that you can return to it when you know precisely how you are going to use it. For another, you want to begin thinking about what you are learning as you read.

Devising a Thesis

Your thesis, the point you wish to make, is the most important element in any paper you write, including the research paper. In a research paper the primary and secondary sources—books, essays, government documents, recordings, films, interviews—are *evidence* for the thesis. The purpose of the paper is not to display sources, but to communicate your ideas, particularly your thesis, to the reader. The sources you refer to, the evidence backing up the thesis, are a means to that end.

Your thesis for this project will be the answer to the question "What *about* the early reaction to rock 'n' roll?" Asking that question will help you clarify what you have learned in your reading. Until you answer that question, you have a collection of individual reactions—attitudes, explanations, predictions—but no particular point to communicate. Here are a few questions you can ask as you go over your notes and comments; they should help you clarify what you have learned and devise a thesis:

- *Are there any significant differences of opinion among my sources?* Describing a controversy (and perhaps its causes) will provide focus for diverse material. For this project you would answer this question by *comparing* and *contrasting* the reactions to rock 'n' roll.
- *What are the dominant concerns of my sources?* You may wish to stress one general reaction—a fear of the effects of rock 'n' roll, for example—and subdivide it into its most common forms. You would not merely describe individual reactions, but classify them and clarify their relationship to one another. In other words, you would *analyze* the response to rock 'n' roll.
- *What were the consequences of the reactions described by my sources?* In this case you are looking for the relationship between the way people felt about rock 'n' roll and the actions they took as a result. Your paper might explain how different reactions to rock 'n' roll led to different actions.
- *How did my sources' reactions change over the years?* The sources in the anthology are arranged chronologically, and you may notice a pattern emerging from your reading. Look at the earliest and the latest articles, noticing any difference, and then review the other articles to find out whether there is a gradual change between the earliest and the latest. You don't have to fit *everything* into the pattern, but you must acknowledge any material that contradicts the pattern.

Your thesis might provide an answer to these or any other questions raised by your reading. Remember, however, that whatever aspect of the subject you choose to write about, the thesis of your paper should be a sentence, not a phrase. "Changes in attitudes toward rock 'n' roll" is satisfactory as a description of your subject, but not as a thesis. Only by answering the question "What *about* the changes in attitudes toward rock 'n' roll?" can you state a thesis.

Generating a Structure

When you are reasonably satisfied with the point you want to make, you are ready to decide what exactly you have to do to prove it. Every thesis carries a commitment to answer the question *What supporting ideas will I have to prove to my readers to convince them of my thesis?* The answers to this question, in sentence form, will provide you with the key ideas of your paper. If you have already worked out the key ideas, you can check them by asking the following questions:

- *Do I have all the ideas necessary to prove my point?* Break down your thesis into its component parts and make sure there are no gaps.
- *Are the ideas in logical order?* Even if you're confident of the order of your ideas, it never hurts to play around with some other possibilities. While doing so, you might think of some new relationships between ideas. This would also be a convenient time to consider the main transitions you will use when you draft the paper. You might even write them down in your list of key ideas.

If you haven't yet worked out your key ideas, there are a number of ways to proceed. You can read over your thesis and any comments you have jotted down and retrace the process that led from your reading to your thesis. Or you can let your analysis of the thesis lead you to the key ideas. If, for example, your thesis points out a difference among people's reactions, the key ideas of your paper will be the various reactions you found. If your thesis has to do with a chronological progression, your key ideas are bound to be the major demarcations along the way.

Taking Notes

Finding and reading sources, formulating a thesis, and taking notes are not separate parts of the writing process. When you read the sources in the anthology, for example, you probably took notes to help you keep track of the material and devise a thesis. You may have underlined the text, written comments in the margin, and jotted down specific ideas. Whatever notes you have taken to this point, you'll now want to return to your sources to take notes on the specific material you will use in your paper.

The specific form of your notes will depend on your instructor. Your instructor may allow you to take notes informally, as you have done in the other projects. If that is the case, you can take notes in any way you wish, making sure, of course, that the source of each note is clear. On the other hand, your instructor may want you to follow the note taking procedures usually recommended for research papers. If that is the case, you will find a discussion of formal note taking on page 419 of the research paper manual in this book.

DRAFTING

Your purpose in this project is to communicate your ideas about the early reaction to rock 'n' roll, using the sources in the anthology as evidence for your thesis. Because you are using several sources as evidence, integrating sources is a more complex procedure in this project than in others in this book. But attribution, the means by which you separate your sources' ideas from one another and from your own ideas, remains a matter of letting your reader know who is responsible for each idea or item of information in your text.

There are a number of ways to do that, and we shall discuss some of them in this section. But the basic rule is *Readers should know who is responsible for each item of information just by reading your text*. Even if there is a separate note page, the reader should know the source of all information without having to turn to that page. *Documentation*—notes, bibliographies, parenthetical references in text—provides details about the *exact* location of the information, but the general origin of each item should be clear in the text.

When people read your paper, the first "reference" they see is your name. Thus, they assume that you are the source of everything—information, ideas, opinions—that follows. When you inform them otherwise by introducing a reference to a source, they assume that everything that follows comes from that source. We can sum this up as two basic principles:

1. Readers assume that everything in your paper is your own, until they are informed otherwise.
2. Once a source is introduced, readers assume that all the material that follows comes from that source, until they are informed otherwise.

Matters of attribution are commonsense applications of these two principles. For example, you must introduce each source you use. Take the following example:

> Many adults were outraged by rock 'n' roll on musical grounds. Dr. Francis J. Braceland, for example, called rock 'n' roll, "cannibalistic and tribalistic."

This simple attribution separates the writer's generalization about adult reaction to rock 'n' roll from Dr. Braceland's comment.

Just how much information is required when you introduce a source? The answer is, as always, it depends. The amount of information you provide about the source depends on how much information you believe is necessary to help your readers appreciate the significance of the source's comments. Take the following case:

> Several educators objected to the appearance of Elvis Presley on the Ed Sullivan Show in 1956. Harry A. Feldman said, "One shudders to contemplate the cultural level of the next generation." Howard Spalding suggested that negative public response might cause broadcasters to reconsider the scheduling of rock 'n' roll performers.

We have applied our two principles here, and the source of each idea is clear. But we would surely enhance our readers' appreciation of these comments if we informed them that Harry A. Feldman was chairman of the Music Department at William C. Bryant High School and Howard Spalding was the principal of A. B. Davis High School.

The same common sense should guide you in all your decisions about attribution. Suppose, for example, that you wish to refer to Kenny Puncerelli's description of the appeal of rock 'n' roll in Gertrude Samuels' article, "Why They Rock 'n' Roll—And Should They?" Is it necessary to introduce the written source, as follows?:

> Teenagers had their own explanation of the phenomenon. In an article by Gertrude Samuels, sixteen-year-old Kenny Puncerelli explained the appeal of rock 'n' roll: "It's the rhythm. It's easy to listen to."

The reference to Gertrude Samuels does not really provide vital information; it merely slows down reading by cluttering the text. In a formal research paper, we will have to cite Samuels, who is the ultimate source of our information. But that citation can be more gracefully presented in a parenthetical reference or in a note than in the text itself. In the text, it is preferable to introduce the immediate source of your information:

> Teenagers had their own explanation of the phenomenon. Sixteen-year-old Kenny Puncerelli explained the appeal of rock 'n' roll: "It's the rhythm. It's easy to listen to."

So far we have concentrated on introducing sources, showing readers precisely where the use of a source begins. But, remembering the second principle, it is equally important to show where the use of a source ends. Often the introduction of another source will take care of the matter:

> Several educators objected to the appearance of Elvis Presley on the Ed Sullivan Show in 1956. Harry A. Feldman, chairman of the Music Department at William C. Bryant High School, said, "One shudders to contemplate the cultural level of the next generation." Howard Spalding, principal of A. B. Davis High School, suggested that negative public response might cause broadcasters to reconsider the scheduling of rock 'n' roll performers.

The introduction of Howard Spalding indicates that we have finished with Harry A. Feldman. Often the place where a source leaves off is obvious:

> Several educators objected to the appearance of Elvis Presley on the Ed Sullivan Show in 1956. Harry A. Feldman, chairman of the Music Department at William C. Bryant High School, said, "One shudders to contemplate the cultural level of the next generation." But other educators were less inclined to worry.

Any reader would recognize that the last sentence is clearly our own comment, not Harry A. Feldman's.

Formally documented papers indicate the end of the use of a source by a parenthetical reference or a note. In the following case, for example, the original page number of the source of the information, placed in parentheses, indicates the end of Howard Spalding's comment:

> Howard Spalding, principal of A. B. Davis High School, suggested that negative public response might cause broadcasters to reconsider the scheduling of rock 'n' roll performers (13).

Whether or not you formally document your sources, and the precise method of documentation you use, will depend on your instructor, who might choose one of the following possibilities:

- Your instructor might not wish you to use formal references in this project at all, but merely to introduce your sources in your text. If that is the case, you need to make sure that it is clear where your use of each source begins and ends. Here is an example:

> Several psychiatrists felt the need to explain the rock 'n' roll phenomenon. A. D. Buchmueller, the executive director of the Child Study Association, described the reaction of teenagers as "a mass kind of hysteria, which is contagious." Dr. Joost A. M. Meerlo compared the effect of rock 'n' roll on teenagers to the effect of St. Vitus Dance.

- Your instructor might wish you to use parenthetical citations to the pages on which your sources appear in this book. In that case you need to provide the page number on which each item of information appears:

> Several psychiatrists felt the need to explain the rock 'n' roll phenomenon. A. D. Buchmueller, the executive director of the Child Study Association, described the reaction of teenagers as "a mass kind of hysteria, which is contagious" (155). Dr. Joost A. M. Meerlo compared the effect of rock 'n' roll on teenagers to the effect of St. Vitus Dance (148).

Note that the parenthetical citation is placed *inside* the punctuation of your own text.

- Your instructor might wish you to document your sources formally. If so, you will document your paper just as you would in a formal research paper. All the information you need for such documentation—including bibliographical information and the original pagination of each item—has been provided with the readings in the anthology. Instruction in formal documentation is provided on p. 438 of the research paper manual. Using the most recent MLA (Modern Language Association) form, our sample paragraph would look like this:

> Several psychiatrists felt the need to explain the rock 'n' roll phenomenon. A. D. Buchmueller, the executive director of the Child Study Association, described the reaction of teenagers as "a mass kind of hysteria, which is contagious" (Samuels 20). Dr. Joost A. M. Meerlo compared the effect of rock 'n' roll on teenagers to the effect of St. Vitus Dance ("Experts Propose Study of 'Craze'" 12).

Whatever style of documentation your instructor assigns, remember that documentation is the way you let readers know the source of the evidence you are using to back up your thesis. Your primary emphasis in drafting this project—as in all writing projects—should be on developing and backing up your argument. Begin with your thesis and key ideas, the overall structure of your paper. Then arrange your source material to back up each idea of your paper. That way you will preserve the proper relationship between your own ideas and the items of information that support them.

REVISING

The revising activities for this project include a set of questions to help you review your own work and a group of activities designed to elicit responses from a reader. The second group of activities stresses a problem particularly relevant to the research paper: integrating your own comments and your source material.

QUESTIONS FOR YOURSELF

1. Is the thesis statement identifiable and clear?
2. Are there clear transitions to each key idea?
3. Is each key idea developed in sufficient detail?
4. Is there a clear transition at the beginning of each paragraph?
5. Are there any sentences that sound awkward as you read them?
6. Are there any mechanical or typographical errors?

GENERAL WRITING STANDARDS

Directions: Read the draft carefully and comment as indicated. If you find any of these operations difficult or impossible to perform, indicate that fact to the writer and, if possible, try to explain the source of the difficulty.

1. Identify the thesis statement of the essay and rewrite it in your own words.
2. List each of the key ideas that develop the thesis.
3. Point out any places where supporting detail is needed.
4. Point out any details without a clear purpose.
5. Indicate any places where the opening of a paragraph does not clearly follow from the conclusion of the previous one.
6. Indicate any sentences that are confusing.

STANDARDS FOR RESEARCH PAPERS

Directions: Read the entire essay carefully and comment as indicated.

1. Indicate any places in the paper where the *responsibility* for an idea or opinion is not clear.

2. Indicate any places where the *purpose* of a quotation or paraphrase is not clear.
3. Check all quotations and indicate any missing end quotation marks.
4. Note down any paraphrases that might be too close to the original text in wording. Indicate any passages that do not sound like the normal "voice" of the writer.

Primary Sources: Early Reactions to Rock 'n' Roll

This anthology consists of a series of newspaper and magazine articles on reactions to rock 'n' roll music during its early years. All the items are primary sources. That is to say, they are sources from the period in question that exemplify reactions of the day. The items are arranged chronologically. The earliest, explaining the nature of rock 'n' roll and the controversy surrounding it, was published in 1955. The latest, two contradictory predictions about the future of rock 'n' roll, appeared in 1960. In between are a variety of reactions from teenagers, parents, critics, and experts of one sort or another.

Since these are primary sources, precisely the sort you might find were you to look up the subject in a library, we are going to let the sources speak for themselves in this anthology. The subject itself requires little background information. In 1955, rock 'n' roll was a new kind of music to most listeners. (The *Reader's Guide to Periodical Literature* still listed it under the title "Jazz" that year.) Elvis Presley did not make his celebrated appearance on the Ed Sullivan Show until 1956, an event which sparked further controversy. By 1960 it seems as if just about everybody had said something on the subject.

We have provided full bibliographic information at the beginning of each source in the anthology, and the original pagination is indicated in brackets within the text.

■

A QUESTION OF QUESTIONABLE MEANINGS

LIFE, APRIL 18, 1955, 168

The heavy-beat and honking-melody tunes of today's rock 'n roll have a clearly defined ancestry in U.S. jazz going back to Louis Armstrong and Bessie Smith of 30 years ago. Once called "race" records, and later "rhythm and blues," the music was first performed by Negroes and sold mostly in Negro communities. During the past years as the big record companies concentrated on mambos and ballads, the country's teen-agers found themselves without snappy dance tunes to their taste. A few disk jockies filled the void with songs like *Ko Ko Mo, Tweedlee Dee, Hearts of Stone, Earth Angel, Flip, Flop, and Fly, Shake, Rattle and Roll,* and the name rock 'n roll took over. On a list of 10 top juke box best-selling records last week, six were r 'n r.

But parents and police were startled by other rock 'n roll records' words, which were frequently suggestive and occasionally lewd. *Variety,* the show business weekly, cranked out indignant stories about "leerics" in the rock 'n roll or rhythm and blues songs. *Cash Box*, the juke box trade journal, countered that much of the suggestiveness was read into the songs by low-minded listeners and challenged anybody to find smut in the top rock 'n roll numbers.

By this time, however, the music had gained such an exaggerated reputation that the worst meanings could be found in the most innocent phrases. Radio, TV and record censors listened not only to rock 'n roll but also—with good reason—to the lyrics of pop records. But hardly a teen-ager afoot had time to listen. They all seemed to be busily and blithely rockin' and rollin' around. [168]

■

ROCK 'N ROLL: A FRENZIED TEEN-AGE MUSIC CRAZE KICKS UP A BIG FUSS

LIFE, APRIL 18, 1955, 166

The nation's teen-agers are dancing their way into an enlarging controversy over rock 'n roll. In New Haven, Conn. the police chief has put a damper on rock 'n roll parties and other towns are following suit. Radio networks are worried over questionable lyrics in rock 'n roll. And some American parents, without quite knowing what it is their kids are up to, are worried that it's something they shouldn't be.

Rock 'n roll is both music and dance. The music has a rhythm often heavily accented on the second and fourth beat. The dance combines the Lindy and Charleston, and, almost anything else. In performing it, hollering helps and a boot banging the floor makes it even better. The over-all result, frequently, is frenzy. [166]

■

ROCK-AND-ROLL CALLED "COMMUNICABLE DISEASE"

NEW YORK TIMES, MARCH 28, 1956, 33

Hartford, Conn., March 27 (UP)—A noted psychiatrist described "rock-and-roll" music today as a "communicable disease" and "another sign of adolescent rebellion."

Dr. Francis J. Braceland, psychiatrist in chief of the Institute of Living, called rock-and-roll a "cannibalistic and tribalistic" form of music. He was commenting on the disturbances that led to eleven arrests during the week-end at a local theatre.

It is insecurity and "rebellion," Dr. Braceland said, that impels teenagers to affect "ducktail" haircuts, wear zootsuits and carry on boisterously at rock-and-roll affairs.

Six of those arrested were fined from $15 to $25 yesterday in Police Court. One hundred more were ejected from the theatre. [33]

SEGREGATIONISTS WOULD BAN ALL ROCK, ROLL HITS

BILLBOARD, APRIL 7, 1956, 130

Birmingham—High school and college students, tavern and restaurant owners, radio stations, and most of all juke box operators, are up in arms over a declaration by a white Citizens' Council leader Thursday that "rock and roll" has got to go.

Asa Carter, executive secretary of the North Alabama Council, said at a rally meeting that "rock and roll" music was inspired by the National Association for the Advancement of Colored People and other pro-integration forces. He indicated that the council would publish the names of music operators and location owners who failed to ban the records.

Operators here in Birmingham were of the general opinion that the idea is fantastic. A survey shows none has been approached by the council.

One operator said: "I won't comment, I won't dignify the proposal by giving my opinion." Another commented: "Suppose we do take this threat seriously, don't think for a minute any of us will take the disks off the machines."

Harry Hurvich, partner of Birmingham Vending, AMI distributor, said: "I consider Carter's proposal an invasion of the freedom of liking what you want to." He said he would not go along with the idea, called it "ridiculous."

A vice-president in charge of programming for a local radio-television station had this to say: "We'd never take r. & b. off the air because any one group didn't like it. The only dictation in our business is that of the tastes of our listeners. Carter's statement that the music is an attempt to destroy the morals of America's young people is absurd."

Teen-agers are unanimous on two points. They like rock and roll and they don't want it taken off the machines. [130]

WHITE COUNCIL VS. ROCK AND ROLL

NEWSWEEK, APRIL 23, 1956, 32

The White Citizens Councils of Alabama, formed to fight desegregation, are equally opposed to jazz, which they consider part of the NAACP "plot to mongrelize America." Asa E. (Ace) Carter, self-appointed leader of the North Alabama Citizens Council, said last week that "bebop," "rock and roll," and all "Negro music" are designed to force "Negro culture" on the South.

"Individual councils have formed action committees to call on owners of establishments with rock-and-roll music on their juke boxes," he said. "We also intend to see the people who sponsor the music, and the people who promote Negro bands to play for teen-agers."

Rock-and-roll music, he said, "is the basic, heavy-beat music of Negroes. It appeals to the base in man, brings out animalism and vulgarity." [32]

■

ELVIS PRESLEY: LACK OF RESPONSIBILITY IS SHOWN BY TV IN EXPLOITING TEEN-AGERS

Jack Gould

NEW YORK TIMES, SEPTEMBER 16, 1956, SEC. II, 13

Television broadcasters cannot be asked to solve life's problems. But they can be expected to display adult leadership and responsibility in areas where they do have some significant influence. This they have hardly done in the case of Elvis Presley, entertainer and phenomenon.

Last Sunday on the Ed Sullivan show Mr. Presley made another of his appearances and attracted a record audience. In some ways it was perhaps the most unpleasant of his recent three performances.

Mr. Presley initially disturbed adult viewers—and instantly became a martyr in the eyes of his teen-age following—for his striptease behavior on last spring's Milton Berle program. Then with Steve Allen he was much more sedate. On the Sullivan program he injected movements of the tongue and indulged in wordless singing that were singularly distasteful.

At least some parents are puzzled or confused by Presley's almost hypnotic power; others are concerned; perhaps most are a shade disgusted and content to permit the Presley fad to play itself out.

Neither criticism of Presley nor of the teen-agers who admire him is particularly to the point. Presley has fallen into a fortune with a routine that in one form or another has always existed on the fringe of show business; in his gyrating figure and suggestive gestures the teen-agers have found something that for the moment seems exciting or important.

Void

Quite possibly Presley just happened to move in where society has failed the teen-ager. Certainly, modern youngsters have been subjected to a great deal of censure and perhaps too little understanding. Greater in their numbers than ever before, they may have found in Presley a rallying point, a nationally prominent figure who seems to be on their side. And, just as surely, there are limitless teenagers who cannot put up with the boy, either vocally or calisthenically.

Family counselors have wisely noted that ours is still a culture in a stage of frantic and tense transition. With even 16-year-olds capable of commanding $20 or $30 a week in their spare time, with access to automobiles at an early age, with communications media of all kinds exposing them to new thoughts very early in life, theirs indeed is a high degree of independence. Inevitably it has been accompanied by a lessening of parental control.

Small wonder, therefore, that the teen-ager is susceptible to overstimulation from the outside. He is at the age when an awareness of sex is both thoroughly natural and normal, when latent rebellion is to be expected. But what is new and a little discouraging is the willingness and indeed eagerness of reputable business men to exploit those critical factors beyond all reasonable grounds.

Television surely is not the only culprit. Exposé magazines, which once were more or less bootleg items, are now carried openly on the best newsstands. The music-publishing business—as Variety most courageously has pointed out—has all but disgraced itself with some of the "rock 'n' roll" songs it has issued. Some of the finest recording companies have been willing to go right along with the trend, too.

Distinctive

Of all these businesses, however, television is in a unique position. First and foremost, it has access directly to the home and its wares are free. Second, the broadcasters are not only addressing themselves to the teen-agers but, much more importantly, also to the lower age groups. When Presley executes his bumps and grinds, it must be remembered by the Columbia Broadcasting System that even the 12-year-old's curiosity may be overstimulated. It is on this score that the adult viewer has every right to expect sympathetic understanding and cooperation from a broadcaster.

A perennial weakness in the executive echelons of the networks is their opportunistic rationalization of television's function. The industry lives fundamentally by the code of giving the public what it wants. This is not the place to argue the artistic foolishness of such a standard; in the case of situation comedies and other escapist diversions it is relatively unimportant.

But when this code is applied to teen-agers just becoming conscious of life's processes, not only is it manifestly without validity but it also is perilous. Catering to the interests of the younger generation is one of television's main jobs; because those interests do not always coincide with parental tastes should not deter the broadcasters. But selfish exploitation and commercialized overstimulation of youth's physical impulses is certainly a gross national disservice.

Sensible

The issue is not one of censorship, which solves nothing; it is one of common sense. It is no impingement on the medium's artistic freedom to ask the broadcaster merely to exercise good sense and display responsibility. It is no blue-nosed suppression of the proper way of depicting life in the theatre to expect stage manners somewhat above the level of the carnival sideshow.

In the long run, perhaps Presley will do everyone a favor by pointing up the need for earlier sex education so that neither his successors nor TV can capitalize on the idea that his type of routine is somehow highly tempting yet forbidden fruit. But that takes time, and meanwhile the broadcasters at least can employ a measure of mature and helpful thoughtfulness in not contributing further to the exploitation of the teen-ager.

With congested schools, early dating, the appeals of the car, military service, acceptance by the right crowd, sex and the normal parental pressures, the teen-ager has all the problems he needs.

Mercenary

To resort to the world's oldest theatrical come-on just to make a fast buck from such a sensitive individual is cheap and tawdry stuff. At least Presley is honest in what he is doing. That the teen-ager sometimes finds it difficult to feel respect for the moralizing older generation may of itself be an encouraging sign of his intelligence. If the profiteering hypocrite is above reproach and Presley isn't, today's youngsters might well ask what God do adults worship. [13]

■

TELEVISION MAILBAG: MR. PRESLEY

NEW YORK TIMES, SEPTEMBER 23, 1956, 13

To the Radio-Television Editor:
Jack Gould's column last Sunday on Elvis Presley was excellent. As a teacher facing youth of today, I cannot help but feel alarmed at the reaction I have noted to this alleged entertainer. And to know that he is aided and abetted by powerful networks is most disturbing.

My quarrel is not with Mr. Presley but with those who push him on further and further.

G. Scott Cree, Syracuse, N.Y.

Responsibility

I am 18 years old and have wide contacts in teen-age circles. My experience would seem to indicate that if it were not for the dubiously sincere moralizing of such men as Mr. Gould, the whole question of Mr. Presley's sexuality might never have arisen and he might not be the national craze that he is today.

Fred Barreiro, Jr., New York

Collaborationists

In aiming his criticism at the recording industry, the music publishers and the television producers, Mr. Gould placed most of the responsibility where it belongs. Let us not, however, overlook the aiders and abettors, like Ed Sullivan and

Steve Allen, who introduce such performers as Elvis Presley with elephantine fanfare.

In order to be accepted by our present-day TV and entertainment entrepreneurs, the performer must be more primitive, more elementary, more mediocre than ever before. One shudders to contemplate the cultural level of the next generation.

Harry A. Feldman, Chairman
Music Department
William C. Bryant High School, New York

Misunderstanding

The teen-age minds reacted toward Elvis Presley as they have toward other American favorites. In no way did they feel a sense of stimulation with a sex-defined attitude. It was puppy love and no more than any admiration that exists between the idol and his fan.

Adults who forever misunderstand the desires of these teen-agers immediately took up the cries of "suggestive performance," "degrading routines" and "sexual gyrations." Believe me, the teen-agers were not aware of this interpretation until it was presented to them by the unhealthy few.

Mrs. Rhoda Frank, New York

Commendation

I want to commend Mr. Gould for his excellent column regarding Elvis Presley. If the adverse public reaction that follows an unfortunate performance such as this were directed at the sponsor as well as the broadcasting industry, would it not cause advertisers to consider more carefully what they wished to present to the public?

Howard Spalding, Principal
A. B. Davis High School
Mount Vernon, N.Y.

Appreciative

I am one of Elvis' frantic fans. I really appreciated the way Mr. Gould outlined the position of teen-agers in this controversy to our parents. Also, I hope and believe that with proper handling Elvis Presley can become a good actor as well as a truly popular singer.

Frances McCarthy, New York

Masterly

Thank you for presenting Jack Gould's masterly arraignment of the Elvis Presley entertainment routine.

Ernest Bristol, New York

Sensible

A line of appreciation for Mr. Gould's fine column. Its common sense should be irresistible to all well-intentioned and thinking people.

Catherine C. Fenzel
Tuckahoe, N.Y. [13]

■

IT ISN'T ALL JUNK

George Marek

GOOD HOUSEKEEPING, OCTOBER 1956, 229–31

To read some of the more lurid newspapers, one would get the impression that today's female teen-ager is a wild thing in blue jeans and the male is a loud lout in white canvas shoes, and that their worthlessness is expressed in the music, the horrible rock 'n' roll, a form of music really beneath contempt.

Love That Rock 'n' Roll

We are not going to pretend that rock 'n' roll is particularly worthy, but why do teen-agers love it so? Partly because of its untrammeled craziness, and partly because of the strong boom-boom of its rhythm, a rhythm that invites dancing (or what could be called dancing!). So you get "Blue Suede Shoes," in which the vocalist will let you do anything to him but please don't step on his blue suede shoes; and "Tutti Frutti," in which the singer shouts frantically, as though he is calling all souls to salvation, except that nobody can figure out just what his message is; and "Why Do Fools Fall in Love?" a song written by a fourteen-year-old and sounding like it. To older ears, rock 'n' roll is nothing but hysterical, raucous shouting. Some of the music is so bad, and much of it so alike, that people in the music business have been saying it will soon wear out its welcome. They have been saying this for two years, yet there is no sign that the fad is abating.

But rock 'n' roll is only a part of today's popular music. Taste is never uniform. One cannot speak glibly of American taste or of what the kids like. Taste is a 1,000-layer cake, with the layers going from best to worst—although the layers' thickness is, to be sure, unequal. The evidence is clear that today's teen-agers like more good music—and more teen-agers like good music—than in the previous generation.

Teens' Taste Is Broadening

The evidence can be found in sales of records in college shops or in stores near high schools; in the number of young people seen at Tanglewood, where the Boston Symphony plays; in the teen-agers playing in the high-school bands. In fact, one can feel everywhere a strong upsurge of interest in all kinds of music. The American Music Conference reports that 8,000,000 youngsters are now studying a musical instrument. And even greater numbers are singing in organized choral groups.

But we needn't get too highbrow on the subject. Within the confines of pop music itself there is a lot of room for different tastes. There is good pop music, there is bad pop music, and there is terrible pop music. There has always been terrible pop music. Some of us are old enough to remember such songs as "Yes! We Have No Bananas" or "Barney Google" or "I'se a-Muggin'."

The Jukeboxes Report

The surest indication of what is popular comes from jukebox operators. From a recent report, I glean that the taste of roadside customers (predominantly boys and girls under twenty-one) is by no means confined to rock 'n' roll. This year the jukeboxes are using twice as many classical and semi-classical records as they did a year ago. Under "classical" they list such numbers as "The Blue Danube Waltz" and Rachmaninoff's "Eighteenth Variation." "Semi-classical" would include selections from *The Student Prince*, and "Jalousie." So-called rhythm and blues songs show increased popularity [229] (they are closely allied to rock 'n' roll). Country and Western music has dropped off considerably, along with old-fashioned country polkas and sentimental torch ballads. It is not true that good melodies haven't got a chance, as some cynical (older) song writers try to claim.

These Were Most Popular

The five most popular jukebox selections in the spring of this year were "Rock 'n' Roll Waltz" by Kay Starr, "The Great Pretender" by The Platters, "Lisbon Antigua" by Nelson Riddle, "Memories Are Made of This" by Dean Martin, and "Poor People of Paris" by Les Baxter.

Of these five, two are rock 'n' roll numbers, more or less: The Kay Starr song is an ingenious novelty that kids the music; "The Great Pretender" has a melody and a good one, although it is sung in typical rock 'n' roll style, with hiccupy phrasing and falsetto tenor. On the other hand, "Lisbon Antigua" and "Poor People of Paris" are both colorful, atmospheric songs, from Portugal and France respectively, and have considerable merit. "Memories Are Made of This" would hardly qualify as a great song; it is an old-fashioned, swingy little ditty that Martin underplays in a gentle, breezy style.

These Are Especially Good

Beyond these five we can name recent successes that, by any standard of taste, are good songs. Among them is a curious melody composed by Kurt Weill for *The Threepenny Opera*. This modern mutation of Gay's eighteenth-century *The Beggar's Opera* was first performed in Berlin in 1928. Recently the work was successfully revived in a little off-Broadway theatre in Greenwich Village, New York City, Dick Hyman recorded one of the numbers from *The Threepenny Opera* called "Moritat," and Weill's 27-year-old music became a hit. Why should youngsters suddenly take up the old song? Well, there seems to be no explanation. [230]

Similarly a very fine French song that had been slumbering for years, and had been recorded in several versions without causing a stir, became, suddenly, a teen-age favorite. That song is "Autumn Leaves," recorded by Roger Williams.

Movies Contribute "Themes"

The movies, which appeal to a larger segment of the population than just the teen-age group, employ good songs—or as good as Hollywood composers can invent—as theme music. So we have the "Theme from *Picnic*," recorded by Morris Toloff, and "Main Title," from *The Man with the Golden Arm*, and both have been highly successful.

We can go back to 1955 and observe that neither "Unchained Melody," that year's top song, recorded by Les Baxter, nor Mitch Miller's "Yellow Rose of Texas" was a rock 'n' roll melody.

Theatre Gives New "Standards"

And we can go forward to "Standing on the Corner," as recorded by the Four Lads, from Frank Loesser's new operetta *The Most Happy Fella*, or to some of the songs from *My Fair Lady*, and predict that they will become "standards" and delight youngsters some years hence. We can point to "Angels in the Sky" or "The Wayward Wind," a ballad with a Western atmosphere sung by Gogi Grant, to observe that folklike tunes can still please. Frank Sinatra has reintroduced a new generation to "My Funny Valentine," one of Richard Rodgers' old tunes. Cole Porter's "I Love Paris," which first appeared in *Can-Can* in 1953, and "From This Moment On," which was heard in his unsuccessful show of 1950, *Out of This World*, are showing sudden new strength on the popularity charts. Let's not forget, either, that the wonderful songs from *Oklahoma!* and *Carousel* keep rolling along.

A song, then, does not *have* to be bad to make a hit with the high-school crowd. [231]

■

THE WAR OF THE GENERATIONS

John Sharnik

HOUSE & GARDEN, OCTOBER 1956, 40–41

Now that Elvis Presley, the baritone Marilyn Monroe, has become a kind of roving minstrel to the courts of television, parents have lost one of their most potent allies in the campaign against the music he exemplifies—that inflammatory cause called Rock 'n' Roll. It must be a temptation for grown-ups to think they also have lost the campaign. Radio, the big record companies, the movies all had defected to the teen-agers; TV seemed to be about the only thing left between us and the wave of adolescent riot that is identified with Rock 'n' Roll and its writing genius, that young man with the guitar.

Well, the TV people are floating downstream with the current. Presley bobs up on one variety show after another, and I may go under with the rest of you. But I honestly don't think that television is to be censured for employing him, or even that Rock 'n' Roll is the thing to be afraid of. It is probably no more than background music in the war between the generations. And, I might as well add, I think we've been defending the wrong ground.

Complicating the Natural

Nobody has suggested banning Miss Monroe from the public platforms—not in my vulgar circle, anyway—and the parallel between her and young Master Presley isn't purely frivolous. One British observer, trying to analyze the peculiar magnetism of America's pet blonde, commented on "the wonderfully complicated business she makes of breathing." It appears to be Presley's special distinction that he makes such excruciating work of singing, another talent that is usually thought to come fairly naturally. The complexities in both cases are similar—which is to say, suggestive. The chief difference seems to be that Miss Monroe addresses herself to the boys, and Mr. Presley, by and large, to the girls. Somehow we accept with amused tolerance the whistles and mutterings of the boys, including a good many boys of rather advanced age. But the squeals of the girls embarrass us, and, in the context of the controversy over Rock 'n' Roll, we are frightened of what we imagine to be the consequences.

We have assurances about these consequences, however, from the psychologists. I don't recommend psychologists as the infallible oracles of our age, but I do find the near-unanimity of their views on this subject quite persuasive. What they seem to be telling us amounts to this:

There is nothing inherently harmful in any sort of music itself, or in the performance of it before audiences of any age. The rhythmic monotony of Rock 'n' Roll, the crudeness of its melodic and harmonic structure, the primitive and often suggestive nature of its lyrics—none of these things in itself incites youngsters to violence, sexual laxness—or any of the other ills that have been blamed on the music. The waltz, after all, produces a certain exhilaration of its own, and, according to social historians, was considered pretty risky stuff for young ladies and gentlemen when it was first introduced in society. It is true enough that some youngsters have acted pretty anti-social (if I may borrow one of those euphemisms of the psychology trade) during or after Rock 'n' Roll performances. But this shows—as one expert said in an on-camera interview during the old, pre-Presley days of television—that there is danger in some youngsters, not in Rock 'n' Roll.

I'm convinced that the suggestiveness is lost on much of the teen-age audience, and that their response to the stimulating rhythm, though physical, is hardly sexual or otherwise anti-social. They are satisfied just to clap their hands and stamp their feet. Any kid who needs to do anything more destructive than that had something bothering him internally long before the band struck up the beat.

What is really bothering us *adults*, I suspect, is not that television has chosen to satisfy this teen-age audience but that such a distinctive audience exists at all, that within our own society there is a large, well defined group whose standards of taste and conduct we find baffling, and even [40] terrifying. These are our children, and we want badly for them to identify themselves with us. But somehow we have failed to inspire in them a respect for our own standards. It is young Presley's air of inarticulate sullenness and suspicion when he talks to the adult M.C. that strikes me as much more symbolic and much more ominous than the gymnastics he performs while singing. It's like that hostile look you get when you've told your 13-year-old daughter that she can't wear lipstick, or stay up to watch the late movie.

Like it or not, a little hostility between generations is a fact of life, and the kids will have their special idols, chosen with not too much discrimination, simply because kids are easily led. You'll hear them squeal, after all, over singers who aren't even trying to *imitate* Presley: and most teenagers' record collections contain a lot of stuff that doesn't sound remotely like Rock 'n' Roll. An acquaintance of mine who had watched, in fascination, while a 16-year-old girl flung herself exultantly out of her seat throughout a Rock 'n' Roll theatre session, asked her afterward what she got out of that particular form of music. "Nothing special," she said blandly. "I don't think it's so hot."

"Comic-Book Music"

Discrimination—the individual exercise of taste—is too much to expect of the young. But it *is* something they can grow into, with guidance, if they are given attractive alternatives to choose. And that, it seems to me, is where we ought to be on guard, because we ourselves too seldom provide intelligent guidance, and because there is too little offered to us all in the way of alternatives.

The real problem, in other words, isn't that Rock 'n' Roll is unique or revolutionary, but that it is so similar to what we accept as perfectly normal. Mitch Miller, probably the outstanding analyst of talent and material in the popular music field and a distinguished musician in his own right, once explained Rock 'n' Roll to me as "comic-book music"—technically crude and emotionally oversimplified. It is, in other words, an especially juvenile form.

Yet these are the very characteristics of most of the material that clutters the airwaves—and the movie screens and much of our popular literature. Youth is almost a national cult: young love, with its easy solutions and its limited, unsubtle range of emotions, is the prevalent idea. Our heroines are button-nosed dolls; our heroes, overgrown adolescents—Henry Aldriches in their fathers' pants. The pallid desires of a *Dungaree Doll*, of *Seventeen*, *A Teen-Age Prayer* and *From the Drugstore on the Corner, to the Chapel on the Hill* are sung to us from the record machines and the TV screens, and sung by grown-ups, with a straight face. Not much here for kids to grow up to. Or adults, if you get right down to it.

Rock 'n' Roll is no threat to any of this. Just the other way around, it's Presley and what little there is of originality in his music that are threatened by television's embrace. You can easily foresee the process of absorption and standardization at the prevailing level.

A few more shots at guest-starring, and Presley will be ripe for *real* exposure. He'll turn up in a couple of spectaculars, with big band, fancy costume, melodramatic lighting, maybe even one of those inevitable ballet choruses—a mass of staging from which Rock 'n' Roll will emerge as indistinguishable from Rodgers and Hammerstein. After a while, Presley will slide into relative obscurity, and Rock 'n' Roll will survive only as an influence on some later phenomenon, just as Rock 'n' Roll itself is a product of previous influences—blues, country music, swing and even Latin-American material.

But wait! Eventually, our hero re-appears, considerably mellowed, as genial host of the weekly "Elvis Presley Show." There, as a kind of middle-aged statesman, he speaks for his generation in the defense against whatever new musical menace has arisen among *its* baffling young. [41]

■

EXPERTS PROPOSE STUDY OF "CRAZE"

Milton Bracker

NEW YORK TIMES, FEBRUARY 23, 1957, 12

Psychologists suggested yesterday that while the rock 'n' roll craze seemed to be related to "rhythmic behavior patterns" as old as the Middle Ages it required full study as a current phenomenon.

One educational psychologist asserted that what happened in and around the Paramount Theatre yesterday struck him as "very much like the medieval type of spontaneous lunacy where one person goes off and lots of other persons go off with him."

A psychopathologist attending a meeting of the American Psychopathological Association at the Park Sheraton Hotel feared that this was just a guess.

Others present noted that a study by Dr. Reginald Lourie of Children's Hospital, Washington, indicated in 1949 that 10 to 20 percent of all children did "some act like rocking or rolling." The study went into detail on the stimulating effects of an intensified musical beat.

Meanwhile, a parallel between rock 'n' roll and St. Vitus Dance has been drawn by Dr. Joost A. M. Meerlo, associate in psychiatry at Columbia University, in a study just completed for publication.

Echo of Fourteenth Century

Dr. Meerlo described the "contagious epidemic of dance fury" that "swept Germany and spread to all of Europe" toward the end of the fourteenth century. It was called St. Vitus Dance (or Chorea Major), he continued, with its victims breaking into dancing and being unable to stop. The same activity in Italy, he noted, was referred to as Tarantism and popularly related to a toxic bite by the hairy spider called tarantula.

"The Children's Crusades and the tale of the Pied Piper of Hamlin," Dr. Meerlo went on, "remind us of these seductive, contagious dance furies."

Dr. Meerlo described his first view of rock 'n' roll this way: Young people were moved by a juke box to dance themselves "more and more into a prehistoric rhythmic trance until it had gone far beyond all the accepted versions of human dancing."

Sweeping the country and even the world, the craze "demonstrated the violent mayhem long repressed everywhere on earth," he asserted.

He also saw possible effects in political terms:

"Why are rhythmical sounds and motions so especially contagious? A rhythmical call to the crowd easily foments mass ecstasy: 'Duce! Duce! Duce!' The call repeats itself into the infinite and liberates the mind of all reasonable inhibitions . . . as in drug addiction, a thousand years of civilization fall away in a moment."

Dr. Meerlo predicted that the craze would pass "as have all paroxysms of exciting music." But he said that the psychic phenomenon was important and dangerous. He concluded in this way:

"Rock 'n' roll is a sign of depersonalization of the individual, of ecstatic veneration of mental decline and passivity.

"If we cannot stem the tide with its waves of rhythmic narcosis and of future waves of vicarious craze, we are preparing our own downfall in the midst of pandemic funeral dances.

"The dance craze is the infantile rage and outlet of our actual world. In this craze the suggestion of deprivation and dissatisfaction is stimulated and advertised day by day. In their automatic need for more people are getting less and less."

"The awareness of this tragic contradiction in our epoch," Dr. Meerlo said, "must bring us back to a new assessment of what value and responsibility are." [12]

■

PASSING FAD

MUSICAL AMERICA, MARCH 1957, 4

A teen-age girl recently wrote a threatening letter to the President of the United States because Elvis Presley was being inducted into the army. A horde of teen-agers, thousands-strong, swarmed into Times Square a couple of weeks ago and created such a commotion in the Paramount Theatre during the showing of a film that there was serious concern that the balcony might collapse under the stamping of their feet. Similar incidents of frenzy and dementia have been occurring in other American communities and—mark this well—simultaneously throughout Europe, including the Soviet Union.

The alleged cause of this mass hysteria is something known as rock 'n' roll music which is being alternately damned and defended from the pulpit, in the press, in the school rooms and in the clinics of the psychiatrists. We have been duly impressed, and even got a bit of perverse satisfaction, perhaps, out of the idea that anything musical could exert such a powerful influence over human behavior. We know, of course, that Verdi's early operas always were carefully screened by government censors because of their riot-producing potential against the Austrian occupation, and we have been present on occasions when hymns like "Onward Christian Soldiers," "The Star-Spangled Banner," "God Save the King" and the "Marseillaise" have moved multitudes to cheers and tears. We know, too, though not at first-hand, about the powerful emotional impact of tribal dances and incantations, and we are titillated by the privilege of grappling with so vital and mercurial a force.

We fear, however, upon inspection, that rock 'n' roll doesn't live up to its billing. We do not find anything in it to move anybody in any spectacular way, and we suspect that the viewers with alarm have been jumping to conclusions and getting the cart before the horse. At best rock 'n' roll is a kind of glorified hillbilly music with a two-beat, the familiar twanging guitar and a grotesquely distorted vocal line picked up from the blues. The insistent rhythm is no different from nor compelling physically or emotionally than any jazz-based idiom, whether dixieland, boogie-woogie, swing, or any other of the manifestations of evolving jazz which succeed each other almost as rapidly as women's fashions.

The rock 'n' roll music in itself can hardly be an incitement to violence. It just isn't that good. More likely it is merely a convenient vent through which a gravely disturbed and uncertain generation can release and externalize its inner tensions. Tomorrow there will be something else. [4]

BRITISH EXPERT UNROCKED BY CURRENT MUSIC TREND

Dorothy Barclay

NEW YORK TIMES, MARCH 1, 1957, 26

Even crowd-happy Times Square was set reeling a week ago when thousands of teen-agers jammed the area, smashed windows and disrupted traffic in their eagerness and determination to see the special rock 'n' roll show at the Paramount Theatre. Police were called out. Barriers set up. Experts proposed a study of the "craze," likening it to medieval lunacy. Educators decried; parents shook their heads.

The British have had their big black headlines about rock 'n' roll "riots" and a spirited defense of the teen-agers has just been presented in, of all places, a publication of the British Medical Association—"Family Doctor," a magazine edited by doctors for parents. In an article titled "There's Nothing Wrong with Rock 'n' Roll," a Dr. J. Macalister Brew analyzes the phenomenon and points at current adult society whatever blame there may be for teen-age excesses.

Then why all the excitement? Dr. Brew holds that becoming upset over adolescent behavior is almost a national pastime in Britain as it is in some circles here. In some individuals it amounts almost to a neurosis, he says, "a neurosis which follows the usual pattern of a refusal to do anything constructive about it."

In newspaper reports, for instance, Dr. Brew points out, "frenzied crowds" are only frenzied crowds—unless they are made up preponderantly of adolescents. In the latter case reports of their misbehavior are followed immediately in the press by indignant letters on the state of modern youth.

Basically No Different

Adolescents today, Dr. Brew declares, are basically no different from those of any other generation. As for their passion for rock 'n' roll, he says, in every era, any new type of dancing has become the fashionable craze of the 15 to 25-year age group. "It is no fault of modern young people that the Charleston, the Bunny Hug and the Turkey Trot of former days were less violent and antisocial. It was a less violent age."

Why do these youngsters dance with abandon until they are ready to drop? "It's jolly good exercise," Dr. Brew quotes them as saying. Why do they allow themselves occasionally to be carried away to the point of creating near-riots? "It seemed so smug and conspicuous not to." Are the jeans and sport shirts and oversized sweaters the rock 'n' rollers affect symbols of moral decay? They have, holds the author, "no more sinister meaning than had the Oxford bags or Norfolk jackets of a former age."

The irritation caused by the Bright Young Things of the Twenties and early Thirties, Dr. Brew observes, was confined to a relatively small group of the well-to-do. Today the inconvenience caused to adults by adolescent enthusiasms is more widely spread "simply because more young people can afford to get 'sent' by the fashionable craze of the moment."

Those most outspoken in their criticism of teenagers' recreational choices are among those least likely to do anything to improve the situation, Dr. Brew holds. He includes in this group many parents of adolescents.

There may come a day, he suggests, when the provision of adequate recreational facilities and trained leaders for youth groups will be regarded "as an essential provision of further education and as a valuable part of preventive medicine." In the meantime, parents might well ask themselves what can be done to provide adolescents "safer and more self-controlled methods of experiencing excitement and physical and emotional release," to insure that children will have "fun with the current crazes" but not be so lonely and unhappy that jazz and jive "become all-absorbing compensatory addictions." [26]

WHY THEY ROCK 'N' ROLL—AND SHOULD THEY?

Gertrude Samuels

NEW YORK TIMES MAGAZINE, JANUARY 12, 1958, 16–17, 19–20

Come on over, baby
Whole lotta shakin' goin' on
Come on over, baby
An' baby you can't go wrong
Ain't nobody fakin'
Whole lotta shakin' goin' on.

"Rocking" the song as though in a life and death struggle with an invisible antagonist was a tall, thin, flaccid youth who pulled his stringy, blond hair over his eyes and down to his chin. He shook his torso about as the beat of the band seemingly goaded him on. Screams from thousands of young throats billowed toward him. In the pandemonium youngsters flailed the air with their arms, jumped from their seats, beckoned madly, lovingly, to the tortured figure onstage.

The song could scarcely be heard over the footlights. No matter. The kids knew the words. They shrilled them with the singer—and kept up their approving, uninhibited screams. The singer finished off at the piano. The applause and yells all but raised the roof. Then a Negro quartet raced onstage, adjusted the microphones, and a new tune brought on a new cascade of screams and energetic hand waves.

This was the teen-age bedlam at the Paramount Theatre in New York where in recent days Alan Freed emceed a rock 'n' roll show. Now the spectacle is moving on to the national scene, to Philadelphia, Washington, Cleveland, Chicago, Detroit, Los Angeles.

What is this thing called rock 'n' roll? What is it that makes teen-agers—mostly children between the ages of 12 and 16—throw off their inhibitions as though at a revivalist meeting? What—who—is responsible for these sorties? And is this generation of teen-agers going to hell?

For some understanding of the rock 'n' roll behavior which has aroused a great deal of controversy, at least in adult circles, one must go to the sources.

An important source, of course, is the music itself. Technically, rock 'n' roll derives from the blues. But rock 'n' roll is an extension of what was known as Rhythm and Blues, a music of the Thirties and Forties that aimed primarily at the Negro market; that music emphasized the second and fourth beats of each measure. Rock 'n' roll exploits this same heavy beat—by making it heavier, lustier and transforming it into what has become known as The Big Beat. It is a tense, monotonous beat that often gives rock 'n' roll music a jungle-like persistence.

In his Encyclopedia Yearbook of Jazz, Leonard Feather comments that "rock 'n' roll bears the same relationship to jazz as wrestling bears to boxing." Freed claims to have invented the term "rock 'n' roll" back in 1951 for a radio show in Cleveland because "of the rocking beat of the music."

Of the top sixty best-selling records in 1957, forty were rock 'n' roll tunes, the biggest seller being Elvis Presley's "All Shook Up" which sold 2,450,000 across the country.

Another rich field for research is found among the children themselves. They come from all economic classes and neighborhoods, sometimes lone-wolfing it, but mostly with their pals, dates, clubs and gangs. Outside the theatre they seem to become one class—rocking the neighborhood with wild and emotional behavior as they break through the wooden police barriers to improve their positions in line or fight toward the box office and their heroes inside.

Like young teen-agers generally, they tend to keep the sexes segregated: girls are mostly with girls, boys with boys. Their clothes and manners bespeak a kind of conformism: so many of the girls wear a sort of uniform—tight revealing sweaters with colorful kerchiefs, skin-tight toreador pants, white woolen socks and loafers; so many of the boys conform to a pattern—leather or sports jackets, blue jeans, loafers and cigarettes.

Physically, it would seem as though [16] the children feared to look different from one another, or lacked confidence in individuality. Indeed, many admit to this cheerfully: "All the kids have this jacket," said one boy, "and I don't want to be different."

Inside the theatre, the emotional conformism is even more obvious. A scream of approval or delight starts—mostly a girl's scream—and everyone starts screaming. An arm shoots up fifth row center, and instantly all arms appear to be flung up and bodies leap up or start swaying crazily. Anyone can touch off the stampede of screaming youngsters who always rush the stage after a show is over. Sometimes, they fling themselves onstage, as did one member of a Brownsville gang who jumped on, zip gun and all, "as though he was Superman," and was firmly ejected.

How do the teen-agers feel about rock 'n' roll?

A black-haired, starry-eyed beauty of 15, emerging from the theatre looks as though she had returned from outer space.

"It's just instinct, that's all," murmured Roseann Chasen of Norfolk, Va., visiting in New York. "I come to hear it because I can sing and scream here. Because it's not like at home where your parents are watching TV and you can't. Here you can scream all you like. And the stars wave to you, and don't act like they don't care whether you're there or not."

Roseann had about fifteen favorite tunes, "but the best are 'Teardrops,' 'At the Hop,' and 'Great Balls of Fire.'"

"He was rocking the house with that 'Great Balls of Fire,'" she said, "did you hear it, when the kids went crazy? It was just instinct with him, that's all," she added dreamily as she went off to join her girl friends. She didn't sound as though she could raise her voice to a scream.

Kenny Puncerelli, a 16-year-old from Englewood, and his two pals, Bob Brennan of Tenafly and Wayne Whalen of Hillsdale, N.J., tried to find words to describe their favorite, Jo-Ann Campbell, the diminutive singer in a shimmering green dress whom no one could have heard over the footlights because of the screams.

"Just say she's the greatest. It's the beat. It's different from any other beat," Kenny said, talking almost with a beat. "It's the rhythm. It's easy to listen to."

"It's the beat," the others confirmed knowingly.

Three 15-year-old girls from Queens, one with braces on her teeth, another in pin curls, the third smoking ("Gee, I wouldn't want my mother to know I was smoking.") had saved their money for the show. Every day they listen to the rock 'n' roll show over Channel 7 "because it's music we can understand."

"And here we can look at the actors and wave to them," one caroled. "They're cute, they're young, and we don't have to do the housework."

The Lords, who called themselves a "sports gang" from Flower Park and Melrose in the Bronx, had been waiting for hours in the queue, lost their place when they went to buy lunches, and failed to persuade a policeman that they deserved their old position in line when they returned. The red-jacketed 15- and 16-year-olds moved to the back, to start waiting anew. Why?

"Because it's great music." "It makes you feel good." "We like to go crazy." "It hops us up. It's different from the records when you can see them and be with them." Some of the boys play instruments. Two were planning college careers (one to be an engineer, another a veterinarian).

Vivian Stoker, 16, and Jerilyn O'Neill, 16, juniors at the Villa Maria Academy in the Bronx, had sat through three shows with Vivian's mother. Both girls "like classical music, too" and have Beethoven, Mozart and Chopin records as well as rock 'n' roll.

"The main thing about this music," said brown-haired Vivian, "is that it's lively—it's not dead. It makes you want to dance. With a waltz you have to be in a good [17] mood to dance to it. But with rock 'n' roll, no matter what your mood is, it gets you."

Did they think the effect of the music, the lyrics, the physical contortions of the actors was making delinquents?

"Some of the kids says that Presley affects them," Jerilyn put in. "My girl friend says he sends chills up her spine. But I think the majority of the girls just like the beat. It's new."

And Mrs. Stoker added: "I like it. The girls have their record collections and keep their minds occupied. They just enjoy it all."

Eddie Cook, 14, and Frankie Mielke, 13, of Queens attend the same parochial school. Eddie wore a religious medal on a chain around his neck. Said Eddie, "I don't like this symphony stuff that my father puts on the radio. My mother doesn't mind rock 'n' roll though."

Frankie said, "In my house they don't mind it as long as they're not around." And Eddie adds reflectively, "If there wasn't this music, we might be getting into trouble . . . you know, there'd be nothing to do at night."

In show business circles there has been bitter controversy about the worth and effects of rock 'n' roll.

Frank Sinatra, a veteran showman, was quoted in a Paris magazine recently as follows: "Rock 'n' roll smells phony and false. It is sung, played and written for the most part by cretinous goons and by means of its almost imbecile reiteration, and sly, lewd, in plain fact, dirty lyrics . . . it manages to be the martial music of every sideburned delinquent on the face of the earth."

Between shows at the Paramount the other day Alan Freed replied to Sinatra and other critics:

"I was shocked when I read what Frank said. He has no business knocking show business. It's been good to him. As for charging that this music is 'dirty' and making delinquents of children, I think I'm helping to combat juvenile delinquency. If my kids are home at night listening to my radio program, and get interested enough to go out and buy records and have a collection to listen to and dance to, I think I'm fighting delinquency.

"This music," he went on, "comes from the levees and the plantations. It's simple to dance to, and to clap your [19] hands to, and the kids know the words to every song. That's why they come. This is an audience-participation kind of music. They come in and pay to sing louder than the performers.

"And it's natural that kids should look for excitement and thrills. Well, I'd rather that they find it in the theatre than in street gangs. I say that if kids have any interest in any kind of music, thank God for it. Because if they have the interest, they can find themselves in it. And as they grow up, they broaden out and come to enjoy all kinds of music."

What does it all prove? One on-the-scene observer, Robert Shapiro, manager of the Paramount Theatre, pointed out that back in the Thirties Bing Crosby, Benny Goodman and Glen Miller were idolized by the young jazz fans. With the advent of Frank Sinatra, Shapiro recalled, teen-agers "swooned, moved and screamed with his every gesture—and now the daughters of those teen-agers are here."

"The young people of all generations," Shapiro said, "are only looking for a chance to express their enthusiasm."

A. D. Buchmueller, a psychiatric social worker and the executive director of the Child Study Association, a national organization working in the field of child development and parent education, said:

"Kids, just like adults, get caught up in a mass kind of hysteria, which is contagious. Some get hurt by it, physically and emotionally.

"But it is not helpful, and may even be harmful, for adults to take a strong and condemning attitude and action toward adolescents in their rock 'n' roll behavior. This behavior is part of their individual as well as collective or group rebellion against the strictness of adult society.

"This doesn't mean that I approve of rock 'n' roll. I don't. I think there are many other kinds of music, more beautiful, and culturally more valuable, that they might be hearing. And also the suggestiveness of a sexual nature in crude and open exhibitionism used by some singers is to be deplored.

"The charge that rock 'n' roll may be an outlet for impulsive behavior or sexual aggression by the youngsters may be true. But this has not been proven by any thorough studies. The charges are mostly hunches that people have been having. The rock 'n' roll behavior seems faddish, as was the behavior for other generations that liked the Charleston, the black bottom, jitterbugging. I don't think it does a bit of good to outlaw it. It will pass, just as the other vogues did."

Finally, Judge Hilda Schwartz, who regularly presides in Adolescents Court and has made many studies of youth problems, had this to say:

"Rock 'n' roll does not produce juvenile delinquents. The causes of delinquency and youth crime are far more complex and varied. But for the disturbed, hostile and insecure youth, the stimulation of the frenzied, abandoned music certainly can't be considered a therapy.

"However, only a tiny proportion of youngsters lining up around the theatre are hostile and insecure. The vast majority are wholesome boys and girls following an adolescent fad as only adolescents can.

"But what a pity that this tremendous hero worship, this yearning for something and someone to look up to, this outpouring of energy and love should have been concentrated on a fad that can only be a passing interest. It is our fault.

We haven't stirred the children with something to live by, to worship, to put their hopes in. They haven't the inspiration because we ourselves haven't put a high value on courage and liberty and working for others. Perhaps we have taken the glamour out of the good life . . . and, because they're young, they're looking for excitement and outlets."

Enthusiasm, hysteria, misguided hero worship? On one thing all experts agree: rock 'n' roll will surely be with us for a while longer. For apprehensive adults who think nothing as alarming as The Big Beat has ever existed, there may be comfort in a college joke of some years back. An Englishman, watching some contorting American dancers in fascination and disbelief, turned to his friend, murmuring, "I say, old boy, they get married afterwards, don't they?"

And that was in the fox-trot and shimmy days, long before rock 'n' roll appeared, amid commotion, on the scene. [20]

■

ROCK 'N' ROLL OPPONENTS ARE DUE FOR BIG BREAK

NEW YORK TIMES, JANUARY 13, 1958, 49

St. Louis, Jan. 12 (AP)—One St. Louis radio station is in revolt against rock 'n' roll music.

Beginning tomorrow, Station KWK will play each such record in its library once—then break it with a sharp snap clearly audible to the listeners. The supply is expected to be exhausted in a week.

Robert T. Convey, KWK president, who gave the order after conferring with his disk jockeys, said they were in agreement that rock 'n' roll "has dominated the music field long enough."

Mr. Convey said he thought what had started as a novelty has "grown to such proportions as to alienate many adult listeners. The majority of listeners will be surprised and pleased at how pleasant radio listening can be [without rock 'n' roll]," Mr. Convey said. [49]

■

EDITORIALLY SPEAKING

MUSICAL JOURNAL, FEBRUARY 1958, 3

In a month which contains the birthdays of two such eminent Americans as George Washington and Abraham Lincoln, not to speak of St. Valentine's Day, dedicated to sentiment of the highest type, it becomes the duty of this magazine to comment on the most disgraceful blasphemy ever committed in the name of music. We refer, obviously, to that popular reversion to savagery known as "Rock 'n' Roll."

Recent newspaper headlines have emphasized the fact that the illiterate gangsters of our younger generation are definitely influenced in their lawlessness by this throw-back to jungle rhythms. Either it actually stirs them to orgies of sex and violence (as its model did for the savages themselves), or they use it as an excuse for the removal of all inhibitions and the complete disregard of the conventions of decency.

In a theatre not long ago an usher and several spectators were stabbed during a general riot of teen-agers. The picture which apparently aroused these violent emotions was something called *Jamboree*. In it various reputable disc jockeys lent themselves to the exploitation of a series of rock 'n' roll specialties featuring imitators of Elvis Presley, whose leering, whining, moaning and suggestive lyrics blandly offered a vicarious sexual experience. If anyone missed the point of these filthy performances, a practically unique naiveté would seem to be indicated.

It has been argued speciously that the public resentment of rock 'n' roll is merely a repetition of similar criticisms of such old-fashioned dances as the Charleston and Black Bottom, even dragging in the waltzes of Johann Strauss. This argument is bad logic, like the claim of the frustrated composer who says, "Wagner was criticized and turned out to be a genius. I am criticized, so I also must be a genius."

Aside from the illiteracy of this vicious "music," it has proved itself definitely a menace to youthful morals and an incitement to juvenile delinquency. There is no point in soft-pedaling these facts any longer. The daily papers provide sufficient proof of their existence.

This is not to say that any youngster who honestly enjoys rock 'n' roll is even potentially a delinquent. That would obviously be an unfair indictment. It is, however, entirely correct to state that every proved delinquent has been definitely influenced by rock 'n' roll, as well as comic books and the more violent movies and television shows.

The direct effect of music on human emotions and behavior is nothing new. The ancient Greeks sincerely believed in the "ethical" powers of their modes or scales, claiming that only the Dorian could inspire true courage, while some others created effeminacy and languor. A Hungarian song some years ago supposedly caused a number of suicides, and the martial influence of such melodies as the *Marseillaise* and *Rakoczy March* is historically famous. Even our modern college songs may be credited with some such psychological significance.

Music, in a variety of forms, can and should be an inspiration to mankind. When it is debased to the service of the lowest animal passions, it becomes a definite threat to civilization.

It may be noted that this issue of *Music Journal* accents the scientific developments in the field of music, from the cover picture, showing young artists in the process of tape recording, through the articles of Coles Doty, Jr., Allegra Gunning, Percy Faith and Jack Dolph, as well as the Music Educators' Round Table, to a passing reference even in Janet Faure's discussion of the exotic music of the Orient. This is in keeping with the spirit of the times, and it is imperative that we remind ourselves of the equal importance of the arts and the sciences in preventing the complete destruction of our civilization.

On the human side, the beloved Danny Kaye (now appearing in the funniest film of his career, *Merry Andrew*) stresses our responsibility toward the children of the world. Helen Fouts Cahoon presents a serious teacher's attitude toward popular singers; Kenneth Berger writes about great bandmasters; Carl Haverlin delves into the music of Washington and Lincoln. Martin Kalmanoff deals with Puccini, Marguerite Tazelaar with libraries and Kathryn Rieder with cowboys, while Howard Mitchell comments on contemporary composition, with practical teaching suggestions from William Zerffi, Herman Rosenthal, Beatrice Chauncey, Josephine Holtgreve and others. [3]

■

ROCK 'N' ROLL STABBING

NEW YORK TIMES, MAY 5, 1958, 48

Boston, May 4 (UP)—Teen-aged brawlers stabbed a sailor and beat and robbed a dozen other persons early today in the aftermath of a rock 'n' roll show at Boston Arena.

The sailor, Albert Reggianni, 19 years old, of Stoughton, was the most seriously injured of those attacked by teen-age gangs after several thousand persons emerged from the music show. Alan Freed and Jerry Lee Lewis were the headliners.

Young Reggianni was taken to City Hospital for emergency treatment and then transferred to Chelsea Naval Hospital. There a spokesman said his condition was not critical. The teen-age brawlers also mauled the boy's two girl companions, Carol Wallace and Jean Austin, both of Stoughton.

Juvenile thugs ripped earrings from Mrs. Julia Talbot, 23, of Somerville who had taken two teen-age girls to the show. [48]

■

BOSTON, NEW HAVEN BAN 'ROCK' SHOWS

NEW YORK TIMES, MAY 6, 1958, 21

Boston, May 5 (UP)—Rock 'n' roll musical shows in public auditoriums were banned in Boston and New Haven today.

Other New England cities braced for the same show that preceded violence in Boston late Saturday night.

Fifteen persons were stabbed, beaten or robbed by gangs of roving teenagers and adults after an Alan Freed show ended at the Boston Arena.

Albert Reggianni, 18-year-old sailor from Stoughton, was stabbed repeatedly in the chest. He was taken to Chelsea Naval Hospital. His condition was reported satisfactory.

Mayor John B. Hynes of Boston said promoters for such shows in the future will not be granted licenses.

"I am not against rock 'n' roll as such," Mr. Hynes said, "and not when it is conducted under the auspices of an established organization. However, I am against rock 'n' roll dances when they are put on by a promoter. This sort of performance attracts the troublemakers and the irresponsible.

"They will not be permitted in Boston."

Mayor Hynes can ban such shows by directing the City Censor not to issue a license to a promoter. [21]

■

ROCK 'N' RIOT

TIME, MAY 19, 1958, 50

Wrapped in a package called "The Big Beat," Disk Jockey Alan Freed has long rolled across the land, introducing rock 'n' roll stars and keynoting gone music, with the express intention of inciting his teen-age followers to happy frenzy. A fortnight ago, the acknowledged "King of Rock 'n' Roll" rolled into Boston and set up shop in its 7,200-seat Arena. Almost 5,000 hip kids poured in the Arena to catch his 17 acts, including four bands, and starring Dreamboat Groaner Jerry Lee Lewis.

Frenzy soon set in. The aisles filled with dancers, and others got into the groove by jumping on their seats. The head of the 20 cops on hand decided that more light on the subject would help curb the crowd's antics. The house lights were turned up. Then, according to Arena Manager Paul Brown, sincere-faced "Deejay" Freed huffed: "I guess the police here in Boston don't want you kids to have a good time." Whatever Freed said, the effect was magical. The Arena really began jumping—while Brown paced his office, "praying it would end."

A while before midnight the wound-up kids spilled into the streets. Just who was responsible for what happened next is a matter of dispute. All around the Arena common citizens were set upon, robbed and sometimes beaten. A young sailor caught a knife in the belly, and two girls with him were thrashed. In all, nine men and six women were roughed up enough to require hospital treatment. Boston police blamed Freed and his frenetic fans, but could not prove it, since they nabbed nobody. Freed's defenders pointed out that the Arena area has been the site of frequent muggings in the past; the toughs might simply have used the crowds pouring out of the Arena as a cover.

But Boston's Mayor John Hynes did not want to hear arguments or evidence. He ordered that no licenses be issued for any more rock 'n' roll shows, and a Boston grand jury returned an indictment against Freed—under an old "anti-anarchy" law—for inciting "the unlawful destruction of property." Professing alarm, and perhaps jumpy over growing criticism of juvenile delinquency, officials in New Haven and Newark seized on the Boston incident as an excuse to ban scheduled Freed appearances.

Freed promptly quit his $25,000-a-year job with Manhattan's radio station WINS because it "failed to stand behind my policies and principles," and returned to his Stamford, Conn. home to contemplate his grievances. Snapped Freed: "Those kids in Boston were the greatest—swell, wonderful kids. But the police were terrible." [50]

YOUR KIDS DIG THAT CRAZY MUSIC, TOO?

CHANGING TIMES, FEBRUARY 1959, 30–32

Every once in a while, half the kids in the country seem to go wild over some sulky, side-burned guitar-twanger in a zooty suit. Usually you can manage to be condescending about these outbursts since, after all, there is no accounting for other people's children. Then one day you discover photographs of the ineffable Elvis himself—or Fats Domino, or Domenico Modugno, or whatever—in your very own daughter's bedroom. Man, you'll flip.

Give a girl a good home, every advantage, a careful upbringing, and she sneaks home pictures of a calf-eyed, no-account singer she wouldn't dare bring to the front door! You resolve on the spot to "do something" about this crazy music. And you mean "crazy" in the precise dictionary sense of the word.

Not that you have anything against music, mind you. Why, you wouldn't worry one second if our kids listened three hours daily to real music—Lawrence Welk, say, or some of those great Benny Goodman or Tommy Dorsey reissues that can be bought without prescription in any drugstore.

But not this rock 'n' roll stuff. It's primitive and brutal, just thump-thump-thump, honking sax and demented wails from people with names like The Teddy Bears or The Five Blobs. Its tastelessness aside, you can't help feeling that this is the music of cheap night spots, tawdry roadhouses, drink, delinquency and, often enough, leering sexual innuendo.

The kids crave it like a narcotic, too, you have noticed. If our girl has to get moony over an entertainer, you wonder, why couldn't it be a nice clean-cut young man like Pat Boone or maybe Ricky Nelson?

Those Words, That Music

You restrain yourself from putting on the Irate Parent act, though. Who wants to be a square in his own family circle? Instead, you go away smoldering, wondering how you can possibly make the kids understand what you find so unacceptable about the music they enjoy.

Well, what is it you object to? Is it the words? Is it the tunes? Both, probably, since they go together. You try to figure it out as best you can with that ungodly racket going on in the recreation room.

Certainly the music itself is bad enough. Monotonous and unmelodic, it is about as musical as a concrete mixer with rocks in its hopper. The vocalizing is so agonized you barely can make out the words. But what little you can comprehend doesn't exactly put your mind at ease. "Lyrics," they call them. Hah!

In sheer horror, you put "My Geiger Counter Heart" and "I'm Going to Sit Right Tight on My Satellite" out of mind. Even the kids won't [30] stand for *that* claptrap. Yet the ones they do dig include several that are plain moronic burblings ("You get that 'Itchy Twitchy Feeling'/You start rocking and a-reeling"). Others celebrate experiences of dubious morality ("You cheated, you lied/You said that you want me"). Still others are shameless wallows in self-teasing sentimentality ("I'm a sad girl, don't say I'm a bad girl/Because I gave my kisses, because I gave my l-o-o-ove").

This, you reflect sadly, is the only poetry today's kids ever meet outside school. Suddenly one critic's remark flashes to mind: "Their effect on American taste makes the jukeboxes a greater danger to American life than the Jukes."

Maybe so. Still, you don't need refined literary tastes to make a go of life. But you do need to have the basic facts of life straight. Imagine how mixed up a kid could be if he faced life knowing no more about love than he had picked up from popular songs!

The main thing wrong with the songs is that they overly idealize boy-and-girl relationships. Love always comes at first sight. Every romance is full-time rapture. There is only one perfect he-or-she for me. Demand instant love; the flavor lasts and ecstasy is guaranteed for life.

That's a pretty fancy expectation to plant in impressionable minds. Suppose love by instantaneous combustion fails to materialize. Or suppose the one perfect he-or-she for me turns out to be regrettably imperfect? Then there will be frustration. And one short step beyond that lies despair.

Sure, there are songs of frustrated love. But they don't say, "You made a mistake." They simply tell the listener that he was unjustly treated, and give the knife an extra turn in the wound. You'll listen a long time before you hear a song saying that once you find your dream-girl or dream-man, your troubles are probably just beginning.

Why the Kids Like It

That's a pretty dismal line of thought. Before you get too depressed by it, perhaps you should recall a more cheerful fact. It is this: There is very little evidence that the kids pay much attention to the misleading messages of the songs they listen to. The kids don't spin rock 'n' roll records for self-education. They have other motives in mind. Right here, an insight once expressed by David Reisman, the sociologist, may be helpful. Movie-going, Reisman pointed out, serves different functions for different people. Some go to see the show, some to neck, some to get in out of the rain. And any individual may go to the movies for different purposes on different occasions.

So it is with popular music. It has several useful functions, and the functions are not always the same for every youngster or on every occasion.

Sometimes it is a socializer, bringing kids together for kid talk, kidding, dancing, sharing enthusiasms. Sometimes it is a ticket of admission, an interest that provides an "in." If the crowd's favorite songs, singers and combos are your favorites, too, you get to be one of the gang instead of an outsider. That's what a youngster means when he tells you, "I like rock 'n' roll because, well, everybody likes it." Music can even help a hep kid become a leader among his contemporaries if he can spot the coming hit or the rising star before the others do.

Nor are the uses of popular music limited to helping a kid get along with others. Some youngsters undoubtedly find it helpful in getting along with themselves.

In moments of loneliness, the group's musical world is as close at hand as the nearest radio or phonograph, ready to provide vicarious companionship. If boredom threatens, there always is a new song or a new musical gimmick to discover and become enthusiastic about. When self-doubt or uncertainty causes trouble, a jaunty tune can offer reassurance that youth is, after all, a carefree time of good friends, fun dates, Coke-party hilarity and infectious good cheer.

Then, too, popular songs do seem to touch deep, dimly felt adolescent emotions. Young people through the ages have yearned for romance and expressed their longing through lyricism of one form or another. "Pussy Cat" or "Mr. Success" may strike your adult ears as pretty pale excuses for lyricism, but there it is. These songs may be reaching some young hearts today as poignantly as "Stardust" or "I'll Never Smile Again" may once have touched yours.

And here is the unkindest cut of all. Youth today, as ever, chafes at the restrictions imposed by parents, school and society at large. It feels the old yen to defy authority and [31] invite disapproval. So it may be—remember this before you reach for the switch—that your youngster likes his Big Beat so much because you like it so little.

What Parents Can Do

If you set out to find an approved cure for your children's addiction to trashy music, you wouldn't get much help from the guidance experts. Most are silent on this subject. This dearth of counsel should be reassuring in itself. If pop music really was about to corrupt our youth and undermine the republic, there would be no lack of Reveres to spread the alarm.

Even so, it is disturbing to see youngsters lavish so much time and enthusiasm on music that really does not deserve such devotion. What then? Well, there are several constructive things a conscientious parent can do.

First, relax. Your child is not going to become a delinquent just because he fancies rock 'n' roll. If he is normal and wholesome in other respects, music can't spoil him. His lamentable tastes simply indicate that he hasn't matured before his time.

And whatever you do, don't put a wrathful taboo on the stuff. Liking the pops is no crime. An unreasonable prohibition will only win you resentment.

Next, get with it. Some months back, one embattled but game parent sat in on a record hop with his children. He was surprised to find them frolicking to a tune right out of his own youth, "I Found a Million Dollar Baby in a Five and Ten Cent Store." What's more, it was sung by a quartet from the same prehistoric era, The Mills Brothers. The punching beat and exuberant bursts of gibberish in the performance were unlike anything he could recall from his own fevered teenhood. Still, he could sense that here was a record worth a spin.

From that moment, his attitude mellowed. He began having fun with his own kids, on their own terms. His sympathetic participation in their listening helped them to become more discriminating without missing any of the fun.

So even though the notion repels you, listen to your kids' music yourself. Try to understand its appeal. See that they have a chance to satisfy their thirst for it in surroundings and with companions you approve. Once you show a basic sympathy, you can get away with poking fun at the worst of it and perhaps come to enjoy the best of it yourself.

Give them good things to admire. Buy them records and take them to concerts so that they can explore other kinds of music than that dished up by the disc jockeys who exploit their enthusiasms by relentlessly programming the top 40 tunes and nothing else. You can't *make* your youngsters like better music. But you can at least give them the chance.

And if you are worried about the delusive notions about romance created by the words that go with the music, try to give them a chance to observe real people coping with love, life and marriage in realistic terms. Your youngsters will learn more about reality in these matters from what is said and done in their own homes—and their friends' homes—than from a million hours at the jukebox.

Finally, don't overact your age. Remember that you, too, once were dewy-eyed and damp-eared. Your musical interests and tastes have been developed and sharpened over the years. What strikes your seasoned ear as dreary banality may reach an inexperienced ear as dramatic revelation. It is unreasonable to expect kids to have the sophisticated musical perceptions at 12 that you needed twice as long to develop.

And incidentally, do count to ten before you sputter indignantly at "The Purple People Eater" or "The Witch Doctor" or this week's successor to leadership on the Nut Parade. Let's see now . . . just who was it that made a national nuisance of "I Faw Down an' Go Boom!," "Let's All Sing Like the Birdies Sing," "The Music Goes 'Round and 'Round," "A-Tisket a-Tasket," "Three Little Fishes" and "Mairzy Doats"? Anybody you know? [32]

R&R STILL BEAMS PLENTY OF LIFE

BILLBOARD, JANUARY 18, 1960, 6, 18

New York—Rock and roll's demise, like that of Mark Twain's, has been greatly exaggerated. For now, even after the payola scandals and the attempt to link all payola with rock and roll recordings, the music with a beat still dominates over 60 per cent of The Billboard's "Hot 100" chart. This is not to say that rock and roll isn't fading, or actually evolving into pop music, but the fade is one of the slowest yet recorded.

Right now the number one rec-chart is "Running Bear," by Johnny Preston on Mercury. The tune was penned by J. P. (Big Bopper) Richardson, and is as much a rock and roll recording as there is. On the charts at the present time are such out-and-out rockers as Frankie Avalon, Freddie Cannon, Jimmy Clanton, Paul Anka, Dion and the Belmonts, Marv Johnson, Fabian, Larry Hall, Bill Black, Bobby Rydell, Duane Eddy, Carl Dobkins, Jack Scott, Conway Twitty, Little Anthony and the Imperials, Rod Lauren, Ricky Nelson, Dee Clark, Lloyd Price, the Crests, Jackie Wilson, the Coasters, Clyde McPhatter, Jerry Wallace,

Joe Turner, Royal Teens, Jimmie Rodgers, Everly Brothers, Fats Domino, the Bluenotes, the Fireballs, Bill Haley, Sammy Turner, Johnny and the Hurricanes, Ray Charles, the Five Satins, the Champs, Tender Sim, the Fleetwoods, Frankie Ford, the Spacemen, and the Rivieras.

This should indicate the still-amazing hold of rock and roll on the younger generation. And is there any doubt that Elvis Presley's first new records, when he is released from the Army, will continue to sell in the millions as his records have consistently done since he joined RCA Victor five years ago?

Rock and roll as such sprung full-fledged upon the scene back in 1954, and has continued to exert its hold on the kids ever since. The reason that it still has the hold is partly due to the economic situation of the record industry itself, in which the youngsters continue to be the biggest market for single records. Even when what is often termed "quality" material is put on disks, adults don't buy the records in any quantity that disk makers hope they might do. An indication of this is the sale of Johnny Mathis singles versus Johnny Mathis albums made up of the same singles. Mathis albums containing "Johnny's Greatest Hits," Vols. 1 and 2, have far outsold the single records of these songs.

Obviously no record company is going to put itself out of the singles business by recording singles that won't sell. And since the largest market is youngsters, it is only logical to aim at this youngish trade. The mistaken belief on the part of even some members of the industry that only rock and roll firms gave out with payola is a belief that is more a fancy than a reality.

The other reason for the continuing hold of rock and roll disks on the kids is simply that they like it. The why and wherefores are questions for folk outside the music business, for inside there is rarely reason to question successful records, or trends, but to go along with them. [18]

■

ROCK 'N' ROLL'S GLOBAL WANE

VARIETY, MARCH 2, 1960, 55, 57

The deemphasis of the rock 'n' roll beat, which has been marked in the U.S. since the start of the various payola probes a few months ago, is being echoed in Europe as well, according to songstress Joni James and her manager-husband, Tony Aquaviva. Recently returned from a swing around Europe, they noted a strong trend to a more standard brand of music among all levels of the population.

A significant straw in the wind is the fact that GI audiences at shows presented at Army bases abroad are no longer screaming for the rocking numbers. Among the Europeans themselves, Miss James stated the big beat never really established a firm hold on the market, except for a few standout artists like Elvis Presley or Bill Haley. Now, the traditional European accent on melodic material is reasserting itself.

In the U.S. Miss James is set for a series of college bookings, teeing off recently with a date at North Carolina U. She said that for the past couple of years the collegians have regarded rock 'n' roll as strictly for the squares and the kids and have been the chief audiences for jazz, folk and standard names.

Miss James, who came up with her first click about eight years ago, recently inked a new deal with MGM Records, involving a [55] substantial annual guarantee and a payoff spread over a long period. It's a five-year pact with the distribution of coin to be allocated over 10 years for maximum tax benefits.

Miss James, who travels around the country in her own twin-engine plane, has mapped an extensive tour of major cities this year with local symphony orchs playing under Aquaviva's baton. It's an extension of her Carnegie Hall, N.Y., date last year and her MGM album project, "100 Strings and Joni." While in England, Miss James cut a religioso album, "100 Voices and Joni." She works through her own production company, J. J. Productions. [57]

PART TWO

READINGS

Women in the Working World

∎

The Nature of Early Human Life

∎

Animal Rights

∎

The Younger Generation

∎

The Impact of Advertising

∎

A Casebook on William Faulkner's
"A Rose for Emily"

WOMEN IN THE WORKING WORLD

AS ONE EXECUTIVE PUT IT, "TO THE AVERAGE American, the term *management* brings to mind one image: short gray hair and a zipper in the front." The image the executive was describing is one aspect of the difficulty women like herself face in corporate America—how to be accepted and treated as equals in a male-dominated world.

Writers have followed the controversial question of the status of women in society at least since the days of the Greek playwright Aristophanes, who wrote *Lysistrata*, a play about a group of women who astounded the men of ancient Athens by putting an end to a war by themselves. Since those days the most significant changes in the socioeconomic status of women have happened during the twentieth century—and especially in the world of business, the changes have occurred largely since the 1960s. It is with these changes in business that the readings in this anthology are concerned.

In the United States the Nineteenth Amendment to the Constitution, ratified in 1920, finally guaranteed the right of women to vote. World Wars I and II introduced many women to the workplace for the first time, yet in the 1950s there was still a very powerful stereotype whose message was, "A woman's place is in the home." The stereotype was embodied in such widely popular television programs as "Father Knows Best," "Ozzie and Harriet," and "Leave It to Beaver," where women were portrayed as essentially cookie bakers and sock menders, economically dependent and not likely to meddle in the "man's world" of business. By the 1960s a variety of social and economic factors were increasing the number of women in the work force. This increase, accompanied by changes in employment discrimination laws and regulations, began to improve job opportunities for women. Two of the most important of the early changes were Title VII of the Civil Rights Act of 1964 and Executive Order 11246, along with their subsequent amendments. As we saw earlier, Michael Moskow points out in his essay (page 22) the significance of the executive order and its 1971 revision.

Through the 1970s and 1980s, issues related to women and work continued to be an important part of public discussion in America. A number of the writers in the anthology treat those issues: equal pay and benefits; recruiting, hiring, and promotion policies; cultural views of the roles of men and women; psychological factors and how they affect women at work. Robin L. Bartlett, Charles Poulton-Callahan, and Patricia Somers look at the struggles women face in the world of corporate management and consider a variety of factors affecting their status and hopes in the business world. They note particularly how the existing structure of business organizations (including their extremely important social structures) can hamper women's chances. One author, Alice Sargent, examines the cultural assumptions about the ways men and women behave as managers and draws the conclusion that the future requires an "androgynous" management style, blending behaviors previously assumed to belong exclusively to men or to women.

Many commentators have pointed to the differences in pay for men and women. One controversial response to the problem is the concept of "comparable worth," which, its advocates say, would level some of the disparities. Michael Evan Gold argues for the concept in his article; Phyllis Schlafly takes the opposing side in hers.

The importance of psychological factors is the focus of one selection. Matina Horner, in a well-known article, explains the peculiar psychological problem facing bright women—the women who should be able to achieve the most. She argues that in our culture bright women are conditioned not only to fear failure but to fear success. The anthology is rounded out by an article by Suzanne Gordon, who sees a conflict between the feminist values that became prominent in the sixties and seventies and the values assumed by women in the corporate world of the eighties. No matter which reading you select for your own project, you will learn something about the present-day problems of women in the working world.

■

WHAT'S HOLDING WOMEN BACK?

Robin L. Bartlett, Charles Poulton-Callahan, and Patricia Somers

When their article appeared in the professional journal *Management World* in 1982, Robin L. Bartlett was an associate professor and Charles Poulton-

Callahan was an assistant professor in the Department of Economics at Denison University in Granville, Ohio. Patricia Somers was director of career life planning at the same school.

Women have made tremendous strides in the workforce in recent years. The labor force participation rate for all women 16 years old and over has increased from 32 percent in 1947 to over 52 percent in 1981, according to U.S. Labor Department statistics. A study conducted in 1977 projected a 51 percent workforce participation rate for women in 1990—which had already been surpassed in 1980.

The rise in the number of women in the workforce involved all ages, although not simultaneously. Three trends emerged. In the 1950s, many older women re-entered the workforce after their children had left home. In the 1960s, many women began leaving the home for paid employment while their children were still in school. In the 1970s, the number of women returning to work soon after childbirth began to increase.

There are many reasons for the large number of women entering the workforce. Higher wages, increased career opportunities, attitudinal changes generated by the women's movement, inflationary pressures, and technological advances have all pushed and pulled women into the workforce. With recent double-digit inflation, high mortgage rates, and high unemployment figures for prime-age males, it takes a two-earner family to assure independence and financial stability.

While not all women left the home willingly, most anticipated fair remunerations and advancement opportunities. Currently, however, women earn, on the average, 60 percent of what men earn, and find themselves segregated into dead-end jobs. In 1950, females constituted 63 percent of all clerical workers. By 1980, this figure had jumped to 80 percent. The same applies to service and low-level professional occupations. In short, while there is a greater number of women in the workforce, they are still confined to the lower echelons of the career ladder. This stems from systemic structural barriers that employers, inadvertently or consciously, construct.

The Individual

Individual characteristics are crucial in determining any worker's first job. In theory, employees with high innate abilities, more education, and more experience will earn more. However, this does not occur fairly across the board. Sex-role stereotyping takes its toll on the judgment of employers.

For instance, it is often assumed that women are better at some tasks and men are better at others. Women are assumed to be less able to think analytically and manage people than men. Women are assumed to be able to tolerate routine, repetitive and boring tasks. A casual glance at the majority of jobs men and women hold indicate that both sets of jobs contain a high element of both qualities—however, men are paid more.

In terms of education, women encountered structural barriers early. Academic counselors channelled women away from subjects such as math, chemistry, and business. Parents encouraged girls to take typing and English courses, in the event they had to work, as a typing or teaching job was always available.

But times have changed, and our economy is no longer generating traditional clerical jobs. Secretaries are being exposed to computer science and are becoming microcomputer specialists, but are not acquiring enough skills to catapult them out of the dead-end clerical job track.

Work experience for men and women also differs. A male and female of comparable age may have significantly different experience and achievement records. A woman will usually lack experience and promotions relative to a man of the same age, therefore further impeding her career progress. However, comparisons need to be made along the lines of experience and not age, since most women still tend to take some time off from working for childbirth and child rearing.

Thus, the stereotypes or myths about women's skills and abilities need to be removed, women's educational efforts need to be redirected towards the traditionally male curriculum, and age or unrelated experience should not be held against a woman applicant. In essence, the problem is a system-wide one that warrants structural, rather than individual, modifications.

Pyramids

Most organizations have a hierarchical decision-making process. This hierarchical structure creates a pyramid of opportunity, which shapes the behavior of employees and colors self-perceptions.

To rise to the top of this pyramid, an employee must make his or her way through several tiers of management. This can be done initially by being placed on a "fast track" or, more often, being placed in one department or division of the company and then moving laterally for experience and exposure—the "be-in-the-right-place-at-the-right-time" route.

However, in traditional organizations, sheer numbers dictate that a substantial proportion of the employees will be blocked in their attempts to reach the top of the corporate pyramid. This is the situation of a majority of all workers. Most women employees, who are at the base of the organizational pyramid in clerical and secretarial jobs, find themselves here.

Bad Sports

While an organizational chart maps out the routes to the top, the informal organization, or "who knows whom," is equally important. In this regard, women suffer because men tend to socialize in activities which exclude women.

For example, men know how to take advantage of activities sponsored by business, service, and athletic clubs which may still formally and legally exclude women. Another opportunity for informal socializing occurs at sporting events, where corporations buy blocks of tickets for sporting events as fringe benefits or to entertain clients. Women, with relatively little previous exposure to athletics, may find such events boring and avoid them. Also, in the office, the rapport built up in sports-buff circles may limit women from acquiring vital information through the informal structure. Moreover, non-participation in athletics may cut women off from the priceless career information obtained at such unlikely places as the golf course or racquetball court.

Mobility in the organization can be blocked in any of these ways. There is also a psychological impact on individuals of blocked opportunity. These effects can be numerous: disengagement, resistance, lowered aspirations, low commitment, non-responsibility, seeking substitute social recognition, chronic criticism and low-risk conservatism. All are traits which prevent movement up the corporate ladder.

Power

Another structural barrier for women is power, or the ability to control resources. Power can be fostered in several ways: outstanding achievement, reorganization, mobility, peer alliances and mentors. Again, these avenues are often barricaded for women. For example, while a promising man may have several volunteers for a mentor, a woman may have difficulty finding one at all.

Attaining power is just as important as having mobility. Primary responses to powerlessness are attempts to control others even less powerful. Low-risk conservatism, heightened territoriality and bureaucratic rule-mindedness are other reactions. In fact, control over minor aspects of the work routine may provide what little power an employee has. This can give rise to the petty, bureaucratic territoriality of employees whose jobs fall low on the hierarchical ladder.

A final structural barrier centers on group dynamics, and particularly on how they affect the few women professionals and managers in a male-dominated environment. Often the focus of much attention, these women are subjected to tremendous performance pressures. They are evaluated against the performance of other women and their male colleagues. Moreover, there is a fine line between acceptable performance and that which is so outstanding that male colleagues are threatened.

There are many different responses by women to this treatment. Some strive to achieve, setting impossible standards of perfection. Others turn against other women. Some women try to turn notoriety to their advantage, or conversely, become invisible.

Men also react to the relative numbers imbalance in numerous ways. The presence of very few women can produce caricatured reactions from the majority group, such as sexual innuendos and lewd behavior. Research on women law students indicates that performance pressures drop dramatically as more women are drawn into the group. This finding supports the notion that organizations must take an active role in alleviating the isolation of women.

Although women have made substantial inroads in absolute numbers in the workforce, only minor progress has been made in managerial ranks. Women have moved into middle management rapidly in the growing high-technology fields, while making slow progress in the troubled auto industry. Thus, women who seek management positions should be aware of the opportunities in growth industries.

In several ways, managers can provide advancement opportunities for women employees. In a corporation's formal organization, jobs can be redesigned, jobs posted, careers counseled, and seniority de-emphasized to clear the career path. Moreover, links between career ladders, uncoupling the status of a secretary from that of her boss, developing multiple competencies through training and task groups to work on projects, and a rotational system for leadership positions are ways to provide more opportunities. Formal mentoring systems and the rehiring of women into certain jobs and locations are two solutions that have been successful.

Employees of a corporation must become aware of the role of the informal structure in acquiring business and career information. Company outings and retreats should be structured to encourage equal participation by male and female employees, and all events should be open to males and females. Also, businesses should discourage the selection of all-male clubs for luncheons.

Although it is more difficult to do, managers should make it clear to job applicants the kind of jobs that are available even if the applicant does not possess the requisite skills. This information allows the applicant to assess his or her skill deficiencies and thus job potential. Information feedback and evaluation is also necessary after entering the corporate environment, so that employees can better themselves and take advantage of opportunities.

Finally, managers need to anticipate the impact of future economic trends on their employees. An upswing in economic activity may generate a whole array of new positions. Employees must be continually upgraded to fit into these positions. On the other hand, an economic downswing may cause undue anxiety and loss of productivity unless creative ways are developed for sharing the burden of less work.

In summary, there are numerous barriers which block women from advancing in organizations. Formal and informal structures need to be examined to determine how they can be changed to bring women up the corporate ranks.

Questions for Comprehension

1. According to the authors, who creates the barriers that confine women to the lower end of the career ladder?
2. According to the authors, what assumptions about women help to limit their opportunities?
3. What is the "pyramid of opportunity," and where are women generally placed in it?
4. What advantage do men have in the "informal organization" of a company?
5. What psychological impact may blocked opportunities have on an individual?
6. In what ways are women blocked from power in organizations, according to the article?
7. What particular "performance pressures" are women subjected to, and in what ways do women respond to these pressures?
8. How do men react to an increase in the relative number of women in their workplace?

9. What steps do the authors recommend managers take to improve advancement opportunities for women employees?

■

WOMEN AND MEN WORKING TOGETHER: TOWARD ANDROGYNY
Alice G. Sargent

Alice G. Sargent is a consultant and trainer in organizational development, managerial effectiveness, and affirmative action. She writes frequently on management topics and is the author of *Beyond Sex Roles* (1977) and *The Androgynous Manager* (1981). In this 1983 article from the *Training and Development Journal* she discusses the need for androgyny in management—that is, a mix of behavioral patterns that were previously assumed to be exclusively male or female.

The movement of women into the managerial work force has created a new culture in organizations, changing men's and women's relationships and generating pressure to find new ways for them to relate.

This calls for a synthesis, a blending of the best of two existing polarities—in this case, the masculine and feminine styles of instrumental and expressive behavior. In organizational leadership, this blend is often called androgynous management—a management approach that blends the best each gender offers. . . .

Both men and women pay heavily for trying to conform to a management style that reflects mostly masculine values. This style emphasizes rationality and solving technical tasks. It accents competition, the use of power to gain the ends of the organization and an external reward system. People's needs often get lost; the organization has top priority. Anger and frustration are the emotions most often expressed in the masculine world of management.

Students of management—and some practitioners—increasingly recognize that focusing on task alone produces ineffective management. The results are isolation and alienation, which are among the major problems confronting organizations today. Managers are learning to deal with relationships among people and to foster cooperation across bureaucratic levels, instead of taking the top-down approach.

The needs of organizations for a model of managerial effectiveness converge with the needs of women and men for different ways of behaving as managers. Women face a discrepancy between how they have been socialized and how they are expected to act as managers. Others see women as bringing "female" qualities to the office when "male" qualities are considered characteristic of good management. Hence, femininity and competence seem in conflict. Acting feminine may mean a woman is not taken seriously. If her ideas are not listened to, her effectiveness as a manager is impaired.

Women have been socialized to be compliant, particularly with males, yet risk-taking is valued and necessary in management. Women in management also experience a conflict between autonomy and learned helplessness. The polarities of passivity and aggressiveness, dependence and independence frequently conflict with managerial expectations.

Research shows that managers of both sexes believe successful managers possess characteristics, attitudes and temperaments ascribed more commonly to men than to women. The impact of such perceptions can be severe for women. They may try to suppress feminine behaviors and enhance or adopt masculine behaviors, or they may seek to preserve their feminine self-image and suppress attributes deemed essential for effective management. They may lose even if they exhibit behaviors regarded as necessary for effective management: Assertiveness is regarded highly in a male manager, but may be seen as pushiness in a woman.

A Navy study on preferred coworkers found that both men and women, when asked directly, said they prefer to work with men. Men are considered, often correctly, to have more access to information and to people with power. It is believed, and often true, that men are listened to more by others. Such expectations show the long road ahead in altering stereotypes and making women full citizens in the work place.

Men, seeming to be in the favored position, pay less obvious penalties than women for adopting and expressing the dominant management style. Men often do not know they are acting "masculine" and do not realize how liberating it might be to have other choices.

Some men, however, see the disadvantages and costs of the masculine style. Stress and related diseases can shave 10 years off a man's life. Unwillingness to express a full range of emotions can impoverish relationships; many men will no longer sacrifice close relationships with members of both sexes.

Fortunately, men and women no longer need to penalize themselves with old behaviors if they are willing to change and to risk some awkwardness and uncertainty.

Blending Old and New

Each sex may need to accentuate the behaviors of the other sex in order to be androgynous. Women need to discuss issues in a linear, systematic style as well as use intuition; to deal with power as well as emotion; to assert themselves and compete, where appropriate, as well as to foster collaboration.

For men, of course, it is the reverse. Men need more than power and competitiveness in order to have a full repertoire of effective behavior. They need to learn to express and deal with emotions other than anger and frustration. They need to engage less in joking and jockeying to establish a position and more in sharing and nurturing to build a team. Thus, a synthesis is necessary, a blending of strong masculine and strong feminine characteristics.

Support Systems and Networks

Any environment can be lonely during change. This may be especially true of organizational, bureaucratic environments, where managers often think they must deal with issues by themselves. When powerful changes overturn management styles and expectations, both women and men may experience uncertainty, self-doubt and fear. Managers of both sexes need support systems through which to share these doubts and networks to provide information, examples for comparison and access to power.

Women, working for effectiveness and acceptance, need support from men and women, without charges of so-called feminine over-dependence.

Some support networks already exist for men through avenues such as business lunches, business travel and sports. But men have little support for change in precisely those areas where they feel most uncomfortable. Men lack structures that support being sensitive, expressing feelings, being vulnerable or comforting others. They need feminine competencies of empathy, dealing with emotion and relating to others to be able to provide support.

Support systems could be built into the organizational structure so that men and women could share experiences and strategies for coping with change.

How Do You Recognize a Competent Woman?

Competent women and men may not act alike. Women gain a sense of identity both through the development of themselves and of others, sometimes too much in the direction of others. Organizations, however, expect effectiveness to be shown through taking action, giving advice, influencing others and having leadership presence.

Many women expect a higher level of expertise from themselves than from others. They won't speak up until completely sure of the facts. They may overuse the power of expertise and underuse the power of their position. Women often express feelings before they arrive at solutions. This may make them appear to be "hysterical" or to lack sufficient problem-solving skills.

Coaching a new manager who was a woman, a male manager said, "You're just not thinking fast enough or putting your ideas out quickly enough for our culture here." The male manager failed to question an organizational style which was competitive, lacking in introspection and reflection—one that devalued feelings and was probably oriented to crisis. The competent woman may not appear able to respond rapidly to new ideas, but her style may work better in certain situations. . . .

Exercise of Power and Control

In the new management environment, cooperation needs to replace competition more often. The old, autocratic management style may be used for fire-fighting, but more consultative styles should be used for decision making and for managing human resources.

Women often draw back from competition or confrontation in policy-making; they may even fail to recognize a power struggle, although power dynamics are rampant (and frequently useful) in every organization. Women managers sometimes give away their power, fail to take power when appropriate and overuse collaboration when inappropriate.

Unlike women, men have been taught to emphasize power, slipping easily into one-up, one-down interactions, even when it is unnecessary. They use power to create distance in many business and social relationships.

Research studies have demonstrated the gender differences surrounding power and control issues. Bartol and Butterfield asked managers and graduate students to rank managerial effectiveness in different situations. The researchers reversed the names of men and women managers in several case studies. A male manager was rated highly effective when he entered an organization, interviewed employees for three weeks and then developed a plan that dictated how employees would operate. When a female manager did exactly the same thing, she was rated ineffective for being too directive and pushy.

But gender prejudice cuts both ways. A woman manager was rated effective for showing consideration for others when she spent time dealing with an employee's personal problems, while a male manager who showed the same behavior was rated as wishy-washy for getting too involved in employee needs.

A woman manager in a federal agency budget department first adopted more masculine approaches and then relaxed into androgynous behavior. It was five years, she said, before she felt comfortable "showing some of my feminine behaviors instead of just focusing on task." Having proved herself in the masculine arena she could reintegrate some of her feminine behavior and become more androgynous. She said, "One reason I've finally been accepted is because I'm high on collaboration. There used to be a lot of staff and line power struggles. I was instrumental in introducing joint accountability. People are working together much more harmoniously."

Dealing with Emotions

In general, women do not find a receptive climate for the expression of emotions in organizations, except anger or frustration. Some women believe men use anger as a weapon, while men sometimes think women use pain and fear in the same manner.

If men and women are to work together effectively, emotional expression is essential. Emotional data is critical to effective problem-solving; feelings are present and have an effect whether expressed or not.

Frequently, men and women differ on how they see interpersonal issues. Women tend to view these issues in the context of a total relationship, consisting of interactions between two people. Many men have learned an organizational style that responds to the message more than the messenger. Therefore, men may be more likely to feel isolated at work and to withdraw from expressions of feelings.

Challenging Dependency

Women are allowed dependency, but men are punished for expressing it. Hence, learned helplessness has been primarily a woman's issue. Dependency has become so closely aligned with femininity that women must work now to overcome this expectation. Often, women give away their independence, seeking help when they do not need it. Indeed, women may run into resistance in the managerial world when they try to be independent.

On the other hand, men often insist on independence, even when it might benefit them or their organization to seek help. Men also tend to resist talking about problems, isolating themselves out of fear of dependency and cutting themselves off from behaviors essential to being fully effective managers. Working through dependency can be important for both men and women, as well as organizations, but it often means taking risks.

Defusing Sexuality

As organizations begin to value androgynous behavior, the feminine behaviors of expressing feelings and touching can become potent issues. Touching needs to be openly negotiated so as not to be misinterpreted. Henley and Mayo point out that when a man touches a woman, it is often regarded as dominance, whereas when a woman touches a man, it is regarded as warmth.

Common business practices may be misinterpreted when they cross gender lines. A lunch invitation may be seen as something other than an act of colleagueship. A man may feel rejected if a woman turns down a dinner invitation because she is too tired or busy, but he may not feel the same if a male colleague gives the same reasons.

Men in one organization felt uncomfortable when they were traveling with women colleagues. The men withdrew, and the women were cut out of an important information and support network.

Issues of sexual attraction are frequently ignored, when simply acknowledging attraction can do much to defuse it. Generally, men and women want and need to relate to each other as colleagues and professionals. Sexuality, if acted out, can complicate a professional relationship and interfere with work effectiveness. Furthermore, the motives for sexual attraction may range from curiosity to a need to impose power.

Conclusion

We are moving slowly toward an androgynous identity for managers. The androgynous manager can deal with power and control in a balanced way; is comfortable with the full range of emotions; can seek support and give it to others; can be independent without becoming isolated; and can acknowledge attraction and choose whether to act on it or not. Such a person is better equipped to face the challenges of these complex, ambiguous times.

Questions for Comprehension

1. Where does Sargent state the thesis of her article?
2. According to Sargent, which values does a mostly male management style emphasize? Which does it neglect?
3. Which "male" patterns of behavior do women need to learn in order to become androgynous managers?
4. To be androgynous managers, which "female" patterns of behavior do men need to learn?
5. Why do both men and women need support systems during the move toward androgynous management?

6. According to Sargent, what problems sometimes arise in recognizing competence in women managers?
7. In what ways do men and women managers differ in expressing emotions?
8. How do both men and women managers face the "challenge of dependency"?
9. How, according to the author, can the issue of sexuality complicate the movement toward androgynous management?

■

THE CASE FOR COMPARABLE WORTH
Michael Evan Gold

Michael Evan Gold is a faculty member in the School of Industrial and Labor Relations at Cornell University. He has published many articles on equal pay and comparable worth. He is the author of A Dialogue on Comparable Worth. The following article appeared in the May/June 1986 issue of The Humanist in opposition to an article by Phyllis Schlafly on the same topic (Schlafly's article follows Gold's in this anthology).

> And the Lord spoke unto Moses, saying, Speak unto the children of Israel, and say unto them:
> When a man shall clearly utter a vow of persons unto the Lord, according to thy evaluation, then thy valuation for the male from twenty years old even unto sixty years old, even thy valuation shall be fifty shekels of silver, after the shekel of the sanctuary. And if be a female, then thy valuation shall be thirty shekels.
> —LEVITICUS 27:4

The value of women's work has not changed over the centuries. Today, as in Moses' day, the average full-time female worker earns only about 60 percent as much as her male counterpart. This figure, calculated by the U.S. Commission on Civil Rights before the commission was captured by the Reagan administration, is adjusted for variables that might legitimately explain the pay gap. If women earned less than men because women worked fewer hours or had less education or seniority, the pay gap would not concern us so urgently. But the 60 percent figure already includes controls for legitimate factors such as weeks and hours worked, education, and age. In the end, women are simply paid less than men.

Blacks have made significant progress in recent years. Women have not. In 1959, the average black man earned 71 percent as much as the average white man; in 1969, the black man earned 75 percent as much as the white; and in 1975, the black man earned 85 percent as much. Black men are catching up. Women are not.

Critics of comparable worth argue that women are being paid fairly now. For example, critics cite a 1976 study showing that the starting salaries of male and female college graduates are equal. But this study ignores what happens to women on the job. A more revealing study examined the pay of graduates of the Stanford Business School. The starting salaries of men and women in 1974 were equal, but by 1978 the women's pay had dropped to less than 80 percent of the men's. Cumulative statistics reveal the pay gap clearly: female household employees earn only 70 percent as much as males; female clericals earn only 66 percent as much as males; female craftworkers earn only 60 percent as much as males; female managers and administrators earn only 58 percent as much as males.

The Cause of the Pay Gap

The pay gap is caused by discrimination against women. One form of discrimination is the universal practice of valuing men's work more highly than women's. As Margaret Mead pointed out, in some societies, men fish and women weave; in other societies, women fish and men weave. Whatever the work the men do, it is valued by that society more highly than the women's work. Examples need not be limited to the developing world. As work loses status, women are allowed to perform it (or, perhaps, as women are allowed to do work, it loses status). Consider lawyers in the Soviet Union: a low status, female job. Consider what has happened to bank tellers in this country.

Critics of comparable worth assert that men's jobs, in fact, require more skill than women's jobs. This assertion was demolished by a study that scored according to skill each of the four thousand jobs in the U.S. Department of Labor's *Dictionary of Occupational Titles*. The study concluded that men's and women's jobs require equal levels of skill overall, but the skills are different. For example, men's and women's jobs require social skills; but men's jobs—like negotiating—call for power skills, while women's jobs—like counseling—call for nurturing skills. When relating skills to compensation, the study found that only about one-third of the pay gap could be explained by the differences in men's and women's skills. Two-thirds of the pay gap could not be explained by differences in skills.

Every working woman knows that her skills are undervalued. A classic example is the case of *Thompson v. Boyle*, in which female bindery workers sued the Government Printing Office, claiming that their work was equal to male bookbinders' work. The government's expert witness studied the jobs and awarded points based upon tasks performed. He gave men four times as many points as women for lifting identical weights. He awarded points to men for handling confidential information, but he gave women no points for handling the same information. Most revealingly, he allowed women no points at all for tasks like hand sewing because most women know how to do it.

Another form of discrimination against women, and another cause of the pay gap, is occupational segregation. An occupation is segregated when one sex holds at least 70 percent of the jobs. Two-thirds of the occupations in this country are segregated by sex. Seventy percent of men and 54 percent of women work in segregated occupations. And, of course, the men's occupations pay better than the women's. A man's earnings curve rises steadily throughout most of his life; a woman's earning curve is flat. The more women in an occupation, the less it pays. All-male occupations pay double what all-female occupations pay.

Critics argue that *segregation* is the wrong word because no one is forced into an occupation in America; they argue that women freely choose jobs that fit in with their familial responsibilities. But the critics ignore the twin forces of occupational exclusion and socialization. The law books are full of cases in which women have been excluded from jobs because of their sex. There may be less exclusion today than twenty years ago, but most women were strictly limited to certain jobs when they began working, and they cannot switch careers now. Thus, the critics' argument that women have freely chosen their jobs is false.

Even if women did choose their jobs, the critics' argument would fail because it ignores the subtle but powerful process of socialization. Women are brainwashed into accepting servile roles in life. It is no accident that little boys play doctor and little girls play nurse. It is no coincidence that big boys engage in competitive sports while big girls help around the house. It is no surprise that men take good jobs and women accept inferior jobs. Socialization continues after a girl grows up. Today, racially mixed marriages are more acceptable than male homemakers.

The Remedy: Comparable Worth

Comparable worth is the doctrine that women should be paid the full value of their work. Comparable worth is the precise remedy for discrimination that results in undervaluation of women's work.

Critics argue that, if women are underpaid, the solution is to enforce equal opportunity laws so that women can have access to better-paying men's jobs. This argument is fallacious, however, because it ignores half of the cause of the problem and almost all of working women. Enforcing equal opportunity may be a proper remedy for the exclusion of women from jobs, but it would do nothing about the undervaluation of women's work. We have noted that the pay of an occupation declines as women move into it. *Enforcing equal opportunity without guaranteeing comparable worth would turn women's careers into a sisyphean game of hopscotch:* women would move into a new occupation and temporarily enjoy the benefit of men's pay, but, as the percentage of women in the occupation increased, the pay would decline and women who wanted pay worthy of their work would be forced to move into another occupation, which the undervaluation process would soon force them to leave, and so on.

Moreover, equal opportunity alone offers no relief to the millions of working women who are locked into undervalued jobs. They took those jobs because a discriminatory society offered no alternatives. Now, as a practical matter, they cannot give up their job security, learn new skills, and start over again at entry-level wages. Only paying women's work its fair value can provide relief to these women. Comparable worth would not compensate these women for past discrimination, but it would save them from injustice in the future.

Implementing comparable worth will not be easy. Significant problems attend all existing proposals to eliminate undervaluation of women's work. But the difficulty of the task should not dissuade us from the effort. We may not be able to foresee the end, but we must not forsake it. The cause is just. Because we will it, we will find a way.

Questions for Comprehension

1. What evidence does Gold cite to support his claim that there is a "universal practice of valuing men's work more highly than women's"?
2. What is "occupational segregation," and what does Gold say is its effect?
3. Why does Gold say that in a sense many women have not freely chosen their jobs?
4. How does the process of socialization limit women's professional opportunities?
5. What happens to compensation when the percentage of women in any occupation increases?
6. What arguments does Gold present to show that simply enforcing equal opportunity laws will not solve the problem of the undervaluation of women's work?

■

COMPARABLE WORTH: UNFAIR TO MEN AND WOMEN
Phyllis Schlafly

Phyllis Schlafly is a lawyer, a syndicated columnist, a radio commentator, and the president of Eagle Forum. She produces a monthly newsletter, *The Phyllis Schlafly Report*. The article printed here, reprinted from the May/June 1986 issue of *The Humanist*, consists of her testimony before a Congressional committee.

My name is Phyllis Schlafly, president of Eagle Forum, a national profamily organization. I am a lawyer, writer, and homemaker.

We oppose the concept called *comparable worth* for two principal reasons: (a) it's unfair to men and (b) it's unfair to women.

The comparable worth advocates are trying to freeze the wages of blue-collar men while forcing employers to raise the wages of *some* white- and pink-collar women above marketplace rates. According to the comparable worth rationale, blue-collar men are overpaid and their wages should be frozen until white- and pink-collar women have their wages artificially raised to the same level. The proof that this is really what the comparable worth debate is all about is in both their rhetoric and their statistics.

I've been debating feminists and listening to their arguments for more than a decade. It is impossible to overlook their rhetoric of envy. I've heard feminist leaders say hundreds of times, "It isn't fair that the man with a high school education earns more money than the women who graduated from college or nursing or secretarial school."

That complaint means that the feminists believe that truck drivers, electricians, plumbers, mechanics, highway workers, maintenance men, policemen, and firemen earn more money than feminists think they are worth. And how do the feminists judge "worth"? By paper credentials instead of by apprenticeship and hard work and by ignoring physical risk and unpleasant working conditions.

So the feminists have devised the slogan *comparable worth* to make the blue-collar man feel guilty for earning more money than women with paper credentials and to trick him into accepting a government-enforced wage freeze while all available funds are used to raise the wages of *some* women.

Statistical proof that the aim of comparable worth is to reduce the relative earning power of blue-collar men is abundantly available in the job evaluations commissioned and approved by the comparable worth advocates. You can prove this to yourself by making a job-by-job examination of *any* study or evaluation made with the approval of comparable worth advocates; it is always an elaborate scheme to devalue the blue-collar man.

For example, look at the Willis evaluation used in the famous case called *AFSCME v. State of Washington*. Willis determined that the electricians and truck drivers were overvalued by the state and that their "worth" was really far less than the "worth" of a registered nurse. More precisely, Willis produced an evaluation chart on which the registered nurse was worth 573 points, whereas the electrician was worth only 193 points (one-third of the nurse), while the truck driver was only worth 97 points (one-sixth of the nurse).

The federal court accepted the Willis evaluation as though it were some kind of divine law (refusing to listen to the Richard Jeanneret "PAQ" evaluation which produced very different estimates of "worth"). The federal court decision (unless it is overturned on appeal) means that the electricians and the truck drivers will probably have their salaries frozen until the state finds a way to pay the registered nurse three times and six times as much, respectively. [In a September 4, 1985, decision, the Ninth U.S. Circuit Court of Appeals overturned the decision.]

How do jobs get certain points? The evaluator invents them. The comparable worth advocates hire under contract an evaluator who is obligated (a) to ignore all marketplace factors and (b) to produce a point scheme to "prove" discrimination against women.

One of the techniques by which this is done is the devaluing of the physical and working-condition factors so important in blue-collar jobs. This devaluation of blue-collar jobs is always an inevitable result of integrating white-collar and blue-collar jobs in the same evaluation. If the federal white-collar and blue-collar pay classifications were integrated, the blue-collar employees would be tremendously devalued because the federal white-collar pay system accords less than 5 percent of the possible points to "physical demands" and "working environment" combined.

The comparable worth advocates and evaluators join in a chorus to claim that it's so "scientific" because "worth" is based on education, training, skills, experience, effort, responsibility, and working conditions. The fact is that, once you throw out marketplace factors, the evaluation is completely subjective and wholly reflective of the bias of the evaluator.

The Willis evaluation determined that the "mental demands" on a nurse are worth 122 points, whereas the mental demands on an electrician are worth only 30 points, and the mental demands on a truck driver are worth only 10 points. That's the view of the profeminist evaluator. For a contrary view, ask the electrician and the truck driver about the worth of their mental demands.

Comparable worth evaluations must be recognized as a racket to get people with your own biases on the evaluation team or to saddle the evaluator with a contract that binds him or her to produce the results you predetermine.

Not only is the comparable worth concept wholly subjective but it is also wholly arbitrary. It proposes to raise only *some* women's pay at the expense of men and other women. This arbitrariness is shown by the fact that *only* those jobs where 70 percent or more of the employees are female would be eligible for comparable worth raises. This was made clear in a devastating analysis of the Wisconsin governor's evaluation made by the Wisconsin Association of Manufacturers and Commerce.

The Wisconsin Governor's Task Force Study lists the job called *institution aide* as having a "C-W Gap" of $5,132. But the employees in this position would not get a comparable worth raise because only 67 percent of the 116 employees are women and institution aide cannot be designated a "woman's job" unless it meets the 70 percent test.

Now suppose that the state needs two more institution aides. If it hires two women, it will cross the 70 percent threshold. The state will then have to give all institution aides a raise, and it will therefore cost the state $595,000 to hire two women. The personnel manager can easily manipulate the system, depending on whether he is profeminist or pro-budget-cutting.

Or, look at the position called *nursing assistant 3*. Because it has 70 percent women, all 104 employees would be scheduled to get a raise of $3,626 to close the so-called C-W Gap. If the personnel manager simply hires one male or fires two females, he or she can avoid comparable worth raises for all and save $377,136 in his budget.

The entire concept of comparable worth hangs on comparisons between male-dominated jobs and female-dominated jobs, so it is impossible to escape the arbitrary nature of the 70 percent.

In addition, comparable worth is unfair to women in that its effect is to squeeze lower-skilled women out of the job market altogether. The respected economist June O'Neill has written lengthy treatises to show how and why this is the result. Clarence Pendleton, chairman of the U.S. Commission on Civil Rights, put this same point succinctly when he said, "Comparable worth would do to low-skilled women what the minimum wage did to black teenagers."

But that's not the only way comparable worth is unfair to women. It also hurts the women who have moved into nontraditional jobs.

When the Illinois nurses sued the state of Illinois, claiming they should be paid equally with the (mostly male) electricians and stationary engineers, eleven female state employees in non-traditional jobs tried to enter the lawsuit as intervenors. They all work in a job classification called *correctional officer*, which is a euphemism for *prison guard*. The evaluation said that these "male-dominated" jobs are not "worth" as much as they are now paid. Illinois was paying prison guards $145 a month more than entry-level secretaries, but the comparable worth evaluation gave secretaries twelve more comparable worth points than prison guards.

[margin note: less offensive →]

The women prison guards claimed that the present system of compensation properly rewards them for their special skills, performance of particularly difficult, dangerous, and unpleasant work, their willingness to challenge stereotypes and perform non-traditional jobs, and the nondiscriminatory market forces of supply and demand. Put another way, the state has found that it must pay more to hire prison guards than office personnel because of the risks on the job and the unpleasant work.

Ask yourself the question, how many women would be willing to be a prison guard if the pay were the same or less than the pay of a secretary?

Women are already flooding into the so-called traditional "women's jobs" by the millions. If the pay is raised for those jobs, even more women will seek those jobs and abandon plans to go into nontraditional lines of work. At the same time, business will eliminate jobs in order to cut costs, and low-skilled women will be laid off. That's why Clarence Pendleton says that comparable worth for women is as self-defeating as saying, twenty years ago, that the way to improve the economic lot of blacks would be to raise the pay of redcaps.

We are all aware that comparable worth has in recent months become a controversial issue in the media. The profeminist bias of the media has meant a pro-comparable-worth bias on most television programs.

So it was with particular interest that I discovered a confidential and copyrighted memorandum on comparable worth distributed by the legal department of the National Association of Broadcasters for the benefit of television and radio station members. This memorandum warns stations to "think very carefully before undertaking any formal study of the relationship between the 'value' or 'difficulty' of the positions held by their employees and the salaries they receive." Be sure to consult your lawyer, the memorandum says. "If an employer's only motive is to protect itself against the hazards of new theories of wage discrimination like comparable worth, it is fair to say that a job evaluation study is far more likely to be a burden than a boon."

That's good advice—not only for television and radio broadcasters but for any employer, including the federal government and state governments.

Questions for Comprehension

1. What single statement of her thesis does Schlafly make?
2. What objection does Schlafly give to the way feminists use the word *worth*?
3. What does Schlafly say is the real aim of the advocates of comparable worth?
4. Why is comparable worth "completely subjective"?

5. What does Schlafly say is illustrated by the point system used to rate the mental demands on nurses, electricians, and truck drivers?
6. According to Schlafly, what is "wholly arbitrary" about comparable worth?
7. What reasons does Schlafly give for saying that comparable worth is unfair to lower-skilled women?
8. How will comparable worth hurt women moving into nontraditional jobs?

■

A BRIGHT WOMAN IS CAUGHT IN A DOUBLE BIND
Matina Horner

After earning a Ph.D. in psychology, Matina Horner (b. 1939) published this widely read and influential article in 1969. It is based on the results of her research into the question of women and success. She describes her findings in the concept of the "double bind." Horner later became the president of Radcliffe College, a position she recently resigned.

> *A woman who is guided by the head and not the heart is a social pestilence: she has all the defects of a passionate and affectionate woman, with none of her compensations: she is without pity, without love, without virtue, without sex.*
> —HONORÉ DE BALZAC

Consider Phil, a bright young college sophomore. He has always done well in school, he is in the honors program, he has wanted to be a doctor as long as he can remember. We ask him to tell us a story based on one clue: *After first-term finals, John finds himself at the top of his medical-school class.* Phil writes:

> John is a conscientious young man who worked hard. He is pleased with himself. John has always wanted to go into medicine and is very dedicated . . . John continues working hard and eventually graduates at the top of his class.

Now consider Monica, another honors student. She too has always done well and she too has visions of a flourishing career. We give her the same clue, but with "Anne" as the successful student—*after first-term finals, Anne finds herself at the top of her medical-school class.* Instead of identifying with Anne's triumph, Monica tells a bizarre tale:

> Anne starts proclaiming her surprise and joy. Her fellow classmates are so disgusted with her behavior that they jump on her in a body and beat her. She is maimed for life.

Next we ask Monica and Phil to work on a series of achievement tests by themselves. Monica scores higher than Phil. Finally we get them together, competing against each other on the same kind of tests. Phil performs magnificently, but Monica dissolves into a bundle of nerves.

The glaring contrast between the two stories and the dramatic changes in performance in competitive situations illustrate important differences between men and women in reacting to achievement.

In 1953, David McClelland, John Atkinson and colleagues published the first major work on the "achievement motive." Through the use of the Thematic Apperception Test (TAT), they were able to isolate the psychological characteristic of a *need to achieve*. This seemed to be an internalized standard of excellence, motivating the individual to do well in any achievement-oriented situation involving intelligence and leadership ability. Subsequent investigators studied innumerable facets of achievement motivation: How it is instilled in children, how it is expressed, how it relates to social class, even how it is connected to the rise and fall of civilizations. The result of all this research is an impressive and a theoretically consistent body of data about the achievement motive—in men.

Women, however, are conspicuously absent from almost all of the studies. In the few cases where the ladies were included, the results were contradictory or confusing. So women were eventually left out altogether. The predominantly male researchers apparently decided, as Freud had before them, that the only way to understand woman was to turn to the poets. Atkinson's 1958 book, *Motives in Fantasy, Action and Society*, is an 800-page compilation of all of the theories and facts on achievement motivation in men. Women got a footnote, reflecting the state of the science.

To help remedy this lopsided state of affairs, I undertook to explore the basis for sex differences in achievement motivation. But where to begin?

My first clue came from the one consistent finding on the women: they get higher test-anxiety scores than do the men. Eleanor Maccoby has suggested that the girl who is motivated to achieve is defying conventions of what girls "should" do. As a result, the intellectual woman pays a price in anxiety. Margaret Mead concurs, noting that intense intellectual striving can be viewed as "competitively aggressive behavior." And of course Freud thought that the whole essence of femininity lay in repressing aggressiveness (and hence intellectuality).

Thus consciously or unconsciously the girl equates intellectual achievement with loss of femininity. A bright woman is caught in a double bind. In testing and other achievement-oriented situations she worries not only about failure, but also about success. If she fails, she is not living up to her own standards of performance; if she succeeds she is not living up to societal expectations about the female role. Men in our society do not experience this kind of ambivalence, because they are not only permitted but actively encouraged to do well.

For women, then, the desire to achieve is often contaminated by what I call the *motive to avoid success*. I define it as the fear that success in competitive achievement situations will lead to negative consequences, such as unpopularity and loss of femininity. This motive, like the achievement motive itself, is a stable disposition within the person, acquired early in life along with other sex-role standards. When fear of success conflicts with a desire to be successful, the result is an inhibition of achievement motivation.

I began my study with several hypotheses about the motive to avoid success:

1. Of course, it would be far more characteristic of women than of men.

2. It would be more characteristic of women who are capable of success and who are career-oriented than of women not so motivated. Women who are not seeking success should not, after all, be threatened by it.
3. I anticipated that the anxiety over success would be greater in competitive situations (when one's intellectual performance is evaluated against someone else's) than in noncompetitive ones (when one works alone). The aggressive, masculine aspects of achievement striving are certainly more pronounced in competitive settings, particularly when the opponent is male. Women's anxiety should therefore be greatest when they compete with men.

I administered the standard TAT achievement motivation measures to a sample of 90 girls and 88 boys, all undergraduates at the University of Michigan. In addition, I asked each to tell a story based on the clue described before: *After first-term finals, John (Anne) finds himself (herself) at the top of his (her) medical-school class.* The girls wrote about Anne, the boys about John.

Their stories were scored for "motive to avoid success" if they expressed any negative imagery that reflected concern about doing well. Generally, such imagery fell into three categories:

1. The most frequent Anne story reflected strong fears of social rejection as a result of success. The girls in this group showed anxiety about becoming unpopular, unmarriageable and lonely.

   Anne is an acne-faced bookworm. She runs to the bulletin board and finds she's at the top. As usual she smarts off. A chorus of groans is the rest of the class's reply . . . She studies 12 hours a day, and lives at home to save money. "Well it certainly paid off. All the Friday and Saturday nights without dates, fun—I'll be the best woman doctor alive." And yet a twinge of sadness comes thru—she wonders what she really has. . . .

   Although Anne is happy with her success she fears what will happen to her social life. The male med. students don't seem to think very highly of a female who has beaten them in their field . . . She will be a proud and successful but also a very *lonely* doctor.

   Anne doesn't want to be number one in her class . . . she feels she shouldn't rank so high because of social reasons. She drops down to ninth in the class and then marries the boy who graduates number one.

   Anne is pretty darn proud of herself, but everyone hates and envies her.

2. Girls in the second category were less concerned with issues of social approval or disapproval; they were more worried about definitions of womanhood. Their stories expressed guilt and despair over success, and doubts about their femininity or normality.

   Unfortunately Anne no longer feels so certain that she really wants to be a doctor. She is worried about herself and wonders if perhaps she isn't normal . . . Anne decides not to continue with her medical work but to take courses that have a deeper personal meaning for her.

Anne feels guilty . . . She will finally have a nervous breakdown and quit medical school and marry a successful young doctor.

Anne is pleased. She had worked extraordinarily hard and her grades showed it. "It is not enough," Anne thinks. "I am not happy." She didn't even want to be a doctor. She is not sure what she wants. Anne says to hell with the whole business and goes into social work—not hardly as glamorous, prestigious or lucrative; but she is happy.

3. The third group of stories did not even try to confront the ambivalence about doing well. Girls in this category simply denied the possibility that any mere woman could be so successful. Some of them completely changed the content of the clue, or distorted it, or refused to believe it, or absolved Anne of responsibility for her success. These stories were remarkable for their psychological ingenuity:

Anne is a *code name* for a nonexistent person created by a group of med. students. They take turns writing exams for Anne. . . .

Anne is really happy she's on top, though *Tom is higher than she*—though that's as it should be . . . Anne doesn't mind Tom winning.

Anne is talking to her counselor. Counselor says she will make a fine *nurse*.

It was *luck* that Anne came out on top because she didn't want to go to medical school anyway.

Fifty-nine girls—over 65 percent—told stories that fell into one or another of the above categories. But only eight boys, fewer than 10 percent, showed evidence of the motive to avoid success. (These differences are significant at better than the .0005 level.) In fact, sometimes I think that most of the young men in the sample were incipient Horatio Algers. They expressed unequivocal delight at John's success (clearly John had worked hard for it), and projected a grand and glorious future for him. There was none of the hostility, bitterness and ambivalence that the girls felt for Anne. In short, the differences between male and female stories based on essentially the same clue were enormous.

Two of the stories are particularly revealing examples of this male-female contrast. The girls insisted that Anne give up her career for marriage:

Anne has a boyfriend, Carl, in the same class and they are quite serious . . . She wants him to be scholastically higher than she is. Anne will deliberately lower her academic standing the next term, while she does all she subtly can to help Carl. His grades come up and Anne soon drops out of medical school. They marry and he goes on in school while she raises their family.

But of course the boys would ask John to do no such thing:

John has worked very hard and his long hours of study have paid off . . . He is thinking about his girl, Cheri, whom he will marry at the end of med. school. He realizes he can give her all the things she desires after he becomes established. He will go on in med. school and be successful in the long run.

Success inhibits social life for the girls; it enhances social life for the boys.

Earlier I suggested that the motive to avoid success is especially aroused in competitive situations. In the second part of this study I wanted to see whether the aggressive overtones of competition against men scared the girls away. Would competition raise their anxiety about success and thus lower their performance?

First I put all of the students together in a large competitive group, and gave them a series of achievement tests (verbal and arithmetic). I then assigned them randomly to one of three other experimental conditions. One-third worked on a similar set of tests, each in competition with a member of the same sex. One-third competed against a member of the opposite sex. The last third worked by themselves, a non-competitive condition.

Ability is an important factor in achievement motivation research. If you want to compare two persons on the strength of their *motivation* to succeed, how do you know that any differences in performance are not due to initial differences in *ability* to succeed? One way of avoiding this problem is to use each subject as his own control; that is, the performance of an individual working alone can be compared with his score in competition. Ability thus remains constant; any change in score must be due to motivational factors. This control over ability was, of course, possible only for the last third of my subjects: the 30 girls and 30 boys who had worked alone *and* in the large group competition. I decided to look at their scores first.

Performance changed dramatically over the two situations. A large number of the men did far better when they were in competition than when they worked alone. For the women the reverse was true. Fewer than one-third of the women, but more than two-thirds of the men, got significantly higher scores in competition.

When we looked at just the girls in terms of the motive to avoid success, the comparisons were even more striking. As predicted, the students who felt ambivalent or anxious about doing well turned in their best scores when they worked by themselves. Seventy-seven percent of the girls who feared success did better alone than in competition. Women who were low on the motive, however, behaved more like the men: 93 percent of them got higher scores in competition. (Results significant at the .005.)

Female Fear of Success & Performance

	perform better working alone	*perform better in competition*
high fear of success	13	4
low fear of success	1	12

As a final test of motivational differences, I asked the students to indicate on a scale from 1 to 100 "How important was it for you to do well in this situation?" The high-fear-of-success girls said that it was much more important for them to do well when they worked alone than when they worked in either kind of competition. For the low-fear girls, such differences were not statistically significant. Their test scores were higher in competition, as we saw, and they thought that it was important to succeed no matter what the setting. And in all experimental conditions—working alone, or in competition against males or females—high-fear women consistently lagged behind their fearless comrades on the importance of doing well.

These findings suggest that most women will fully explore their intellectual potential only when they do not need to compete—and least of all when they are competing with men. This was most true of women with a strong anxiety about success. Unfortunately, these are often the same women who could be very successful if they were free from that anxiety. The girls in my sample who feared success also tended to have high intellectual ability and histories of academic success. (It is interesting to note that all but two of these girls were majoring in the humanities and in spite of very high grade points aspired to traditional female careers: housewife, mother, nurse, schoolteacher. Girls who did not fear success, however, were aspiring to graduate degrees, and careers in such scientific areas as math, physics and chemistry.)

We can see from this small study that achievement motivation in women is much more complex than the same drive in men. Most men do not find many inhibiting forces in their path if they are able and motivated to succeed. As a result, they are not threatened by competition; in fact, surpassing an opponent is a source of pride and enhanced masculinity.

If a woman sets out to do well, however, she bumps into a number of obstacles. She learns that it really isn't ladylike to be too intellectual. She is warned that men will treat her with distrustful tolerance at best, and outright prejudice at worst, if she pursues a career. She learns the truth of Samuel Johnson's comment, "A man is in general better pleased when he has a good dinner upon his table, than when his wife talks Greek." So she doesn't learn Greek, and the motive to avoid success is born.

In recent years many legal and educational barriers to female achievement have been removed; but it is clear that a psychological barrier remains. The motive to avoid success has an all-too-important influence on the intellectual and professional lives of women in our society. But perhaps there is cause for optimism. Monica may have seen Anne maimed for life, but a few of the girls forecast a happier future for our medical student. Said one:

> Anne is quite a lady—not only is she tops academically, but she is liked and admired by her fellow students—quite a trick in a man-dominated field. She is brilliant—but she is also a woman. She will continue to be at or near the top. And . . . always a lady.

Questions for Comprehension

1. What does the story of Phil and Monica illustrate?
2. Why was the 1953 achievement study, as well as other similar ones, inadequate, according to Horner?
3. What general conclusion does Horner reach about bright women and achievement?
4. What is the "motive to avoid success"?

5. What are the three major categories used to classify the responses students gave to the story of the high-achieving girl named Anne?
6. What did Horner want to find out in the second part of her study?
7. What circumstances may prevent women from fully exploring their intellectual potential?
8. Why is achievement motivation more complex in women than men?

■

THE NEW CORPORATE FEMINISM
Suzanne Gordon

Suzanne Gordon is associate editor of *Working Papers* magazine and is the author of *Off Balance: The Real World of Ballet*. In the following article, published in *The Nation* in 1983, she argues that the "radical feminism" of the past has been transformed in the business world into what she calls "corporate feminism."

About four weeks ago a friend of mine, who is an editor at a major New York City publishing house, went to one of her company's biannual sales conferences. She departed full of ideas about books on feminism—books about feminist psychology, about socialist feminism, about women and culture. After a week in Puerto Rico, she returned well tanned and well deflated. She told me that when she explained her ideas to the company's salespeople, they did not respond enthusiastically. They insisted that women's books were still high on their list and so was feminism. But the kinds of books they felt would sell and the feminism they described had little to do with my friend's political ideals.

What publishers are looking for these days isn't radical feminism. It's corporate feminism—a brand of feminism designed to sell books and magazines, three-piece suits, airline tickets, Scotch, cigarettes and, most important, corporate America's message, which runs: Yes, women were discriminated against in the past, but that unfortunate mistake has been remedied; now every woman can attain wealth, prestige and power by dint of individual rather than collective effort.

At a time when hundreds of thousands of women are still trying to realize the ideals of radical feminism, business has set about redefining and depoliticizing one of the most compelling social movements of the late twentieth century. Indeed, what has happened to reformist feminism in the past decade is perhaps the most dramatic example of American capitalism's genius at defusing protest by winning the protesters over to the very values and institutions they once attacked.

Evidence of the success of this effort is not hard to find. Ten years ago, you could walk into any large bookstore and browse among shelves of books and magazines carrying the kind of message my editor friend longs to publish. Today, things are different. Walk into any large bookstore and you'll find racks of primers on appropriate managerial and entrepreneurial conduct. Covers with clenched fists and feminist symbols are no longer in vogue. Now we have photographs of smartly dressed women standing in front of imposing desks in elegant but efficiently furnished offices. This role model of success—a tailored Charlie's Angel who carries an attaché case instead of a .38—will teach her sisters about the virtues of action, as well as how to "network," cut deals, make killings, be the boss and get to the top of the corporate heap.

The helpful tips our sisters in business provide are necessary, they say, because women face serious obstacles as they travel the road to success. First, they must overcome their feminine socialization. Their upbringing has, sadly, made them nurturers rather than predators and thus ill suited for the marketplace. More important, women must also overcome the scruples instilled by their feminist education, for feminism and the radical movements from which it sprang had little positive to say about corporate America and the power relations and values that prevail therein. In the late 1960s and early 1970s, women who came to feminism from the antiwar and civil rights movements shared certain ideals and goals: they shared the desire, as Eugene Debs so aptly put it, "to rise with the ranks, rather than from the ranks." Wealth, ambition, jockeying for power, the subordination of one's personal life to one's professional life and the delight in wielding authority—in short, precisely what many women are now choosing to pursue—were not highly regarded. Now many of the same women who once hoped to revolutionize the system are being trained as its administrators, and they need a corporate education as well as an ideology that will allow them to reconcile the hopes of the past with the realities of the present.

That is exactly what book after book and article after article, not to mention the myriad seminars on entrepreneurial feminism, are offering them. To draw the fainthearted or skeptical woman into the fray, these voices of corporate America start by calming her fear that she must become a "company woman." The first lesson the would-be managerial woman receives is that she can be totally committed to both her sisters and herself. For the managerial woman will be less competitive and callous, more humane and supportive, than the managerial man.

"Today women managers are bringing a new dimension to the administrative process," writes Margaret Fenn in *In the Spotlight: Women Executives in a Changing Environment*. "Women managers are helping to move business toward the adoption of an administrative philosophy that provides the opportunity for all members to participate and contribute their skills and knowledge to the processes affecting them." "Women," writes Nancy Lee in *Targeting the Top*, "have generally trained themselves to pay close attention to others in order to understand their motivations and predict what is apt to happen. Intuition or accurately reading verbal and non-verbal signals, coupled with genuine concern for other people, are the great strengths that women are bringing with them into the organization."

Lest women worry that wielding power will corrupt them as it has corrupted so many men, *Ms.* magazine's recent issue on power reassures them that "the solidarity fostered by the women's movement" is "setting precedents for the next generation and they [powerful women] are creating a reality, a way to think about and perceive powerful women, where before we only had myths and caricatures."

The question, of course, is what kind of reality are these women creating? Are women in business any different from their male counterparts?

The women's movement grew out of a critique of male power and out of a close accounting of the price men pay for their dominant position. Feminists argued that men have forfeited the ability to lead a life that can bring both personal and professional fulfillment; feminism's promise was a life that balanced love, friendship and work. Yet the same corporate feminists who spout volumes about the need to combine personal and professional fulfillment also write that the woman manager must, like so many men before her, subordinate the personal to the professional. Margaret V. Higginson and Thomas L. Quick in *The Ambitious Woman's Guide to a Successful Career* make it quite clear that if a woman is to succeed in business she must play by the rules: "The separation of personal, private self from public self may be distasteful but most managers find it necessary. Managerial performance requires that the manager be where the action is. This requirement may entail long hours, travel movement outside work hours and public review of one's action."

"Managerial performance" also involves making one's personal life serve one's professional goals. "Your relationships with former associates," say Higginson and Quick, "must reflect position not emotion." "Women," they complain, "seem to have a special problem in this area. In the company cafeteria, for example, they will sit down with other women—even if these women are on a lower job level, rather than joining the men who are now their peers."

Margaret Fenn put it even more bluntly: "Associations and friendships reflect managerial values. These imply a degree of social distancing from subordinates." And according to Gay Norton Edelman, in an article on office politics, "The fact is, you were hired to get the job done, not to win friends, fulfill needs left from your childhood or work out unresolved conflicts from your past. You don't have to be a cold fish or a cutthroat . . . but it's good politics to avoid becoming too people-oriented. You don't want personal relationships in the office to harm your work and career." In other words, the recognition that we all need intimacy is not a strength but a weakness, a holdover from childhood that must be shed by women seeking to take their places in the adult world.

Thus friendships are inappropriate and sticking together must give way to looking out for number one, say the corporate Machiavellis. When one troubled executive wrote to *Savvy* magazine's column "Ideas and Strategies for Doing Better Business," she learned that better business is simply business as usual. New to her company, she had been beset by a gang of employees who challenged her authority. What was *Savvy*'s solution? "Divide and conquer. The way your gang is acting, the time for group talk is over. Now you must deal with each one privately. You must make each see that her future self-interest is linked to pleasing you and not to pleasing others in the group."

In the same issue, a disgruntled employee who had joined her co-workers to fight an authoritarian boss was given similar counsel: "You have probably already hurt yourself by joining the grumblers, but it's still not too late to do what you should have done in the beginning. Request a private meeting and tell her that you are committed to working with her. As for your colleagues—remember, old alliances often go through radical swings during the first months under a new leadership. . . . One thing you can depend on: Change at the top provides opportunities for new alliances."

These new alliances, of course, should be alliances with the powerful, and the effect of them is to maintain that power, not redistribute it. And so it is no surprise that these books and articles place great emphasis on the virtues of networking and role-modeling. Indeed, the adoption of networking by women in business has been lauded as one of modern feminism's foremost achievements. Women realized that affirmative action suits would take them only so far. What they needed was contact with the rich and powerful, so they began to form replicas of the "old boy networks" through which powerful men have traditionally passed on their power to a select few. As a result of these networks, more women are now in, or near, positions of power and can thus serve as role models who, according to Ms., pave the road that millions of other women will travel.

In reality, however, the relationships cemented in the old girl networks are no different from those the old boy networks foster. For no matter which sex uses it, the network is a vehicle for the advancement of an elite. Moreover, the role-model concept turns feminist politics into fantasy: women cease to be the architects of a radical vision of the world and become spectators, watching the drama of other women's success.

The power of collective action, these books and articles say, is no longer the goal; corporate feminism seeks the legitimation of the individual manager's power over others. And so Fenn informs us:

> An effective manager recognizes that power and influence are parts of everyday life. It's true that all organizational members are positioned in a hierarchy which implies unequal power distribution. But such distribution emerges naturally from ideas about social organization and behavior. As a condition of employment employees accept as legitimate the exercise of authority over areas related to performance and are indifferent to the fact that they have the ability to choose other alternatives.

If they're not worried about your authority, why should you be?

The message of these self-help books is expounded with great enthusiasm when businesswomen gather to march off into the corporate sunset. At the third Women in Business Conference in New York City, attended by 3,000 executives, entrepreneurs and owners of small and large businesses, the participants were treated to seminars on business skills that emphasized the virtues of wealth and status. Women were not told how to nurture their subordinates, how to fight for the underprivileged or how to imbue the corporation with radical feminist values. They were schooled in the arts of adaptation.

In a seminar entitled "Dressing for Success," women were taught that the way they present themselves is no less important than the business equipment they purchase. Four panelists—Beverly Stephen, a syndicated columnist for the New York *Daily News*; Maria Rios, a psychotherapist; Ruth McCarthy Manton, president of a design management company; and Barbara Munder, a high-level executive at McGraw-Hill—explained that finding a "self and self-style" appropriate to the corporate world involves change and risk. They also pointed out that one's clothes, like one's friendships, must reflect managerial values. "In corporate or financial institutions you can show some individuality, but not too much,"

Munder said candidly. "You can't show too much individuality, not even at the top. I would never go into a presentation without a suit."

While most of the conference participants were trying to make contacts, I talked with Marie Robinson, who owns a business and is an avid proponent of the corporate feminist success gospel. I asked her if she thinks women function differently from men in the business world. She answered unequivocally in the affirmative: "Women's leadership style is to reach a consensus rather than be authoritarian. My style is generally to reach a consensus, to build a team.

"I think women generally have tremendous empathy for the women working under them. They're part of the family women create." This means, she elaborated, that if you "make them feel they belong," they'll be willing to work longer hours without demanding overtime.

Grace Fippinger, a vice president at New York Telephone and honorary chair of the conference, amiably informed me that she wants all women in business to consider themselves part of her team. But she feels she has a responsibility only to women at her own level. When I asked if she thought she should help her female subordinates advance, she was aghast: "I wouldn't treat a woman who reports to me any different than a man. That wouldn't be fair."

A reading of the literature on corporate feminism and an examination of corporate feminist values lead to one inescapable conclusion: women exercising their entrepreneurial skills, wielding power and flexing their financial muscles are joining the system, not changing it. Some women have noted this with dismay and exhorted feminists to return to their roots. In an article in *The New York Times Magazine*, for example, Anne Taylor Flemming ruefully reported the sad fact that women have not responded to success as feminists had hoped they would. On their "way to the top," women are not being "as gentle with one another as we once hoped we'd be," she wrote, and recalled the promise of feminism—that women would "be tender with one another because our wombs had somehow bequeathed us an extra empathy, a kind of biologic tenderness." She doesn't question the pursuit of careerist goals; she merely seeks a "gentler jungle."

This Victorian vision of femininity is precisely the vision that fuels corporate feminism. Femininity, the corporate feminists argue, is a kind of armor that magically protects women from the compromises the business world forces men to make every day of their professional lives. Because of femininity—and corporate feminism—women can enter that world and remain pure; they can manage and administer without power corrupting them because it is the sex, not the system, that determines what people believe and how they act.

The reality, of course, is quite the opposite. As these books and articles and seminars show, it is the system, not the sex, that determines values and behavior. For centuries men have been in charge, and so feminism has associated capitalism's ills with masculinity. But putting a corporate feminist in charge won't cure those ills; she'll simply perpetuate them—though her rhetoric will be more gentle.

Women cannot do it differently because they're not allowed to. They cannot live by the values of radical feminism (or any other ism—except, of course, capitalism) in the business world because no one in corporate America has the freedom to live by values other than those of corporate America. As Barbara

Munder said in her disquisition on dress: women in business can't even escape the uniform when they're on top. Ostensibly, she was referring only to appearances. In fact, standardization in fashion is indicative of a more extensive standardization. When women—or men for that matter—enter the business world, they must shed their politics, their emotions and their ideals, and they must standardize their attire, their attitudes, their behavior and even their skills.

Given the current state of the women's movement and the fragmentation of progressive politics, this is hardly surprising. If reform feminism had chosen to be an aggressive partner in a strong progressive movement for broad social change, the outlook would not be so grim. One could safely counsel women to take their places at all levels of economic and political life, knowing that a political community would reinforce their ideals, help them withstand the institutional pressures to adapt to the status quo and encourage action that might lead to changes within America's major institutions.

Without such a movement, and in the face of reformist feminism's affair with careerism, it is hard to imagine a scenario other than the one thousands of women are enacting today. For once collective ideals are abandoned, everything else—the fine feelings and fond wishes—goes with it. Women must become company women because there is nothing left to be.

Questions for Comprehension

1. List the basic differences between what Gordon calls "corporate feminism" and "radical feminism." Where are the author's sympathies?
2. What are the causes of the new corporate feminism?
3. What is "networking"? According to its advocates, how does it help women?
4. What criticism does Gordon make of "networking"?
5. How do "collective ideals" and "collective action" by women conflict with the values of what Gordon calls "corporate feminism"?
6. What criticism does Gordon make of the attitude of the "corporate Machiavellis" toward friendship and sticking together?
7. What general conclusion has Gordon reached from her reading of the literature of corporate feminism?

ADDITIONAL WRITING ASSIGNMENTS

1. Compare the articles by Phyllis Schlafly and Michael Evan Gold on the subject of comparable worth. Gold believes that comparable worth offers a way to correct some of the noticeable disparities in pay between men and women, while Schlafly sees the concept as harmful to both men and women. After you discover the key ideas each author uses, determine what point you can make to your readers on the subject. When you draft your paper, use the relevant points of similarity and difference to prove your own point.
2. In "The New Corporate Feminism" Suzanne Gordon asserts that a conflict exists between the feminist values of the 1960s and 1970s and the values

assumed by women in the corporate world of the 1980s. What do you think of Gordon's assertion? What assumptions does she make? Does she take into account all the relevant evidence?

3. After reading Alice Sargent's article "Women and Men Working Together: Toward Androgyny," write a paper in which you explain to an appropriate audience what the basic principles of androgyny are, and show how they would or would not be of use in any business or profession employing men and women. You might begin your prewriting by focusing your reading on Sargent's discussion of the cultural assumptions people make about men and women as managers and her conclusions about the need for a new, "androgynous" management style. Then list for yourself the major features of such a style—one combining behaviors previously assumed to belong exclusively to either men or women.

4. For this assignment assume your audience is a corporation interested in improving its use of female executives. Your job is to prepare a consultant's report to help take appropriate action. Write a report in which you explain the major problems involving women in management and offer a solution of at least one of them. Base your report on at least two of the articles in this anthology. "What's Holding Women Back?" is one useful source of information about the problems. The solution you offer may come from one or both articles or may be one of your own.

5. Read Matina Horner's 1969 article "A Bright Woman Is Caught in a Double Bind," making sure you understand her thesis (the discussion of Horner's essay in the summary project can help). Then consider the present-day status of intelligent women in our society: How much have things changed, and how much have they stayed the same? Write an essay in which you explain to what extent you believe being an intelligent woman is or isn't still a handicap. Support your conclusion with information from your own experience or from external sources—your reading, television, and so on.

The Nature of Early Human Life

MOST CHILDREN AT SOME TIME OR OTHER BEGIN TO wonder, "Where did I come from?" Though phrased in the simple language of a child, the question expresses longing for knowledge of the ultimate source of personal identity: Who *am* I?

That same question has long haunted human beings collectively. The question of identity is often expressed as a question of origin: Where did human culture come from? What were human beings like at the very beginning? On the answers to these questions rest many ideas about human nature, progress, freedom, and responsibility.

It is no wonder, then, that the question of the nature of early human life has been raised so often in religious, philosophical, scientific, and literary contexts; in cultural monuments (Milton's *Paradise Lost*) and in popular entertainment ("The Flintstones"). The essays in this anthology attempt to examine the nature of early humankind from the point of view of the social science that studies the origin and cultural development of human beings—anthropology.

Three of the essays belong to one school of thought. Raymond Dart (whose essay appears on page 39), Desmond Morris, and Robert Ardrey paint a picture of our early ancestors as aggressive, bloodthirsty predators. None of these writers were trained as anthropologists, but their views, particularly as expressed in Ardrey's best-seller *African Genesis*, created an image that many people take for granted. It was largely to counter that image and present a more balanced view that Ashley Montague wrote his essay (part of a collection of essays he edited in response to the growing popularity of Ardrey's definition of human nature). In a similar vein, the essay by Richard Leakey and Roger Lewin attempts to debunk the view of evolution and human nature put forth by Dart, Ardrey, and the ethologist Konrad Lorenz. The anthology concludes with two attempts to provide models of early human behavior. Nancy Tanner counters the "hunting model" of human nature, and its inherent sexism, with a model that stresses the equality of the sexes. Finally, Glynn Isaac presents a model in which food gathering is the essential activity of our protohuman ancestors.

You should be familiar with a few scientific terms before reading the essays. There have been many recent discoveries in the field of paleoanthropology, the study of creatures more primitive than *Homo sapiens*, and the terminology used by older writers such as Dart can be confusing. The following brief review may be helpful.

Each of us is a *Homo sapiens*—that is, human beings are of the genus *Homo* and the species *sapiens*. Any erect-walking primate is known as a *hominid*, a category that includes our ancestors, collateral relatives, and, of course, ourselves. Working backwards from *Homo sapiens* through the other hominids, we have the Neanderthal man (who may or may not have been a *Homo sapiens*), *Homo erectus*, and *Homo habilis*. It is these creatures whom the writers in this anthology mean when they refer to "early mankind."

A hominid not of the genus *Homo* is known as an *australopithecine*, an erect-walking near-human (what Dart refers to as a "proto-man"). Dart discovered the first australopithecine, the so-called Tuang Baby, and named the genus. There are two varieties of australopithecines: *Australopithecus africanus* and *Australopithecus gracilis*.

■

CAIN'S CHILDREN

Robert Ardrey

Robert Ardrey (1908–80) was a playwright, novelist, and author of books on anthropology, among them *African Genesis* (1961), *The Territorial Imperative* (1966), and *The Social Contract* (1970). Ardrey's views on the nature of early humanity were influenced by his friendship with Raymond Dart. In his books Ardrey expresses his view that man is an innately aggressive being driven by the desire to protect his property and control others. The following essay is an excerpt from *African Genesis*.

What are the things that we know about man? How much have the natural sciences brought to us, so far, in the course of a silent, unfinished revolution? What has been added to our comprehension of ourselves that can support us in our staggering, lighten our burdens in our carrying, add to our hopes, subtract from our anxieties, and direct us through hazard and fog and predicament? Or should the natural sciences have stayed in bed?

We know above all that man is a portion of the natural world and that much of the human reality lies hidden in times past. We are an iceberg floating like a gleaming jewel down the cold blue waters of the Denmark Strait; most of our presence is submerged in the sea. We are a moonlit temple in a Guatemala jungle; our foundations are the secret of darkness and old creepers. We are a thriving, scrambling, elbowing city; but no one can find his way through our labyrinthine streets without awareness of the cities that have stood here before. And so for the moment let us excavate man.

What stands above the surface? His mind, I suppose. The mind is the city whose streets we get lost in, the most recent construction on a very old site. After seventy million years of most gradual primate enlargement, the brain nearly trebled in size in a very few hundreds of thousands of years. Our city is spacious and not lacking in magnificence, but it has the problems of any boom town. Let us dig.

We are Cain's children. The union of the enlarging brain and the carnivorous way produced man as a genetic possibility. The tightly packed weapons of the predator form the highest, final, and most immediate foundation on which we stand. How deep does it extend? A few million, five million, ten million years? We do not know. But it is the material of our immediate foundation as it is the basic material of our city. And we have so far been unable to build without it.

Man is a predator whose natural instinct is to kill with a weapon. The sudden addition of the enlarged brain to the equipment of an armed already-successful predatory animal created not only the human being but also the human predicament. But the final foundation on which we stand has a strange cement. We are bad-weather animals. The deposit was laid down in a time of stress. It is no mere rubble of carnage and cunning. City and foundation alike are compacted by a mortar of mysterious strength, the capacity to survive no matter what the storm. The quality of the mortar may hold future significance far exceeding that of the material it binds.

Let us dig deeper. Layer upon layer of primate preparation lies buried beneath the predatory foundation. As the addition of a suddenly enlarged brain to the way of the hunting primate multiplied both the problems and the promises of the sum total, man, so the addition of carnivorous demands to the non-aggressive, vegetarian primate way multiplied the problems and promises of the sum total, our ancestral hunting primate. He came into his Pliocene time no more immaculately conceived than did we into ours.

The primate has instincts demanding the maintenance and defence of territories; an attitude of perpetual hostility for the territorial neighbour; the formation of social bands as the principal means of survival for a physically vulnerable creature; an attitude of amity and loyalty for the social partner; and varying but universal systems of dominance to insure the efficiency of his social instrument and to promote the natural selection of the more fit from the less. Upon this deeply-buried, complex, primate instinctual bundle were added the necessities and the opportunities of the hunting life.

The non-aggressive primate is rarely called upon to die in defence of his territory. But death from territorial conflict is second among the causes of lion mortality in the Kruger reserve. The non-aggressive primate seldom suffers much beyond humiliation in his quarrels for dominance. The lion dies of such conflicts more than of all other causes. The forest primate suppresses many an individual demand in the interests of his society. But nothing in the animal world can compare with the organization and the discipline of the lion's hunting pride or the wolf's hunting pack.

We can only presume that when the necessities of the hunting life encountered the basic primate instincts, then all were intensified. Conflicts became lethal, territorial arguments minor wars. The social band as a hunting and defensive unit became harsher in its codes whether of amity or enmity. The dominant became more dominant, the subordinate more disciplined. Overshadowing all other qualitative changes, however, was the coming of the aggressive imperative. The creature who had once killed only through circumstance killed now for a living.

As we glimpsed in the predatory foundation of man's nature the mysterious strength of the bad-weather animal, so we may see in the coming of the carnivorous way something new and immense and perhaps more significant than the killing necessity. The hunting primate was free. He was free of the forest prison; wherever game roamed the world was his. His hands were freed from the earth or the bough; erect carriage opened new and unguessed opportunities for manual answers to ancient quadruped problems. His daily life was freed from the eternal munching; the capacity to digest high-calorie food meant a life more diverse than one endless meal-time. And his wits were freed. Behind him lay the forest orthodoxies. Ahead of him lay freedom of choice and invention as a new imperative if a revolutionary creature were to meet the unpredictable challenges of a revolutionary way of life. Freedom—as the human being means freedom—was the first gift of the predatory way.

We may excavate man deeply and ever more deeply as we dig down through pre-primate, pre-mammal, and even pre-land-life levels of experience. We shall pass through the beginnings of sexual activity as a year-around affair, and the consequent beginnings of the primate family. But all the other instincts will be there still deeper down: the instinct to dominate one's fellows, to defend what one deems one's own, to form societies, to mate, to eat and avoid being eaten. The record will grow dim and the outlines blurred. But even in the earliest deposits of our nature where death and the individual have their start, we shall still find traces of animal nostalgia, of fear and dominance and order.

Here is our heritage, so far as we know it today. Here is the excavated mound of our nature with *Homo sapiens'* boom town on top. But whatever tall towers reason may fling against the storms and the promises of the human future, their foundations must rest on the beds of our past for there is nowhere else to build.

Cain's children have their problems. It is difficult to describe the invention of the radiant weapon as anything but the consummation of a species. Our history reveals the development and contest of superior weapons as *Homo sapiens'* single, universal cultural preoccupation. Peoples may perish, nations dwindle, empires fall; one civilization may surrender its memories to another civilization's sands. But mankind as a whole, with an instinct as true as a meadow-lark's song, has never in a single instance allowed local failure to impede the progress of the weapon, its most significant cultural endowment.

Must the city of man therefore perish in a blinding moment of universal annihilation? Was the sudden union of the predatory way and the enlarged brain so ill-starred that a guarantee of sudden and magnificent disaster was written into our species' conception? Are we so far from being nature's most glorious triumph that we are in fact evolution's most tragic error, doomed to bring extinction not just to ourselves but to all life on our planet?

It may be so; or it may not. We shall brood about this in a moment. But to reach such a conclusion too easily is to oversimplify both our human future and our animal past. Cain's children may have many an ancestor beyond *Australopithecus africanus*, and many a problem beyond war. And the first of our problems is to comprehend our own nature. For we shall fashion no miracles in our city's sky until we know the names of the streets where we live.

Questions for Comprehension

1. What does Ardrey mean when he says "let us excavate man"? How does the image of excavation predict the structure of his essay?
2. What are the distinct "layers" Ardrey finds in his excavation? In what paragraphs does each appear?
3. What two factors, according to Ardrey, brought humanity as we know it into being?
4. What particular primate instincts were added to the necessities of the hunting life in early human beings? How did these instincts and necessities interact?
5. What does Ardrey mean when he claims that "freedom—as the human being means freedom—was the first gift of the predatory way"?
6. What are the "instincts" Ardrey believes characteristic of human beings from the beginning of the evolutionary process?
7. What is "*Homo sapiens*' single, universal cultural preoccupation"? To what question does that preoccupation inevitably lead?

■

THE NAKED APE

Desmond Morris

Desmond Morris (b. 1928) is an English zoologist educated at Birmingham University and Oxford University. He is well known for his best-sellers *The Naked Ape* and *The Human Zoo*, in which he describes contemporary society in terms of innate animal behavior. The following essay is excerpted from *The Naked Ape* (1967).

What happened to the early apes? We know that the climate began to work against them and that, by a point somewhere around fifteen million years ago, their forest strongholds had become seriously reduced in size. The ancestral apes were forced to do one of two things: either they had to cling on to what was left of their old forest homes, or, in an almost biblical sense, they had to face expulsion from the Garden. The ancestors of the chimpanzees, gorillas, gibbons and orangs stayed put, and their numbers have been slowly dwindling ever since. The ancestors of the only other surviving ape—the naked ape—struck out, left the forests, and threw themselves into competition with the already efficiently adapted ground-dwellers. It was a risky business, but in terms of evolutionary success it paid dividends.

The naked ape's success story from this point on is well known, but a brief summary will help, because it is vital to keep in mind the events which followed if we are to gain an objective understanding of the present-day behaviour of the species.

Faced with a new environment, our ancestors encountered a bleak prospect. They had to become either better killers than the old-time carnivores, or better grazers than the old-time herbivores. We know today that, in a sense, success has been won on both scores; but agriculture is only a few thousand years old, and we are dealing in millions of years. Specialized exploitation of the plant life of the open country was beyond the capacity of our early ancestors and had to await the development of advanced techniques of modern times. The digestive system necessary for a direct conquest of the grassland food supply was lacking. The fruit and nut diet of the forest could be adapted to a root and bulb diet at ground level, but the limitations were severe. Instead of lazily reaching out to the end of the branch for a luscious ripe fruit, the vegetable-seeking ground ape would be forced to scratch and scrape painstakingly in the hard earth for his precious food.

His old forest diet, however, was not all fruit and nut. Animal proteins were undoubtedly of great importance to him. He came originally, after all, from basic insectivore stock, and his ancient arboreal home had always been rich in insect life. Juicy bugs, eggs, young helpless nestlings, tree-frogs and small reptiles were all grist to his mill. What is more, they posed no great problems for his rather generalized digestive system. Down on the ground this source of food supply was by no means absent and there was nothing to stop him increasing this part of his diet. At first, he was no match for the professional killer of the carnivore world. Even a small mongoose, not to mention a big cat, could beat him to the kill. But young animals of all kinds, helpless ones or sick ones, were there for the taking, and the first step on the road to major meat-eating was an easy one. The really big prizes, however, were poised on long, stilt-like legs, ready to flee at a moment's notice at quite impossible speeds. The protein-laden ungulates were beyond his grasp.

This brings us to the last million or so years of the naked ape's ancestral history, and to a series of shattering and increasingly dramatic developments. Several things happened together, and it is important to realize this. All too often, when the story is told, the separate parts of it are spread out as if one major advance led to another, but this is misleading. The ancestral ground-apes already had large and high-quality brains. They had good eyes and efficient grasping hands. They inevitably, as primates, had some degree of social organization. With strong pressure on them to increase their prey-killing prowess, vital changes began to take place. They became more upright—fast, better runners. Their hands became freed from locomotion duties—strong, efficient weapon-holders. Their brains became more complex—brighter, quicker decision-makers. These things did not follow one another in a major, set sequence; they blossomed together, minute advances being made first in one quality and then in another, each urging the other on. A hunting ape, a killer ape, was in the making.

It could be argued that evolution might have favoured the less drastic step of developing a more typical cat- or dog-like killer, a kind of cat-ape or dog-ape, by the simple process of enlarging the teeth and nails into savage fang-like and claw-like weapons. But this would have put the ancestral ground-ape into direct competition with the already highly specialized cat and dog killers. It would have meant competing with them on their own terms, and the outcome would no doubt have been disastrous for the primates in question. (For all we know, this may actually have been tried and failed so badly that the evidence has not been found.) Instead, an entirely new approach was made, using artificial weapons instead of natural ones, and it worked.

From tool-using to tool-making was the next step, and alongside this development went improved hunting techniques, not only in terms of weapons, but also in terms of social co-operation. The hunting apes were pack-hunters, and as their techniques of killing were improved, so were their methods of social organization. Wolves in a pack deploy themselves, but the hunting ape already had a much better brain than a wolf and could turn it to such problems as group communication and co-operation. Increasingly complex manoeuvres could be developed. The growth of the brain surged on.

Essentially this was a hunting-group of males. The females were too busy rearing the young to be able to play a major role in chasing and catching prey. As the complexity of the hunt increased and the forays became more prolonged, it became essential for the hunting ape to abandon the meandering, nomadic ways of its ancestors. A home base was necessary, a place to come back to with the spoils, where the females and young would be waiting and could share the food. This step, as we shall see in later chapters, has had profound effects on many aspects of the behaviour of even the most sophisticated naked apes of today.

So the hunting ape became a territorial ape. His whole sexual, parental and social pattern began to be affected. His old wandering, fruit-plucking way of life was fading rapidly. He had now really left his forest of Eden. He was an ape with responsibilities. He began to worry about the prehistoric equivalent of washing machines and refrigerators. He began to develop the home comforts—fire, food storage, artificial shelters. But this is where we must stop for the moment, for we are moving out of the realms of biology and into the realms of culture. The biological basis of these advanced steps lies in the development of a brain large and complex enough to enable the hunting ape to take them, but the exact form they assume is no longer a matter of specific genetic control. The forest ape that became a ground ape that became a hunting ape that became a territorial ape has become a cultural ape, and we must call a temporary halt.

. . . To what extent was he able to modify himself, to blend his frugivorous heritage with his newly adopted carnivory? Exactly what kind of an animal did this cause him to become?

To start with, he had the wrong kind of sensory equipment for life on the ground. His nose was too weak and his ears not sharp enough. His physique was hopelessly inadequate for arduous endurance tests and for lightning sprints. In personality he was more competitive than co-operative and no doubt poor on planning and concentration. But fortunately he had an excellent brain, already better in terms of general intelligence than that of his carnivore rivals. By bringing his body up into a vertical position, modifying his hands in one way and his feet in another, and by improving his brain still further and using it as hard as he could, he stood a chance.

12   This is easy to say, but it took a long time to do, and it had all kinds of repercussions on other aspects of his daily life, as we shall see in later chapters. All we need concern ourselves with for the moment is how it was achieved and how it affected his hunting and feeding behaviour.

13   As the battle was to be won by brain rather than brawn, some kind of dramatic evolutionary step had to be taken to greatly increase his brain-power. What happened was rather odd: the hunting ape became an infantile ape. This evolutionary trick is not unique; it has happened in a number of quite separate cases. Put very simply, it is a process (called neoteny) by which certain juvenile or infantile characters are retained and prolonged into adult life. (A famous example is the axolotl, a kind of salamander that may remain a tadpole all its life and is capable of breeding in this condition.)

14   The way in which this process of neoteny helps the primate brain to grow and develop is best understood if we consider the unborn infant of a typical monkey. Before birth the brain of the monkey foetus increases rapidly in size and complexity. When the animal is born its brain has already attained seventy per cent of its final adult size. The remaining thirty per cent of growth is quickly completed in the first six months of life. Even a young chimpanzee completes its brain-growth within twelve months after birth. Our own species, by contrast, has at birth a brain which is only twenty-three per cent of its final adult size. Rapid growth continues for a further six years after birth, and the whole growing process is not complete until about the twenty-third year of life.

15   For you and me, then, brain-growth continues for about ten years *after* we have attained sexual maturity, but for the chimpanzee it is completed six or seven years *before* the animal becomes reproductively active. This explains very clearly what is meant by saying that we became infantile apes, but it is essential to qualify this statement. We (or rather, our hunting ape ancestors) became infantile in certain ways, but not in others. The rates of development of our various properties got out of phase. While our reproductive systems raced ahead, our brain-growth dawdled behind. And so it was with various other parts of our make-up, some being greatly slowed down, others a little, and still others not at all. In other words, there was a process of differential infantilism. Once the trend was under way, natural selection would favour the slowing down of any parts of the animal's make-up that helped it to survive in its hostile and difficult new environment. The brain was not the only part of the body affected: the body posture was also influenced in the same way. An unborn mammal has the axis of its head at right angles to the axis of its trunk. If it were born in this condition its head would point down at the ground as it moved along on all fours, but before birth occurs the head rotates backwards so that its axis is in line with that of the trunk. Then, when it is born and walking along, its head points forwards in the approved

manner. If such an animal began to walk along on its hind legs in a vertical posture, its head would point upwards, looking at the sky. For a vertical animal, like the hunting ape, it is important therefore to retain the foetal angle of the head, keeping it at right angles to the body so that, despite the new locomotion position, the head faces forwards. This is, of course, what has happened and, once again, it is an example of neoteny, the pre-birth stage being retained into the post-birth and adult life.

Many of the other special physical characters of the hunting ape can be accounted for in this way: the long slender neck, the flatness of the face, the small size of the teeth and their late eruption, the absence of heavy brow ridges and the nonrotation of the big toe.

The fact that so many separate embryonic characteristics were potentially valuable to the hunting ape in his new role was the evolutionary breakthrough that he needed. In one neotenous stroke he was able to acquire both the brain he needed and the body to go with it. He could run vertically with his hands free to wield weapons, and at the same time he developed the brain that could develop the weapons. More than that, he not only became brainier at manipulating objects, but he also had a longer childhood during which he could learn from his parents and other adults. Infant monkeys and chimpanzees are playful, exploratory, and inventive, but this phase dies quickly. The naked ape's infancy was, in these respects, extended right through into his sexually adult life. There was plenty of time to imitate and learn the special techniques that had been devised by previous generations. His weaknesses as a physical and instinctive hunter could be more than compensated for by his intelligence and his imitative abilities. He could be taught by his parents as no animal had even been taught before.

But teaching alone was not enough. Genetic assistance was required. Basic biological changes in the nature of the hunting ape had to accompany this process. If one simply took a typical, forest-living, fruit-picking primate of the kind described earlier, and gave it a big brain and a hunting body, it would be difficult for it to become a successful hunting ape without some other modifications. Its basic behaviour patterns would be wrong. It might be able to think things out and plan in a very clever way, but its more fundamental animal urges would be of the wrong type. The teaching would be working *against* its natural tendencies, not only in its feeding behaviour, but also in its general social, aggressive, and sexual behaviour, and in all the other basic behavioural aspects of its earlier primate existence. If genetically controlled changes were not wrought here too, then the new education of the young hunting ape would be an impossibly uphill task. Cultural training can achieve a great deal, but no matter how brilliant the machinery of the higher centres of the brain, it needs a considerable degree of support from the lower regions.

If we look back now at the differences between the typical "pure" carnivore and the typical "pure" primate, we can see how this probably came about. The advanced carnivore separates the actions of food-seeking (hunting and killing) from the actions of eating. They have become two distinct motivational systems with only partial dependence one on the other. This has come about because the whole sequence is so lengthy and arduous. The act of feeding is too remote, and so the action of killing has to become a reward in itself. Researches with cats have even indicated that the sequence there has become further subdivided. Catching the prey, killing it, preparing it (plucking it), and eating it, each have their own partially independent motivational systems. If one of these patterns of behaviour is satiated, it does not automatically satiate the others.

For the fruit-picking primate the situation is entirely different. Each feeding sequence, comprising simple food-searching and then immediate eating, is comparatively so brief that no splitting up into separate motivational systems is necessary. This is something that would have to be changed, and changed radically, in the case of the hunting ape. Hunting would have to bring its own reward, it could no longer simply act as an appetitive sequence leading up to the consummatory meal. Perhaps, as in the cat, hunting, killing, and preparing the food would each develop their own separate, independent goals, would each become ends in themselves. Each would then have to find expression and one could not be damped down by satisfying another. If we examine—as we shall be doing in a later chapter—the feeding behaviour of present-day naked apes, we shall see that there are plenty of indications that something like this did occur.

In addition to becoming a biological (as opposed to a cultural) killer, the hunting ape also had to modify the timing arrangements of his eating behaviour. Minute-by-minute snacks were out and big, spaced meals were in. Food storage was practised. A basic tendency to return to a fixed home base had to be built in to the behavioural system. Orientation and homing abilities had to be improved. Defecation had to become a spatially organized pattern of behaviour, a private (carnivore) activity instead of a communal (primate) one.

I mentioned earlier that one outcome of using a fixed home base is that it makes parasitization by fleas possible. I also said that carnivores have fleas, but primates do not. If the hunting ape was unique amongst primates in having a fixed base, then we would also expect him to break the primate rule concerning fleas, and this certainly seems to be the case. We know that today our species is parasitized by these insects and that we have our own special kind of flea—one that belongs to a different species from other fleas, one that has evolved with us. If it had sufficient time to develop into a new species, then it must have been with us for a very long while indeed, long enough to have been an unwelcome companion right back in our earliest hunting-ape days.

Questions for Comprehension

1. What were the evolutionary changes that turned our ancestors into the "naked ape"?
2. Why was it necessary for the "hunting ape" to become a "territorial ape"?
3. In what ways was the naked ape at a disadvantage with respect to the other carnivores?
4. What is neoteny? In what ways was neoteny crucial in the evolution of the human brain and body?
5. Why did the separation of hunting and feeding make it necessary for hunting to become its own reward?

6. How does the fact that human beings are parasitized by fleas back up Morris's argument?
7. What is Morris's view of the relationship between men and women in early hominid society?

■

THE NEW LITANY OF "INNATE DEPRAVITY"

M. F. Ashley Montague

Ashley Montague (b. 1905), one of the world's best-known anthropologists, was born in London. He emigrated to the United States in 1927 and received a doctorate from Columbia University in 1937. Among his numerous publications are *Man's Most Dangerous Myth: The Fallacy of Race* (1942), *On Being Human* (1950), and *The Natural Superiority of Women* (1953). The following essay is excerpted from the preface to *Man and Aggression* (1968).

It is said that when the Bishop of Worcester returned from the Oxford meeting of the British Association in 1860, he informed his wife, at tea, that the horrid Professor Huxley* had declared that man was descended from the apes. Whereupon the dear lady is said to have exclaimed, "Descended from the apes! Let us hope it is not true, but if it is, let us pray that it will not become generally known."

It would seem that the last forty years of anthropological research and discovery in the field and in the laboratory, taken together with the findings of the behavioral sciences, place us in much the same position as the Bishop's lady, for while the findings of these disciplines are wholly opposed to the deeply entrenched view that man is an innately aggressive creature, most people tend to dismiss these findings out of hand or ridicule them as a rather eccentric idealistic heterodoxy, which do not deserve to become generally known. In preference to examining the scientific findings they choose to cast their lot with such "authorities" as William Golding who, in his novel *Lord of the Flies*, offers a colorful account of the allegedly innate nastiness of human nature, and Robert Ardrey who, in *African Genesis* and more recently in *The Territorial Imperative*, similarly seeks to show that man is an innately aggressive creature.

The first part of *African Genesis* is devoted to a demonstration, which the author brings off quite convincingly and with éclat, of the validity of Professor Raymond Dart's claims for an osteodontokeratic culture among the australopithecines. It is in the second part that Mr. Ardrey makes one of the most remarkable extrapolations from the first part I have ever encountered in any work. Mr. Ardrey argues that since the australopithecines made use of tools, and employed some of them as implements with which to bash in the skulls of baboons, the australopithecines were therefore "killers," and that *therefore* human beings are "killers"

---

* Editor's note: Thomas Henry Huxley (1825–95) was an eminent British biologist and early supporter of Charles Darwin's theory of evolution.

by nature! Mr. Ardrey's book constitutes, perhaps, the most illuminating example of the manner in which a man's prejudices may get in the way of his reason and distort his view of the evidence. Mr. Ardrey refers to some of his early personal experiences of violence which convinced him of the murderousness of human nature. Hence, when through the distorting glass of his prejudgments he looks at a tool it becomes not simply a scraper but a weapon, a knife becomes a dagger, and even a large canine tooth becomes "the natural dagger that is the hallmark of all hunting mammals," while in "the armed hunting primate" it becomes "a redundant instrument." "With the advent of the lethal weapon natural selection turned from the armament of the jaw to the armament of the hand."

But the teeth are no more an armament than is the hand, and it is entirely to beg the question to call them so. Virtually all the members of the order of primates, other than man, have large canine teeth, and these animals, with the exception of the baboons, are predominantly vegetarians, and it is because they are vegetarians that they require large canine teeth; that such teeth may, on occasion, serve a protective purpose is entirely secondary to their main function, which is to rip and shred the hard outer coverings of plant foods. Primates are not usually belligerent unless provoked, and the more carefully they are observed the more remarkably revealing do their unquarrelsomeness and cooperativeness become. The myth of the ferocity of "wild animals" constitutes one of Western man's supreme rationalizations, for it not only has served to "explain" to him the origins of his own aggressiveness, but also to relieve him of the responsibility for it—for since it is "innate," derived from his early apelike ancestors, he can hardly, so he rationalizes, be blamed for it! And some have gone so far as to add that nothing can be done about it, and that therefore wars and juvenile delinquents, as Mr. Ardrey among others tells us, will always be with us! From one not-so-minor error to another Mr. Ardrey sweeps on to the grand fallacy.

At this point it needs to be said that Mr. Ardrey's views are firmly based on and derived from those of Professor Raymond Dart, who in an article entitled, "The Predatory Transition from Ape to Man," published in 1953, argued that man's animal ancestry was carnivorous, predatory, and cannibalistic in origin, and went on to add that "The blood-bespattered, slaughter-gutted archives of human history from the earliest Egyptian and Sumerian records to the most recent atrocities of the Second World War accord with early universal cannibalism, with animal and human sacrificial practices or their substitutes in formalized religions and with the world-wide scalping, head-hunting, body-mutilating and necrophiliac practices of mankind in proclaiming this common bloodlust differentiator, this predaceous habit, this mark of Cain that separates man dietetically from his anthropoidal relatives and allies him rather with the deadliest of Carnivora."

Mr. Ardrey puts this in the following words: "The human being in the most fundamental aspects of his soul and body is nature's last if temporary word on the subject of the armed predator. And human history must be read in these terms."

In furtherance of this argument "tools" for Mr. Ardrey are not only identified as "weapons," but, he goes on to imply, nay, indeed, he states, "that when any scientist writes the word, 'tool,' as a rule he refers to weapons. This is a euphemism" (306).

Perhaps this opportunity should be taken to assure Mr. Ardrey that when scientists write the word "tool" they mean exactly what they say, and that euphemisms are not, as Mr. Ardrey says, "normal to all natural science" (306). Some tools may be used as weapons and even manufactured as such, but most tools of prehistoric man, from his earliest days, were most certainly not designed primarily to serve as weapons. Knives were designed to cut, scrapers to scrape, choppers to chop, and hammers to hammer. That such tools could be used as weapons is true, but to serve as weapons was not their primary purpose nor the reason for which they were devised.

"Man," Mr. Ardrey tells us, "is a predator whose natural instinct is to kill with a weapon" (316). But man has no instincts, and if he had, they could hardly include the use of weapons in their psychophysical structure.

Early man's hunting, according to Mr. Ardrey, was due to instinctive belligerence, not to the hunger for food. "When the necessities of the hunting life encountered the basic primate instincts, then all were intensified. Conflicts became lethal, territorial arguments minor wars. . . . The creature who had once killed only through circumstance now killed for a living" (317). This was "the aggressive imperative."

The evidence does not support Mr. Ardrey's theories. Whatever "the basic primate instincts" may be, they are not what Mr. Ardrey implies. Indeed, when he forgets himself, he writes of "the nonaggressive, vegetarian primate," which is precisely what all primates tend to be. But Mr. Ardrey would have us believe the contrary: the basic primate instincts according to him are aggressive. And, of course, with the assumption of hunting as a way of life, these, according to him, would become intensified. But in previous pages, and at greater length elsewhere, I have given the evidence for the contrary view. This evidence renders Mr. Ardrey's interpretations quite unacceptable. Everything points to the nonviolence of the greater part of early man's life, to the contribution made by the increasing development of cooperative activities, the very social process of hunting itself, the invention of speech, the development of food-getting and food-preparing tools, and the like. These facts are never once mentioned by Mr. Ardrey, except perhaps obliquely as a doctrine which scheming scientists have foisted upon an unsuspecting world. The truth is that Mr. Ardrey is arguing a thesis. It is the thesis of "innate depravity." It is an unsound thesis, and it is a dangerous one, because it perpetuates unsound views which justify, and even tend to sanction, the violence which man is capable of learning, but which Mr. Ardrey erroneously believes to be inherited from man's australopithecine ancestors.

When man hunts he is the predator and the hunted animal is the prey. But prehistoric man did not hunt for pleasure, in order to satisfy his "predatory instincts." He hunted for food, to satisfy his hunger, and the hunger of those who were dependent upon him. He did not hunt because he was a "killer," any more than contemporary men are "killers" who kill animals in abattoirs so that others may eat them. Prehistoric man was no more a "killer" than we are "killers" when we sit down at table to consume a chicken or a steak which, by proxy, someone else has "killed" for us. It would be interesting to know who are the "murderers," the men who are paid to slaughter the animals we eat, or we who pay the cashier at the supermarket? Or perhaps it is really the owner of the store in which we buy meat who is the "murderer," the "killer"? Prehistoric man hunted because he desired to live—*that* hardly makes him a killer, any more than our continuing in the habit of eating meat makes us killers.

Works Cited

Ardrey, Robert. *African Genesis*. New York: Atheneum, 1961.
———. *The Territorial Imperative*. New York: Atheneum, 1966.
Dart, Raymond A. "The Predatory Transition from Ape to Man." *International Anthropological and Linguistic Review* 1 (1953): 201–08.
Golding, William. *Lord of the Flies*. New York: Harcourt, Brace & Co., 1954.

Questions for Comprehension

1. What is Montague's attitude toward "the deeply entrenched view that man is an innately aggressive creature"?
2. What logical error does Montague accuse Ardrey of? How does he account for the error?
3. What different accounts do Montague and Ardrey offer for primates' large canine teeth?
4. How does Montague account for the popularity of "the myth of the ferocity of 'wild animals'"?
5. How do Montague and Ardrey differ on the nature of tools?
6. What does Montague mean by "the thesis of 'innate depravity'"? Why does he believe it to be unsound and dangerous?
7. How does Montague's disagreement with Ardrey on the nature and purpose of hunting reflect their basic disagreement on human nature itself?

■

IS IT OUR CULTURE, NOT OUR GENES, THAT MAKES US KILLERS?

Richard E. Leakey and Roger Lewin

Richard E. Leakey, born in Kenya in 1944, is the son of the celebrated anthropologists Louis and Mary Leakey. Though not formally educated in anthropology, Leakey is one of the best known and most influential figures in the field. In a series of excavations at Lake Turkana he uncovered a number of important hominid remains, some dating back over two million years. Leakey is the author of several books, including *Origins* (1977) and *People of the Lake* (1978). Roger Lewin, science editor of *The New Scientist*, is the author of a number of books on biology. The following essay first appeared in *Smithsonian* in 1977.

"The blood-bespattered, slaughter-gutted archives of human history from the earliest Egyptian and Sumerian records to the most recent atrocities of the Second World War accord with early universal cannibalism, with animal and human sacrificial practices or their substitutes in formalized religions, and with the worldwide scalping, head-hunting, body-mutilating and necrophilic practices of mankind in proclaiming this common bloodlust differentiator, this predaceous habit, this mark of Cain that separates man dietetically from his anthropoidal relatives and allies him rather with the deadliest of Carnivora." The message of these stirring words, written by Paleoanthropologist Raymond Dart, is clear: humans are unswervingly brutal, possessed of an innate drive to kill each other.

On the same subject, the Nobel Prize winner Konrad Lorenz, one of the founders of modern ethology, wrote with even more eloquence: "There is evidence that the first inventors of pebble tools—the African australopithecines—promptly used their weapons to kill not only game, but fellow members of their species as well. Peking Man, the Prometheus* who learned to preserve fire, used it to roast his brothers: beside the first traces of the regular use of fire lie the . . . roasted bones of *Sinanthropus pekinensis* himself."

Lorenz sounded these dramatic phrases 14 years ago in his celebrated book *On Aggression*, the main burden of which is that the human species carries with it an inescapable legacy of territoriality and aggression, instincts which must be ventilated lest they spill over in ugly fashion. All these—archaeological evidence of cannibalism, the notion of territorial and aggressive instincts, of an evolutionary career as killer apes—were woven together to form one of the most dangerously persuasive myths of our time: mankind is incorrigibly belligerent; war and violence are in our genes.

This essentially pessimistic view of human nature was assimilated with unseemly haste into a popular conventional wisdom, an assimilation that was further enhanced by Desmond Morris (with *The Naked Ape*) and Robert Ardrey (with *African Genesis, The Territorial Imperative, Social Contract,* and more recently *The Hunting Hypothesis*). We emphatically reject this conventional wisdom for three reasons: first, on the very general premise that no theory of human nature can be so firmly proved as its proponents imply; second, that much of the evidence used to erect this aggression theory is simply not relevant to human behavior; and last, the clues that do impinge on the basic elements of human nature argue much more persuasively that we are a cooperative rather than an aggressive animal.

The rules for human behavior are simple, we believe, precisely because they offer such a wide scope for expression. By contrast, the proponents of innate aggression try to tie us down to narrow, well-defined paths of behavior: humans are aggressive, they propose, because there is a universal territorial instinct in biology; territories are established and maintained by displays of aggression; our ancestors acquired weapons, turning ritual displays into bloody combat, a development that was exacerbated through a lust for killing. And according to the Lorenzian school, aggression is such a crucial part of the territorial animal's survival kit that it is backed up by a steady rise in pressure for its expression. Aggression may be released by an appropriate cue, such as a threat by another

---

* Editor's note: In Greek mythology Prometheus was the god who gave human beings the gift of fire.

animal, but in the protracted absence of such cues the pressure eventually reaches a critical point at which the behavior bursts out spontaneously. The difference between a piece of behavior that is elicited by a particular type of stimulus, and one that will be expressed whether or not cues occur is enormous, and that difference is central to understanding aggression in the human context.

6 There is no doubt that aggression and territoriality are part of modern life: vandalism is a distressingly familiar part of the urban scene, and there is war, an apparent display of territoriality and aggression on a grand scale. Are these unsavory aspects of modern living simply part of an inescapable legacy of our animal origins? Or are they phenomena which have entirely different causes?

7 To begin with, it is worth taking a broad view of territoriality and aggression in the animal world. Why are some animals territorial? Simply to protect resources, such as food, a nest or a similar reproductive area. Many birds defend one piece of real estate in which a male may attract and court a female, and then move off to another one, also to be defended, in which they build a nest and rear young. Intruders are soon met with territorial displays, the intention of which is quite clear. The clarity of the defender's response, and also of the intruder's prowess, is the secret of nature's success with these so-called aggressive encounters.

8 Such confrontations are strictly ritualized, so that on all but the rarest occasions the biologically fitter of the two wins without the infliction of physical damage on either one. This "aggression" is in fact an exercise in competitive display rather than physical violence. The biological common sense implicit in this simple behavioral device is reiterated again and again throughout the animal kingdom. For a species to transgress, there must be extremely unusual circumstances. We cannot deny that with the invention of tools, an impulse to employ them occasionally as weapons might have caused serious injury, there being no stereotyped behavior patterns to deflect their risk. And it is possible that our increasingly intelligent prehuman ancestors may have understood the implications of power over others through the delivery of one swift blow with a sharpened pebble tool. But is it likely?

9 The answer must be no. An animal that develops a proclivity for killing its fellows thrusts itself into an evolutionarily disadvantageous position. Because our ancestors almost always lived in small bands, in which individuals were closely related to one another, and had as neighbors similar bands which also contained blood relations, in most acts of murder the victim would more than likely have been kin to the murderer. As the evolutionary success is in the production and well-being of as many descendants as possible, an undifferentiated innate drive for killing individuals of one's own species would soon have wiped that species out. Humans, as we know, did not blunder up an evolutionary blind alley, a fate that innate, unrestrained aggressiveness would undoubtedly have produced.

10 To argue, as we do, that humans are innately nonaggressive toward one another is not to imply that we are of necessity innately good-natured toward our fellows. In the lower echelons of the animal kingdom the management of conflict is largely through genetically-seated mock battles. But farther along the evolu-

tionary path, carrying out the appropriate avoidance behavior comes to depend more and more on learning, and in social animals, the channel of learning is social education. The capacity for that behavior is rooted in the animal's genes, it is true, but its elaboration depends also on learning.

For instance, among the Micronesian Ifaluk of the western Pacific, real violence is now so thoroughly condemned that "ritual" management of conflict is taught in childhood. The children play boisterously, as any normal children do; however a child who feels that he or she is being treated unfairly will set off in pursuit of the offender—but at a pace that will not permit catching up. As other children stand around, showing looks of disapproval, the chase may end with the plaintiff throwing pieces of coconut at the accused—once again with sufficient care so as to miss the target! This is ritual conflict, culturally based, not genetic.

Animal conflict occurs both between animals of different species and between individuals of the same species, and under differing environmental conditions. Anyone who argues for inbuilt aggression in Homo sapiens must see aggression as a universal instinct in the animal kingdom. It is no such thing. Much of the research on territoriality and aggression concerns birds. Because they usually must build nests, in which they will then spend a good deal of time incubating eggs, and still longer rearing their young, it is a biological necessity for them to protect their territory. It is therefore not surprising that most birds possess a strong territorial drive. But simply because greylag geese and mockingbirds, for instance, enthusiastically defend their territory, we should not infer that all animals do so. And it is not surprising that hummingbirds show considerably more territorial aggression than lions, even though the king of beasts is a lethal hunter. Our closest animal relatives, the chimpanzees and gorillas, are notably nonterritorial. Both of these species are relatively mobile and so they can forage for food over a wide area.

The animal kingdom therefore offers a broad spectrum of territoriality, whose basic determining factor is the mode of reproduction and style of daily life. Indeed, an animal may find it necessary to assert ownership of land in one situation and not in another.

That territoriality is flexible should not be surprising. If food resources and space are scarce, then there may well be conspicuous territorial behavior. Some individuals will fail to secure sufficient food or a place in which to rear a brood. These individuals are, of course, the weakest, and this is what survival of the fittest through natural selection really means.

Territorial behavior is therefore triggered when it is required and remains dormant when it is not. The Lorenzians, however, take a different view: aggression, they say, builds up inexorably, to be released either by appropriate cues or spontaneously in the absence of appropriate cues. A safety valve suggested by Lorenzians for human societies is competitive sport. But such a suggestion neglects the high correlation between highly competitive encounters and associated vandalism and physical violence—as players, referees and crowds know to their cost through Europe and the Americas. More significantly, research now shows a close match between warlike behavior in countries and a devotion to sport. Far from defusing aggression, highly organized, emotionally charged sporting events generate even more aggression and reflect the degree to which humans' deep propensity to group identity and cohesion can be manipulated.

We can say therefore that territoriality and aggression are not universal instincts as such. Rather they are pieces of behavior that are tuned to particular life-styles and to changes in the availability of important resources in the environment.

When the practice of hunting and gathering was becoming firmly rooted in the fertile soil of prehuman society, our ancestors would of course not have operated sophisticated kinship networks. But we do know that chimpanzees know who are their brothers and sisters and who are not. And we know too that chimpanzees and baboons do migrate between their various troops. The biological benefits of reducing tension and conflict between groups through exogamy almost certainly would have been achieved early in hominid evolution. The notion of hostile neighboring hordes is an image born of the mistaken belief in a belligerence written ineradicably into the human genetic blueprint.

Food shortage, either on the hoof or rooted in the ground, must nevertheless have been a cause of potential conflict between bands. Indeed, severe famine may well have forced hominids into belligerent confrontation with one another in open competition for the scarce food. And the band that lost out may even have ended as the victors' supper. But there is neither evidence nor any reason to suggest that hominid flesh, either roasted or raw, appeared on our ancestors' diet, specifically as a source of food, in any but the most extreme circumstances. A much more likely consequence of conflict over food resources, so far as can be judged from what we know of both animals and present-day hunter-gatherers, would have been the dispersal of bands and even the temporary scattering of individuals, a practice that ensures the best use of the limited food that is available.

Along with lions, humans are one of the few mammals who on occasion deliberately eat each other. When a male lion wins control of a pride, he will often consume the young cubs and set about producing offspring of his own. Ruthless and wasteful though it may appear, the biological reason for the dominant male's behavior is evident: the offspring produced by the pride will have been sired by a very powerful animal, providing a brutal but efficient method of natural selection. Cannibalism in humans, however, takes place for different reasons.

Two Kinds of Human Cannibalism

Broadly, there are two sorts of cannibalism and the distinction between them is crucial. First, there is the eating of members of one tribe of individuals by another—usually as the end result of raids; such is the conventional version of the practice, and it is known as exocannibalism. In the second form, known as endocannibalism, people eat members of their own tribe.

Human cannibalism takes place primarily as part of some kind of ritual. Even among the infamous tribes in the highlands of New Guinea, the context is one of extensive tribal ritual. Months of preparation—weaving symbolic adornments and the carving of elaborate wooden images—precede a raid, and it is abundantly clear that the entire exercise has a powerful unifying effect on the tribe. The habits of the New Guinea tribes are, in any event, extremely rare, and as against cannibalism manifested in this extreme form we may set the other extreme, in which people swallow a small morsel of a dead relative as a mark of love and respect.

Altogether, then, the notion that humans are inherently aggressive is simply not tenable. We cannot deny that 20th-century humans display a good deal of aggression, but we cannot point to our evolutionary past either to explain its origins or to excuse it. There are many reasons why a youth may "spontaneously" smash a window or attack an old lady, but an inborn drive inherited from our animal origins is probably not one of them. Human behavior is extraordinarily sensitive to the nature of the environment, and so it should not be particularly surprising that a person reared in unpleasant surroundings, perhaps subjected to material insecurity and emotional deprivation, should later behave in a way that people blessed with a more fortunate life might regard as unpleasant. Urban problems will not be solved by pointing to supposed defects in our genes while ignoring real [defects] in social justice.

The fallacy of thus adducing our animal origins should be evident for wars as well. Wars are planned and organized by leaders intent on increasing their power. In war men are more like sheep than wolves: they may be led to manufacture munitions at home, to release bombs from 10,000 feet up, or to fire long-range guns and rockets—all as part of one great cooperative effort. It is not insignificant that those soldiers who engage in hand-to-hand fighting are subjected to an intense process of desensitization before they can do it.

With the growth of agriculture and of materially based societies, warfare has increased steadily in ferocity, culminating in our current capability to destroy even the planet. We should not look to our genes for the seeds of war; those seeds were planted when, 10,000 years ago, our ancestors for the first time planted crops and began to be farmers. The transition from the nomadic hunting way of life to the sedentary one of farmers and industrialists made war possible and potentially profitable.

Possible, but not inevitable. For what has transformed the possible into reality is the same factor that has made human beings special in the biological kingdom: culture. Because of our seemingly limitless inventiveness and our vast capacity for learning, there is an endless potential for difference among human cultures, as indeed may be witnessed throughout the world. An important element of culture, however, consists in those central values that make up an ideology. It is social and political ideologies, and the tolerance or lack of it between them, that brings human nations to bloody conflict. Those who argue that war is in our genes not only are wrong, but in addition they commit the crime of diverting attention from the real cause of war.

One supreme biological irony underlies the entire issue of organized war in modern societies—the cooperative nature of human beings. Throughout our recent evolutionary history, particularly since the rise of a hunting way of life, there must have been extreme selective pressures in favor of our ability to cooperate as a group: organized food-gathering and hunts are successful only if each member of the band knows his task and joins in with the activity of his fellows. The degree of selective pressure toward cooperation, group awareness and identification was so strong, and the period over which it operated was so extended, that it can hardly have failed to have become embedded to some degree in our genetic makeup.

We are not suggesting that the human animal is a cooperative, group-oriented automaton. That would negate what is the prime evolutionary heritage of humans: their ability to acquire culture through education and learning. We are essentially cultural animals with the capacity to formulate many kinds of social structures; but a deep-seated urge toward cooperation, toward working as a group, provides a basic framework for those structures.

Unfortunately, it is our deeply rooted urge for group cooperation that makes large-scale wars not only possible, but unique in their destructiveness. Animals that are essentially self-centered and untutored in coordinated activity could neither hunt large prey nor make war. Equally, however, massive warfare would not be possible without the inventive intelligence that has produced the increasingly sophisticated hardware of human conflict. It is therefore as unhelpful to blame the scourge of war on our cooperativeness as it would be to blame it on our intelligence. To do either is to evade the real issue—those ideological values and behavioral habits on which nations are based, through which governments manipulate their people.

If we wish to, we can change our social structures without any fear of some primal urge welling to the surface and sucking us back into some atavistic pattern. We are, after all, the ultimate expression of a cultural animal; we have not totally broken free of our biological roots, but neither are we ruled by them.

Questions for Comprehension

1. What is the position against which Leakey and Lewin are arguing?
2. What are their three reasons for opposing this position? In which paragraphs in their essay is each reason found?
3. How do Leakey and Lewin account for territoriality and aggression in the animal world? How does their view differ from Konrad Lorenz's?
4. Why does a "proclivity for killing" put an animal into a disadvantageous position?
5. Why is it significant that Leakey and Lewin find human cannibalism to be essentially ritualistic?
6. How do Leakey and Lewin account for the origin of war?
7. What is the relationship between "our deeply rooted urge for group cooperation" and the implementation of massive warfare? Does the one *cause* the other?
8. In what ways is Leakey and Lewin's final paragraph a summation of all that has preceded it?

ON BECOMING HUMAN
Nancy Tanner

Nancy Tanner, an associate professor of anthropology at the University of California, Santa Cruz, was educated at the University of Chicago and the University of California, Berkeley. The following is an excerpt from On Becoming Human (1981).

Although others have mentioned that early hominids probably gathered much of their food, until quite recently the prevailing idea underlying reconstructions of social behavior has been that *Australopithecus* was primarily a hunter. There are, however, considerable data that are anomalous from a hunting perspective. For their small size, all australopithecines—even the early basal hominids and the so-called gracile line—had powerful chewing and grinding capacities. This kind of chewing apparatus is best understood as an adaptation to a diet including a high proportion of tough, uncooked plant food. Further, given their small size and still very simple technology, it is improbable that they pursued, captured, and killed large dangerous animals with tools. The data on size, tools, and teeth do not fit a hunting model but make a great deal of sense when viewed within a gathering context.

There has been a misemphasis on hunting—that is, using tools to stop and kill moving animals—at this early stage of hominid evolution. Along with the premature emphasis on hunting has come a plethora of dubious assumptions: for example, the supposition of male-male bonding, assumed to have been developed for cooperation in hunting and in defense; similarly, the belief that males provided meat for and protection to females with whom they had fathered offspring, and so to their own young. The presumption that females did not provide a significant degree of food or protection for themselves and their offspring apparently then followed. Reconstructions largely fail to make note of females in these contexts.

With the supposition that males were the providers of meat and were the defenders of females and young in the face of danger, the idea of a pair bond became intimately interwoven into the evolutionary saga, with our earliest hominid female forebears—much like American women of the 1940s and 1950s—relegated to a passive role in sexual, economic, technological, protective, and even most social behaviors. Here is the evolutionist version of the Adam and Eve story: a pair-bond mating system, with coterminous economic and mating units.

Male tool use related to hunting and protection frequently is referred to in popular and scholarly writing alike; female tool use has seldom been mentioned. Yet it seems highly probable that early hominid females made and used tools for digging up vegetable food, knocking down fruit and nuts, collecting insects and their products such as honey, and dividing plant and animal food. They also may have invented a simple container for carrying gathered food and a device for supporting infants. And it is very likely indeed that both sexes used tools for protection and eventually some butchering and that neither males nor females used tools in extensive big game hunting.

Here, in terms of the hunting model, is a case where popular writing has greatly exaggerated anything ever put forward by students of human evolution. Yet, in terms of model building, it is a question of emphasis. The assumption of male tool use for hunting has—like the use of some of Darwin's phrases in Social Darwinism—become part of Western society's modern evolutionary "origin myth." For example, male hunting with tools has been seen as male killing with tools from very early in the human past and has been used to explain and, in a sense, legitimize male involvement in warfare. Warfare does indeed need study and explanation. The explanations will be far more complex, however, and warfare itself is probably quite a recent human invention—one that is associated with fairly large, organized human societies such as tribes and, in particular, nation-states. At any rate, we have here an example of one sort of modern evolutionary myth making that has been associated with a hunting model.

Tight social organization has been supposed necessary for protection on the "exposed" savanna. The argument that there is safety in numbers has had as its implicit corollary that males, and cooperation among them, were necessary for protection. But what about the surprise that upright hominid posture gave to predators and, especially, what about the use of tools for defense?

If tools are used for defense—and such "tools" may be as simple as readily available sticks, branches, stones, and wads of grass—then both females and males can frighten away carnivores. At one australopithecine site, Swartkrans in southern Africa, there is evidence that the early hominids may have occasionally been killed and eaten by leopards. There was, then, need for defense. If australopithecines were as intelligent as chimpanzees, and if females were as self-protective and protective of their infants as are chimpanzee females, then both female and male hominids would learn to use such tools for protection. The group therefore did not always need to be large or to have an adult male accompanying females and young. Group flexibility could be maintained, with changes in both size and composition occurring in response to variable ecological conditions.

Intelligence usually has been discussed relative to hunting—in turn assumed to be a male activity. By implication, then, there is no selection pressure for female intelligence. The list could go on and on, but that is hardly necessary. The point is not to dwell on all the gaps in past reconstructions but to develop a model that corrects the imbalance. Even now, when a role for gathering is often acknowledged, the far-reaching implications of this major innovation are rarely explored.

The approach taken here obviously is not without assumptions: The perspective is evolutionary. From this it follows that selection operated on all ages and both sexes for effective behaviors. As a corollary, females as well as males were intelligent and active. They were not so encumbered by being pregnant or carrying a young child that they were prevented from tool making and using, thinking about where to find food, gathering it, or defending themselves and their children. Indeed, it is assumed that there was selection for all adult females to possess these capacities and consistently utilize their abilities. The children with the best survival chances were those whose mothers most effectively exercised such capabilities. Even among modern gatherer-hunters living long after the invention of hunting with tools, women still consistently provide a large proportion of the food and have an essential economic as well as social role in the group.

Questions for Comprehension

1. What is the position Tanner is arguing against?
2. Why does Tanner believe gathering to be a more likely model for the behavior of early hominids than hunting?
3. What are the "dubious assumptions" that arise from the "misemphasis on hunting"?
4. How does Tanner's discussion of tool use relate to the thesis of her essay?
5. Why does the hunting model of early human activity necessarily involve an imbalance in the importance of men and women?
6. What is the significance of Tanner's assertion that "the group therefore did not always need to be large or to have an adult male accompanying females and the young"? How does the assertion relate to her position on the relationship between males and females in early hominid society?

THE FOOD SHARING BEHAVIOR OF PROTOHUMAN HOMINIDS

Glynn Isaac

Glynn Isaac is a professor of anthropology at the University of California, Berkeley. A native of South Africa, Isaac was educated at the University of Cape Town and Cambridge University. In 1961 he began working with the celebrated anthropologist Louis Leakey in East Africa and has been working with Richard Leakey since 1970. The following essay is the final section of an article first published in *Scientific American* in 1978. Earlier in the article, Isaac has discussed the recent evidence for hominid behavior.

Model Strategies

These archaeological facts and indications allow the construction of a theoretical model that shows how at least some aspects of early hominid social existence may have been organized. Critical to the validity of the model is the inference that the various clusters of remains we have uncovered reflect social and economic modes in the lives of the toolmakers who left behind these ancient patches of litter. Because of the evidence suggestive of the transport of food to certain focal points, the first question that the model must confront is why early hominid social groups departed from the norm among living subhuman primates, whose social groups feed as they range. To put it another way, what ecological and evolutionary advantages are there in postponing some food consumption and transporting the food?

Several possible answers to this question have been advanced. For example, Adrienne Zihlman and Nancy Tanner of the University of California at Santa Cruz suggest that when the protohumans acquired edible plants out on the open grasslands, away from the shelter of trees, it would have been advantageous for them to seize the plant products quickly and withdraw to places sheltered from menacing predators. Others have proposed that when the early hominids foraged, they left their young behind at "nest" or "den" sites in the manner of birds, wild dogs and hyenas and returned to these locales at intervals, bringing food with them to help feed and wean the young.

If we look to the recorded data concerning primitive human societies, a third possibility arises. Among extant and recently extinct primitive human societies the transport of food is associated with a division of labor. The society is divided by age and sex into classes that characteristically make different contributions to the total food supply. One significant result of such a division is an increase in the variety of foodstuffs consumed by the group. To generalize on the basis of many different enthnographic reports, the adult females of the society contribute the majority of the "gathered" foods; such foods are mainly plant products but may include shellfish, amphibians and small reptiles, eggs, insects and the like. The adult males usually, although not invariably, contribute most of the "hunted" foodstuffs: the flesh of mammals, fishes, birds and so forth. Characteristically the males and females range in separate groups and each sex eventually brings back to a home base at least the surplus of its foraging.

Could this simple mechanism, a division of the subsistence effort, have initiated food carrying by early hominids? One cannot dismiss out of hand the models that suggest safety from competitors or the feeding of nesting young as the initiating mechanisms for food carrying. Nevertheless, neither model seems to me as plausible as one that has division of labor as the primary initiating mechanism. Even if no other argument favored the model, we know for a fact that somewhere along the line in the evolution of human behavior two patterns became established: food sharing and a division of labor. If we include both patterns in our model of early hominid society, we will at least be parsimonious.

Other arguments can be advanced in favor of an early development of a division of labor. For example, the East African evidence shows that the protohuman toolmakers consumed meat from a far greater range of species and sizes of animals than are eaten by such living primates as the chimpanzee and the baboon. Among recent human hunter-gatherers the existence of a division of labor seems clearly related to the females being encumbered with children, a handicap that bars them from hunting or scavenging activities that require speed afoot or long-range mobility. For the protohumans too the incorporation of meat in the diet in significant quantities may well have been a key factor in the development not only of a division of labor but also of the organization of movements around a home base and the transport and sharing of food.

The model I propose for testing visualizes food sharing as the behavior central to a novel complex of adaptations that include as critical components hunting and/or scavenging, gathering and carrying. Speaking metaphorically, food sharing provides the model with a kind of central platform. The adaptive system I visualize, however, could only have functioned through the use of tools and other equipment. For example, without the aid of a carrying device primates such as ourselves or our ancestors could not have transported from the field to the home base a sufficient amount of plant food to be worth sharing. An object as uncomplicated as a bark tray would have served the purpose, but some such item of equipment would have been mandatory. In fact, Richard Borshay Lee of the University of Toronto has suggested that a carrying device was the basic invention that made human evolution possible.

What about stone tools? Our ancestors, like ourselves, could probably break up the body of a small animal as chimpanzees do, with nothing but their hands and teeth. It is hard to visualize them or us, however, eating the meat of an elephant, a hippopotamus or some other large mammal without the aid of a cutting implement. As the archaeological evidence demonstrates abundantly, the protohumans of East Africa not only knew how to produce such stone flakes by percussion but also found them so useful that they carried the raw materials needed to make the implements with them from place to place. Thus whereas the existence of a carrying device required by the model remains hypothetical as far as archaeological evidence is concerned, the fact that tools were used and carried about is amply attested to.

In this connection it should be stressed that the archaeological evidence is also silent with regard to protohuman consumption of plant foods. Both the morphology and the patterns of wear observable on hominid teeth suggest such a plant component in the diet, and so does the weight of comparative data on subsistence patterns among living nonhuman primates and among nonfarming human societies. Nevertheless, if positive evidence is to be found, we shall have to sharpen our ingenuity, perhaps by turning to organic geochemical analyses. It is clear that as long as we do not correct for the imbalance created by the durability of bone as compared with that of plant residues, studies of human evolution will tend to have a male bias.

As far as the model is concerned the key question is not whether collectable foods—fruits, nuts, tubers, greens and even insects—were eaten. It is whether these protohumans carried such foods about. Lacking any evidence for the consumption of plant foods, I shall fall back on the argument that the system I visualize would have worked best if the mobile hunter-scavenger contribution of meat to the social group was balanced by the gatherer-carrier collection of high-grade plant foods. What is certain is that at some time during the past several million years just such a division of labor came to be a standard kind of behavior among the ancestors of modern man.

A final cautionary word about the model: The reader may have noted that I have been careful about the use of the words "hunter" and "hunting." This is because we cannot judge how much of the meat taken by the protohumans of East Africa came from opportunistic scavenging and how much was obtained by hunting. It is reasonable to assume that the carcasses of animals killed by carnivores and those of animals that had otherwise died or been disabled would always have provided active scavengers a certain amount of meat. For the present it seems less reasonable to assume that protohumans, armed primitively if at all, would be particularly effective hunters. Attempts are now under way, notably by Elizabeth Vrba of South Africa, to distinguish between assemblages of bones attributable to scavenging and assemblages attributable to hunting, but no findings from East Africa are yet available. For the present I am inclined to accept the verdict of J. Desmond Clark of the University of California at Berkeley and Lewis R. Binford of the University of New Mexico. In their view the earliest meat-eaters might have obtained the flesh of animals weighing up to 30 kilograms by deliberate hunting, but the flesh of larger animals was probably available only through scavenging.

Tools as Testimony

Of course, the adaptive model I have advanced here reflects only a working hypothesis and not established fact. Nevertheless, there is sufficient evidence in its favor to justify looking further at its possible implications for the course of human evolution. For example, the model clearly implies that early toolmaking hominids displayed certain patterns of behavior that, among the patterns of behavior of all primates, uniquely characterize our own species and set it apart from its closest living relatives, the great apes. Does this mean that the toolmaking hominids of 1.5 to 2 million years ago were in fact "human"? 11

I would surmise that it does not, and I have been at pains to characterize these East African pioneers as protohumans. In summarizing the contrasts between living men and living apes, I put high on the list language and the cultural phenomena that are dependent on it. We have no direct means of learning whether or not any of these early hominids had language. It is my suspicion, however, that the principal evolutionary change in the hominid line leading to full humanity over the past two million years has been the great expansion of language and communication abilities, together with the cognitive and cultural capabilities integrally related to language. What is the evidence in support of this surmise? 12

One humble indicator of expanding mental capacities is the series of changes that appears in the most durable material record available to us: the stone tools. The earlier tools from the period under consideration here seem to me to show a simple and opportunistic range of forms that reflect no more than an uncomplicated empirical grasp of one skill; how to fracture stone by percussion in such a way as to obtain fragments with sharp edges. At that stage of toolmaking the maker imposed a minimum of culturally dictated forms on his artifacts. Stone tools as simple as these perform perfectly well the basic functions that support progress in the direction of becoming human, for example the shaping of a digging stick, a spear and a bark tray, or the butchering of an animal carcass. 13

The fact is that exactly such simple stone tools have been made and used ever since their first invention, right down to the present day. Archaeology also shows, however, that over the past several hundred thousand years some assemblages of stone tools began to reflect a greater cultural complexity on the part of their makers. The complexity is first shown in the imposition of more arbitrary 14 tool forms; these changes were followed by increases in the number of such forms. There is a marked contrast between the pure opportunism apparent in the shapes of the earliest stone tools and the orderly array of forms that appear later in the Old Stone Age, when each form is represented by numerous standardized examples in each assemblage of tools. The contrast strongly suggests that the first toolmakers lacked the highly developed mental and cultural abilities of more recent humans.

The evidence of the hominid fossils and the evidence of the artifacts together suggest that these early artisans were nonhuman hominids. I imagine that if we had a time machine and could visit a place such as the Kay Behrensmeyer site at the time of its original occupation, we would find hominids that were living in social groups much like those of other higher primates. The differences would be apparent only after prolonged observation. Perhaps at the start of each day we would observe a group splitting up as some of its members went off in one direction and some in another. All these subgroups would very probably feed intermittently as they moved about and encountered ubiquitous low-grade plant foods such as berries, but we might well observe that some of the higher-grade materials—large tubers or the haunch of a scavenged carcass—were being reserved for group consumption when the foraging parties reconvened at their starting point.

Social Advances

To the observer in the time machine, behavior of this kind, taken in context with the early hominids' practice of making tools and equipment, would seem familarly "human." If, as I suppose, the hominids under observation communicated only as chimpanzees do or perhaps by means of very rudimentary protolinguistic signals, then the observer might feel he was witnessing the activities of some kind of fascinating bipedal ape. When one is relying on archaeology to reconstruct protohuman life, one must strongly resist the temptation to project too much of ourselves into the past. As Jane B. Lancaster of the University of Oklahoma has pointed out, the hominid life systems of two million years ago have no living counterparts.

My model of early hominid adaptation can do more than indicate that the first toolmakers were culturally protohuman. It can also help to explain the dyamics of certain significant advances in the long course of mankind's development. For example, one can imagine that a hominid social organization involving some division of labor and a degree of food sharing might well have been able to function even if it had communicative abilities little more advanced than those of living chimpanzees. In such a simple subsistence system, however, any group with members that were able not only to exchange food but also to exchange information would have gained a critical selective advantage over all the rest. Such a group's gatherers could report on scavenging or hunting opportunities they had observed, and its hunters could tell the gatherers about any plant foods they had encountered.

By the same token the fine adjustment of social relations, always a matter of importance among primates, becomes doubly important in a social system that involves food exchange. Language serves in modern human societies not only for the exchange of information but also as an instrument for social adjustment and even for the exchange of misinformation.

Food sharing and the kinds of behavior associated with it probably played an important part in the development of systems of reciprocal social obligations that characterize all human societies we know about. Anthropological research shows that each human being in a group is ordinarily linked to many other members of the group by ties that are both social and economic. The French anthropologist Marcel Mauss, in a classic essay "The Gift," published in 1925, showed that social ties are usually reciprocal in the sense that whereas benefits from a relationship may initially pass in only one direction, there is an expectation of a future return of help in time of need. The formation and management of such ties calls for an ability to calculate complex chains of contingencies that reach far into the future. After food sharing had become a part of protohuman behavior the need for such an ability to plan and calculate must have provided an important part of the biological basis for the evolution of the human intellect.

The model may also help explain the development of human marriage arrangements. It assumes that in early protohuman populations the males and females divided subsistence labor between them so that each sex was preferentially tapping a different kind of food resource and then sharing within a social group some of what had been obtained. In such circumstances a mating system that involved at least one male in "family" food procurement on behalf of each child-rearing female in the group would have a clear selective advantage over, for example, the chimpanzees' pattern of opportunistic relations between the sexes.

I have emphasized food sharing as a principle that is central to an understanding of human evolution over the past two million years or so. I have also set forth archaeological evidence that food sharing was an established kind of behavior among early protohumans. The notion is far from novel; it is implicit in many philosophical speculations and in many writings on paleoanthropology. What is novel is that I have undertaken to make the hypothesis explicit so that it can be tested and revised.

Thus the food sharing hypothesis now joins other hypotheses that have been put forward to account for the course of human evolution. Each of these hypotheses tends to maintain that one or another innovation in protohuman behavior was the critical driving force of change. For example, the argument has been advanced that tools were the "prime movers." Here the underlying implication is that in each successive generation the more capable individuals made better tools and thereby gained advantages that favored the transmission of their genes through natural selection: it is supposed that these greater capabilities would later be applied in aspects of life other than technology. Another hypothesis regards hunting as being the driving force. Here the argument is that hunting requires intelligence, cunning, skilled neuromuscular coordination and, in the case of group hunting, cooperation. Among other suggested prime movers are such practices as carrying and gathering.

If we compare the food sharing explanation with these alternative explanations we see that in fact food sharing incorporates many aspects of each of the others. It will also be seen that in the food sharing model the isolated elements are treated as being integral parts of a complex, flexible system. The model itself is probably an oversimplified version of what actually happened, but it seems sufficiently realistic to be worthy of testing through further archaeological and paleontology research.

Lastly, the food sharing model can be seen to have interconnections with the physical implications of fossil hominid anatomy. For example, a prerequisite of food sharing is the ability to carry things. This ability in turn is greatly facilitated by a habitual two-legged posture. As Gordon W. Hewes of the University of Colorado has pointed out, an important part of the initial evolutionary divergence of hominids from their primate relatives may have been the propensity and the ability to carry things about. To me it seems equally plausible that the physical selection pressures that promoted an increase in the size of the protohuman brain, thereby surely enhancing the hominid capacity for communication, are a consequence of the shift from individual foraging to food sharing some two million years ago.

Questions for Comprehension

1. How does Isaac explain the fact that early hominids collected their food in certain focal locations?
2. What were the different contributions to the food supply made by men and women in primitive human societies? Why does the fact that bone is more durable than plant residues create a "male bias" in studies of human evolution?
3. How does the manner in which early hominids used tools indicate that they were protohumans and not humans?
4. In what way was food gathering and sharing instrumental in the development of "systems of reciprocal social obligations that characterize all human societies we know about"?
5. Why is marriage an advantage in a food sharing culture?
6. How is the food sharing hypothesis for the course of human evolution related to the tool making and hunting hypotheses?

ADDITIONAL WRITING ASSIGNMENTS

1. Summarize the essay by Desmond Morris. You may find the Questions for Comprehension at the end of the essay helpful in finding the thesis and key ideas of his essay.
2. Contrast the two basic images of the nature of early human life that appear in the readings in this anthology. Use specific sources to exemplify each image.
3. Early human life is often depicted—both seriously and humorously—in books, movies, television programs, comic strips, and cartoons. Choose one such representation and describe the image of early human life it projects. See if you can relate that representation to one of the readings in the anthology.

4. Take one of the essays in the anthology and explain the author's conception of human nature. What, according to the author, are the defining characteristics of the human race? Is the author's view of human nature optimistic or pessimistic? How accurately does the author's view depict human nature as you know it?

Animal Rights

GATHERING THE ESSAYS IN THIS ANTHOLOGY UNder the title "Animal Rights" may be jumping the gun somewhat; one of the questions debated by the authors of these essays is whether or not animals have moral rights. We must not, however, confuse this question with another one, whether or not animals ought to be treated with kindness. Few people, and none of the writers in our anthology, have disputed that animals ought to be treated humanely. But many have questioned what is meant by "humane treatment." For some people humane treatment consists essentially of taking care not to inflict unnecessary pain on animals. For other people, however, experimenting on animals and killing them for food are inhumane, regardless of whether or not we avoid inflicting "unnecessary" pain. Everyone agrees on the formula, but what exactly does it mean?

This is not an uncommon situation to find ourselves in when we ask ethical questions, when we consider the nature of moral and immoral conduct. Before we can decide on a moral course of action, we often find it necessary to dig deeper and ask more basic questions. In this case, before we can define what specific behavior constitutes the proper treatment of animals, we must consider the nature of our relationship to animals. For example, if we believe that animals are to be regarded as beings put on Earth for our benefit, we will justify any treatment of animals that benefits human beings (though we will still have to define precisely what we mean by a benefit). If we believe, on the other hand, that the relationship between animals and humans is one of moral equality, we are likely to find any treatment that causes harm to animals to be repugnant, in spite of any benefits to humans. The point is that if we are to make serious decisions about our behavior toward animals, we must delve into basic questions about the nature of animals and their relationship to us. These are the questions explored by the philosophers whose essays appear in this anthology.

The anthology opens with two contrasting essays from the early twentieth century. Humanitarian and social reformer Henry S. Salt considers what he terms the "logic of the larder," the set of rationalizations people employ to justify their appetite for flesh consumption. The Jesuit philosopher Joseph Rickaby, on the other hand, uses biblical evidence and the writings of the church fathers to prove that human beings have no duties to animals. The question of whether or not animals have moral rights is addressed more recently by Peter Singer (page 56), James Rachels, and Michael Fox. Singer, as we have seen, argues that the capacity to suffer is a sufficient condition for moral rights, a view disputed by Fox, who believes that participation in a moral community must be added to the capacity to suffer if a creature is to have moral rights. Rachels uses the distinction between "being alive" and "having a life" to determine whether or not an animal has a right to life.

Thomas L. Benson takes up the issue of human attitudes toward animals, analyzing the various stereotypes people have created over the years. These stereotypes, he believes, prevent human beings from considering animals in a realistic light and justify immoral behavior toward them. Tom Regan discusses the use of animals in educational settings, in particular the practice of dissecting live animals in high school and college biology courses. Finally, Michael Levin casts a critical eye on the entire animal rights movement.

■

THE LOGIC OF THE LARDER

Henry S. Salt

> Henry S. Salt (1851–1939), though largely forgotten today, was an English humanitarian who wrote many books on social reform and campaigned actively in favor of animal rights. His personality and writings influenced the thought of such reformers as George Bernard Shaw and Gandhi. The following essay originally appeared in 1914.

It is often said, as an excuse for the slaughter of animals, that it is better for them to live and to be butchered than not to live at all. Now, obviously, if such reasoning justifies the practice of flesh-eating, it must equally justify *all* breeding of animals for profit or pastime, when their life is a fairly happy one. The argument is frequently used by sportsmen, on the ground that the fox would long ago have become extinct in this country had not they, his true friends, "preserved" him for purposes of sport. Vivisectors, who breed guinea-pigs for experimentation, also have used it, and they have as much right to it as flesh-eaters; for how, they may say, can a few hours of suffering be set in the balance against the enormous benefit of life? In fact, if we once admit that it is an *advantage* to an animal to be brought into the world, there is hardly any treatment that cannot be justified by the supposed terms of such a contract.

Also, the argument must apply to mankind. It has, in fact, been the plea of the slave-breeder; and it is logically just as good an excuse for slave-holding as for flesh-eating. It would justify parents in almost any treatment of their children, who owe them, for the great boon of life, a debt of gratitude which no subsequent services can repay. We could hardly deny the same merit to cannibals, if they were to breed their human victims for the table, as the early Peruvians are said to have done.

It is on record, in no less authentic a work than "Hansard"* (March 7, 1883), that when Sir Herbert Maxwell argued in Parliament that a "blue rock" would prefer to be sport for pigeon-shooters than not to exist at all, Mr. W. E. Forster satirically remarked that what we have to consider is not a blue rock *before* existence, but a blue rock *in* existence. There, in brief, is the key to the whole matter. The fallacy lies in the confusion of thought which attempts to compare existence with non-existence. A person who is already in existence may feel that he would rather have lived than not, but he must first have the *terra firma* of existence to argue from; the moment he begins to argue as if from the abyss of the non-existent, he talks nonsense, by predicating good or evil, happiness or unhappiness, of that of which we can predicate nothing.

When, therefore, we talk of "bringing a being," as we vaguely express it, "into the world," we cannot claim from that being any *gratitude* for our action, or drive a bargain with him, and a very shabby one, on that account; nor can our duties to him be evaded by any such quibble, in which the wish is so obviously father to the thought. Nor, in this connection, is it necessary to enter on the question of ante-natal existence, because, if such existence there be, we have no reason for assuming that it is less happy than the present existence; and thus equally the argument falls to the ground. It is absurd to compare a supposed preexistence, or non-existence, with actual individual life as known to us here. All reasoning based on such comparison must necessarily be false, and will lead to grotesque conclusions.

Take the case, as it stands, between the Philosopher and the Pig. Is it not adding insult to injury that this much-massacred animal should not only be *eaten* by the Philosopher, but should also be made the subject of a far from disinterested beatification—"Blessed is the Pig, for the Philosopher is fond of bacon." . . . We can imagine how the Philosopher, when he passes a butcher's shop, which, according to his showing, is a very shrine and centre of humaneness, since without it there "would be no pigs at all," must pause in serene self-satisfaction to felicitate the pallid carcase laid out there, with the mockery of an ornamental orange in its

---

* Editor's note: The Hansard was the official report of the proceedings of the British Parliament.

mouth. "I have been a benefactor to this Pig," he must say, "inasmuch as I ate a portion of his predecessor; and now I will be a benefactor to some yet unborn pig, by eating a portion of this one."

This, then, is the benign attitude of the Philosopher towards the Pig; and what shall be the reply of the Pig to the Philosopher? "Revered moralist," he might plead, "it were unseemly for me, who am to-day a pig, and to-morrow but ham and sausages, to dispute with a master of ethics, yet to my porcine intellect it appeareth that having first determined to kill and devour me, thou hast afterwards bestirred thee to find a moral reason. For mark, I pray thee, that in my entry into the world my own predilection was in no wise considered, nor did I purchase life on condition of my own butchery. If, then, thou art firm set on pork, so be it, for pork I am: but though thou hast not spared my life, at least spare me thy sophistry. It is not for *his* sake, but for *thine*, that in his life the Pig is filthily housed and fed, and at the end barbarously butchered."

From whatever point one looks at this sophism, it is seen to be equally hollow. For even apart from the philosophical flaw which vitiates it, there is the practical consideration that a far greater number of human lives can be supported on a grain and fruit-growing district than on one which rears cattle; so that if a larger area of England were devoted to the rearing of "livestock," we should actually be lessening human life that there might be more beef and mutton; that is, we should be increasing the lower existence at the expense of the higher. It is worth noting, too, that the life of animals doomed to the slaughter is of a far lower quality than it would be if the same animals were either entirely wild, or domesticated to some rational purpose by friendly association with man; the very fact that an animal is going to be eaten seems to remove it from the category of intelligent beings, and causes it to be regarded as mere animated "meat." "To keep a man, slave, or servant," says Edward Carpenter, "for your own advantage merely, to keep an animal, that you may *eat* it, is a lie; you cannot look that animal in the face." The existence of bullocks, for example, can scarcely be called life; they are "live-stock," but they do not *live*. And what of the "fat beasts" that are yearly exhibited at the Agricultural Hall, and elsewhere, at the season of peace and goodwill? Are these wretched victims of human gluttony to be grateful for the boon of life? Are crammed fowls and Strasburg geese to be grateful? And the calf and the lamb—are *they* to be felicitated on the rather short term allowed them in the ghoulish contract, or must we except the eaters of veal and lamb from the list of animal benefactors?

Let us heartily accept all that may be said of "the joyfulness of life." But what is the moral to be drawn from that fact? Surely not that we are justified in outraging and destroying life, to pamper our selfish appetites, because forsooth we shall then produce more of it! But rather that we should respect the beauty and sanctity of life in others as in ourselves, and strive as far as possible to secure its fullest natural development. This logic of the larder is the very negation of a true reverence for life; for it implies that the real lover of animals is he whose larder is fullest of them:

> He prayeth best, who *eateth* best
> All things both great and small.

It is the philosophy of the wolf, the shark, the cannibal. If there be any truth in such an argument, let those who believe it have the courage of their convictions, and face the inevitable conclusion. The Ogre has hitherto been a much misunderstood character, but now at last Philosophy and Science are doing justice to his beneficence. His organization has been defective, perhaps, but his spirit has been wholly commendable. He is *par excellence* the zoophilist, the philanthropist, the saint. . . .

But enough of this quibbling! Vegetarianism would save the actual animals, who have been brought into this actual world, from the very real suffering that is inseparable from the cattle-ship and the slaughter-house; and if its only inhumanity is that which it perpetrates on non-existent races by not arranging for their birth, it may bear the charge with equanimity. If there were any unkindness, or any lack of kindness, in *not* breeding animals, the enormity of our sins of omission would be more than the human conscience could endure, for the number of the unborn is limitless, and to wade through slaughter to a throne, "and shut the gates of mercy on mankind," would be a trifle in comparison with this cold-blooded shutting of the gates of life on the poor, neglected non-existent!

It is interesting to note that this fallacy—the assumption that it is a *kindness* to bring a being into the world—is as old as the time of Lucretius, who deals with it, in another connection, in a passage of his great philosophical poem, *De Rerum Natura** (v. 176–180), which may be rendered thus:

> What loss were ours, if we had known not birth?
> Let living men to longer life aspire,
> While fond affection binds their hearts to earth:
> But whoso ne'er hath tasted life's desire,
> Unborn, impersonal, can feel no dearth.

We see, then, that a vulgar sophism of to-day was clearly exposed nearly two thousand years ago. It is quite possible that fools may be repeating it two thousand years hence.

Questions for Comprehension

1. What is the argument Salt is attacking at the beginning of his essay? What is the "conflict of thought" Salt finds in the argument?
2. How does the Philosopher justify eating meat? How does the Pig's response clarify Salt's position?
3. What is the "practical consideration" in favor of vegetarianism?
4. What is the moral Salt would have us draw from "the joyfulness of life"?
5. What is "the logic of the larder"? In what sense is it "the very negation of a true reverence for life"?
6. What is a "sophism"? How do the lines from Lucretius expose the "vulgar sophism" against which Salt argues in his essay?

---

* Editor's note: *On the Nature of the Universe*, written in the first century B.C.

OF THE SO-CALLED RIGHTS OF ANIMALS

Joseph Rickaby

Joseph Rickaby, S.J. (1845–1932), was a Jesuit philosopher whose book *Moral Philosophy* was an influential text in numerous Catholic colleges. In the following essay, published in 1901, he considers the issue of animal rights from the perspective of the Bible and the church fathers.

Brute beasts, not having understanding and therefore not being persons, cannot have any rights. The conclusion is clear. They are not autocentric. They are of the number of *things*, which are another's: they are chattels, or cattle. We have no duties to them,—not of justice, as is shown: not of religion, unless we are to worship them, like the Egyptians of old; not of fidelity, for they are incapable of accepting a promise. The only question can be of charity. Have we duties of charity to the lower animals? Charity is an extension of the love of ourselves to beings like ourselves, in view of our common nature and our common destiny to happiness in God. . . . It is not for the present treatise to prove, but to assume, that our nature is not common to brute beasts, but immeasurably above theirs, higher indeed above them than we are below the angels. Man alone speaks, man alone worships, man alone hopes to contemplate for ever, if not—in the natural order—the Face of his Father in Heaven, at least the reflected brightness of that Divine Face. . . . We have then no duties of charity, nor duties of any kind, to the lower animals, as neither to sticks and stones.

Still we have duties *about* stones, not to fling them through our neighbour's windows; and we have duties *about* brute beasts. We must not harm them, when they are our neighbour's property. We must not break out into paroxysms of rage and impatience in dealing with them. It is a miserable way of showing off human pre-eminence, to torture poor brutes in malevolent glee at their pain and helplessness. Such wanton cruelty is especially deplorable, because it disposes the perpetrators to be cruel also to men. As St. Thomas* says . . . :

"Because the passion of pity arises from the afflictions of others, and it happens even to brute animals to feel pain, the affection of pity may arise in man even about the afflictions of animals. Obviously, whoever is practised in the affection of pity towards animals, is thereby more disposed to the affection of pity towards men: whence it is said in Proverbs xii. 10: 'The just regardeth the lives of his beasts, but the bowels of the wicked are cruel.' And therefore the Lord, seeing the Jewish people to be cruel, that He might reclaim them to pity, wished to train them to pity even towards brute beasts, forbidding certain things to be done to animals which seem to touch upon cruelty. And therefore He forbad them to seethe the kid in the mother's milk (Deut. xiv. 21), or to muzzle the treading ox (Deut. xxv. 4), or to kill the old bird with the young (Deut. xxii. 6, 7)."

It is wanton cruelty to vex and annoy a brute beast *for sport*. This is

---

* Editor's note: St. Thomas Aquinas (1225–74), foremost Catholic theologian.

unworthy of man, and disposes him to inhumanity towards his own species. Yet the converse is not to be relied on: there have been cruel men who have made pets of the brute creation. But there is no shadow of evil resting on the practice of causing pain to brutes *in sport*, where the pain is not the sport itself, but an incidental concomitant of it. Much more in all that conduces to the sustenance of man may we give pain to brutes, as also in the pursuit of science. Nor are we bound to any anxious care to make this pain as little as may be. Brutes are as *things* in our regard: so far as they are useful to us, they exist for us, not for themselves; and we do right in using them unsparingly for our need and convenience, though not for our wantonness. If then any special case of pain to a brute creature be a fact of considerable value for observation in biological science or the medical art, no reasoned considerations of morality can stand in the way of man making the experiment, yet so that even in the quest of science he be mindful of mercy.

Altogether it will be found that a sedulous observance of the rights and claims of other men, a mastery over one's own passions, and a reverence for the Creator, give the best assurance of a wise and humane treatment of the lower animals. But to preach kindness to brutes as a primary obligation, and capital point of amendment in the conversion of a sinner, is to treat the symptom and leave unchecked the inward malady.

Questions for Comprehension

1. Why does Rickaby believe that "brute beasts" have no rights?
2. On what basis does Rickaby conclude that "we have then no duties of charity, nor duties of any kind, to lower animals, as neither to sticks and stones"?
3. What is the difference between having duties *to* animals and having duties *about* animals?
4. What specifically are our duties about animals?
5. Why, according to St. Thomas Aquinas, ought we to be kind to animals?
6. What precisely is Rickaby's attitude toward using animals for sport?
7. What is Rickaby's attitude toward the use of animals in scientific experimentation?
8. How does Rickaby's last paragraph serve as a unifying idea?

■

DO ANIMALS HAVE A RIGHT TO LIFE?

James Rachels

James Rachels is University Professor at the University of Alabama at Birmingham. He is the author of *The Elements of Moral Philosophy* and *The End of Life*. The following is an excerpt from an essay published in 1983.

With respect to the characteristics that qualify one for a right to life, I wish to offer the following thesis: an individual has a right to life if that individual has a life. Like many philosophical claims, this one is more complicated than it first appears to be.

2 "Having a life" is different from merely being alive. . . . The latter is merely a biological notion; to be alive is just to be a functioning biological organism. A life, in the sense in which it concerns us here, is a notion of biography rather than biology. "The Life of Babe Ruth" will be concerned not with the biological facts of Ruth's existence—he had a heart and liver and blood and kidneys—but with facts about his attitudes, beliefs, actions, and relationships. It will say that he was born in Baltimore in 1895; that he was the troubled child of a poor family, sent to live at St. Mary's School when he was eight; that he learned baseball at the school and started pitching for the Red Sox at 19; that he was a fine pitcher for six seasons before switching to the Yankee outfield and going on to become the most idolized slugger in the history of the game; that he was the beer-guzzling friend of Lou Gehrig, and married to Claire; that he died of cancer at age 53; and much more.

3 The contingencies of human existence determine the general shape of our lives. Because we are born physically weak and without knowledge or skills, the first part of our lives is a process of growth, learning, and general maturation. Because we will not live much longer than 75 years, and because in the last years we will decline mentally and physically, the projects and activities that will fill our lives cannot be planned for much longer than that. The forms of life within human society are adjusted to these dimensions: in our society, families care for children while they are small and are acquiring a basic understanding of the world; schools continue the educational process; careers last about 40 years; and people retire when they are 65 or 70.

4 The stages of a life are not isolated or self-contained parts. They bear relations to one another that must be understood if any part of the life is to be understood. We cannot understand what a medical student is doing, for example, if we do not appreciate the way in which his or her present activity is preparation for the stages of life that will come later. Moreover, the *evaluation* of one stage of a life may require reference to what came before: to be a doorkeeper, with a small but steady income sufficient to pay the rent on a one-room apartment, might be a laudable achievement for one who previously was a homeless drunk; but for one who was a vice-president of the United States, caught taking bribes, the same existence might be a sign of failure and disgrace. (This is of course a fictitious example, since this is not what happens to vice-presidents caught taking bribes.) Thus the fact that people have memories, and are able to contemplate their futures, in a fairly sophisticated way, is important to explaining why they are able to have lives. Those philosophers who have sought to explain the continuing identity of *persons* by reference to memory may have been barking up the wrong tree since it is more plausible to think that the connections of memory are necessary for the unity of a *life*.

5 The concept of a life is useful, too, in explaining the kinds of goods and evils to which people are susceptible. Consider the plight of a young concert pianist who loses the use of his hands: why is this a bad thing for him? It is not a sufficient explanation to say that it is bad because it will cause him pain, frustration, worry, and the like. The tragedy consists in the fact that important possibil-

ities for his life have been foreclosed; he could have had a career as a pianist, and now he cannot. If he is frustrated or depressed, he has something to be depressed about. It is not as though the mental anguish associated with his misfortune were only an accidental byproduct; on the contrary, it is a perfectly rational response to a situation that is, independently of his response, bad. We will not have eliminated the evil by eliminating the response to it: we cannot make things all right by getting him to cheer up. It is the loss of the possibility for him, and not simply its effects on his consciousness, that is the evil.

The evil of death is like this. Epicurus*, who believed that all good and evil consists in pleasant or unpleasant sensation, thought that death is not an evil because when dead a person experiences no sensations. He failed to appreciate that a person can be the subject of good or evil, not only because he has the capacity for enjoyment or suffering, but also because he may have hopes or aspirations that go unfulfilled, and because he is the subject of a life with possibilities that may go unrealized. . . . When Frank Ramsey† died, it was a tragedy, for Ramsey was a young man whose life was only beginning; when Bertrand Russell‡ died, after a full life, things seemed different. Epicurus could not account for the difference. (If death, at even an advanced age, is thought to be evil, it must be because we are able to view a life as in principle open-ended, always having possibilities that still might be realized, if only it could go on.)

Death is an evil when it puts an end to a life. Some humans, tragically, do not have lives and never will. An infant with Tay-Sachs disease will never develop beyond about six months of age, there may be some regression at that point, and it will die. Suppose such an infant contracts pneumonia: the decision might be made not to treat the pneumonia, and allow the baby to die. The decision seems justified because, in the absence of any possibility of a life in the biographical sense, life in the biological sense has little value. The same sort of consideration explains why it seems so pointless to maintain persons in irreversible coma. The families of such patients are quick to realize that merely being alive is unimportant. The mother of a man who died after six years in a coma told a newspaper reporter, "My son died at age 34 after having lived for 28 years." . . . It was a melodramatic remark, and on the surface a paradoxical one—how can one die at 34 and have lived only 28 years?—yet what she meant is clear enough. The man's *life* was over when he entered the coma, even though he *was alive* for six years longer. The temporal boundaries of one's being alive need not be the same as the temporal boundaries of one's life.

Therefore, I believe that it is unwise to insist that any animal, human or nonhuman, has a right to life simply because it is a living being. The doctrine of the sanctity of life, interpreted as applying merely to biological life, has little to recommend it. My thesis about the right to life is that an individual has a right to life if that being has a life in the biographical sense. By this criterion, at least some nonhuman animals would have such a right. Monkeys, to take the most

---

* Editor's note: Epicurus (ca. 342–270 B.C.), Greek philosopher and originator of epicureanism.
† Editor's note: Frank Ramsey (1903–30), brilliant British mathematician.
‡ Editor's note: Bertrand Russell (1872–1970), British philosopher, mathematician, and social critic.

obvious example, have lives that are quite complex. They are remarkably intelligent, they have families and live together in social groups, and they apparently have forward-looking and backward-looking attitudes. Their lives do not appear to be as emotionally or intellectually complex as the lives of humans; but the more we learn about them, the more impressed we are with the similarities between them and us. . . .

Of course we do not know a great deal about the lives of the members of most other species. To make intelligent judgments about them we need the sort of information that could be gained by observing animals in their natural homes, rather than in the laboratory—although laboratory-acquired information can be helpful. When baboons, dogs, and wolves have been studied in "the wild," it has been found that the lives of individual animals, carried out within pack societies, are surprisingly diverse. But we are only beginning to appreciate the richness of the animal kingdom. Take the octopus, for example. It is a mollusk—like a clam—but it has the most complex central nervous system of all invertebrates, apparently developed originally to control the many gripping-pads along its tentacles. It has a home, stakes out a territory, and fights other octopuses that invade its territory, but not to the death. Observers believe that it shows emotions like fear and anger by changing its skin color (the ability to change color also allows it to blend with its surroundings when natural enemies are nearby). When fighting its prey, it shows no emotion, but when fighting other octopuses it does show emotion. Its intelligence has been tested in such ways as giving it food in a jar to see whether it can figure out how to screw the top off. The animal does figure this out, within a couple of minutes. Now we do not know very much about octopuses, and I am not mentioning all this in order to argue that they have lives and therefore a right to life. I only want to point out the way in which new information can make a difference to our view of animals' lives. Speaking for myself at least, even this meager information makes the octopus seem very different from before. 9

In our present state of semi-ignorance about other species, the situation seems to be this. When we consider the mammals with which we are most familiar, it is reasonable to believe that they do have lives in the biographical sense. They have emotions and cares and social systems and the rest, although perhaps not in just the way that humans do. Then the further down the phylogenetic scale we go, the less confidence we have that there is anything resembling a life. When we come to bugs, or shrimp, the animals pretty clearly lack the mental capacities necessary for a life, although they certainly are alive. (But being alive is not so important, even for us humans, except in that it is necessary for the continuation of our lives.) Most of us already recognize the importance of this— we think that killing a human is worse than killing a monkey, but we also think that killing a monkey is a more morally serious matter than swatting a fly. And when we come to plants, which are alive, but where the notion of a biographical life has no application whatever, the moral qualms about killing have vanished altogether. If the thesis that I have suggested is correct, these feelings have a rational basis: in so far as we have reason to view other creatures as having lives, as we do, we have reason to view them as having a right to life, if we do. 10

One final question: If humans have a right to life, and some other animals do also, does this mean that all their lives are equally valuable and have equal 11 moral protection? No. In a situation of forced choice, in which two lives are at stake and only one may be saved, it is reasonable to give preference to the life of the more mentally complex being. That is why human life may rightly be regarded as in general more valuable than nonhuman life (although *some* humans are mentally less complex than some nonhumans, and so should not be given preference).

Philosophers sometimes doubt whether mental complexity has this kind of importance. . . . Some explanation should therefore be provided of why complexity matters. Complexity matters because, when a mentally sophisticated being dies, there are more reasons why the death is a bad thing. A young writer who dies in a car-accident will not get to finish her novel; she will not see her children grow up; her talents will remain forever undeveloped, her aspirations unfulfilled. In the case of a simpler being, not nearly so much of this kind can be said, and so its death, while a bad thing, is not comparably tragic.

Questions for Comprehension

1. What is the difference between "having a life" and "being alive"?
2. Why does Rachels believe that "the doctrine of the sanctity of life, interpreted as applying merely to biological life, has little to recommend it"?
3. On what basis does Rachels conclude that monkeys have a right to life?
4. Why are the facts of octopus life relevant to Rachels' thesis?
5. What is the rational basis for believing that "killing a monkey is a more morally serious matter than swatting a fly"? How does this comment derive from Rachels' distinction between "having a life" and "being alive"?
6. Why is the death of a mentally complex being more tragic than the death of a simpler being?

■

ANIMALS DO NOT HAVE MORAL RIGHTS

Michael Fox

Michael Fox (b. 1940) is a member of the philosophy department at Queens College in Canada. A frequent speaker and consultant on the subject of animal experimentation, his publications include *The Case for Animal Experimentation: An Evolutionary and Ethical Perspective* (1986) and *Conceptual Foundations of Environmental Ethics* (1988). The following essay, first published in 1978, is part of a critique of the writings of Peter Singer and Tom Regan. In it, Fox develops his own conception that autonomy is necessary for the possession of moral rights.

What other characteristics, then, that humans share in general should be cited in order to give an adequate account of the reasons why they have, and animals lack, moral rights? A complete list of these would have to include at least the following: the capacities to be critically self-aware, manipulate concepts, use a sophisticated language, reflect, plan, deliberate, choose, and accept responsibility for acting. In a similar vein, McCloskey suggests that the crucial morally relevant characteristics of humans which we are seeking here are those which manifest the attributes of truly autonomous beings, where this entails being capable of acting freely, choosing and deciding rationally in the fullest sense, creating and self-making (self-realizing). I have drawn attention to certain cognitive capacities (critical self-awareness, concept manipulation, and the use of a sophisticated language) because these are the essential tools or vehicles by means of which an agent's autonomy is evolved, made known to himself reflexively, and manifested or expressed. The possession of these cognitive capacities, therefore, is a necessary prerequisite for autonomy, which is the capacity for self-conscious, voluntary and deliberate action, in the fullest sense of these words. Autonomy, which thus entails certain cognitive capacities, is necessary (and, together with the capacity to enjoy and suffer, sufficient) for the possession of moral rights. It follows that all (and only) those beings which are members of a species of which it is true in general (i.e., typically the case at maturity, assuming normal development) that members of the species in question can be considered autonomous agents are beings endowed with moral rights.

2   Now how can the above entailments be defended? I cannot give full treatment to this important topic here, but I should like to suggest that only autonomous beings, as just described, can and do belong to a moral community, which is the sort of social group within which (and only within which) such concepts as those of rights and duties have any meaning and application. For it is only in a community of interacting autonomous beings of this sort that there can be the kind of mutual recognition required for these concepts to evolve and be understood. Obligations and rights, as well as the moral discourse generated by these and ancillary notions, are functions of mutual recognition and accountability and are, consequently, inapplicable outside the context specified. It should be made clear that the foregoing is not an attempt merely to legislate concerning the kinds of beings which qualify as possessors of moral rights. Rather, my analysis is meant to suggest that, since the only species we know of that has developed the concepts of rights and obligations (and the institutions associated with them) is *Homo sapiens*, there must be something about this peculiar sort of social being that accounts for the phenomenon in question. And my argument is that the relevant features of humans (other than their capacity to suffer and enjoy) that explain why they have rights are their possession of a certain kind of consciousness, particular cognitive and linguistic abilities, and the capacity to comprehend, undertake, and carry out obligations and to expect the same of like beings.

3   The considerations taken up briefly here should suffice to show that regarding the cognitive capacities of human beings as relevant to the question of possessing moral rights is not tantamount to invoking some simplistic notion of humans' rationality to settle a vastly more complex set of issues as proponents of animal rights frequently suppose. Singer and Regan just conveniently leave the capacities I have mentioned out of the picture or else systematically misunderstand and underrate their significance.

4   I conclude, then, that it is difficult to see how an argument for ascribing specifically moral rights to animals can get started. And if it cannot get off the ground, then there also appears to be no case for saying either that animals ought

not to be treated as means to human ends, provided that they are treated in as humane a manner as possible in the process, or that they have a right to live. But it seems to me that the overall obligation to prevent or minimize animal suffering should suffice as a moral basis for prohibiting the atrocious conditions of crowding and confinement that prevail on modern factory farms, for drastically curtailing the use of animals in excruciating but pointless experiments in product testing, and for ending other inhumane practices (in slaughtering, trapping, the keeping of pets, hunting, racing, and so on). Undoubtedly animals should not be maltreated. They should not be made to suffer needlessly or excessively. Singer and Regan are surely correct to single out animals' capacity to suffer as the reason why we should treat them humanely. But it is no more clear how this extends moral rights to them than how our dawning ecological sense that we ought not to waste natural resources and systematically ravage the environment would establish moral rights for trees, lakes, or mineral deposits. What should be said is that we have an obligation to avoid mistreating animals, but that this is an obligation without a corresponding right on the part of the beings affected by our behavior.

Is speciesism immoral, then? The only sensible verdict, I think, is "not proven." The effort to establish speciesism, on the one hand, and racism and sexism, on the other, as identical forms of unjust discrimination which flout basic moral rights cannot succeed because neither Singer nor Regan has shown any meaningful sense in which rights can and should be ascribed to animals to begin with.

It would seem, therefore, that while the issue of the infliction of unnecessary and excessive pain and suffering upon animals, which is not offset by a significant long-term gain in pleasure for humans or for animals, is a matter that ought to concern every thoughtful and caring person, the question of animals' rights in which it has unfortunately become embroiled—and hence, that of "animal liberation"—is a nonstarter. But Regan and Singer have an important moral to teach. As Regan rightly notes, "The onus of justification is always on anyone who supports a practice that is known to inflict nontrivial, undeserved pain on a sentient creature to show that, in doing so, he is not doing anything wrong" (202). The point implicit here, it seems to me, is not that everyone who finds great animal suffering odious to contemplate should rush to dump the contents of his frozen meat locker and medicine cabinet or makeup kit in the garbage pail and don the nearest available (synthetic) hair shirt. Rather, it is that each concerned person should consider carefully the amount of meat a sensible diet, the world food crisis, and the cost of living really should allow him or her, and what sorts of drugs and cosmetics are really essential, and begin lobbying for the elimination of factory farms and for more stringent regulation of the use of animals in experiments and product testing.

Works Cited

McCloskey, H. J. "The Right to Life." *Mind* 84 (1975): 410–13.

Regan, Tom. "The Moral Basis of Vegetarianism." *Canadian Journal of Philosophy* 5.2 (1975): 181–214.

Singer, Peter. *Animal Liberation*. New York: New York Review, 1975.

Questions for Comprehension

1. According to Fox, autonomy is necessary if a creature is to have moral rights. How does he define autonomy?
2. What does Fox mean when he states that the concepts of rights and duties have meaning only within a "moral community"? Why must members of a moral community be autonomous?
3. Why can't animals be part of a moral community?
4. Does Fox believe that humans have any obligations toward animals?
5. What, according to Fox, is the important moral that Peter Singer and Tom Regan have to teach?

■

THE CLOUDED MIRROR: ANIMAL STEREOTYPES AND HUMAN CRUELTY

Thomas L. Benson

Thomas L. Benson is vice president and dean of Saint Andrews College in Laurinburg, North Carolina. Trained as a philosopher, he has published a number of articles dealing with topics in moral philosophy, religion, and educational theory. In this essay he examines the nature and consequences of our stereotyped views of animals.

Misdeeds and moral illusions keep close company. Acts of cruelty may pass for something better where the victims can be seen as either undeserving or of no moral account. In turn, low estimations of another's moral worth do little to discourage hostile conduct. The long history of injustice to women and the sordid traditions of racial and ethnic discrimination amply illustrate this pattern. In each case a system of degrading stereotypes has served both to legitimate and to stimulate immoral conduct. Somewhat less recognized, but no less potent are the stereotypes that shape and are shaped by the traditions of human cruelty to animals.

Walter Lippmann referred to stereotypes as pictures we "carry about in our heads,"—*a priori* representations all too often at odds with complex reality (59). Their function, according to Gordon Allport, is to justify categorical acceptance or rejection of select groups and to screen out unwelcome details that threaten simplicity in perception and thinking (187). Not surprisingly, stereotypes have their greatest currency with respect to groups that are at best vaguely understood and, more often than not, thoroughly mistrusted. The stereotype defines the status of such groups as being either second class or beyond the pale of moral accounting altogether. As such, these groups may be denied the full protection of the society's legal and moral sanctions. In the case of animals, a cluster of tenacious stereotypes has served to maintain widespread indifference to their suffering at the hands of humans. Having been hunted, roped, and penned-in by our stereotypes, animals face such treatment all over again in nonmetaphorical terms.

The stereotype enjoys a shadowy existence, influencing perceptions and shaping ideas from behind the scenes. The controlling picture is, typically, quite unflattering. Its grip on the imagination is registered in a wide range of hostile behaviors, from acts of physical cruelty to psychological abuse and derisive speech. Among the group of dominant animal stereotypes, however, there are some interesting exceptions to this pattern. As we shall see, not all of the stereotypes associated with animals are obviously pejorative. Indeed, some of them involve apparently innocuous or even idealized versions of animal nature. Unflattering or not, however, each of the stereotypes responds more to human needs than to the realities of animal nature. Such stereotypes are, quite simply, lies told at the expense of animals; and here, as elsewhere, deception acquires its own momentum. One lie tends to beget another. The seemingly benign distortion is all too easily replaced by an unmistakably vicious one. There is, thus, an essential instability among the animal stereotypes. Cut adrift from the demands of discovering and responding to animals as they present themselves to us, we are free to invent their natures, floating at the impulse of need and fantasy from one false image to another.

The full range and variety of animal stereotypes defies neat and rapid review. We can do no more than note some of the more popular and influential ones. In examining each of these stereotypes, it should be kept in mind that none of them dominates the field nor functions in isolation. The attitude that many people have toward animals appears to be a composite of several of the stereotypes, with some animals being viewed according to one, and others according to another. Moreover, the stereotypes associated with a particular species may vary with changing circumstances. The five stereotypes I shall discuss in the following pages are *alien, child, moral paragon, demon,* and *machine.* Although the first of these is, perhaps, the most formidable and far-reaching stereotype and the last the most recently developed, no significance should be assigned to the order of presentation.

The Animal as Alien

There is between the human and the nonhuman animal what John Berger has called an "abyss of noncomprehension" (3). Beyond the distractions of scent, sound, form, and movement, there is a lack of focus in the eyes, an inability to slice through the fog of species separation. It is not simply that the animals cannot talk with us; rather, it is the deeper, more sobering realization that, as Wittgenstein noted, "If a lion could talk, we could not understand him" (223). The encounter of the human and the nonhuman animal is always a meeting of radically different forms of life. It is not surprising, then, that humans have been tempted to regard animals as aliens. An animal is, after all, like many aliens, on leave from a strange region and possessed of unfamiliar habits. And, as with human aliens, there are always ugly flashes of the sentiment: "He doesn't really belong here." The alien comes to us an intruder or a guest—in either case as one without widely acknowledged rights to freedom or the resources of the land. Moreover, like the human alien, the animal inspires both fascination and suspicion. Contrary to expectations, the fascination appears to derive from the margin of dissimilarity between the animal and the human, while the suspicion owes to the perception of crucial similarities. We are attracted by the novelties of appearance and behavior, and, at the same time, unnerved by the possibility that these features mask evils we have discovered in ourselves.

As aliens, animals are dimly thought capable of the same greed and treachery humans too often visit on one another. Our repertory of metaphorical epithets reflects this distrust of animals. A human may be censured as a "snake," "vulture," "rat," "pig," "turkey," "shark," "leech," and much more. It is suspicion, then, that dominates the response to the animal as alien. This suspicion, in turn, stimulates the desire to control the animal's behavior. Such control tends to fall into one or the other of three broad categories: assimilation, confinement, or banishment. In the case of diverse immigrant groups and the Native American "alien," it is not difficult to trace these categories—and the pattern is no more mysterious with respect to animals. The direct or indirect extermination of hundreds of species of wild animals, the domestication of others, and the confinement of a wide variety of animals in game preserves, zoos, and, more benignly, in animal sanctuaries, all conform to the categories of control.

In zoos and safari parks, there remains, of course, a fascination with the peculiar appearance and behavior of the animal, but this interest is indulged only within a framework of strict controls. It is these controls and the larger process of subjugation that leads to disappointment at such places of amusement, for what we encounter at the zoo or the safari park are, at best, imitation animals, possessing the genes and broad forms of their kinds, but behaviorally transformed. John Berger refers to zoos as monuments to an historic loss. Through the centuries of accelerating control of animals, humans have succeeded in marginalizing animal life—to the point of nearly total dependence upon favorable human behavior. Berger writes: "Looking at each animal, the unaccompanied zoo visitor is alone. As for the crowds, they belong to a species which has at last been isolated" (26).

The Animal as Child

The tendency to view the animal as a child—cute, cuddly, and dependent—is, like the institution of human childhood, a relatively modern development (see Aries). Although we can find some isolated anticipations of this attitude in earlier periods, e.g., the paternalistic attitude shared by St. Godric of Finchale and St. Francis of Assisi, the roots of the child/animal stereotype are to be found in the romantic ideals of the late eighteenth and early nineteenth centuries. At a time of unprecedented growth in the cities and in the experimental sciences and technology, animal life was being exploited and sacrificed at an alarming rate. In reaction to these depredations, the humane movement arose and began to exercise a growing influence on public policy and private habits, advocating a wide range of reforms, from anti-cruelty statutes to vegetarian diets. Much of the thought and literature associated with the early humane movement is intensely anthropomorphic and sentimental. Appeals for reform were based, more often than not, on the plight of the defenseless and innocent animal, engulfed in a gathering tide of human abuses (see Turner). In the ensuing years and struggles, many wings of the humane movement have retained this paternalistic, somewhat sentimentalized outlook. The remarks of Hans Ruesch, in his recently published attack on vivisection, reflect the persistence of this attitude: "The desire to protect animals derives from better acquaintance with them, from the realization that they are sensitive and intelligent creatures, affectionate and seeking affection, powerless in a cruel and incomprehensible world, exposed to all the whims of the master species" (45).

In our time, the notion of the animal as a dependent child has acquired considerable popularity, with the media of film, television, and photography providing animal images of great sentimental appeal. A culture of cuteness now surrounds many animal species. Every nursery is equipped with a menagerie of stuffed animals; and children's literature, films, and television programs are nearly monopolized by winsome child/animals. This partnership of children and anthropomorphized animals may well be desirable from a psychological point of view. The vulnerable, dependent, and frequently incompetent child/animal may approximate the child's own experience of himself and may invite the exploration of attitudes of trust and responsibility toward others. The unthreatening companionship of a puppy or of a soft teddy bear may be just what Dr. Spock ordered. Nevertheless, some cautionary notes are in order. It should be observed, for example, that the child/animal stereotype is selectively imposed. Not all animals are cute and cuddly. And many of those who are cute soon become less so, thereby losing their appeal. The cute duckling/ugly duck pattern is tragically familiar to animal welfare workers who must cope each spring with the suddenly matured and no longer wanted Easter presents. The same story can be told even more dramatically with respect to puppies and kittens. Whatever its psychological value, the commercially driven emphasis on the cute and cuddly animal predisposes the human child to relate to animals on an unrealistic and anthropocentric basis. The value of the animal consists in its docility, playfulness, and charm as a human companion. Animals that fail to meet such standards may be written off as of no account.

The sentimental paternalism associated with the child/animal stereotype may be, in some respects, unwholesome for the favored species as well. In his book on social values and human childhood, *Escape from Childhood*, John Holt argues that cuteness is the handmaiden of subjugation. Children are usually held to be most cute when they are exhibiting ignorance and incompetence. The intelligent and thoroughly competent child seldom strikes us as cute (85). Moreover, Holt argues that there is a direct connection between sentimental perceptions of children as cute and cruelty towards them:

> The trouble with sentimentality, and the reason it always leads to callousness and cruelty, is that it is abstract and unreal. We look at the lives and concerns and troubles of children as we might look at actors on a stage, a comedy as long as it does not become a nuisance. And so, since their feelings and their

pain are neither serious nor real, any pain we may cause them is not real either. In any conflict of interest with us, they must give way; only our needs are real. (81)

The ease with which some people are able to move from Mickey Mouse cartoons to the setting of spring action mouse traps, from a chorus of "Old MacDonald Had a Farm" to a round of hamburgers at the local fast food outlet, suggests the applicability of Holt's argument to the child/animal stereotype. At bottom, as Holt observes, it is the abstractness, the unreality of the cute child image that creates the difficulties. So also with the child/animal stereotype. The sentimentalized representations of animals provide a distorted picture of their natures and needs. Children reared in an environment that portrays animals exclusively as cute, docile, and innocent are ill-prepared to appreciate the complex behavior and very real suffering of mature and, from a human standpoint, not always attractive animals.

In registering these points of caution about the child/animal stereotype, there need be no concern about the imminent exile of Winnie the Pooh or Kermit the Frog from the crib or nursery cupboard. It would be foolish to deny or attempt to suppress the charm and appeal that many animals and animal-like toys hold for us. Similarly, abandonment of the sentimentalizing excesses associated with the child/animal stereotype need not and should not cause us to discount our custodial responsibilities toward domestic animals and endangered and threatened species. Indeed, in outgrowing our tendency to regard animals as docile and dependent children, we may discover fresh possibilities for more responsible and satisfying companionship with them.

The Animal as Moral Paragon

If the child is frequently confronted with images of the animal as helpless and cuddly, he also becomes well-acquainted with images of the animal as protective older brother or surrogate parent. Lassie, Rin Tin Tin, Rikki Tikki Tavi, Flipper, Flicka, Lobo, the parade of gallant and plucky animal heroes goes on and on, trailing back into the childhood library and the neighborhood moviehouse. In each case, the animal hero, while retaining much of the charm and appeal of the child/animal, models some virtue or cluster of moral ideals. In the preface to *Lives of the Hunted*, Ernest Thompson Seton, a storyteller with few rivals in the representation of animals as moral heroes, claims that his aim has always been "to emphasize our kinship with animals by showing that in them we can find the virtues most admired in Man" (9). Seton provides an inventory of the virtues associated with his animal heroes: "Lobo stands for Dignity and Love-constancy; Silverspot, for Sagacity; Redruff, for Obedience; Bingo, for Fidelity; Vixen and Molly Cottontail, for Mother-Love; Wahb, for Physical Force; and the Pacing Mustang, for the Love of Liberty" (9).

There is, of course, nothing new in the latter-day representations of animals as moral exemplars. Kenneth Clark suggests that the ancient cave-paintings at sites such as Lascaux in Southwest France were motivated primarily by admiration for animals and by a humility before their strength and speed (72). Indeed, reverence for certain animals as supremely gifted and/or virtuous appears to underlie both totemistic worship practices and the ample use of animal symbols in many primitive religious traditions. In the Psalms of David and the preaching of Jesus, as well as in the Buddhist Sutras and the teachings of Lao Tzu and Chuang Tzu, animals appear as models of diverse moral and spiritual virtues. It is also an idealized view of animal nature that inspired the early animal fables and the development of the *Physiologus*, the most significant of the early bestiaries.

In all of these traditions, old and new, there is boundless anthropomorphism. The virtues manifested by the animals are distinctly human ideals. What the animals do effortlessly and consistently, humans achieve only sporadically and with much effort. On this account, the exemplary animals are seen as innocent and, in some accounts, beatific. Catherine Roberts advances such a view in her recently published book, *Science, Animals, and Evolution*. Animals are uniquely virtuous, Roberts claims, and incapable of immoral conduct. "Nature thinks no evil and does no evil. How blessed is man to live in an environment of purity" (182). The difficulties posed by crediting animals with both virtue and the inability to do wrong appear to trouble Roberts no more than all the others before her who extol animals as moral paragons.

The moral paragon stereotype presupposes that animals are moral agents, capable of understanding, however dimly, the principles of right conduct and equally capable of pursuing such principles. To this extent, it is misleadingly anthropomorphic and inaccurate. Although animals may possess moral rights, there is no good reason to include them in the class of moral agents. There is, nevertheless, something to be said for one of the other, perhaps more fundamental, presuppositions of the moral paragon stereotype—the notion that we can draw moral lessons from animal behavior. The restraint shown by most animals in intraspecies conflict and the economies practiced by animals in manipulating the means of survival have clear instructional value for us, given our long history of internecine conflict and our reckless wasting of precious natural resources. Our greed and destructiveness cannot be written off to biology. It is within our power to adapt more harmoniously to each other and to the environment.

In evaluating the moral paragon stereotype, it should also be noted that there is a dark side to the picture. A pattern of species favoritism is built into the stereotype. Not all animals are regarded as virtuous. The animal kingdom includes both the virtuous and the derelict. From Aesop to Disney, the sheep and the wolf, the ant and the grasshopper divisions persist. With only rare exceptions, the virtuous animals are docile and attractive, while the ranks of the morally errant are filled by animals perceived as ugly or menacing. As long as lines are drawn in this arbitrary and anthropomorphic manner, it will remain difficult to win broad support for efforts to improve the lot of the laboratory mouse, the pork farm pig, or the endangered red wolf—among scores of maligned species—none of whom is conventionally thought of as morally exemplary.

The moral paragon stereotype poses still another problem. In the sometimes romantic representations of animals as heroes (and villains), there is a tendency to deprive them of their natural identities. The objections that feminists and Native American activists have leveled at efforts to place them on pedestals, as guileless and innately wise, are relevant here. The latter groups have recognized the potential for mischief in such romantic portraits. To be set apart as morally exemplary by means of patently distorted characterizations is to run the risk of being set apart and, indeed, left out—on the basis of other distorted characterizations—when it is a matter of distributing rights and opportunities. As noted earlier, one lie begets another; one false characterization, even if inoffensive on its face, invites another. The distorted picture of animals conveyed by the moral paragon stereotype may well hold comparable risks for animals. Animals have suffered enormously at the hands of humans who have insisted on viewing animals according to one nature-distorting stereotype or another. The sooner animals are recognized as animals, nothing less and nothing more, the better their fortunes will be.

The Animal as Demon

Beyond the traditions that regard some animals as morally derelict, there is a still grimmer view, one that represents some animals as demonic beings, utterly outside the pale of decency. Rats, snakes, sharks, spiders, vultures, bats, and crocodiles, among other species, are sometimes viewed in this manner. They are seen as treacherous predators who compound their crimes of greed and destruction by resorting to methods of stealth and cruel surprise. The representation of such animals as demonic serves to legitimate programs of annihilation. There is, after all, only one proper disposition for demons, devils, and witches. Such was the logic used in the persecution of dissident and eccentric women in seventeenth century New England. Still another application of this logic, and of the underlying demon stereotype, is discussed by J. Glenn Gray in his classic study of men in battle, *The Warriors*. Gray writes: 18

> There is another image of the enemy . . . even more abstract and deadly in its psychological effects. In this the enemy is conceived to be not merely a loathsome animal, below the human level, but also above it in being a devil or at least demon-possessed and, as such, an enemy of God. (163)

Gray adds that this image of the enemy leads to one policy—annihilation: "Killing them becomes a kind of sacrament; after enough of it, the killers come to feel like high priests" (154).

Although the demon/animal stereotype is often associated with widespread fears concerning such animals as snakes and rats, it may derive from deeper currents of distrust in all animals. In the mythic traditions of many cultures, the animal is a symbol of chaos and the irrational. A number of primitive cosmogonies, such as the Babylonian Epic of Creation, the *Enuma elish*, represent the world as having been fashioned out of the remains of a slain chaos-monster. The ritual sacrifices of animals in some ancient societies can be understood as commemorating the primordial conquest of the chaos-monster (Eliade, 54–58). In contemporary life, there are grim resonances of such sacrifice in the spectacles of the bullfight and the rodeo, as well as in large game hunting and deep sea fishing. 19

Secular philosophical traditions in both the East and the West have also contributed to the notion of the animal as an irrational being. In the West, Aristotelian thought excluded animals from the class of rational beings, while in the East, the Confucian ethic regarded "birds and beasts" as proceeding in the opposite direction from the ideal man, the *chün tzu*. Additional sources of suspicion concerning animal nature may be found in the Gnostic and Manichaean traditions, with their radical rejection of things earthly and carnal. Here the animals, devoid of *nous*, are seen as minions of darkness and evil. These and other intellectual currents have created a legacy of profound distrust toward animals and have inclined some to view them as inherently defective and evil.

The terms "animal" and "beast" are widely used to refer to people who are utterly lacking in decency and respect for others. Not infrequently, we will hear an advocate of the death penalty speak of criminals as "animals who should be taken out and shot." Lost in the racing flood of metaphor is the fact that, for the most part, the *beasts* are simply not *beastly*. The human animal, on the other hand, too often is—especially in his conduct toward animals. Rats, sharks, snakes, bats, and spiders—however much they may frighten or appear to menace us—are not models of lechery, greed, treachery, and the like. We must look to the annals of human behavior for proper examples of such conduct. Mary Midgley has exposed the distortions and covert anthropomorphism underlying what I have called the demon stereotype. She points out that ". . . man has always been unwilling to admit his own ferocity, and has tried to deflect attention from it by making animals out more ferocious than they are" (99).

Humans have an abiding fascination with the terrible and the macabre. It is no accident that monster movies and horror stories featuring giant spiders, armies of rats, and beachcombing sharks are perennial favorites. At the roots of this taste for terror may lie apprehensions, not about dread monsters and demonic animals, but about our own, distinctly human capacities to inflict and to experience evil. Perhaps, it is the beast within ourselves who parades and prowls through these suspenseful stories. And that inner beast is *not* our "animal nature," that which we share with the other species, but rather the uniquely human potential for irrationality and moral corruption. In still broader terms, it may be argued that the appeal of the demon/animal stereotype owes substantially to our unwillingness to face our own demonic tendencies. And thus, the animals are mustered once again; this time, as Richard Lewinsohn observes, ". . . to pay by being made to mirror man's depravity" (191).

The Animal as Machine

Although Rene Descartes' notion of the animal automaton stimulated a great deal of heated discussion, its influence on the rise of what Konrad Lorenz has called the "mechanomorphic" view of animals is negligible. It was the imperatives of industrialization and urbanization, rather than metaphysics, that gave currency to the image of the animal as a machine. The new era brought a fresh emphasis on the rationalization of productive processes—a striving for greater control over the elements in such processes and increasing efficiency in manipulating them. As elements in a large number of productive processes, animals came to be seen more and more in mechanistic terms.

Throughout much of human history, animals have been used for food, clothing, labor, transportation, companionship, religious ritual, and entertainment. In most of these associations—however cruel and onerous—some trace of recognition of the animals' "creatureliness" remained. Such rudimentary respect for animal life derived, in part, from a sober realization of the vulnerability and value of animals and, in part, from a spiritual sense, here faint and there distinct, of the intrinsic worth of animals. The new atmosphere in the age of the machine was much less hospitable to such considerations. Nicholas Berdyaev accounts for this important shift in attitudes:

> The supremacy of technique and the machine is primarily a transition from organic to organized life, from growth to construction. From the viewpoint of organic life, technique spells disincarnation. . . . Technique destroys ancient bodies and the new ones it creates do not resemble organic bodies; they are organized bodies. (39)

The animal/machine stereotype is associated almost exclusively with farm and laboratory animals. The breeding, maintenance, and feeding of these groups is usually controlled according to strict standards. Most farm and laboratory animals are bred to fulfill quite specific roles in diverse productive processes. In the case of the farm animals, it is usually the production of foodstuffs and a wide range of organic byproducts. The laboratory animal, on the other hand, is involved in a quite different manufacturing process: the production of experimental data. Just as machines are designed, tested, and maintained according to precisely defined production standards, so also the fortunes of farm and laboratory animals depend increasingly on their levels of performance, judged in terms of strict reliability and cost-effectiveness standards. Irregularities in performance, stress reactions, diseases, and other difficulties are understood and treated as engineering problems.

In *Animal Factories*, a survey of recent developments in agricultural technology, Jim Mason and Peter Singer reveal some of the neglected "moral costs" associated with the treatment of animals as machines. Noting the expanding application of such Brave New Farm concepts as the mechanized total-confinement system, synthetic environmental control, reproductive engineering, and chemical manipulation of animal growth and behavior, Mason and Singer conclude:

> Productivity for and catering to the whims of the market may be all right in the plastics or automobile industries, but it can be cruel and abusive when the factory method is applied to animals. . . . Animal factories are one more sign of the extent to which our technological capacities have advanced faster than our ethics. (125)

The animal/machine stereotype represents the last stop on the way to the total marginalization of animal life. However unhappy and defeating the other stereotypes may be, they allow for some measure of feeling, some organic kinship, faint or not, between animal and human life. Seen in mechanistic terms, the animal becomes merely a thing, an object to be manipulated according to the designs of the human technician. The advantages in this for the laboratory researcher and the factory farm operator seem to be considerable. Freed of the sometimes inconvenient moral constraints that regulate our behavior toward sentient beings, he can concentrate on the efficiency and productivity of his enterprise.

The tendency to reduce animals to the level of cogs in a productive system is not without parallels in relations among human beings. The development of modern industry, with its assembly lines, engineered environments, and systems management approaches to personnel issues, has stimulated much social criticism and moral concern. Alarm over the mechanization of human life is also to be found in recent controversies involving such matters as behavior modification strategies in the schools, health care technology, city planning concepts, and the expanding role of the computer in everyday affairs. Although some of the concern may be unwarranted, there can be no doubt that an earnest struggle is underway between the human and his muscle-flexing machines. At stake is the domestication of the machine or the subjugation of man. In the face of such difficulties, the animal/machine stereotype is even less welcome. To disregard the animal's manifest capacity for suffering, treating it, at best, as so much noise in the machine, may facilitate a comparable attitude toward human beings. We would do well to remember Kant's cautionary words: "If (a man) is not to stifle his human feelings, he must practice kindness toward animals, for he who is cruel to animals becomes hard also in dealing with men. We can judge the heart of a man by his treatment of animals" (240).

Beyond the Stereotypes: The Animal as Animal

How animals are seen and how they are treated are interrelated matters. As long as the stereotypes we have examined persist, there is little prospect for meaningful changes in human conduct toward animal life. What, then, is the ideal attitude toward animals? How are they to be seen? Any answer will be inadequate that fails to acknowledge the mystery of animal nature. As noted earlier, there is an "abyss of noncomprehension" dividing us, and it is unlikely to yield to any amount of zoological and ethological research. We cannot know the animals, however much we may know *about* them. Much of the clatter and dither of anthropomorphic stereotyping derives from an inability to accept the essential inaccessibility of the myriad forms of animal life. Rather than contriving false identities for animals, identities that serve human interests, we must make peace with the mystery of animal life. At the same time, we must appreciate the importance of what we do know about the animals—that they are active, complex, sentient, and valuable neighbors. In short, we must come to accept animals as animals. Such an attitude will do justice both to what we know and what we cannot know.

Although we may succeed in adopting this new attitude toward animals, we will, inescapably, continue to employ many anthropomorphic categories. Some animal behavior will appear admirable, some ignoble. Some animals will strike us as lovable, others as aloof and unlikable. We will be frightened by some animals, and moved by paternalistic impulses toward others. Movement beyond the animal stereotypes requires some vigilance in our indulgence of such sentiments, but it does not mean the eradication of all vestiges of anthropomorphism. It does mean, however, the renunciation of anthropocentrism, those modes of viewing animals that serve only to justify patterns of exploitation by humans. To perceive animals nonanthropocentrically is, above all else, to regard them as possessing worth independently of any uses we may have for them.

Given the extraordinary involvement of the diverse animal stereotypes in popular attitudes and contemporary institutions, the task of transforming attitudes toward animals will not be easy. The continuing struggles of many minority and feminist groups in this area provide only moderate encouragement. Nevertheless, if we are serious about achieving substantial reforms in human conduct toward animals, we cannot avoid such work. As the effort is begun, it may be useful to attempt to rekindle that awareness of a common cause that motivated some of the early advocates of abolitionism, women's rights, and animal welfare reforms. The traditions of bigotry and injustice are joined in complex and mutually reinforcing patterns. As we have seen, the stereotypes that promote indifference to animal suffering are closely related to modes of racist and sexist thought. If genuine and lasting changes are to be made, we must recognize anew that the degradation of life anywhere threatens the dignity of life everywhere.

Works Cited

Allport, G. W. *The Nature of Prejudice*. Garden City, N.Y.: Doubleday Anchor, 1958.
Aries, P. *Centuries of Childhood*. New York: Vintage, 1962.
Berdyaev, N. "Man and Machine." In *The Bourgeois Mind and Other Essays*. New York: Books for Libraries Press, 1934.
Berger, J. *About Looking*. New York: Pantheon Books, 1979.
Clark, K. *Animals and Men*. New York: William Morrow and Co., 1977.
Eliade, M. *The Sacred and the Profane*. Trans. W. R. Trask. New York: Harper & Row, 1961.
Gray, J. G. *The Warriors*. New York: Harper & Row, 1967.
Holt, J. *Escape from Childhood*. New York: Ballantine Books, 1975.
Kant, I. "Duties to Animals and Spirits." In *Lectures on Ethics*. Trans. L. Infield. New York: Harper & Row, 1963.
Lewinsohn, R. *Animals, Men and Myths*. New York: Harper, 1954.
Lippmann, W. *Public Opinion*. New York: Free Press, 1922.
Mason, J. and P. Singer. *Animal Factories*. New York: Crown Publishers, 1980.
Midgley, M. "The Concept of Beastliness." In *Animal Rights and Human Obligations*. Ed. Tom Regan and Peter Singer. Englewood Cliffs, N.J.: Prentice-Hall, 1976.
Roberts, C. *Science, Animals, and Evolution*. Westport, Conn.: Greenwood Press, 1980.
Ruesch, H. *Slaughter of the Innocent*. New York: Bantam Books, 1978.
Seton, E. T. *Lives of the Hunted*. New York: New American Library, 1901.
Turner, E. S. *All Heaven in a Rage*. London: Michael Joseph, Ltd., 1964.
Wittgenstein, L. *Philosophical Investigations*. 2nd ed. Trans. G. E. M. Anscombe. New York: Macmillan, 1958.

Questions for Comprehension

1. Why, according to Benson, are stereotypes so dangerous?
2. What are the sources of the fascination and suspicion inspired by the stereotype of the animal as alien?

3. How does Benson account for the origin of the stereotype of the animal as child?
4. What does Benson mean when he says, agreeing with John Holt, that "cuteness is the handmaiden of subjugation"?
5. What are the two consequences that Benson refers to as the "dark side" of the stereotype of the animal as moral paragon?
6. What does Benson mean when he says that "in still broader terms, it may be argued that the appeal of the demon/animal stereotype owes substantially to our unwillingness to face our own demonic tendencies"?
7. How does the breeding, maintenance, and feeding of farm and laboratory animals contribute to the stereotype of the animal as machine?
8. How is it possible for human beings to "accept animals as animals"?

■

THE USE OF ANIMALS IN EDUCATIONAL SETTINGS
Tom Regan

Tom Regan (b. 1938) is a member of the philosophy department at North Carolina State University. He has written a number of philosophical studies, including *The Case for Animal Rights* and *The Expanding Circle*.

Animals of many kinds and descriptions are used in a variety of ways in educational settings, including science fairs, standard laboratory sections for high school and university courses in biology, zoology and related disciplines, in student-conducted research projects, in practice surgery in both medical and veterinary schools—the list goes on. Nothing approaching a complete examination of the many uses is possible. By concentrating on one use (namely, the dissection of live animals in high school and university lab sections), what the rights view's position would be regarding these remaining uses should be clear enough not to require separate treatment, especially in light of this view's position about the use of animals in toxicology and research.

As farm and wild animals are not to be viewed as mere receptacles or renewable resources whose rights can be overridden on the basis of aggregating human benefits, so mammalian laboratory animals are not to be viewed in these ways. The acquisition of knowledge is a good thing, but the value of knowledge does not by itself justify harming others, the less so when this knowledge is obtainable by other means. In the case of knowledge of the anatomy and physiology of mammalian animals studied in lab sections in high school and university biology, zoology and related courses, this knowledge is obtainable without relying on hands-on experience. Students do not need to dissect any known animals to learn facts about their anatomy and physiology. Detailed drawings of animal anatomy and physiology exist in abundance and are usually included in the very texts used in such courses. On the rights view, to continue to include standard lab sections involving dissection of live mammalian animals is as unnecessary as it is unjustified.

Three objections can be anticipated. (1) The first claims that, while these facts can be obtained without dissecting any living animal, *the experience of dissecting* cannot be had by this means. That experience can only be had by dissecting. This is true, but not to the point. Morally, one cannot justify doing something merely on the grounds that one cannot have the experience of doing it without doing it. If that were sufficient, one could justify doing anything and everything, from rape to murder; for it is only if I participate in a rape or if I murder someone that I can have the experience of doing so. The general point is the simple one—namely, that to justify doing something, one has to justify what one does independently of pointing out that one could not experience it without doing it. Thus, while it is true that students could not have the experience of dissecting a living animal without dissecting one, that fact by itself goes no way toward justifying their doing it, let alone requiring that they do it. One must ask whether there are any reasons for viewing what is done as wrong, or as not wrong, and this will involve asking whether the value of having the experience is sufficient to justify doing what is necessary to have it. The rights view holds that the reasons against doing it outweigh the reasons for. Since dissecting a living mammalian animal harms that animal, frequently causing it pain and customarily being a prelude to that animal's untimely death, to defend dissection by appeal to the value of the experience of dissecting commits one to viewing these animals as if they were mere receptacles or renewable resources, a profound mistake according to the rights view. It is wrong because unjust to dissect living animals so one can have the experience of dissecting.

(2) In reply, the following might be urged. Even granting that the harm done to *mammalian* animals in lab sections is unjustified, most of the animals used in such courses are *not* mammals. Now, since, on the rights view, nonmammalian animals are not claimed to be the subjects-of-a-life, in the sense in which this notion is understood by the rights view, the proponents of that view should have no principled objection to the use of these animals.

The rights view's response begins by noting that even if nonmammalian animals are not the subjects-of-a-life in the sense explained, it is possible that many of these animals are conscious and capable of experiencing pain. As has been conceded on more than one occasion in the above . . . *where one draws the line* regarding the presence of consciousness is in some ways analogous to where one draws the line in other cases (e.g., how tall one has to be to be tall, or how old one must be to be old). There is no precise height or exact age one must be to be tall or old, respectively; but there are clear cases nonetheless. Similarly, it may not be possible to say, with anything approaching certitude, whether a given individual is or is not conscious or does or does not experience pain, despite the fact that there are clear cases where individuals are conscious and sentient. But though analogous in some respects, the two cases differ in others. Normally, nothing of moral significance turns on whether an individual is tall or is old. A great deal that is morally significant turns on whether an individual is conscious and can experience pain. Because we are uncertain where the boundaries of consciousness lie, it is not unreasonable to advocate a policy that bespeaks moral caution. Such a policy would have us act *as if* nonmammalian animals are conscious and are capable of experiencing pain unless a convincing case can be made to the contrary. In the absence of the case to the contrary, that is, it is not unreasonable to advocate a policy that gives the benefit of the doubt to animals that, though not mammals, nevertheless share relevant anatomical and physiological properties with mammalian animals (for example, a central nervous system). The adoption of this policy would make a significant difference to whether we should permit or require dissection of live, unanesthetized animals that are relevantly like paradigm conscious beings. If we give these animals the benefit of the doubt, we will operate on the assumption that these animals are conscious and do experience pain; and if we operate on that assumption, we will view dissection, when they are unanesthetized, as causing them pain and thus as standing in need of moral defense. That defense is not supplied by pointing to the knowledge gained. Since this knowledge is obtainable without causing pain to anyone, the presumptive pain caused those animals to whom we have given the benefit of the doubt, caused in the name of acquiring knowledge, is morally too great. Nor is the required justification supplied by alluding to the value of having the experience of dissecting, when this causes presumptive pain, since that experience can be had without risking causing any pain. Without the use of anesthetics, the policy of giving these animals the benefit of the doubt assumes that the animals *are* caused pain *and* pain that is unnecessary. To require or allow students to dissect "lower" animals without the use of anesthetics is morally unjustified.

But what of cases where "lower" animals are anesthetized? The same considerations apply. Though nonmammalian animals differ from us anatomically and physiologically in some respects, they resemble us in others, and it may be that the resemblances in some cases are more important than the differences. We simply do not know enough to justify dismissing, *out of hand*, the idea that a frog, say, may be the subject-of-a-life, replete with desires, goals, beliefs, intentions, and the like. When our ignorance is so great, and the possible moral price so large, it is not unreasonable to give these animals the benefit of the doubt, treating them *as if* they are subjects, due our respectful treatment, especially when doing so causes no harm to us. Adoption of this policy would make a difference, one that taking care to administer anesthesia to frogs, say, would not fully accommodate. For since the untimely death of an animal who is the subject-of-a-life *harms* the animal, the routine death caused those animals in lab sections becomes morally relevant. If we are genuinely to give the frog the benefit of the doubt, we will not only take care to spare frogs unnecessary pain by using anesthesia, we will also take care not to kill them, or allow them to die, unnecessarily. We will, that is, not use them for purposes of dissection.

(3) A critic might protest that frogs *just aren't worth* giving the benefit of the doubt to, claiming that stirring our conscience over the remote possibility that "frogs have rights" is to carry things too far. Let us, then, this critic maintains, prohibit use of mammalian animals but allow unlimited use of those who are not mammals, though with the recommendation that anesthesia be used. This reply occasions the third point. What transpires in, say, a biology lab doesn't occur in a vacuum. It is both an effect and a contributing cause of prevailing

cultural beliefs, attitudes, and traditions about nonhumans. The acquisition of these beliefs and attitudes and the introduction into these traditions are part of our acculturation. The rights view has implications that challenge some of these beliefs, attitudes, and traditions. It rejects the view that mammalian animals, at least, are mere receptacles or convenient renewable resources and affirms that they have a value of their own, independent of human interests. Now, the cultural acceptance of the rights view obviously in part turns on how well it is received and transmitted in our culture's system of education, including courses in science. Indeed, it is these courses, more than any others, that have the greatest potential to encourage cultural acceptance of the rights view. Pedagogically, how might this potential be developed most fully? Not by continuing to require students to dissect living animals, whether anesthetized or not, and whether mammalian or not, especially when the knowledge gained is obtainable without doing this. To require this is to help encourage the belief that *nonhuman animals don't count morally*, a belief that the dominant cultural influences outside the lab encourage enough without the need of any further assistance. Outside the lab is the world of Big Macs, Kentucky Fried Chicken, the weekend hunting trip, commercial whaling, fur coats, rodeos, cock fights, animal shelters—all symptoms of our culture's throw-away attitude toward animals, as if these sensitive creatures were commodities or *things*. To require students to dissect animals, when the knowledge acquired can be gained without doing this, is to feed into this throw-away attitude. To cease to require this is to take an important step in the opposite direction.

A variant of Kant's psychological speculations is apt in this regard. Kant's position, it will be recalled . . . is that "cruelty to animals" ought to be discouraged, not because we owe it to animals themselves not to be cruel to them, but because people who are cruel to animals develop habits of cruelty that in time lead them to maltreat human beings. However likely Kant's speculation about the connection between "cruelty to animals" and "cruelty to human beings" might be, it is more likely that requiring students to treat some animals as if they were of no direct moral significance will encourage them to form this habit of thought and action toward animals generally, the more so given that the dominant cultural influences already are heavily inclined in this direction. Even if it is true, then, that the animals most frequently dissected in high school and university lab sections lack rights, to continue to require dissecting them is likely to help foster habits that will lead persons to engage in practices that violate the rights of those animals who do have them—or to acquiesce by supporting those who do so. One way (and this a not unimportant way) to check the development of these habits is to cease to require students to dissect *any* animal, explaining that the knowledge acquired by doing it is obtainable without doing it and pointing out that the sciences of biology, zoology, and the like do not take the view that the animals they study are so insignificant, so "valueless," that they may be dissected and disposed of when it is unnecessary to do this. . . .

These judgments are unlikely to meet with much enthusiasm on the part of some of those who teach high school and university courses in the life sciences. Like academicians generally, they will treasure their academic freedom, and rightly so. To challenge what they require or permit in their laboratories is likely to be viewed as an invasion of this freedom. "We don't tell philosophers how they should teach their courses," it may be said, "so philosophers shouldn't tell us how we ought to teach ours!" The point is well taken, up to a point. Philosophers obviously are not in a position to select what text should be used in science courses, or what scientific ideas should be stressed, or in what order these ideas should be presented. Nothing said in the above implies otherwise. What a philosopher may legitimately do is challenge common practices on moral grounds, with reasons that do not require expertise in one or another scientific discipline. And scientists can do the same, if they find practices in the classrooms of philosophy that they consider morally objectionable. *It is the soundness of the moral arguments given, not who gives them, that should be decisive.* The preceding attempts to show how, by relying on the rights view, a commonly accepted practice in scientific education can be challenged. Reasons for accepting the rights view have been set forth at length in the preceding chapters. If that view has reason on its side, and if its application in the present case is sound, then lab sections that require or permit dissection of live animals ought to cease. For teachers to call a halt to this customary part of our education in the life sciences would not be to abdicate their academic freedom; it would be to exercise it. . . .

Questions for Comprehension

1. How useful does Regan believe mammalian animals to be in high school and college biology courses?
2. How does Regan counter the argument that the experience of dissecting can only be obtained by the performing of dissections?
3. On what basis does Regan reject the dissection of nonmammalian animals? What are the relevant criteria for determining how an animal may be used in a laboratory setting?
4. How does the use of animals in the laboratory reflect our attitudes toward them in everyday life?

■

ANIMAL RIGHTS EVALUATED

Michael E. Levin

Michael E. Levin teaches philosophy at the City College of the City University of New York. In the following essay he critically evaluates the bases upon which the claims of animal rights rest.

On the face of it, rights are created by special features of beings and situations; unless animals satisfy these special conditions, there are no grounds for ascribing rights to them. What, then are characteristic rights-creating situations? One obvious and broad basis for rights is consent. A vast selection of the rights we enjoy are created by voluntary transactions and explicit or implicit contractual agreement. Most property rights fall into this class, and many philosophers . . . have argued that we are obligated to obey the laws of a society because, by accepting the benefits of others' obedience to these laws, we have tacitly consented to do so. Now this certainly cannot be the basis for any animal rights, since no one has, or ever could have, entered into an agreement with an animal. Moreover, even though we obviously benefit from our relations with animals, these benefits do not arise from animals obeying certain rules in the expectation that we will reciprocate. Man has never done anything remotely like tacitly consenting to treat animals one way rather than another. Animals do not have the conceptual equipment to be party to such a reciprocal agreement.

There are, to be sure, some rights that apply to all men, not because of special arrangements, but as "natural." All men are said to have the right to be free, for example. Perhaps, then, animals have "natural" rights. The trouble with supposing this is that such rights pertain to a man, it seems, in virtue of just those traits that distinguish him from animals: the ability to reason abstractly, to conceive of himself as an enduring entity and to pursue life goals. . . . Indeed, animals clearly fail to meet all the suggested criteria: they cannot reason abstractly and do not conceive of themselves as enduring entities with histories and prospects, nor do they entertain goals beyond the promptings of instinct and immediate appetite.

At this point, however, the philosophical vegetarian deploys what is perhaps his key argument. He wants to know why possession of *those* traits exempt our fellowmen from certain kinds of treatment, while lack of them makes such treatment permissible for animals. What is so special, he asks, about the capacity to reason? If we say, with Kant, that only with the capacity to reason can a being conform his behavior to the concept of law, we will be asked what is so special about the ability to conform one's behavior to the concept of law. And, admittedly, there comes a point at which we cannot answer, because we have reached an ultimate moral premise incapable of further justification. . . . Now this argument may seem effective, but in fact it cuts so many different ways that it proves nothing. If any point at which we draw the line can be challenged, then the same challenge can be lodged at whatever point the animal-rights advocate wants to draw the line. If one says (as does Singer) that we have obligations toward all sentient beings, he must tell us what is so special about sentience. Perhaps bricks, even though insentient, have a right not to be cemented into walls. If our moral consciousness is to be expanded to include cows and cats, why not bricks? Indeed, why not draw the line at advocates of animal rights? We may be told that it is self-evident that sentience is what counts—but, historically, philosophers have tended to find rationality the self-evident demarcation. The philosophical vegetarian has left unexplained why some appeals to self-evidence are less satisfactory than others. Every normative position has an ultimate normative premise, that is neither a strength nor a weakness of normative positions.

Another popular basis for the claim that animals (and even trees) have rights . . . is legal ascriptivism. This view holds that rights are not properties of beings in the way, say, that their size is, but are *ascribed* to rights-holders by some recognized social mechanism. For you to have a right to X is tantamount to the existence of an enforceable legal prohibition against interference with your doing X. Since nothing prevents the enactment of a law that punishes anyone who acts in certain ways toward animals, perhaps legal ascription is the ultimate basis of animal rights. . . . But such an argument quite puts the cart before the horse. Whenever a legislator proposes to "create a legal right," he is presumably motivated by the desire to guarantee a *pre-existent* right of the prospective right holder. No legislator would dream of creating a legal right to random killing, precisely because nobody has that right, morally speaking, in the first place. Similarly, one justifies laws against unreasonable search on the grounds that they protect the right people already have to a secure home. One cannot justify the claim that one has a moral right to X from the fact that one does or can have a legal right to X. Scrutiny of legal rights reveals only those rights legislators believe rights-holders possess antecedent to law-making (and deserve enforcement). Similarly, two words cannot be synonymous because they are so listed in a dictionary, since a dictionary is simply the lexicographer's best guess about the preexisting synonymies of the language he is studying.

In short, I am not denying that any possible action toward animals can be *made* legally obligatory (or forbidden). I am just pointing out that proponents of animal rights need something stronger—that such actions *deserve* to be made legally obligatory *because* they are already morally obligatory. Since this is the very thing they are trying to show, appeal to legal ascriptivism gets them nowhere.

Nozick and others have appealed to the golden rule: surely I (or a researcher) would not like it if roles were reversed and I were a test animal. The trouble with this seemingly plausible appeal is that it is not clear what it means to ask "What if I were a test animal?" After all, I am a human being, and while I may coherently suppose myself to have been taller or shorter than I am, would I not cease being *me* were I an animal? In traditional terminology, I am *essentially* human. Asking me to imagine a situation in which I were an animal is asking me to imagine what is logically impossible, and it is a commonplace that no conclusions can be drawn from what would happen in a logically impossible situation. The philosophical vegetarian might contend that he can imagine what it would be like were he a dog, and that my failure to follow his lead is due to a weakness of my imagination (or perhaps that of sympathy). But it must still be recognized that there is no way of settling our disagreement, and when appeals to imagination become this obscure, it is best to abandon them altogether. It is worth remarking, incidentally, that if I were a test animal—granting one knows what this means—I would not mind being a test animal, since I would be unable to conceptualize this status. The golden-rule test seems to be applicable only because it appeals to just those human traits—my ability to understand being a subject of an experiment—that I would not have were I in the situation the test envisions. The golden-rule test works only *within* the human community, where imaginative role-reversal makes sense.

Consider, finally, the absurdities entailed by animal rights. If animals have rights, they are violated every time one creature kills another in the wild. If I don't have the right to kill a mouse for research, a cat does not have the right to kill a mouse for food. It will not do to say that we alone are obligated to refrain because we alone know what we are doing, for we cannot know that what we are doing is wrong unless it is wrong independently of our knowing it. The wrongness of an act cannot consist in the fact that someone knows it is wrong. An especially guilt-ridden philosophical vegetarian might argue that, while all killing in nature is wrong, only man is *blameworthy* for the killing he does for food. (Are predators, like sharks, who cannot be conditioned to leave other animals alone, to be considered criminally insane?) While this is a logically consistent position, it leaves its advocate saddled with the claim, absurd to anyone not already a philosophical vegetarian, that a tiger who eats an antelope has violated the antelope's rights.

Moreover, if animals are to be given consideration *equal* to that we give to man, consider the case of a man and a wolf trapped on a mountaintop. It would, then, be wrong to make a greater effort to rescue the man. Is not the absurdity of this as clear as any moral intuition we have? Am I saddling the philosophical vegetarian with consequences he would not draw? Well, suppose we say that we owe *some* consideration to animals, although not consideration equal to that we owe our fellowman. Suppose the obligation is, say, one one-hundredth as strong. Then if a man and a pack of one hundred wolves were trapped on a mountaintop, it would be wrong to make a greater effort to rescue the man. 8

If such consequences do not reduce the case for animal rights to absurdity, I cannot imagine what a true *reductio* would be like. And I cannot see that the philosophical vegetarian can back away from these consequences without altogether abandoning the language of rights. 9

. . . It is appropriate that Singer links "animal liberation" to the women's liberation movement. Thus he writes "I ask you to recognize that your attitudes to members of other species are a form of prejudice no less objectionable than prejudice about a person's race or sex." And certainly Singer's coinage of "speciesism" is as aggressively ugly as the feminists' "sexism." And, in truth, the last decade has seen an eruption of irrationality combined with a deep respect accorded to protest and "liberation" per se. Anyone who perceives women's liberation as the boundless self-assertion of its female protagonists and the grotesque self-abasement of its male protagonists will appreciate Singer's analogy. For what is women's liberation but an appeal to guilt about being a man and acting in such ways as manhood demands? And what is this new discovery of rights of animals other than guilt about being *human* and doing those things necessary for a satisfactory human life? 10

The common core of this progressive generalization of guilt, from guilt about one's race to guilt about one's sex to guilt about one's species—will it end with guilt about being a carbon-based life-form?—is a progressive weakening in American society of the convictions that what we do, and what we are, are *worth* something. One can speculate about the deeper sources of this new failure of nerve and loss of a sense of value: the disintegration of the family, perhaps, or a turning away from reality to the aesthetics of experience. Whatever the cause, what else can explain the widespread conviction that such social institutions as police, government, and the university exist not to do difficult and necessary jobs 11 but to offer "equal opportunities" to any sufficiently noisy protest group? What else can explain the growing conviction that the necessity of the family and unobstructed scientific research for our survival is *no presumption at all* in their favor?

Women's liberation presents a world in which genderless "persons" have identical nature, inclinations, and expectations. Proponents of animal rights present a world in which all creatures can coexist without having to kill to survive. These worlds may be nicer than the one we have, but the gap between reality and fantasy did not used to trouble us so. Because we have lost all conviction about the value and necessity of our actions in the world as it actually is, such fantasies have been parlayed into rights claims that in some cases are almost universally respected. It is bad enough when such claims cause the imposition of race and gender quotas in employment and in schools. In the animal-rights movement, we are beginning to see the use of such claims to frustrate the supreme value of Western civilization, arguably the supreme value that man has attained: the unimpeded pursuit of scientific knowledge for its own sake and for the good of mankind. When our convictions here are undermined, we are lost.

Questions for Comprehension

1. How does "consent" serve as a basis for rights? Why does Levin eliminate animals on this basis?
2. Why do animals fail to meet the criteria for natural rights?
3. What is the meaning of "legal ascriptivism"? What is the basis of rights in this view?
4. What is the proper relationship between moral and legal rights? Which come first?
5. Why does Levin believe the Golden Rule to be inapplicable to animals?
6. What, according to Levin, are the absurd consequences of the animal rights position?
7. What is Levin's attitude toward the women's liberation movement? How are his comments on women's liberation related to his attack on the animal rights movement?

ADDITIONAL WRITING ASSIGNMENTS

1. Summarize "Do Animals Have a Right To Life?" by James Rachels. You'll want to pay particular attention to the distinction between being alive and having a life.
2. According to Thomas Benson, "a system of degrading stereotypes has served both to legitimate and to stimulate immoral conduct." Identify one group of human beings who have been victimized by stereotyping and describe in detail the main features of the stereotype. Then explain how this stereotype can be used or has been used to justify immoral behavior toward the group. You might consider one of the following: religious, racial, regional, national, political, economic groups.

3. Write an essay in which you explain your own position on the use of animals for experimental purposes. Under what circumstances should animals be used experimentally? What limits, if any, should be placed on the use of animals in the laboratory? Use any of the essays in the anthology to back up your position.

The Younger Generation

A FAMOUS COMMENT GOES "YOUTH IS WASTED ON the young." The remark, obviously by a member of the older generation, brings up an inexhaustible topic—the young and the old and how they see each other. Commentators frequently label the young, and sometimes the labels become the permanent identification of a whole generation—the so-called Silent Generation, for example. Often, younger generations are identified with decades; thus many writers discuss the generation of the 1920s or the generation of the 1960s as if each ten-year period necessarily defined a distinct group. In fact, the next "younger generation" is often singled out as soon as commentators can find a few clear-cut differences from the young of a few years before. If you are using the readings in this section for a comparison paper, that tendency means that you don't have to select generations fifty years apart to write a successful comparison. If you want to compare the young of the early 1960s with those of the late 1960s, there's no reason not to do so.

In selecting sources for your comparison, you may find it useful to spend some time previewing the kinds of articles available in the anthology. The articles were written at different times by a variety of authors—scholars, recent college graduates, journalists. Some of the selections appeared in scholarly journals for academic audiences; others were published in mass circulation magazines. Some are comprehensive, cataloging a wide variety of characteristics of a younger generation, while others focus on a few issues.

In the prewriting section of "Comparing Sources" we discussed a 1951 *Time* magazine article, "The Younger Generation" (page 79), in which *Time*'s correspondents focus on a wide variety of characteristics of the group of young people who came to be known as the "Silent Generation." There are seven additional articles in the anthology, each about a different younger generation. In the first selection Paula Fass analyzes the tensions in young people's behavior in the 1920s—an analysis that does not support the stereotype of a wildly rebellious generation. Irwin Ross's 1941 article, "What They Really Think, and Why," focuses on young people's values and their attitudes toward democracy, the Depression, and the approaching war.

Reuel Denney, a well-known poet and teacher, gives a sociologist's view of the young at the beginning of the 1960s. His article helps readers see the forces at work in shaping the character of the younger generation. Tad Szulc's article, "Youth in America," discusses the complex elements of the revolutionary generation of the mid- and late 1960s. From the perspective of a college president, Rolf A. Weil sketches eleven characteristics of the same generation in his 1971 article "College Youth Attitudes Today." He also suggests how society ought to respond to the young. *Time* magazine affixes a new label to youth in "Now, the Self-Centered Generation," a comprehensive article about the seventies generation now better known as the Me Generation. Finally, David Wank's "Who Are We? A Self-Portrait of College Students Today" describes a wide variety of characteristics of the college culture of the mid-1980s.

■

CHANGE AND STABILITY: YOUTH IN THE 1920's

Paula S. Fass

> During her academic career, Paula S. Fass has been associated with the history departments of Columbia University and the University of California at Berkeley. Her book *The Damned and the Beautiful: American Youth in the 1920's*, published in 1977, is a carefully detailed study of young people in a time when American culture was being remade. In the selection reprinted here, Fass singles out two important elements that helped shape a generation usually regarded as an example of rebellion.

"We are all more or less self-centered residents of Main Street," remarked a Trinity College editor. And truly, much remained about the lives of college youths in the twenties that bound them securely to their time and place. Fraternities were imbued with the same boosterism familiar to the lodges and clubs which dominated the social lives and cultural horizons of the contemporary middle classes. Indeed, more often than not, Kiwani or Rotarian met collegian at the same athletic events and matched him cheer for cheer. And the self-advertisement of universities was not so very different from the efforts of many small-city Chambers of Commerce out to put their towns on the map. Students eagerly read Lewis' *Main Street*,* carelessly imitated Mencken,† and often cultivated worldly airs sorely belied by the facts of their lives. The provincial still tainted the modern, and beneath the brushed-up and sophisticated exterior of most collegiate fraternity pins beat the sterling heart of a Babbitt.‡ "George F. Jr. is going to college," an Ohio State editor noted, "and he is even more secure in college than in the world of business, if we are to believe our eyes and ears and the college papers."

It would have been strange had it been otherwise. The young lived in the world and most emphatically of it. Their reading matter was of a piece with the fare found in most middle-class living rooms, with the possible difference that they read fewer newspapers and more humor magazines: the *American, Saturday Evening Post, Life* (a humor magazine in the twenties), *Ladies' Home Journal, True Romance, Cosmopolitan*. Occasionally, they attended to an article recommended to them in the *Atlantic* or *Scribner's*; much more rarely they read the *New Republic* or the *Nation*; and sometimes, the *American Mercury*. They saw the films their parents saw and admired the same actors. They voted for the same politicians, with perhaps more skepticism and less general approval, but with the same overall majorities supporting Harding and Coolidge and Hoover. "As the colleges go," the *Ohio State Lantern* accurately reported about the elections, "so goes the nation."

Living in a culture that valued business success and denied intellectual endeavors the laurels granted the creative geniuses of the Chamber of Commerce, the young had no desire to reorder priorities. Very few were interested in emulating the lives of their professors or in caring intensely for books or ideas. While the social structure of the peer system had adjusted the success myth to twentieth-century dimensions with its valuation of style within conformity and its dependence on prestige and association, it still enthusiastically embraced the business ethic and the American system. Although mating choices, sexual expression, and cultural forms had been newly tuned to an emerging American life style, they were still very much within the main line of the culture. Marriage was for the coed what business was in the imagination of her male partner. The young had liberated many behaviors and values from a conventional morality, but they had not separated themselves from the roles and responsibilities that they would soon assume. They had no reason to doubt that the future held anything but opportunities. They could not have foreseen, nor would they have believed, that it would be otherwise. Because they were secure in their present freedoms and in their future hopes, they were neither lax nor cynical. They were malleable, practical, and profoundly oblivious of the defects of American society, except for the superficial way in which they decried corruption in government, the existence of which

---

* Editor's note: Sinclair Lewis's 1920 novel, which satirized small-town life.
† Editor's note: H. L. Mencken (1880–1956) often wrote ironically about middle-class American habits and values.
‡ Editor's note: George Babbitt, a businessman character in Sinclair Lewis's 1922 satirical novel *Babbitt*, represents unthinking conformity to middle-class standards.

was daily shouted at them from the headlines. It was, after all, for the roles of worker, wife, citizen, and consumer that youth was a preparation.

And yet, there was a difference, and it was a difference in substance as well as tone. In good part, that difference was a new latitude in experience; in part, it was also a broadening in attitude. The young had experienced an increase in personal freedoms, a newly expressive nurture, more schooling, more room for experimentation, and a greater sensitivity to the need for personal expression within themselves and for others. At home, they had enjoyed a person-oriented nurture; among peers, they were encouraged toward group-supported experimentation. And they had leisure. Thus at a time when values were not yet fixed and when youth could most readily test the limits of freedom, they were responsible only to each other.

They were more tolerant in attitude as well as freer in behavior, and in this the schools played their part, for education had exposed them to the relativism of philosophers, writers, and scientists who had long been preparing the ground for youth's beliefs and values. Not that the majority of college youths studied hard, but rather they necessarily were in contact with thinkers and innovators who colored their world view and their view of each other. Every college newspaper was unyielding in its denunciation of isolationism, fundamentalism, anti-evolutionism, censorship, and repression. Every editor took issue with the cult of moral reform. "College is the place to broaden out and to assimilate ideas from the classroom and the campus which tend to widen the scope of conception," Berkeley's *Daily Californian* proclaimed. "It is the place to balance old ideals against new experience; to test the value of former principles in the light of recent knowledge." And while students often complained that their studies were all too irrelevant to their lives, their lives had become more related to their studies. For it was their experience which made the difference, and that experience made the tolerance so urgently contained in their books more meaningful and real.

This new latitude in experience separated the young from their parents and from the American past. Moreover, like the widening circles in an agitated pond, it was reaching farther and farther into the society. For the experience of the youth of the twenties was becoming increasingly institutionalized as more families became smaller, more youths were sent to school rather than to work, and more adjustments were required at a time when older attitudes toward sex, religion, and manners gave way to newer habits, to dating, movies, corporate work patterns, and Sunday golf. The young turned readily to what was new in the culture, and they did it with a delight and excitement that could only have made their elders both fearful and envious. The young could adjust, were forced to adjust, and were eager to adjust. And as they did so, they drew the culture with them.

They were a generation in tension. In a culture slowly moving toward the future, they were caught between those encroaching Main Street roles that they would soon assume and those innovations that had twisted their lives into new directions. So they were optimistic about business and naughty about sex. They could tolerate latitude in the behavior of others but most prudently guard against suspicion in their own. They could sneer with the cynic but harbor bright hopes for their own future success. The women smoked and the men drank, but neither were in any doubt about their decency and respectability. They could pet and denounce repression but carefully guard against too great indulgence in instinct. They were flamboyant about their rights and careful in their dress. They had charted the course for the new century as they prepared to assume adult lives in Zenith,* U.S.A., *circa* 1929.

The peer group and the college peer society helped to direct the young both to effective stability in their own lives and to vital change in the society. At its most elementary level, the peer society provided company for young men and women freed from the need for work, released from obligations to the families from which they came, not yet engaged with families of their own, and endowed with energies unconsumed by the assigned work of the classroom. Though simple, this function of the peer group is basic to its very existence. Without leisure and without the formal structure provided by the schools, youth would have had neither so much time nor so many occasions for intense peer-group interaction. But the peer culture did more than provide fellowship for the individual. It developed an intricate set of work and play relationships, provided a sense of solidarity and identification, and asked in turn for obedience to its rules and conformity to its standards. The peer group had adapted the individual to a society largely of its own making and carefully protected from adult interference.

Ultimately, of course, it was the specific relationship between the youth society and the larger culture that was most crucial. At a time when affectionate person-centered nurture was growing in the family while other social relations were more and more governed by impersonal roles and performance demands, youth peers socialized individuals to accept group standards and thus provided a necessary transition from childhood to adulthood. From individuals reared to expect unqualified love and security just as a result of being, peers demanded performance and made approval and affiliation contingent on active behavior. Peer groups redirected expectations, providing the primary emotional security of group belonging in return for approved performance. Campus peer groups had thus become part of a new network of socialization in which schools and peers bridged the gap between family and marketplace.

When youth in the twenties changed adult standards of respectability in sexual behavior and when they expanded the possibilities of women's behavior, they were effectively directing individuals away from adult norms and creating and approving new social patterns. When they opposed Prohibition and drank liquor, they were at once denying the urgency of adult norms, rejecting the notion of an unchanging standard of morality, and questioning the validity of adult laws. In adjusting to adult standards, they thus became by those standards immoral and law-breakers. They moreover asked for a latitude in behavior to be determined not by impersonal criteria but by personal preference. If peer groups trained only to an acceptance of standards, then youth groups in the twenties should not have

---

* Editor's note: The fictional middle-American town where George Babbitt lived.

denied that in certain areas there should be no standards. To explain such major variations in terms of deviancy, especially in relation to a generation in other ways stable and responsible, is not useful.

The tensions in youth's behavior can be understood only if we recognize that in many ways college peers in the 1920's continued the person-oriented conditioning of the family. In certain areas, the young believed that personal expression, style, and need—not objective standards—should govern conduct. This was especially true in moral matters and was very effective as a value in sexuality and mating. But beyond the enunciated ideal of preference, many of the actual criteria of acceptability in the peer society were largely those of personal congeniality. Each group selected congenial associates within certain broad racial and class limitations and then proceeded to instruct members in those qualities which would increase that congeniality. Many of the tasks that members were required to perform concerned sociability. Personal conformity and not work performance was most highly valued. Despite the emphasis placed upon active competition in extra-curricular activities, it was personal rating, prestigious association, and collegiate style that dominated the social world of the young. Those values were latent in the whole network of peer relations. Amiability, sociability, congeniality, personal plasticity, these and not objective products were prime assets in the youth society, which was highly leisure-oriented. Many of the personal qualities were directed toward mating, but they were also valued as a means for business success.

Moreover, deviation from adult standards was built into peer relationships in the 1920's. One of the things the peer society on the campus encouraged was experimentation and partial socialization to a variety of minority ethics. This is a result of the comparative freedom that prevails during adolescence. Unhindered by responsibilities and obligations except to his own needs and isolated from adult values, the individual is during this period least required to conform to adult standards and freest of adult control. Youth is a period of manifest irresponsibility that Kenneth Keniston has called "belligerently non-adult"; a period when, according to Erik Erikson, a youth is at once directed toward future roles and intensely engaged in immediate enthusiasms. . . . Contradictions abound as the individual becomes intensely critical of previously respected adult models, oriented toward new ones, and uneasy about his own future. Youths in the twenties embodied many of these contradictions. The peer group permitted the individual to experiment without making him personally responsible for all his decisions. Devotion to the group and group enthusiasms mobilized an individual's energies, fulfilled his need for direction, and relieved him of personal responsibility for bad choices. The group as a whole, rather than the individual, provided models for imitation that filled the need for experimentation and commitment and assisted the process of self-definition. The peer group thus encouraged irresponsibility or impropriety as the adult world defined it. The individual was able to experience the freedom of anti-parental value choices without losing the security of group support.

In the twenties, this experimentation with values and behaviors was fostered by what David Matza has called the "subterranean traditions of youth."

Matza has identified three major subterranean tendencies in youth societies—delinquency, radicalism, and bohemianism. And this concept of youth's traditional choice of anti-social models of behavior can help to illuminate certain tendencies among the young of the twenties, despite the fact that I have stressed that the young in the twenties were both anti-radical and anti-Bohemian and although I have been concerned with normative and not delinquent groups.

There was among the mass of college youths in the twenties a very real infatuation with playing naughty-boy roles, an inclination toward affectations of sophistication and worldliness. It was not quite bohemian, but it was not quite respectable either. In this attitude they were amply provided with adult models. To name just a few is to recognize the varieties of the cultural history of the twenties, especially as it demonstrated disaffection from normative values and provided romantic alternatives: H. L. Mencken, Randolph Bourne, Emma Goldman, Floyd Dell, Edna St. Vincent Millay, F. Scott Fitzgerald, Scott Nearing, Theda Bara, Rudolph Valentino, Clara Bow.* The list is endless. Each represents in a different way the possibilities of unconventional conduct and values. Each served as a well-advertised model upon which to base a tendency toward non-conformity. On the whole, these tendencies were developed to an important degree only among small minorities, but their influence as potential models for imitation was general, and all youth appear to have felt it to some degree. The "deviates" in adult society gave youth a host of patterns that could and did affect the tone or style of youth life. This variety expanded the possibilities of approved experimentation, now supported by active peer mediation, and was a way of assimilating change to the generally conservative (but not traditional) standards that prevailed. These models were, of course, available to adults as well, and no doubt they influenced the behavior of some. But the young in the 1920's were more vulnerable to their example because during a period of search and experimental role-playing, when values were plastic and imitative, the young had group support for experimentation.

There is another potential peer-group function that does not seem on the whole to have affected college youth in the twenties. The peer group can encourage or condone self-conscious conflicts with adult society and adult authority. The potential of adolescence as a period of hostility between adults and youth, parents and children, was well known in the twenties. The more sanguine critics used the age-old conflict of the generations as an explanation for what they interpreted as the rebelliousness of youth. The young also used the generation gap as a convenient way of countering criticism.

The young in the twenties were rather more optimistic than idealistic, and they were also notoriously pragmatic. With a shrewd eye for the limits of acceptable conduct and belief, youth rarely provoked adult authority on the high ground of theory. When they were idealistic, it was about very specific issues not as a general orientation. They could argue against the stupidities of war or denounce the inanities of censorship. But they condemned pacifism and radicalism and were

---

* Editor's note: Well-known writers, entertainers, and social activists.

bigoted and nationalistic. The young were plastic, but this is not the same as being naturally idealistic. That plasticity simply made them more vulnerable to change. When the young believed their vital interests were at stake, they became flamboyantly idealistic, but it was idealism that always betrayed their sense of what was convenient as well as what was good. Moreover, even when they were idealistic in theory, very few indeed were willing to pledge themselves unreservedly to pacifism, or to claim that Prohibition laws should be disobeyed, or, regarding the double standard of sexual morality, to test the limits of equality. Indeed, the young were, if anything, consciously hard-nosed, prudent, and pragmatic. No doubt, the young adapted more easily to the rapid social changes that were transforming American society and culture than their elders. But they did so not from some primary idealism directed toward a more liberal future but because peers were helping to liberate each other from the greater confines of parents and past and because peer groups were using the very instruments of the new culture, like fads and movies, to effect new social controls on behavior.

The college youth of the twenties were not a generation that deliberately denied the moral or intellectual competence of its elders. They were "naughty," not angry. They knew that they lived in a changing world that demanded new understanding, new conventions, and constant readjustments. And they conceived of their behavior and attitudes as positively responsive to these conditions. They were sometimes accused of ignoring adults and of denying them an influence in their lives. If this was so, it was because adults did have less influence in their lives and not because they chose to deny them authority. The college papers show an avid concern with adult opinion, and students usually cared enough to attempt to explain themselves. Acutely aware of being observed and criticized, the young would often artfully accentuate certain qualities to which they knew adults would react, usually with horror or outrage. As a form of self-defense, the pose itself was serious, but the implications usually less than wholly sincere. And it all betrayed a wispy self-mockery which belied their cocky self-assurance.

The *New Student* had been intent on developing a youth consciousness grounded in political commitment that would confront the adult world and contend with it on the basis of generations. There were moves to mobilize youth on political matters throughout the decade, best illustrated in the student conferences and leagues, but they affected a minority of students and found no real momentum. The one area in which the young seemed to find a voice was in cultural matters, or rather in matters of style. They conceived of themselves as modern in dress, manners, and interest, and they were proud of it. They opposed all attempts to return American life to an impossible past that would condemn their new liberties in sex, thought, and interest. This was a diffuse kind of sentiment, a tone, an inclination, but it was strong enough to lend a certain self-consciousness to the college youth of the twenties.

There was no hostility toward the world of the elders, only a sense of difference. The problem with cultural differences is that they are vague and easily appropriated. And so it was with the youth of the twenties. Their identifying symbols—their clothes, their music, their athletics, and their slang—merged into the consciousness of a decade. The adult population hounded their every step, and where some came to condemn, others stayed to imitate. For many, the path of the damned had become the way of the beautiful.

Questions for Comprehension

1. According to Fass, what are some of the specific ways in which the young of the 1920s were *like* their parents?
2. In what ways were college students of the 1920s a tolerant group, and what was the cause of their tolerance?
3. What was the result of the "increasingly institutionalized" experience of youth in the 1920s?
4. What were the two broad influences of the college peer group society?
5. What values dominated the social world of the young?
6. How did the college peer group contribute to the "anti-parental value choices" made by the young?
7. What does Fass say about idealism and the younger generation of the 1920s?
8. How much open hostility toward the older generation was present among the young?

■

WHAT THEY REALLY THINK, AND WHY

Irwin Ross

The following article appeared in *Harper's* magazine in January 1941, a little less than one year before the United States entered World War II. The successes of the German armies in Europe had aroused a great deal of public interest in America in how the younger generation felt about democracy, justice, and freedom. After *Harper's* published two articles critical of the young, the magazine's mail was so heavy its editors decided to publish more articles along with a sampling of the mail. One of those articles was this one, written by a member of the younger generation, Irwin Ross, who had graduated from Harvard in June of 1940.

There is a widespread notion that American young people are cowardly, cynical, and indifferent to the fate of their country. Let us look at the facts.

It is generally agreed that the first peace-time conscription bill in the history of this country was enacted because the American people suddenly recognized their danger and understood the need for resolute action. No shortsighted isolationism, little specious immunity here. Naturally, if American youth were wandering in the pacifist fairyland one would expect them to bridle at the bill. The opposite was true. During last July Dr. Gallup's American Institute of Public Opinion conducted a nation-wide survey of youth's opinion of conscription. He asked: "Do you think that every able-bodied young man should be made to serve in the Army, Navy, or air force for one year?" Young people 15 to 20 years of age answered "Yes" to the tune of 67 per cent, while those between the ages of 21 and 29 favored conscription to the tune of 62 per cent. The older people were polled on the same question. Interestingly enough, they favored conscription in the same proportion as the 15- to 20-year group—67 per cent.

When passage of the conscription bill became imminent the youth of the land were interviewed once again. This time the question was: "If the draft law is passed, will you, personally, have any objection to spending a year in some branch of the military service?" Of the men 21 to 24 years old, 68 percent had no objection. Those between the ages of 16 and 21 were even more resoundingly in favor: 81 per cent were quite willing to serve, only 19 per cent demurred.

Two years ago the American Youth Commission published a survey of 13,528 Maryland young people between the ages of 16 and 24. This sampling was so selected as to be an accurate cross-section of the 21,000,000 American youth in the same age group: the same percentages of farm and city, negro and white, rich and poor youth, were interviewed. The poll covered a variety of subjects—family background, employment, education, church attendance, attitudes on contemporary problems—and is without doubt the most complete inventory of facts about American youth that we possess.

The Maryland youngsters were asked what action they would take in case of war. Of the boys, 76 per cent replied that they would volunteer or fight if drafted. Another 12 per cent would answer the call only if invasion threatened. Eleven per cent would refuse under any circumstances. The remainder could not make up their minds. If we remember that this poll was taken two years ago, when the question was still academic to many people, we must agree that anti-war propaganda had had scant success in promoting conscientious objection.

If the great majority of young people are not indifferent to defense and express a willingness to fight when called upon, why all the alarm? Is it because they apparently do not favor entrance into the European war? ("Apparently" is used advisedly, since nobody has taken a poll on the subject.) Even granting a 90 per cent objection to a war declaration, such a feeling is strongly seconded by the older generation. According to Dr. Gallup as of mid-October, only 17 per cent of the American people favor entry into the war; the other 83 per cent are resolutely opposed. In common fairness, youth cannot be whipped and the oldsters left beyond the range of the birch rod.

Perhaps the objection is not to youth's disinclination to fight in Europe, but only to a suspected disapproval of aiding England. The American people, there seems no doubt, are in favor of such aid. What youth thinks nobody really knows. The only young people who circulate petitions with any frequency seem to be college students. One day fifteen hundred Yale undergraduates denounce aid to England, the next day another fifteen hundred petition for such aid. Curiously enough, a few individuals sign both petitions.

Or perhaps the oldsters are distressed by the fact that while American youth is still willing to do its duty, the old bravado and full-throated enthusiasm have departed. Few youngsters, apparently, really want to fight for fighting's sake; the old itch is gone. When Dr. Gallup asked the young men if they favored conscription the affirmative responses were without exception nonbelligerent and merely stressed the need for preparedness: "So if we had a war they wouldn't be greenhorns." "We would not be caught the way others were if we are trained." "So as to preserve the United States as a democracy and a dominant world power."

What causes surprise is not that 81 per cent are willing to serve in the armed forces, but that all of 19 per cent do object to conscription.

The 19 per cent are very vocal too. But for this very reason, the rumpus they make can easily promote an exaggerated estimate of their numerical strength.

But while the radicals indubitably monopolize the headlines, it is also true that a large segment of intelligent youth opinion is isolationist: pro-Ally, but hesitating to lift a hand to help lest such generosity draw us into war. From this undeniable fact too many of our older generation of democratic stalwarts jump to the conclusion that at least these youths are non-believers in democracy and the American heritage, indifferent to moral values, cynics before their time, a callow and heartless lot.

Equally misunderstood are the progressive and quite commendable mainsprings of much of this isolationism. It is not an isolationism of inertia, retreat, or plain lack of perception. Short-sighted it may be, yet it is worthy of respectful consideration. True-blue pacifism of course commends itself to only a small group of young people; but none of these even can be accused of a lack of idealism. They are courageous to a fault, as witness the eight Union Theological students and two socialists in New York who braved five-year jail terms by refusing to register for the draft. The religious groups preach nonviolence as a way of life and are quite zealous in keeping their ranks free of individuals whose convictions are less hardy. When the Fellowship of Reconciliation sponsored an anti-conscription march in New York City on registration day no one was allowed to participate who was not experienced in the tactics of nonviolent action and would not be certain to "turn the other cheek" to provocation.

The majority of isolationists do not have these scruples about fighting. They merely object to participation in a war whose outward aspects do not present to them an unblurred picture of black and white. Mistrust of England is an understandable, if unjustifiable, hangover from pre-Churchill appeasement days. Subsequent events have shaken the faith of many in the democratic pretensions of the Allied cause.

Similarly with the defense effort of the United States. These young men and women believe they see business obtaining countless concessions as the price of its grudging co-operation, while labor is constantly stepped on. While democratic oratory reaches new heights of eloquence, they see drastic infringements on our traditional liberties occurring throughout the land. Minority parties are ruled off the ballot, religious sects are persecuted, alertness to the fifth column verges on anti-alien hysteria. Looking beyond our frontiers, they see us talking of a good neighbor policy and then putting the screws on Mexico; planning to win the Western Hemisphere for democracy and simultaneously supporting what look to them like native fascist regimes in South America. Our actions belie our words, they argue: is this a war for democracy?

Finally many young people are dubious about defending a society which in peacetime has no need for them. If they are asked to fight they want to enjoy the privileges as well as the liabilities of American citizenship. That means jobs, educational opportunities, as well as the other recognized amenities of our civilization.

The Welfare Council of New York recently published the results of a survey of one million New York City young people between the ages of 16 and 24. (McGill and Matthews, *The Youth of New York City*, The Macmillan Co.) The same cross-section sampling was employed as in the Maryland study by the American Youth Commission. The interviewers asked if the depression interfered with marriage plans; 32 percent of the young men, 21 percent of the young women, over 21, replied that it did. "Things were too bad and my girl refused to wait any longer," one chap said. Another was blunter: "We broke off—no money." An economic silver cord was revealed by a third: "My money was needed at home, so I gave my girl up." Some of the girls were too poor to get dates. "I can't get a guy—I don't have the clothes to go out in." Another recurrent note: "Since moving to a poor neighborhood I won't invite people."

If one bears these facts in mind, does there not seem something insensitive in the plea that the young people get tough, tighten their belt-lines, put aside the luxuries of an effete society? Roy Helton* wrote in the September issue of *Harper's*: "We indulge our children illimitably. Instead of rearing a race of lusty, weather-conditioned sons and daughters of democracy, we exhaust our private purses to buy gasoline for our racing youth, and strain the resources of our schools and colleges to erect stadia unparalleled since the days of degenerating Rome." One wonders how many of our four million unemployed youth enjoy the luxury of a private car or can afford $3.85 to witness a big-time football match. The sacrifice of these inessentials would be little to ask if the gain were the strengthening of democracy. But when words like "sacrifice" or that other great desideratum—"discipline"—are so vaguely bandied about, the unsophisticated can only conclude that not alone our upper- and middle-class youth are being discussed, but our entire younger generation—a spoiled and pampered lot, who should forthwith be denied the extravagances of NYA and CCC. Talk such as this will gain few recruits for democracy and runs the risk of alienating many still loyal.

According to Dr. Mortimer J. Adler,† youth has no faith in the moral verities, since these are not susceptible of scientific proof. As a consequence, young people will believe in democracy only if it works—if it provides material benefits—not because it is morally correct. Dr. Adler offers scant evidence to support this thesis. But granting its validity for argument's sake, the solution he proposes—revamping our all-pervasive educational philosophy, chucking out decadent "scientism," and enthroning moral intuition—seems unrealistic in the extreme. There is insufficient time to save democracy merely by persuading people of its moral soundness. If Americans are essentially pragmatic, as Dr. Adler says they are, meet them on their own ground: make democracy work. There is one trustworthy specific: give youth a stake in the country—jobs, hope in the future.

Youth doesn't ask much. Dr. Gallup recently polled young people on their chief ambition in life; few were extravagant. Only about 11 per cent of the boys and girls agreed with the 20-year-old Kentucky youth who wanted to "accumulate

---

* Editor's note: Lecturer, poet, novelist (not the coauthor of this text).
† Editor's note: Philosopher, author, educator—associated with the Great Books program.

wealth" or with the 23-year-old clerical secretary in New York whose greatest desire was to be "a lady of leisure." Over two-thirds merely wanted to improve themselves in a modest fashion. One 23-year-old girl who was a cashier in Nebraska wanted to be a stenographer; another wanted to be a nurse; a third, a typist in a Minnesota department store, said she "hoped to live a happy life," but gave no specifications. The males were similarly undemanding. Typical responses were: a parking-lot attendant in California: "I'd like to be in the Marine Air Corps"; an unemployed Virginian, 18 years old: "To be an undertaker"; a Pennsylvania youth of 24, now working in the lithography business: "To be comfortable, secure and to do some good in the world."

The National Youth Administration and the Civilian Conservation Corps have made a start in the right direction. The CCC semiannually takes 250,000 young men off the streets of the nation, feeds and clothes them, builds up their bodies, develops their manual abilities. The out-of-school work program of the NYA has been expanded, by virtue of a recent appropriation of $32,500,000, and now accommodates 500,000 young people, who work on projects that provide an elementary kind of vocational training. They do not learn a specific trade, but they get enough experience at different tasks so that they are not green when they secure a job in private industry.

NYA and CCC, however, care for only 750,000 of the 4,000,000 unemployed youth. Much, much more is needed. Last spring President Roosevelt proposed a youth-training program which would have enrolled 2,000,000 boys in the service of the nation. There were many cogent objections to the plan, mainly that compulsion was unnecessary. Let jobs be offered and the youth will flock to them. But the President's plan had the merit of recognizing that a large-scale effort was demanded.

It may be true that the youth problem cannot be solved apart from our general unemployment problem. If that is so, and alienation of youth's loyalties is feared, there is all the more reason to doctor our ailing economy. One way or another, jobs must be provided for the vast multitude of unemployed youth. It is the only solution.

Questions for Comprehension

1. What charge against the younger generation does the author identify at the beginning of his essay?
2. What does the author call an "insensitive" attitude toward the young by some members of the older generation?
3. What charge did Mortimer Adler make against the young?
4. What attitude toward money do the young have?
5. In what ways does the author see the American economy as the key to the attitudes of the younger generation?
6. How had an article in the September issue of *Harper's* characterized the younger generation?
7. What role does "isolationism" play in the picture the author creates of the young?

AMERICAN YOUTH TODAY: A BIGGER CAST, A WIDER SCREEN

Reuel N. Denney

Reuel Denney (b. 1913) has had distinguished careers in a number of fields. A prize-winning poet and critic, he has also taught and written about the humanities and the social sciences. His books include *The Connecticut River and Other Poems* (1939), *The Astonished Muse* (1957), and *Conrad Aiken* (1964). With David Riesman and Nathan Glazer, he is coauthor of *The Lonely Crowd* (1950), a major study of American society. The selection printed here is from an article that originally appeared in the journal *Daedalus* in 1962.

It takes a kind of shabby arrogance to survive in our time, and a fairly romantic nature to want to. These are scarce resources, but more abundant among adolescents than elsewhere, at least to begin with.

Spies moving delicately among the enemy,
The younger sons, the fools.

Gertrude Stein* once explained that the United States is the oldest country in the world. The United States, she meant, has acquired the longest experience of modern society. In a *New Yorker* article of a few years back, Dwight Macdonald† told us that the United States had been the first to develop the concept (not yet accepted in Europe) of the "teen-ager." His article suggested that the United States had by now acquired the longest experience with the subculture of youth as it develops in a modern society: our densely populated youth culture is in some ways the oldest, the most advanced, and the most distinctive in the world. It has also been said, almost in the same breath, that one reason the young in the United States do not organize themselves as a social and political movement is that they are already organized by our society as a body of affluent consumers.

How much these youthful social forms of ours will become a model for other societies is still uncertain. Meanwhile, there is agreement that American young people constitute something of a new social type, even while there is disagreement as to what that type is. In the years after World War II, American self-consciousness invented so many new "generations" of the young that the word itself now suggests a period hardly longer than the college life of a college class. Yet it is agreed about the American young that their numbers, homogeneity, prosperity, relatively prolonged dependency, socialization and education (full career comes much later for most, even if marriage comes earlier for many), and

---

* Editor's note: Gertrude Stein (1874–1946), American expatriate writer, frequent commentator on American culture.
† Editor's note: Dwight Macdonald (1906–82), publicist, author, literary critic.

their increasing specialization in the labor force constitute their basic and unique generational experiences. Whether they are being prompted by this encounter to substitute new values for old or whether they are simply casting older values in newer forms, is another question.

Isn't it easier to call to mind a typical young person in the United States today than it would have been when I was between twelve and nineteen, from 1925 to 1930? There were not nearly so many of us then, nor did we bulk so large as a proportion of the total population. Yet through no fault of our own we were more diverse. Differences in family income were greater than they are today, and they were reinforced by distinct class, ethnic, and generational styles of life. Today the bilingual and the foreign-accent family, for example (except among the Latins), are becoming pressed flowers in the American album of nostalgias. The very speech of the American young, with its centripetal drift toward the mid-Western speech pattern that has become the American standard, tells what has happened. Within the great internal market of the nation, the automobile, the electronic wave, and a variety of other forces have served an equalitarian tropism by making young people richer than they have ever been, and rather more like each other than they have been since the Civil War. That date marks the last previous era when American young people, with the exception of Negroes and Indians, constituted a homogeneous population: North European and English-speaking farm-bred folk with lower grammar-school literacy and a predominantly Protestant world view.

For the more than 61 million people under eighteen to constitute such a large percentage of the total population under sixty-five as they do today is also a cyclical return to an aspect of earlier historical experience. At the time of the signing of the Declaration of Independence, half the nation was under eighteen. We do not touch this proportion today. But the infant and first-year mortality rate has fallen from one out of three in 1880 to a few in a thousand. By 1965, when the great 1947 peak in the postwar birth rate must be felt even more than it is now, it will have the effect of doubling within a decade the number of people annually arriving at the age of eighteen—from two million in 1956 to four million in 1965. Within the next few years, about eighty percent of this group will be in high school. About one-third of these will leave high school without graduating, the boys to enter the army or the labor market, the girls to enter the labor market or to marry without entering it. Of the more than one and one-half million who graduate from high school, about half will go on to register at college, more young men than young women. It can be expected that the roughly twenty-five percent of the sixteen to twenty-four age group who now are registered in college will increase. The age of extended socialization is in full swing.

One of the odd effects of extended socialization is that it seems to us older ones to be connected as much with a downward extension of age-graded roles and a general widening of privileges as it does with the postponement of a full career as an adult. In my day, it was chiefly the farm youth who learned as a matter of course to drive a car early in life, and not many of the young were car-owners. Today, driving and car-ownership are fully accepted and more or less unexciting stages in the rites of passage of almost all young men and women. The high-school student of today has taken up the ceremonial burden of graduating in a manner befitting the college graduate of earlier years. He expects to be equipped with the cars, white jackets, carnations, orders for corsages, and all the other equipment of role and status that in my day as a stripling were reserved by the Florist's Association, the Cadillac ads, the pages of *Vanity Fair*, and the apparel shops, for well-off adults and a small number of country club sprouts. In 1925, the earliest pairs of trousers were provided for sons of the family as they were readying for college or a job. Today, the earliest pairs of trousers are tailored for infant girls who do not even know enough syllables to protest the absence of a working fly. All these precocious privileges appear at the lower end of the age scale, even while the upper end is displaying the novelty of the father of three who is being worked through college by his father-in-law and through his graduate thesis by his wife. The downward shift of age privileges may be a narrowly middle-class occurrence. It is conservatively resisted by some upper-income groups. In some lower-income groups on the move, the shift works in the other direction. But the largesse of male privilege to both sexes seems general and as strong in South Harlem as in Scottsdale, Arizona.

For the youth as student and as worker in the very near future, two trends that would once have had to be regarded as contradictory will be felt at the same time. Because of our postwar growth in population, the number of persons under twenty-four in the work force will far exceed any previous figures for this group. On the other hand, because of our enlarged educational goals and ambitions, more young people than ever before will be held until a later age out of the labor market. The educational preparation of the young poses three issues of great importance that are troubling us now: inequality of opportunity, premature specialization, and the glorification of the average. The young boy or girl in the United States today is offered an education whose high-average achievements are marred by segregation, compromised by the belief that all vocational talents can and should be identified at an early age, and clouded by the number of high schools in which the best is too close to the average. Segregation is present in the North as well as the South, of course. Northern segregation is based on class rather than caste and is not openly defended by many. These are cold comforts to progressive school districts whose standards can be lowered by ill-prepared Negro students; they are even colder comforts to Negroes lined up to get something better than substandard treatment by the public purse.

As for specialization, it is notable that American high schools offend less in this respect than do many colleges. The American high school student can find basic disciplines and teachers of great ability in many places today. Yet more public high schools might be even better than they are, resembling New Trier, in Winnetka, Illinois, for example, if their parent constituencies were more informed, and if their core curriculum were more loyally classical. There is an increasing belief among some middle-class parents that a first-rate secondary school may be even more important than a good college.

American higher education presents a widely mixed scene in which vocationalism still runs strong. More students take degrees in business than in either the sciences or the humanities, and the average college graduate in the United States is culturally illiterate. More than half of them, for example, read less than seven books a year. Graduate and professional schools are of good but varied quality, and it is natural that they should tend to seek narrowly professional competences in their graduates. They show disloyalty to the general educational scene when they insist (as they often do) that their preconceptions and prerequisites should divert students from a broad education in the earlier school years.

In the face of the educational bureaucracy, with its persistently laggard standards in both private and public schools, the better college student of today often feels in lock step. He knows that most American higher education is too industrially organized around classrooms, grades, and hastily contrived examinations. Moreover, the American habit of interference in the private lives of students, induced partly by American coeducation, partly by public education, partly by the theory of *in loco parentis*,* is undignified for those who run universities and unedifying for students. It has now been complicated by shocking governmental pressures on universities to supply information about students which they have received in professional confidence. The comparative dependency of American college youth is a scandal in the Western world: in California recently, young university students were indifferently treated as infants and as swine by police assigned to keep order at hearings of the House Un-American Activities Committee. It is perhaps for partial escape from these conditions that many a student of today turns toward a college culture of work-study-sociability. This sector, if one takes into account the large number of students who are involved, the scale of their efforts, the variety of their part-time occupations, and the linkage of their work with the newer leisure in the United States, amounts to a new thing on the American scene.

Even the recent recession did not prevent about two million students from finding summer work and thus continuing that dramatic re-entrance of youth into the labor force that occurred during and after World War II, reversing the youthful joblessness of the Depression. The new employment of the American student on a part-time basis involves every industry, skill, and role, but much of its impetus comes from the seasonal, the service, and the tourist trades. The young American student in high school or college bases his expenditures on a budget in which public scholarship, private scholarship, family support, and self-earnings are often all present. This youthful work economy is not, by and large, vocationally directed, even though it may serve as a way of trying out possible occupations. It is rather a form of paid sociability combined with study, an existence in which the student-waiter brings some of the campus to the resort and uses the pool after hours. Even if it does not reach these pleasant heights, it possesses a general, national quality that is to be recognized anywhere. It is dependent upon the newer service-centered economy that we associate with the resort, the marina, the bowling alley, the camp, the summer campus, the summer music school, the baby-sitting guild, the campus research project, the young straw-hat theater, the youth hostel, and all the rest.

These new social scenes of experience-seeking youth have been created by public education, the increase of the average family income, the rise of leisure expenditures, the urban public programs of recreation, the national parks, the

---

* Editor's note: *in loco parentis*—theory that schools act "in the place of parents."

extension works of the farm bureaus and the state universities, the expansion of audiences for art and music, the increasing "brow" tone of resorts, the rise of the conference trade (every topic has its conference, just as every trade has its convention), and a variety of other forces that seem to have dropped a Chautauqua tent over the country from Eastport to San Diego. It is no chore for the nation to support thousands of young ski-bums, some from mansions and some from shanty towns. The right to self-supporting adventure at work, taken away from youth by automation and unionization at the beginning of the century, has been given back with a premium in the latter part of the century. Thousands are still excluded from this subsidized playground by reason of race or other conditions of servitude, but the remarkable thing is how many are in. Even without the glamor, there are more spots in the United States today where kids can work in a beanery in the morning and study Sanskrit or folk dancing in the afternoon than there were saloons in the Old West or sweat shops in the Old East Side.

12   These scenes of youthful work-play-and-study are pervasive but not universal, and even the young who enjoy them most are prone to anxiety. The reasons vary. One of the main reasons seems to be that, although wealthy and conservative nations such as the United States want their children to be responsible and obedient rather than aggressive and full of initiative, they hesitate to admit it. The extraordinary interest of the American parent in the early occupational specialization of the young male is one sign of this. With the decline of status associated with class and family the vacuum has been filled by status associated with the professional badge. Again, in *The Lonely Crowd*, David Riesman, Nathan Glazer, and I observed that many young people seemed to care more about "fitting in" with their friends and their society than ever before. A study of this theme among both students and their parents, by John and Mathilda Riley, seems to show that parents are hardly less interested in the conformity of their young than the young themselves. What lies under these appearances of complaisance?

13   In search of the self concept, some of the young prefer to be known, after seventeen or so, by the somewhat starchy title of "young adults." On the other hand, a fluent loose-jointedness, restlessness alternating with catatonic repose, can be found in all classes of the young. "Like *this* or like that, *man*," so popular a construction in their speech, suggests a feeling for life that is both tentative and metaphorical. Youth can be so different from itself, as it moves from role to role, that it still maintains, even in a society devoted to publicity, a great capacity for concealment. This masquerade, and the range of youth, and the pace of change, make it difficult to generalize about the young. There was the young high-school graduate who recently dared the disapproval of his community by rejecting the award of a veterans' group whose attitudes he did not honor. On the other hand, there are the hot-rodders who perpetually hum "Transfusion," by Nervous Norbus:

> Toolin' down the highway doin' 79
> I'm a twin-pipe poppa
> And I'm feelin' fine.
> Hey, dig that!
> Was that a red stop sign?

(Sound of crash)
Transfusion, Transfusion!

It seems that young people are living through a change in the character structure of our society and that they show it in their response to public events. The modern mass media have made it possible for a glamorous academic to use cribbed answers on a TV show. Seven-eighths of the students polled at his own school (Columbia University) sympathized with the fallen hero, and many found occasions to make excuses for him. An almost equal number of mid-Western high-school students responded in more or less the same way. Many of the grounds offered by the students for minimizing the star's offense seem lax and complacent. On the other hand, there is something worthy of attention in the observation by some of these students that the difference between entertaining fiction and intellectual fraud in the mass media is an ambiguous matter. The difference depends in part on conventions linking the program with the audience and on the sophistication of the audience itself. It seemed fantastic to many of these young people that the audience could take the quiz programs as anything but a circus in which the phoney was an admitted part of the game.

A comment by Edgar Z. Friedenberg in *The Vanishing Adolescent* seems to me to be very much to the point here. "It must be taken for granted that in many respects our conception of integrity is obsolete; we include in it many ways of feeling and acting that acquired their social significance under social conditions that no longer exist." He goes on to say that "individualism, which led to success in a society dominated by the economic necessities of industrialization and empire, is a poor model for the young today." I myself am particularly impressed by the difficulties in judgement induced by the unequal socialization of the older and the younger people in the mass media. The older people are the more literal, more censorship-minded, and more out of touch in their response to the mass media. They often label as cynical a youthful response to the mass media that is based on skills they do not possess. This occurs in each generation, of course, but there is reason to think that the very rapid increase in the younger educated groups has recently widened the gap between the fifteen-year-old and the fifty-year-old in our society. The second most popular public visiting place for service men in New York, after the Empire State Building, is the Museum of Modern Art. This suggests that young people in general are increasingly the participants in a cosmopolitan culture from which most older members of the society, because of provincialism and lack of training, are excluded. An apt illustration of this is the fact that young people have generally had ample opportunity to enjoy the *double entendre* of a new jazz or calypso record by the time adult ears have understood it and banned it from the air.

Admittedly, there is much evidence that many of the youthful population are notable chiefly for their traditionalism. Readers of reports by H. H. Remmers and D. H. Radler of Purdue University have been shocked by their findings in recent years. They show that a general, low evaluation of tolerance for diverse viewpoints in the adult population (as shown by Samuel A. Stouffer in *Communism, Conformity and Civil Liberties*) is also quite widely distributed among the high-school students of the country. These young people are "traditional" in the sense that they continue a habit of disrespect for traditional American liberties of conscience, free speech, and the press. Even if it is not quite clear whether they always understood what they were saying in their answers to Remmers and Radler, the number of them who took an authoritarian position is disturbing. There are so many of them for each one of the Southern white girls who followed their beliefs about the sit-ins right into the sheriff's office. Indeed, it is quite possible that a hell-fearing intensity in personal morality can cool off, not toward a greater liberality in view of the self and of others, but toward a defensive self-righteousness. This apparently defensive form of illiberality, as found among the youth of some rural areas, is perhaps associated with the strain between facts and appearances in the political life of the regions. The co-authors of *Small Town in Mass Society* suggest that the less these towns control their own political destiny, the more they talk about the virtues of local self-rule. In such situations, the young are presented with adult models who preach nineteenth-century individualism while reaching for twentieth-century subsidies.

17 The question of the general character structure of the young, in contrast to previous generations, is complicated, of course, by changes in the sexes' roles. The convergence in these roles makes it possible to say that much of what has been suggested in this article so far is as true for young women as for young men. The intersexual, like the interethnic, feelings of the young used to play across a social and sociable space rather crudely organized in terms of class and ethnic endogamy, economic values, and an array of class-spaced and sex-separated church-goings, sports, and other occasions for entertainment. Today the sociable activities in which the sexes are separated still continue their long decline. Such things as the men's club are retained more firmly by the few Greek-Americans of the city corner than they are by the rich or the educated.

18 The slow but steady increase in privileges for women (including the privilege of working hard both at home and on the job) is a mixed matter in the United States. For one thing, it derives partly from a frontier scarcity of women which no longer prevails. For another, it is marked by considerable inequalities for women of various social and ethnic groups. What is even more important, the newer freedoms of women, including young women, has been vitiated by the absence of ideal types. The adulation of Mrs. Roosevelt among widely varying social groups might be considered evidence for the hunger felt by American women (and men too) for what an aristocratic tradition might have bequeathed to American women had it ever existed in strength. The most general development for young women is that they are increasingly permitted to enter the labor force at higher and higher levels, but that few have the resources, especially economic ones, to control both a job and a home. Despite the movement toward younger marriages, a declining divorce rate, and the newer "cooperative" marriage (in which the family life gets rationalized like a business, or parceled out in roles like an *atelier*) many young women seem to regard caring for husbands and trotting after children as the unexciting payments they make on an insurance policy. The tendency toward younger marriages also seems to have threatened the postschool period of work-and-leisure that women's magazines define as every American girl's birthright as a single person.

There are some signs of relief in the younger feminine generation at the widened range of interests of American middle-class males. Nothing seems to have failed so grandly on the American scene of the last twenty years as the frontier, rural, hair-on-the-chest version of masculinity. This is surely related to the declining demand for labor in the extractive and farming enterprises—we can produce with less than ten percent of our work force enough food to make young Americans, like their parents, generally overweight. If the muscular pose still persists on the more or less rural and Western co-ed school scene, it is on the defensive even there. Young men and women are aware that the ambitious young fellow of today is as likely to be aiming for a position on the charity or ballet board as he is for a golf club membership—the more so the higher his corporate ambitions are.

They are also aware that scientists consider themselves licensed to feel bored with other scientists who do not play the classical guitar or translate verse. The culture of the small town, the range states, and the small business enclave still fights for the old male ideal by dint of bars furnished with longhorns and fast talk about oil wells. Although some of this is a genuine remnant of frontier culture and not a sagebrush stage set for the farm lobby, it is remarkable how much it needs to be sustained by mythology. No young males enjoy the imagery of the ruggedly individualistic more than those of the arid rural states do—states that would hardly break even were it not for federal subsidies of farm products, metal and water resources, and the returns of tourist bars, dude ranches, gambling tables, and graft on the public lands. One of the most observable shifts of fashion among young people since World War II is that toward the subtle, the Italianate, the pale, and the pensive. The wholesome frontier blonde and the stubbled football player have gone out of fashion as hero and heroine.

As a drama, the life of American youth today presents itself in a bigger cast than ever, playing on a wider screen. Youth plays a role to which the word "juvenile" can no longer be applied, because, while this word once meant someone up to fourteen or so, it now means a grammar-school youngster—or a book written for one. There is evidence as to young people in the decline of books intended for the twelve- to sixteen-year-old—today *Tom Swift* would not pass much muster with much younger readers, and *Ann of Green Gables* could not compete with *Mademoiselle*.

Questions for Comprehension

1. In paragraph 2 how does the author generalize about the young?
2. What does the author mean by "the age of extended socialization"?
3. What is the "widening of privileges" Denney sees among the young at the time he is writing?
4. What are the two trends that Denney says will be felt by the young at the same time?
5. According to the author, what are the major effects of education on the young?

6. What does the author mean by the "comparative dependency" of college youth?
7. How are *work* and *leisure* linked for American young people?
8. According to Denney, what are some of the reasons for anxiety among the young?
9. What roles does traditionalism play among the young?
10. What changes are taking place in the role of women, according to the author?

■

YOUTH IN AMERICA

Tad Szulc

Born in Poland in 1926, Tad Szulc was for nearly twenty years a correspondent in Southeast Asia, Latin America, Spain, eastern Europe, the Middle East, and Washington for the *New York Times*. Since then, he has lectured widely on foreign affairs and American culture. A prolific author, his books include *Twilight of the Tyrants* (1959), *The Dominican Diary* (1965), *Compulsive Spy* (1973), and *The Illusion of Peace: Foreign Policy in the Nixon Years* (1978). "Youth in America" is taken from Szulc's 1974 book about American culture, *Innocents at Home*. In the selection reprinted here, he discusses the younger generation of the late 1960s.

I am not sure I know precisely what aroused American youth in the 1960s to become a rebel generation. These boys and girls, born during the beginning of the cold war and the Korean war, were reaching adolescence and young adulthood and replacing the "silent generation" of the 1950s, the last children of the Great Depression and the first war babies. (Nowadays, this "silent generation" is fully parental and at the threshold of middle age. I daresay they were as perplexed by the emergence of the rebels as we were in our somewhat more advanced age.) It was an astonishingly varied and multifaceted phenomenon, particularly when one considers that it was carried out by a minority of the nation's youth, perhaps just a few million of them.

Yet the youth rebellion had an enormous influence on America's thinking and policies. It pushed the political parties into a new round of social concerns and commitments—the 1972 presidential campaign made this quite evident, even if after his reelection President Nixon backpedaled on the nation's social problems—and forced the first fundamental changes in the philosophy of higher education since the days of John Dewey,* along with a major cultural revival.

Young Americans questioned the authority of a government that ill-governed and cared not enough, that was lost in an endless Asian war and its own bureaucratic bigness. They questioned the power of corporations and the relevance of teachers who did not teach and considered little about anything except their own tenure and the compulsion to "publish or perish." At first, these young-

---

* Editor's note: American philosopher and educator (1859–1952).

sters were perceived as destructive; in time it dawned on a great many people that, disorderly as it seemed, their protest was an essentially constructive process. Thus the young gained a voice in the fashioning of their own destinies.

Like everything in America, the youth rebellion had a touch of the sublime and a touch of the ridiculous. It reeked of contradiction, it was dizzyingly mercurial, it abhorred any form of leadership, it displayed intellectual brilliance and deep naiveté, and, inevitably, it blended inspiring idealism with cheap and irresponsible opportunism. It had to shout out everything "like it is," leaving nothing to imagination. It was irreverent and enamored of freedom, if not of duty. It talked incessantly of love, its members were "brothers and sisters," yet it was cruel. There was nothing quite like young Americans anywhere in the world—and they were quickly imitated everywhere.

Everything overlapped. The youth revolt had something for everybody, but not always enough for most. The rebellion was politics when it came to the Vietnam war or racial relations. It was "student power" and the rejection of the "irrelevant" in education. It was the need to "relate" to people in an alienated society. It was attire, hair, sex, drugs, the discovery of nature and beauty and art and natural foods, new life styles without end. And, of course, the young were used by anybody who had any kind of axe to grind.

The initial political position taken up in advocacy of the civil-rights movement touched off a national youth rebellion which, in short order, turned against the Vietnam war and then against the entire structure of the American state. So short-circuited had the pattern of ideas become that support for the Vietcong and North Vietnam—expressed in adolescent chants about "Uncle Ho" and the defiant hoisting of red-and-blue Vietcong flags—was quickly transmuted into ideological positions taken up against American "imperialism," "corporate state," and capitalism. Hence bomb and arson attacks on banks, police stations, corporate offices, ROTC centers, and armories—the "centers of imperialism." Strongly influenced by the SDS,* the only seriously structured movement to emerge briefly from an otherwise unorchestrated political rebellion (SDS split in 1968 into the armed-action Weatherpeople faction and the quasi-Maoist-Marxist-Leninist Progressive Labor faction, rapidly losing its national influence), uncounted thousands chaotically joined New Left and neo-New Left groups. There were Yippies, factions of rampaging "Crazies," and, later, "Zippies." The large Socialist Youth Alliance, key in the antiwar movement, quarreled with the pro-terror Weatherpeople and the class-conscious "Revolutionary Marxists."

Support for blacks at home soon extended to all minorities and, quickly, to the "Third World" and to an infatuation with revolutionary Cuba and every "liberation movement" in the world. Several thousand young Americans traveled to Cuba individually or as members of the "Venceremos" brigades to cut cane and harvest vegetables for the Cubans, gain ideological indoctrination, and, allegedly but unprovably, receive guerrilla and sabotage training. It is a matter of record, however, that a number of those who had gone to Cuba were later implicated in bombings and other terrorist acts at home. (The National Committee of the

---

* Editor's note: Students for a Democratic Society.

Venceremos Brigades was a dedicated and highly ideological extreme leftist group. Its members bought, sold, and read *Granma*, the Cuban government's official newspaper—it could be obtained openly in New York, Berkeley, and elsewhere—and disseminated propaganda in favor of revolutionary Cuba.)

In this affinity with the Third World, an old American humanist tradition was present, though probably not consciously accepted. Defenders of Asian, African, and Latin American freedoms were the heirs to the Americans who had once gone overseas as missionaries, doctors, and nurses. Their immediate forerunners were the Peace Corps volunteers whom John F. Kennedy had energized into helping the poor and the sick abroad in an American mission for humanity. It made absolute sense to me that in 1965 the Peace Corps volunteers actively aided the rebels in the Dominican Republic against right-wing military forces and the U.S. troops sent there to back the generals. I saw them at work in Dominican hospitals (one of them was a blind volunteer) under air and artillery bombardment, and I was never so impressed by a group of young Americans as in those grim days in Santo Domingo.

The great political battle fought by the young rebels in support of Senator Eugene McCarthy* during the "Days of Rage" at the Democratic National Convention in Chicago in 1968 was the most violent and the ugliest American confrontation between kids and Establishment. The youthful workers for Senator George McGovern† in 1972 were the calmer and more pragmatic successors of the Chicago warriors. But now, having talked to scores of Chicago veterans, I have my doubts as to what extent those young people really wanted McCarthy nominated back in 1968. I'm inclined to think that the convention simply provided them with a perfect setting for protest against the war and the Establishment. Would they, I wondered, have worked in the campaign for Robert Kennedy had he lived and been nominated? Chatting with McCarthy late in 1971, just before he announced his short-lived candidacy for 1972, I found him so totally detached and aloof from his one-time constituency that it was almost impossible to visualize him as their champion only three years earlier.

In any event, the Establishment, which has a demonstrable talent for overreaction and overkill, played right into the hands of the rebels by having them brutalized by the Chicago police and staging politically motivated trials against their seven more mature leaders. This proved to young people (and to many others) that brute force is the only response of which the Establishment is capable when it is challenged—which, of course, it was. Other challenges came at Berkeley's "People's Park," Kent State, and Jackson in 1970, bringing deaths to students at the hands of those charged with intelligently maintaining peace and order. Chicago, Berkeley, Kent, Jackson, Lawrence, Baton Rouge,‡ and so many other events of these years deepened their cynicism and alienation. Their political candidates had been defeated, the government would not end the Indochina war, racism could not be eliminated overnight, the government went on ignoring

---

* Editor's note: Antiwar senator (b. 1916) who sought the Democratic presidential nomination in 1968.
† Editor's note: Democratic candidate for president in 1972 (b. 1922).
‡ Editor's note: Scenes of violent confrontations between established authority and youth.

misery and injustice and applying maximal police power against dissidents in the streets. So the "pig"—the policeman—became the official enemy of the young, and, inevitably, the harried police perceived the young as their enemy.

Another major ingredient of the youth rebellion was concern with environment and ecology. Young people who were aghast over the erosion of moral values in America—they believed these were being destroyed by the ruling generation's materialism, opportunism, and obeisance before the almighty dollar—now came to believe that for decades the country was being physically fouled by every conceivable type of pollution of land, water, and air. They became aware that much of the United States was being turned into a gigantic garbage dump, that the nation's beautiful land and seascapes were being mutilated by urban honky-tonks, gray impersonal superhighways, and overwhelming works of industry. They saw the huge open-pit mines in the midst of wilderness, offshore drilling rigs, oil spills on the beaches, and fluvial transportation canals slashing across wildlife preserves. They saw the rats in the streets of the ghettos, and dead fish and dead birds on the beaches.

Defense of the environment and of ecological balance became, at least for a while, one of the loudest battle cries. Consumerism was another popular cause, intimately related to the protection of the environment. And all these concerns fed into the overriding opposition to the bigness and impersonality of American corporate and political structures.

Questions for Comprehension

1. What broad effects did the youth rebellion of the late 1960s have on "American thinking and politics"?
2. In what ways did the youth rebellion have a "touch of the sublime and a touch of the ridiculous"?
3. What was the significance of the "Days of Rage" in 1968 for the younger generation?
4. What does Szulc mean by saying that "everything overlapped" in the youth rebellion?
5. What were the major targets of the youth rebellion?
6. How did the young feel about materialism?
7. What other concerns does Szulc list as important to young people in the late 1960s?

■

COLLEGE YOUTH ATTITUDES TODAY

Rolf A. Weil

Rolf A. Weil, born in Germany in 1921, holds a Ph.D. from the University of Chicago. He began his career doing research in economics for private industry and government. In 1946 he joined the faculty of Roosevelt University in Chicago and remained there, frequently publishing articles in professional journals. In 1966 Weil was named president of Roosevelt University.

The article reprinted here from the educational journal *School and Society* gives Weil's portrait of the younger generation in 1971.

This is the age of the behavioral scientist who, armed with attitude scales and other complex tools contained in his black bag of tricks, attempts to uncover the secrets of attitude development. Perhaps such scholars could give greater enlightenment on the perplexing youth culture of today than could a university administrator who has a functional responsibility that calls for quick judgment and immediate action. However, I shall attempt to catalog objectively the important attitudes of college youth as I know them. Where possible, I shall try to explain the evolution of these attitudes and indicate intelligent societal responses.

Questioning of Values and Authority
This generation, for better or for worse, has been raised in a highly permissive environment. Values are not accepted on faith or by parental authority. There is an experimental and questioning spirit and a desire to learn from experience. It may be costly to reject the wisdom of the ages, but the young have a fervent desire to "make it on their own," even if it means rediscovering the wheel.

Rejection of Materialism
The youths of today tend to reject materialism, at least during their college years. This is particularly true of young people from middle- and upper-class backgrounds who can enjoy a short period of simulated poverty secure in the knowledge that their families will be standing by to shower them lovingly with necessities or luxuries whenever called upon to do so.

Commitment to Tolerance
This generation of students, compared to ours, is much more liberal in its attitudes, on sex, drugs, or religion. There is no adequate evidence to support the contention of some that there is more promiscuity among young people today, but they are more open and honest about sexual matters. It also is not established that college youths take more drugs than others in society, but again, the drug user is tolerated and society's laws in this respect are questioned. Both the atheist and the Christian fundamentalist are respected for "doing their own thing." Even cultists do not face ostracism.

Genuine Idealism
There is no doubt that this generation of college students is more idealistic and more genuinely honest with regard to the need for righting the wrongs of society. Racial and ethnic discrimination are denounced almost universally and, what is more, not practiced. Unemployment, pollution, restrictions on birth control, excessive nationalism, and militarism are denounced and opposed.

Challenging the "Establishment"
Students with youthful vigor enjoy challenging the older generation's assumed virtues. Taking pot-shots at the establishment has become a competitive sport.

The young have become masters of the "put on" and the "needle" and love to demolish the lip-service idealism and occasional hypocrisy of the older generation.

The Claim of Individualism
Young people like to think of themselves as individuals, but they actually have become highly conformist themselves as evidenced by the fashion and hair style rebellion, as well as in the use of their new code language in which they seem to find semantic security.

The Trend to One-Way Communication
We hear a great deal about the need for communication with the older generation and that generation's willingness to listen, but youth tends to be intolerant of the other fellow's point of view. As far as the young are concerned, "listening" frequently means agreeing with their values.

The Search for Self-Fulfillment
Our young men and women deeply are concerned with finding themselves and "rap" endlessly about romantic notions regarding the pastoral life, communal living, and utopias of all types.

Ambivalence about Violence
In general, college youths sincerely are opposed to war and violence, but an increasing number of nonviolent people seem to be justifying the use of terrorist methods by those who have given up on the system. There is a tendency to rationalize the use of coercive means to attain "just" ends. The definition of violence also has become dangerously flexible—building take-overs, bomb threats, false fire alarms, implied threats of physical harm, and the use of weapons for "defense," etc., often are termed "nonviolent."

Realism Among Black Youths
Although black college youths share in most of the general characteristics of students, there exists among them greater realism, more bitterness about past injustice, and greater disappointment about as yet unrealized aspirations. As a result, black rhetoric seems more threatening in a physical sense, and demands have more of a bread-and-butter orientation.

Loyalty to the Youth Culture
There has developed among college students a deep loyalty to the youth culture which transcends racial and political lines. Loyalty to each other frequently has driven young people of divergent views into solidarity against the rules of the "establishment."

    I have tried to list some of the prevalent attitudes of the youths of America today. Obviously, there are great deviations from these generalizations, but I believe we must start with these in order to understand the youth culture.

These attitudes evolved as a result of the environment in which this generation of college students has grown to maturity. I would emphasize the following factors as particularly important: permissive upbringing; war as a constant during their lifetime, with the U.S. engaged since 1950 in almost uninterrupted combat; the logic and rhetoric of the civil rights movement; affluence and its impact on success motivation; the boredom and emptiness of the lives of many adults; and the emphasis on technology and the absence of religious or ethical commitment.

What lessons can we learn from a study of these youth attitudes? Obviously, I only can speculate, but here are a few tentative conclusions.

Society—especially parents, school, church, and government—must be totally honest, with greater consistency than ever before. This does not mean that we necessarily must substitute the values of the young for ours, but we must mean what we preach or stop preaching. Universities, particularly, consistently must reexamine rules and regulations and must bring them into conformity with the realities of campus life. Curricula must conform increasingly to the needs of a new type of student population resulting from society's decision for universal higher education. Curricular emphasis may have to be restructured to meet the changes in taste from the technological to the humane and from the theoretical to the applied. We must be firm in our commitment to freedom of expression for all and equally firm in suppressing the will of those who want to accomplish their objectives through coercive techniques. We must stop pretending that the universities are either like corporations or like governments. Participatory democracy as some propose is a practical impossibility and incompatible with *bona fide* education.

In conclusion, I am confident that this generation of bright young people will meet the challenges of the future at least as successfully as we have met the challenges of the past. I suspect that they will raise their children with less permissiveness, that they will be more open and honest, and that they will make as many mistakes as we have made. They will survive, and I hope that we also can live through the difficult transition in our system of values.

Questions for Comprehension

1. What does Weil announce as the purpose of his essay?
2. What contradiction can you find in the essay to the "commitment to tolerance" Weil mentions?
3. What does the author say about youth's claims of individualism?
4. What attitude does the younger generation have toward authority and established values?
5. What are the consequences of the loyalty young people display toward the "youth culture"?
6. What does Weil say are the causes of the attitudes of the younger generation?
7. According to Weil, how should society respond to the younger generation?
8. What does the author see in the future for the young people he is discussing?

NOW, THE SELF-CENTERED GENERATION

The Editors of Time

Time magazine regularly covers the young people of the day for its readers. Like the 1951 article included in the comparison project, this September 23, 1974, article gives a wide-ranging list of characteristics of the younger generation. It also suggests some comparisons with the younger generations of the fifties and sixties.

A new spirit clearly dominates U.S. college campuses as 8.6 million young people begin the fall term this month. Not since the 1950s have students been so pragmatic in their outlook, so highly oriented toward careers and financial security. Deeply worried about an economy that is fraught with future uncertainties, overwhelmingly concerned with preparing for lucrative and satisfying jobs, today's college students can be fairly characterized as the Self-Centered Generation.

Once the draft and the threat of the Viet Nam War ended, American campuses reverted to a normality of sorts. The old political activism and revolutionary fervor have disappeared entirely. Indeed, the shifts in student attitudes and outlook since the late 1960s are so startling that they clearly mark the end of an old era and the beginning of a new one.

"Unwanted Group"
The mood is strikingly similar to that of the 1950s Silent Generation, in that today's students are chiefly concerned with their own personal lives. Says Senior Steve Ainsworth, 21, former editor of the *Daily Bruin*, the student newspaper at the University of California at Los Angeles: "The mood is, 'I'm here for me.' The kids are preoccupied with going into the mainstream of economic life."

But the analogy to the 1950s is only partly valid. Studies by Daniel Yankelovich, the public-opinion analyst who periodically surveys American youth, document the fact that the social and moral values that flourished on campus in the 1960s "have grown stronger and more powerful." More liberal sexual mores, a lessening of automatic obedience to established authority and skepticism about the U.S. political process seem to have become fixed characteristics of most American young people.

The overriding influence on student attitudes today is the economy. *Time* reporters recently visited two dozen campuses and found that the greatest worry among students is that there will be no jobs for them after graduation. Says Princeton Junior Peter Seldin: "It's depressing to be part of an unwanted group." Moreover, as part of the enduring heritage of the 1960s, students want their careers to provide them with greater self-expression and self-fulfillment as well as high salaries. That is a significant departure from what young people sought in the 1950s and substantially narrows their future job options.

Students are most interested in preparing for professions like law, medicine and architecture. Claims Senior Judy Wandzilak, 21, of Boston University, "The gut [easy] course is no longer avidly sought. Students can't afford to waste their time and money. They are seeking tangible, not spiritual returns for their investment in a university."

More often than not, freshmen (or "freshpersons" as some feminists solemnly call them) enter college with firm ideas about what courses will prepare them for their chosen careers. Nearly everywhere, chemistry, biology, engineering and business administration classes are packed while enrollments are dwindling in history, philosophy and the other liberal arts. Quips Tony Peyser, 20, a student in film making at U.C.L.A.: "English is the best prerequisite for unemployment." Black studies courses are being cut back at some campuses because most black students prefer majors that lead directly to a career.

Young people are approaching their studies with newfound seriousness, crowding into college libraries and competing feverishly for grades. Observes Yale Philosophy Professor Michael Williams, 27: "There's not much goofing off these days." At Brandeis University in Waltham, Mass., close to a third of the 690 freshmen told school officials that they hope to be medical doctors. Shoving matches broke out among some students in the crush to register for pre-med courses. In one dormitory at the University of Kansas, some 250 students expressed interest in a remedial clinic that aims to raise their grades by improving their reading and study skills. Last year only six students wanted to take the optional course.

No Regulations

Inflation has contributed significantly to students' newly sober attitude toward higher education. A year's average tuition and room and board at a private college costs about $3,200; at many schools the total is close to $5,000. "One of the first things the students do is look for part-time jobs," says Eileen Roberson, director of student employment at Simmons College in Boston. Among the most common jobs: waiting on table, manning switchboards and doing research for professors.

Partly because students want to save money, there is a renewed interest in communal living in dormitories as an alternative to more expensive off-campus apartments. Quite a few colleges have abolished most dormitory rules. At Berkeley, says Ben Leifer, 21, a graduate student in public health, "there are virtually no regulations except be discreet, mind your own business and don't bother anyone." Hampshire College in Amherst, Mass., permits students in dormitory suites to choose their own roommates—of whatever sex.

The desire for communal living, as well as the return to normality, has been chiefly responsible for the resurgence of college fraternities and sororities. At the University of California at Berkeley, which gave birth to the student counterculture with the Free Speech Movement ten years ago, the number of fraternities has risen from 24 in 1971 to 28 now; ten others want to reopen chapters that were closed in the 1960s for lack of members.

"Prudes' Palace"

At most colleges, the sexual revolution is over, premarital sex and cohabitation among unmarried students are accepted as a matter of course. More recently, students at many campuses have become highly tolerant of homosexual and bisexual behavior. Among the most extreme avant-garde students at Berkeley and Columbia, it has become fashionable to have a homosexual or bisexual experience. On the other hand, at some campuses there has been a noticeable reaction against the new permissiveness. For example, one women's dormitory at the University of Michigan used to be sniggeringly called "Prudes' Palace" or the "Virgin Vault" because men were banned above the first floor during weekdays. This year, however, it has a waiting list of more than 50 coeds.

The student orientation toward jobs has even contributed to the comeback on campus of beer and liquor, since many students fear that a drug arrest might ruin their chances for a successful career. Moreover, they often find alcohol to be cheaper than drugs, which have been hard hit by inflation. At Boston University, Quaaludes have gone from 30 cents a tablet to as high as $3, at the University of Michigan, an ounce of marijuana costs as much as $15, up from $12 last year.

For all their new seriousness, students still blow off steam. They have rediscovered some old fads—panty raids at the University of Michigan and the twist at Houston's Rice University—and some other fancies as well. Among undergraduates at Wake Forest University in Winston-Salem, N.C., rides in large coin-operated clothes dryers are the latest thrill—with the door open or, more dangerously because of the heat, with it closed. Admits Junior Steve Wildey, 20: "It sounds kind of dumb. But after a few beers, it seems like an entirely reasonable thing to do."

Most disturbing for the nation's future, students demonstrate almost no interest in political activities, on or off campus. There are rare exceptions. In 21 states, small numbers of student activists operate public-interest research groups, which lobby for education bills in state legislatures and try to influence state politics. For example, New York's group recently published pamphlet-size political profiles of each of the 60 senators and 150 assemblymen who are running for re-election to the state legislature.

Moreover, many young people still follow and react to big political developments, though not to the rancorous extremes of a few years ago. Not surprisingly, President Ford's promise of limited amnesty for Viet Nam War–era deserters and draft dodgers won him a measure of popularity in campus communities, while his full pardon of former President Nixon produced cries of outrage. On a Sunday evening a student called a talk show in Lawrence, Kansas, and suggested that instead of pardoning Nixon, Ford should have urged him to go to Canada.

Afraid to Believe
For the most part, however, students seem unwilling to involve themselves directly in the U.S. political process. A recent survey showed that half of the students polled at the University of Missouri are not even registered to vote. At the University of Kansas, campus Democrats concluded after a poll that large numbers of students did not know that State Attorney General Vern Miller was a candidate for Governor, even though he had gained much notoriety for his flamboyant drug arrests of Kansas students. At the University of Wisconsin, says Tim Tully, 28, a graduate student and veteran radical of the 1960s, "all the activity of late in Madison, political or otherwise, would fit in a shot glass."

Indeed, not even Watergate reignited students' interest in politics. According to Yankelovich, more than six out of ten young people believe that "special interests" run the nation's political machinery. Similarly, George Mihaly, president of Gilbert Youth Research of New York City, recently found that only about 1% of students are thinking of politics as a career. "We know that people and movements are fallible," observes Margie Corbett, 21, a junior at American University in Washington. "We're afraid to believe too much in anything or anyone." Thus the overwhelming majority of students today are far more intent on using their college education as a means of entering the American system than as preparation for reforming it.

Questions for Comprehension

1. What dominant impression do the authors have of the younger generation of 1974?
2. To what do they attribute the change they see?
3. What similarity do the authors see between the youth of their day and the youth of the 1950s?
4. What is the "overriding influence on student attitudes," and how have students reacted to it?
5. What has changed in the attitudes of students to their studies?
6. What has been the impact of economic inflation on student attitudes toward higher education?
7. What attitudes toward sex seem prevalent to the authors?
8. How does the younger generation "blow off steam"?
9. How does the younger generation feel about political involvement?

■

WHO ARE WE? A SELF-PORTRAIT OF COLLEGE STUDENTS TODAY

David Wank

David Wank graduated from Oberlin College four years before he wrote this article. At the time the article appeared in Ms. magazine in 1984, he had taught and studied in China for two years and had worked as a daily reporter in Washington and New Orleans.

The persistent beat of the GoGo's sets the pace at campus parties, and beer, lots of it, is the thing to drink. Nautilus rooms are where the chic and the sweaty socialize. Guest speakers lecture on job trends, and *In Search of Excellence*, a book touting the glories of corporate America, is a best-seller in campus bookstores. Ethnic studies and soc majors are "out"; computer programming and marketing are "in." But a look behind the music and the machines reveals a different side. Students are forming more political organizations than ever before. Attendance in campus churches and synagogues is skyrocketing. And classes on war and peace issues are now being offered in response to student fears of nuclear war. A concern for personal success rivals an equally strong concern for global survival.

In my interviews with dozens of students on a variety of campuses, I was struck by contradictions, confusion, and most of all, diversity. Their answers to questions about goals, values, lifestyles, and politics defy easy generalization. Pragmatism exists alongside idealism. Concerns for high salaries are tempered by dreams for self-fulfillment. Apathy and activism are both present. On many campuses, promiscuity coexists with chastity (and both are tolerated). There is a sense among students that a new kind of society is emerging but has yet to take shape. The issues of the day—the role of women, America's economic decline, the nuclear arms race, the place of computers in society—raise questions students know they will have to resolve. While pushing ahead in their personal lives, they are still in search of answers to these larger questions. "I'm always open to hearing both sides of an issue," said Janet Friday, at Dartmouth. "But everything is so complicated. I'm not ready to take a stand on anything yet."

High Ideals, High Salaries, or High Times?

"Students have a sense that this is not four years to waste," said Jim Newton, publisher of a student newspaper at Dartmouth College. "They want to choose a path that will pay off." An annual survey on freshmen attitudes by the American Council on Education bears this out. Last year 76.2 percent of all freshmen said they went to college to get a better job. Business administration and accounting were the most popular majors. Almost 70 percent of the freshmen hoped to become very well-off financially. "I call it the 'Titanic ethic': there's a feeling that if the ship is going down why not go first-class?" said Dr. Arthur Levine, president of Bradford College and author of *When Dreams and Heroes Died* (Jossey-Bass) and other works on student attitudes.

Students are bringing their job angst to campus career offices in record numbers. "If you looked into our career library, you'd find yourself tripping over the bodies," said Lanna Hagge, director of the Office of Career Development and Placement at Oberlin College.

To enhance their job prospects, students are mastering computers. "If you want to be successful, you've got to learn computers," said Dazon Dixon of Spelman College. "I've already taken one class and I'm still trying to catch up." But some modern day Luddites are spurning computers. "Everyone's dependence on machines just drives me up a wall," said Kirsten Speidel of Oberlin College. Speidel is studying Russian, Korean, French, and Chinese but refuses to plunge into BASIC.

Some students plan to postpone marriage in order to concentrate on their careers. "I don't see myself getting married until after I'm thirty," said Michelle Pinsky of Dickinson College. "I'd rather have a career." But many women students worry about combining a marriage and career. More realistic than their counterparts five years ago, they no longer buy the myth of "having it all." "They read about all these successful women who have gotten divorced," said Eleanor Bender, a teacher and administrator at Stephens College. "These students haven't even graduated, and they're already worrying about divorce."

Other students worry about the growth of pre-professionalism on campus. "I know people who are trying to resolve what they think they should be doing to make this world a better place and what they are being told to do to guarantee a comfortable life for themselves," said Steve Mines of Dartmouth College. For David Seidenberg of Dartmouth College, the question is one of job fulfillment, not future salary. "I have enough confidence to know I can earn a living. But I am worried about finding something that I'll enjoy doing for a long time."

Daphne Goodson of Spelman College reflects a sixties' idealism in her career choice combined with an eighties' realism of getting there. A drama and mass communications major, Goodson is gaining practical experience by working on voter registration drives and acting in theater productions. "When I get where I'm going, people will hear me," said Goodson. And one of the issues she will speak out on is diminishing opportunities for black college graduates: "The doors that have been opening for blacks since the late 1960s are now closing. The companies have all filled their minority quotas. Now blacks have to work twice as hard and be twice as good to beat out the white man."

Sex, Religion, and Rules

Students sought personal values in the works of social thinkers like Marx, Nietzsche, and Marcuse during the politically charged sixties. In today's more moderate climate, many students are turning to the Bible, Koran, and Talmud in their quest for purpose. A recent Gallup poll shows that 50 percent of all college students feel that religion is important—up from 39 percent five years ago. The chapel at Louisiana State University has grown from a dozen members in 1973 to 1,500 today. Students at the University of New Hampshire have called for the reinstitution of Wednesday-night mass, which was canceled in 1979 for lack of student interest. Jewish students at New York University have formed two new clubs: Chabad, an Orthodox-based youth organization, and the Flame, which teaches Judaic observances. Some link this rebirth of religion to the economy. "In an economic depression, people tend to turn back to traditional institutions," said Katherine Dvorak, a religious studies instructor at Franklin and Marshall College. "They're looking for security."

Students are flocking to classes on religion as well. Enrollment in religion classes at Michigan State University has almost doubled in the past two years. At Dartmouth College religion is the fastest growing department at the school. "Women students come into classes with a more complex agenda for working out issues such as reproduction and family structure," said Dvorak. "And more women are taking classes because of new opportunities opening up for them in religion."

The revolutionary social values of the 1960s have become "mainstreamed," and students are free to choose from a wide array of lifestyles. Sex is now a personal issue. "In the fifties you couldn't say 'yes' and in the sixties you couldn't say 'no'," said Jamie Kahl, a junior at Pennsylvania State University. "Now you're likely to be respected for either choice." A decision to abstain from sex might have nothing to do with traditional morality. "Relationships are draining," said Katherine Kleine of Penn State. "You spend so much energy just going to school. One-night stands can be exhausting and long-term relationships take so much energy to keep together." "I think it is important to allot some sacred space in our lives," explained a Dartmouth senior. "Virginity is my space." Celibacy has indeed become a valid choice.

"There's still a double standard," said a senior woman. "Let's face it: one-night stands are better physically for men than they are for us. Women hope for some kind of closeness to emerge from the experience, but when the guy doesn't call, or is indifferent, it's just another failed attempt at intimacy. And as cynical as this might sound, you feel as if you've given something of yourself for no return."

Long-term relationships still exist, but they are changing. At Wesleyan University, students held a workshop where couples met to talk about problems and contradictions they were having in working toward equality. "Our four-year relationship is exceptional," said a senior from Wesleyan, "but he still feels the pressure to act in charge and to ogle women when he's with his friends. I have enough of that kind of thing every day and don't need to battle him as well."

"I would love to sleep with some of my male friends," said a female student at the University of California at Los Angeles. "But in my group of friends, we don't pair off into couples. It spoils the sense of easy and equal friendship among everyone, and little jealousies pop up. And expectations—like knowing he might call but not minding if he didn't—become tense and self-conscious."

"Of course in college you're free to experiment with all kinds of identities, including sexual ones," said one freshman. In fact, on some campuses bisexuality is chic. "But there's a difference between playful experimentation with other women and being openly lesbian," said a senior woman, who still changes "she" to "he" when talking with straight friends about her lover. Many colleges now have gay/lesbian awareness weeks or dorm raps which dispel some of the myths and animosities about homosexuality. "Away from parental restrictions, I saw a whole spectrum of sexuality and could think about where I fit in," said a sophomore at a small coed school. "I had always had close emotional relations with women, but in college I felt free to act on my erotic feelings as well." There's definitely support on campus. "When you see other women who've made the decision, it's no longer a hypothetical situation—you see a real person you can identify with and know what it meant to her," she added.

But students want a few rules in this too unstructured social climate. They want quiet hours so that they can study in the dorms. Some would like dorm parents to go to for advice. Colleges are also reorganizing the dorms, making it easier for students to meet each other. Dartmouth College is setting up residential clusters in each dorm with spaces for cooking and socializing. "This is the best idea that Dartmouth has had in years," said junior Margaret Pappano. "It's a chance for students to get to know one another in a nonalcoholic, nonpickup atmosphere."

At the large state universities, fraternities and sororities are booming as students seek the security of ersatz families. "This is such a big campus," said Brenda Bogut of Penn State. "It's nice to have the girls in my sorority to turn to."

But Jill Holwager, a senior at the University of California at Los Angeles, who labeled herself an "embittered survivor of the Greek system" took a different view. "Women are grouped together under the auspices of 'sisterhood' and 'support,' but competition, exclusivity, and selfishness are fostered instead." And the administrations at some small colleges agree with this outlook and are pressuring fraternities to halt their drunken, noisy excesses and conform to the intellectual atmosphere on campus. For the eight fraternities and two sororities at Colby college, it's too late: they were shut down last spring.

Feminism's New Face

Feminist gains are taken for granted on many college campuses, though women's centers, nurtured by women's studies programs, are still vital. About 700 schools have women's centers that offer counseling services, bring speakers to campus, and run feminist libraries. Other women's groups, formed spontaneously by students, are showing a new political savvy. Two years ago in the Boston area, women's groups at eight colleges formed the Intercollegiate Women's Coalition (IWC) to pool their numbers. "We discovered that women at different colleges faced the same issues—sexual harassment, campus pornography," said IWC member Barbara Findlen of Boston University. The IWC, which includes Brandeis, MIT, and Wellesley, is presently trying to stop MIT's tradition of showing a pornographic film during registration week.

At black colleges, sororities are often the focal point for feminist activities. "We don't want to separate Greekdom from black sisterhood," said Daphne Goodson, a member of the Delta Sigma Theta Sorority, Inc., at Spelman College. Her sorority works with a rape-crisis center, tutors underprivileged children, and coordinates voter registration drives. "It's a tradition for black sororities to share their education with the community," said Goodson.

Feminists at Dartmouth are being politic about coping with an image problem. "Feminists are seen in two lights," said junior Janet Friday. On the one hand, "they are man-haters who can't deal with relationships with men"; on the other hand, "they believe in equality with men and are fighting for themselves." Because of this image, many women on campus do not call themselves feminist, even though they support feminist positions.

"In the past, women's groups at Dartmouth didn't last long," said Margaret Pappano, a member of the new Dartmouth Women's Issues League. "They would get a radical reputation and membership would dwindle. I joined a sorority," said Pappano, "now I'm seen as a sister—not as a sproutsy type. And as a mainstream woman, I can do more things." To broaden its appeal, the league invites speakers to come and discuss health topics.

Last year, rather than picket fraternities, the league sought legislation to stop a frat practice. Each year fraternities pick attractive women from the freshmen handbook and invite them to serve as hostesses to entice freshmen pledges during rush week. "It might seem like a petty issue, but it's typical of the whole frat brother attitude toward women," said Pappano. "At first the sorority council supported us but backed down when the issue was perceived as a leftist cause." But the league still scored a partial victory; women were still invited, but fewer accepted than in previous years.

The tendency of male professors to favor male students was an issue at Penn State last year. "I get furious when I see male students with closer intellectual relationships to professors than I have even though I'm a better student. The professors just quietly brush me aside and call me 'young lady,'" said a junior woman. The Penn State newspaper ran a series of articles last year called "Chilly Classroom Climate" that explored the problems of women in the classroom. One result of the series was greater student awareness of sexual harassment by professors. "There's a new consciousness among women at Penn," said Whitney Henry, a recent graduate. "Women are more serious about getting on with life. They're not going to stand for getting shortchanged in their education."

Activism '80s Style

"Why It's All Quiet on the Campus Front" headlined an article on college students in *U.S. News and World Report* last year. Many students feel their image as "apathetic," "cynical," or "grinds" is a media creation that results from unfair comparisons with students in the 1960s. Said Paul Chiland, a student photographer for the Penn State newspaper, "In the 1960s, students were demonstrating in the streets. It was a good story and students were labeled political. Now the press has returned to campus. Since they don't see anyone manning the barricades, they've decided we're not political." "The media use 1960s' style activism as a yardstick to measure political activity today," said Dr. Levine. "Students are still active, but they are concerned with different issues and are doing things that are less visible. For example, there's an increase in student litigation."

However, it is true that students as a group are paying less attention to politics today. According to an American Council on Education freshman survey, only 35.1 percent of the 1983 freshman class felt it was important to keep up with politics compared to 54.7 percent in 1970. Some students maintain this is not apathy, but simply alienation from politics. "We keep informed and we discuss the news. Most of my friends voted in the primaries," said David Edwards, a senior at Franklin and Marshall College. "But the issues to get us marching just aren't around any more. The antinuke movement is too abstract." Students may not be marching, but they aren't ignoring the issue of nuclear proliferation either. A course called "Nuclear War and Its Prevention" was offered last year at New York University. And a new course, "Introduction to Peace and War Studies," is being offered at Franklin and Marshall College this fall.

In fact, the number of political groups on campus has almost doubled. The political umbrella groups of the 1960s such as Students for a Democratic Society have broken up, spawning a host of groups focused on single issues—minority opportunity, price-checking in drugstores, save the whales, and so on. "These organizations are less overtly political," said Carol Wilson, editor of *National On-Campus Review*, "and are often concerned with issues that are nonideological."

Many student governments have been transformed from havens for ineffective groups of résumé padders into dynamic organizations with real muscle. Part of this is careerism—budding young lawyers, politicians, and businesspeople want to hone their political and managerial skills. But many student governments actually have a greater responsibility in the 1980s: as a result of the student movement in the 1960s they now control substantial student activity fees. At the University of Connecticut, the student government runs a credit union for students. The student government at the University of Texas at Austin, which now handles $7.5 million, regularly lobbies the state legislature; operates a nightly student escort service; publishes banking and off-campus housing guides; and has just launched a pilot program for peer counseling.

National organizations also figure prominently on the campus political scene. The Ralph Nader-inspired Public Interest Research Groups (PIRG) has branches on more than 100 colleges. The campus PIRGs do things as diverse as evaluating local banking services to warning residents on the dangers of acid rain. Last spring, PIRG organized thousands of students in the first national voter registration drive on campuses since the early seventies. The volunteer intensive drive has a goal of registering one million students.

For students at state schools, concerns over tuition increases, hiring policies, and civil rights violations are no longer dealt with through street demonstrations. Instead, student lobbies in 15 state capitols play legislative politics to get the best deal for the students. The University of California Student Lobby, formed in 1972, was recently rated the twelfth most effective lobby in California. "That makes us tie with Bank-America. Not bad when you consider how much money they have," said director Ron Balestrieri.

However, some issues lend themselves to demonstrations; for example, sit-ins for divestment in South Africa have forced almost 40 schools either to freeze their investments or to partially divest. But most demonstrations are on issues that affect students directly, such as Take Back the Night marches against rape. In fact, very local issues that have an immediate impact on students often incite the most heated outbursts, from the trivial—students at the University of Notre Dame blocking the cafeteria aisles to get back their favorite Cap'n Crunch cereal—to the serious: hundreds of Oberlin College students occupying the administration building last May to protest the dismissal of an activist campus minister.

Students feel their political style is a break with the past. Their "new ideas, new style" is an as yet undefined political philosophy that they are developing from their own social experiences in the 1980s. "We're not runny-nosed liberals," said David Edwards of Franklin and Marshall College. "But we're not coldhearted conservatives either." "We'll get to problems and we'll work on them in our own way," said Jane Greenwell of Franklin and Marshall College. "But we have our whole lives ahead of us."

Questions for Comprehension

1. What is Wank's overall impression of the younger generation in 1984?
2. What is the major interest of students in going to college?
3. What problems do women face regarding careers?
4. To what sources do young people turn in their search for personal and moral values?

5. What attitudes toward sex are apparent in the young?
6. What are some consequences of the desire for security in the younger generation?
7. What is the prevailing attitude toward feminists on college campuses?
8. Characterize the attitude of the younger generation toward politics.
9. What kinds of issues cause the students Wank discusses to conduct demonstrations?

ADDITIONAL WRITING ASSIGNMENTS

1. Summarize Irwin Ross's essay, "What They Really Think, and Why," being sure to clarify for your readers the dominant impression of the younger generation conveyed by the article.
2. Each of the readings in this section characterizes the younger generation of a particular era. Write a description that could serve as a similar source for someone wanting to know about your own generation. Your readers will need to know what your dominant impression of your own generation is and what major characteristics contribute to that impression.
3. Every generation has its worries; the question is whether everybody's problems are basically the same. Using at least two of the sources in the anthology, look at the worries and anxieties expressed by the young of other eras. Then think about the things that bother your own generation. What similarities or differences do you see? What overall conclusion can you draw from your comparison? Write an essay in which you present your conclusion and the evidence for it.
4. Read the article by Paula Fass about the younger generation of the 1920s, in which the author points out a number of ways the young were *like* their parents. Write an essay in which you explain the ways today's college students are like or unlike their parents. What values, interests, activities, and aspirations do the two groups have in common?
5. In his article "Who Are We? A Self-Portrait of College Students Today" David Wank describes the dispute over whether or not college students of the mid-1980s were apathetic about politics and social causes, both nationally and on local campuses. Write an essay in which you show your readers the degree to which college students today are either politically and socially active or inactive.

The Impact of Advertising

ONE OF THE MOST DISTINCTIVE AND PERVASIVE ELEments of our culture, advertising is also one of the most frequently discussed. The essays in this anthology focus on three aspects of the subject. Paul Stevens and the editors of *Consumer Reports* call attention to the deceptive use of language employed by advertisers. Stevens discusses what he calls "weasel words," words whose purpose is to get consumers "to accept as truth things that have only been implied." The editors of *Consumer Reports* explain how producers use two loosely defined words—*natural* and *organic*—to suggest nutritional value, often nonexistent, in their products. Maurine Christopher and Frank McConnell are concerned with the negative effects of television advertising. Christopher explains why she believes that political advertising on television degrades our democratic system and ought to be banned. McConnell, a recovering alcoholic, concentrates on "the fictions of alcohol," the images advertisers use to push alcohol on television. Finally, William Meyers and Michael Schudson consider relationships between advertising and consumers. Meyers describes the techniques advertisers use to categorize and appeal to consumers. Schudson considers the nature and extent of the influence of advertising in our society.

WEASEL WORDS
Paul Stevens

Paul Stevens (b. 1937), a former teacher of English and music, has written television commercials for an advertising agency. In the following essay, first published in Stevens' book *I Can Sell You Anything* (1972), he describes one of the tools of the trade.

First of all, you know what a weasel is, right? It's a small, slimy animal that eats small birds and other animals, and is especially fond of devouring vermin. Now, consider for a moment the kind of winning personality he must have. I mean, what kind of guy would get his jollies eating rats and mice? Would you invite him to a party? Take him home to meet your mother? This is one of the slyest and most cunning of all creatures; sneaky, slippery, and thoroughly obnoxious. And so it is with great and warm personal regard for these attributes that we humbly award this King of All Devious the honor of bestowing his name upon our golden sword: the weasel word.

A weasel word is "a word used in order to evade or retreat from a direct or forthright statement or position" (Webster). In other words, if we can't say it, we'll weasel it. And, in fact, a weasel word has become more than just an evasion or retreat. We've trained our weasels. They can do anything. They can make you hear things that aren't being said, accept as truths things that have only been implied, and believe things that have only been suggested. Come to think of it, not only do we have our weasels trained, but they, in turn, have got you trained. When *you* hear a weasel word, you automatically hear the implication. Not the real meaning, but the meaning *it* wants *you* to hear. So if you're ready for a little re-education, let's take a good look under a strong light at the two kinds of weasel words.

1. Words That Mean Things They Really Don't Mean

Help That's it. "Help." It means "aid" or "assist." Nothing more. Yet, "help" is the one single word which, in all the annals of advertising, has done the most to say something that couldn't be said. Because "help" is the great qualifier; once you say it, you can say almost anything after it. In short, "help" has helped help us the most.

> Helps keep you young
> Helps prevent cavities
> Helps keep your house germ-free

"Help" qualifies everything. You've never heard anyone say, "This product will keep you young," or "This toothpaste will positively prevent cavities for all time." Obviously, we can't say anything like that, because there aren't any products like that made. But by adding that one little word, "help," in front, we can use the strongest language possible afterward. And the most fascinating part of it is, you are immune to the word. You literally don't hear the word "help." You only hear what comes after it. And why not? That's strong language, and likely to be much more important to you than the silly little word at the front end.

I would guess that 75 percent of all advertising uses the word "help." Think, for a minute, about how many times each day you hear these phrases:

> Helps stop . . .
> Helps prevent . . .
> Helps fight . . .
> Helps overcome . . .
> Helps you feel . . .
> Helps you look . . .

I could go on and on, but so could you. Just as a simple exercise, call it homework if you wish, tonight when you plop down in front of the boob tube for your customary three and a half hours of violence and/or situation comedies, take a pad and pencil, and keep score. See if you can count how many times the word "help" comes up during the commercials. Instead of going to the bathroom during the pause before Marcus Welby operates, or raiding the refrigerator prior to witnessing the Mob Squad wipe out a nest of dope pushers, stick with it. Count the "helps," and discover just how dirty a four-letter word can be.

Like Coming in second, but only losing out by a nose, is the word "like," used in comparison. Watch:

> It's like getting one bar free
> Cleans like a white tornado
> It's like taking a trip to Portugal

Okay. "Like" is a qualifier, and is used in much the same way as "help." But "like" is also a comparative element, with a very specific purpose; we use "like" to get you to stop thinking about the product per se, and to get you thinking about something that is bigger or better or different from the product we're selling. In other words, we can make you believe that the product is more than it is by likening it to something else.

Take a look at that first phrase, straight out of recent Ivory Soap advertising. On the surface of it, they tell you that four bars of Ivory cost about the same as three bars of most other soaps. So, if you're going to spend a certain amount of money on soap, you can buy four bars instead of three. Therefore, it's like getting one bar free. Now, the question you have to ask yourself is, "Why the weasel? Why do they say 'like'? Why don't they just come out and say, 'You get one bar free'?" The answer is, of course, that for one reason or another, you really don't. Here are two possible reasons. One: sure, you get four bars, but in terms of the actual amount of soap that you get, it may very well be the same as in three bars of another brand. Remember, Ivory has a lot of air in it—that's what makes it float. And air takes up room. Room that could otherwise be occupied by more soap. So, in terms of pure product, the amount of actual soap in four bars of Ivory may be only as much as the actual amount of soap in three bars of most others. That's why we can't—or won't—come out with a straightforward declaration such as, "You get 25 percent more soap," or "Buy three bars, and get the fourth one free."

Reason number two: the actual cost and value of the product. Did it ever occur to you that Ivory may simply be a cheaper soap to make and, therefore, a cheaper soap to sell? After all, it doesn't have any perfume, or hexachlorophene, or other additives that can raise the cost of manufacturing. It's plain, simple, cheap soap, and so it can be sold for less money while still maintaining a profit margin as great as more expensive soaps. By way of illustrating this, suppose you were trying to decide whether to buy a Mercedes-Benz or a Ford. Let's say the Mercedes cost $7,000, and the Ford $3,500. Now the Ford salesman comes up to you with this deal: as long as you're considering spending $7,000 on a car, buy my Ford for $7,000 and I'll give you a second Ford, free! Well, the same principle can apply to Ivory: as long as you're considering spending 35 cents on soap, buy my cheaper soap, and I'll give you more of it.

I'm sure there are other reasons why Ivory uses the weasel "like." Perhaps you've thought of one or two yourself. That's good. You're starting to think.

Now, what about that wonderful white tornado? Ajax pulled that one out of the hat some eight years ago, and you're still buying it. It's a classic example of the use of the word "like" in which we can force you to think, not about the product itself, but about something bigger, more exciting, certainly more powerful than a bottle of fancy ammonia. The word "like" is used here as a transfer word, which gets you away from the obvious—the odious job of getting down on your hands and knees and scrubbing your kitchen floor—and into the world of fantasy, where we can imply that this little bottle of miracles will supply all the elbow grease you need. Isn't that the name of the game? The whirlwind activity of the tornado replacing the whirlwind motion of your arm? Think about the swirling of the tornado, and all the work it will save you. Think about the power of that devastating windstorm; able to lift houses, overturn cars, and now, pick the dirt up off your floor. And we get the license to do it simply by using the word "like."

It's a copywriter's dream, because we don't have to substantiate anything. When we compare our product to "another leading brand," we'd better be able to prove what we say. But how can you compare ammonia to a windstorm? It's ludicrous. It can't be done. The whole statement is so ridiculous it couldn't be challenged by the government or the networks. So it went on the air, and it worked. Because the little word "like" let us take you out of the world of reality, and into your own fantasies.

Speaking of fantasies, how about that trip to Portugal? Mateus Rosé is actually trying to tell you that you will be transported clear across the Atlantic Ocean merely by sipping their wine. "Oh, come on," you say. "You don't expect me to believe that." Actually, we don't expect you to believe it. But we do expect you to get our meaning. This is called "romancing the product," and it is made possible by the dear little "like." In this case, we deliberately bring attention to the word, and we ask you to join us in setting reality aside for a moment. We take your hand and gently lead you down the path of moonlit nights, graceful dancers, and mysterious women. Are we saying that these things are all contained inside our wine? Of course not. But what we mean is, our wine is part of all this, and with a little help from "like," we'll get you to feel that way, too. So don't think of us as a bunch of peasants squashing a bunch of grapes. As a matter of fact, don't think of us at all. Feel with us.

"Like" is a virus that kills. You'd better get immune to it.

Other Weasels

"Help" and "like" are the two weasels so powerful that they can stand on their own. There are countless other words, not quite so potent, but equally effective when used in conjunction with our two basic weasels, or with each other. Let me show you a few.

Virtual or *virtually* How many times have you responded to an ad that said:

> Virtually trouble-free . . .
> Virtually foolproof . . .
> Virtually never needs service . . .

Ever remember what "virtual" means? It means "in essence or effect, but not in fact." Important—"but not in fact." Yet today the word "virtually" is interpreted by you as meaning "almost or just about the same as. . . ." Well, gang, it just isn't true. "Not," in fact, means not, in fact. I was scanning, rather longingly I must confess, through the brochure Chevrolet publishes for its Corvette, and I came to this phrase: "The seats in the 1972 Corvette are virtually handmade." They had me, for a minute. I almost took the bait of that lovely little weasel. I almost decided that those seats were just about completely handmade. And then I remembered. Those seats were not, *in fact*, handmade. Remember, "virtually" means "not, in fact," or you will, in fact, get sold down the river.

Acts or *works* These two action words are rarely used alone, and are generally accompanied by "like." They need help to work, mostly because they are verbs, but their implied meaning is deadly, nonetheless. Here are the key phrases:

> Acts like . . .
> Acts against . . .
> Works like . . .
> Works against . . .
> Works to prevent (*or* help prevent) . . .

You see what happens? "Acts" or "works" brings an action to the product that might not otherwise be there. When we say that a certain cough syrup "acts on the cough control center," the implication is that the syrup goes to this mysterious organ and immediately makes it better. But the implication here far exceeds what the truthful promise should be. An act is simply a deed. So the claim "acts on" simply means it performs a deed on. What that deed is, we may never know.

The rule of thumb is this: if we can't say "cures" or "fixes" or use any other positive word, we'll nail you with "acts like" or "works against," and get you thinking about something else. Don't.

Miscellaneous Weasels

Can be This is for comparison, and what we do is to find an announcer who can really make it sound positive. But keep your ears open. "Crest can be of significant value when used in . . . ," etc., is indicative of an ideal situation, and most of us don't live in ideal situations.

Up to Here's another way of expressing an ideal situation. Remember the cigarette that said it was aged, or "cured for up to eight long, lazy weeks"? Well, that could, and should, be interpreted as meaning that the tobaccos used were cured anywhere from one hour to eight weeks. We like to glamorize the ideal situation; it's up to you to bring it back to reality.

As much as More of the same. "As much as 20 percent greater mileage" with our gasoline again promises the ideal, but qualifies it.

Refreshes, comforts, tackles, fights, comes on Just a handful of the same action weasels, in the same category as "acts" and "works," though not as frequently used. The way to complete the thought here is to ask the simple question, "How?" Usually, you won't get an answer. That's because, usually, the weasel will run and hide.

Feel or *the feel of* This is the first of our subjective weasels. When we deal with a subjective word, it is simply a matter of opinion. In our opinion, Naugahyde has the feel of real leather. So we can say it. And, indeed, if you were to touch leather, and then touch Naugahyde, you may very well agree with us. But that doesn't mean it is real leather, only that it feels the same. The best way to handle subjective weasels is to complete the thought yourself, by simply saying, "But it isn't." At least that way you can remain grounded in reality.

The look of or *looks like* "Look" is the same as "feel," our subjective opinion. Did you ever walk into a Woolworth's and see those $29.95 masterpieces hanging in their "Art Gallery"? "The look of a real oil painting," it will say. "But it isn't," you will now reply. And probably be $29.95 richer for it.

2. Words That Have No Specific Meaning

If you have kids, then you have all kinds of breakfast cereals in the house. When I was a kid, it was Rice Krispies, the breakfast cereal that went snap, crackle, and pop. (One hell of a claim for a product that is supposed to offer nutritional benefits.) Or Wheaties, the breakfast of champions, whatever that means. Nowadays, we're forced to a confrontation with Quisp, Quake, Lucky Stars, Cocoa-Puffs, Clunkers, Blooies, Snarkles and Razzmatazz. And they all have one thing in common: they're all "fortified." Some are simply "fortified with vitamin D," or some other letter. But what does it all mean?

"Fortified" means "added on to." But "fortified," like so many other weasel words of indefinite meaning, simply doesn't tell us enough. If, for instance, a cereal were to contain one unit of vitamin D, and the manufacturers added some chemical which would produce two units of vitamin D, they could then claim that the cereal was "fortified with twice as much vitamin D." So what? It would still be about as nutritional as sawdust.

The point is, weasel words with no specific meaning don't tell us enough, but we have come to accept them as factual statements closely associated with something good that has been done to the product. Here's another example.

Enriched We use this one when we have a product that starts out with nothing. You mostly find it in bread, where the bleaching process combined with the chemicals used as preservatives render the loaves totally void of anything but filler. So the manufacturer puts a couple of drops of vitamins into the batter, and presto! It's enriched. Sounds great when you say it. Looks great when you read it. But what you have to determine is, is it really great? Figure out what information is missing, and then try to supply that information. The odds are, you won't. Even the breakfast cereals that are playing it straight, like Kellogg's Special K, leave something to be desired. They tell you what vitamins you get, and how much of each in one serving. The catch is, what constitutes a serving? They say, one ounce. So now you have to whip out your baby scale and weigh one serving. Do you have any idea how much that is? Maybe you do. Maybe you don't care. Okay, so you polish off this mound of dried stuff, and now what? You have ostensibly received the minimum, repeat, minimum dosage of certain vitamins for the day. One day. And you still have to go find the vitamins you didn't get. Try looking it up on a box of frozen peas. Bet you won't find it. But do be alert to "fortified" and "enriched." Asking the right questions will prove beneficial.

Did you buy that last sentence? Too bad, because I weaseled you, with the word "beneficial." Think about it.

Flavor and *taste* These are two totally subjective words that allow us to claim marvelous things about products that are edible. Every cigarette in the world has claimed the best taste. Every supermarket has advertised the most flavorful meat. And let's not forget "aroma," a subdivision of this category. Wouldn't you like to have a nickel for every time a room freshener (a weasel in itself) told you it would make your home "smell fresh as all outdoors"? Well, they can say it, because smell, like taste and flavor, is a subjective thing. And, incidentally, there are no less than three weasels in that phrase. "Smell" is the first. Then, there's "as" (a substitute for the ever-popular "like"), and, finally, "fresh," which, in context, is a subjective comparison, rather than the primary definition of "new."

Now we can use an unlimited number of combinations of these weasels for added impact. "Fresher-smelling clothes." "Fresher-tasting tobacco." "Tastes like grandma used to make." Unfortunately, there's no sure way of bringing these weasels down to size, simply because you can't define them accurately. Trying to ascertain the meaning of "taste" in any context is like trying to push a rope up a hill. All you can do is be aware that these words are subjective, and represent only one opinion—usually that of the manufacturer.

Style and *good looks* Anyone for buying a new car? Okay, which is the one with the good looks? The smart new styling? What's that you say? All of them? Well, you're right. Because this is another group of subjective opinions. And it is the subjective and collective opinion of both Detroit and Madison Avenue that the following cars have "bold new styling": Buick Riviera, Plymouth Satellite, Dodge Monaco, Mercury Brougham, and you can fill in the spaces for the rest. Subjectively, you have to decide on which bold new styling is, indeed, bold new styling. Then, you might spend a minute or two trying to determine what's going on under that styling. The rest I leave to Ralph Nader.

Different, special, and *exclusive* To be different, you have to be not the same as. Here, you must rely on your own good judgment and common sense. Exclusive formulas and special combinations of ingredients are coming at you every day, in every way. You must constantly assure yourself that, basically, all products in any given category are the same. So when you hear "special," "exclusive," or "different," you have to establish two things: on what basis are they different, and is that difference an important one? Let me give you a hypothetical example.

All so-called "permanent" antifreeze is basically the same. It is made from a liquid known as ethylene glycol, which has two amazing properties: It has a lower freezing point than water, and a higher boiling point than water. It does not break down (lose its properties), nor will it boil away. And every permanent antifreeze starts with it as a base. Also, just about every antifreeze has now got antileak ingredients, as well as antirust and anticorrosion ingredients. Now, let's suppose that, in formulating the product, one of the companies comes up with a solution that is pink in color, as opposed to all the others, which are blue. Presto—an exclusivity claim. "Nothing else looks like it, nothing else performs like it." Or, how about, "Look at ours, and look at anyone else's. You can see the difference our exclusive formula makes." Granted, I'm exaggerating. But did I prove a point?

A Few More Goodies

> At Phillips 66, it's performance that counts
> Whisk puts its strength where the dirt is
> At Bird's Eye, we've got quality in our corner
> Delicious and long-lasting, too

Very quickly now, let's deflate those four lines. First, what the hell does "performance" mean? It means that this product will do what any other product in its category will do. Kind of a back-handed reassurance that this gasoline will function properly in your car. That's it, and nothing more. To perform means to function at a standard consistent with the rest of the industry. All products in a category are basically the same.

Second line: What does "strength" or "strong" mean? Does it mean "not weak"? Or "superior in power"? No, it means consistent with the norms of the business. You can bet your first-born that if Whisk were superior in power to other detergents, they'd be saying it, loud and clear. So strength is merely a description of a property inherent in all similar products in its class. If you really want to poke a pin in a bubble, substitute the word "ingredients" for the word "strength." That'll do it every time.

Third line: The old "quality" claim, and you fell for it. "Quality" is not a comparison. In order to do that, we'd have to say, "We've got better quality in our corner than any other frozen food." Quality relates only to the subjective opinion that Bird's Eye has of its own products, and to which it is entitled. The word "quality" is what we call a "parity" statement; that is, it tells you that it is as good as any other. Want a substitute? Try "equals," meaning "the same as."

Fourth line: How delicious is delicious? About the same as good-tasting is good-tasting, or fresher smelling is fresher smelling. A subjective opinion regarding taste, which you can either accept or reject. More fun, though, is "long-lasting." You might want to consider writing a note to Mr. Wrigley, inquiring as to the standard length of time which a piece of gum is supposed to last. Surely there must be a guideline covering it. The longest lasting piece of gum I ever encountered lasted just over four hours, which is the amount of time it took me to get it off the sole of my shoe. Try expressing the line this way: "It has a definite taste, and you may chew it as long as you wish." Does that place it in perspective?

There are two other aspects of weasel words that I should mention here. The first one represents the pinnacle of the copywriter's craft, and I call it the "Weasel of Omission." Let me demonstrate:

> Of America's best-tasting gums, Trident is sugar-free

Disregard, for a moment, the obvious subjective weasel "best-tasting." Look again at the line. Something has been left out. Omitted very deliberately. Do you know what that word is? The word that's missing is the word "only," which should come right before the name of the product. But it doesn't. It's gone. Left out. And the question is, why? The answer is, the government wouldn't let them. You see, they start out by making a subjective judgment, that their gum is among the best-tasting. That's fine, as far as it goes. That's their opinion. But it is also the opinion of every other maker of sugar-free gum that his product is also among the best-tasting. And, since both of their opinions must be regarded as having equal value, neither one is allowed the superiority claim, which is what the word "only" would do. So Trident left it out. But the sentence is so brilliantly constructed, the word "only" is so heavily implied, that most people hear it, even though it hasn't been said. That's the Weasel of Omission. Constructing a set of words that forces you to a conclusion that otherwise could not have been drawn. Be on the lookout for what isn't said, and try to fill the gaps realistically.

The other aspect of weasels is the use of all those great, groovy, swinging, wonderful, fantastic, exciting and fun-filled words known as adjectives. Your eyes, ears, mind, and soul have been bombarded by adjectives for so long that you are probably numb to most of them by now. If I were to give you a list of adjectives to look out for, it would require the next five hundred pages, and it wouldn't do you any good, anyway. More important is to bear in mind what adjectives do, and then to be able to sweep them aside and distinguish only the facts.

An adjective modifies a noun, and is generally used to denote the quality or a quality of the thing named. And that's our grammar lesson for today. Realistically, an adjective enhances or makes more of the product being discussed. It's the difference between "Come visit Copenhagen," and "Come visit beautiful Copenhagen." Adjectives are used so freely these days that we feel almost naked, robbed, if we don't get at least a couple. Try speaking without adjectives. Try describing something; you can't do it. The words are too stark, too bare-boned, too factual. And that's the key to judging advertising. There is a direct, inverse proportion between the number of adjectives and the number of facts. To put it succinctly, the more adjectives we use, the less we have to say.

You can almost make a scale, based on that simple mathematical premise. At one end you have cosmetics, soft drinks, cigarettes, products that have little or nothing of any value to say. So we get them all dressed up with lavish word and thought images, and present you with thirty or sixty seconds of adjectival puffery. The other end of the scale is much harder to find. Usually, it will be occupied by a new product that is truly new or different. Our craving for adjectives has become so overriding that we simply cannot listen to what is known as "nuts and bolts" advertising. The rest falls somewhere in the middle; a combination of adjectives, weasels, and semitruths. All I can tell you is, try to brush the description aside, and see what's really at the bottom.

Summary

A weasel word is a word that's used to imply a meaning that cannot be truthfully stated. Some weasels imply meanings that are not the same as their actual definition, such as "help," "like," or "fortified." They can act as qualifiers and/or comparatives. Other weasels, such as "taste" and "flavor," have no definite meanings, and are simply subjective opinions offered by the manufacturer. A weasel of omission is one that implies a claim so strongly that it forces you to supply the bogus fact. Adjectives are weasels used to convey feelings and emotions to a greater extent than the product itself can.

In dealing with weasels, you must strip away the innuendos and try to ascertain the facts, if any. To do this, you need to ask questions such as: How? Why? How many? How much? Stick to basic definitions of words. Look them up if you have to. Then, apply the strict definition to the text of the advertisement or commercial. "Like" means similar to, but not the same as. "Virtually" means the same in essence, but not in fact.

Above all, never underestimate the devious qualities of a weasel. Weasels twist and turn and hide in dark shadows. You must come to grips with them, or advertising will rule you forever.

My advice to you is: Beware of weasels. They are nasty and untrainable, and they attack pocketbooks.

Questions for Comprehension

1. What is a weasel word?
2. How has the word *help* enabled advertisers to "say something that couldn't be said"?
3. Why is the word *like* a "copywriter's dream"?
4. How do advertisers use vague words to confer nonexistent virtues on their products?
5. What is a "Weasel of Omission"?
6. According to Stevens, how can we deal successfully with weasel words?

IT'S NATURAL! IT'S ORGANIC! OR IS IT?

The Editors of Consumer Reports

Consumer Reports is a publication of Consumer's Union, a nonprofit organization that provides consumers with information about available products and services. The following article was first published in 1980.

1 "No artificial flavors or colors!" reads the Nabisco advertisement in *Progressive Grocer*, a grocery trade magazine. "And research shows that's exactly what consumers are eager to buy."

2 The ad, promoting Nabisco's *Sesame Wheats* as "a natural whole wheat cracker," might raise a few eyebrows among thoughtful consumers of Nabisco's *Wheat Thins* and *Cheese Nips*, which contain artificial colors, or of its *Ginger Snaps* and *Oreo Cookies*, which have artificial flavors. But Nabisco has not suddenly become a champion of "natural" foods. Like other giants of the food industry, the company is merely keeping its eye on what will produce a profit.

3 Nabisco's trade ad, which was headlined "A Natural for Profits," is simply a routine effort by a food processor to capitalize on the concerns that consumers have about the safety of the food they buy.

4 Supermarket shelves are being flooded with "natural" products, some of them containing a long list of chemical additives. And some products that never did contain additives have suddenly sprouted "natural" or "no preservative" labels. Along with the new formulations and labels have come higher prices, since the food industry has realized that consumers are willing to pay more for products they think are especially healthful.

5 The mass merchandising of "natural" foods is a spillover onto supermarket shelves of a phenomenon once confined to health-food stores, as major food manufacturers enter what was once the exclusive territory of small entrepreneurs. Health-food stores were the first to foster and capitalize on the growing consumer interest in nutrition and are still thriving. Along with honey-sweetened snacks, "natural" vitamins, and other "natural" food products, the health-food stores frequently feature "organic" produce and other "organic" foods.

6 Like the new merchandise in supermarkets, the products sold at health-food stores carry the implication that they're somehow better for you—safer or more nutritious. In this report, we'll examine that premise, looking at both "natural" foods, which are widely sold, and "organic" foods, which are sold primarily at health-food stores. While the terms "natural" and "organic" are often used loosely, "organic" generally refers to the way food is grown (without pesticides or chemical fertilizers) and "natural" to the character of the ingredients (no preservatives or artificial additives) and to the fact that the food product has undergone minimal processing.

7 *Langendorf Natural Lemon Flavored Creme Pie* contains no cream. It does contain sodium propionate, certified food colors, sodium benzoate, and vegetable gum.

8 That's natural?

Yes indeed, says L.A. Cushman Jr., chairman of American Bakeries Co., the Chicago firm that owns Langendorf. The word "natural," he explains, modifies "lemon flavored," and the pie contains oil from lemon rinds. "The lemon flavor," Cushman states, "comes from natural lemon flavor as opposed to artificial lemon flavor, assuming there is such a thing as artificial lemon flavor."

Welcome to the world of natural foods.

You can eat your "natural" way from one end of the supermarket to the other. Make yourself a sandwich of *Kraft Cracker Barrel Natural Cheddar Cheese* on *Better Way Natural Whole Grain Wheat Nugget Bread* spread with *Autumn Natural Margarine*. Wash it down with *Anheuser-Busch Natural Light Beer* or *Rich-Life Natural Orange NutriPop*. Snack on any number of brands of "natural" potato chips and "natural" candy bars. And don't exclude your pet: Feed your dog *Gravy Train Dog Food With Natural Beef Flavor* or, if it's a puppy, try *Blue Mountain Natural Style Puppy Food*.

The "natural" bandwagon doesn't end at the kitchen. You can bathe in *Batherapy Natural Mineral Bath* (sodium sesquicarbonate, isopropyl myristate, fragrance, D & C Green No. 5, D & C Yellow No. 10 among its ingredients), using *Queene Helene "All-Natural" Amino Peptide Shampoo* (propylene glycol, hydroxyethyl cellulose, methylparaben, D & C Red No. 3, D & C Brown No. 1) and *Organic Aid Natural Clear Soaps*. Then, if you're so inclined, you can apply *Naturade Conditioning Mascara with Natural Protein* (stearic acid, PVP, butylene glycol, sorbitan sesquioleate, triethanolamine, imidazolidinyl urea, methylparaben, propylparaben).

At its ridiculous extreme, the "natural" ploy extends to furniture, cigarettes, denture adhesives, and shoes.

The Selling of a Word

The word "natural" does not have to be synonymous with "ripoff." Over the years, the safety of many food additives has been questioned. And a consumer who reads labels carefully can in fact find some foods in supermarkets that have been processed without additives.

But the word "natural" does not guarantee that. All too often, as the above examples indicate, the word is used more as a key to higher profits. Often, it implies a health benefit that does not really exist.

Co-op News, the publication of the Berkeley Co-op, the nation's largest consumer-cooperative store chain, reported on "two 15-ounce cans of tomato sauce, available side-by-side" at one of its stores. One sauce, called *Health Valley*, claimed on its label to have "no citric acid, no sugars, no preservatives, no artificial colors or flavors." There were none of those ingredients in the Co-op's house brand, either, but their absence was hardly worth noting on the label, since canned tomato sauce almost never contains artificial colors or flavors and doesn't need preservatives after being heated in the canning process. The visible difference between the two products was price, not ingredients. The *Health Valley* tomato sauce was selling for 85 cents; the Co-op house brand, for only 29 cents.

One supermarket industry consultant estimates that 7 percent of all processed food products now sold are touted as "natural." And that could be just the beginning. A Federal Trade Commission report noted that 63 percent of people polled in a survey agreed with the statement, "Natural foods are more nutritious than other foods." Thirty-nine percent said they regularly buy food because it is "natural," and 47 percent said they are willing to pay 10 percent more for a food that is "natural."

According to those who have studied the trend, the consumer's desire for "natural" foods goes beyond the fear of specific chemicals. "There is a mistrust of technology," says Howard Moskowitz, a taste researcher and consultant to the food industry. "There is a movement afoot to return to simplicity in all aspects of life." A spokeswoman for Lever Bros., one of the nation's major food merchandisers, adds: "'Natural' is a psychological thing of everyone wanting to get out of the industrial world."

Because consumers are acting out of such vague, undefined feelings, they aren't sure what they should be getting when they buy a product labeled "natural." William Wittenberg, president of Grandma's Food Inc., comments: "Manufacturers and marketers are making an attempt to appeal to a consumer who feels he should be eating something natural, but doesn't know why. I think the marketers of the country in effect mirror back to the people what they want to hear. People have to look to themselves for their own protection." Grandma's makes a *Whole Grain Date Filled Fruit 'n Oatmeal Bar* labeled "naturally Good Flavor." The ingredients include "artificial flavor."

Is "Natural" Better?

"Natural" foods are not necessarily preferable nor, as we have seen, necessarily natural.

Consider "natural" potato chips. They are often cut thick from unpeeled potatoes, packaged without preservatives in heavy foil bags with fancy lettering, and sold at a premium price. Sometimes, such chips include "sea salt," a product whose advantage over conventional "land" salt has not been demonstrated. The packaging is intended to give the impression that "natural" potato chips are less of a junk food than regular chips. But nutritionally there is no difference. Both are made from the same food, the potato, and both have been processed so that they are high in salt and in calories.

Sometimes the "natural" products may have ingredients you'd prefer to avoid. *Quaker 100% Natural* cereal, for example, contains 24 percent sugars, a high percentage, considering it's not promoted as a sugared cereal. (*Kellogg's Corn Flakes* has 7.8 percent sugar.) Many similar "natural" granola-type cereals have oil added, giving them a much higher fat content than conventional cereals.

Taste researcher Moskowitz notes that food processors are "trying to signal to the consumer a sensory impact that can be called natural." Two of the most popular signals, says Moskowitz, are honey and coconut. But honey is just another sugar, with no significant nutrients other than calories . . . and coconut is especially high in saturated fats.

While many processed foods are less nutritious than their fresh counterparts, processing can sometimes help foods: Freezing preserves nutrients that can be lost if fresh foods are not consumed quickly; pasteurization kills potentially dangerous bacteria in milk. Some additives are also both safe and useful. Sorbic acid, for instance, prevents the growth of potentially harmful molds in cheese and other products, and sodium benzoate has been used for more than 70 years to prevent the growth of microorganisms in acidic foods.

"Preservative" has become a dirty word, to judge from the number of "no preservative" labels on food products. Calcium propionate might sound terrible on a bread label, but this mildew-retarding substance occurs naturally in both raisins and Swiss cheese. "Bread without preservatives could well cost you more than bread with them," says Vernal S. Packard Jr., a University of Minnesota nutrition professor. "Without preservatives, the bread gets stale faster; it may go moldy with the production of hazardous aflatoxin. And already we in the United States return [to producers] 100 million pounds of bread of each year—this in a world nagged by hunger and malnutrition."

Nor are all the "natural" substances safe. Sassafras tea was banned by the U.S. Food and Drug Administration several years ago because it contains safrole, which has produced liver cancer in laboratory animals. Kelp, a seaweed that is becoming increasingly fashionable as a dietary supplement, can have a high arsenic content. Aflatoxin, produced by a mold that can grow on improperly stored peanuts, corn, and grains, is a known carcinogen.

To complicate matters, our palates have become attuned to many unnatural tastes. "We don't have receptors on our tongues that signal 'natural'," says taste researcher Moskowitz. He points out, for instance, that a panel of consumers would almost certainly reject a natural lemonade "in favor of a lemonade scientifically designed to taste natural. If you put real lemon, sugar, and water together, people would reject it as harsh. They are used to flavors developed by flavor houses." Similarly, Moskowitz points out, many consumers say that for health reasons they prefer less salty food—but the results of various taste tests have contradicted this, too.

The Tactics of Deception

In the midst of all this confusion, it's not surprising that the food industry is having a promotional field day. Companies are using various tactics to convince the consumer that a food product is "natural"—and hence preferable. Here are some of the most common:

The indeterminate modifier. Use a string of adjectives and claim that "natural" modifies only the next adjective in line, not the product itself. Take *Pillsbury Natural Chocolate Flavored Chocolate Chip Cookies.* Many a buyer might be surprised to learn from the fine print that these cookies contain artificial flavor, as well as the chemical antioxidant BHA. But Pillsbury doesn't bat an eyelash at this. "We're not trying to mislead anybody," says a company representative, explaining that the word "natural" modifies only "chocolate flavored," while the artificial flavoring is vanilla. Then why not call the product "Chocolate Chip Cookies with Natural Chocolate Flavoring"? "From a labeling point of view, we're trying to use a limited amount of space" was the answer.

Innocence by association. Put nature on your side. *Life Cinnamon Flavor High Protein Cereal,* a Quaker Oats Co. product, contains BHA and artificial color, among other things. How could the company imply the cereal was "natural" and still be truthful? One series of *Life* boxes solves the problem neatly. The back panel has an instructional lesson for children entitled "Nature." The box uses the word "Nature" four times and "natural" once—but never actually to describe the cereal inside. Other products surround themselves with a "natural" aura by picturing outdoor or farm scenes on their packages.

The "printer's error." From time to time, readers send us food wrappers making a "natural" claim directly contradicted by the ingredients list. We have, for example, received a batch of individually wrapped *Devonsheer* crackers with a big red label saying: "A Natural Product, no preservatives." The ingredients list includes "calcium propionate (to retard spoilage)."

How could a manufacturer defend that? "At a given printing, the printer was instructed to remove 'no preservatives, natural product' when we changed ingredients, but he didn't do it," says Curtis Marshall, vice president for operations at Devonsheer Melba Corp.

The best defense. Don't defend yourself; attack the competition. Sometimes the use of the word "natural" is, well, just plain unnatural. Take the battle that has been brewing between the nation's two largest beer makers, Miller Brewing Co. and Anheuser-Busch. The latter's product, *Anheuser-Busch Natural Light Beer*, has been the object of considerable derision by Miller.

Miller wants the word "natural" dropped from Anheuser-Busch's advertisements because beers are "highly processed, complex products, made with chemical additives and other components not in their natural form."

Anheuser-Busch has responded only with some digs at Miller, charging Miller with using artificial foam stabilizer and adding an industrial enzyme instead of natural malt to reduce the caloric content of its *Miller Lite* beer.

No victor has yet emerged from the great beer war, but the industry is obviously getting edgy.

"Other brewers say it's time for the two companies to shut up," the Wall Street Journal reported. "One thing they [the other brewers] are worried about," says William T. Elliot, president of C. Schmidt & Sons, a Philadelphia brewery, "is all the fuss over ingredients. Publicity about that issue is disclosing to beer drinkers that their suds may include sulfuric acid, calcium sulfate, alginic acid, or amyloglucosidase."

The negative pitch. Point out in big letters on the label that the product doesn't contain something it wouldn't contain anyway. The "no artificial preservatives" label stuck on a jar of jam or jelly is true and always has been—since sugar is all the preservative jams and jellies need. Canned goods, likewise, are preserved in their manufacture—by the heat of the canning process. Then there is the "no cholesterol" claim of vegetable oils, margarines, and even (in a radio commercial) canned pineapple. Those are also true, but beside the point, since cholesterol is found only in animal products.

An Approach to Regulation

What can be done about such all-but-deceptive practices? One might suggest that the word "natural" is so vague as to be inherently deceptive, and therefore should not be available for promotional use. Indeed, the FTC staff suggested precisely that a few years ago but later backed away from the idea. The California legislature last year passed a weak bill defining the word "organic," but decided that political realities argued against tackling the word "natural."

"If we had included the word 'natural' in the bill, it most likely would not have gotten out of the legislature," says one legislative staff member. "When you've got large economic interests in certain areas, the tendency is to guard those interests very carefully."

Under the revised FTC staff proposal, which had not been acted on by the full commission as we went to press, the word "natural" can be used if the product has undergone only minimal processing and doesn't have artificial ingredients. That would eliminate the outright frauds, as well as the labeling of such products as Lever Bros.' *Autumn Natural Margarine*, which obviously has been highly processed from its original vegetable-oil state. But the FTC proposal might run into difficulty in defining exactly what "minimal processing" means. And it would also allow some deceptive implications. For instance, a product containing honey might be called "natural," while a food with refined sugar might not, thus implying that honey is superior to other sugars, which it is not.

A law incorporating similar regulations went into effect in Maine at the beginning of this year. If a product is to be labeled "natural" and sold in Maine, it must have undergone only minimal processing and have no additives, preservatives, or refined additions such as white flour and sugar.

Questions for Comprehension

1. What attracts people to the word *natural* on product labels?
2. How do the Editors of *Consumer Reports* back up their assertion that "'Natural' foods are not necessarily preferable nor, as we have seen, necessarily natural"?
3. What are the most common tactics companies use to convince consumers that a food is natural?
4. What definition of *natural* did the FTC suggest?

WHEN TV ADS BECOME MOST DISREPUTABLE

Maurine Christopher

Maurine Christopher has been a reporter for the *Baltimore Sun* and *Advertising Age*. She has also moderated and produced the radio program "Admen." The following article was first pubished in the November 5, 1984, issue of *Advertising Age*.

Contrary to Thomas Wolfe, North Carolina's celebrated novelist, you can go home again to the South and be treated handsomely.

I found this out last week when I visited Kingsport, Tenn., to speak to the Tri-City Metro Advertising Federation. They were friendly throughout my stay, even though my topic, "The Credibility Gap in Advertising," meant that most of my time would be devoted to what's wrong, rather than what's right, with their chosen field. They appeared interested in what I had to say and asked a number of provocative questions afterwards—assurance, at least, that I had not put them to sleep.

Speaking to the media, advertiser and agency professionals from Kingsport, Bristol and Johnson City brought back a flood of memories. It was the first time I had been to a formal meeting in this fast-growing little East Tennessee town since I left during World War II to go North to pursue my career as a journalist. My first post-college job was at the *Kingsport Times-News*, where I was entertainment editor, among many other assignments, including sports coverage.

The occasion was a reminder that I've been in the news business all my life, having started as a carrier at the age of 12 in partnership with my young brother, Jack. As the tough, big sister, I carried the now defunct *Knoxville Times* and the still very much alive *News-Sentinel* on Fridays in order to collect. I also made the rounds on Sundays when the papers were too heavy for a small boy. We were successful enough to have some money in the bank to lose when most of them failed in the Great Depression.

Since the trauma of the Vietnam War and Watergate, the American public has become increasingly skeptical of all the major institutions in society—religion, medicine, education, business, labor unions and certainly advertising. This skepticism is more pronounced than elsewhere in East Tennessee, a region with a proud mountain tradition for independent thinking and a tolerance for talented neurotics and unconventional characters.

As I told the Tri-City Federation, the advertising credibility gap is worsening and the trend will be accelerated by the shrillness, rudeness and distortions of this election year political campaigns. Advertising has only itself to blame for this predicament.

Take the case of ads that overpromise. Who was kidding whom when David Mahoney, former chairman of Norton Simon Inc., appeared in the commercials for Avis and made it sound as though he personally was waiting at the airport to make sure the customer got good treatment and the requested car?

Lee Iacocca, chairman of Chrysler, has worked wonders with that company, but even his excellent commercials can mislead. Several months ago I received a letter from an irate auto owner who had bought a lemon. He said he had tried in vain to get satisfaction at the dealer and factory level.

Then, he thought, "I'll write to the friendly Mr. Iacocca I keep seeing on tv." The unhappy car owner did just that. In a classic case of inept public relations, the Chrysler chairman didn't even go through the motions of answering personally. The disgruntled customer was bucked back down to the same people with whom he already had been struggling in vain.

What of the ads for jeans? Does anyone think very many of today's bright teen agers believe the secret to popularity and success to be an upscale label on form-fitting pants covering a shapely backside? (The *Kingsport Times-News* business writer who interviewed me after the speech noted that people of all ages are buying millions of those jeans. "You're right," I responded. "They are good, comfortable clothes. They sell despite an inane, sexist advertising approach.")

Too often, in my opinion, the tv commercials for headache, cough and cold medicine confuse rather than guide the potential customers. And isn't there a nagging worry about overdependence on drugs if one chooses Extra-Strength Anacin? Formula 44 requires self-diagnosis to select one of four cough categories to know what syrup to take. Any skeptic would be suspicious of how different those formulations are.

I also feel that an agency insults the customers' intelligence with an overworked creative crutch. The new product come-on, as in the case of the new Bounty towels or the new Cottonelle toilet tissue, should be bounced. Surely the creative people can come up with a better, less overworked approach.

Whatever their shortcomings, product ads rarely sink as low as some of the concoctions for the politicos. Political strategists deserve the top awards for misleading and downright dishonest ads.

Remember the infamous Lyndon B. Johnson spot in the 1960s. A little girl, a daisy and a dissolve into the world being blown up. The macho Texan had nailed his opponent, Sen. Barry Goldwater (R., Ariz.), as a quick-on-the-trigger warmonger. Unfortunately, people old enough to recall *those days* know LBJ was the President who escalated the war and bogged down America in Vietnam where President and former Gen. Eisenhower had warned the U.S. not to fight.

(Since I've returned to New York, I understand Walter Mondale is running a similar explosive ad to argue for a verifiable nuclear freeze. Should he be elected and then dispatch American troops to Central America, this commercial might chalk up a negative score to match LBJ's daisy spot. If he were elected and started a dialog going with the Russians and began to insist on cost controls at the Pentagon, the approach would be honest and honorable. Since most experts expect him to lose, the question may be moot.)

I am baffled by a variety of balanced budget-deficit spots for President Reagan and Republican congressional candidates. Here's the President who has bulldozed through the spineless, two-party Congress the most monumental deficit in history—much of it for enough exotic military weapons to kill everybody in the world several times over—and he's hitting the opposition party over the head with the balanced budget issue.

Weird!

(During my trip to Tennessee the *Knoxville News-Sentinel*, convinced of the president's vitality following a 30-minute Scripps-Howard editorial session with him, endorsed Mr. Reagan for reelection. At the same time, the paper demonstrated its integrity by front-paging the latest federal deficit report. That story noted the U.S. is now $1.69 trillion in debt, one-third of it accumulated during four years of the Reagan administration. George Washington and all the rest were pikers by comparison.)

Political advertising on tv degrades advertising and damages politicians, government and society in general. Like England and the other European democracies, America should ban it. Instead, major party candidates should be given a modest amount of free time, not for slick ads, but in longer periods of a half hour or so for straightforward presentations of their views to the voters. For tv, as Young & Rubicam chairman Ed Ney has suggested, that would be it, except for talk shows, news, debates and interviews. As in Europe, candidates would be allowed to purchase ads in other media if they wish.

If tv were placed off limits, the budgets that now hit obscene levels of $20 million and up for senators and $46 million-plus for Presidents, could be trimmed sharply. It would be hard to spend tv-size budgets elsewhere; there just aren't that many appropriate alternate vehicles.

America no longer would be ridiculed as a country with the best government money can buy. As voters, individually, we would no longer need to wonder which political action committee—the dairy pac, the conservative pac, the union pac, the fundamental religion pac, the chamber of commerce pac—owns our representative.

During the q&a portion of the program in Kingsport, a broadcaster asked me why tv should be deprived of political advertising support, if newspapers and other media were not. I would ban tv and not other media because tv is so much more expensive, persuasive and influential.

Telecasters, like all thoughtful citizens, should be concerned about the damaging impact of unbridled, disreputable advertising on the American government.

Questions for Comprehension

1. What does Christopher mean by "the advertising credibility gap"? Why is it worsened by the Avis and Chrysler advertisements she cites?
2. How do commercials for medicine contribute to skepticism about advertising?
3. What is the basis of Christopher's criticism of Lyndon B. Johnson's advertisements during the 1964 presidential campaign?
4. What does Christopher find deceptive about Ronald Reagan's advertisements during the 1984 presidential campaign?
5. How does Christopher propose to solve the problem of deceptive political advertising?
6. What would be the advantages of a ban on political advertising on TV?
7. Why does Christopher believe television to be different from other advertising media?

■

ADS & ADDICTIONS: BOOZE ON THE TUBE

Frank McConnell

Frank McConnell (b. 1942) is a professor of English at the University of California, Santa Barbara. He is the author of numerous books and articles on British and American literature. The following essay was first published in the Catholic journal *Commonweal* in 1983.

"Don't take the car, you'll kill yourself!" Who hasn't seen that commercial by the National Council on Alcoholism—the drunk husband lurching toward his car and the panicked wife shouting from the porch? And who does not know that it has become virtually a standard punch-line for every standup comic on the circuit? When in trouble, play with that line, and the audience roars (one reason, of course, being that probably half of them are snockered, so the joke becomes self-defense: that poor boob, thank God we're not like *him*, we can handle the stuff, can't we?)

But: "If you've got the time, we've got the beer." A group of healthy, shiny-faced American males go out for a day's Marlin fishing (Hemingway sport), or mountain climbing, or hang-glider flying, just all buddies together and having a *heck* of a good, invigorating time. And, inevitably, what do you do at the end of a great day like that? Why, you gather at your favorite bar, and you start calling for the beer, probably with that most *macho* of American phrases, "Run a tab, Rosie."

As a slogan, it's about as broad and silly as "Don't take the car, etc." So why isn't anybody laughing?

Any recovering alcoholic (and yes, I'm a member of the club) can tell you. It's because the use—and abuse—of alcohol is so deeply ingrained in, and sanctioned by, our culture that *not* drinking is perceived as the abnormal, and of course only the abnormal, the outsider, can be the clown or the fool and get a laugh.

Now this is a media column, and I am concerned with the ways media reflect both the national self-image and the national self-delusions: I am not, fear not, about to preach you a sermon on the evil of demon rum. But this time around, my subject is liquor and anti-liquor advertising in America, which is to say the ways we try to come to terms with (or don't try to come to terms with) a disease which is among the major causes of death in this country. If statistics mean anything, three out of ten of you reading this piece will contract or have contracted the sickness. In fact, given the demographics of *Commonweal*'s readership—heavily Irish and German—it is probably more like four or five in ten, since the evidence is that a predisposition, at least, to the sickness is genetically transmitted, sorry. And ten out of every ten will find themselves, their lives, their loves, affected and probably affected severely, by someone who *has* the sickness. Now *that's* what I call a disease.

It is a curious disease, moreover. Like tooth decay and hypertension, it is a disease of civilization; only when men have become civilized enough to ferment grain, precipitate sugar from cane, or evolve the profession of insurance salesmen do these ailments become possible.

It is also a disease one of whose prime constituents is secrecy. *No* drinker wants to admit that he (or she) drinks too much, so the heavy drinker goes to elaborate, and sometimes rather brilliant lengths to invent proofs that he (or she) doesn't drink too much. I have sometimes thought, indeed, that as much intellectual energy has been expended by drinkers demonstrating that they don't drink as was expended by Scholastic theologians demonstrating the existence of God.

Not that everyone is fooled, of course. In adultery, runs the cliché, the wife (or husband) is always the last one to know. But alcoholism is a disease, not a sin, and in that condition it is the victim who is always the last to know—if, that is, he is lucky enough to find out.

Do you know a beer commercial that *doesn't* include a group? Do you know a brandy or bourbon ad that shows one person alone drinking? I'll answer for you: you don't, and the reason you don't is that the people who sell us our booze are smart enough to realize that it is a private addiction sanctioned by public, social acceptability. Imagine the commercials if heroin (an equivalently dangerous drug) were legal: four old pals, sitting around the apartment, setting up their gimmicks, spoon, match, hypodermic: "This skin-pop's for you."

Not that the people who run the distilleries or write the liquor ads are vampires sucking self-respect and productivity out of the soul of the Republic. They are, like the rest of us, poor souls struggling between heaven and earth and trying to make a buck on route. But the way they write the ads reflects a great deal about the way we think about alcohol abuse, and the ways we invent to convince ourselves—actually, to con ourselves—to believe there really is no such thing.

Think about booze as a metaphor for social and sexual roles. In a very serious way, we use liquor not only as social lubricant ("Ice is nice, but liquor is quicker"—Ogden Nash), but as a way of *validating* ourselves socially. James Bond—the last public school gentleman or the first punk rocker—can consume infinite vodka martinis per diem and still be razor-sharp when he confronts the vile machinations of SPECTRE. "I'll drink till I drop down, with one eye on my clothes," sings Roger Daltrey in the Who's brilliant punk-opera, *Quadrophenia*. And no American private eye would be worth his salt (and his lime and tequila?) if he did not keep a bottle of something in his lower desk drawer.

We are always in control: that is the message of the fictions of alcohol, and of the advertisements for alcohol. It is, I am convinced, the real root of the disease—the desire for total control of the environment, and the denial that there are things that can happen to us over which we have *no* control. "You have the *right* to feel rotten," said my alcohol counselor, and it was an insight and a revelation of some cultural as well as personal import. Because the liberal myth of American society is precisely that you *needn't* feel rotten: and if you do, if you happen to be black in a white world or female in a male world or chemically addicted in a "normal" world, then there must be something wrong with you. How to fix it? Well you know, you can always have a drink.

Booze—since it tried so hard to kill me, I enjoy calling it by its vulgarest name—is a kind of inverted sacrament. It is a chemically-authenticated denial of the Fall (after the third beer, do you feel that anything is *wrong* with you?) and it is marketed as such. Lately I understand why bread and wine are the materials of the Eucharist—as opposed, say, to water and roast beef; because bread and wine *are* products of civilization, unimaginable to pre-Neolithic, which is to say, pre-urban man, and the Eucharist is a blessing, a *baruch*, on the chances for urban man to exchange his urbanity for something like transcendence. But Eucharist is not euphoria, and what liquor advertising in America sells is euphoria: the camaraderie of ex-football players downing lite beer after lite beer, the romanticism of a man in a tuxedo and a woman in an evening dress sharing a snifter of brandy, or the pure success-myth of a wealthy entertainer and businesswoman extolling the virtues of her favorite brand of vodka. The point of this sacrament is not that it conduces toward transcendence, but precisely that it reintroduces us into the secular city where, already, we felt so hopeless and alone. The real horror of alcoholism, said Malcolm Lowry, a great novelist (*Under the Volcano*) and a drunk of Olympic-class proportions, is the terrible sterility of existence as *sold* to you.

And sold to whom? we might ask. Very few liquor ads involve women alone (except for sherry, which, as we all know, is "downright upright," right?). But the percentage of female alcoholism is—again, if statistics mean anything—rather rapidly approaching fifty percent of the total addicted population. Why the reticence, then? Just because, I think, we find the image of a woman drunk still more offensive than the image of a man drunk: sexist perhaps, but also an index of the degree to which we remain faintly embarrassed about using our drug of choice. And it is also significant, surely, that the most powerful of anti-alcohol ads on television are those which show us the suburban housewife asleep at noon on the sofa, with an empty bottle overturned at her feet and a cigarette smoldering in the ashtray. It is melodramatic stuff, to be sure; a second-rate Dickens couldn't have done worse. But it is also supremely intelligent, since, for a number of people, this is really what the specious glamor of the liquor ads comes down to.

Mack Sennett, the master of silent slapstick comedy, said that he always wanted to make a film where the Keystone Kops would, predictably, drive their car into a ditch, and then leave the camera rolling, so that the audience could—*would have to*—watch the cops crawl, bloody and broken, out of that terrible accident. They never let him do it. I, for one, would like to see one of those brandy or sherry commercials where the elegant man and woman congregate over their bottle and glasses, with a slow dissolve to the next morning: sprawled on the bed, hair dishevelled and sweaty, dry mouth, and unable to get up before noon.

I try not to be a moralist in these columns and I am not—repeat *not*— advocating a new prohibition or a ban on liquor advertising. But I am saying that a great deal of national distress is attributable to the way in which we market and mythicize this *very* dangerous substance. I am also, I suppose, suggesting that a large part of our natural and national growing-up process might be to realize that we *are* an addicted society, and that at least the first step toward a greater sanity might be facing up to that addiction. At the very least, we ought to be able to train ourselves to laugh as hard at "If you've got the time, we've got the beer" as we do at "Don't take your car, you'll kill yourself." The first one, after all, *is* the sillier line.

Questions for Comprehension

1. What do the two commercials McConnell cites tell us about our culture's attitude toward drinking?
2. What are the unusual features of alcoholism as a disease?
3. Why do people always drink in groups in beer commercials? How does this fact serve to legitimize drinking?

4. In what way is "the denial that there are things that can happen to us over which we have *no* control" the root of alcoholism? How do people use liquor to deny their helplessness?
5. What does McConnell mean when he asserts that alcohol "is a chemically-authenticated denial of the Fall"? How do the images advertisers associate with drinking sell a "euphoria" that denies human weakness?
6. Why does McConnell believe that people find the image of a drunken woman more offensive than the image of a drunken man?

■

PSYCHOGRAPHICS: ADVERTISING DISCOVERS THE WORLD ACCORDING TO VALS

William Meyers

William Meyers (b. 1951), a former advertising executive, is a journalist who specializes in advertising. The following essay is taken from his book *The Image Makers: Power and Persuasion on Madison Avenue* (1984).

Madison Avenue was in deep trouble a decade ago. After almost twenty-five years of unparalleled prosperity and growth—due in large part to the emergence of television as a powerful sales tool—it was no longer able to persuade the American public to purchase its clients' goods and services. Like a star pitcher who mysteriously loses the control of his fastball, the advertising industry's deft marketing touch had vanished.

The sudden disappearance of Ad Alley's consumer clout during the early 1970s shocked and alarmed advertisers across the country. Once-prosperous companies, realizing that their commercials were having little or no impact on potential customers, watched in dismay as their sales dropped, inventories grew, and bottom lines shrank.

The Age of Affluence, begun in the afterglow of World War II, was over. Buffeted by repeated bouts of inflation and recession, the average citizen was more concerned with coping and surviving than consuming and shopping. Even when marketers pushed America's BUY button—as they did frequently—it was often difficult for people to pay for advertised products and still make the monthly mortgage payments.

Between 1970 and 1981, stagflation slashed the purchasing power of a dollar by nearly 60 percent; productivity plummeted, and foreign competition took more than 2 million industrial jobs away from American workers, more and more of whom went on unemployment. And, naturally, debt deepened—from 35 percent of after-tax income in 1955 to 85 percent in 1975—as consumers tried to keep up with both the Joneses and the Consumer Price Index.

The Age of Leisure ended, too, as an increasing number of American women began making the daily trek to the office or factory. Stay-at-home females had traditionally been the advertising executive's favorite audience—chauvinists in the business called them "sitting ducks"—easy to reach on the tube via morning game shows or afternoon soap operas. These ladies, who had once welcomed visits from the Man from Glad and other Madison Avenue sales surrogates, were suddenly unavailable to advertisers during most of the day. They had exchanged the coffee klatch for the executive lunch, and the cleansing power of suds didn't matter so much anymore.

The Age of Innocence also came to a close, and the Age of Cynicism dawned. Skeptical and hostile consumers, wounded by Vietnam and wary after Watergate, turned against Madison Avenue and its version of the American Dream. Ralph Nader led the revolt against advertising's hidden persuaders and hucksters by pointing out their propensity for half-truth, exaggeration, and misrepresentation. He wasn't all wrong.

During the 1950s, executives up and down Ad Alley had created commercials that played fast and loose with the public. They put marbles in a bowl of soup so the few vegetables it contained would float to the top; they sprayed shaving cream, rather than real whipped cream, on a dessert to make it look richer; and they dressed actors as doctors and let them endorse drugs.

The advertising industry wasn't above using scare tactics to move goods thirty years ago either. One commercial warned of the "dangers" of heartburn and the "benefits" of an antacid tablet by pouring "stomach acid" over a handkerchief until it burned a hole in the cloth. Other phony demonstrations were common, too. One razor blade manufacturer had a piece of sandpaper "shaved" as smooth as silk on television to con men into buying its product.

The ads of the 1960s were equally hollow, although they were a bit more sophisticated. Consumers were still taken for granted and treated like ten-year-olds by Madison Avenue, which now relied on the gimmick instead of the trick as its primary tool of persuasion. Braniff Airlines painted its planes in bold, colorful patterns designed by the artist Alexander Calder and dressed its stewardesses in uniforms by Emilio Pucci. The advertising campaign crowed that this marked "The End of the Plain Plane," but it never mentioned what was in it for passengers. Hathaway threw a black eyepatch on a model to help make its shirts seem more stylish, and a bearded Commander Whitehead from Britain was recruited to make the drinking of tonic water appear cosmopolitan.

The 1960s were also the days when Tony the Tiger roared loudly to kids that Kellogg's Frosted Flakes were *G-r-r-reat*, even if they did contain an overdose of sugar, and the Pillsbury Doughboy waddled about on behalf of frozen rolls that were kept alive with chemicals and preservatives. And a rugged, healthy-looking cowboy became Marlboro's enduring symbol, riding off into the sunset inhaling the clean, fresh air of the Wild West between puffs on cancer-causing cigarettes. With a track record like this, it's no wonder that by the 1970s advertising executives regularly appeared at the bottom of the public's "most respected profession" list—below insurance salesmen and pawnshop proprietors.

Madison Avenue received its lowest marks from the members of the Woodstock Generation, who in the 1970s were dropping out of the consumer culture that Ad Alley had taken such pains to create. This group, of about 50 million disillusioned people between the ages of twenty-five and forty, constitutes approximately 20 percent of the total United States population today. Advertisers had been counting on these post–World War II baby-boomers to follow in the footsteps of their upwardly mobile parents, to become the strivers of tomorrow. But the stress and strain required for success made no sense to the children of the counterculture. They refused to accept the burden of ambition, and they rejected materialism. They sought inner growth rather than goods, meaning instead of money, personal fulfillment over power, and liberty over luxury. And this drove advertising executives crazy.

With their backs to the wall, advertising agency people were forced to examine where they had gone wrong and why consumers had begun to resist their sales pitches. After intensive study and research, the executives finally concluded that America was undergoing fundamental changes that were dramatically altering our society's values, attitudes, and beliefs. It became clear that Madison Avenue's old-fashioned gimmicks and stunts were no longer relevant to the average citizen. In short, we were living in a new age.

To get the rebellious public purchasing again, Ad Alley devised a new marketing technique: image transformation. This approach, known along Madison Avenue as the "face lift," sought to increase the value and worth of mundane mass products in the consumer's mind. By performing "plastic surgery" on various items and making them seem more appealing, advertising executives believed they could recycle and sell a host of goods and services that people said—or thought—they didn't want. Based on sophisticated psychological principles, this subtle form of manipulation linked products to people's most pressing vulnerabilities while offering them easy remedies for their anxieties and insecurities. A campaign that offered people an emotional reward improved their perception of an item. By associating blue jeans with sex appeal or cigarettes with peer approval, for example, Ad Alley was able to cajole recalcitrant citizens into buying. What's important to a potential customer on the verge of purchasing is how he feels about a product—not how, or whether, it works. Brand personality triumphs over brand performance.

To implement this innovative and insightful marketing strategy, Madison Avenue began dividing up Americans according to their innermost needs—their fears, desires, and prejudices. It adopted *psychographics*, as opposed to the Census Bureau's traditional demographics, to ensure that its sales pitches were aimed at the most susceptible consumer targets. Ad executives no longer relied exclusively on mere statistics to assess their audience. Instead, they developed detailed profiles of each population segment's attitudes and beliefs.

Agency-employed psychologists and sociologists refined this art of emotional exploitation by using a variety of psychographic research systems. For example, several shops conducted extensive interviews with consumers and partitioned the public into Resistant, Successful, and Traditional adapters—people who were either open to change and new ideas or tied to conventional standards. One firm broke the country down into Easy Streeters, Service Seekers, Environmentally Concerned, and The Resigned. Another company labeled post–World War II baby-boomers the "Sensation Generation," because its findings revealed that these consumers yearned for a rich and varied life-style.

One of the most widely used psychographic approaches on Ad Alley today, however, is VALS (Values and Life-Styles), designed by SRI International (formerly known as Stanford Research Institute) in Northern California. The world according to VALS is simple. There are essentially five basic groups of citizens in this nation—Belongers, Emulators, Emulator-Achievers, Societally Conscious Achievers, and the Need-Directed. Each segment of VALSociety is driven by its own special demons, demons that the advertising industry seeks to exorcise with its 30-second television commercials and print ads.

Whether today's marketers use the actual VALS terminology or another psychographic system, SRI's research approach accurately represents the way Madison Avenue divides America's consuming public into easily defined segments. The VALS labels are used throughout this book.

VALS tells us that almost one out of three citizens in the United States today is a *Belonger*—the typical traditionalist, the cautious and conforming conservative. Archie Bunker is a Belonger; he believes in God, country, and family. The lifeblood of the Belonger's world is a strong community consciousness. Change is his archenemy. Without a secure, stable, and structured society, this staunch defender of the status quo is unable to cope.

The Belonger's consumer profile reflects his old-fashioned view of things. He usually drives a Dodge or a Plymouth; he drinks Coke, Pepsi, or Budweiser; he eats at McDonald's with the family; he loves Jell-O; and his wife scrubs the bathroom tiles with Lestoil or Spic and Span.

In the 1970s, Belongers were caught by surprise as their sheltered environment, so carefully constructed through the years, was dismantled bit by bit. The cherished concept of a happy home and hearth withered over the decade as nonfamilial living in America increased by 75 percent, largely because of divorce and the flight of young adults from the nest at an earlier age. By 1980, one out of four American households was headed by a single man or woman. The spirit of community camaraderie faded away as approximately 50 percent of all Americans hit the road, often moving from the densely populated inner-city neighborhoods of the Northeast and Midwest to the sprawling suburbs and rural ranges of the Sunbelt. A sense of self-sufficiency also evaporated during these ten years; paychecks from industrial jobs and hard manual labor, which had once fueled the Belonger's faith in the American Dream, were gradually lost as the industrial economy shriveled and a service economy took its place.

Madison Avenue rescues Belongers and helps bind their psychic wounds with commercials that offer a world of idealized images. McDonald's, for example, uses the Big Mac in its ad campaigns to lure the shattered family back together. Pepsi and Coke have traditionally featured picnics and Frisbee flings. Ma Bell eases the loneliness of long-distance relationships with its "Reach Out and Touch Someone" campaign. And Miller Beer's advertising reinforces the warm glow of fraternity to help lessen the pressures of the workplace.

Emulators are not so set in their ways. They are a small but impressionable group of young people in desperate search of an identity and a place in the adult working world. These kids, who represent about 15 percent of the American population, will do almost anything to fit in. Most of them lack self-confidence and are discouraged about their prospects. They envision little future for themselves in our society. They compensate for this pessimism with unabashed personal hedonism. Confused and vulnerable, Emulators will purchase products from advertisers who offer solutions to their postadolescent dilemmas. In dealing with Emulators, advertisers prey on their insecurity.

Chevrolet, for example, has sold hundreds of thousands of Camaros to these uncertain youngsters by positioning the vehicle as the coolest car on the market. Dr. Pepper became a major soft drink in this country with its "Be a Pepper" campaign, which offered teenagers the reassurance of group acceptance and friendship. The tobacco business also capitalized on this segment's precarious sense of self-worth.

During the 1970s, the cigarette industry became a tough-but-tender authority figure for Emulators. With most adult smokers already hooked on their favorite brands, the growth of individual tobacco companies depends on the uninitiated. That's why cigarette manufacturers spend almost $2 billion a year trying to get youngsters to light up. By law, these corporations can't harness the power of television to advertise, so instead they have created a striking iconography in newspapers and magazines.

Tobacco ads featuring heroes and heroines, Madison Avenue's idea of role models, help unsure Emulators to find themselves. The solitary cowboy's message for young men is to smoke Marlboro if they want to be independent and strong. The macho outdoorsmen from Camel and Winston seem to say, "Take a puff of this and you'll be tough like us." The Kool campaign, associating that brand with a hip jazz ensemble, lets young blacks know that it's cool to smoke Kools.

Fashionable ladies symbolizing Virgina Slims inject young women with the positive spirit of accomplishment. If this is your cigarette, they seem to be saying, all good things are possible—especially a glamorous and profitable career. The message must be getting through. Despite medical studies linking tobacco to cancer, the number of female teenage smokers in this country has increased by 40 percent since 1975.

Emulator-Achievers, America's materialists, have already made it. These acquisitive consumers often own a Mercedes; they feel most comfortable with such "uptown" brand names as Dom Pérignon, Tiffany, or Gucci; and they have to have the latest in high-tech toys—Sony's Betamax or Casio's wristwatch television.

Although they have reached a prosperous plateau of middle-class success and status, Emulator-Achievers still want to derive even greater financial rewards from the system. But the new era of limits has cramped their hard-driving style, making additional monetary gains next to impossible. Emulator-Achievers, approximately 20 percent of the population, are in a funk. Once they believed the sky was the limit; today they feel frustrated, perhaps a bit cheated, stuck just below the top rung of the economic ladder. Despite their relative affluence, three-quarters of these striving citizens said they were dissatisfied with the quality of their lives in the early 1980s. Over 50 percent of them feared they wouldn't be able to attain their fiscal goals during the coming decade.

Madison Avenue cheers up Emulator-Achievers with commercials that transform everyday items into accouterments of accomplishment, success, and taste. Advertisers convince these compulsive consumers that by purchasing certain products they will be seen as the modern aristocrats they seek to be.

Clothing manufacturers such as Ralph Lauren and Izod, who put little polo players and alligators on the breast pockets of cotton shirts, offer simple togs with fancy prices that give consumers a sense of upper-crust respectability. And one recent ad for Johnnie Walker Black showed a picture of a mansion with a lawn stretching as far as the eye could see. The caption informed covetous Emulator-Achievers, "On the way up, the work may not get easier, but the rewards get better." The message was clear: Serve this scotch to your friends, and you'll be just like the landed gentry—even if you do live on half an acre in the suburbs. Ad executives know that to get Emulator-Achievers into the stores, you've got to offer them the opportunity to be king or queen for a day.

Societally Conscious Achievers are the flower children of America's consumer culture. They are members of the post–World War II baby-boom generation who care more about inner peace and environmental safety than about financial success and elegant surroundings. Personal, not professional, fulfillment matters most to these individualists. Societally Conscious Achievers, constituting approximately 20 percent of the U.S. population, are experimental—they will try anything from acupuncture to Zen, as long as it fits into their uncomplicated lifestyle. Unlike the Emulator-Achievers, whose materialistic drives are constrained by the economy, these gradually graying hippies are self-constrained in their purchasing behavior. Many of them are dropouts from the world of commerce—reformed strivers who no longer see the need for conspicuous consumption.

A typical Societally Conscious Achiever might be an antiques dealer living in a nineteenth-century barn he restored himself. Instead of spending his weekends carousing at the country club with doctors, lawyers, or stockbrokers, he's busy tending to his organic garden. A lover of the outdoors, he wants to share this experience with his kids, who spend their free time hiking through the woods rather than playing video games.

Societally Conscious Achievers often shop for their clothing by mail, choosing L. L. Bean moccasins over Gucci loafers, and they usually drive small foreign cars—Mazda, Honda, Volvo, or Subaru. Lighter wines or such wholesome beverages as herbal tea, fruit juice, or bottled water are preferred by these inner-directed citizens to the scotch, vodka, or gin that their parents drink. If they smoke at all, counterculturalists generally puff on "healthy" low-tar Merits. These fitness-oriented citizens also take their exercise seriously; Nike and New Balance running shoes are essential parts of their athletic wardrobe.

Societally Conscious Achievers are the ad industry's toughest challenge. They turn a deaf ear to advertising unless it whispers softly. They need to be told in their own iconoclastic language that their low-key values and attitudes make sense. Several imported car manufacturers have won the confidence of Societally Conscious Achievers by emphasizing such counterculture buzzwords as "simplicity" and "integrity." Volvo calls itself "a car you can believe in." Subaru says it's "inexpensive, and built to stay that way."

Societally Conscious Achievers are elusive, but they are the fastest-growing and most influential group of citizens in the country. It is estimated that by 1990 almost one-third of the United States will share their practical world view. As a result, an increasing number of marketers are quickly learning the new vocabulary and switching from high-tech to high-touch commercials.

Need-Directed Americans are the survivors, the people struggling to sustain themselves on subsistence incomes. Mostly welfare recipients, Social Security beneficiaries, and minimum-wage earners, these citizens, who represent close to 15 percent of the country, aren't consumers in the true sense of the word. They're so busy trying to make ends meet that they really don't have time to worry about the type of beer they drink or the image projected by the cigarettes they smoke. The Need-Directed aren't driving new cars or acquiring state-of-the-art personal computers, and they rarely have enough money to take the family out for even a fast-food meal.

As far as Ad Alley is concerned, the Need-Directed don't exist. They are the people who are least affected by television commercials in this country. When you're dirt-poor, a dollar will stretch only so far, and you buy what you can afford. Even the wizards of Madison Avenue can't find a cure for poverty.

Questions for Comprehension

1. How does Meyers account for the declining influence of advertising in the seventies? How did the end of the Age of Affluence, the Age of Leisure, and the Age of Innocence all contribute to the decline?
2. What is "image transformation"? How does it sell products?
3. What is "psychographics"? Why is the information provided by psychographics necessary for advertisers using the technique of image transformation?
4. What are the values of Belongers? How were those values undermined in the 1970s? How do advertisers help bind the "psychic wounds" of Belongers?
5. What kinds of people are Emulators? How do advertisers exploit their insecurities?
6. What are the values of Emulator-Achievers? What accounts for the feeling of frustration many of them feel? How do advertisers exploit this feeling?
7. What are the values of Societally Conscious Achievers? How does the advertising industry meet the challenge they represent?
8. What kinds of people are Need-Directed? What is the advertising industry's attitude toward them?

■

ADVERTISING SAYS, "LET US FEEL GOOD ABOUT OURSELVES"

Michael Schudson

Michael Schudson (b. 1946), educated at Swarthmore College and Harvard University, is professor of sociology and communication at the University of California, San Diego. He has written extensively on advertising and journalism. The following article, which reports an interview with Schudson, was first published in *U.S. News & World Report* in 1985.

"Commercials don't create a consumerist world"

Television commercials that depict a rich, leisured lifestyle reinforce attitudes and desires toward materialism, but they don't create a consumerist world. If we think of advertising as art, and we're surrounded not by icons and paintings of the saints, as people were at one time, but by icons and paintings of commercially manufactured products day after day and hour after hour, we are led to believe that everyone around us is living well and gaining some satisfaction by using advertised products. We are not persuaded that we are going to have a wonderful sex life if we go out and buy a particular cologne, but the weight of advertising makes us more aware of and disposed to the world of consumption.

Yet people's aspirations are not simply created by ads. The whole style of life, the high-intensity capitalist culture, has come about for a variety of reasons—urbanization, the growth of the media, the shifting of family patterns and the like. One thing that has been very important in shaping trends in consumer products in the past decade is that a lot more people are living alone. Did advertising create that? No. But once that trend was established, companies tried to capitalize on it by designing cups of soup and meals for one and then advertising them to meet the needs of a new category of person.

"Advertisers are like surfers"

Advertising is socially conservative; it doesn't want to associate a product with some trend so new that it might not be accepted. Advertisers are like surfers: They want to catch a wave as it's rising. They'd like to get on that wave ahead of everybody else, but only after they are sure that it is going to be a big one. They don't want to get stuck in a little trough.

A good example relates to women smoking cigarettes back in the 1920s. Tobacco companies self-consciously avoided advertising to women until it was clear that tens of thousands of them were smoking and the trend was accelerating.

But there is one way in which advertising enlarges on social trends. Ad experts, who tend to live in places such as New York, Chicago and Los Angeles, may take note of a new development that they see around them before the trend reaches places more removed from the cultural centers. Maybe the middle-class folks in Wichita don't become aware of break dancing until they see it in a soft-drink commercial. The ad brings it to their attention and helps to spread break dancing.

One way for society to "affirm its values"

Any social system needs to affirm itself and its values. It needs to say, "This is who we are, and we feel good about it." Advertising is a way we do this. Ads remind us that this is a country of private people, private ambitions, individual achievement and purportedly infinite material possibility. Ads remind us day after day of a world of choice, abundance and freedom. This focuses on very limited aspects of our lives, and the choice, freedom and abundance exist within very circumscribed, commercial categories. In that sense, ads are misleading but in a way that says, "Let us affirm ourselves, and let us feel good about ourselves."

Do ads really persuade?

Businesses use advertising, hope it works, but rely as little as possible on its persuasive powers. They want ads to inform people about new products, but they really don't believe that this will turn anyone's head around who already knows about some product category. So they tend to put their advertising behind products that are already doing well. And they put their advertising most heavily in front of audiences or subpopulations already inclined toward the product.

In the very way they marshal their forces, businesses indicate that they think ads are going to work most of all by reminding people who already know what they want rather than by persuading people of something new.

Questions for Comprehension

1. What are the forces apart from advertising that help create people's aspirations?
2. In what way are advertisers like surfers? How does Schudson's simile help to clarify the relationship between advertising and social trends?
3. How can advertising enlarge upon social trends?
4. What values does advertising affirm?
5. What is the attitude of businesses toward advertising?

ADDITIONAL WRITING ASSIGNMENTS

1. Summarize either Frank McConnell's article "Ads & Addictions: Booze on the Tube," or Maurine Christopher's article "When TV Ads Become Most Disreputable," remembering that the readers of your summary need the thesis of the original and the key supporting ideas.
2. Paul Stevens' classic essay on deceptive language in advertising was first published in 1972. After reading the article, skim some present-day advertising to see if Stevens' analysis is still accurate. Write an essay in which you demonstrate to your readers how "weasel words" are still used today, or else how you think things have changed.
3. Read Maurine Christopher's article "When TV Ads Become Most Disreputable." Based on advertising you have seen, describe the approaches (or types) of ads you find objectionable. Then propose to your readers what you believe is an appropriate response to such ads. (Christopher, for example, suggests what she thinks should be done about political advertising.)
4. As you read William Meyers' article on psychographics, note the five basic groups of consumers as defined by the VALS system. Select one of the groups

and write an essay in which you identify the group you've selected and then illustrate for your readers how current ads are designed for this particular segment of consumers. You can draw examples and evidence from radio, television, and print advertisements to prove your point.

5. In "Advertising Says, 'Let Us Feel Good About Ourselves'" Michael Schudson claims that advertising is a way we affirm our values and say who we are collectively. Assume that someone's knowledge of the United States was limited entirely to advertisements. What picture of Americans, their interests, and their values would that person form on the basis of ads? You will want to focus on the general conclusions such a person would draw.

A Casebook on William Faulkner's "A Rose for Emily"

THE FOLLOWING CASEBOOK IS A SUPPLEMENTAL anthology that your instructor may wish to use as source material for one of the projects in the text. The anthology consists of a series of essays about a literary work, William Faulkner's short story "A Rose for Emily." We have included a number of writing assignments that stress the skills discussed in the projects. The first writing assignment, for example, is a summary, and the second a simple synthesis. Most of the assignments, however, emphasize the primary use of literary criticism—to help readers gain insight into a literary work.

William Faulkner's "A Rose for Emily" was first published in 1930. Its author, one of the greatest American writers, was born in New Albany, Mississippi in 1897, the descendant (like Emily Grierson in the story) of a Southern aristocratic family that had seen better days. In 1902 Faulkner's family moved to Oxford, Mississippi, where Faulkner lived most of his life. After a succession of odd jobs (including a brief stint in the Royal Canadian Air Force) Faulkner enrolled at the University of Mississippi, dropping out after two years to pursue his own writing interests.

William Faulkner is most celebrated for the great series of novels set in the fictional Mississippi county of Yoknapatawpha, beginning with *Sartoris* in 1929 and including *The Sound and the Fury* (1929), *As I Lay Dying* (1930), *Light in August* (1932), *Absalom, Absalom!* (1936), and *The Hamlet* (1940). He also worked in Hollywood as a screenwriter for MGM, producing scripts for such memorable films as *To Have and Have Not* and *The Big Sleep*. In 1949 Faulkner was awarded the Nobel Prize for literature. He died of a heart attack in Oxford, Mississippi, in 1962.

Since its publication in 1930, "A Rose for Emily" has fascinated readers in much the way that Emily Grierson herself seems to have dominated conversation in Jefferson, Mississippi. The essays below reflect a variety of interpretations and approaches to the story. Naturally, most of these interpretations emphasize the personality of Emily Grierson. In an essay from their influential textbook *Understanding Fiction*, Cleanth Brooks and Robert Penn Warren discuss Emily's paradoxical position as "idol and scapegoat for the community," stressing, finally, the tragic aspects of her personality. Ray B. West, Jr., on the other hand, stresses the "monstrous and inhuman" results of Emily's failure to come to terms with the passing of time. West's view of the story is in turn challenged by William Van O'Conner, who disagrees with West's view that Emily's rejection of the passing of time represents a conflict between the Old and New South. Jack Scherting takes a psychoanalytic approach to Emily's character, finding in her relationship to Homer Barron a sublimation of her Oedipal feelings toward her own father. Judith Fetterley brings a feminist perspective to the story, exploring "the violence done to a woman by making her a lady."

The last three essays in the anthology discuss specific aspects of the story. T. J. Stafford explains the significance of an often-overlooked character, Emily Grierson's black servant Tobe. Helen E. Nebeker offers a startling interpretation of the relationship between Emily and the narrator of the story. Finally, Robert Crosman employs a "reader response" approach, assigning the creation of meaning in a literary work to readers, not authors.

■

A ROSE FOR EMILY

William Faulkner

I

When Miss Emily Grierson died, our whole town went to her funeral: the men through a sort of respectful affection for a fallen monument, the women mostly out of curiosity to see the inside of her house, which no one save an old manservant—a combined gardener and cook—had seen in at least ten years.

It was a big, squarish frame house that had once been white, decorated with cupolas and spires and scrolled balconies in the heavily lightsome style of the seventies, set on what had once been our most select street. But garages and cotton gins had encroached and obliterated even the august names of that neighborhood; only Miss Emily's house was left, lifting its stubborn and coquettish decay above the cotton wagons and the gasoline pumps—an eyesore among eyesores. And now Miss Emily had gone to join the representatives of those august names where they lay in the cedar-bemused cemetery among the ranked and anonymous graves of Union and Confederate soldiers who fell at the battle of Jefferson.

Alive, Miss Emily had been a tradition, a duty, and a care; a sort of hereditary obligation upon the town, dating from that day in 1894 when Colonel Sartoris, the mayor—he who fathered the edict that no Negro woman should appear on the streets without an apron—remitted her taxes, the dispensation dating from the death of her father on into perpetuity. Not that Miss Emily would have accepted charity. Colonel Sartoris invented an involved tale to the effect that Miss Emily's father had loaned money to the town, which the town, as a matter of business, preferred this way of repaying. Only a man of Colonel Sartoris' generation and thought could have invented it, and only a woman could have believed it.

When the next generation, with its more modern ideas, became mayors and aldermen, this arrangement created some little dissatisfaction. On the first of the year they mailed her a tax notice. February came, and there was no reply. They wrote her a formal letter, asking her to call at the sheriff's office at her convenience. A week later the mayor wrote her himself, offering to call or to send his car for her, and received in reply a note on paper of an archaic shape, in a thin, flowing calligraphy in faded ink, to the effect that she no longer went out at all. The tax notice was also enclosed, without comment.

They called a special meeting of the Board of Aldermen. A deputation waited upon her, knocked at the door through which no visitor had passed since she ceased giving china-painting lessons eight or ten years earlier. They were admitted by the old Negro into a dim hall from which a stairway mounted into still more shadow. It smelled of dust and disuse—a close, dank smell. The Negro led them into the parlor. It was furnished in heavy, leather-covered furniture. When the Negro opened the blinds of one window, a faint dust rose sluggishly about their thighs, spinning with slow motes in the single sun-ray. On a tarnished gilt easel before the fireplace stood a crayon portrait of Miss Emily's father.

They rose when she entered—a small, fat woman in black, with a thin gold chain descending to her waist and vanishing into her belt, leaning on an ebony cane with a tarnished gold head. Her skeleton was small and spare; perhaps that was why what would have been merely plumpness in another was obesity in her. She looked bloated, like a body long submerged in motionless water, and of that pallid hue. Her eyes, lost in the fatty ridges of her face, looked like two small pieces of coal pressed into a lump of dough as they moved from one face to another while the visitors stated their errand.

She did not ask them to sit. She just stood in the door and listened quietly until the spokesman came to a stumbling halt. Then they could hear the invisible watch ticking at the end of the gold chain.

Her voice was dry and cold. "I have no taxes in Jefferson. Colonel Sartoris explained it to me. Perhaps one of you can gain access to the city records and satisfy yourselves."

"But we have. We are the city authorities, Miss Emily. Didn't you get a notice from the sheriff, signed by him?"

"I received a paper, yes," Miss Emily said. "Perhaps he considers himself the sheriff. . . . I have no taxes in Jefferson."

"But there is nothing on the books to show that, you see. We must go by the—"

"See Colonel Sartoris. I have no taxes in Jefferson."

"But, Miss Emily—"

"See Colonel Sartoris." (Colonel Sartoris had been dead almost ten years.) "I have no taxes in Jefferson. Tobe!" The Negro appeared. "Show these gentlemen out."

II

So she vanquished them, horse and foot, just as she had vanquished their fathers thirty years before about the smell. That was two years after her father's death and a short time after her sweetheart—the one we believed would marry her—had deserted her. After her father's death she went out very little; after her sweetheart went away, people hardly saw her at all. A few of the ladies had the temerity to call, but were not received, and the only sign of life about the place was the Negro man—a young man then—going in and out with a market basket.

"Just as if a man—any man—could keep a kitchen properly," the ladies said; so they were not surprised when the smell developed. It was another link between the gross, teeming world and the high and mighty Griersons.

A neighbor, a woman, complained to the mayor, Judge Stevens, eighty years old.

"But what will you have me do about it, madam?" he said.

"Why, send her word to stop it," the woman said. "Isn't there a law?"

"I'm sure that won't be necessary," Judge Stevens said. "It's probably just a snake or a rat that nigger of hers killed in the yard. I'll speak to him about it."

The next day he received two more complaints, one from a man who came in diffident deprecation. "We really must do something about it, Judge. I'd be the last one in the world to bother Miss Emily, but we've got to do something." That night the Board of Aldermen met—three graybeards and one younger man, a member of the rising generation.

"It's simple enough," he said. "Send her word to have her place cleaned up. Give her a certain time to do it in, and if she don't . . ."

"Dammit, sir," Judge Stevens said, "will you accuse a lady to her face of smelling bad?"

So the next night, after midnight, four men crossed Miss Emily's lawn and slunk about the house like burglars, sniffing along the base of the brickwork and at the cellar openings while one of them performed a regular sowing motion with his hand out of a sack slung from his shoulder. They broke open the cellar door and sprinkled lime there, and in all the outbuildings. As they recrossed the lawn, a window that had been dark was lighted and Miss Emily sat in it, the light behind her, and her upright torso motionless as that of an idol. They crept quietly across the lawn and into the shadow of the locusts that lined the street. After a week or two the smell went away.

That was when people had begun to feel really sorry for her. People in our town, remembering how old lady Wyatt, her great-aunt, had gone completely crazy at last, believed that the Griersons held themselves a little too high for what they really were. None of the young men were quite good enough for Miss Emily and such. We had long thought of them as a tableau; Miss Emily a slender figure in white in the background, her father a spraddled silhouette in the foreground, his back to her and clutching a horsewhip, the two of them framed by the back-flung front door. So when she got to be thirty and was still single, we were not pleased exactly, but vindicated; even with insanity in the family she wouldn't have turned down all of her chances if they had really materialized.

When her father died, it got about that the house was all that was left to her; and in a way, people were glad. At last they could pity Miss Emily. Being left alone, and a pauper, she had become humanized. Now she too would know the old thrill and the old despair of a penny more or less.

The day after his death all the ladies prepared to call at the house and offer condolence and aid, as is our custom. Miss Emily met them at the door, dressed as usual and with no trace of grief on her face. She told them that her father was not dead. She did that for three days, with the ministers calling on her, and the doctors, trying to persuade her to let them dispose of the body. Just as they were about to resort to law and force, she broke down, and they buried her father quickly.

We did not say she was crazy then. We believed she had to do that. We remembered all the young men her father had driven away, and we knew that with nothing left, she would have to cling to that which had robbed her, as people will.

III

She was sick for a long time. When we saw her again, her hair was cut short, making her look like a girl, with a vague resemblance to those angels in colored church windows—sort of tragic and serene.

The town had just let the contracts for paving the sidewalks, and in the summer after her father's death they began to work. The construction company came with niggers and mules and machinery, and a foreman named Homer Barron, a Yankee—a big, dark, ready man, with a big voice and eyes lighter than his face. The little boys would follow in groups to hear him cuss the niggers, and the niggers singing in time to the rise and fall of picks. Pretty soon he knew everybody in town. Whenever you heard a lot of laughing anywhere about the square, Homer Barron would be in the center of the group. Presently we began to see him and Miss Emily on Sunday afternoons driving in the yellow-wheeled buggy and the matched team of bays from the livery stable.

At first we were glad that Miss Emily would have an interest, because the ladies all said, "Of course a Grierson would not think seriously of a Northerner, a day laborer." But there were still others, older people, who said that even grief could not cause a real lady to forget *noblesse oblige*—without calling it *noblesse oblige*. They just said, "Poor Emily. Her kinsfolk should come to her." She had some kin in Alabama; but years ago her father had fallen out with them over the estate of old lady Wyatt, the crazy woman, and there was no communication between the two families. They had not even been represented at the funeral.

And as soon as the old people said, "Poor Emily," the whispering began. "Do you suppose it's really so?" they said to one another. "Of course it is. What else could . . ." This behind their hands; rustling of craned silk and satin behind jalousies closed upon the sun of Sunday afternoon as the thin, swift clop-clop-clop of the matched team passed: "Poor Emily."

She carried her head high enough—even when we believed that she was fallen. It was as if she demanded more than ever the recognition of her dignity as the last Grierson; as if it had wanted that touch of earthiness to reaffirm her imperviousness. Like when she bought the rat poison, the arsenic. That was over a year after they had begun to say "Poor Emily," and while the two female cousins were visiting her.

"I want some poison," she said to the druggist. She was over thirty then, still a slight woman, though thinner than usual, with cold, haughty black eyes in a face the flesh of which was strained across the temples and about the eyesockets as you imagine a lighthouse-keeper's face ought to look. "I want some poison," she said.

"Yes, Miss Emily. What kind? For rats and such? I'd recom—"

"I want the best you have. I don't care what kind."

The druggist named several. "They'll kill anything up to an elephant. But what you want is—"

"Arsenic," Miss Emily said. "Is that a good one?"

"Is . . . arsenic? Yes ma'am. But what you want—"

"I want arsenic."

The druggist looked down at her. She looked back at him, erect, her face like a strained flag. "Why, of course," the druggist said. "If that's what you want. But the law requires you to tell what you are going to use it for."

Miss Emily just stared at him, her head tilted back in order to look him eye for eye, until he looked away and went and got the arsenic and wrapped it up. The Negro delivery boy brought her the package; the druggist didn't come back. When she opened the package at home there was written on the box, under the skull and bones: "For rats."

IV

So the next day we all said, "She will kill herself"; and we said it would be the best thing. When she had first begun to be seen with Homer Barron, we had said, "She will marry him." Then we said, "She will persuade him yet," because Homer himself had remarked—he liked men, and it was known that he drank with the younger men in the Elk's Club—that he was not a marrying man. Later we said, "Poor Emily" behind the jalousies as they passed on Sunday afternoon in the glittering buggy, Miss Emily with her head high and Homer Barron with his hat cocked and a cigar in his teeth, reins and whip in a yellow glove.

Then some of the ladies began to say that it was a disgrace to the town and a bad example to the young people. The men did not want to interfere, but at last the ladies forced the Baptist minister—Miss Emily's people were Episcopal—to call upon her. He would never divulge what happened during that interview, but he refused to go back again. The next Sunday they again drove about the streets, and the following day the minister's wife wrote to Miss Emily's relations in Alabama.

So she had blood-kin under her roof again and we sat back to watch developments. At first nothing happened. Then we were sure that they were to be married. We learned that Miss Emily had been to the jeweler's and ordered a man's toilet set in silver, with the letters H.B. on each piece. Two days later we learned that she had bought a complete outfit of men's clothing, including a nightshirt, and we said, "They are married." We were really glad. We were glad because the two female cousins were even more Grierson than Miss Emily had ever been.

So we were not surprised when Homer Barron—the streets had been finished some time since—was gone. We were a little disappointed that there was not a public blowing-off, but we believed that he had gone on to prepare for Miss Emily's coming, or to give her a chance to get rid of the cousins. (By that time it was a cabal, and we were all Miss Emily's allies to help circumvent the cousins.) Sure enough, after another week they departed. And, as we had expected all along, within three days Homer Barron was back in town. A neighbor saw the Negro man admit him at the kitchen door at dusk one evening.

And that was the last we saw of Homer Barron. And of Miss Emily for some time. The Negro man went in and out with the market basket, but the front door remained closed. Now and then we would see her at a window for a moment, as the men did that night when they sprinkled the lime, but for almost six months she did not appear on the streets. Then we knew that this was to be expected too; as if that quality of her father which had thwarted her woman's life so many times had been too virulent and too furious to die.

When we next saw Miss Emily, she had grown fat and her hair was turning gray. During the next few years it grew grayer and grayer until it attained an even pepper-and-salt iron-gray, when it ceased turning. Up to the day of her death at seventy-four it was still that vigorous iron-gray, like the hair of an active man.

From that time on her front door remained closed, save for a period of six or seven years, when she was about forty, during which she gave lessons in china-painting. She fitted up a studio in one of the downstairs rooms, where the daughters and granddaughters of Colonel Sartoris' contemporaries were sent to her with the same regularity and in the same spirit that they were sent to church on Sundays with a twenty-five-cent piece for the collection plate. Meanwhile her taxes had been remitted.

Then the newer generation became the backbone and the spirit of the town, and the painting pupils grew up and fell away and did not send their children to her with boxes of color and tedious brushes and pictures cut from the ladies' magazines. The front door closed upon the last one and remained closed for good. When the town got free postal delivery Miss Emily alone refused to let them fasten the metal numbers above her door and attach a mailbox to it. She would not listen to them.

Daily, monthly, yearly we watched the Negro grow grayer and more stooped, going in and out with the market basket. Each December we sent her a tax notice, which would be returned by the post office a week later, unclaimed. Now and then we would see her in one of the downstairs windows—she had evidently shut up the top floor of the house—like the carven torso of an idol in a niche, looking or not looking at us, we could never tell which. Thus she passed from generation to generation—dear, inescapable, impervious, tranquil, and perverse.

And so she died. Fell ill in the house filled with dust and shadows, with only a doddering Negro man to wait on her. We did not even know she was sick; we had long since given up trying to get any information from the Negro. He talked to no one, probably not even to her, for his voice had grown harsh and rusty, as if from disuse.

She died in one of the downstairs rooms, in a heavy walnut bed with a curtain, her gray head propped on a pillow yellow and moldy with age and lack of sunlight.

V

The Negro met the first of the ladies at the front door and let them in, with their hushed, sibilant voices and their quick, curious glances, and then he disappeared. He walked right through the house and out the back and was not seen again.

The two female cousins came at once. They held the funeral on the second day, with the town coming to look at Miss Emily beneath a mass of bought flowers, with the crayon face of her father musing profoundly above the bier and the ladies sibilant and macabre; and the very old men—some in their brushed Confederate uniforms—on the porch and the lawn, talking of Miss Emily as if she had been a contemporary of theirs, believing that they had danced with her and courted her perhaps, confusing time with its mathematical progression, as the old do, to whom all the past is not a diminishing road but, instead, a huge meadow which no winter ever quite touches, divided from them now by the narrow bottleneck of the most recent decade of years.

Already we knew that there was one room in that region above stairs which no one had seen in forty years, and which would have to be forced. They waited until Miss Emily was decently in the ground before they opened it.

The violence of breaking down the door seemed to fill this room with pervading dust. A thin, acrid pall as of the tomb seemed to lie everywhere upon this room decked and furnished as for a bridal: upon the valance curtains of faded rose color, upon the rose-shaded lights, upon the dressing table, upon the delicate array of crystal and the man's toilet things backed with tarnished silver, silver so tarnished that the monogram was obscured. Among them lay a collar and tie, as if they had just been removed, which, lifted, left upon the surface a pale crescent in the dust. Upon a chair hung the suit, carefully folded; beneath it the two mute shoes and the discarded socks.

The man himself lay in the bed.

For a long while we just stood there, looking down at the profound and fleshless grin. The body had apparently once lain in the attitude of an embrace, but now the long sleep that outlasts love, that conquers even the grimace of love, had cuckolded him. What was left of him, rotted beneath what was left of the nightshirt, had become inextricable from the bed in which he lay; and upon him and upon the pillow beside him lay that even coating of the patient and biding dust.

Then we noticed that in the second pillow was the indentation of a head. One of us lifted something from it, and leaning forward, that faint and invisible dust dry and acrid in the nostrils, we saw a long strand of iron-gray hair.

AN INTERPRETATION OF "A ROSE FOR EMILY"

Cleanth Brooks and Robert Penn Warren

Cleanth Brooks (b. 1906) is one of the most influential American literary critics and a leading figure in the critical movement known as the New Criticism. Robert Penn Warren (b. 1905) is a novelist, poet, essayist, and literary critic. He is perhaps best known for his Pulitzer Prize–winning novel *All the King's Men*. The following essay was published in Brooks and Warren's *Understanding Fiction* in 1943.

1   This is a story of horror. We have a decaying mansion in which the protagonist, shut away from the world, grows into something monstrous, and becomes as divorced from the human as some fungus growing in the dark on a damp wall. Miss Emily Grierson remains in voluntary isolation (or perhaps fettered by some inner compulsion) away from the bustle and dust and sunshine of the human world of normal affairs, and what in the end is found in the upstairs room gives perhaps a sense of penetrating and gruesome horror.

2   Has this sense of horror been conjured up for its own sake? If not, then why has the author contrived to insert so much of the monstrous into the story? In other words, does the horror contribute to the theme of Faulkner's story? Is the horror meaningful?

3   In order to answer this question, we shall have to examine rather carefully some of the items earlier in the story. In the first place, why does Miss Emily commit her monstrous act? Is she supplied with a proper motivation? Faulkner has, we can see, been rather careful to prepare for his dénouement. Miss Emily, it becomes obvious fairly early in the story, is one of those persons for whom the distinction between reality and illusion has blurred out. For example, she refuses to admit that she owes any taxes. When the mayor protests, she does not recognize him as mayor. Instead, she refers the committee to Colonel Sartoris, who, as the reader is told, has been dead for nearly ten years. For Miss Emily, apparently, Colonel Sartoris is still alive. Most specific preparation of all, when her father dies, she denies to the townspeople for three days that he is dead. "Just as they were about to resort to law and force, she broke down, and they buried her father quickly."

4   Miss Emily is obviously a pathological case. The narrator indicates plainly enough that people felt that she was crazy. All of this explanation prepares us for what Miss Emily does in order to hold her lover—the dead lover is in one sense still alive for her—the realms of reality and appearance merge. But having said

this, we have got no nearer to justifying the story: for, if Faulkner is merely interested in relating a case history of abnormal psychology, the story lacks meaning and justification as a story. . . . If the story is to be justified, there must be what may be called a moral significance, a meaning in moral terms—not merely psychological terms.

Incidentally, it is very easy to misread the story as merely a horrible case history, presented in order to titillate the reader. Faulkner has been frequently judged to be doing nothing more than this in his work.

The lapse of the distinction between illusion and reality, between life and death, is important, therefore, in helping to account for Miss Emily's motivation, but merely to note this lapse is not fully to account for the theme of the story.

Suppose we approach the motivation again in these terms: what is Miss Emily like? What are the mainsprings of her character? What causes the distinction between illusion and reality to blur out for her? She is obviously a woman of tremendous firmness of will. In the matter of the taxes, crazed though she is, she is never at a loss. She is utterly composed. She dominates the rather frightened committee of officers who see her. In the matter of her purchase of the poison, she completely overawes the clerk. She makes no pretense. She refuses to tell him what she wants the poison for. And yet this firmness of will and iron pride have not kept her from being thwarted and hurt. Her father has run off the young men who came to call upon her, and for the man who tells the story, Miss Emily and her father form a tableau: "Miss Emily a slender figure in white in the background, her father a spraddled silhouette in the foreground, his back to her and clutching a horsewhip, the two of them framed by the backflung front door." Whether the picture is a remembered scene, or merely a symbolic construct, this is the picture which remains in the storyteller's mind.

We have indicated that her pride is connected with her contempt for public opinion. This comes to the fore, of course, when she rides around about the town with the foreman whom everybody believes is beneath her. And it is her proud refusal to admit an external set of codes, or conventions, or other wills which contradict her own will, which makes her capable at the end of keeping her lover from going away. Confronted with his jilting her, she tries to override not only his will and the opinion of other people, but the laws of death and decay themselves.

But this, still, hardly gives the meaning of the story. For in all that has been said thus far, we are still merely accounting for a psychological aberration—we are still merely dealing with a case history in abnormal psychology. In order to make a case for the story as "meaningful," we shall have to tie Miss Emily's thoughts and actions back into the normal life of the community, and establish some sort of relationship between them. And just here one pervasive element in the narration suggests a clue. The story is told by one of the townspeople. And in it, as a constant factor, is the reference to what the community thought of Miss Emily. Continually through the story is it what "we" said, and then what "we" did, and what seemed true to "us," and so on. The narrator puts the matter even more sharply still. He says, in the course of the story, that to the community Miss Emily seemed "dear, inescapable, impervious, tranquil, and perverse." Each of the adjectives is important and meaningful. In a sense, Miss Emily because of her very fact of isolation and perversity belongs to the whole community. She is even something treasured by it. Ironically, because of Emily's perversion of an aristocratic independence of mores and because of her contempt for "what people say," her life is public, even communal. And various phrases used by the narrator underline this view of her position. For example, her face looks "as you imagine a lighthouse-keeper's face ought to look," like the face of a person who lives in the kind of isolation imposed on a lighthouse-keeper, who looks out into the blackness and whose light serves a public function. Or, again, after her father's death, she becomes very ill, and when she appears after the illness, she has "a vague resemblance to those angels in colored church windows—sort of tragic and serene." Whatever we make of these descriptions, certainly the author is trying to suggest a kind of calm and dignity which is supermundane, unearthly, or "over-earthly," such as an angel might possess.

10 Miss Emily, then, is a combination of idol and scapegoat for the community. On the one hand, the community feels admiration for Miss Emily—she represents something in the past of the community which the community is proud of. They feel a sort of awe of her, as is illustrated by the behavior of the mayor and the committee in her presence. On the other hand, her queerness, the fact that she cannot compete with them in their ordinary life, the fact that she is hopelessly out of touch with the modern world—all of these things make them feel superior to her, and also to that past which she represents. It is, then, Miss Emily's complete detachment which gives her actions their special meaning for the community.

11 Miss Emily, since she is the conscious aristocrat, since she is consciously "better" than other people, since she is above and outside their canons of behavior, can, at the same time, be worse than other people; and she *is* worse, horribly so. She is worse than other people, but at the same time, as the narrator implies, she remains somehow admirable. This raises a fundamental question: why is this true?

12 Perhaps the horrible and the admirable aspects of Miss Emily's final deed arise from the same basic fact of her character: she insists on meeting the world on her own terms. She never cringes, she never begs for sympathy, she refuses to shrink into an amiable old maid, she never accepts the community's ordinary judgments or values. This independence of spirit and pride can, and does in her case, twist the individual into a sort of monster, but, at the same time, this refusal to accept the herd values carries with it a dignity and courage. The community senses this, as we gather from the fact that the community carries out the decencies of the funeral before breaking in the door of the upper room. There is, as it were, a kind of secret understanding that she has won her right of privacy, until she herself has entered history. Furthermore, despite the fact that, as the narrator says, "already we knew that there was one room in that region above stairs which no one had seen in forty years, and which would have to be forced," her funeral is something of a state occasion with "the very old men—some in their brushed Confederate uniforms—on the porch and the lawn, talking of Miss Emily as if

she had been a contemporary of theirs, believing that they had danced with her and courted her perhaps . . ." In other words, the community accepts her into its honored history. All of this works as a kind of tacit recognition of Miss Emily's triumph of will. The community, we are told earlier, had wanted to pity Miss Emily when she had lost her money, just as they had wanted to commiserate over her when they believed that she had actually become a fallen woman, but she had triumphed over their pity and commiseration and condemnation, just as she had triumphed over all their other attitudes.

But, as we have indicated earlier, it may be said that Miss Emily is mad. This may be true, but there are two things to consider in this connection. First, one must consider the special terms which her "madness" takes. Her madness is simply a development of her pride and her refusal to submit to ordinary standards of behavior. So, because of this fact, her "madness" is meaningful after all. It involves issues which in themselves are really important and have to do with the world of conscious moral choice. Second, the community interprets her "madness" as meaningful. They admire her, even if they are disappointed by her refusals to let herself be pitied, and the narrator, who is a spokesman for the community, recognizes the last grim revelation as an instance of her having carried her own values to their ultimate conclusion. She would marry the common laborer, Homer Barron, let the community think what it would. She would not be jilted. And she would hold him as a lover. But it would all be on her own terms. She remains completely dominant, and contemptuous of the day-to-day world.

It has been suggested by many critics that tragedy implies a hero who is completely himself, who insists on meeting the world on his own terms, who wants something so intensely, or lives so intensely, that he cannot accept any compromise. It cannot be maintained that this story is comparable to any of the great tragedies, such as *Hamlet* or *King Lear*, but it can be pointed out that this story, in its own way, involves some of the same basic elements. Certainly, Miss Emily's pride, isolation, and independence remind one of factors in the character of the typical tragic hero. And it can be pointed out that, just as the horror of her deed lies outside the ordinary life of the community, so the magnificence of her independence lies outside its ordinary virtues.

Questions for Comprehension

1. What evidence do Brooks and Warren offer of Emily's inability to distinguish between illusion and reality?
2. What do Brooks and Warren say is required for the story to justify itself as being more than a mere case history of abnormal psychology?
3. What are the characteristics that Brooks and Warren call the "mainsprings" of Emily's character?
4. According to the authors, what special function does the narrator of the story serve?
5. To what traits in her character do the authors attribute Emily's madness?
6. What characteristics make Emily a tragic hero?

ATMOSPHERE AND THEME IN FAULKNER'S "A ROSE FOR EMILY"

Ray B. West, Jr.

Ray B. West, Jr. (b. 1908) is Professor Emeritus of English at San Francisco State University. He has published poetry and fiction in addition to numerous scholarly books and articles. The following essay was first published in *Perspective* in 1949.

The first clues to meaning in a short story usually arise from a detection of the principal contrasts which an author sets up. The most common, perhaps, are contrasts of character, but when characters are contrasted there is usually also a resultant contrast in terms of action. Since action reflects a moral or ethical state, contrasting action points to a contrast in ideological perspectives and hence toward the theme.

The principal contrast in William Faulkner's short story "A Rose for Emily" is between past time and present time: the past as represented in Emily herself, in Colonel Sartoris, in the old Negro servant, and in the Board of Aldermen who accepted the Colonel's attitude toward Emily and rescinded her taxes; the present is depicted through the unnamed narrator and is represented in the *new* Board of Aldermen, in Homer Barron (the representative of Yankee attitudes toward the Griersons and through them toward the entire South), and in what is called "the next generation with its more modern ideas."

Atmosphere is defined in the *Dictionary of World Literature* as "The particular world in which the events of a story or a play occur: time, place, conditions, and the attendant mood." When, as in "A Rose for Emily," the world depicted is a confusion between the past and the present, the atmosphere is one of distortion—of unreality. This unreal world results from the suspension of a natural time order. Normality consists in a decorous progression of the human being from birth, through youth, to age and finally death. Preciocity in children is as monstrous as idiocy in the adult, because both are *unnatural*. Monstrosity, however, is a sentimental subject for fiction unless it is the result of human action—the result of a willful attempt to circumvent time. When such circumvention produces acts of violence, as in "A Rose for Emily," the atmosphere becomes one of horror.

Horror, however, represents only the extreme form of maladjusted nature. It is not produced in "A Rose for Emily" until the final act of violence has been disclosed. All that has gone before has prepared us by producing a general tone of mystery, foreboding, decay, etc., so that we may say the entire series of events that have gone before are "in key"—that is, they are depicted in a mood in which the final violence does not appear too shocking or horrible. We are inclined to say, "In such an atmosphere, anything may happen." Foreshadowing is often accomplished through atmosphere, and in this case the atmosphere prepares us for Emily's unnatural act at the end of the story. Actually, such preparation begins in the very first sentence:

> When Miss Emily Grierson died, our whole town went to her funeral: the men through a sort of respectful affection for a fallen monument, the women mostly out of curiosity to see the inside of her house, which no one save an old manservant—a combined gardener and cook—had seen in at least ten years.

Emily is portrayed as "a fallen monument," a *monument* for reasons which we shall examine later, *fallen* because she has shown herself susceptible to death (and decay) after all. In the mention of death, we are conditioned (as the psychologist says) for the more specific concern with it later on. The second paragraph depicts the essential ugliness of the contrast: the description of Miss Emily's house "lifting its stubborn and coquettish decay above the cotton wagons and the gasoline pumps—an eyesore among eyesores." (A juxtaposition of past and present.) We recognize this scene as an emblematic presentation of Miss Emily herself, suggested as it is through the words "stubborn and coquettish." The tone—and the contrast—is preserved in a description of the note which Miss Emily sent to the mayor, "a note on paper of an archaic shape, in a thin, flowing calligraphy in faded ink," and in the description of the interior of the house when the deputation from the Board of Aldermen visit her: "They were admitted by the old Negro into a dim hall from which a stairway mounted into still more shadow. It smelled of dust and disuse—a close, dank smell." In the next paragraph a description of Emily discloses her similarity to the house: "She looked bloated, like a body long submerged in motionless water, and of that pallid hue."

Emily had not always looked like this. When she was young and part of the world with which she was contemporary, she was, we are told, "a slender figure in white," as contrasted with her father, who is described as "a spraddled silhouette." In the picture of Emily and her father together, framed by the door, she frail and apparently hungering to participate in the life of her time, we have a reversal of the contrast which has already been presented and which is to be developed later. Even after her father's death, Emily is not monstrous, but rather looked like a girl "with a vague resemblance to those angels in colored church windows—sort of tragic and serene." The suggestion is that she had already begun her entrance into that nether-world (a world which is depicted later as "rose-tinted"), but that she might even yet have been saved, had Homer Barron been another kind of man.

By the time the deputation from the new, progressive Board of Aldermen wait upon her concerning her delinquent taxes, however, she has completely retreated into her world of the past. There is no communication possible between her and them:

> Her voice was dry and cold. "I have no taxes in Jefferson. Colonel Sartoris explained it to me. Perhaps one of you can gain access to the city records and satisfy yourselves."
>
> "But we have. We are the city authorities, Miss Emily. Didn't you get a notice from the sheriff, signed by him?"

"I received a paper, yes," Miss Emily said. "Perhaps he considers himself the sheriff. . . . I have no taxes in Jefferson."

"But there is nothing on the books to show that, you see. We must go by them—"

"See Colonel Sartoris. I have no taxes in Jefferson."

"But Miss Emily—"

"See Colonel Sartoris." (Colonel Sartoris had been dead almost ten years.)

"I have no taxes in Jefferson. Tobe!" The Negro appeared. "Show these gentlemen out."

Just as Emily refused to acknowledge the death of her father, she now refuses to recognize the death of Colonel Sartoris. He had given his word, and according to the traditional view, "his word" knew no death. It is the Past pitted against the Present—the Past with its social decorum, the Present with everything set down in "the books." Emily dwells in the Past, always a world of unreality to us of the Present. Here are the facts which set the tone of the story and which create the atmosphere of unreality which surrounds it.

Such contrasts are used over and over again: the difference between the attitude of Judge Stevens (who is over eighty years old) and the attitude of the young man who comes to him about the "smell" at Emily's place. For the young man (who is a member of the "rising generation") it is easy. For him, Miss Emily's world has ceased to exist. The city's health regulations are on the books. "Dammit, sir," Judge Stevens replied, "will you accuse a lady to her face of smelling bad?" Emily had given in to social pressure when she allowed them to bury her father, but she triumphed over society in the matter of the smell. She had won already when she bought the poison, refusing to comply with the requirements of the law, because for her they did not exist.

Such incidents seem, however, mere preparation for the final, more important contrast between Emily and Homer Barron. Emily is the town's aristocrat; Homer is a day laborer. Homer is an active man dealing with machinery and workman—a man's man. He is a Yankee—a Northerner. Emily is a "monument" of Southern gentility. As such she is common property of the town, but in a special way—as an ideal of *past* values. Here the author seems to be commenting upon the complex relationship between the Southerner and his past and between the Southerner of the present and the Yankee from the North. She is unreal to her compatriots, yet she impresses them with her station, even at a time when they considered her *fallen*: "as if [her dignity] had wanted that touch of earthiness to reaffirm her imperviousness." It appeared for a time that Homer had won her over, as though the demands of reality as depicted in him (earthiness) had triumphed over her withdrawal and seclusion. This is the conflict that is not resolved until the final scene. We can imagine, however, what the outcome might have been had Homer Barron, who was not a marrying man, succeeded, in the town's eyes, in seducing her (violating her world) and then deserted her. The view of Emily as a monument would have been destroyed. Emily might have become the object of continued gossip, but she would have become susceptible to the town's pity—therefore, human. Emily's world, however, continues to be the Past (in its extreme form it is death), and when she is threatened with desertion and disgrace, she not only takes refuge in that world, but she also takes Homer with her, in the only manner possible.

It is important, too, to realize that during the period of Emily's courtship, the town became Emily's allies in a contest between Emily and her Grierson cousins, "because the two female cousins were even more Grierson than Miss Emily had ever been." The cousins were protecting the general proprieties against which the town (and the times) was in gradual rebellion. Just as each succeeding generation rebels against its elders, so the town took sides with Emily against her relations. Had Homer Barron been the proper kind of man, it is implied, Miss Emily might have escaped both horns of the dilemma (her cousins' traditionalism and Homer's immorality) and become an accepted and respected member of the community. The town's attitude toward the Grierson cousins represents the usual ambiguous attitude of man toward the past: a mixture of veneration and rebelliousness. The unfaithfulness of Homer represents the final act in the drama of Emily's struggle to escape from the past. From the moment that she realizes that he will desert her, tradition becomes magnified out of all proportion to life and death, and she conducts herself as though Homer really had been faithful—as though this view represented reality.

Miss Emily's position in regard to the specific problem of time is suggested in the scene where the old soldiers appear at her funeral. There are, we are told, two views of time: (1) the world of the present, viewing time as a mechanical progression in which the past is a diminishing road, never to be encountered again; (2) the world of tradition, viewing the past as a huge meadow which no winter ever quite touches, divided from (us) now by the narrow bottleneck of the most recent decade of years. The first is the view of Homer Barron and the modern generation in Jefferson. The second is the view of the older members of the Board of Aldermen and of the confederate soldiers. Emily holds the second view, except that for her there is no bottleneck dividing her from the meadow of the past.

Emily's small room above stairs has become that timeless meadow. In it, the living Emily and the dead Homer have remained together as though not even death could separate them. It is the monstrousness of this view which creates the final atmosphere of horror, and the scene is intensified by the portrayal of the unchanged objects which have surrounded Homer in life. Here he lay in the roseate atmosphere of Emily's death-in-life: "What was left of him, rotted beneath what was left of the nightshirt, had become inextricable from the bed in which he lay; and upon him and upon the pillow beside him lay that even coating of the patient and biding dust." The symbols of Homer's life of action have become mute and silent. Contrariwise, Emily's world, though it had been inviolate while she was alive, has been invaded after her death—the whole gruesome and unlovely tale unfolded.

In its simplest sense, the story says that death conquers all. But what is death? Upon one level, death is the past, tradition, whatever is opposite to the present. In the specific setting of this story, it is the past of the South in which the retrospective survivors of the War deny changing customs and the passage of time. Homer Barron, the Yankee, lived in the present, ready to take his pleasure and depart, apparently unwilling to consider the possibility of defeat, either by tradition (the Griersons) or by time (death) itself. In a sense, Emily conquered time, but only briefly and by retreating into her rose-tinted world of the past, a world in which death was denied at the same time that it is shown to have existed. Such retreat, the story implies, is hopeless, since everyone (even Emily) is finally subjected to death and the invasion of his world by the clamorous and curious inhabitants of the world of the present.

14 In these terms, it might seem that the story is a comment upon tradition and upon those people who live in a dream world of the past. But is it not also a comment upon the present? There is some justification for Emily's actions. She is a tragic—and heroic—figure. In the first place, she has been frustrated by her father, prevented from participating in the life of her contemporaries. When she attempts to achieve freedom, she is betrayed by a man who represents the new morality, threatened by disclosure and humiliation. The grounds of the tragedy is depicted in the scene already referred to between Emily and the deputation from the Board of Aldermen: for the new generation, the word of Colonel Sartoris meant nothing. This was a new age, a different time; the present was not bound by the promises of the past. For Emily, however, the word of the Colonel was everything. The tax notice was but a scrap of paper.

15 Atmosphere, we might say, is nothing but the fictional reflection of man's attitude toward the state of the universe. The atmosphere of classic tragedy inveighed against the ethical dislocation of the Grecian world merely by portraying such dislocation and depicting man's tragic efforts to conform both to the will of the gods and to the demands of his own contemporary society. Such dislocation in the modern world is likely to be seen mirrored in the natural universe, with problems of death and time representing that flaw in the golden bowl of eighteenth- and nineteenth-century natural philosophy which is the inheritance of our times. Perhaps our specific dilemma is the conflict of the pragmatic present against the set mores of the past. Homer Barron was an unheroic figure who put too much dependence upon his self-centered and rootless philosophy, a belief which suggested that he could take whatever he wanted without considering any obligation to the past (tradition) or to the future (death). Emily's resistance is heroic. Her tragic flaw is the conventional pride: she undertook to regulate the natural time-universe. She acted as though death did not exist, as though she could retain her unfaithful lover by poisoning him and holding his physical self prisoner in a world which had all of the appearances of reality except that most necessary of all things—life.

16 The extraction of a statement of theme from so complex a subject matter is dangerous and never wholly satisfactory. The subject, as we have seen, is concerned not alone with man's relationship to death, but with his relationship as it refers to all the facets of social intercourse. The theme is not one directed at presenting an attitude of Southerner to Yankee, or Yankee to Southerner, as has been hinted at in so many discussions of William Faulkner. The Southern Problem is one of the objective facts with which the theme is concerned, but the theme itself transcends it. Wallace Stevens is certainly right when he says that a theme may be emotive as well as intellectual and logical, and it is this recognition which

explains why the extraction of a logical statement of theme is so delicate and dangerous an operation: the story *is* its theme as the life of the body *is* the body.

Nevertheless, in so far as a theme represents the *meaning* of a story, it can be observed in logical terms; indeed, these are the only terms in which it can be observed for those who, at a first or even a repeated reading, fail to recognize the implications of the total story. The logical statement, in other words, may be a clue to the total, emotive content. In these terms, "A Rose for Emily" would seem to be saying that man must come to terms both with the past and the present; for to ignore the first is to be guilty of a foolish innocence, to ignore the second is to become monstrous and inhuman, above all to betray an excessive pride (such as Emily Grierson's) before the humbling fact of death. The total story says what has been said in so much successful literature, that man's plight is tragic, but that there is heroism in an attempt to rise above it.

17

Questions for Comprehension

1. What does West say is the value of contrast in a literary work? What does he identify as the principal contrast in "A Rose for Emily"?
2. According to West, what is the "unreal world" of the story?
3. What forces or events drive Emily to take refuge in the past?
4. What case does West make for calling the past an "extreme form of death"?
5. What point does West make about the connection between tradition and death in the story?
6. What reasons does West give for saying that Emily is a tragic and heroic figure?
7. What conclusion does West draw about the function of atmosphere in a literary work, especially a tragedy?

■

HISTORY IN "A ROSE FOR EMILY"
William Van O'Conner

William Van O'Conner (1915–1966), a literary critic and scholar, was professor of English at the University of California, Davis. He published extensively on American literature. The following is an excerpt from an essay published in *Sewanee Review* in 1952.

My point is that stressing or rather over-stressing historical and sociological, or regional, aspects of Faulkner's fiction, even when the mythic qualities are acknowledged, leads to distorting the more basic intention of many, perhaps most, of the stories—to reading them somehow as documents in a legendary history of the South. (I am not of course trying to say that one can ignore these aspects. They are inevitably and powerfully interwoven with the themes; they may have brought some of the themes sharply to his consciousness; and certainly the regional characteristics modify and qualify the ways in which the themes are developed.) Perhaps a review of Ray West's account of "A Rose for Emily" will indicate the dangers in the "historical" emphasis. West reads the story as a conflict between the values of the Old South and the new order, business-like, pragmatic, self-centered. But it can't be read in these terms because the Old South and the new order are merely a part of the flavor and tone of the story, *not* the poles of conflict. The theme is that a denial of normal emotions invites retreat into a marginal world, into fantasy. The severity of Miss Emily's father was the cause of her frustrations and her retreat. The past becomes a part of her fantasies, just as the present does. It is incidental that her relationship to the Old South makes her a part of the town's nostalgia; it was the nostalgia, not her being a "lady," which caused her to be treated reverently by the town's board when she refused to acknowledge her taxes; presumably even ladies paid their taxes in the Old South. If the conflict is between the two orders it seems curious indeed that Miss Emily would choose Homer Barron, Yankee, amoral, and without loyalty, as her beloved. And her murder of the new order, Homer Barron, is the reverse of what actually happened, the destruction of the old order by the new. The story is simple enough when read as an account of Miss Emily's becoming mad as a consequence of her frustrations, the denial to her of normal emotional relations. That the Old South, which as a physical presence (in its houses, memories, and so on) lingers in the new order and in doing so seems unreal, has its parallel, obviously, in Miss Emily, who was most strangely detached from reality. But this is a parallel only—it is not the dramatic pull or struggle that composes the action.

Questions for Comprehension

1. What does O'Conner say is the result of overstressing the historical and sociological aspects of Faulkner's work?
2. What reason does the author give to explain why Ray West's interpretation of the story can't be right?
3. What does O'Conner say is the real theme of the story?

EMILY GRIERSON'S OEDIPUS COMPLEX: MOTIF, MOTIVE, AND MEANING IN FAULKNER'S "A ROSE FOR EMILY"

Jack Scherting

Jack Scherting (b. 1934) is associate professor and director of the American Studies Program at Utah State University. He has published many articles on American literature. The following essay first appeared in *Studies in Short Fiction* in 1980.

Most readers of Faulkner's story "A Rose for Emily" would agree that its meaning is somehow connected with the motive which prompts Emily Grierson to poison her lover and conceal his corpse from the public for some forty years. Most readers would also agree that the problem of identifying this motive and relating it to the meaning of the story is complicated by the manner in which Faulkner has narrated his tale. "A Rose for Emily" is related by an anonymous narrator in the first person plural. Faulkner uses the "we" point of view to indicate that the events are being described by a resident of Jefferson[1]—a representative of the community's collective understanding of Emily's life. His desultory narrative, which incorporates a substantial amount of local gossip, is of necessity incomplete because Emily seldom left her house and because the only person who could have described what actually went on inside that house—her Negro servant—ran off immediately after her death. By limiting access to the facts this way, Faulkner forces the reader to search beyond the surface of the narrative for an explanation of Emily's behavior.

This is a formidable task because Faulkner, through his narrator, is obviously describing a psychotic personality. The narrator recognizes and comments perceptively on the superficial aspects of Emily's bizarre conduct, but he does not attempt to explain the nature of Emily's derangement nor is he able to offer a motive which would clear up the mystery. In this sense he is a naive raconteur. Moreover, his retrospective narration scrambles the chronology of the story, leaving readers with the task of reconstructing the sequence of events from casual references to time.

Much of the appeal of "A Rose for Emily" resides in the challenges which this mode of narration poses for anyone attempting to interpret the story. For assistance in untangling the chronology, readers can check Paul D. McGlynn's careful study[2]; but once this obstacle is surmounted, there remains the central question: Why did Emily Grierson murder her lover? This thematically significant question has not been satisfactorily answered. The generally accepted explanation was first proposed by Brooks and Warren: "Confronted with his jilting her, she tries to override not only his will and the opinion of other people, but the laws of death and decay themselves. . . . She would not be jilted."[3] This is an appealing explanation of Emily's motive, but it has one serious defect—the evidence contradicts rather than supports the assertion that Emily was jilted by her lover. A brief review of the evidence will show that this popular interpretation of motive has, at best, a weak factual basis.

Miss Emily and her lover, Homer Barron, had been carrying on for the better part of two years. We know this because Emily met Homer in the summer following her father's death and because the smell of Homer's decaying corpse was noticed about two years *after* her father died. During these two years, Homer visited Emily on a regular basis. This is evident in section 4 of the story, the first paragraphs of which summarize the townspeople's attitude toward Emily's conduct. At first they accepted her affair with benign tolerance, expecting it soon to

---

[1] The narrator is evidently a male of about the same age as Emily. In section 4 of the story, paragraph two, a distinction is made between the attitude of the ladies and the men, the latter favoring nonintervention in Emily's affair. The narrator identifies himself with the male faction two paragraphs later: "we were all Miss Emily's allies to help circumvent the cousins." His first-hand knowledge of Emily's life indicates that he is about her age.
[2] "The Chronology of 'A Rose for Emily,'" *Studies in Short Fiction*, 6 (Summer 1969), 461–462.
[3] Cleanth Brooks and Robert Penn Warren, *Understanding Fiction* (2nd ed.; New York: F. S. Crofts, 1959), pp. 352; 354.

be "ratified" by marriage. But when some two years had lapsed, tolerance gave way to indignation. The affair was temporarily interrupted during the visit of Emily's cousins, summoned by the minister's wife in a final effort to end the scandal.

If Faulkner had intended readers to infer that Homer Barron had jilted Emily or that he intended to jilt her, we would expect the author to provide some substantive evidence as a basis for such an inference. There is only one allusion to jilting in the history of this protracted affair. Noting Homer's disappearance, the people of Jefferson assumed that he "had deserted her. . . . after her sweetheart went away, people hardly saw her at all."[4] That assumption is not reinforced anywhere else in the story. To the contrary, the evidence strongly suggests that Homer had *not* deserted her, that he was in fact taking a "long sleep" in an upstairs bedroom of the Grierson house: Emily purchased poison during her cousins' visit (3); Homer re-entered the Grierson house "within three days" of their departure and "that was the last we saw of Homer Barron" (4); "a short time after" Homer disappeared, a very disagreeable smell developed around the Grierson house (2); about forty years later, Homer's remains are discovered.

If, as the evidence suggests, Homer did not jilt Emily, what motive would she have for murdering him? To answer this question we need at least a glimpse into the recesses of her pathological mind. Unless Faulkner was simply presenting for us an incomprehensible mystery of demented behavior, he must, through his naive raconteur, have provided readers with the clues necessary to comprehend, however dimly, the contorted psyche which conceived and executed this singular murder/marriage. He did provide such clues. Deliberately and with consummate skill Faulkner employed the Freudian principle of Oedipal[5] fixation as a means of depicting Emily's character and informing the story with its powerful theme, a theme intimately connected with the incestuous nature of Emily's love for Homer. Emily Grierson was possessed by an unresolved Oedipal complex. Her libidinal desires for her father were transferred, after his death, to a male surrogate—Homer Barron. Fortunately we need not superimpose this Freudian structure on the story because there is ample evidence—external as well as internal—to show that Faulkner consciously used the Oedipal motif in composing his story.

First a look at the external evidence. Sigmund Freud's theories on sex had been pretty well assimilated (often half-digested) by the time "A Rose for Emily" was published in April of 1930. Like many other American authors, Faulkner was very much aware of and influenced by the literary possibilities inherent in the new psychological approach to maladjusted personalities.[6] In view of this, it seems

---

[4] Instead of citing references to one of the many editions of "A Rose for Emily," I will indicate in parenthesis which of the story's five numbered sections the information was taken from. These sections are brief, and the source can be quickly located in any edition the reader may have at hand. Thus the quote above is from (4).

[5] The daughter/father relationship is often referred to as the Electra complex; however, for stylistic reasons I have employed the broader usage evident in Freud's discussions of Oedipal behavior.

[6] See William Richard Brown's doctoral dissertation "Faulkner's Use of the Materials of Abnormal Psychology in Characterization," University of Arkansas, 1965.

curious that the relationship between Emily Grierson and her father has not been scrutinized with the care it deserves. In later years, Faulkner himself suggested the significance of that relationship, using a Freudian concept (repression) in his remarks [italics mine]:

> In this case there was a young girl with a young girl's *normal* aspirations to find love and then a husband and family, who was browbeaten and kept down by her father, a selfish man who didn't want her to leave home because he wanted a housekeeper, and it was a *natural instinct* of—*repressed* which—you can't repress it—you can mash it down but it comes up somewhere else and very likely in a tragic form. . . .[7]

Because Faulkner stressed the significance of the father/daughter relationship, his comments should be given careful consideration. In doing so, I will paraphrase and analyze Faulkner's remarks in order to develop fully the meaning implicit in them. Emily's father had prevented her from maturing sexually in the normal and natural way. Thus repressed, her sexual drives emerged in a tragic form—that is to say, in abnormal and unnatural behavior. The affair between Emily and Homer is illicit, yes, but would Faulkner describe this situation—a situation in which a woman facing spinsterhood at last finds a lover—as tragic? Not likely. When he said that the repressed natural instinct comes up "somewhere else," he could only have meant somewhere *other than* a normal man/woman relationship. On the surface, Emily's affair with Homer falls well within the scope of sexual normalcy; however, if we start with the postulate that Emily was never allowed to outgrow her Oedipal attachment to her father and that Homer was, libidinally, a surrogate for her father, then the affair does indeed become abnormal and tragic. A closer look at the story itself will reveal the extent to which the Oedipal motif pervades Faulkner's tale.

Readers will recall that Emily's father—an imperious man, proud of his Southern heritage and of his family's status in Jefferson—had constantly interposed himself between Emily and any male interested in courting her. The narrator describes the situation in this way: "We had long thought of them as a tableau; Miss Emily a slender figure in white in the background, her father a spraddled silhouette in the foreground, his back to her and clutching a horsewhip, the two of them framed by the back-flung front door" (2). Emily, already past thirty, had been denied normal contacts with the opposite sex. To use Freudian terminology, the father had prevented his daughter from transferring her libido to an outside object, thus intensifying her libidinal dependence upon him. Understandably, then, his death was an extremely traumatic event in her life—so traumatic that she could not consciously cope with it.

Emily's subsequent behavior clearly shows that the death of her father was a piece of reality disavowed by her ego. The narrator recalls that when neighbors came by to offer condolences the day after Mr. Grierson's death, "Miss Emily met them at the door, dressed as usual and with no trace of grief on her face. She told

---

[7] Frederick L. Gwynn and Joseph L. Blotner, eds., *Faulkner in the University* (Charlottesville: University of Virginia Press, 1959), p. 138.

them that her father was not dead." For three days Emily guarded her father's corpse, turning away those who would take him from her. Finally, "just as they were about to resort to law and force, she broke down, and they buried her father quickly" (2). Faulkner's use of the phrase "broke down" does not mean that Emily consciously acknowledged the reality of her father's death; on the contrary, her breakdown signalled a retreat from that reality into the defenses of her own psyche. Emily regressed into her childhood. This explains why she was "sick for a long time" after her father's death and why, during her seclusion, she cut her hair short, "making her look like a girl" (3). Emily became an emotional orphan in search of the father who had been taken from her.

Through his narrator, Faulkner offered a key observation concerning Emily's relationship with her father and her refusal to give up his corpse: "We remembered all the young men her father had driven away, and we knew that with nothing left, she would have to cling to that which had robbed her, as people will" (2). Indeed, Emily's father had robbed her of a normal sex life, preventing her from resolving the childhood Oedipal complex. And the people of Jefferson, in removing his corpse, had robbed her of the only man in her life. Under the circumstances, it is not at all surprising that Miss Emily's libidinal attachment to her father was soon transferred to a surrogate male.

In the summer following her father's death and Emily's long illness, Homer Barron—a Northerner—arrived in Jefferson and began work as a foreman of a sidewalk paving crew. Much to the surprise of the townfolk, Emily began an affair with Homer, an affair which lasted the better part of two years. Emily's conduct during that time baffled the people of Jefferson: How could she—a well-bred Southern lady—abide an intimate relationship with this common laborer, this Yankee? Though they "believed she had fallen," still Emily proudly "carried her head high" (3) on her buggy rides with Homer each Sunday. This apparently inexplicable behavior becomes comprehensible when we recognize that Homer Barron is a surrogate for Emily's father. The deceased father was the *subject* of her sublimated desire, Homer merely a living *object* on which that desire had been fixed and from which she evidently received considerable gratification. Faulkner offers hints of this parallel between Mr. Grierson and Emily's lover. Both are characterized as strong-willed men, and in separate scenes, both are described holding horsewhips. Of greater significance, however, is the fact that Emily replaces the corpse of her father with that of his objective counterpart, Homer Barron. As we shall see later, Faulkner re-enforces this father/lover parallel by careful word choice and by ambiguous phrasing in the final scene.

We cannot, of course, unravel Emily's convoluted psyche and explain every aspect of her demented behavior. But it is evident that Emily perceives reality in a most peculiar way. She is unable to discriminate between a Southern gentleman and a Yankee laborer, between past and present, between sleep and death, between that which is vital and that which is decaying. With this background, we are in a position to examine more closely the motive which drove Emily to murder Homer and immure his corpse in the Grierson house for some forty years.

Emily's affair becomes complicated when the ladies of Jefferson, determined to end the scandal, encourage the Baptist minister to reason with Emily. Though we do not know what took place during his visit with Emily, we do know that the minister's efforts were futile and that he was somehow stunned by what he learned, for "he would never divulge what happened during that interview," and he "refused to go back again" (4). The minister's wife then wrote to Emily's cousins in hopes that they would be able to deal with the deranged woman. Their arrival intensified rather than resolved Emily's problems. The narrator does not tell us what transpired during the cousins' brief visit with Emily. It was a private matter, and quite likely the people of Jefferson did not know the particulars. Obviously, however, what the cousins said precipitated a crisis in Emily's life, for she murdered her lover as soon as they left. We can only speculate on what they might have told her. Given the circumstances, it is logical to assume that they forced her to make a choice: either marry Homer or stop carrying on with him. If in fact they confronted Emily in this way, it would explain why she subsequently murdered her lover. Such a choice would place Emily in a terrible dilemma because "Homer himself had remarked . . . that he was not a marrying man" (4). He preferred the male companionship of the local Elk's Club to the confines of the family circle. Still Emily could not bear parting with Homer, as society demanded, any more than she could bear parting with her beloved father. How did she respond when the security of her fragile universe was threatened in this way? The lover/father would not marry Miss Emily, so Emily took the initiative. She made preparations to marry Homer. During her cousins' visit, Emily purchased "a man's toilet set in silver, with the letters H. B. on each piece," as well as "a complete outfit of men's clothing, including a nightshirt" (4). She also bought some arsenic.

Three days after Emily's cousins left, Homer returned to the Grierson house and remained there for some forty years. The people of Jefferson assumed that "he had deserted her" (2), but Miss Emily had outsmarted them. She simultaneously murdered and "married" Homer Barron. Because the people of Jefferson had taken her beloved father's body from the Grierson house, Emily insured that they would not take away its surrogate by concealing, in an upstairs bedroom, the corpse of the man who gratified her unresolved Oedipal desires. Now he would never leave her bed; he would always be there to comfort her.

At the conclusion of his story, Faulkner re-enforces this connection between Emily's father and her lover. He does it first by using the word "profound" to suggest the parallel. Those who attended Emily's funeral some forty years after Homer's death saw a crayon portrait of her father "musing profoundly" over her coffin. And those who later entered the upstairs bedroom gazed upon Homer's remains, his skull confronting them with a "profound and fleshless grin" (5). Why is this portrait of Emily's father standing "on a tarnished gilt easel before the fireplace," mentioned at the beginning as well as at the end of the story? The portrait may have been the work of an ante-bellum artist; or it may be that Emily, who later took up china painting, did the portrait herself, using the antiquated crayon technique. Whatever the case may have been, the repeated reference to the portrait is an effective way of suggesting that the spirit of Mr. Grierson so preoccupied Emily's distorted universe that it dominated the personal identity of Homer Barron. The initials which Emily had ordered engraved on Homer's toilet set, a "wedding" gift, are now obscured by tarnish, what was once a face is now a featureless skull, heightening by contrast the lifelike image of her father standing vigil over Emily's coffin.

Another important key to the connection between Mr. Grierson and Homer Barron is contained in the ambiguity of a sentence which Faulkner carefully constructed. Commenting on Homer's fate, the narrator says, "Now the long sleep that outlasts love, that conquers even the grimace of love, had cuckolded him" (5). One meaning of this sentence—the meaning understood by the narrator and the community he represents—is that death, the long sleep, has stolen Emily from Homer, that is, cuckolded him. But Faulkner's choice of phrases gives that sentence a second and far more significant meaning. To perceive this meaning we must remember that Emily could not distinguish sleep and death and that Homer Barron was merely a surrogate male who gratified her Oedipal desires. When placed against this background, the sentence can also be interpreted as follows: "The long sleep that outlasts love" refers to the interim—about forty-two years—between the death of her father and that of Emily. Even during this long sleep, Emily's father maintained the dominance over her sexuality which he had established in her formative years, outlasting by far Homer's two-year affair with his daughter. Faulkner's choice of the word "cuckold" also sheds light on this bizarre affair. Strange as it may seem, Homer Barron was cuckolded by Emily's deceased father every time he went to bed with her. And after Homer's death the spirit of Emily's ever-vigilant father, in some peculiar way, continued to live for Emily in the corpse she had lain with at least twice during her forty-year honeymoon.[8] This interpretation of the sentence is re-enforced by a second look at an earlier passage: "that quality of her father which had thwarted her woman's life so many times had been too virulent and too furious to die" (4).

---

[8] This assertion is based upon two elements of the story. In the first place, Homer's remains "had apparently once lain in the attitude of an embrace" (3). In view of the tormenting spasms associated with death by arsenic poisoning, Emily herself must have positioned Homer's corpse in this posture. Secondly, there is a "strand of iron-gray hair" found on the pillow next to the skeleton. The pillow has the "indentation of a head" (5) and is covered by an even coating of dust. The fact that the strand of hair is iron-gray indicates almost certainly that Emily had also lain with Homer's remains, at least once, several years after his death. Emily's hair "was turning gray" when the townfolk saw her once again six months after Homer's disappearance. "During the next few years it grew grayer and grayer until it attained an even pepper-and-salt iron-gray, when it ceased turning" (4). Since Emily's hair did not turn iron-gray until several years after Homer's death, that strand of hair found on the pillow could not have been left there earlier. Paul McGlynn ["The Chronology of 'A Rose for Emily'"] asserts that "Emily's hair turns gray during her six-month retreat after Homer's disappearance, so the strand of hair found on the pillow . . . has been there since the period between 1896 and 1898, the time from Homer's disappearance to the closing of the room." McGlynn overlooks the present continuous tense of the verb in Faulkner's phrase "was turning gray," concluding that Emily's hair had turned to the iron-gray shade of the strand found on the pillow. He also assumes that "Homer's bedroom has been closed for forty years, . . ." Granted, the narrator reports that "there was one room in that region above stairs which no one had seen in forty years" (3), but this is an assumption on the narrator's part which is contradicted by his own facts. Emily had to have entered the room during that period; moreover, the strand of iron-gray hair and the "indentation of a head" on the pillow are the strongest possible evidence that she must have lain with Homer's corpse—how many times, we have no way of knowing. The fact that her pillow is found covered with dust indicates that she had ceased doing so some time earlier.

The title of Faulkner's story, like every facet of this carefully wrought gem, perfectly matches the overall design.[9] Roses had a definite symbolic meaning for couples and are still offered as a pledge of fidelity in passion. Though Emily slept with Homer and with his corpse in that rose-tinted bedroom, "furnished as for a bridal," yet she was psychically incapable of being unfaithful in her pathetic love for her own father. The rose symbol—by chance if not by design—can also be related to another meaning which helps to illuminate this dark side of Faulkner's tale. In ancient Rome, a rose suspended in a room signified that nothing which transpired *sub rosa* was to be divulged to the outside world. The Oedipal desires expressed in Emily's affair with Homer were never recognized by the people of Jefferson, and Emily herself was aware of them only as subconscious longings. This secret is inclosed within an intricately constructed story which, like a Chinese puzzle-box, challenges and at the same time frustrates our efforts to open it. Yet it is a secret which must be disclosed to appreciate the magnitude of Faulkner's achievement and the meaning of his story.

At this point, I feel obliged to apologize for my protracted analysis of the Oedipal motif inherent in "A Rose for Emily." Faulkner's story is of course not merely a case history of a pathological mind. I have treated the Oedipal motif in such detail to establish it as the primary vehicle which the author used to convey the broader meaning of his story. That meaning is inextricably bound to the incestuous nature of Emily's love affair with Homer and the necrophilia inherent in her relationship with Homer's corpse.

Questions for Comprehension

1. What reasons does Scherting offer for rejecting the Brooks and Warren interpretation that Emily was jilted by Homer Barron?
2. What does the author mean by the "incestuous" nature of the love between Emily and Homer?
3. What evidence is presented to explain why Emily is suffering from repressed sexuality?
4. According to Scherting, what events triggered Emily's murder of Homer?
5. What choices does Scherting suggest Emily's cousins presented to her?
6. What does Scherting say is the best interpretation of the sentence that says of Homer Barron, "Now the long sleep that outlasts love, that conquers even the grimace of love, had cuckolded him"?

■

A ROSE FOR "A ROSE FOR EMILY"

Judith Fetterley

Judith Fetterley (b. 1938) is professor of English at the State University of New York, Albany. The following essay was first published in *The Resisting Reader* in 1978.

---

[9] Faulkner's response to a question about the meaning of the title was not particularly enlightening: "It was just 'A Rose for Emily'—that's all." (*Faulkner in the University*, p. 88.)

. . . Justifying Faulkner's use of the grotesque has been a major concern of critics who have written on the story. If, however, one approaches "A Rose for Emily" from a feminist perspective, one notices that the grotesque aspects of the story are a result of its violation of the expectations generated by the conventions of sexual politics. The ending shocks us not simply by its hint of necrophilia; more shocking is the fact that it is a woman who provides the hint. It is one thing for Poe* to spend his nights in the tomb of Annabel Lee and another thing for Miss Emily Grierson to deposit a strand of iron-gray hair on the pillow beside the rotted corpse of Homer Barron. Further, we do not expect to discover that a woman has murdered a man. The conventions of sexual politics have familiarized us with the image of Georgiana† nobly accepting death at her husband's hand. To reverse this "natural" pattern inevitably produces the grotesque.

Faulkner, however, is not interested in invoking the kind of grotesque which is the consequence of reversing the clichés of sexism for the sake of a cheap thrill; that is left to writers like Mickey Spillane. (Indeed, Spillane's ready willingness to capitalize on the shock value provided by the image of woman as killer in I, the Jury suggests, by contrast, how little such a sexist gambit is Faulkner's intent.) Rather, Faulkner invokes the grotesque in order to illuminate and define the true nature of the conventions on which it depends. "A Rose for Emily" is a story not of a conflict between the South and the North or between the old order and the new; it is a story of the patriarchy North and South, new and old, and of the sexual conflict within it. As Faulkner himself has implied . . . it is a story of a woman victimized and betrayed by the system of sexual politics, who nevertheless has discovered, within the structures that victimize her, sources of power for herself. If "The Birthmark" is the story of how to murder your wife and get away with it, "A Rose for Emily" is the story of how to murder your gentleman caller and get away with it. Faulkner's story is an analysis of how men's attitudes toward women turn back upon themselves; it is a demonstration of the thesis that it is impossible to oppress without in turn being oppressed, it is impossible to kill without creating the conditions for your own murder. "A Rose for Emily" is the story of a *lady* and of her revenge for that grotesque identity.

"When Miss Emily Grierson died, our whole town went to her funeral." The public and communal nature of Emily's funeral, a festival that brings the town together, clarifying its social relationships and revitalizing its sense of the past, indicates her central role in Jefferson. Alive, Emily is town property and the subject of shared speculation; dead, she is town history and the subject of legend. It is her value as a symbol, however obscure and however ambivalent, of something that is of central significance to the identity of Jefferson and to the meaning of its history that compels the narrator to assume a communal voice to tell her story. For Emily, like Georgiana, is a man-made object, a cultural artifact, and what she is reflects and defines the culture that has produced her.

The history the narrator relates to us reveals Jefferson's continuous emotional involvement with Emily. Indeed, though she shuts herself up in a house

---

* Editor's note: Edgar Allan Poe (1809–49), American poet, critic, and short story writer. The reference is to his poem "Annabel Lee."
† Editor's note: A character in "The Birthmark," a short story by Nathaniel Hawthorne.

which she rarely leaves and which no one enters, her furious isolation is in direct proportion to the town's obsession with her. Like Georgiana, she is the object of incessant attention; her every act is immediately consumed by the town for gossip and seized on to justify their interference in her affairs. Her private life becomes a public document that the town folk feel free to interpret at will, and they are alternately curious, jealous, spiteful, pitying, partisan, proud, disapproving, admiring, and vindicated. Her funeral is not simply a communal ceremony; it is also the climax of their invasion of her private life and the logical extension of their voyeuristic attitude toward her. Despite the narrator's demurral, getting inside Emily's house is the all-consuming desire of the town's population, both male and female; while the men may wait a little longer, their motive is still prurient curiosity: "Already we knew that there was one room in that region above stairs which no one had seen in forty years, and which would have to be forced. They waited until Miss Emily was decently in the ground before they opened it."

In a context in which the overtones of violation and invasion are so palpable, the word "decently" has that ironic ring which gives the game away. When the men finally do break down the door, they find that Emily has satisfied their prurience with a vengeance and in doing so has created for them a mirror image of themselves. The true nature of Emily's relation to Jefferson is contained in the analogies between what those who break open that room see in it and what has brought them there to see it. The perverse, violent, and grotesque aspects of the sight of Homer Barron's rotted corpse in a room decked out for a bridal and now faded and covered in dust reflects back to them the perverseness of their own prurient interest in Emily, the violence implicit in their continued invasions of her life, and the grotesqueness of the symbolic artifact they have made of her—their monument, their idol, their lady. Thus, the figure that Jefferson places at the center of its legendary history does indeed contain the clue to the meaning of that history—a history which began long before Emily's funeral and long before Homer Barron's disappearance or appearance and long before Colonel Sartoris' fathering of edicts and remittances. It is recorded in that emblem which lies at the heart of the town's memory and at the heart of patriarchal culture: "We had long thought of them as a tableau, Miss Emily a slender figure in white in the background, her father a spraddled silhouette in the foreground, his back to her and clutching a horsewhip, the two of them framed by the back-flung front door."

The importance of Emily's father in shaping the quality of her life is insistent throughout the story. Even in her death the force of his presence is felt; above her dead body sits "the crayon face of her father musing profoundly," symbolic of the degree to which he has dominated and shadowed her life, "as if that quality of her father which had thwarted her woman's life so many times had been too virulent and too furious to die." The violence of this consuming relationship is made explicit in the imagery of the tableau. Although the violence is apparently directed outward—the upraised horsewhip against the would-be suitor—the real object of it is the woman-daughter, forced into the background and dominated by the phallic figure of the spraddled father whose back is turned on her and who prevents her from getting out at the same time that he prevents them from getting in. Like Georgiana's spatial confinement in "Birthmark," Emily's is a metaphor for her psychic confinement: her identity is determined by the constructs of her father's mind, and she can no more escape from his creation of her as "a slender figure in white" than she can escape his house.

What is true for Emily in relation to her father is equally true for her in relation to Jefferson: her status as a lady is a cage from which she cannot escape. To them she is always *Miss* Emily; she is never referred to and never thought of as otherwise. In omitting her title from his, Faulkner emphasizes the point that the real violence done to Emily is in making her a "Miss"; the omission is one of his roses for her. Because she is *Miss* Emily *Grierson*, Emily's father dresses her in white, places her in the background, and drives away her suitors. Because she is Miss Emily Grierson, the town invests her with that communal significance which makes her the object of their obsession and the subject of their incessant scrutiny. And because she is a lady, the town is able to impose a particular code of behavior on her ("But there were still others, older people, who said that even grief could not cause a real lady to forget *noblesse oblige*") and to see in her failure to live up to that code an excuse for interfering in her life. As a lady, Emily is venerated, but veneration results in the more telling emotions of envy and spite: "It was another link between the gross, teeming world and the high and mighty Griersons"; "People . . . believed that the Griersons held themselves a little too high for what they really were." The violence implicit in the desire to see the monument fall and reveal itself for clay suggests the violence inherent in the original impulse to venerate.

The violence behind veneration is emphasized through another telling emblem in the story. Emily's position as an hereditary obligation upon the town dates from "that day in 1894 when Colonel Sartoris, the mayor—he who fathered the edict that no Negro woman should appear on the streets without an apron on—remitted her taxes, the dispensation dating from the death of her father on into perpetuity." The conjunction of these two actions in the same syntactic unit is crucial, for it insists on their essential similarity. It indicates that the impulse to exempt is analogous to the desire to restrict, and that what appears to be a kindness or an act of veneration is in fact an insult. Sartoris' remission of Emily's taxes is a public declaration of the fact that a lady is not considered to be, and hence not allowed or enabled to be, economically independent (consider, in this connection, Emily's lessons in china painting; they are a latter-day version of Sartoris' "charity" and a brilliant image of Emily's economic uselessness). His act is a public statement of the fact that a lady, if she is to survive, must have either husband or father, and that, because Emily has neither, the town must assume responsibility for her. The remission of taxes that defines Emily's status dates from the death of her father, and she is handed over from one patron to the next, the town instead of husband taking on the role of father. Indeed, the use of the word "fathered" in describing Sartoris' behavior as mayor underlines the fact that his chivalric attitude toward Emily is simply a subtler and more dishonest version of her father's horsewhip.

The narrator is the last of the patriarchs who take upon themselves the burden of defining Emily's life, and his violence toward her is the most subtle of all. His tone of incantatory reminiscence and nostalgic veneration seems free of the taint of horsewhip and edict. Yet a thoroughgoing contempt for the "ladies" who spy and pry and gossip out of their petty jealousy and curiosity is one of the clearest strands in the narrator's consciousness. Emily is exempted from the general indictment because she is a *real* lady—that is, eccentric, slightly crazy, obsolete, a "stubborn and coquettish decay," absurd but indulged; "dear, inescapable, impervious, tranquil, and perverse"; indeed, anything and everything but human.

Not only does "A Rose for Emily" expose the violence done to a woman by making her a lady; it also explores the particular form of power the victim gains from this position and can use on those who enact this violence. "A Rose for Emily" is concerned with the consequences of violence for both the violated and the violators. One of the most striking aspects of the story is the disparity between Miss Emily Grierson and the Emily to whom Faulkner gives his rose in ironic imitation of the chivalric behavior the story exposes. The form of Faulkner's title establishes a camaraderie between author and protagonist and signals that a distinction must be made between the story Faulkner is telling and the story the narrator is telling. This distinction is of major importance because it suggests, of course, that the narrator, looking through a patriarchal lens, does not see Emily at all but rather a figment of his own imagination created in conjunction with the cumulative imagination of the town. Like Ellison's invisible man,* nobody sees *Emily*. And because nobody sees *her*, she can literally get away with murder. Emily is characterized by her ability to understand and utilize the power that accrues to her from the fact that men do not see her but rather their concept of her: "'I have no taxes in Jefferson. Colonel Sartoris explained it to me. . . . Tobe! . . . Show these gentlemen out.'" Relying on the conventional assumptions about ladies who are expected to be neither reasonable nor in touch with reality, Emily presents an impregnable front that vanquishes the men "horse and foot, just as she had vanquished their fathers thirty years before." In spite of their "modern" ideas, this new generation, when faced with Miss Emily, are as much bound by the code of gentlemanly behavior as their fathers were ("They rose when she entered"). This code gives Emily a power that renders the gentlemen unable to function in a situation in which a lady neither sits down herself nor asks them to. They are brought to a "stumbling halt" and can do nothing when confronted with her refusal to engage in rational discourse. Their only recourse in the face of such eccentricity is to engage in behavior unbecoming to gentlemen, and Emily can count on their continuing to see themselves as gentlemen and her as a lady and on their returning a verdict of helpless noninterference.

It is in relation to Emily's disposal of Homer Barron, however, that Faulkner demonstrates most clearly the power of conventional assumptions about the nature of ladies to blind the town to what is going on and to allow Emily to murder with impunity. When Emily buys the poison, it never occurs to anyone that she intends to use it on Homer, so strong is the presumption that ladies when jilted commit suicide, not murder. And when her house begins to smell, the women

---

* Editor's note: A reference to the novel *Invisible Man* by Ralph Ellison.

blame it on the eccentricity of having a man servant rather than a woman, "as if a man—any man—could keep a kitchen properly." And then they hint that her eccentricity may have shaded over into madness, "remembering how old lady Wyatt, her great aunt, had gone completely crazy at last." The presumption of madness, that preeminently female response to bereavement, can be used to explain away much in the behavior of ladies whose activities seem a bit odd.

But even more pointed is what happens when the men try not to explain but to do something about the smell: "'Dammit, sir,' Judge Stevens said, 'will you accuse a lady to her face of smelling bad?'" But if a lady cannot be told that she smells, then the cause of the smell cannot be discovered and so her crime is "perfect." Clearly, the assumptions behind the Judge's outraged retort go beyond the myth that ladies are out of touch with reality. His outburst insists that it is the responsibility of gentlemen to make them so. Ladies must not be confronted with facts; they must be shielded from all that is unpleasant. Thus Colonel Sartoris remits Emily's taxes with a palpably absurd story, designed to protect her from an awareness of her poverty and her dependence on charity, and to protect him from having to confront her with it. And thus Judge Stevens will not confront Emily with the fact that her house stinks, though she is living in it and can hardly be unaware of the odor. Committed as they are to the myth that ladies and bad smells cannot coexist, these gentlemen insulate themselves from reality. And by defining a lady as a subhuman and hence sublegal entity, they have created a situation their laws can't touch. They have made it possible for Emily to be extra-legal: "'Why, of course,' the druggist said, 'If that's what you want. But the law requires you to tell what you are going to use it for.' Miss Emily just stared at him, her head tilted back in order to look him eye for eye, until he looked away and went and got the arsenic and wrapped it up." And, finally, they have created a situation in which they become the criminals: "So the next night, after midnight, four men crossed Miss Emily's lawn and slunk about the house like burglars." Above them, "her upright torso motionless as that of an idol," sits Emily, observing them act out their charade of chivalry. As they leave, she confronts them with the reality they are trying to protect her from: she turns on the light so that they may see her watching them. One can only wonder at the fact, and regret, that she didn't call the sheriff and have them arrested for trespassing.

Not only is "A Rose for Emily" a supreme analysis of what men do to women by making them ladies; it is also an exposure of how this act in turn defines and recoils upon men. This is the significance of the dynamic that Faulkner establishes between Emily and Jefferson. And it is equally the point of the dynamic implied between the tableau of Emily and her father and the tableau which greets the men who break down the door of that room in the region above the stairs. When the would-be "suitors" finally get into her father's house, they discover the consequences of his oppression of her, for the violence contained in the rotted corpse of Homer Barron is the mirror image of the violence represented in the tableau, the back-flung front door flung back with a vengeance. Having been consumed by her father, Emily in turn feeds off Homer Barron, becoming, after his death, suspiciously fat. Or, to put it another way, it is as if, after her father's death, she has reversed his act of incorporating her by incorporating and becoming him, metamorphosed from the slender figure in white to the obese figure in black whose hair is "a vigorous iron-gray, like the hair of an active man." She has taken into herself the violence in him which thwarted her and has reenacted it upon Homer Barron.

That final encounter, however, is not simply an image of the reciprocity of violence. Its power of definition also derives from its grotesqueness, which makes finally explicit the grotesqueness that has been latent in the description of Emily throughout the story: "Her skeleton was small and spare; perhaps that was why what would have been merely plumpness in another was obesity in her. She looked bloated, like a body long submerged in motionless water, and of that pallid hue. Her eyes, lost in the fatty ridges of her face, looked like two small pieces of coal pressed into a lump of dough." The impact of this description depends on the contrast it establishes between Emily's reality as a fat, bloated figure in black and the conventional image of a lady—expectations that are fostered in the town by its emblematic memory of Emily as a slender figure in white and in us by the narrator's tone of romantic invocation and by the passage itself. Were she not expected to look so different, were her skeleton not small and spare, Emily would not be so grotesque. Thus, the focus is on the grotesqueness that results when stereotypes are imposed upon reality. And the implication of this focus is that the real grotesque is the stereotype itself. If Emily is both lady and grotesque, then the syllogism must be completed thus: the idea of a lady is grotesque. So Emily is metaphor and mirror for the town of Jefferson; and when, at the end, the town folk finally discover who and what she is, they have in fact encountered who and what they are.

Questions for Comprehension

1. How does Fetterley characterize the attitude of the townspeople toward Emily Grierson during her lifetime? How is this attitude reflected in their behavior after her death?
2. In what ways is the tableau of Emily and her father an emblem of Jefferson's "patriarchal culture"?
3. According to Fetterley, Emily's "status as a lady is a cage from which she cannot escape." What is the meaning of "lady" in this context? Why is this status a "cage"? Who has locked Emily in this cage?
4. How do the actions of various town leaders exemplify Fetterley's assertion that "what appears to be a kindness or an act of veneration is in fact an insult"?
5. In what way does the narrator exemplify the patriarchal attitude toward Emily?
6. How does the patriarchal attitude that oppresses Emily also give her power? How is this power exemplified by the murder of Homer Barron and its aftermath?
7. How does the change in Emily's appearance after the murder, and particularly her physical resemblance to her father, exemplify the process by which "men's attitudes toward women turn back upon themselves"?
8. What is the ultimate source of the grotesqueness of Emily's appearance? How does that grotesqueness underline the theme of the story?

TOBE'S SIGNIFICANCE IN "A ROSE FOR EMILY"
T. J. Stafford

T. J. Stafford is professor of English at the University of Texas, El Paso. The following essay first appeared in the 1968–69 issue of Modern Fiction Studies.

In William Faulkner's "A Rose for Emily," a search for the motivation of Emily Grierson's murder of Homer Barron usually begins with an effort to understand Miss Emily herself. Until she is understood, everything remains an enigma. In trying to solve the puzzle, Brooks and Warren conclude that her behavior reflects a pride and independence of spirit which are highly regarded by Faulkner. Such a view, however, fails to account for the disparity between the admirable qualities motivating the action and the ignominy of the act. To view Miss Emily in this way is to come to the story with a presupposition about what Faulkner is doing and not to look at the story as it actually operates, for the fact remains that Miss Emily's relation with Homer is an abnormal, degenerate, and meaningless human association which is unworthy of the pride it took to attain it.

In a work of art, one cannot always isolate the part he wishes to understand, for other parts may offer a necessary perspective. In this case, Faulkner's purpose becomes more clear by seeing Miss Emily in contrast to her Negro servant. While Emily occupies the foreground and provides the primary movement (a movement toward decay), the servant hovers in the background and offers a countermovement of purposeful activity. Although only ten separate references are made to the Negro, each is strategically placed and richly suggestive of his contrast with Miss Emily.

Faulkner gives a rather full impression of the servant's activities. He does the gardening, marketing, and cooking, all of which sustain Miss Emily physically. He conducts the townsmen in and shows them out when she is finished with them, and later he admits Homer at the kitchen door. He is, as protector of Miss Emily, thought of as having killed a snake or a rat. He thus engages in purposeful and altruistic action. Miss Emily, by contrast, gives an impression of immobility, "motionless as that of an idol," an image which Faulkner reiterates. In only one section (III) is Emily able to perform action, courting Homer Barron, riding about town, and buying arsenic. Ironically, it is the only section in which the Negro does not appear, and Emily's one set of deeds, performed without the servant's being present in the story, results in violence and destruction.

The servant offers Miss Emily the means for contact with humanity in two ways. On the one hand, his errands furnish a link between her deteriorating world and human society, while on the other hand, he is in himself a whole and healthy human (a fact established by his ability to perform and to remain in contact with the world). But his provision for an access to the human heart for Miss Emily also contrasts with her condition. First, his sallies forth to the marketplace, his meeting the world that comes to her door (and turning it away only at her command), and his final liberation into the world after her death, all stand in juxtaposition to her isolation and alienation. Second, although he is himself a human, she does not even talk with him, for, as the narrator says, his voice "had grown harsh and rusty, as if from disuse."

The Negro servant's importance actually lies beyond the story's end. Faulkner suggests this meaning through the choice of name, "Tobe," emphasized by avoiding the usual spelling of "Toby" and clearly implying that he is "to be," that once he is liberated from the foul atmosphere of Miss Emily's alienation and paralysis, his fulfillment will be. The ending reinforces this suggestion, for, while exposing Miss Emily's inability to engage in meaningful human associations, it frees Tobe from her decayed sphere into a world that is to be.

Tobe's significance becomes even more clear in the broader frame of Faulkner's work. Dilsey is like Tobe in that she is the only person in *The Sound and the Fury* who is able to engage in meaningful action and who provides a moral center to the story. Also like Tobe, she sustains and protects her white masters, outlives them, and suggests the indomitability of the human spirit. Tobe also relates to certain views expressed by Faulkner. In *The Bear*, for example, Ike McCaslin tells Lucas Beauchamp that the white man has had his turn and that someday "your peoples' turn will come because we have forfeited ours." Later Ike says that the Negro people "will endure. They will outlast us. . . . They are better than we are. Stronger than we are." It is the same idea implied in Faulkner's Appendix to *The Sound and the Fury* which ends with the simple description of Dilsey, "they endured."

Tobe, like Dilsey is to the Compsons, has thus been more than a servant to Miss Emily's physical needs. While serving as cook and gardener, he has demonstrated the possibility of meaningful action; while meeting the world for her, he has provided her with the means for contact with it. But she has been unable to avail herself of his humanity and in so failing she suggests the explanation for her abnormal and depraved relation with Homer Barron, which is in itself symbolic of her relationship with the human heart, her own, Tobe's, and human kind's.

While it may be true, as Brooks and Warren say, that Emily reveals pride and independence of spirit, qualities which Faulkner greatly valued, it is even more clear that in Miss Emily they do not lead to a richer life but are perverted into destruction and decay. Thus, Faulkner here qualifies his feelings about pride, demonstrating that it is insufficient in itself and that other qualities are needed to humanize it. These qualities are shown through Tobe, who reveals humility, patience, endurance, courage, and pity. A clearer picture of Miss Emily's true nature is therefore given by her sharp contrast with Tobe's wholeness. Toward the end, a feeling of release is associated with Tobe as he disappears into the future and the narrator turns to lead the reader into the room of dust, death, and decay which Emily Grierson has created.

Questions for Comprehension

1. What is the basis of Stafford's criticism of the position taken by Brooks and Warren?
2. How does Tobe's "purposeful activity" contrast with Emily Grierson's way of life?

3. What significance does Stafford attach to Tobe's name?
4. How does Emily's relationship to Tobe suggest the explanation for her "abnormal and depraved" relationships?
5. How does the contrast between Emily and Tobe clarify Faulkner's attitude toward Emily?

■

EMILY'S ROSE OF LOVE: THEMATIC IMPLICATIONS OF POINT OF VIEW IN FAULKNER'S "A ROSE FOR EMILY"

Helen E. Nebeker

Helen E. Nebeker (b. 1927) teaches English at Arizona State University. The following essay first appeared in the *Bulletin of the Rocky Mountain Modern Language Association* in 1970.

The thesis of this paper, simply stated, is that forty years of critical study of Faulkner's short story, "A Rose for Emily," has failed to come to grips with the problem of its narrative focus or point of view. Furthermore, I will contend that this failure to fully explore the significance of the narrative voice has obscured several essential points of the story, chief of which is the underlying horror of Faulkner's real theme, a theme which he has kept successfully hidden through the years within his deliberate structural ambiguity and behind his anonymous narrator.

As most readers are no doubt aware, the general view of critics regarding the anonymous, ubiquitous narrator is that he is a kind of innocuous, naive, passive citizen of Jefferson, who relates for the reader the story of Miss Emily's life and death. Or, in the words of one critic summing up the prevailing view, he is ". . . a townsman, gifted in the art of storytale-telling, shifting his identity imaginatively as he moves through the story." Or, as another group of critics states, the narrator simply records ". . . the progress or advance in the . . . knowledge of Emily's townsmen . . . a growth from bemused tolerance, to suspicion, to knowledge, to horror . . ." at Emily's crime. From these more or less similar views of the narrator, the critics proceed to develop their interpretations of Miss Emily as the proud, unbending monument of the Old South who somehow triumphs over time and change, thereby evoking admiration conjoined with pity.[1]

On the surface, such explanation of both narrator and theme may suffice. But if one looks sharply and critically at the point of view chosen by Faulkner, remembering that the basic structural resource of a writer is point of view which

---

1. For a few useful and interesting references to these interpretations, see: Cleanth Brooks and R. P. Warren, *The Scope of Fiction* (New York: Appleton-Century-Crofts, 1980), pp. 302–306. Donald Heiney, *Recent American Literature* (Great Neck, N.Y.: Barron's Educational Series, Inc., 1958), pp. 221–225. Ray B. West, Jr., *Reading the Short Story* (New York: Thomas Y. Crowell Co., 1968), pp. 82–85. Explicators: VI (May, 1948), item 45; VII (Oct., 1948), item 8; XIX (Jan., 1961), item 26; XX (May, 1962), item 78; XXII (April, 1964), item 68.

becomes, in the words of Mark Schorer, a mode of thematic definition, and if one acknowledges the mastery of Faulkner in merging person, time, place, and events, the importance of his chosen point of view should not be so lightly dismissed. However in just such dismissal, readers and critics alike have permitted themselves to be fooled by a master story-teller who lays out point by point the details of a horror far more monstrous than that of a poor demented woman who kills her lover.

For the truth of the Miss Emily episode lies, not in the character and motivation of Miss Emily, but in the identity of the narrator. And to arrive at that identity, the reader must untangle the deliberate ambiguity of the various pronoun references which control the point of view. Once this is done, the implicit horror of the story is clearly revealed, and from that horror, a new, more subtle theme emerges, revealing starkly and undeniably the significance of the "rose" of the title.

The reader of "A Rose for Emily" realizes immediately the vagueness of the pronoun focus within this story. Within all five sections we note a continual shifting of person, from *our* to *they* to *we* (all italics added). And this shift is further complicated by implied shifts of referents for the various pronouns. That is, *our* does not always have the same referent, nor do *they* and *we*! For example, in Section I, this shifting ranges from the *our* of the opening sentence (*our* whole town), which we easily equate with the townspeople, to the *they* of the fourth paragraph (*they* mailed her a tax notice), equated at this point in the story with the generation of mayors and aldermen who took power after the paternal despotism of Colonel Sartoris, the man who abrogated the taxes of Miss Emily.

In Section II, we are told that ". . . she vanquished *them*" (the generation indicated above) "just as she had vanquished *their* fathers thirty years before . . ." (another previous generation). And in the shifting chronology of events in this passage, their *fathers* becomes the *they* of the Board of Aldermen, "three gray beards and one younger man, a member of the rising generation," who confer about the odor at Miss Emily's house. Thus, in the first two sections, we have ambiguously but definably presented before us three groups—the general townspeople of the inclusive *our*; the *they* of a contemporary society functioning when Miss Emily was in her late 50s or early 60s and to whom she refused to pay taxes; and the *they* of an earlier group. This last group would have been a chronologically overlapping group composed of Emily's post-war contemporaries as well as the older pre-Civil War generation—men such as Colonel Sartoris who, unable to affront a needy lady with charity, concocted a story which permitted Miss Emily to accept charity in the form of remitted taxes and a Judge Stevens, eighty years old and unable to "accuse a lady to her face of smelling bad." Predictable Faulknerian generations: the autocratic pre-Civil War hierarchy to whom a lady is always a lady; the generation this hierarchy breeds, Emily's generation, characterized by decay, ruin, but also reverence for the past; the unknowing, uncaring, opportunistic new breed which will dun a lady for her taxes.

But challenging this convenient categorization is the introduction in Section II of a different pronoun, the *we* who thought of Emily and her father as a tableau: "Miss Emily a slender figure in white in the background, her father a spraddled silhouette in the foreground, his back to her, clutching a horse-whip . . ."; the *we* who were not pleased but *vindicated* when she reached thirty and was still single; the *we* who did not say she was crazy then because they remembered all the young men her father had driven away. Traditionally this has been accepted as a universal *we*, referring to the townspeople as a whole; as indicated by the previous "our whole town" it supposedly is the *we* of public rumor, piecemeal hearsay. But this interpretation avoids an extremely pertinent question: why is this *we* separated from the *they* who, still in Section II of the story, began to feel sorry for Emily after Homer's disappearance, remembering her great aunt's madness; the *they* who pity her, alone and destitute at her father's death; the *they* who buried her father quickly?

Upon careful consideration it seems obvious that, in this *we*, another group has been introduced into the personae of the story—a smaller group whose members have personally seen the tableau of daughter and father with upraised whip. Whip upraised against what? The town and life in general? Or young men in particular?—young men of Emily's own generation, none of whom "were quite good enough for Miss Emily" and who are "vindicated" (avenged?) by her spinsterhood. It is conceivable that this *we*, in the context in which it is presented, is the disappointed but still devoted group of suitors that surrounded every belle of the Southern myth, suitors not socially prominent enough to be acceptable to the Old Aristocracy but of a breeding, position, and means superior to the *they*—the general townspeople—who must reduce Emily from an untouchable monument to an impoverished pitiable human. Is this *we* a select group to whom Emily is a "care" (paragraph 3) as opposed to the *they* to whom she is a "duty" (the older generation which believes in the protection of Southern Womanhood)? Structurally this is more than just a defensible supposition.

Entertaining this possibility, and holding in abeyance momentarily the final intriguing paragraph of Section II, let us pursue the pronoun shifting a little further.

Section III introduces Barron, the Northern Outsider, gross, arrogant, dynamic; and in connection with him, again the *we*. We saw Miss Emily after her illness as girlish and somewhat angelic with her short hair; *we* were glad she had an interest; *we* believed she was fallen. Juxtaposed with this *we* is the *they* of the older tradition-bound people who knew that even grief could not account for Emily's lapse with Homer (the implication in the light of the various references to insanity is, of course, that Emily must be mad) and who began to say "Poor Emily." And then the *they* of a younger and less aristocratic group who began to whisper about Emily and Homer after the older people had set the precedent. Here again is the grouping previously mentioned (without, of course, the youngest group which is not yet grown)—the Old Order, Emily's contemporaries, and the small, exclusive group of *we*.

Concluding this same Section III is an accurate, knowledgeable revelation of Miss Emily buying the arsenic, a scene dramatic in presentation, without equivocation. What observer witnessed that scene? Who remembered and repeated the exact words? Who could possibly report that when Miss Emily opened the box of poison at home she found written on it the notation, "For rats"? To explain this knowledge as public rumor, common gossip, is to ignore the care of Faulkner as an artist and to grossly oversimplify the narrative structure of this story. Reasonably, only the druggist could have known the facts of the rat poison episode and it seems obvious that it was the druggist who looked down at her and saw her face like a "strained flag." Now would the druggist, having tacitly violated the law (and even believing that Emily would commit suicide),[2] have made this episode public gossip? If so, he not only indicts himself, but the whole town quite literally connives at murder. Thus this interpretation seems unlikely. He might, however, have revealed it confidentially to an intimate or two, those who, like him, "*watched over*" (and spied upon) Miss Emily.

With this idea in mind, refer back to Section II which relates an episode which took place two years after the death of Emily's father, after her purchase of the poison, and a short time after the disappearance of Homer Barron. Because of complaints about the smell at Emily's house, the Board of Aldermen, "three graybeards and one younger man, a member of the rising generation," have met. Subsequently four men skulked about her house, sniffing, sowing lime. In a week or two the smell went away. Interesting questions are raised here. First of all, who are the four men prowling outside Miss Emily's house, even breaking into the cellar to sprinkle the lime? The Board of Aldermen, spied upon by an outsider who later reveals the episode? But how would an outsider know of the earlier Board meeting in such detail? Is it just possible that the younger man of the Board, assisted by three cohorts who have been alerted to the situation, acts to forestall further investigation? Do we have at least a tenable clue to the ambiguous *we* when we link this episode with that of the rat poison? Can we imagine the rising young alderman and the druggist (with at least two others) as conspirators who speculate, discuss the events of Emily's life among themselves? At any rate, whatever their identity, these four men act to protect Miss Emily. Why? What do these men suspect? And why, "after a week or two," does the smell go away? It takes *weeks* for the smell of a decomposing body to dissipate—and we the readers know that the lime has never touched the source of the corruption! What happens to stop the odor unless the body is either completely destroyed or sealed off in an airless room? And who seals it: Miss Emily alerted by the skulking men? Cohorts in crime who advise Miss Emily that something must be done to prevent public action? Hold these points in reserve temporarily.

Now we must look for a moment at the structural and chronological significance of Section II. As we have already discovered, in this section the various groups within Jefferson have been carefully, if obscurely, introduced. But more than this, every major episode except Emily's death has also been introduced, merged within a kind of ebbing and flowing continuum of time—a structural technique essential to Faulkner's purpose. Note that in the first paragraph we start with a reference to a fairly recent occurrence, the attempt to collect Emily's taxes,

---

2. Note in the light of the rest of this discussion, the implications of the druggist's willingness to let her commit suicide—or perhaps to suggest by means of his label that the poison might better be used on someone else.

and shift in the same sentence to a reference concerning the smell which occurred after her father's death and Homer's disappearance. Then we slip back to her father's death (interestingly juxtaposed by a semicolon to her sweetheart's going away), the consequent visit of the ladies, the reference to the Negro servant who is Emily's lone retainer, and from him to the smell again, which is accepted *by the ladies* as conclusive proof that no man could keep a kitchen properly. All of this in ten lines. And from this chronological jump-off, we learn of the secret night visit by the four men.

Then, in the eleventh paragraph of Section II, we read, "That was when people had begun to feel really sorry for her," remembering how insanity ran in Emily's family. But in the confusing chronological sequence just indicated, to what time period does that sentence refer? Surely not to the preceding line, "After a week or two the smell went away." Does it refer to her father's death? To Homer's disappearance? It is impossible to tell in the merging of events presented to our view. But two paragraphs later we are told about Emily's refusal to admit her father's death, and how *they*, about to resort to force, were finally permitted by Miss Emily to dispose of the body. Then that curious last paragraph which we were holding in abeyance:

> We did not say that she was crazy then. We believed she had to do that. We remembered all the young men her father had driven away, and we knew that with nothing left, she would have to cling to that which had robbed her, as people will.

Again *we* carefully separated from *they*. And again the question, to what period of time does that paragraph refer? I suggest that it not only refers to Emily's attempt to keep her father's body, but, in an already established pattern of time transformance, to events following his death—the purchase of the poison, the disappearance of Homer, and the development of the smell. In other words, we did not admit that she was crazy *then*—when she kept the body of her father, when she bought the poison; we knew she had to do *that*—keep her father's body, buy the poison. But note the full implications of *then* and *that*. When did we say that she was crazy? After we realized the significance of the smell? When we knew that she had murdered Homer? We knew she had to do that—deny the death of her father, keep her lover's body, her lover who had robbed her of even her pride (her father having deprived her of all hope of an acceptable form of love because of his family pride). In the unfolding horror of these possibilities lies the defense for what has been criticized as an unneccessarily complicated structure and chronology. Through this structure and chronology with its merging and confusing of events and participants, Faulkner permits his first person narrator to mask not only his identity but also to conceal from us the knowledge he or rather they have concerning Emily's horrible crime. This is the genius of Faulkner. The clues are all there as early as the second section, even though we will continue through three more sections, still unaware of the magnitude of the horror unfolding before us.

In Section IV, the merging of time and events continues. Following the purchase of the poison, "we all said" (note the clue here that the select *we* group is larger than the two already identified) that Emily would kill herself "*and that would be the best thing.*" (That is, the tradition of aristocratic honor must not be violated.) Time then telescopes to the whole affair between Emily and Homer. The pronouns in this section are much less confusing. The whole town knows about the affair; everyone sees Emily and Homer. The minority *we* becomes more or less a part of the general *we*, and all of us side with Miss Emily against the outside Griersons who "were even more Grierson than Miss Emily had ever been." And then Homer disappears after having been seen entering the kitchen door at dusk—the front door is closed and Miss Emily does not appear on the street for six months. Then when *we* next see her, she has grown fat and gray; her front door remains closed for some years until she opens it to give painting lessons to a few of her contemporaries and their children. (Chronologically, Emily is approximately thirty-two when Homer disappears, forty-ish when she fits up her studio.)

17   Then, the "newer generation"—a second generation from Emily—succeeds as the "spirit of the town," a generation to whom Emily is neither "tradition" nor "duty" and certainly not "care" in the sense of any kind of attention or personal involvement, and so the front door closes irrevocably. When the town gets free postal delivery (symbolic of the new order), Emily will not let *them* attach the numbers and mailbox above her door. Years pass as *we* watch her Negro grow older. Now *we*—not *they*—send her a tax notice each December. With the passage of years, only Emily, symbolic of the indomitable but dying Old South in all its decadence, pride, refusal to admit the changing order, remains distinguishable, definable. *We* have admitted the change, accepted it, merged into it, become a part of the *they*. Only Emily "passed from generation to generation—dear [to the old order], inescapable [to her contemporary protectors], impervious [to the new order], tranquil [in her madness], and perverse [turned to the illusory past instead of reality]." And so she dies, alone, *scarcely remembered*, "in the house filled with dust and shadows . . ."

18   And with her death, the town gathers. The Negro attendant admits the first visitors and then, knowing the horrible secret of that upper room, walks out of the house and disappears forever. The female cousins arrive. The very old men, last of the Great Confederacy, gather to pay honor to a myth of the past, convincing themselves that they had danced with and courted Emily, although she had in reality belonged to a younger generation. They reminisce, "confusing time with its mathematical progression, as the old do, to whom all the past is not a diminishing road, but, instead, a huge meadow . . ." (Note that in these lines Faulkner has clearly revealed his structural intent and his narrative secret.) Emily lies beneath a mass of "bought flowers," not flowers gathered by caring hands from lovingly tended gardens, but "bought flowers" tendered by a crass, unknowing, uncaring generation. Symbolically, the New South has triumphed.

19   But in the midst of this triumph, once more, clearly and finally, the emergence of that separate *we*. "Already we knew that there was *one room* in that region above stairs which no one had seen in forty years and which would have to be forced." The implications here are overwhelming. *We* knew what was in that room; *we* had known it for forty years! Emily died at seventy-four; her father had died when she was approximately thirty-one or thirty-two; Homer had disap-

peared two years later. And someone had seen that room after his death, forty years earlier, or had suspected what it contained. Now the reader understands clearly what has been suggested earlier—that the room had been sealed shortly after decomposition of Homer's body had begun, either by Miss Emily herself or by accomplices after-the-fact.[3] Someone had locked that door; someone had disposed of the key so that *they* would have to break down the door after Miss Emily was decently in the ground. Now if Miss Emily had locked the door herself and thrown away the key, how do *we* know that the room must be forced; how do *we* know that no one has seen that room in forty years? Have not *we*, knowing her horrible crime, concurring in it, even abetting it, stood guard, protected, cherished these many years this putrescent symbol of a way of life long dead, almost forgotten? Do *we*, almost as lovers, offer this last appalling act of devotion—the keeping of her ghastly secret—as a final tribute, as our "rose for Emily"? A rose in sharp, poignant, horrible contrast to the "bought flowers" of a new generation? In other words, as alien outside forces seemingly triumph over Emily in death, have not *we*, in reality, finally cuckolded *they* in the keeping of our macabre secret? And in preserving—or using—Emily,[4] *we* have kept untarnished the honor and myth of the South!

Now, in this last act of the drama, as *they* force the door, *we* note the remembered (or anticipated) details of the room, almost as though a camera slowly moved from point to point. The violence of the falling door seems to fill the room with dust. The smell of the tomb pervades the bridal room, lying upon the faded rose of the bed curtains, the rose-shaded lights, the tarnished silver of the toilet articles, the men's clothes. And then the body. Rotting, grimacing, "cuckolded" by death (as well as by aged lovers?) lies Homer Barron. No shock, no surprise as *we* view the scene, just careful attention to every detail. And then, "one of us" lifts something from the pillow, a long strand of Emily's iron-gray hair.

Now, upon the threshold of that room and from the obscurities and complexities of structure and personae, the truth of time and circumstance emerges for the reader. From that room the odor of death and corruption assaults our senses and we, the readers, know the final horror. The guilt of a crazed old lady is clear, horrible but comprehensible in the light of her loss, her insanity. But the odor of the "rose of love" proffered Emily by those aged lovers, sickens, suffocates, is beyond our comprehension. The composite *we* looms monstrous, corrupt. And through that monstrous *we*, Faulkner offers us a frightening comment on the moral fabric of the Southern social structure.

For thus he tells us that the immediate post-war remnant of the Old Southern hierarchy—symbolized in the person of Emily—lies dead, buried, even pardoned in the light of her heritage, her madness, her incorruptible endurance. But another remnant of this Old South—symbolized in the persons of the anonymous

---

3. This writer's mother recalls clearly, as a child in the South, the sealing up of a room in which a sister had died of diphtheria. She remembers that it was a time-consuming and difficult task for her father and believes it would have been impossible for the strength of her mother.
4. See footnote 2.

ancient suitors—lives on, linked only tenuously and superficially to that now-dead, indomitable aristocracy. Inferior in every way to the clans of Sartoris and Grierson (perhaps even to the minor aristocracy of Barrons), this order yet lusts and covets consummation. Torn between envy and revulsion, love and hate, it protects and extends the myth of its idol. Robbed of everything else, even as Emily had been robbed, it clings to the rotting body of the loved one—just as Emily had clung to the dead body of her father (the past) and the rotted body of her lover (the present and future)—cherishing it even as it putrefies and maddens before its eyes, even as it dies.

Insidious, monstrous, unforgivably corrupt, this sub-culture merges into the innocuous *they* of respectability and modernity. In the form of Emily's secret protectors, sane, deliberate, knowing, this group stands self-righteously and horribly amid the final debacle, proffering to Emily—at once its victim and its care—its loathsome rose of love.

Addendum

To those who respond to the thesis of this paper with the question, "But how do you explain the gray hair on the pillow?" may I point out that forty years of critical attention has not been able to settle this problem. Nor can this question, in the context of the story, ever be fully clarified.

However, three specific points can be made. First of all, this critical question of the gray hair has served as a red herring for Faulkner through the years, almost completely diverting attention from the real problem of the story, the narrative focus. Secondly, we can point out that there is one obvious point of confusion in the critical studies in relation to the time at which Miss Emily's hair turned gray. This error is rooted in Section IV of the story, after Homer had been admitted at dusk and Miss Emily disappears from public view for "almost six months." There follows another sentence and then the next paragraph begins,

> When we next saw Miss Emily, she had grown fat and her hair was turning gray. During the next few years it grew grayer and grayer until it obtained an even pepper-and-salt iron gray, when it ceased turning. Up to the day of her death at seventy-four it was still that vigorous iron-gray . . .

Critics have confused Miss Emily's appearance after the six-month interval with the time when *we* (in the context of this paper's thesis) *next* saw her. There is no way of absolutely equating the references nor of accurately pin-pointing how long after Homer's death Emily's hair began to turn. We can say, however, that at some time subsequent to the sealing up of the room and after the smell of the corpse had dissipated, Emily had found a way to enter the room and had lain—whether briefly or often we cannot know (because the narrator cannot know!)—beside the corpse. When that room is entered, the only thing seemingly unanticipated by the narrator-group is that long strand of iron-gray hair which one of *us* lifts from the pillow.

Thus, carrying my thesis to its furthest conclusion: just as *we* (the Old South) have cuckolded *they* (the new), triumphing over them in this moment of death, so has Emily ultimately cuckolded *us* (the old lovers) and Faulkner's theme is brought full circle. We, the readers, are left in complete knowledge that Emily's South, though dead and buried and forgiven, has left its horror imprinted forever on the structure and in the persons of the present.

Chronology of "A Rose for Emily"

1863 (ca.)	Emily born.
1893	Emily's father dies. (Emily is just past thirty.)
1894	Taxes are remitted by Colonel Sartoris *retroactive* to his death. (Probably a time lapse of approximately a year for tax notices.)
1895–96	Homer disappears, the smell develops. Emily is past thirty, her father has been dead two years. Emily is not seen on the streets for almost six months. Contrary to general criticism, taken contextually one cannot assume definitely that Emily was turning gray when she appeared after six months. Although the paragraph following this reference to the six-month time lapse begins, "When we next saw Miss Emily, she had grown fat and her hair was turning gray," we have no way of knowing whether a further time lapse is involved or not.
1895–96	N.B.: The room must have been sealed almost immediately following the sprinkling of the lime. No lime ever touches the body and the smell of a rotting corpse lingers for weeks!
1902–10	Emily is about forty when she begins to give china-painting lessons. This would be one of the few genteel avenues of income for a destitute "lady" of her time.
1910	Colonel Sartoris dies about this time. This would account for the falling off of her pupils—he can no longer influence his children and friends to subsidize Miss Emily, just as he will no longer be able to control the matter of her taxes.
1920–25	A second Board of Aldermen calls upon her personally about her taxes. This is thirty years after their fathers had dealt with the problem of the smell (approx. 1925) or eight to ten years after she ceased giving painting lessons (approx. 1920). Emily would be between fifty-seven and sixty-two.
1937 (ca.)	Emily dies. Although the narrator tells us that no one had entered her house for at least ten years, since no mention is made of any specific visit, we might assume that in the chronology of the seventy-four years of Emily's life and the forty-four years encompassed since her father's death some discrepancy of time is to be expected—especially when one recognizes the secret of the narrator—and that the visit by the tax collectors was the last time her doors were opened.

Overlapping (Predictably Faulknerian) Generations (ca.) 1830–1936

I. Old Aristocracy—Pre–Civil War (The proud, indomitable autocracy with its belief in "its flower of Southern Womanhood"; *those to whom Emily is "a duty"*)

Colonel Sartoris
  Grierson
  Judge Stevens
  The "very old men" in their Confederate uniforms at the funeral
  They who know that even grief cannot account for Emily's lapse with Homer
II. Post-War Generation (*those to whom Emily is "a care"*)
  A. Aristocratic descendants of Old Aristocracy
    Emily
  B. Less socially acceptable but "spiritual heirs" of the Old South
    1. The *they* "who meet about the smell"
      (a) three old graybeards (Judge Stevens)
      (b) one younger man, a member of the rising generation
    2. The *they* who begin to whisper about Emily and Homer after the older people set the precedent
    3. The "narrative we," obviously a chronological if not social peer group
      (a) *we* see Emily and her father as a tableau—note sexual overtones of that scene
      (b) *we* are "vindicated" when she is not married at 30
      (c) *we* are there at her death and when the room is opened
      (d) *we* (one of us) lift the hair from the pillow
  C. The Negro servant
    A young male Negro who serves Miss Emily until her death at 74, when he, "a doddering old man," disappears. He obviously knows the horrid secret, but we can forgive him for not betraying his mistress in the tradition of the old Negro servitor—just as we can forgive her in the knowledge of her madness. But, can he be the only one who knows the horror of that upstairs room?
III. A Newer Rising Generation (*Those to whom Emily is "a tradition"*)
  A. *They* mailed her tax notices but treated her respectfully, and Emily "vanquished them" when *they* called on her (again, an overlapping age group)
  B. The daughters and granddaughters of Colonel Sartoris' contemporaries who "were sent" to her as painting pupils
IV. A Newer Second Generation (*Those to whom Emily is neither duty nor tradition nor care*)
  A. *They* become the backbone and spirit of the town (Section IV)
  B. The granddaughters (See III-B above) who grow up and do not send their children to her
  C. *They* try to fasten the numbers over her door and attach a mailbox to it
  D. *They* send "bought" flowers (not *carefully nurtured*, garden-grown flowers)
V. A Composite Product
    A sub-culture *we*, which is linked tenuously and superficially to the Old Aristocracy; which is a product of the Post-War Generation; which

becomes a part of the Newer Rising Generation, which, in turn, ultimately merges with the Newer Second Generation to become the innocuous *they* of respectability and modernity. This *we* now sends her tax notices in the name of civic duty even as *we* had dutifully compounded her crime in the name of Southern honor.

Questions for Comprehension

1. According to Nebeker, to whom does the pronoun *we* refer at the beginning of "A Rose for Emily"? (See paragraph 8.) How does the episode involving Emily Grierson and the druggist help to back up this identification?
2. According to Nebeker, how was the odor of Homer Barron's decomposing body taken care of? (See paragraph 12.)
3. Why does the pronoun *we* eventually come to refer to the whole town? (See paragraphs 16–17.)
4. How does Nebeker explain the significance of the title of the story?
5. How does the identification of *we* explain Faulkner's attitude toward "the old Southern hierarchy" in the story?
6. How does Nebeker account for the gray hair on the pillow?

■

HOW READERS MAKE MEANING

Robert Crosman

Robert Crosman (b. 1940), educated at the University of California, Berkeley, and Columbia University, teaches English at Tufts University. The following essay first appeared in *College Literature* in 1982.

For a number of years now I have been arguing that readers make the meanings of literary texts, and that accordingly there is no such thing as "right reading." Such a conclusion troubles most students of literature, and raises a host of questions, some of which—like "By what authority can I tell a student his interpretation is wrong?" or "How then can English be called a discipline?"—are questions of campus politics that are, theoretically at least, very easily answered. The problem for us is to answer the much more complex question of *how* readers make meaning: under what impulses or constraints, following what conventions or strategies? Beyond this lies a second thorny question: are different readers' results all equally valid?

I want to try answering these general questions by looking at a specific text—William Faulkner's short story "A Rose for Emily"—and two antithetical interpretations of it. My contention is that although these interpretations contradict each other, both are valid. How this can be, it will be my task to explain. The two readers are myself and one of the students in a course called "Responses to Literature" that I taught at Trinity College in 1976. Our procedure was to read a text, and then immediately to write in our journals about our thoughts, feelings, and fantasies during and after reading. Here first is my journal entry, warts and all, exactly as I wrote it:

> This is a story I had never actually read, though I had heard of it, read something about it, and in particular knew its ending, which kept me from feeling the pure shock that the reader must feel who knows nothing of what is coming. Even so I felt a shock, and reacted with an audible cry of mingled loathing and pleasure at the final and most shocking discovery: that Emily has slept with this cadaver for forty years. The loathing is easy enough to explain: the problem is to explain the pleasure. But before trying, let me record other parts of my "response."
>
> I found my mind wandering as I read this story; there were paragraphs I had to reread several times. For one reason or another I was "uninvolved" with the story, perhaps a product of the circumstances under which I read it, but possibly also a response to the story itself. There are various reasons why I might tonight shun wrestling with a "serious" story, but perhaps I also shrank from the "horror" I knew was coming. Perhaps the story of a woman killing her faithless lover is not one I particularly want to hear. I've known about this story for years, yet had no urge to read it, perhaps because I knew what it contained.
>
> She kills him. What do I care about him?—he's hardly in the story at all. But I noticed the repeated differentiation at the story's beginning between men and women, and the put-downs of women. The story seemed to be setting me up for some attitude toward women, and even though I noticed this, I did take the attitude: women are mean, ill-willed, and therefore (though not men's equals) menacing. Miss Emily is menacing. But at first she seems grotesque and stupid: her house smells bad; she's fat, with a dead look; she faces down the fathers [i.e. the aldermen] by (apparently) missing their point. Only gradually do I see the force of her will, that just because she doesn't go out or *do* anything doesn't mean that she isn't in control.
>
> The scene with the rat-poison is crucial here: Miss Emily got her way, and the fact that her way is inscrutable, though surely menacing (arsenic), only makes it worse. The whole feeling of the story is of a mystery, something to do with male-female relationships, as well as time, perhaps, but a mystery one doesn't entirely want solved. Perhaps because I knew what was coming my mind wandered, putting even further distance between myself and the disgusting (but fascinating) revelation of the "bedroom" scene at the end. But the distancing is there in the story itself. The time-lags, the mysteriousness, the indirection, all put barriers between you and the story's subject.
>
> So this is what I'd say at first reading, anyway. As far as response goes, mine is a considerable *fear* of the discovery I know is waiting, the sex-and-death thing, though there is a *fascination*, too. As far as the story's technique goes, I think it sets up shields of various sorts, that hide the ultimate truth, yet that have chinks that give us inklings, and the effect of secrets-not-entirely-hidden, of horrible-premonitions-defended-against, is what I'd guess is the technique that seems to arouse my feelings.

Now let me admit, right off, that this isn't an "unmediated" response to Faulkner's story. It was written not during but immediately after reading the story, by a relatively sophisticated, self-conscious reader, who also had some foreknowledge of the story's shocking climax. Most of all, it is a *written account* of a response, and so subject to all kinds of misrepresentation on my part *as I wrote it*. Also it was written by someone who has had considerable exposure to psychotherapy, and who therefore is somewhat at ease when expressing a taboo pleasure at contemplating necrophilia, an activity that is widely considered (and no doubt really is) loathsome to engage in.

Nonetheless, all this said, my response should give comfort to literary Freudians. For what I saw in "A Rose for Emily" was pretty certainly a "primal scene." Both my fear and my interest, my loathing and pleasure, derived, at least in part, from remembered childish speculation as to what went on in the parental bedroom. The structure of the story's plot is to set up a dark and impenetrable mystery—what is troubling Emily?—and to penetrate deeper and deeper into her past in hopes of getting an answer. Formally the pleasure is derived from solving the mystery, but the solution is a shocking one. My unconscious *knew* all along that nothing good went on behind a locked bedroom door, but now it has proof, and has won a victory over my conscious mind, which assured me it was none of my business. My conscious mind, meanwhile, has to content itself with solving a puzzle, with the self-evident reflection that after all Emily and Homer aren't Mom and Dad, and that, anyway, "it's only a story."

Beyond the illicit pleasure of letting a taboo thought become momentarily conscious, there was more bad news for my conscious mind in my response to "A Rose for Emily," for it turns out that my unconscious is a nasty little sexist, as I dutifully though rather reluctantly reported in my journal: "women are mean, ill-willed, men's inferiors, and menacing." I don't approve of such feelings, or consciously agree with them—some of my best friends are women—but they are *there* lying in wait for me when I read Faulkner. My shocked response to the imagined scene of Emily bedding down with Homer Barron's decomposing body, and my related interest at male/female antagonism and conflict in the story are only the beginnings of an interpretation, of course, but any class I would teach, or essay I would write on the story would feature such interests prominently.

In sharp contrast to my response was that of my student, Stacy. Since her notebook remained in her possession, I will summarize from memory her entry on "A Rose for Emily." Surprisingly, Stacy did not mention the terrible denouement of the story—the discovery of Homer Barron's remains in Emily's bed. On questioning, she said that Emily's poisoning of Homer remained shadowy and hypothetical in her mind, and she had completely missed the implication of the strand of Emily's hair found on the pillow next to the corpse. Instead, Stacy had written a rather poetic reverie about her *grandmother*, of whom she was strongly reminded by Emily. The grandmother lived, Stacy wrote, shut away in a house full of relics and mementos of the past. Events of long ago, and people long dead, were more real to her than the world of the present, but Stacy found very positive things in her grandmother, and (by implication) in Emily as well: endurance, faith, love. She even identified the frail, pretty woman with Faulkner's picture of Emily when young: "a slender figure in white."

The contrast between our two reactions to the story was striking, and cause for discussion in class. In a more conventional course, I might have been tearing my hair over a student who "missed the point" of the story as to ignore in her interpretation the terrifying climax of Emily's story, and who did not even notice the grizzly implications of that strand of iron-grey hair on the pillow beside Homer Barron. But what I found myself doing, instead, was to go back over the story and see how much of its meaning *I* had missed, how much there was in Faulkner's picture of Emily that *was* attractive, noble, tragic. Deprived of all normal suitors by a domineering father, she had clung to that father, even in death; deprived of her father, she had found a suitor outside the limits of respectability for a woman of her class and background; threatened with his loss as well she found a way to keep him, and then she remained true to him all the days of her life. Certainly it is hard entirely to like a Juliet who poisons her Romeo, yet remember that this is an extraordinarily evasive, indirect story, in which the reader can easily overlook unwanted implications. No poisoning actually occurs in its pages; the deed is left for the reader to infer. Stacy found it easy to ignore, and when confronted with it, accepted it as a qualification, but not a refutation of her admiration for Emily: just as I was able to modify my interpretation of the story without giving up my spontaneous horror, so Stacy could acknowledge the horror, without surrendering her view of Emily as embodying positive values.

What happened between Stacy and me is a perfectly familiar event in the lives of all of us: we communicated our differing interpretations to each other and both learned from the exchange. I wasn't right and she wrong, nor *vice versa*. Nor did we emerge from the exchange with identical interpretations of the story: Emily will doubtless never be as noble a character for me as she is for Stacy. Nonetheless, each of us improved his or her sense of understanding the story by sharing it with the other. Similarly, I can imagine no essay that I might read on "A Rose for Emily" that would leave my sense of the story entirely unchanged, nor any essay that would completely obliterate my old sense of the story. Meaning, as David Bleich has so eloquently argued, is constituted by individual readers as response, and is then negotiated by them into group knowledge. Readers, first individually and then collectively, make meaning.

Now what, we might want to ask, must Faulkner's text be like, if Stacy's interpretation and mine are both "right"—both defensible, that is, under the laws of logic and evidence? The obvious answer is that the text must be ambiguous. Indeed we have already seen its ambiguity with reference to Emily's own character. A figure of pathos as a young girl under her father's thumb, she develops in later years into a formidable figure herself. Victimized first by her father and then by Homer Barron, she turns the tables and becomes a victimizer; but even in this latter role she is ambiguous—the villainous-heroic resolver of an impossible situation. Even physically our imaginations must hover between the picture of Emily as a slender, girlish, angelic creature, and that of the older Emily: "She looked bloated, like a body long submerged in motionless water, and of that pallid hue." To complicate matters still further, the advanced-age description occurs earlier in the story.

The ambiguities of Emily's character are echoed in those of the other people portrayed in the story. The fact is that, like Emily, all characters in this story are seen through such a veil of vagueness, of mysteriousness, of innuendo pointing in no clearly defined direction, that whatever stance a reader takes toward any of the characters is conjecture based on little real information.

Equally vague and contradictory are the subjects and themes that we find in the story. Take the issue that spoke to me most at first reading: the man/woman polarity. The narrator (although typically given no name, age, sex, or other distinguishing characteristic) begins in the first sentence to distinguish between the sexes:

> When Miss Emily Grierson died, our whole town went to her funeral: the men through a sort of respectful affection for a fallen monument, the women mostly out of curiosity to see the inside of her house. . . .

In contrast to women, men seem high-minded here, capable of a gallantry echoed in Judge Stevens' refusal to force Emily to clean her house: "'Dammit, sir,' Judge Stevens said, 'will you accuse a lady to her face of smelling bad?'" When Emily begins her "affair" with Homer Barron (the exact nature of which is, to put it mildly, unclear) it is "the ladies" who try to meddle, while "the men did not want to interfere." Struggle is certainly there between men and women, but my initial interpretation of the story as "bad woman destroys good man" suppresses a good deal of evidence that it is the men, father and lover, who are ultimately responsible for Emily's pitiful condition. If she later turns the tables on them and wins a series of victories, isn't this an instance of the underdog triumphing? Emily's "victories" are, in any case, utterly grotesque (she succeeds in buying arsenic from the reluctant druggist, she succeeds in "keeping" her faithless lover) and could as easily be called *moral defeats*. If there is a battle of the sexes in "A Rose for Emily," the reader must decide who wins.

Other polarities are equally ambiguous. The story sets up tensions—or allows tensions to be felt—between age and youth, parent and child, black and white, individual and group, North and South, past and present, love and hate, and perhaps most of all between life and death. The picture (not actually in the story, but imperatively implied by it in my experience) of "bloated" corpselike Emily lying with her decomposing lover is as vivid an image of death-in-life as I know: Emily already dead in a sense, Homer still alive to her (despite the stink, the "fleshless grin"). Which one of them is deader? Which one would you rather be? Nowhere in literature do I remember the line between death and life so definitively rubbed out.

Indeed, I find it tempting to picture Faulkner's story as a series of widening concentric rings, with the dead/alive lovers at their center. As we move outward, we reach progressively wider polarities: the family (Emily/Father), the community (individual/group; men/women; older/younger generations), the nation (North/South: "And now Miss Emily had gone to join the representatives of those august names where they lay in the cedar-bemused cemetery among the ranked and anonymous graves of Union and Confederate soldiers who fell at the battle of Jefferson"), and the universe (past/present; life/death). "What is true at the center," the story seems to say, "is equally true at every wider circumference." But what (I ask) is true at the center? Those lovers on their bed seem to be a hieroglyph of some profound truth about life, death, time—about *everything*, in fact. But any attempt to pin it down, to state its meaning, excludes other equally possible interpretations—which doesn't mean that we shouldn't interpret, but only that we should have some humility about the status of our results.

Finally, with respect to the story's technique, we find the same sort of ambiguities. I mentioned in my original journal entry the extraordinary indirection with which the story is told. The narrator is anything but omniscient, reporting only what is common knowledge in Jefferson, and even then withholding foreknowledge of earlier events—such as the cause of the bad smell emanating from Emily's house in the months following Homer's disappearance—until the right moment comes to spring it on the reader.

The narrator is himself a "reader" of Emily's story, trying to put together from fragments a complete picture, trying to find the meaning of her life in its impact upon an audience, the citizens of Jefferson, of which he is a member. He disregards chronology, working generally backward from recent events to ever-earlier ones, as if seeking their explanation in a receding past that never throws quite enough light. Displaced chronology and the narrator's carefully limited point of view are two sources of the story's murkiness, which leaves us constantly guessing about events—What caused the smell? Why did Emily buy arsenic? What happened to Homer? Yet the narrator can be wonderfully, or cruelly, explicit too in his handling of details.

To read Faulkner's story, then, is to negotiate a series of oppositions that the text itself has left unresolved. We feel compelled to resolve its ambiguities, but however we do so, some of the evidence will have to be ignored. Small wonder if Stacy and I each constructed our interpretations out of different bits of this conflicting, shifting, and incomplete mass of evidence, each of us ignoring what didn't fit.

It is often argued, when this point is reached, that the text in question is in a special (though daily widening) category of texts whose meaning is, in effect, "everything is ambiguous." Modern critics—New Critical, Structuralist, semiotic, deconstructive—are fond of finding this message everywhere they look. I confess a fondness for it myself, yet I remember that at first "A Rose for Emily" had a definite meaning for me; that only second, more "mature" thoughts softened it into a structure of irresolvable ambiguities. I am not convinced, in other words, that ambiguity is the *meaning* of Faulkner's story. I think, rather, that it is the *nature* of this text to be ambiguous, and that meaning is what the reader makes, by choosing among its paired, antithetical elements. I hope to have demonstrated this contention with respect to "A Rose for Emily." I cannot hope to prove here, but do affirm my belief that all literary texts are by nature ambiguous, and that the reader makes their meaning.

In his extensive inquiry into the psychology of reading, *5 Readers Reading*, Norman Holland asks what is the nature of a text, and then shrugs his shoulders:

> A reader reads something, certainly, but if one cannot separate his "subjective" response from its "objective" basis, there seems no way to find out what that "something" is in any impersonal sense. It is visible only in the psychological processes the reader creates in himself by means of the literary work.
> (p. 40)

Certainly Holland has a point: it is impossible to discover a situation in which a text can be observed without an observer (a reader) being present. Yet it is well to remember that this predicament is shared by all the sciences, even by particle physics, which nonetheless goes on finding leptons and quarks, the sub-subatomic particles of matter. Moreover, if it is impossible to describe the *text* with certainty, that same limitation applies, in spades, to describing with certainty the reader's "psychological processes"—approximation and plausibility are the most we can hope for in either enterprise.

Holland writes as if a solitary reader confronted a solitary text in a void, equipped only by the internal psychological processes described by Freud. This is for Holland a fruitful hypothesis; yet, from another, equally sound, point of view, the individual reader is a member of a society, a product of a lifetime of education whose substance is the learning of conventions shared by other members of society. The very language in which the literary text is written is the product not of his own psyche but of a human community ongoing over millennia. It seems clear that the individual reader reads, in part at least, according to conventions, strategies, and expectations that he has learned from other human beings and that he shares with them.

Remember, for example, that though Stacy and I interpreted Emily in antithetical ways, we both shared a reading strategy: call it reading-for-character. It would seem that the text could accordingly be described as embodying the "character-reading code," put there by Faulkner, who knew the code as well as anyone. This is the approach of the relatively new discipline of Semiotics, whose goal is to specify all the codes operating in a text and thus to read "scientifically." In practice, though, the name and nature of the codes are variable with the critic and the work, and the codes become so numerous and so redundant that instead of achieving with their help a specific meaning we are left, once again, contemplating the universal aesthetic message of ambiguity.

We are on firmer ground, I think, when we think of the "codes" as in the reader, not in the text, and call them "reading conventions" or "reading strategies." Stacy and I (and many others) read "A Rose for Emily" as a portrait of its heroine's character, but that's not *all* we read it as, and other readers will apply entirely different strategies: the Marxist will read for (and find) representations of a decaying class-structure and social victimization, a deconstructionist will read it as a self-consuming artifact, allegorizing readers of all sorts will read for all sorts of symbols, a Structuralist will read for structures; and in no case (except perhaps by majority-rule) can we exclude any of these strategies from validity, though some will interest us more than others.

But if the "codes" are in the reader, what is in the text? I suggest that when we look closely at texts what we find are not "codes"—consistent, coherent, smoothly concatenated—but a jumble of "features" or "elements." The maddening thing is that these elements seem to spring into being only when a reader is present—that is, when a reading strategy is being applied. The reader's freedom is limited both by the elements in the story, and by the codes he has learned from his culture, but since he *is* free to select which codes he applies, which elements he constitutes, he is in practice no more constrained by them than putting on a pair of sneakers compels me to run. What he *is* forced to do is to apply *some* strategy, look at *some* elements of the text (since that, after all, is what reading is) and in so doing he joins a community of which all other readers, and the author himself, are members—he enters, that is, a dialogue, all of whose voices speak within him, all of whose roles he plays.

It is my conclusion—a tentative conclusion, as always—that such issues are never definitively settled; that since literary texts are richly ambiguous, individual readers do resolve those ambiguities, fill in the hermeneutic gaps, with their own individual psychological makeups, their own "identity themes," to borrow Holland's phrase. But reader and text do not exist in a void. Rather, they are framed by a vast series of linguistic, literary, and cultural conventions of interpretation, some of which, at least, readers cannot help knowing and using, since that is what "reading" is. These conventions, or codes, are *so* numerous, however, and so mutually contradictory, that the individual reader still exercises considerable freedom in the way he interprets, merely by his choice and emphasis among the conventions.

Reading is *both* a solitary *and* a communal enterprise; we read *both* for self-discovery *and* to learn about the world; and we go on learning, after we have read a text, by sharing our interpretation with others, and by letting their interpretations enrich our own.

I won't pretend that disagreements, even violent disagreements, can't occur. Many of them are due to the pernicious belief in "right reading": the idea that if you and I disagree, one of us is wrong, and it better not be me! But disagreements can also result from real moral or political differences. Even here, though, negotiation and compromise may be a more useful approach than the verbal equivalent of war, however stimulating and entertaining a quarrel may be.

Still, it helps to remember that these disagreements are not epistemological but political, whether on or off the campus. I had only to *offer* my interpretation of "A Rose for Emily" for Stacy to change hers, but if she had resisted mine completely, I would still have listened to hers and learned from it, confident that sooner or later she would follow my example. Telling her that she was "wrong" would have been not only unhelpful but untrue. Her interpretation was *not* wrong; it was merely partial, incomplete, and *all* interpretations are incomplete. Literary study *is* a discipline not because it gives *certain* answers—no field of inquiry does that—but because it is eternally in the business of developing procedures for assembling evidence and answering questions about an area of human experience that human beings collectively judge to be important and worthy of inquiry. Literary theory, I submit, is nothing more nor less than the study, with regard to literary texts, of how readers make meaning.

Questions for Comprehension

1. How does Crosman's response to "A Rose for Emily" reveal his "considerable exposure to psychotherapy"?
2. What are the different responses of Crosman and his student to Emily Grierson? How does Crosman account for the difference?
3. What ambiguities in Faulkner's depiction of Emily account for the different responses Crosman cites?

4. How does the narrator's technique contribute to the ambiguity of "A Rose for Emily"?
5. How do Crosman and Holland differ about the nature of the reading experience?
6. To what extent do "conventions of interpretation" limit a reader's freedom?
7. In what sense is literary study a discipline?

WRITING PROJECTS

1. Write a 500–700 word summary of either Cleanth Brooks and Robert Penn Warren's "An Interpretation of 'A Rose for Emily'" or Judith Fetterley's "A Rose for 'A Rose for Emily'," being sure to include the authors' central point and main supporting details.
2. According to Brooks and Warren it is very easy to misread "A Rose for Emily" as "merely a horrible case history, presented in order to titillate the reader." A number of critics in this anthology agree that there is some purpose to the story beyond the shocking revelation of Emily Grierson's bizarre behavior. Select two articles from those by the following authors: Brooks and Warren, Helen E. Nebeker, Judith Fetterley, and Ray B. West, Jr. Write a simple synthesis explaining how the two critics you select define that purpose.
3. William Van O'Conner believes that the historical and social contexts of the story provide nothing more than background for Emily's own inner conflict. Some critics (Brooks and Warren, Stafford) agree with O'Conner in regarding "A Rose for Emily" as a character study of Emily Grierson, whereas others (West, Fetterley, Nebeker) believe the story explains the effect of social environment on character. Using one critic from each side, write an essay that shows how the story may be viewed from either perspective.
4. Write an essay in which you apply Brooks and Warren's definition of a tragic hero to a character in a literary work you have read. Begin by explaining Brooks and Warren's definition of a tragic hero. Then show how the character you select exemplifies that definition.
5. Judith Fetterley says that Emily's "status as a lady is a cage from which she cannot escape." To what extent is this observation valid in the world outside the story? Write an essay describing your own response to Fetterley's comment.
6. Write an essay answering the following question: Why is it of value to read a story that seems like a lot of gossip about a crazy old lady? Use any of the critics in the anthology to help you answer the question.

PART THREE

WRITING THE RESEARCH PAPER: A MANUAL

Finding a Topic

Narrowing the Topic

Gathering a Working Bibliography

Taking Notes from Sources

Devising a Thesis

Generating a Structure

Drafting the Research Paper

Documenting Sources

Preparing the Finished Copy

A Sample Research Paper

The best thing about writing a research paper—also called a library paper—is that it is fundamentally like the other kinds of writing you are already familiar with. In any research project your basic aim is to learn something worth knowing about a subject and then to communicate it to readers. The purpose of this manual is, on the one hand, to remind you of the basic principles and procedures for using multiple sources in a paper and, on the other, to explain the features of a research paper that set it apart from other writing projects.

Let's clarify the process you're about to begin as a researcher. Although we will be describing a number of distinct research activities throughout the manual, you shouldn't think of the research process as merely a set of steps to be mechanically followed. Writing a research paper is not like building a model airplane. You can build the airplane successfully just by reading the instructions and completing each step in the prescribed order, adding one piece at a time to produce the final product. Following instructions is all that is necessary to reach your goal. In a research project your first goal is to learn something about your subject that you didn't know before. As you begin the initial phase of your project, keep in mind that each activity is a means to an end—finding something worth telling somebody else about.

Some research projects begin with a narrowly defined focus to investigate; others may be so broadly stated that they require you to do a good bit of preliminary work just to define the limits of your topic. Quite often in college courses the subject matter is supplied for you. Your instructor may assign either a broad or a limited area for your investigation: a work by an author in your literature course, a revolutionary movement in your political science course, a successful ad campaign in your marketing course, a new respiratory therapy in your medical technology course. With such projects, your immediate task is to find a way to narrow the focus of the assigned subject, something we'll consider shortly.

Occasionally, your assignment may be quite open-ended, calling on you to find your own subject matter and focus: "Each student will do a research paper. Check with me when you think you have found a workable topic," your instructor might say. In such cases it is up to you to determine what broad subject matter you want to explore in your research. Then, as with an assigned subject, you can begin to define more narrowly what you want to cover in your paper. Once you have sharpened the focus, you can begin some preliminary reading to give yourself a general idea of the scope of your subject. You can also use this preliminary reading to help you devise a set of investigative questions to help you learn about your subject.

Finding a Topic

Let's first consider what to do when the assignment at hand is the open-ended kind that requires you to come up with your own topic for research. Although there is no prescribed formula for producing a research topic in such circumstances, there are some practical procedures to try. Begin by taking an inventory of the things you already know about or would like to know more about. Do a bit of brainstorming and write down whatever comes to mind: books, movies, hobbies, controversies, people, movements, popular culture, sports, historical events, and so on. When you finish your brainstorming, look over your list to see if anything catches your eye. After all, that's all you need at this point—something promising enough to investigate.

If brainstorming doesn't work, try looking through the table of contents or the index of a book on a subject that interests you. The headings and subdivisions you find can reveal a topic worth investigating.

In any case, don't overestimate the importance of topic selection. Students often place so much emphasis on finding the "right topic" that they keep themselves from starting their research. The important thing in a research paper is not so much the topic itself as what the researcher does with the topic, so the best advice is to settle on something that seems promising and prepare to move on.

Narrowing the Topic

Whether you have an assigned topic or have had to discover a topic on your own, you will need to limit it. As in any writing assignment, the broader the topic, the more difficult it is to cover it in adequate detail. Limiting your topic at this early stage of your research also pays off by making your search for sources more efficient. With a very broad topic like "the Union Army in the Civil War" you could spend your time looking through hundreds of sources. With a limited, specific topic like "the use of observation balloons during the Civil War" you can more quickly zero in on relevant books and articles.

Here are several procedures that may help you limit your own topic:

1. *Analyze the topic.* One way to limit a topic is to analyze it—to divide it and then see if one aspect can be investigated on its own. If you've selected an event, for example, consider focusing on causes of the event (obvious ones or underlying ones), effects of the event, reactions to it (both at the time and later), or the stages of the event as it happened. Or if your assignment were to write about a novel such as *The Sun Also Rises*, you might begin by considering the ways the novel is typical or atypical of its time period, the way its author uses imagery or any other technical resource of a novelist, the relationship of this work to others by Hemingway, or the relationship of the work to novels by other writers.

2. *Look up the topic in the index of a book.* For another kind of help in narrowing the focus of your research project, you can again turn to the index of a book on your subject and skim the headings for promising

entries. Indexes, after all, are designed to subdivide topics for easy reference, and you can take advantage of the arrangement to see what the components of your topic are. If you were interested in the broad issue of environmental pollution, you might look in the index of a book like *Only One Earth*. There you would find—along with entries on air and water pollution, atomic energy, and chemical dumps—the following heading and subdivisions:

> Pesticides
>   alternatives to
>   control
>   toxicity

You might decide that although you hadn't given much thought to the alternatives to pesticides before, that focus looked promising. The more ways you can see your topic divided in an index, the better you will be able to see the possibilities for your own research.

3. *Look up the topic in a reference index.* Another useful way to narrow a topic is to turn to a different kind of index, a bibliographical index such as *Readers' Guide to Periodical Literature*. By reading the subheadings and cross-references under your topic, you can see additional possibilities for narrowing your focus. Then, as you skim the lists of specific articles, you can look for titles suggesting even more ways writers have focused on your topic. You'll also be able to make efficient use of your research time because you will see in the listings which aspects of the topic have been written about. There is certainly nothing to keep you from writing down several possibilities for a limited topic. If one doesn't pan out, then you will have another ready in its place.

Suppose you have begun a research project dealing with crime and you are interested in focusing on burglary. If you look up the heading "burglary" in *Readers' Guide*, Figure 1 shows what you would find in the 1985 volume. The entries in the first section are fairly mixed—a couple of specific cases and an article about violence. But under the heading "Burglary protection" things look more interesting. There you discover no less than seven articles about ways to combat burglars, and they appear in a wide range of magazines—*Popular Science, Ladies' Home Journal, Business Week,* and *Harper's Bazaar*. You might begin to suspect, if you did not already know it, that there was a widespread fear of burglary in the United States in 1985. At least you would have good reason to investigate that possibility. You might want to consider as well the range of solutions being offered anxious homeowners.

4. *Do some preliminary reading.* Still another way to narrow a topic is to do some preliminary reading, preferably in a brief, general format such as an encyclopedia article or an introductory chapter of a book. Look for and write down any aspect of your topic that you might want to dig into

> **Burglar alarms** *See* Alarms
> **Burglary and burglars**
> > *See also*
> > Art thefts
>
> After a burglary. A. Scardino. il *N Y Times Mag* p 74 Je 2 '85
> I won't call the sheriff [burglary of rural home] E. Pullen-Hoff. il *Ladies Home J* 102:22+ Ap '85
> N.C. basketball star gets probation in theft case [C. Washburn] por *Jet* 67:48 F 25 '85
> Violence is part of most burglaries: study. *Jet* 67:38 Ja 28 '85
> The woman who wanted justice [P. Simpson chases men who robbed her home] J. Ward. il pors *Good Housekeep* 200:80+ Ja '85
> > **Anecdotes, facetiae, satire, etc.**
>
> A shaggy duck story. C. Simmons. il *Harpers* 271:68-9 Ag '85
> **Burglary** protection
> > *See also*
> > Alarms
> > Locks and keys
> > Safes
>
> Bluff the burglars. Install these automatic draperies. C. M. Swenson. il *Pop Sci* 226:77 Mr '85
> Four new burglar-foilers. S. Renner-Smith. il *Pop Sci* 226:42 Ap '85
> Home & auto security: how much is enough? [special section] il *Home Mech* 80:77-88 Ja '85
> How to prevent home burglaries. L. Werner. *Ladies Home J* 102:73 N '85
> Keeping burglars at bay. B. Hitchings. il *Bus Week* p 154-6 My 27 '85
> Lock yourself up. *Harpers Bazaar* 118:80 Ap '85
> New security systems. il *Home Mech* 80:107-8 Ja '85
> **Burgoyne's Invasion**, 1777 *See* Saratoga Campaign, 1777
> **Burgundy (France)**

FIGURE 1

further. Remember, the purpose of this kind of reading is not to take notes for writing your paper, but to look for ways to narrow a broad topic.

Developing Investigative Questions You can also use your preliminary reading to help plan an investigative strategy to follow throughout your research. Since your purpose in research is to learn something worth knowing about your topic, the best procedure is to write down some questions to investigate as you do your research. Decide what kinds of things would probably be important for your reader to know about your topic. Of course, you haven't learned enough about your topic to make any final decisions about such matters yet, but you can use the reading you have done so far to make some reasonably intelligent guesses. Suppose you had started with the broad general topic of the First World War and had already used your reading to narrow the scope of your research to the American involvement in the war. What questions might you ask? Some factual questions would quickly occur to you:

1. When did the United States become involved in World War I?
2. Who were the American commanders?

3. How many men were involved, and what kinds of war supplies were furnished?
4. Which major battles were American troops involved in?
5. How did the American troops fit into the battle plans of the allies?
6. What were the casualties suffered by the American troops?

How would these questions help you explore your topic? What kinds of answers would they yield? As you can see by looking at them, these questions would lead to limited, factual answers that would be dead ends for continuing research. They are not the *appropriate* questions. The most useful questions for research papers are analytical and open-ended, not factual; that is, they require understanding of the topic and not merely specific, concrete bits of information to answer them. Here are some questions that are more speculative and thought-provoking and therefore more likely to open up your investigation of your topic:

1. Why did the United States wait from 1914 until 1917 to enter the war?
2. Why did the United States finally enter the war?
3. What attitudes did the American people have toward Germany and its allies before the United States entered the war?
4. How was the American contribution to the war viewed by America's allies?
5. How have later analysts and commentators viewed the American contribution to the war?
6. What did the American people expect the world to be like at the end of the war?
7. What kind of relationship did American soldiers have with the other allied soldiers?

The analytical questions you pose at this early stage of your research will help give you some idea of the divisions of the topic and of the possibilities for continuing to narrow your focus. In fact, you could easily keep in mind each of the questions about American involvement in the war as a potential topic on its own. By asking such questions now and continuing to ask them (and others that occur to you later) throughout your research, you help ensure that you will learn something worth knowing about your topic. Your investigative strategy, then, is to find the significant questions that should be asked about your topic, write them down, and then attempt to find the answers.

GATHERING A WORKING BIBLIOGRAPHY

As part of your work in selecting and narrowing a topic, you did some general, preliminary reading to gain a sense of the scope of your subject and to narrow the focus of your research. Now it is time to prepare a *working bibliography*, a list of the sources from which you will gather information for writing your research paper. At the same time, you will want to continue looking for ways to sharpen the focus of your writing project.

Your work will begin in the reference department of your library, where you will find the standard indexes and bibliographies needed for your search. Indexes such as the card catalog, the *Readers' Guide*, the *Social Sciences and Humanities Index*, the *New York Times Index*, and others provide the authors, titles, and publication data for thousands of books, articles, pamphlets, and reports. Your purpose is to list in your working bibliography any source that sounds as if it might contain useful information on your topic. It's a good idea to compile a fairly extensive bibliography before you actually begin going to the sources because not everything in your original bibliography will turn out to be useful or available.

Making a List of Subject Headings

The keys that unlock any index are the *subject headings* used to classify entries. You can increase your chances of finding the sources you will need by turning to the *Library of Congress Subject Heading Catalog*, which provides the specific headings employed by almost all indexes and bibliographies in English. Look in the *Subject Heading Catalog* under almost any of the words you associate with your topic, and you will find the exact headings used for your subject. The catalog can also provide valuable clues for focusing a topic as well. Suppose you are interested in doing a paper on the general subject of pollution, that you have done some reading, and that you have narrowed the focus somewhat to chemical pollution. If you go directly to the card catalog or other indexes, you will not find the heading *chemical pollution*, but if you look in the *Subject Heading Catalog* under the general heading "pollution," you will find the listing shown in Figure 2 (p. 398).

All the terms listed under *sa* are headings used in indexes and can be written down for your own use in checking the indexes. Those designated *x* are not used at all in the indexes, and those labeled *xx* are broader, related headings that you could look under in the *Subject Heading Catalog* if the *sa* headings don't lead to useful sources. You could also use the catalog to help narrow your general topic of chemical pollution. If one of the headings, say "spraying and dusting residues in agriculture," should catch your eye, you could look it up separately in the *Subject Heading Catalog*. There you would find new headings related to this limited subject. As you begin your own research project, consult the *Subject Heading Catalog* and write down a list of the headings for your topic. Then you can use the list as you search through indexes for sources for your research paper.

Using Indexes and Bibliographies

Most library reference departments contain hundreds, and even thousands, of indexes and bibliographies. You must decide which of these many books to consult in compiling your preliminary bibliography. The indexes

> **Pollution** *(Indirect)* *(TD180)*
> Here are entered works on the condition resulting from the action of environmental contaminants. Works on the substances which contaminate or degrade the environment are entered under Pollutants.
> *sa* Air—Pollution
> Air—Pollution potential
> Electric power-plants—Environmental aspects
> Environmental engineering
> Factory and trade waste
> Factory and trade waste—Environmental aspects
> Hazardous wastes
> Irrigation water—Pollution
> Marine pollution
> Noise pollution
> Pollutants
> Pollution control industry
> Radioactive pollution
> Refuse and refuse disposal
> Soil pollution
> Spraying and dusting residues in agriculture
> Waste spills
> Water—Pollution
> Water, Underground—Pollution
> *subdivision* Environmental aspects *under individual environmental pollutants, e.g.* Copper—Environmental aspects
> *x* Chemical pollution
> Contamination of environment
> Environmental pollution
> Pollution—Control
> Pollution—Prevention
> *xx* Contamination (Technology)
> Environmental engineering
> Environmental health
> Environmental policy
> Factory and trade waste
> Factory and trade waste—Environmental aspects
> Hazardous wastes
> Man—Influence on nature
> Pollutants
> Public health
> Refuse and refuse disposal
> Sanitary engineering
> Sanitation

FIGURE 2

that follow are the most important ones, covering all the basic types of source materials. If you take your list of subject headings and consult the appropriate indexes, you can be sure that you have a broad base for your research.

The Card Catalog Almost everyone is familiar with the card catalog, which is simply an index to the library, containing cards for all the books in the library. Although the card catalog contains separate cards listing each book under its author's name, its title, and its subject, the most useful listing for your purposes will be the *subject heading*. You will want to look in the card catalog under each possible heading on the list you prepared during your preliminary reading. In fact, you can even use the card catalog itself as a key-word subject index to add additional headings to your list. Suppose you were interested in the general subject of earth satellites and your preliminary reading focused your attention on the problem of "space junk"—all the worn out rockets and satellites that eventually fall back to earth. You might first look in the card catalog under "satellites." (The subject headings, by the way, are often typed in red at the top of the cards in the catalog.) When you look up that heading, you may find one of several things:

1. The first subject heading may be on a card that says only "see" and gives you another heading to consult—for example,

    satellites

    see

    artificial satellites

    In such cases, of course, consult the heading or headings listed on the card.
2. You may find this first subject used on several potential sources. If so, copy each of these sources down in your working bibliography.
3. Under the first subject heading, you may find cards for several sources, and the cards may include typed "see also" references giving you still more headings to consult. Add these "see also" words to your list of subject headings and then consult each one in the card catalog.
4. Even if there are no typed headings at the bottom of the card, there will probably be several printed headings numbered 1., 2., 3., and so on. These are additional card catalog headings under which you will find the particular book on this card. If you check these headings, you may discover related books that were not under the original subject heading.

As you can see, you can use the cards in the card catalog to expand your list of key headings, which will help you in making full use of other indexes. In addition, any one of the specific headings you find may be the very one that helps you toward the final focus of your paper. For example, the original heading "satellites" may have led you through several other headings to "artificial satellites—orbits," which in turn may have helped you find a book on the physics of orbiting satellites. At this point you may have found not only a book title to put on a bibliography card, you may have found an idea: Why not focus on the mechanics of satellites and why they become "junk" that falls back to earth?

```
574.19      Biological physics
Sn27b       Snell, Fred M
              Biophysical principles of structure and function
            [by] Fred M. Snell [and others] Palo Alto,
            Addison-Wesley Pub. Co. [1965]

                    x, 390 p. illus. 24 cm. (The Addison-Wesley series in the life
                  sciences)
                    Includes bibliographies.



                  1. Biological physics.  2. Molecular biology.    I. Title.

            QH505.S6              574.19              65–14745

            Library of Congress
```

FIGURE 3

How to read the catalog card The sample card shown in Figure 3 is a subject heading card (the kind you will most frequently be using). Here's how to translate each part of the card:

- *Biological physics:* This is the subject heading (possibly one of several) under which this book can be found in the card catalog.
- *574.19*
  Sn27b: This is the Dewey decimal system call number to help you locate the book in your library.
- *Snell, Fred M:* The author's name.
- *Biophysical principles of structure and function:* The full title of the book.
- *[by] Fred M. Snell [and others]:* This shows the author's name and the fact that there are additional authors.
- *Palo Alto:* The place of publication.
- *Addison-Wesley Pub. Co.:* The name of the publisher.
- *1965:* The original date of publication.
- *x, 390 p. illus. 24 cm.:* The book has ten (Roman numeral x) pages of prefatory material and 390 pages of text. The book is illustrated. Its size is 24 centimeters high.
- *(The Addison-Wesley series in the life sciences):* The title of the series of which the book is a part (something you will want to write down).
- *Includes bibliographies:* The book has its own bibliographies, which you should remember to check for additional source listings.
- *1. Biological physics. 2. Molecular biology. I. Title:* These are three card catalog headings under which you can expect to find the book listed—two

subject headings and the title heading for this book. You might wish to check the subject heading "Molecular biology" to see if books related to Snell's are included there.
- *QH505.S6:* Library of Congress System call number.
- *574.19:* Dewey Decimal System call number.
- *65-14745:* Order number.
- *Library of Congress:* Publisher of this card.

Periodical Indexes Magazines and journals are very productive sources of information on almost any topic. You can locate relevant articles by using both general and specialized periodical indexes in the reference department of your library. The best known of these indexes is the *Readers' Guide to Periodical Literature*.

Readers' Guide to Periodical Literature, *1900–present. Readers' Guide* includes listings of articles from approximately 160 general, nontechnical American magazines. It will be especially useful to you whenever you have a research topic that is likely to have been written about in general, widely-circulated magazines. Topics such as religious cults, cable television, the debate over gun control, the Vietnam protest movement of the 1960s, developments in automobile safety, or world famine should certainly send you to *Readers' Guide*. Even though you might be working on a topic that could be considered highly technical, such as heart transplants, the subject is one that has been widely discussed in nontechnical as well as technical periodicals, and *Readers' Guide* will therefore prove useful. In addition, *Readers' Guide* contains listings of reviews of plays, movies, TV productions, and books. In general, if you think your topic might have been discussed in such magazines as *Time, Newsweek, McCall's, Ebony, Popular Mechanics, Field and Stream, National Geographic, Business Week,* or similar publications, then be sure to consult *Readers' Guide*.

How to read the index Because *Readers' Guide* indexes magazine articles year by year, you cannot confine your search to one volume; you will need to go through as many years as seem appropriate to your topic. For a paper on gangsters in the Roaring Twenties you would, of course, consult the volumes covering the 1920s, but you also would need to search the volumes since the 1920s because people have continued to write about the topic. For a paper on the relatively new topic of biological cloning, you might decide to start with the most recent volume of *Readers' Guide* and work your way back for five or ten years. Going through the volumes of thirty or forty years ago would almost certainly be fruitless.

In the sample listing from *Readers' Guide 1978* (Figure 4, p. 402), you can find several entries under the subject heading CLONES. Here's how to read the first entry:

- *All about clones:* The title of the magazine article.

> CLONES (biology)
>   All about clones. P. Gwynne and others. il por Newsweek 91:68-9 Mr 20 '78
>   Baby born without a mother. R. Morgan. Ms 6:19 My '78
>   British scientist sues over clone book. C. Holden. Science 201:326 Jl 28 '78
>   Can science make carbon copies of you? H. Johnson. il Ebony 33:95-6+ Jl '78
>   Cloning around; controversy surrounding book of D. Rorvik. N. Wade. New Repub 178:9-10 Ap 22 '78
>   Cloning caper makes it to the halls of Congress. B. J. Culliton. Science 200:1250-2 Je 16 '78
>   Cloning controversy. J. Randal. Progressive 42:11-12 My '78
>   Cloning era is almost here. G. Bylinsky. il Fortune 97:100-4+ Je 19 '78
>   Cloning: has man's reach exceeded his grasp? J. Dobbie. il Macleans 91:68-9 Ap 3 '78
>   Cloning of a man: debate begins. Sci News 113:164 Mr 18 '78
>   Cloning of an antibody. J. A. Miller. il por Sci News 114:444-7 D 23 '78
>   Cloning: the picture today; symposium. Sci Digest 83:9-14 Je '78
>   Coexistence of clones in a heterogeneous environment. R. C. Vrijenhoek. bibl il map Science 199:549-52 F 3 '78
>   Costly hoax? lawsuit brought against Lippincott's clone book. Time 112:47 Jl 24 '78
>   Human cloning: an apathetic view; letter. J. J. Swetnam. Science 201:572+ Ag 18 '78; Same with title Cloneconomics. Psychol Today 12:127 N '78
>   In his own words; interview, ed by C. P. Andersen. J. Watson. il pors People 9:93-4+ Ap 17 '78
>   Responsibility of publishers; controversy surrounding work of D. Rorvik. W. Arnold. Sat R 5:37 Jl 8 '78
>   Road to cloning. il Chemistry 51:25-7 O '78
>   Scientist sues Lippincott over cloning book. M. Reuter. Pub W 124:18+ Jl 31 '78
>   Scientists dispute book's claim that human clone has been born. B. J. Culliton. Science 199:1314-16 Mr 24 '78; Reply, P. R. Gross. 200:126+ Ap 14 '78
>   Test tube baby is not a clone. Time 112:65 Jl 31 '78
>   Test-tube potatoes. Sci Am 238:83-4+ Je '78
>   To clone—or not to clone. D. M. Rorvik. Sci Digest 83:63 My '78
>   Anecdotes, facetiae, satire, etc.
>   Literary cloning scandal. R. R. Lingeman. Nation 226:544-5 My 6 '78
> CLONES (botany)
>   Clones in your garden. R. Rodale. il Org Gard 25:32-4 Ag '78
>   Test-tube baby plants are coming into fashion. D. Seibert. Sci Digest 84:69-72 N '78

FIGURE 4

- *P. Gwynne and others:* The authors of the article. Some articles may have no author given.
- *il por:* The article is illustrated and it contains a portrait.
- *Newsweek:* The name of the magazine in which the article appears. Longer names are abbreviated.
- *91:68-9:* The number before the colon is the volume number of the magazine. The numbers following the colon are the page numbers of the article.
- *Mr 20 '78:* The date of the issue of the magazine in which the article appears.

Though some entries may contain less information than this sample, and some may contain additional symbols and abbreviations, the basic order is similar in all entries. Moreover, the form of entries in *Readers' Guide* is virtually identical to the form in almost all the periodical indexes. For a key to symbols and abbreviations and for complete information on reading an entry, simply look in the front of the index.

New York Times Index, *1913–present.* The *New York Times Index* is a subject index to a newspaper whose wide coverage makes it a useful source of factual and opinion articles on many subjects. Whether you are writing about social reform in the 1930s, the stock market crash of 1929, the Second World War, the problems of small farmers, the movement of killer bees toward North America, or virtually any other topic, the *New York Times Index* can provide you with listings of relevant articles. To use the index efficiently, you must know at least an approximate date to suggest which volumes to check.

Most newspapers do not have indexes of their own, but you can use the *New York Times Index* to help locate information in them. Once you know the dates on which articles were published in the *New York Times*, you can locate similar articles in other newspapers, some of which may be more readily available to you than the *New York Times* itself.

A separate index, published by R. R. Bowker Company, covers the *New York Times* from 1851 to 1905. As you can tell from the dates, there is presently a gap in the indexing from 1905 to 1912, but that deficiency may be remedied in the future.

How to read the index In each volume of the *New York Times Index* individual subject headings are followed by a listing of all the articles on that subject for the year. Articles are arranged chronologically under the subject headings, thus providing a kind of running narrative of the developing story. The articles are briefly summarized, making it easy for you to judge their relevance.

Assume that you were doing research on artificial sweeteners. As you can see in the sample from the 1983 *Times* index (Figure 5, p. 404), the sweetener aspartame (Nutrasweet) was an immediate and huge success (stories from July 2 to December 23), but created at least some controversy as well (July 13). Here's how to translate the final entry:

- SWEETENERS, *artificial:* The subject heading that helped you locate the article.
- *G D Searle & Co enters into agreement with General Foods Corp to supply Nutrasweet for use in variety of food and beverage products:* A description of the contents of the article—*not* the title of the article. To find the title or headline of a *New York Times* article, you need to see the article itself.
- *(S):* Indicates that the article is short.
- *D 23:* The date of the article is December 23. Note: The index entry gives

A MANUAL **403**

> **SWEETENERS, Artificial**
> Diet Coke, made by Coca-Cola Co. has gone national and become fastest-selling soft drink in shortest amount of time; new Diet Coke's success linked to Coke name, large budget and distribution network capable of getting product to 155 countries; illustration; chart ranking diet soft drinks by number of cases shipped (M), Mr 1,IV,1:3
> 18 Coca-Cola bottling companies accuse Coca-Cola Co of overcharging for syrup used to produce Diet Coke, suit, Federal District Court, Wilmington, Del; say they were pressured to pay more for Diet Coke syrup than syrup used in regular Coke, even though Diet Coke syrup is far less expensive to produce; new suit is part of running price battle between Coca-Cola and some of its 530 bottlers (M), Mr 2,IV,4:3
> Four brief articles on food regulation, including saccharin controversy; sketches, Ap 24,III,15:1
> FDA approves use of aspartame, low-calorie sweetener of G D Searle & Co, for use in soft drinks in US; aspartame, first sweetener to be approved in 25 years, now becomes only rival to saccharin in $4 billion diet soft-drink market (M), Jl 2,II,31:1
> Approval of aspartame, artificial sweetener, as soft-drink additive culminates decadelong effort of scientific uncertainty and controversy over its potential risks, and extreme caution on part of Food and Drug Administration, which banned cyclamates as possible cancer risk and tried to ban saccharin for same reason; Dr Michael Jacobson claims lack of any known cancer risk makes aspartame far preferable to saccharin, but warns that experience with aspartame in people is limited; drawing (M), Jl 13,III,1:1
> Correction: July 2 article on new artificial sweetener aspartame incorrectly reported its potency, Jl 22,II,1:6
> Genex Corp enters into contract with Searle Food Resources Inc, subsidiary of G D Searle & Co, calling for sale to Searle of quantities of L-phenylalanine, compound used in Nutrasweet, Searle's low-calorie sweetener (S), Ag 16,IV,3:6
> Article on new artificial sweetener Aspartame, which has opened up vast new consumer market since introduction in Spring of 1983: new sweetener, discovered accidentally by chemist at G D Searle & Co in 1965, is being used by increasing number of companies; competes with sugar in taste and saccharin in calories; photograph (M), S 3,I,29:3
> G D Searle & Company says Pepsico Inc, Dr Pepper and Seven-Up Company have signed contracts to use Searle's protein-based, low-calorie sweetener aspartame in their diet soft drinks; Seven-Up declines comment (M), S 20,IV,4:5
> Researchers rept that artificial sweetener Nutra-Sweet will lower blood pressure in lab animals and may someday be used as 'medical food' in people (S), N 6,I,56:5
> G D Searle & Co enters into agreement with General Foods Corp to supply Nutrasweet for use in variety of food and beverage products (S), D 23,IV,3:1

FIGURE 5

only the month and day of publication; you must check the top of the page (or the cover) of the volume you are using to determine the year of the item—in this case, 1983.

- *IV, 3:1:* The Roman numeral indicates the section of the *New York Times*. (Not all issues are divided with section designations.) The 3 indicates the page number of the article, and the 1 indicates the column number. (Each page is divided into eight vertical columns, numbered from the left-hand side.)

If you discover any other symbols or abbreviations, consult the front of the volume for a full explanation.

Humanities Index, *1974–.* This index covers more than 250 magazines not indexed in *Readers' Guide* and includes such subjects as language, literature, philosophy, history, folklore, archaeology, classics, and religion. It contains a separate section of book reviews.

Social Sciences Index, *1974–.* This index lists articles in journals in the fields of anthropology, sociology, psychology, law, economics, political science, and other social sciences. It also lists book reviews. From 1965 to 1974 the *Humanities Index* and the *Social Sciences Index* were published together as the *Social Sciences and Humanities Index,* and from 1907 until 1965 they were titled the *International Index.*

Poole's Index to Periodical Literature, *1802–1906.* You might think of *Poole's Index* as the grandfather of *Readers' Guide* and other magazine indexes. In fact, it is the only index to nineteenth-century periodicals up to 1890. It is a subject index to a wide variety of popular and scholarly magazines, most of which have long since dropped from circulation, but which are often available on microfilm in college libraries.

Nineteenth Century Readers' Guide, *1890–1899.* Although the time period this index covers overlaps *Poole's,* the indexes do not list the same magazines and therefore supplement each other.

Public Affairs Information Service Index *(P.A.I.S.), 1915–.* The *P.A.I.S.* is a subject index to works published in English throughout the world. It covers materials on economic and social conditions, public administration, and international relations and includes a great deal of material not listed anywhere else.

America: History and Life, *1964–.* This index is a particularly good source of articles on any aspect of American life, culture, or history. Its listings include *abstracts* of sources—brief summaries that can give you a clear idea of the possible usefulness of a source.

Many other indexes cover specialized fields, listing material that is not included in the general indexes. Select the ones that are appropriate for your subject. The following are some of the specialized indexes:

> *Applied Science and Technology Index,* 1913–
>   (before 1958 called the *Industrial Arts Index*)
> *Art Index,* 1929–
> *Bibliographic Index,* 1937–
>   (lists books and articles with bibliographies of their own)
> *Biography Index,* 1946–
> *Biological and Agricultural Index,* 1964–
> *Business Periodicals Index,* 1953–
>   (before 1958 covered in the *Industrial Arts Index*)
> *Catholic Periodical and Literature Index,* 1968–

Current Index to Journals in Education, 1969–
Education Index, 1929–
Engineering Index, 1884–
Essay and General Literature Index, 1934–
   (lists essays and articles appearing in book-length studies)
Film Literature Index, 1973–
MLA International Bibliography, 1921–
   (language and literature)
Music Index, 1949–
United States Government Publications, Monthly Catalog, 1895–

Other Types of Indexes

Book review indexes. Book reviews can be helpful in two ways. First, you can use them to evaluate the reliability of a book you are considering as a source for your paper. Reviews can tell you how the book was regarded at the time of its publication. And, of course, if your topic itself is about a particular book, then the reviews will be important as you take notes for your paper. Here are four general indexes to book reviews:

- *Book Review Digest,* 1905–. Lists reviews in more than seventy general periodicals. Includes brief excerpts from some of the reviews to show the balance of opinion on the book being reviewed.
- *Book Review Index,* 1965–. Lists reviews from more than two hundred periodicals and can be used to supplement *Book Review Digest.*
- *Index to Book Reviews in the Humanities,* 1960–. Lists reviews from about seven hundred magazines and journals.
- *New York Times Book Review Index,* 1896–1970. Lists reviews that appeared in this famous weekly book review section.

On-line searching. More and more, the bibliographical listings that have always been found in printed volumes in the reference departments of libraries are being collected as databases, computer files that can be electronically scanned for entries. If your library subscribes to any of the databases, such as the *Population Bibliography* or *Pollution Abstracts,* you can use the system to list for you the relevant articles in that database. In using a database, you must have the right key terms; the computer can't browse through an index the way you can. It looks only for the key terms you furnish it, but it does so with great speed and can save a researcher much time. Consult your library's reference department for available databases.

Sources as indexes. Your search for bibliography entries doesn't end with the indexes in the reference department. You should remain ready to add items to your bibliography later as you do your reading and note taking. You might find that one of the sources you located has a bibliography of its own. Take advantage of the author's skill as a researcher by checking your bibliography against the one in the source to see if it includes any items you have overlooked.

Preparing Bibliography Cards

By now you know how to use appropriate indexes and bibliographies to find sources for your project and to continue the process of focusing your ideas on your topic. The only remaining step in this phase of your research is the preparation of bibliography cards listing all the specific sources you will want to read for your paper. These cards will be your *working bibliography*—the one you will use in *searching* for material—as opposed to the one you will later include in your completed paper to show which sources you finally used.

Your first purpose in this phase of your research is to find usable sources for your paper, but at the same time you can make things much easier for yourself later by using the standard bibliographical forms on your bibliography cards now. The forms you find in the indexes are not the same as the ones you will use in the bibliography in your finished paper. The forms in indexes, in fact, are highly condensed, using many abbreviations and symbols that would not appear in your paper. If you use the standard bibliographical forms now on your cards, then when you are ready to write out the final bibliography for your research paper, all you will have to do is alphabetize the cards you used and type out the entries. Besides, the more you use the standard forms, the easier they become to remember. In fact, using them becomes almost second nature after a while.

You should prepare your working bibliography on three-by-five-inch index cards—ruled or unruled, white or in color, as you prefer. Cards of this size easily contain the necessary information for each entry, and they are easy to handle and sort. Separate slips of paper are less durable, and sheets of notebook paper containing multiple entries are almost impossible to use efficiently.

Each bibliography card should contain the following information:

1. An identification number in the upper right corner. The first card you prepare will be number 1, the second number 2, and so on. Use each number only once, and be sure that each card has a number. These numbers will make your later note taking easier and will help guarantee accurate identification of the sources of notes.
2. The bibliographical entry for the source itself. Be sure to use the standard forms as they appear in the models in the next section.
3. If you are listing a book that you found in the card catalog, put the call number of the book in the upper left corner of the bibliography card. Having the call number will save time when you try to locate the book later.
4. At the bottom of the card you may put in brackets any personal notes or additional information that does not properly belong in the bibliographical entry itself.

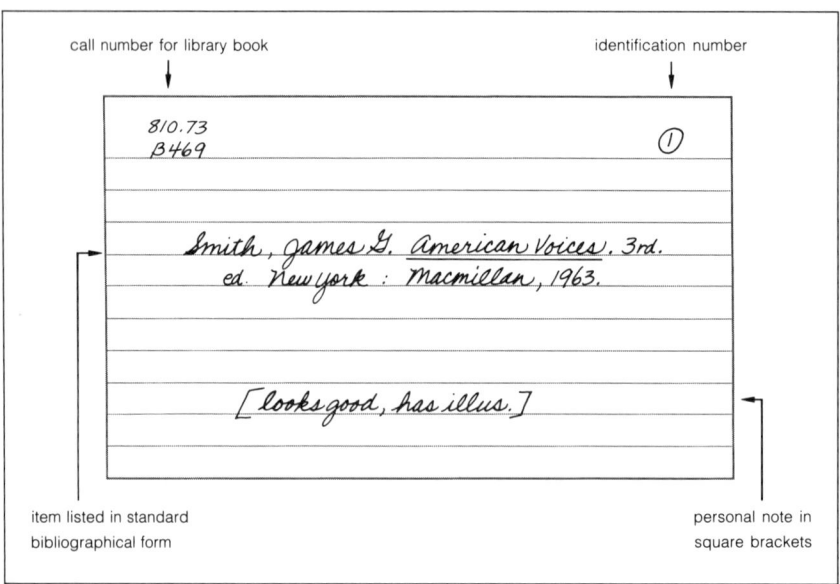

FIGURE 6

A typical bibliography card for a book is shown in Figure 6.

Here are some practical pointers to keep in mind about the mechanics of writing and collecting bibliography cards:

1. Write up and number the cards in whatever order you find the items in your search of indexes and bibliographies. You do not have to do all books first, then articles. Neither do you have to worry about alphabetizing cards at this time.
2. Put only one bibliographical entry on a card. If you have several articles from one magazine or newspaper or several essays from one anthology, make a separate card for each.
3. Try to avoid writing anything on the back of a card. The odds are that if you do, you will not see it again.
4. You will encounter some entries in indexes that do not give you all the information you need for a full bibliographical entry. When you do, you should leave a blank space in the entry on your bibliography card for the missing information. The *New York Times Index*, for example, lists brief descriptions of the contents of articles rather than the titles of articles. On your bibliography card, list all the information you are given according to the standard form, placing the contents description in brackets at the bottom of the card and leaving a space in the entry for the actual title. You can fill in the blank later when you actually find the source to take notes from it.
5. Keep cards for items that you discover are useless or unavailable to avoid duplicating them in later research and to prevent trying to find them more than once in the library. Mark the card to show it has already been checked.

Bibliographical Forms

Although writing bibliography items is essentially a mechanical operation, even here there is room for intelligence and imagination. The best way to perform this task is to learn the basic forms first. It will take a certain amount of time and practice, but once you have learned them, you can write up cards very quickly.

The forms you will find described in this section are known as the "MLA style," described in the *MLA Handbook* published by the Modern Language Association in 1984. It is one of a number of accepted styles of documentation. No single system of bibliographical notation is used in all fields. Your instructor might require, for example, the documentation style recommended in Kate Turabian's *Manual for Writers of Term Papers, Theses, and Dissertations*, the University of Chicago Press's *The Chicago Manual of Style*, or the *Publication Manual of the American Psychological Association*. In addition, many other style manuals are available. The important thing is to use one style consistently so that readers will be able to follow your paper with ease. In the examples that follow, the models follow the MLA standards.

Forms for Books

The basic bibliographical form for books is divided into four parts:

1. Author or authors (with first author's last name first) plus period, then two spaces.
2. Title (underlined) plus period, then two spaces.
3. Miscellaneous information in the following order:
   a. Translator and/or editor (name in normal order) preceded by *Ed.* or *Trans.* plus period.
   b. Edition (if not the first edition) in Arabic numerals plus *ed.*
   c. Number of volumes with this particular title (in Arabic numerals) plus *vols.*
   d. If part of a series, the name of the series plus comma followed by the number in the series (in Arabic numerals) plus period. If unnumbered, place a period after the name of the series.
4. Publication information consisting of:
   a. Place of publication plus colon, then one space.
   b. Name of publisher plus comma, then one space.
   c. Copyright date plus period.

You will find publication information in the first few pages of the book. Use the shortest forms possible, shortening publisher's names when you can. For example, Harcourt Brace Jovanovich can become Harcourt, and Harvard University Press can become Harvard UP.

If a part of the entry is not applicable (for example, if the book is published anonymously and therefore has no information on authorship, or if there is no editor or translator), simply go on to the next piece of information in the model. The core of information in the model entry for a book consists of items 1, 2, and 4, and this may be considered the most basic bibliography form:

>Sagan, Carl. The Cosmic Connection. New York: Doubleday, 1973.

The items subject to most variation are those listed under "miscellaneous information." All, or any of these items may be applicable. An entry with such miscellaneous information might look like this:

>Cassatt, Jean L. The Philosophy of Hegel. Trans. Nicholas T. Rankin. 2nd ed. 2 vols. Literary Masterpieces series 5. New York: Arrowsmith P, 1938.

A book by a single author

>Carson, Rachel. Silent Spring. Boston: Houghton Mifflin, 1962.

A book by two or three authors

>Patterson, Barbara, Nancy Meadows, and Carol Dreger. The Successful Woman. Englewood Cliffs: Prentice-Hall, 1982.

Give the names in the order they appear on the title page. Only the name of the first-listed author is given with last name first.

A book with more than three authors

>Baugh, Albert C., et al. A Literary History of England. New York: Appleton, 1948.

Use the name of the first-listed author and the Latin abbreviation *et al.*, which means "and others."

A book with corporate authorship

>American Humane Association. Child Abuse Legislation in the 1970's. Denver: American Humane Association, 1970.

If there is no individual listed as author, you may use the name of an organization or institution.

A book with no author given

>Virgina: The Old Dominion in Pictures. New York: Fleming, 1941.

Do not use the word *anonymous* or a string of hyphens to indicate a work with no listed author. Just begin with the title.

A book with an author and an editor

>Poe, Edgar Allan. Selected Writings of Edgar Allan Poe.
>Ed. Edward H. Davidson. Boston: Houghton Mifflin,
>1956.

A book with an editor

>Denenberg, Victor H., ed. Education of the Infant and
>Young Child. New York: Academic P, 1970.

A preface, introduction, foreword, or afterword

>Storrow, James J. Jr. Introduction. The State of the
>Nation. Ed. David Boroff. Englewood Cliffs:
>Prentice-Hall, 1965. vii–x.

A later edition

>Heward, William L., and Michael D. Orlansky. Exceptional
>Children. 2nd ed. Columbus: Charles Merrill, 1984.

A work in more than one volume

>Sewall, Richard B. The Life of Emily Dickinson. 2 vols.
>New York: Farrar, Straus & Giroux, 1944.

For a work published in more than one volume include the total number of volumes immediately after the title.

>Sewall, Richard B. The Life of Emily Dickinson. 2 vols.
>New York: Farrar, Straus & Giroux, 1944. Vol. 1.

If you are using only one volume, place that information at the end of the entry.

A book in a series

>Middleton, John, ed. Myth and Cosmos: Readings in
>Mythology and Symbolism. American Museum Sourcebooks
>in Anthropology. Garden City: Natural History P,
>1967.

A series title follows the title of the work and is not underlined.

A republished work

>Lorenz, Konrad Z. King Solomon's Ring. 1952. New York:
>Time, 1962.

If you list a republished work—perhaps a book first published in hardback and later republished in paperback—give the publication information for the edition you are actually using, but insert the original date of publication after the title. Do not include the original publisher or place of publication. You'll find the information you need following the title page in the reprinted version.

A translation

>Homer. The Iliad. Trans. Richmond Lattimore. Chicago: U of Chicago P, 1951.

A selection from an edited anthology

>Schlegel, Richard. "Time and Thermodynamics." The Voices of Time. Ed. J. T. Fraser. New York: Braziller, 1966. 500–23.

Begin with the author and title of the selection you are using. Enclose its title in quotation marks. Then give the title of the anthology and the name of its editor (*Ed.* means "edited by"). At the end of the entry give the page numbers for the selection. If you use several selections from one anthology, treat each one as a separate source.

Reference works

>Powers, Philip N. "Nuclear Power." Encyclopaedia Britannica. Macropaedia. 1974 ed.

Give the author only when the individual article is signed in the reference work. Otherwise, begin with the title of the article. The only publication information needed besides the work's title is the edition (if there is one) and the date of publication.

Pamphlets, brochures, and manuals

>Franklin Ace 1000 User Reference Manual. Cherry Hill: Franklin Computer Corp., 1983.

>American Council on Education. College Teaching as a Career. Washington D.C.: American Council on Education, 1958.

Pamphlets, brochures, and manuals often have corporate authorship or no author listed, but if the source has an author, begin with that information. The titles of such works should be underlined.

Government documents

>United States. Committee on Economic Security. Social Security in America. Social Security Board Pub. No. 20. Washington D.C.: GPO, 1937.

> United States. Cong. Senate. Committee on the Judiciary.
> Subcommittee to Investigate Juvenile Delinquency.
> <u>Television and Juvenile Delinquency</u>. Report No.
> 1466. 84th Cong. 2nd sess. Washington D.C.: GPO,
> 1956.

If an author is given, begin with that information. Otherwise, give the appropriate agency as the author, going from the broadest (here, United States) down to the most specific (the subcommittee in the second example). For Congressional documents include the number and session of Congress.

Forms for Periodicals
The basic form for periodicals is divided into three parts:

1. Author or authors (with first author's last name first) plus period, then two spaces.
2. Full title of the article in quotation marks, plus period (inside the quotation mark), then two spaces.
3. Publication information in this order: title of periodical (underlined), volume and/or issue number (in Arabic numerals), date of publication, page numbers for entire article (with no abbreviation *pp*). Individual variations involving volume numbers and dates are covered in the following examples.

Article in journal with continuous pagination throughout the annual volume

> Keniston, Kenneth. "Alienation and the Decline of
> Utopia." <u>American Scholar</u> 39 (1960): 161–200.

> Stafford, T. J. "Tobe's Significance in 'A Rose for
> Emily.'" <u>Modern Fiction Studies</u> 14 (1968–69):
> 451–53.

Some journals number their pages continuously as one volume, usually from the first issue of the year through the last issue. For such journals give the volume number (in Arabic numerals) after the title, followed by the year only in parentheses. End with the page numbers of the whole article. Notice particularly the punctuation in the entries.

Article in journal with pages numbered separately throughout the annual volume

> Macklin, M.C., and R. H. Kolbe. "Sex Role Stereotyping in
> Children's Advertising: Current and Past Trends."
> <u>Journal of Advertising</u> 13.2 (1984): 34–42.

For an article in a journal that numbers the pages in each issue separately throughout the annual volume, follow the basic form for a journal with continuous pagination, but include the volume and issue number separated by a period (13.2).

An article in a monthly or bimonthly magazine

>Lageman, John K. "If Robots Run the Works." <u>Nation's Business</u> Mar. 1951: 31-33+.

If the article is not printed consecutively—for example, begins on pages 31 to 33 and concludes later in the issue—list the page numbers where it begins, followed by a plus sign.

>Ridenour, Louis N. "The Role of the Computer." <u>Scientific American</u> Sept. 1952: 116-30.

Follow the title of the magazine with the month (abbreviated) and year of the issue (not separated by a comma). Do not include a volume or issue number or place parentheses around the date.

An article in a weekly or biweekly magazine

>"Pesticides: The Price for Progress." <u>Time</u> 28 Sept. 1962: 45-46.

>Edman, Irwin. "Mind and Matter." <u>New Yorker</u> 14 Oct. 1950: 139-42.

Follow the title of the magazine with the day, month (abbreviated), and year of the issue. (The military date style simplifies punctuation.) Do not include a volume or issue number or place parentheses around the date.

A newspaper article

>"One Million Children Crowd Job Market." <u>New York Times</u> 7 Dec. 1931: 7.

>Lee, John M. "'Silent Spring' Is Now Noisy Summer." <u>New York Times</u> 22 July 1962: 1+.

>Connolly, Patrick. "Up, Up and Away: Flying Without Jitters." <u>Nashville Tennessean</u> 21 Dec. 1986: F1+.

The form is the same as for a weekly or biweekly magazine with one exception. If the paper is divided into separately labeled sections, include that information with the page number (*F1+* in the third example).

An editorial or letter to the editor

>"A Fine Play Reveals a Need." Editorial. <u>Life</u> 18 May 1959: 42.

>Jonas, Gerald. "DDT in Dry Cleaning." Letter. <u>New York Times</u> 26 July 1972: 26.

If the editorial or letter has an author or title given, include the information. If there is no author or title, use either the word "Editorial" or "Letter" to begin the entry.

A review

> Kanfer, Stefan. "Feather Complex." Rev. of <u>S. J. Perelman: A Life</u>, by Dorothy Herrman. <u>Time</u> 13 Oct. 1986: 100.

Other Sources

Unpublished dissertations and theses

> Jones, Daryl E. "The Dime Novel Western: The Evolution of a Popular Formula." Diss. Michigan State U, 1974.

Use quotation marks for the title, followed by "Diss." for dissertation, followed by the institution granting the degree, followed by the date.

Plays, concerts, performances

> <u>Doubles</u>. By Neil Simon. With Gabe Kaplan and Martin Milner. Tennessee Performing Arts Center, Nashville. 16 Dec. 1986.

Begin with the title and author, followed by other information about performers and the theater, city, and date.

Recordings

> Springsteen, Bruce. <u>Born in the U.S.A.</u> Columbia, QC 38653, 1984.

Begin with the name of the person whose recorded work you are using, followed by the title, followed by the manufacturer's catalog number and the copyright date that appear on the recording or audio or videotape. If there is no date given, use the abbreviation *n.d.*

Unpublished letters

> Parham, Robert. Letter. 6 July 1971.

Lectures and speeches

> Rogers, Stuart C. "Freedom Needs Advertising." Washington, D.C., 19 Sept. 1984.

> Duncan, E. H. Class lecture. Vanderbilt U. Nashville, 20 Oct. 1965.

Computer software

> Mass Production Unit. Computer software. Micorp, 1985.
>   MS-DOS. 256 KB, disk.

Give the title, writer, manufacturer, and copyright date. Information about operating systems or memory is optional.

Interviews

> Lansing, Edward. Conversation With Edward Lansing. With
>   Robert Adams. Boston: Beecham P, 1927.

For a published interview, begin with the name of the person interviewed, followed by the title of the interview and the name of the interviewer—if given—followed by publication information.

> Warren, Robert Penn. Personal interview. 8 Apr. 1966.

If you conducted the interview yourself, give the name of the person you interviewed, indicate whether it was a personal or telephone interview, and give the date of the interview.

Bibliographical Forms in APA Format Some disciplines follow the style of documentation developed by the American Psychological Association (APA). If you are writing a paper in a field such as anthropology, psychology, education, political science, business, linguistics, home economics, physical education, or sociology, your instructor may ask you to use the APA style. The following examples illustrate the basic APA bibliographical forms. For more detailed listings, consult the *Publication Manual of the American Psychological Association*.

APA model for a book The basic bibliography entry for a book includes the following:

1. Author or authors, last name first (for all authors), followed by initials rather than first names. Follow names with two spaces. Use an ampersand (&) in place of the word *and* with multiple authors.
2. Date of publication in parentheses, plus period. Follow with two spaces.
3. Title of book, underlined, plus period, then two spaces. Capitalize only the first word, proper nouns, and the first word of any subtitle.
4. Miscellaneous information such as translator, edition, volume numbers, or series title.
5. Publication information: city, plus colon, followed by name of publisher, plus period.

> Patterson, B., Meadows, N., & Dreger, C. (1982). The
>   successful woman. Englewood Cliffs: Prentice-Hall.

APA model for a journal article The basic model for an article in a journal paginated continuously throughout the year or volume includes the following:

1. Author or authors, last name first, followed by initials rather than first names. Follow names with two spaces. Use an ampersand (&) in place of the word *and* with multiple authors.
2. Date of publication in parentheses, plus period. Follow with two spaces.
3. Title of article, plus period, then two spaces. Capitalize only the first word, proper nouns, and the first word of any subtitle. Place *no* quotation marks around article titles.
4. Publication information:
    a. Name of the journal, underlined, plus comma. Capitalize the main words.
    b. Volume number, underlined, plus comma.
    c. Page numbers for the article, plus period. Do not use *p.* or *pp.* abbreviations.

```
Keniston, K. Alienation and the cost of utopia. (1960).
    American Scholar, 39, 161-200.
```

APA model for a magazine article The basic model for an article in a weekly or monthly magazine paginated separately for each issue includes the following:

1. Author or authors, last name first, followed by initials rather than first names. Follow names with two spaces. Use an ampersand (&) in place of the word *and* with multiple authors.
2. Date of publication in parentheses. Within parentheses give year first, plus comma, followed by month. If day of publication is given, follow month with the day. Parentheses followed by period, then two spaces.
3. Title of article, plus period, then two spaces. Capitalize only the first word, proper nouns, and the first word of any subtitle. Place *no* quotation marks around article titles.
4. Publication information:
    a. Name of the magazine, underlined, plus comma. Capitalize the main words.
    b. Page numbers for the article, plus period. Use *p.* or *pp.* abbreviations.

```
Edman, E. (1950, October 14). Mind and matter. New Yorker,
    pp. 139-42.
```

Taking Notes from Sources

With a set of bibliography cards to help you find promising sources, you are now ready to take notes, to gather the information from which the paper itself will be written. You have a topic and some idea of what you will be looking for in your reading (the investigative questions you have already written). But beyond that it is difficult to generalize. The relationship between those early, tentative ideas about a topic and the final thesis from which the paper is developed varies greatly with different writers and with different assignments. At this stage in the process some writers have found in their reading a clear focus for organizing the final paper. Others may see several possibilities and remain uncertain as to which one to pursue. But most do not find a usable thesis idea until later in the process.

This state of affairs is to be expected. There are too many variables in this process to permit a single statement that applies to all writers in all situations. It is important, however, to keep in mind that note taking is really three separate activities all going on in this learning phase of a research project. You continuously move back and forth from reading to writing down notes to thinking about a possible thesis. You read to discover answers to the questions you have developed about the subject. As you discover answers—or perhaps previously unsuspected ideas—you record them as notes. In turn, as you take notes, you learn more and more about the subject and you begin to formulate the point you want to make about it.

Thus the reading and note taking enable you to narrow down your topic and focus your reading and thinking more specifically. In this manner you move from particular pieces of information to a more precise conception of how those pieces relate to one another—that is, to a thesis. With a trial thesis in mind, you can concentrate in your further reading on information that relates specifically to the narrowed focus. You concentrate on finding particular facts to back up the tentative thesis. This process then begins again as you continue reading and learning about the subject. You may find it necessary to look at the same information more than once, each time from a different point of view. This being the case, it is best at the beginning of note taking not to be too committed to any single conclusion. The important thing to remember is that note taking involves more than just piling up cards—it is a vital part of your effort to develop your own conclusions about the subject you are investigating.

Trial Thesis and Outline

Throughout your note taking, you should provide yourself with a summary of your position, a running commentary on where you have been, where you are, and where you might be heading. Such a summary will help you as you begin to draw your own conclusions, and later as you prepare the outline from which you will write your paper. Some people can simply remember such information, but most of us tend to forget ideas that might prove fruitful later on. Putting your information together in this preliminary way as a kind of trial outline will also enable you to see connections between isolated pieces of information that you might not otherwise have noticed. The act of writing things down has the advantage of forcing you to test various ways of relating information.

As you look at the material in this trial outline—which will probably resemble a list more than the traditional outline with formal headings and subheadings—decide what conclusions you can draw at this point in your investigation. Write down as a complete sentence what you believe to be the most significant overall conclusion; this sentence will serve as your trial thesis. In fact, there is nothing wrong with listing more than one possible thesis at this stage of your work. Naturally, such conclusions will be tentative, based as they are on a limited amount of research, but they are important because they help focus on what you have learned so far and they provide ideas to investigate as you continue reading.

The trial thesis and outline will enable you to see the relationship of the specific items of information in your notes. *It is best not to think of the trial thesis and outline as one step in the process but as a continuing mental operation that is put into writing from time to time.* In a sense, then, the mental activity involved in composing a tentative thesis and outline is more significant than the product itself.

Note Card Format

Most students ask, "Exactly how many note cards do I need for a research paper?" Rather than thinking about a specific number, you should understand that what makes note cards valuable is their *quality*, not their *quantity*. Obviously, you are going to need a sufficient number of note cards to write your paper, and that number can only be determined by the nature of the assignment. It is certain that some cards will prove worthless, so you should be generous in estimating your needs. But you should always remember that the notes serve two purposes: They provide information when you draft the paper, and they help you now as you formulate a thesis. When you read anything, make a guess as to whether or not you will be able to use it—either because it supports your trial thesis or because it suggests a new possibility for refining or modifying that thesis—and then take notes accordingly. In the earlier parts of your research, when you may not have a clear idea of your thesis, you may find this a difficult decision to make, but as you continue to take notes and continue to write out your trial thesis and outline, you will find the decision easier and easier to make. The point is that you want to do more than just collect note cards; you want to use note taking to help stimulate your thinking.

The notes you take must serve a number of functions, and those functions dictate the best techniques for preparing them. First of all, the cards will serve as your memory of what you have read. For this reason they should be easy to read. The cards will help you when you decide on your method of organizing the paper, and since at this point in the process you are not sure what that method will be, they should be flexible. Finally, the cards will help you as you draft your paper and integrate your source material into your text. Thus, at the drafting stage, as well as all other stages of the process, your note cards should be accurate, the most important characteristic of all.

Being systematic about the forms you use in taking notes will pay off by making your notes easy to read, flexible, and accurate. Here are some tips to help in note taking.

1. The most flexible way to take notes is on four-by-six-inch cards. The three-by-five-inch cards are sufficient for bibliography cards, which contain relatively little information, but the larger size accommodates more extensive notes. Sheets of paper are more difficult to handle and more likely to become damaged by repeated handling. Cards allow you to sort and rearrange your notes with ease, making it a simple task to try out new ways of organizing your material. All you have to do is shuffle the cards into whatever order you prefer.

2. To make it easy to read and rearrange the note cards, record the general subject matter of the note in a phrase in the top left corner of the card. Make sure that the phrase you select is not too broad. If you label all your note cards for a paper about the Battle of Gettysburg either "North" or "South," you will have done little to help yourself arrange the notes efficiently. On the other hand, if you use such specific labels that almost every card has a different caption, you won't be able to group related ideas. You might want to use the headings from your trial outline to label your notes. In any case, remember that you can change the headings later, when you learn more precisely how you are going to use them.

3. Identify the source of the information in your note in the upper right corner of the card. First enter the identification number you previously put on the bibliography card for the source. Also enter the last name of the author of the source. If the source has no author, give its title instead. If the source has a corporate author (that is, an organization is listed as the author), enter the name of the organization. Listing the author not only helps identify the source, it also makes it easier for you to integrate the information on the card into the text of your paper. You can refer to the author's name in the text of your draft without having to hunt for the bibliography card while you are in the middle of composing a paragraph.

4. Do not put information from more than one source on the same note card, even though the material is closely related or fits under the same heading on the tentative outline. Each note card should be identified with only one bibliography card. This procedure makes documenting sources in the final text much easier.

5. Do not put information for two subject headings on one note card, even though they are found in the same source. Instead, put the information on two cards. This will make it easy to group the note cards later.

6. Be careful to put the exact source page number for the information on each note card, whether the information is summarized or quoted directly. If the

material on one card is from several different pages in the source, mark the card to indicate which part came from which page. Putting a double slash mark (//) in your note at the location of a page break is a good way to ensure such accuracy. When you eventually draft your paper, you may use only part of the information on a note card, and you must be able to cite precisely where you got it.

In short, a note card should contain just enough material to provide you with all the information you need for organizing and writing the paper and just enough to lead you quickly to the bibliography card for documenting your source. You should let this general purpose guide your specific procedure. For example, if the title of an article or the place it appeared is significant, do not neglect to put that information in the right-hand corner along with the author's name and the bibliography card identification number. A typical note card and the bibliography card for its source are shown in Figure 7, p. 422.

Writing the Notes

As you write note cards, you learn about your subject and work at formulating a thesis about it. Later, in the drafting phase of your research project, the notes will serve as substitutes for the sources themselves. To avoid wasting time by going back to the sources, you should put information on the note cards in the most usable form. When you draft your paper, you will use your sources in one of two ways—either by paraphrasing them or by quoting them directly. These are the two basic ways to take notes as well.

Most of your notes should be taken in paraphrased form—using the facts and opinions in the sources, but expressing them in your own words and sentence structure. It might seem easier to take all notes as direct quotations, simply copying sources down verbatim, but that procedure would be self-defeating. Your role in a research project includes more than just finding a topic and recording a collection of information about it. Your primary responsibility is to show your reader that you have something of your own to say about the topic. Your sources furnish supporting evidence for your own ideas. Thus, drafting the paper is much easier if you have paraphrased most of your notes from the beginning.

Nevertheless, it is appropriate to quote the exact words of a source for specific reasons such as the following:

1. If the source's words are striking and original or if a brief passage is succinct and brings the meaning of the whole selection into focus, then you may want to quote the passage.
2. If you find that a paraphrase will somehow distort the passage, quote it. The tone of a passage—comic, ironic, tragic—is often as significant as its content, and it is sometimes impossible to duplicate this tone in a paraphrase. Consider the following passage from A Modest Proposal, in which Jonathan

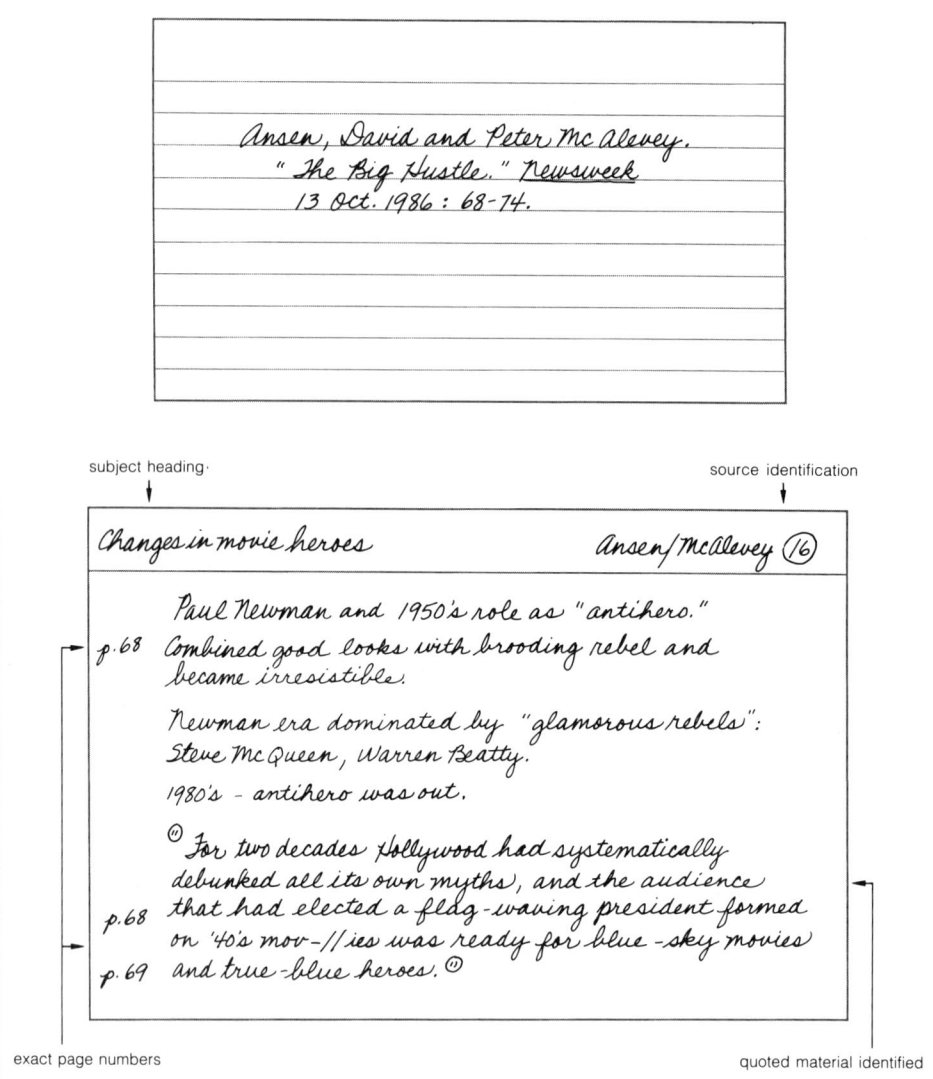

FIGURE 7

Swift writes in ironic and bitter terms of the plight of the poor in eighteenth century Ireland:

Some persons of a desponding Spirit are in great concern about the vast number of poor People, who are Aged, Diseased, or Maimed, and I have been desired to imploy my Thoughts what Course may be taken, to ease the Nation of so grievous an Incumberance. But I am not in the least Pain upon that matter, because it is very well known, that they are every Day dying, and rotting, by cold and famine, and filth, and vermin, as fast as can reasonably be expected.

Swift's feelings are conveyed through the bitter contrasts in language, but it would be impossible to indicate that this was the case in a paraphrase. A paraphrase might make it appear that Swift was truly unconcerned about the misery he described.

3. If the words themselves are what you are writing about, you should quote them. A paper about a writer's style or an analysis of a literary work requires quotation of the words you are analyzing.
4. If you are going to refute the specific words of an author, you should quote those words. You will be fairer and more effective by allowing the author to speak in his or her own voice.

Paraphrased Notes Here's an excerpt from a sample source. A note card paraphrasing the excerpt is shown in Figure 8, p. 424.

> The spread of gambling across the U.S. is certain to sharpen the debate about its social effects and spur efforts to analyze its roots in human behavior. One explanation for its pervasiveness is offered by James Ritchie, executive director of the Gambling Commission. "There is in the breast of every person," he observes, "a desire to risk. It may be a desire to run for political office, or a desire by a farmer to plant wheat and see if the elements allow him to reap a crop, or a desire to buy stock or commodity futures. Or maybe it comes from a person who decides he has some disposable income and he's going to risk that money because he has a feeling he'll come away with more money, which is called gambling. It's the desire to risk."
>
> It can even be argued that betting, within reason, has redeeming social value. Felicia Campbell, a University of Nevada behaviorist who earned her Ph.D. with a thesis on "Gambling Mythologies and Typologies" (and was once married to a croupier), insists that gambling permits many people—especially the elderly—to "lose themselves in the action of the moment." She adds: Even though the final result is often negative, it's a positive impulse. The peak experience is almost more important than winning. When he grabs the dice, a blue-collar worker is in control of his destiny. For the businessman, gambling can be cathartic because it can produce an altered state of consciousness.
>
> "Gambling Goes Legit," *Time*, Dec. 6, 1975, 65.

There are two basic procedures for writing a usable paraphrase:

1. First, read and, if necessary, reread the source to be certain you understand what it says, and then write down what the source says in your own words. Obviously, a few isolated key words of the original author will appear in

> Legal Gambling – Pro   "Gambling Goes Legit"   (12)
>
> Increased gambling will result in increased analysis of its cause and effects. James Ritchie (Exec. Dir. of Gambling Commission) says everyone has a secret desire to take risks. Examples: people who run for
> p.65 public office, farmers who plant crops in hope of future payoff, purchasers of stocks and commodity futures. Felicia Campbell (psych. at U. Nevada) says value of gambling is that it allows people to become absorbed in present moment. The desire to gamble gives a positive feeling.

FIGURE 8

your paraphrase; you could not paraphrase this article without incuding *gamble, risk, value, blue-collar worker,* and so on. But the vocabulary and sentence structure must be essentially your own. You must do more than make a few verbal changes: a few omissions, a few substitutions of synonyms, a few verb changes, a few rearrangements of words. The simplest way to paraphrase is to look away from the source and write your note as if you were turning from your reading to tell someone else what you had just read.

2. Take steps to ensure the accuracy of your paraphrase. After completing a paraphrase, always check your note card against the source to make certain that you have retained not only the facts of the source but also its emphasis. For example, you would misrepresent the source we've just read if you wrote, "James Ritchie advocates legalized gambling by arguing that most people like to take risks." Certainly, you will also want to verify that names, dates, and figures in your paraphrase are correct.

    Make sure that you have not inadvertently included your own interpretation or opinion as if it were part of the original. If your paraphrase of the source in the example said, "Felicia Campbell is wrong when she says gambling is good for old people," you would be adding your interpretation to what is supposed to be an objective summary of the source.

    When you paraphrase a passage that contains the ideas or opinions of several people, you should take special care to attribute each idea to the particular person responsible for it. Make certain (as the example in Figure 8 does) to indicate precisely which parts of the paraphrase are from the author of the article and which parts are from each of the other authorities.

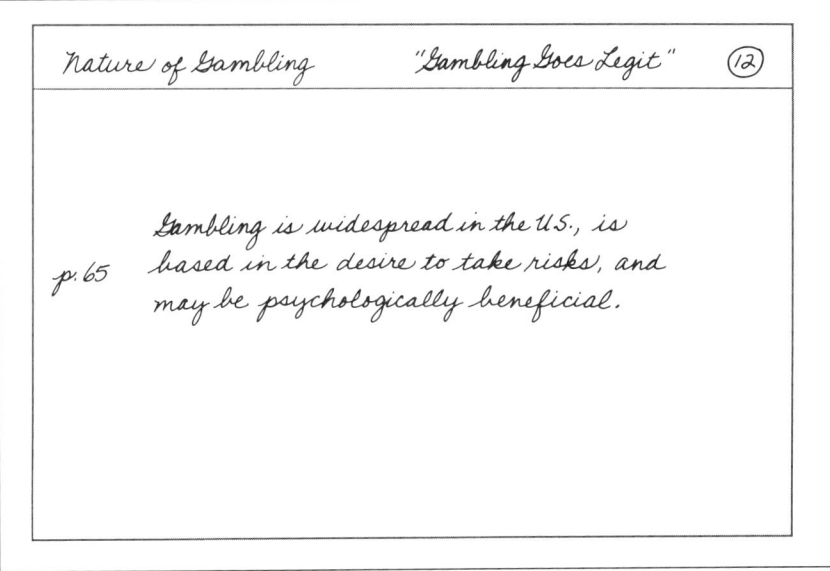

FIGURE 9

Sometimes you may find source material related to your research topic, but you may decide that you don't really need a detailed summary of it. In such a case you may wish to write a *précis* of the source—a statement of its thesis. A detailed paraphrase of a source includes not only the thesis, but also at least some of the supporting evidence; a précis omits these details. The précis may prove to be the most effective type of note in several situations. For example, you may find a source that appears useful but is simply too long to paraphrase. In that case you can confine your note taking to recording the gist of what the source says. Or your topic may focus on a person, event, or idea that generated a number of different reactions by individuals or groups. In your paper you would probably wish simply to mention the general reactions without going into detail. Finally, you may not be sure as you are reading and taking notes that you will be able to use the material at all. But rather than ignoring completely something that has a chance of proving useful, you might wish at least to write down a précis. After all, you can always go back to the source if it should turn out to be more important than you expected. Figure 9 shows a précis note of the passage in the preceding example.

Quoted Notes Sometimes, when you decide you have good reason to use the exact words of a source, you will want to record the entire passage you are reading. At other times you may be interested in preserving only a few choice phrases on a note card that is otherwise paraphrased. In either situation the basic format for the note card is the one illustrated for

```
┌─────────────────────────────────────────────┐
│  Ethics of Future              Ramsey    ⑬  │
│  ┌───────────────────────────────────────┐  │
│  │    ⁽¹⁾ This burden of proof has to be  │  │
│  │    assumed if it is proposed that,    │  │
│  │    for the sake of the remote         │  │
│  │ p.129 future, present moral values or │  │
│  │    claims are to be overridden or     │  │
│  │    changed. It has not been           │  │
│  │    assumed because no such            │  │
│  │    conclusion can be given sufficient │  │
│  │    support by // rational             │  │
│  │ p.130 argument.⁽¹⁾                     │  │
│  └───────────────────────────────────────┘  │
└─────────────────────────────────────────────┘
```

FIGURE 10

paraphrases. Here is a sample passage from a book by Paul Ramsey on the ethics of genetic engineering. A note card quoting from the passage is shown in Figure 10.

> This burden of proof has to be assumed if it is proposed that, for the sake of the remote future, present moral values or claims are to be overridden or changed. It has not been assumed because no such conclusion can be given sufficient support by rational argument. The promotion of certain qualities could easily "be undesirable unless we could also determine the conditions of life in the community of the future, including its values."[*] No one knows, for example, whether an increase in the number of intelligent men would be a good thing unless he could guarantee a comparable increase in the number of altruists. One, therefore, now knows that he does not and cannot know that an increase in intelligence would be desirable in the community of the remote future.

So far we have concentrated on notes that are entirely quoted. In most cases, however, you will find that a source contains only a few phrases or clauses that justify direct quotation, and your note card will combine

---

[*] Quoting Martin P. Golding, "Ethical Issues in Biological Engineering," *UCLA Law Review* 15 (Feb., 1968).

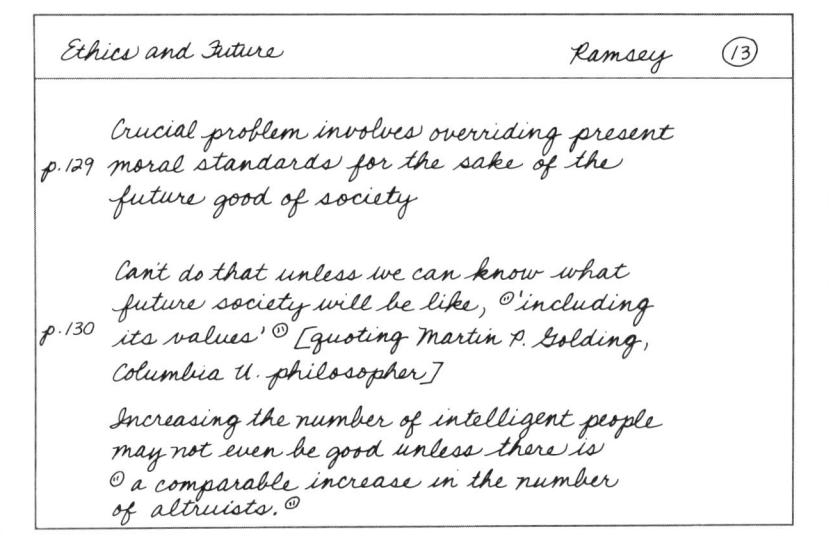

FIGURE 11

paraphrased material with the quoted material. An example of such a note card, based on the Ramsey selection, is shown in Figure 11. Some special techniques ensure that note cards containing quoted material are easy to read, flexible, and accurate.

1. Accuracy is most important in direct quotation. Be certain to copy exactly what is in the original—spelling, capitalization, punctuation, italics, and all. (Italics are indicated in your handwritten notes by underlining.) It is a good idea to stop and check a note card quotation word by word as soon as you have completed it.
2. Put quotation marks around everything you quote verbatim, whether whole sentences or parts of sentences. Don't forget the ending quotation marks, and to guarantee that you do not miss them when you use the quotation in your paper, circle the quotation marks on the note card.
3. If the passage you are quoting already contains quotation marks, change them to single quotation marks on the note card. You can see such a change in the sample note card in Figure 11. Double (or primary) quotation marks are used at the beginning and end of the quotation. Single (or secondary) quotation marks designate the words that were already in quotation marks in the source.
4. Record the exact page number in the source for every quoted sentence or part of a sentence. If you quote something that goes from one page to the next, follow the example of the Ramsey note card (Figure 10) and use the double slash marks (or some other mark) to indicate where the break occurs.

Devising a Thesis

Before you began to take notes, you developed a trial thesis and outline to focus your thinking about your topic, and during your reading you continued to look for ways to connect the materials you found. By now you may have developed and refined your trial thesis so that you have a clear idea of what you want to say, and you can begin arranging the evidence you will need to support your conclusion. If, however, your efforts haven't led you to a thesis yet, now is the time to take stock of the material you have at hand. Devising a thesis often is just a matter of clarifying for yourself what you have learned. In fact, you may already have a thesis without recognizing it. Remember that the thesis is the basic point that you want to make to your readers about your subject. Although there is no prescribed model to follow in devising a thesis, there are a number of things you can do to help yourself focus on this basic point:

1. Write down the subject headings from your trial outline or from your note cards. Then review the headings to see if they suggest any conclusions. You can ask of each heading on the list, "What *about*———?" Your answer will be a conclusion you have drawn.
2. Try shuffling your note cards and then skimming through them. Seeing your notes in a new order can sometimes help you discover relationships you would otherwise miss.
3. Ask yourself, "Did I discover anything unexpected or surprising in my research?" What surprises you will probably surprise your readers, too. Describing what has commonly been assumed about a topic by most people and then revealing what is actually the case both interests readers and represents a real insight on your part.
4. Ask yourself, "Are there any significant differences of opinion among my sources?" Describing a controversy and perhaps its causes or outcome will provide focus for diverse material.
5. Ask yourself, "What is the single most important thing someone should know about my topic?" In answering this question you necessarily focus attention on the key to understanding your topic, whether it is the stock market crash of 1929 or the treatment of terminally ill hospital patients.

Any of these techniques might generate a usable thesis. However you arrive at your thesis, remember these basic requirements: *A thesis is a complete sentence making a coherent comment that unifies various aspects of a subject.* In the sample research paper about the impact of Rachel Carson's book *Silent Spring* (page 445) the student writer's thesis came from the combination of an unexpected discovery on her part and her conclusion about what was most important for her readers to understand. She decided that the most important point was that the publication of *Silent Spring* led to the banning of DDT and that the most surprising thing she had learned was that before the publication of the book, DDT had been highly regarded by most people. The result was her thesis: "The publication of

Rachel Carson's *Silent Spring* in 1962 helped reverse public acceptance of DDT and initiated a chain reaction that eventually led to the banning of the pesticide in the United States."

GENERATING A STRUCTURE

Once you have formulated your own thesis, you can turn your attention to selecting and arranging the evidence you will need to prove your point to your readers. Begin by clarifying for yourself exactly what you will have to prove. Every thesis brings with it a commitment to answer the question "What will I have to prove to my readers to convince them of my thesis?" The answers to this basic question—in the form of complete sentences—will provide you with the *key ideas* for your paper. Analyzing your thesis for its commitment serves two purposes: it enables you to make sure that you have the material you need to prove your point, and it provides the outline of key points you will need when you draft your paper.

If, however, you haven't yet worked out the key ideas needed to develop your thesis, there are two ways to proceed:

1. You can read over your thesis and any comments or notes you have jotted down and retrace the process that led from your reading to your thesis. The steps along the way may represent the key ideas from which you drew your conclusion.
2. You can let your analysis of the thesis lead you to the key ideas you have to prove. For example, if your thesis points out the various ways people responded to the changes in women's appearance during the "Flapper Era" of the 1920s, the key ideas will be the differing reactions you found. If your thesis comments on the forces that brought about a change in the child labor laws in the 1930s, the key ideas will be the various factions at work in causing the change. Or if your thesis concerns the future of computers in education, the key ideas will be the categories of uses that your sources have revealed.

Carefully studying your thesis should lead you to the main ideas for your paper. When you write down these ideas in the order you want to present them, you will have the basis of a sentence outline from which to draft your paper. A sentence outline (one in which every heading and subheading in the outline is a grammatically complete sentence) will be useful to you because it requires you to express fully each key idea. Each complete sentence will stand out as a claim you intend to prove to your readers, making it possible for you to see just what you are committing yourself to accomplish in your paper. Then you can go on to subdivide each key idea into the main supporting details needed to support it. For example, here is the thesis for the sample research paper on the impact of

Silent Spring, followed by the key ideas the student writer decided were needed to develop it:

> *Thesis:* The publication of Rachel Carson's *Silent Spring* in 1962 helped reverse public acceptance of DDT and initiated a chain reaction that eventually led to the banning of the pesticide in the United States.
> *Key Ideas:*
>   I. Rachel Carson began the book after seeing the results of DDT use.
>   II. Carson's book painted a bleak picture of America's future with DDT.
>   III. DDT had long been used with high public regard.
>   IV. Carson's discussion of the negative effects of DDT produced immediate and extensive criticism.
>   V. *Silent Spring* changed attitudes and stimulated inquiry about DDT.
>   VI. The investigations led to major reforms.

With this set of key ideas in hand, the writer went on to subdivide each idea so she would have a record of exactly which important details from her notes she would use in writing her first draft. At this stage your outline is for *you*, to guide you in drafting the paper. Later you may be asked to include the outline in your finished paper as a guide for readers. Here's the way the sentence outline looked when fleshed out:

> Outline
> *Thesis:* The publication of Rachel Carson's *Silent Spring* in 1962 helped reverse public acceptance of DDT and initiated a chain reaction that eventually led to the banning of the pesticide in the United States.
>   I. Rachel Carson began the book after seeing the results of DDT use.
>   A. In 1958 Carson saw animals killed by DDT.
>   B. Following a friend's urging, Carson spent four years doing research on pesticide use.
>   II. Carson's book painted a bleak picture of America's future with DDT.
>   A. Carson described a hypothetical town dying from pesticide use.
>   B. Carson based all the descriptions on actual cases.
>   III. DDT had long been used with high public regard.
>   A. DDT played an important role in disease control in WWII.
>   B. After the war DDT continued to be used to control disease and to raise food production.
>   C. DDT continued with ever-wider use into the 1960s.
>   IV. Carson's discussion of the negative effects of DDT produced immediate and extensive criticism.
>   A. *Silent Spring* was attacked by the pesticide industry.
>   B. Carson was accused of trying to frighten readers.
>   C. Some government officials called Carson an alarmist.
>   V. *Silent Spring* changed attitudes and stimulated inquiry about DDT.
>   A. Carson's descriptions stimulated questions and investigations.

          1. Government agencies began new tests and sought increased budgets.
          2. Private groups and writers turned their attention to the topic.
     B. Investigative results confirmed Carson's warnings.
          1. The Agriculture Department and Public Health Service confirmed the severe health hazards of DDT.
          2. The Science Advisory Committee urged immediate cutback and elimination of the use of DDT.
VI. The investigations led to major reforms.
     A. The changes came slowly.
     B. The EPA finally banned DDT ten years after *Silent Spring*.

In constructing an outline, you will need to follow several basic principles:

1. The outline should follow the standard format for headings and subdivisions:

   I.
      A.
         1.
            a.
            b.
         2.
      B.
   II.

   You are not bound to divide your outline into the third and fourth levels (Arabic numerals and lowercase letters) shown here. The first two levels are often sufficient.

2. The divisions of the outline should show which ideas are primary and which are subordinate. The Roman numeral headings are limited to the key ideas needed to prove the thesis. When one of those headings is subdivided, the capital letter subheadings must be separate, distinct ideas or details related to the single key idea (Roman numeral heading) above them. In turn, each subdivision of an A or B level must be a separate supporting detail for that A or B level idea.

3. Avoid single subheadings at any level because they suggest the odd notion that something can be divided into one part.

Later, if you include an outline with your finished paper, your instructor may ask for a topic outline—one using phrases instead of sentences. In that case you can easily convert the sentence outline headings into phrases. But for now you have devised a thesis and developed a working outline in sentence form, and you're ready to begin drafting the text of your paper.

Drafting the Research Paper

When you draft your paper, you move from the learning phase of the writing process, in which your main task is to discover a point you wish to make about your subject, to the communication phase. Your goal now is to communicate your thesis and back it up with the evidence derived from your reading. A good way to begin arranging your evidence is to sort your note cards according to the subject headings you previously put on them. Each group of cards will provide the supporting details you need to develop the key ideas in your outline. As you begin drafting your text, however, be prepared to follow up ideas that did not occur to you when you wrote your outline. Don't hesitate to make alterations.

Integrating Sources into Your Text

In making your point, you will encounter some drafting problems common to all papers using multiple sources. Your aim is to communicate your ideas about your topic, using sources as evidence for your thesis. When you took notes originally, you did not know the context in which you would eventually use them. But now that you have a context, you will need to make specific adjustments to fit your sources into your paper. However complex the use of sources in a project, your job is to keep perspective straight—that is, to separate your sources' ideas from one another and from your own ideas. In other words, you must give credit where credit is due by attributing each fact or idea to its original author.

There are a number of ways to attribute ideas to their sources, but whatever means you choose, the basic requirement remains the same: *Readers should know who is responsible for each item of information just by reading your text.* This principle holds true for all forms of documentation. Although your research paper may have a separate note page to identify your sources, your readers should know the source of all information without having to turn to the note page. Notes and bibliographies (pages formally listing the sources you used) provide the exact location—book, article—of the information in the source, but the general origin of each item should be clear from reading the text.

The reason for taking care to distinguish what you say from what your sources say is simple. When readers read something with your name on it, they make the natural assumption that you are the source of everything—information, ideas, opinions—that follows. When you tell them otherwise by introducing a reference to a source, they assume that everything that follows comes from that source. There are, then, two basic principles for using sources in a paper:

1. *Readers assume that everything in your paper is your own, until they are informed otherwise.*

2. *Once a source is introduced, readers assume that all of the material that follows is from that source, until they are informed otherwise.*

Attributing Ideas to Sources

Matters of attribution (separating your source's ideas from one another and from your own ideas) are commonsense applications of these two principles. For instance, when you use an idea from a source, you should refer to that source. Take the following example:

```
Political advertising has, in recent years, been
subjected to increasingly sharp criticism on many fronts.
Maurine Christopher, for example, has called on
telecasters to "be concerned about the damaging impact of
unbridled, disreputable advertising on the American
government" (61).
```

The phrase "Maurine Christopher, for example" separates the writer's generalization about the status of political advertising from Maurine Christopher's specific appeal to telecasters. The information at the end of the passage—the "(61)"—is an example of the parenthetical style for formally documenting sources. It tells readers the page location of the information you are using; a list at the end of your paper gives full bibliographical details for each source you have used. You will find a full discussion of such citations in the section on documentation. Note: Place final punctuation *after* the parenthetical citation.

Just how much information is required when you introduce a source? The answer depends on how much information you believe is needed to convince your readers of the significance of the source's comments. Take the following case:

```
Prison inmates in the 1880s were often controlled through
relentless humiliation. Henry J. W. Dam observed that
inmates were often stripped of their clothing and
searched by guards (515). A reporter for the New York
Times wrote that striped prison suits were degrading to
inmates but that officials insisted the suits were needed
to control prisoners and to prevent escapes ("Prison
Wardens" 3). Another newspaper report described a prison
in which naked inmates went through the still greater
humiliation of being forced to wear heavy chains and iron
rings around their waists and ankles ("Prison" 3).
```

Information identifying Henry J. W. Dam—a prisoner? a guard? a visitor?—would have been useful for helping readers understand and appreciate his observations.

Common sense should guide all your decisions about attribution. When you introduce any source, avoid bogging down your text with more information than is really necessary. Suppose, for example, that you wish to refer to a young promotion manager's remarks in a *Time* magazine article. You might introduce the source as follows:

> Many of the younger generation at the beginning of the 1950s placed a high priority on money and security. In a May 1951 Time article entitled "The Younger Generation" a 26-year-old promotion manager is quoted as saying, "Sure, I'd like to do something on my own, but I want to get well fixed first—make plenty of money and then maybe start some innovations" (26).

The detailed reference to the *Time* article slows down reading by cluttering the text.

In your research paper you would, of course, have to provide a citation to the article, which is the ultimate source of your information. But that citation can be more gracefully presented in a parenthetical reference or in a note than in the text itself. In the text it is preferable to introduce the immediate source of your information:

> Many of the younger generation at the beginning of the 1950s placed a high priority on money and security. A 26-year-old Dallas promotion manager said, "Sure, I'd like to do something on my own, but I want to get well fixed first—make plenty of money and then maybe start some innovations" ("Younger Generation" 26).

The examples thus far have concentrated on introducing sources, showing readers precisely where the use of a source *begins*. But the second principle for using sources makes it equally important to clarify where the use of a source *ends*. Often the introduction of another source will take care of the matter:

> There were many opinions about how the FCC should react to the "War of the Worlds" broadcast. FCC Chairman Frank R. McNinch called the broadcast "regrettable" but would not comment on what action the FCC would take ("FCC" 26). Commissioner C. A. M. Craven strongly opposed censorship, saying, "The public does not want a spineless radio" ("Scare Script" 1).

The introduction of Commissioner Craven indicates the writer has finished with Chairman McNinch.

Frequently your wording can make the place where a source leaves off obvious:

> U.S. News reported in October of 1961 that its staff believed the Communists in Vietnam would have to become much stronger before American involvement became

>compelling ("U.S. Troops" 65). Many other print reporters
>at that time and even later shared the opinion expressed
>by the magazine. Virtually all commentators at the time
>agreed that the Vietnamese must want help before any help
>would be given.

Readers would recognize that the last two sentences are clearly your own comments, not those of the *U.S. News* editors. Most important, readers can make that distinction without reference to the parenthetical citation.

When you write a paragraph containing a number of sentences paraphrased from the same source, you must make sure the perspective remains clear *throughout* the passage:

>At a meeting of the Society of Automotive Engineers
>in 1935, Commander Charles E. Rosendahl called for the
>continued building of dirigibles. He argued that
>accidents shouldn't be permitted to thwart new
>experimentation and development. In fact, Rosendahl said
>that knowledge gained from accidents actually contributed
>to improving airships. He also argued that submarines,
>ships, trains, and automobiles individually caused more
>loss of life than did dirigibles. However, Rosendahl's
>last-ditch eforts came too late to save the dirigible
>("Launching" 18, 29).

The wording allows readers to follow the perspective through the whole passage.

Integrating Direct Quotations

Using direct quotations often requires some additional effort on your part to ensure the effectiveness and accuracy of the quoted material. Whenever you quote from a source, there are four things to remember:

1. *Keep the perspective clear.* Quotation marks, of course, immediately signal readers of a switch in perspective, but they give no other information readers may need to understand the source and significance of the quoted words. Take the following example:

>A British doctor urged parents to "ask themselves what can
>be done to provide adolescents 'safer and more self-
>controlled methods of experiencing excitement and
>physical and emotional release'" ("Adolescents" 27).

Notice that single quotation marks here replace the double quotation marks that were in the original source. But we are left wondering who spoke (or wrote) the words enclosed in single quotation marks.

2. *Integrate all quoted material smoothly into your text with some of your own wording.* Quotation marks set your source's words apart from your own, so there's a particular need to smooth the transition into each quotation. You can accomplish such transitions and at the same time clarify perspective. The following is an example:

> Concerning his fellow passengers on the Titanic, Colonel Archibald Gracie later wrote, "I saw nothing but unexampled self-sacrifice and self-control and the greatest courage under the most harrowing circumstances" ("Tidings" 3).

3. *Ensure the accuracy of quotations.* Readers assume that everything between quotation marks is exactly as it appeared in the original source. Accuracy is thus partly a matter of carefully copying wording (spelling, capitalization, punctuation, and all). Sometimes, however, you may need to make alterations in a quoted passage to fit it into your paper, and so accuracy also includes clearly marking for your readers any such additions, deletions, or other changes you decide to make in a quotation.

A. *Omissions from quotations.* If you omit some words from a quotation, you usually should show the deletion by an *ellipsis* (or ellipsis points), three spaced dots (. . .). Brief quoted phrases that are obviously fragments do not require the use of an ellipsis. Notice that readers would have no difficulty realizing that the two phrases quoted in this example are not complete sentences:

> Irwin Ross writes of a younger generation missing "the old bravado and full-throated enthusiasm" and lacking much desire for "defending a society which in peacetime has no need for them" (367).

Do, however, use an ellipsis to show an omission *within* a quoted sentence. Here is a passage from a source, followed by an incomplete quotation from that source:

> One sees clearly in accounts that are contemporary with the change in the parts of Europe that exported toward America, how the Anglo's prejudice developed when he deduced a man's nature from his circumstances.
> —Ben Maddow, *A Sunday Between Wars*

> Discussing that period, Maddow writes, "One sees clearly . . . how the Anglo's prejudice developed when he deduced a man's nature from his circumstances" (182).

If the omitted wording is at the *end* of a quoted sentence, include a period, making a four-dot ellipsis (. . . .). Look at the following original and the quotation taken from it:

> Youth is almost a national cult: young love, with its easy solutions and its limited, unsubtle range of emotions, is the prevalent idea. Our heroines are button-nosed dolls; our heroes, overgrown adolescents—Henry Aldriches in their fathers' pants.
> —John Sharnik, "The War of the Generations"

```
The phenomenon was already noticeable in 1956 when John
Sharnik wrote, "Youth is almost a national cult. . . . Our
heroines are button-nosed dolls; our heroes, overgrown
adolescents . . ." (41).
```

Each ellipsis in the example tells readers that the end of the quoted sentence was omitted, something that would not otherwise be obvious. Note: With an ending ellipsis, the period (fourth dot) goes outside the parenthetical citation.

B. *Additions to quotations.* A basic principle for quotations is that everything inside the quotation marks should be from the original source. On some occasions, however, you may need to insert a word or phrase of your own into a quotation (1) for clarity, (2) to smooth the transition into the quotation, or (3) to indicate an error in the source. All such additions must be enclosed in square brackets [ ] and not with parentheses ( ), which are used for other purposes.

In this example the inserted wording helps clarify the pronoun *he* in the original source:

```
As one modern historian has written, "In the safer field
of psychology he [Aristotle] writes more originally and
to the point, and almost creates the study of esthetics,
the theory of beauty and art" (Brandon 284).
```

Sometimes it is necessary to insert a word or to change the tense of a verb in order to fit a quotation into your own sentence. Here the verb *is* in the original is changed to *was* to make the quotation fit its new context:

```
Writing on this issue in 1941, one contemporary
commentator was moved to insist that "there [was]
insufficient time to save democracy merely by persuading
people of its moral soundness" (Ross 454).
```

Use brackets and the Latin abbreviation *sic* ("thus") to tell readers that an error in a quotation was actually in the original. For instance:

```
Smith argues that "the election of Abraham Lincoln in 1850
[sic] was the most crucial presidential choice in
American history" (232).
```

4. *Use block form for long quotations.* If the material you are quoting will take five or more lines in your paper, treat it as a *block quotation,* indenting it and omitting quotation marks. Use such lengthy quotations sparingly, and employ the form illustrated here:

> The order finally came for Japanese Americans to move to the internment camps. One man, a boy of eleven at the time, describes the scene:
> > I also remember the day we had to leave our house and walk to this assembly point at San Mateo and then get on the bus and go to Tanforan which was that racetrack. I remember those posters, all of a sudden on every telephone pole. The posters again made us feel guilty and that we better again stick closely together. We were just fearful. (Tateishi 243)
>
> Many others shared his feelings of confusion and fear during those early months of the war.

Here are the rules for block quotations:

1. Introduce the quotation with some of your own wording followed by a colon.
2. Indent the whole quotation ten spaces from the left margin. If the quoted material begins at the opening of a paragraph in the original, indent the first line in the block quotation fifteen spaces from the left margin.
3. Do not put quotation marks at the beginning and end of a block quotation. Do include quotation marks that were in the original; do not change them to single quotation marks.
4. Double-space within the block quotation.
5. Place the final punctuation *before* the parenthetical citation.

Documenting Sources

Whenever you borrow facts, opinions, ideas, or words from any source, you must acknowledge that source in your paper. If you borrow a chart, diagram, illustration, or a quoted passage, you readily recognize and acknowledge your indebtedness to your source. With paraphrased material, however, it is sometimes easy to forget that although the wording is yours, the facts and ideas you are summarizing are borrowed and must be attributed to their source. The best general principle to follow is that you must acknowledge *every* quotation or paraphrase, no matter what the length. And if you should use the same material at several different places in your paper, you must cite the source each time you use it.

You inform your readers of borrowed material, first of all, by the wording you use to integrate each paraphrase or direct quotation into your text. The second way to signal your use of sources is to employ one of the standard systems of documentation. You may use either internal, parenthetical documentation or notes (either footnotes or endnotes) to indicate your sources of information. Parenthetical documentation cites sources by using brief identifying information within the text itself. In the note system, numbers in the text refer to notes at the bottoms of pages or at the end of the paper, in which your sources of information are acknowledged.

The most widely recognized documentation systems in the sciences and the humanities now use internal citations of sources rather than footnotes or endnotes. This simple and direct style is the one recommended in the 1984 *MLA Handbook* and is the basis for the models in this manual. To use this style, you need give only a minimum of identification for your sources in the text itself, followed at the end of the paper by a list of works cited to provide readers with full bibliographical details.

What to Document

You should provide a source citation for every quotation, for all paraphrased opinions and ideas, and for any facts that are not general (or common) knowledge. You will run into some cases in which it is unclear whether a particular fact requires a citation. Just remember that you need not document the kinds of facts found in standard reference works such as encyclopedias. For example, you don't have to document the fact that the United States entered World War II after the Japanese attacked Pearl Harbor on December 7, 1941, or that Franklin D. Roosevelt was president at the time. You would, however, document less commonly known facts such as details of the Japanese battle plans at Pearl Harbor or the amount of intelligence information Roosevelt may have had prior to the attack. Decisions about whether to cite such facts are often judgment calls and subject to dispute; a good rule is *If in doubt, document.*

Using Parenthetical Citations

The MLA approach to documentation uses brief parenthetical references in the text. Each parenthetical citation should include the minimum amount of information needed (1) to refer readers to the appropriate bibliographical entry in the list of works cited and (2) to enable them to find the source page location of the borrowed material. In most cases the minimum required for a citation will be the author's last name and the appropriate page number or numbers.

If the author's name does not appear in the text itself, include it in the parenthetical citation. For example:

```
Defenders of DDT and other pesticides insisted that
discontinuing their use would inevitably result in a
decrease in the world's food supply and an increase in
diseases (Ehrlich 117).
```

This citation directs readers to the alphabetical list of works cited at the end of the paper, where they would find a full bibliographical entry for *The Population Bomb* by Paul Ehrlich. The page number 117 indicates the exact location of the material being cited. If the source is only one page, omit the page number within the parentheses. For the sake of clarity and accuracy, place the citation as close as possible to the borrowed material, as in the example.

If the author's name appears in the text itself, do not include it in the parenthetical citation. For example:

> Roderick Nash argues that "most American intellectuals followed Dewey's reasoning in attempting to explain how a wrong could so suddenly become a right" (36).

If the author's name is used as part of a general reference to the *whole work* rather than to any particular passage, you do not need a parenthetical citation. For example:

> Roderick Nash analyzes American thought during the period from 1917 to 1930.

Simply include the bibliographical entry for this work by Nash in the list at the end of the paper.

Sometimes the author's name and a page reference will not provide the minimum required for clearly and accurately identifying the source of your information. Although it is not possible to provide examples of all possible variations, the following models illustrate the ones that occur most frequently:

A single article or book in one volume

A single article:

> One analyst has called on telecasters to "be concerned about the damaging impact of unbridled, disreputable advertising on the American government" (Christopher 96).

A book in one volume:

> The authors claim that "a certain amount of tension and stress can, in fact, be healthy" (Patterson, Meadows, and Dreger 200).

With two or three authors, list all the names. With more than three, give the name of the first-listed author, followed by the abbreviation *et al.*

A multivolume work

> In retelling the story of Odysseus and the blinding of the Cyclops, Graves uses the expression "the eyes hissed" to evoke the emotion of the scene (2: 356).

The number before the colon indicates which volume of a multivolume work by Robert Graves is being cited; the number after the colon is the page.

> He begins with the story of Oedipus and concludes with the
> homecoming of Odysseus (Graves, vol. 2).

The reference is to a whole volume of a multivolume series and not to any specific pages.

A work without an author

> A panel of students offered their services to speak to
> clubs, high schools, plants, and other organizations
> about how contemporary college students viewed the world
> ("How it Feels").

For a parenthetical reference to an unsigned work, use the title (or a shortened version if the title is lengthy) and the page number. Because this article is on only one page, omit the page number.

A work with corporate authorship

> A 1968 American Civil Liberties Union report stated that
> secondary school students could best be prepared to
> become good citizens by being given a real chance to
> participate in the life of the school and community (9).

Treat the name of the organization or agency as the author. If the name of the organization is long, work it into the text to avoid a clumsy parenthetical reference.

Two or more works by the same author

> The Blackfoot Indian story of creation begins with the Old
> Man who travels up from the south, making birds and
> animals as he goes (Campbell, The Hero 289–91). Campbell
> argues that the function of ritual is "to give form to
> human life, not in the way of a mere surface arrangement,
> but in depth" (Myths to Live By 43).

If your list of works cited includes more than one work by the same author, you must alert your reader in your parenthetical citation by giving the title as well as the author's last name. If the title is long, use a shortened version. The title of the first work in the example is *The Hero with a Thousand Faces*. As with citations to other works, put the author's name in the parenthetical reference only if it is not mentioned in your text.

More than one work in a single reference

> Of all the groups opposed to reforms in child labor laws
> in the 1930s, two of the most active and vocal were the
> National Association of Manufacturers and the various
> agricultural interests (Lampkin and Douglas 228; Hayhurst
> 160–61).

Use semicolons to separate works when it is necessary to cite more than one work in the same parenthetical reference.

An indirect source

> At one point Woodrow Wilson wrote to Roosevelt to protest the planned "memorial" that made it sound as if Wilson were already dead. He said, "I hope in the near future to give frequent evidences I am not dead" (qtd. in Smith 216).

You should try to take material from the original sources when possible. When you must rely on an indirect source, use the abbreviation *qtd.* in the parenthetical reference. Here the name Smith identifies a biography of President Wilson, in which the original letter is quoted.

Parenthetical Citation in APA Style Like the MLA approach to documentation, the system recommended by the American Psychological Association uses brief parenthetical references in the text to direct readers to a list of sources at the end of the paper. Just as in MLA style, each parenthetical citation should include the minimum amount of information needed (1) to refer readers to the appropriate bibliographical entry in the reference list and (2) enable them to find the exact page location of the material you have borrowed. The most obvious difference between the MLA and APA forms is that the APA system uses what is called the *name-year style*, which includes the year of publication as part of the minimum information in each citation.

The following models illustrate the basic features of documentation in APA style:

When the author's name is not mentioned in the text:

> In 1945 there was a great demand for food worldwide, and DDT, according to its advocates, could "increase production more than any other insecticide" (Davis, 1971, p. 47).

Notice that the citation includes within the parentheses the author's name, the date of publication, and the page number(s) with the abbreviation *p.* or *pp.* as appropriate. The period for the sentence follows the parenthesis.

When the author's name is mentioned in the text:

> Davis (1971) reports that in 1945 there was a great demand for food worldwide, and DDT, according to its advocates, could "increase production more than any other insecticide" (p. 47).

The author's name in the text is followed by the date of the work. The parenthesis at the end includes only the essential information not already given in the text itself.

When the source has two authors:

> The effectiveness of the proposed therapy for new patients has been widely and loudly debated since it was first proposed in 1985 (Williams & Sneed, 1987, p. 348).

With two authors, use both names either in text or parenthetical citation. Notice that an ampersand (&) is used in place of the word *and*.

When the source has three or more authors:

> The proposal for legislative redistricting has been given little chance of passing in any of the state legislatures where it has been introduced (Rankin, Taylor, & Levi, 1978, pp. 142–45).

List all authors in the first citation. Use the abbreviation *et al.* ("and others") in subsequent citations.

> (Rankin et al., 1978)

When the author has more than one source written in the same year:

> The most challenging problem at the outset of the project was met with a strong and united response (Rang, 1974a, p. 3), yet by the final stages almost no one could agree on any common strategy (Rang, 1974b, p. 376).

You avoid confusion by citing each source with a letter designation. Readers will be able to identify the appropriate source in the references easily. The reference list is arranged alphabetically according to authors' last names. When you have several articles by the same author in one year, list them alphabetically by title within the year, designating each with the year and a letter.

At the end of a paper in the MLA style you provide a list of works cited in the text. You provide a similar list when you use APA style, heading it "References." The list is arranged alphabetically by author and treats the titles of anonymous works as if they were the authors' names. The models for the bibliographical forms used on the reference sheet are described on p. 416.

Using Footnotes or Endnotes

Prior to 1984 the *MLA Handbook* recommended footnotes and endnotes for acknowledging sources. Despite its present emphasis on parenthetical citation, the *Handbook* still explains the note system for those who wish to use it. Some writers, for example, believe that footnotes or endnotes are less distracting to readers than parenthetical citations within the text.

To use either footnotes or endnotes, first place a raised numeral in the text at the end of the material you are acknowledging, and continue numbering citations consecutively throughout the paper. For footnotes the citations themselves appear at the bottom of the appropriate pages. Footnotes begin four lines below the text, are single-spaced within each note, and are double-spaced between notes. For endnotes the citations are listed in numerical order on a page at the end of the paper, double-spaced within and between notes. Details concerning the appearance of an endnote page are given in the following section on research paper format.

The format for notes is based on the bibliographical forms you encountered when you wrote bibliography cards. There are, however, some differences:

Bibliography entry

  Sagan, Carl. <u>The Cosmic Connection</u>. New York: Doubleday, 1973.

Footnote form

  [1] Carl Sagan, <u>The Cosmic Connection</u> (New York: Doubleday, 1973) 102.

The bibliographical entry indents the second and subsequent lines five spaces; the footnote indents the first line but not the subsequent lines. Note form places the author's name in normal order, uses commas instead of periods, and puts publication information inside parentheses. The note includes the page number(s) being cited.

The following note models use the same sources as the bibliographical models given earlier. As with the previous models, some types of sources require special information.

Forms for Books

A book by a single author

  [1] Rachel Carson, <u>Silent Spring</u> (Boston: Houghton Mifflin, 1962) 29.

A book by two or three authors

  [2] Barbara Paterson, Nancy Meadows, and Carol Dreger, <u>The Successful Woman</u> (Englewood Cliffs: Prentice-Hall, 1982) 64-68.

A book with more than three authors

  [3] Albert C. Baugh et al., <u>A Literary History of England</u> (New York: Appleton, 1948) 239-42.

A book with corporate authorship

    [4] American Humane Association, <u>Child Abuse Legislation in the 1970's</u> (Denver: American Humane Association, 1970) 12–13.

A book with no author given

    [5] <u>Virginia: The Old Dominion in Pictures</u> (New York: Fleming, 1941) 3.

A book with an author and an editor

    [6] Edgar Allan Poe, <u>Selected Writings of Edgar Allan Poe</u>, ed. Edward H. Davidson (Boston: Houghton Mifflin, 1956) 131–33.

A book with an editor

    [7] Victor H. Denenberg, ed., <u>Education of the Infant and Young Child</u> (New York: Academic P, 1970) 67.

A preface, introduction, foreword, or afterword

    [8] James J. Storrow Jr., introduction, <u>The State of the Nation</u>, ed. David Boroff (Englewood Cliffs: Prentice-Hall, 1965) vi–vii.

A later edition

    [9] William L. Heward and Michael D. Orlansky, <u>Exceptional Children</u>, 2nd ed. (Columbus: Charles Merrill, 1984) 123–26.

A work in more than one volume

    [10] Richard B. Sewell, <u>The Life of Emily Dickinson</u>, 2 vols. (New York: Farrar, Strauss & Giroux, 1944) 2: 236.

A book in a series

    [11] John Middleton, ed., <u>Myth and Cosmos: Readings in Mythology and Symbolism</u>, American Museum Sourcebooks in Anthropology (Garden City: Natural History P, 1967) 66.

A republished work

    [12] Konrad Z. Lorenz, <u>King Solomon's Ring</u> (1952: New York: Time, 1962) 98–99.

A translation

    [13] Homer, <u>The Iliad</u>, trans. Richmond Lattimore (Chicago: U of Chicago P, 1951) 122.

A selection from an edited anthology

> [14] Richard Schlegel, "Time and Thermodynamics," <u>The Voices of Time</u>, ed. J.T. Fraser (New York: Braziller, 1966) 522.

Reference works

> [15] Philip N. Powers, "Nuclear Power," <u>Encyclopaedia Britannica: Macropaedia</u>, 1974 ed.

Pamphlets, brochures, and manuals

> [16] <u>Franklin Ace 1000 User Reference Manual</u> (Cherry Hill, N.J.: Franklin Computer Corp., 1983) 29–31.

Government documents

> [17] United States, Committee on Economic Security, <u>Social Security in America</u>, Social Security Board Pub. Number 20 (Washington, D.C.: GPO, 1937) 10.

Forms for Periodicals

Article in journal with continuous pagination throughout the annual volume

> [18] Kenneth Keniston, "Alienation and the Decline of Utopia," <u>American Scholar</u> 39 (1960) 162.

Article in journal with pages numbered separately throughout the annual volume

> [19] M. C. Macklin and R. H. Kolbe, "Sex Role Stereotyping in Children's Advertising: Current and Past Trends," <u>Journal of Advertising</u> 13.2 (1984) 35.

An article in a monthly or bimonthly magazine

> [20] John K. Lageman, "If Robots Run the Works," <u>Nation's Business</u> Mar. 1951: 32–33.

An article in a weekly or biweekly magazine

> [21] "Pesticides: The Price for Progress," <u>Time</u> 28 Sept. 1962: 45.

> [22] Irwin Edman, "Mind and Matter," <u>New Yorker</u> 14 Oct. 1950: 140.

A newspaper article

> [23] Patrick Connolly, "Up, Up and Away: Flying Without Jitters," <u>Nashville Tennessean</u> 21 Dec. 1986: F1.

An editorial or letter to the editor

> [24] "A Fine Play Reveals a Need," editorial, <u>Life</u> 18 May 1959: 42.

[25] Gerald Jonas, "DDT in Dry Cleaning," letter, <u>New York Times</u> 26 July 1972: 26.

A review

[26] Stefan Kanfer, "Feather Complex," rev. of <u>S. J. Perelman: A Life</u>, by Dorothy Herrman, <u>Time</u> 13 Oct. 1986: 100.

Forms for Other Sources

Unpublished dissertations and theses

[27] Daryl E. Jones, "The Dime Novel Western: The Evolution of a Popular Formula," diss., Michigan State U, 1974: 68–69.

Plays, concerts, performances

[28] <u>Doubles</u>, by Neil Simon, with Gabe Kaplan and Martin Milner, Tennessee Performing Arts Center, Nashville, 16 Dec. 1986.

Recordings

[29] Bruce Springsteen, <u>Born in the U.S.A.</u>, Columbia, QC 38653, 1984.

Interviews

[30] Robert Penn Warren, personal interview, 8 April 1966.

Unpublished letters

[31] Robert Parham, letter, 6 July 1971.

Lectures and speeches

[32] E. H. Duncan, class lecture, Vanderbilt U, Nashville, 20 Oct. 1965.

Computer software

[33] <u>Mass Production Unit</u>, computer software, Micorp, 1985, MS-DOS, 256 KB, disk.

Subsequent References to the Same Source

Use the full documentation form the *first* time you cite a source in a note. All later notes to the same source can use a shortened form. As with parenthetical references, you should give the minimum information needed to allow readers to find your source in the list of works cited and to know the exact page(s) you are citing. In most instances the last name of the author and the page number(s) will suffice.

> [34] Carson 125–27.

If you use two or more works by the same author, the minimum requirement for accuracy and clarity will be the name and title.

> [35] Campbell, <u>The Hero</u> 222.
>
> [36] Campbell, <u>Myths to Live By</u> 23–26.

Use a title when no author is given.

> [37] "Pesticides: The Price for Progress" 45.

Repeat the information even when the succeeding note is to the same source.

> [38] Macklin and Kolbe 34.
>
> [39] Macklin and Kolbe 35–36.

Preparing the Finished Copy

When you have completed drafting and revising the text of your research paper, you will want to prepare a final manuscript that does justice to your efforts. The suggestions on formatting given here will help give your manuscript the look you want it to have:

1. Type your paper on 8½-by-11-inch white paper.
2. Do not use script or any other nonstandard typeface. Avoid using erasable paper, which, despite its convenience in typing, tends to smudge and leave ink on readers' fingers.
3. Unless your instructor tells you to use a plastic binder or other folder for your paper, just staple it in the upper left corner or paper clip it.
4. Make corrections neatly by typing them in or writing them in ink. Avoid making corrections in the margins of your paper, and if corrections are numerous, retype the page.

The Sections of the Paper

The following are the sections of a research paper in the order they occur in the finished manuscript:

1. *Title Page* If your instructor requires a separate title page for your paper, include three pieces of information on the page: the title, your name, and the course identification called for by your instructor. Type the title about a third of the way down the page, then your name, then course

> Laurie Wheeler
> Professor Earnest
> Eng. 102-4
> April 25, 1986
>
> <u>Silent Spring</u> and the Banning of DDT
>
> In 1962, Rachel Carson's book <u>Silent Spring</u> stimulated a complacent public to consider seriously the connection between pesticides and public health.

FIGURE 12

information. Center each line and leave space between items to create a balanced appearance. See the sample research paper for an example of a title page.

If your instructor does not call for a separate title page, follow the recommendations in the *MLA Handbook* and place identifying information at the top of the first page of text as illustrated below in Figure 12.

2. Formal Outline If your instructor requires a formal outline with your finished paper, place it between the title page and the first page of text. The formal outline should include the thesis of your paper and the outline itself. Number the pages of the outline in lowercase Roman numerals in the upper right-hand corner of the page, one-half inch from the top of the page. Precede the page number with your last name, a bit of insurance in case the pages become separated. Center the word *Outline* one inch from the top of the page. Double space throughout the outline. (See sample research paper.)

The sentence outline you used in writing your paper can serve as the formal outline in the finished copy. Check it to make sure that it accurately reflects any changes you made in drafting your text. Your instructor may prefer that you submit a *topic outline*, using brief phrases rather than whole sentences. In that case, you can easily prepare a topic outline by substituting phrases for the sentence headings. Keep in mind two points: (1) Each topic heading must be clear to someone who has not already read your

```
                                                        Wheeler i
                              Outline
Thesis:  The publication of Rachel Carson's Silent Spring in
         1962 helped reverse public acceptance of DDT and
         initiated a chain reaction that eventually led to
         the banning of the pesticide in the United States.

    I.  Carson's motivations for book
        A.  Animals' deaths from DDT
        B.  Four years of research
   II.  Book's bleak picture
        A.  Fictional dying town
        B.  Descriptions of actual cases
  III.  DDT's previous good reputation
        A.  Disease control in WWII
        B.  Postwar disease control and food production
        C.  Wider use in 1960s
   IV.  Critical reaction to book
        A.  Attacks by pesticide industry
        B.  Accusations of fright tactics
        C.  Charges by government officials
    V.  Effects of book
        A.  Investigations, reactions
            1.  Government
            2.  Private
        B.  Warnings confirmed
            1.  Agriculture Department and Public Health
                Service
            2.  Science Advisory Committee
   VI.  Reforms
        A.  Slow change
        B.  EPA ban
```

FIGURE 13

paper. (2) The headings within each level—Roman numeral, capital letter, Arabic numeral—must be grammatically parallel. For example, if point A is a prepositional phrase, points B and C and so on must also be prepositional phrases.

The example in Figure 13 shows the sentence outline from Laurie Wheeler's paper as it would appear after being converted to topic form.

3. The Text of the Paper In papers with a separate title page, the first page of text begins with the title of the paper centered one inch from the top of the page. Use one-inch margins on all sides of the pages throughout the text. Use Arabic numerals for page numbers and place them in the upper right corner, one-half inch from the top. As in the outline, precede the page number with your last name. Type the text of the paper double-spaced throughout, including block quotations.

Tables, charts, illustrations If you plan to include a table in your text, when you reach the place in the text where you want the table to appear, begin with the words *Table 1* (for the first table), typed flush with the left margin of the page. Double-space and type a caption or title line for the table, not underlined or in quotation marks. Follow with the table itself, double-spaced throughout. Give the source of the table under it, flush with the left margin.

Table 1

Female Percentage of the Labor Force:
Soviet Union and the United States, 1957

	Soviet Union	United States
Total	53	32
Major types of employment:		
Industry	45	26
Construction	31	3
Agriculture	59	19
Transportation and communication	32	18
Trade and supply	65	39
Government and administration	51	27

Source: Joint Economic Committee, Congress of the United States, <u>Comparisons of the United States and Soviet Economies</u> (1959).

To include drawings, graphs, maps, or photographs, place the item on the page near the section of the text that refers to it. Under the illustration, type *Figure 1* (for the first illustration), flush with the left margin of the page, followed by caption or title and the source.

Fig. 1. Etana Flying to Heaven. From a cylinder seal formerly in the collection of Lord Southesk. Rpt. in Theodore H. Gaster, <u>The Oldest Stories in the World</u> (Boston: Beacon P, 1952) 79.

4. Endnotes If you are not using parenthetical documentation, place all of the notes for your paper in a separate section at the end of your text. (Your instructor may prefer footnotes, with the notes placed at the bottoms of the pages in the text.) Number the endnote page in sequence with the preceding page of text, placing your last name and the page number in the upper right corner. Type the word *Notes* one inch from the top of the page, centered. Then double-space, indent five spaces from the left margin, and begin the first note by typing the number 1, elevated halfway above the line level. Using the models for footnotes/endnotes given in the section on documentation, list the notes consecutively, double-spacing within and between them. Figure 14 shows how Laurie Wheeler's paper would look if she had used endnotes rather than parenthetical citations.

Supplementary endnotes with parenthetical documentation Even if you use parenthetical documentation, you may find you need some notes to provide readers with information that doesn't fit very well into the text itself. You might wish to add background, provide interesting sidelights, note exceptions, or list additional references. You can place such informative notes at the bottom of the pages to which they refer, or put all of them on an endnote page as the Wheeler paper does. (Wheeler used only one supplementary note in her paper.)

5. List of Works Cited Your list of works cited should include a bibliographical entry for each work you have cited in a parenthetical note (or

> typhus, and dysentery and typhoid fever respectively. DDT was also a tremendous aid in food production. In 1945 there was a great demand for food worldwide and DDT, according to its advocates, could "increase production more than any other insecticide."[4] Muller was awarded the Nobel Prize in Medicine for DDT in 1948, further attesting to the high status accorded the chemical. By 1950 the use of DDT had saved millions of lives that would have been lost to malaria and starvation worldwide.[5] Its use

---

> Notes
>
> [1] Rachel Carson, Silent Spring (Boston: Houghton Mifflin, 1962) 1.
>
> [2] Carson 2.
>
> [3] Carson 1–3.
>
> [4] Kenneth S. Davis, "Deadly Dust: The Unhappy History of DDT," American Heritage 22.2 (1971) 47.
>
> [5] Davis 44–47.

FIGURE 14

footnote/endnote if you used that system). If you also list other works you read even though you did not specifically cite them, use the title *Works Consulted*. In the upper right corner continue the pagination from the preceding page, one-half inch from the top of the page. Type *Works Cited* (or *Works Consulted*) one inch from the top, centered; then double-space before the first entry. Arrange all entries alphabetically according to the author's last name, using the same bibliography forms you used in preparing your bibliography cards. For a work with no author given, alphabetize by the first important word in the title (not counting the words *a*, *an*, and *the*). If you cite more than one work by the same author, give the name in the first entry only. In subsequent entries, in place of the author's name, type three hyphens and a period. Then skip two spaces and begin the title. Start the first line of each entry flush with the left margin. Indent any additional lines in the entry five spaces. Double-space within and between entries. The Wheeler paper illustrates the form of a list of works cited.

A Sample Research Paper Using MLA Parenthetical Documentation

Silent Spring and the Banning of DDT

By
Laurie Wheeler
English 102-04
Professor Earnest
April 25, 1986

Outline

Thesis: The publication of Rachel Carson's <u>Silent Spring</u> in 1962 helped reverse public acceptance of DDT and initiated a chain reaction that eventually led to the banning of the pesticide in the United States.

I. Rachel Carson began the book after seeing the results of DDT use.
   A. In 1958 Carson saw animals killed by DDT.
   B. Following a friend's urging, Carson spent four years doing research on pesticide use.
II. Carson's book painted a bleak picture of America's future with DDT.
   A. Carson described a hypothetical town dying from pesticide use.
   B. Carson based all the descriptions on actual cases.
III. DDT had long been used with high public regard.
   A. DDT played an important role in disease control in WWII.
   B. After the war DDT continued to be used to control disease and to raise food production.
   C. DDT continued with ever-wider use into the

1960s.

IV. Carson's discussion of the negative effects of DDT produced immediate and extensive criticism.
   A. _Silent Spring_ was attacked by the pesticide industry.
   B. Carson was accused of trying to frighten readers.
   C. Some government officials called Carson an alarmist.

V. _Silent Spring_ changed attitudes and stimulated inquiry about DDT.
   A. Carson's descriptions stimulated questions and investigations.
      1. Government agencies began new tests and sought increased budgets.
      2. Private groups and writers turned their attention to the topic.
   B. Investigative results confirmed Carson's warnings.
      1. The Agriculture Department and Public Health Service confirmed severe health hazards of DDT.
      2. The Science Advisory Committee urged immediate cutback and elimination of the use of DDT.

VI. The investigations led to major reforms.
   A. The changes came slowly.
   B. The EPA finally banned DDT 10 years after *Silent Spring*.

Wheeler 1

<u>Silent Spring</u> and the Banning of DDT

    In 1962, Rachel Carson's book <u>Silent Spring</u> stimulated a complacent public to consider seriously the connection between pesticides and public health. <u>Silent Spring</u> was the first major public attack on DDT and other pesticides. By the early sixties DDT was the most commonly known and widely used pesticide in the world, and Carson's book was the first step in a chain reaction which led to its banning in the United States. The general public received a preview of <u>Silent Spring</u> when three issues of <u>The New Yorker</u> ran excerpts from the book before it was published in October of 1962. Carson's book argued that the use of DDT and other pesticides was killing wildlife, polluting the environment, and creating the possibility of extinction for the human race.

    It was a direct personal experience with the effects of DDT that prompted Rachel Carson to write <u>Silent Spring</u>. At the beginning of 1958, Carson received a letter from her friend Olga Huckins describing the effects of a recent DDT spraying on her bird sanctuary. Carson visited her friend and witnessed a spraying of DDT for mosquito control during her visit. The sight of the dead and dying birds and fish on her friend's property after the spraying appalled Carson. Huckins even suggested to Carson that she write about this serious problem (Davis 47+). Carson, after witnessing first hand the severity of the problem, followed her friend's suggestion. For four years after that visit Rachel researched the pesticide situation and then wrote her famous book.

In the first chapter of <u>Silent Spring</u>, entitled "A Fable for Tomorrow," Carson tells the story of a hypothetical American town "where all life seemed to live in harmony with its surroundings" (1). Then Carson reports that "a strange blight crept over the area and everything began to change" (2). The livestock died, and several townspeople became sick and died as well. The birds disappeared, and the streams no longer contained fish. The roadsides no longer were lined with flowers, and barren ground replaced plentiful crops. Carson determined that the townspeople's use of pesticides caused the mishaps. Even though the town presented did not exist on a map, Carson demonstrated that each incident she used to create the town had actually occurred in various places in the world (1-3).

Pesticides had been used for many years before <u>Silent Spring</u> was written, though. A 1971 <u>American Heritage</u> article, "Deadly Dust: The Unhappy History of DDT," describes the previous uses of the pesticide. DDT (dichlorodiphenyltrichloroethane) dates back to 1874 when a German student, Othmar Zeidler, synthesized it as an exercise in pure chemistry. DDT was synthesized again in 1939 by Dr. Paul Herman Muller, an employee at the time of the dye-manufacturing firm of J. R. Geigy, S.A., of Basel. Muller later discovered DDT's potential as an insecticide, and Geigy patented the DDT formula in 1940. Patent descriptions were sent to Geigy's branches in Britain and the United States in early 1942, and wide distribution of DDT began. The insecticide was widely used in World War II for disease control. DDT was effective against mosquitos, body lice, and houseflies, which carried malaria, typhus, and dysentery and typhoid fever respectively. DDT was also a tremendous aid in food production. In 1945 there was a great demand for food worldwide and DDT, according to its advocates, could "increase production more than any other insecticide" (Davis 47). Muller was awarded a Nobel Prize in Medicine for DDT in 1948, further attesting to the high status accorded the chemical. By 1950, the use of DDT had saved millions of lives that would have been lost to malaria and starvation worldwide (Davis 44-47). Its use continued into the 1960s, and by then, DDT was even being used in a mothproofing solution by dry cleaners in New York (Jonas).[1]

Rachel Carson did not write another celebration of DDT and the other pesticides that the world had become so thankful for, though. She chose to write about the unpublicized, harmful side of pesticide use, and the result for Silent Spring was a tremendous amount of criticism. An article in the New York Times, "'Silent Spring' Is Now Noisy Summer," voiced the criticism of the pesticide industry: "The industry feels that she has presented a one-sided case and has chosen to ignore the enormous benefits . . . from the development and use of modern pesticides" (Lee 11). John Lee, the author of the article, reported that the pesticide makers were "crying foul" (1). An article in Time magazine carried the charge that "Miss Carson has taken up her pen in alarm and anger [against pesticides], putting literary skill second to the task of frightening and arousing her readers" ("Pesticides: The Price for Progress" 45). The Business Week article "Are We Poisoning Ourselves?" reported, "Government officials . . . regard Miss Carson's presentation as somewhat alarmist . . ." (36). Many people were vocal in their reactions to Carson's negative view of pesticides.

Even though most of Silent Spring's reception was negative, the book still managed to have a positive result. The compelling arguments of Carson's book caused people who knew little about DDT and other pesticides to start asking questions. Everyone seemed to be demanding answers. Government agencies and local groups alike began taking action. The FDA began testing three times as many products as it had before for pesticide residues. The USDA quickly requested a $250,000 increase to strengthen pesticide control and asked Congress for stronger control legislation. Pesticides became the main topic at garden club meetings, and Rachel Carson reported that she was receiving enormous numbers of letters telling of action taken by small-town groups to defend their communities from further negligent pesticide use. Many pamphlets and magazine articles appeared debating the general issue of pesticide use ("Pesticides: Attack and Counterattack" 39). The majority of these debates focused directly on DDT.

All the effort being expended on trying to discover the extent of problems Carson had pointed out seemed promising. Results from DDT testings were made public, and scientists continued to draw their own conclusions about the pesticide, conclusions which were similar to Carson's as to the detrimental effects of widespread DDT use. The Department of Agriculture and the U.S. Public Health Service willingly acknowledged that some insecticides were not only toxic to insects, but to man as well ("Pesticides: The Price for Progress" 45). DDT was one of those insecticides. In 1963, Dr. William C. H. Huper of the National Cancer Institute determined that DDT was "cancer producing according to presently available evidence," and he accused DDT of causing "production of benign and malignant tumors of the liver, cancers of the lung, and leukemias" (qtd. in Davis 93). In the same year, President Kennedy's Science Advisory Committee urged a cutback of DDT use "with a view to its total elimination as quickly as possible" (Davis 93).

Even though statements like these were being made in the wake of Silent Spring in the early 1960s, DDT's use continued into the 1970s, and so the process of reducing DDT use was a very slow one. In "A Celebration of Silent Spring," Kevin Shea makes a similar point: "In spite of the public furor brought on by its publication," Shea reasons, "Silent Spring did not cause a stampede to reform the use and control of pesticides" (4). It is true that Silent Spring did not cause an immediate change in the regulation and control of pesticides, but it did have a very definite effect on the issue. Carson brought attention to a subject that was not widely known; everyone had heard of the lifesaving role that DDT played, but few were aware that this miracle pesticide was also a killer in disguise. So much emphasis was put on the usefulness of DDT that hardly any testing was done for long-range side effects until <u>Silent Spring</u> was published. Carson opened the public's eyes to a growing problem that was simply going unnoticed. Without <u>Silent Spring</u> it is difficult to imagine how much longer it would have taken for the DDT problem to be openly acknowledged and ultimately solved.

Finally, the solution to the DDT problem was initiated; the Environmental Protection Agency ordered an almost total ban on DDT, which became effective as of December 31, 1972. There were three exceptions to the ban. The first allowed DDT to be used in case of a sudden epidemic caused by disease-carrying insects. The second allowed DDT to be used in certain locations on onions, green peppers, and sweet potatoes. The third allowed DDT to be exported to other countries ("Verdict on DDT"). These exceptions were slight, so as far as America was concerned the war against DDT was won. Carson should be given the credit for the victory because she realized the problem with DDT and other pesticides early and tried to do something about it. <u>Silent Spring</u> was her successful attempt to make the pesticide problem known. An article in <u>Time</u> magazine which appeared after the EPA ban characterized the status DDT had once had and acknowledged Rachel Carson's pivotal role in its banning:

> When DDT first appeared in the U.S. in 1942, it seemed almost like a miracle drug. Cheap and efficient, it destroyed pests, reduced such insect-borne diseases as malaria, and brought bumper harvests. But over the years scientists found disturbing evidence, first publicized in Rachel Carson's <u>Silent Spring</u>, that DDT was harmful to animals too, and might threaten man as well. ("Verdict on DDT" 43)

The EPA did, in fact, find DDT harmful enough to ban it, and it is fair to say that <u>Silent Spring</u> was the first step in a ten-year effort to awaken a country to its peril.

Note

[1] Gerald Jonas was curious and concerned about the use of DDT in dry cleaning establishments. In a 1962 letter to the *New York Times*, Jonas voices his curiosity. He states, "When I called one distributor of the mothproofing product to ask what strength the DDT solution was he told me it was none of my business and hung up."

Works Cited

"Are We Poisoning Ourselves?" *Business Week* 8 Sept. 1962: 36+.

Carson, Rachel Louis. *Silent Spring*. Boston: Houghton Mifflin, 1962.

Davis, Kenneth S. "Deadly Dust: The Unhappy History of DDT." *American Heritage* 22.2 (1971): 44–47+.

Jonas, Gerald. "Letters to the Times: DDT in Dry Cleaning." *New York Times* 26 July 1962, 26:5.

Lee, John M. "'Silent Spring' Is Now Noisy Summer." *New York Times* 22 July 1962, sec. 3: 1+.

"Pesticides: Attack and Counterattack." *Consumer Reports* 28 (1963): 37–39.

"Pesticides: The Price for Progress." *Time* 28 Sept. 1962: 45–46+.

Shea, Kevin P. "A Celebration of *Silent Spring*." *Environment* 15 (1973): 4–5.

"Verdict on DDT." *Time* 26 June 1972: 43.

ACKNOWLEDGMENTS

p. 11: Abridged from Michael H. Moskow, "Government in the Lead," in *Corporate Lib: Women's Challenge to Management*, ed. by Eli Ginzberg and Alice M. Yohalme. Reprinted by permission of Johns Hopkins University Press.

p. 56: From Peter Singer, "All Animals Are Equal," from *Philosophic Exchange* 1 (1977). Reprinted by permission of the author and publisher.

p. 79: "The Younger Generation" Copyright 1951 Time Inc. All rights reserved. Reprinted by permission from *TIME*.

p. 92. From "Are Today's Young a Disillusioned Generation?" *U.S. News & World Report* (January 23, 1984) p. 40. Reprinted by permission of the publisher.

p. 92: From Joseph N. Bell, "Silence on Campus," *Harper's* 252 (March 1976). Reprinted by permission of the publisher.

p. 105: From Jeff Greenfield, "Boob Rubes," reprinted from the *Columbia Journalism Review* (Sept/Oct) © 1975. Reprinted by permission of the author and publisher.

p. 136: From "A Question of Questionable Meanings," in *Life*, April 18, 1955. Reprinted by permission of the publisher.

p. 137: From "Rock & Roll: A Frenzied Teenage Craze Kicks Up a Big Fuss," in *Life*, April 18, 1955. Used by permission of the publisher.

p. 137: From "Rock-and-Roll Called 'Communicable Disease'." Reprinted with permission of United Press International, Copyright 1956.

p. 138: From "White Council vs. Rock and Roll," *Newsweek*, April 23, 1956, p. 32. Copyright 1956 by Newsweek, Inc. All rights reserved. Reprinted by permission of the publisher.

p. 139: From Jack Gould, "Elvis Presley/Lack of Responsibility Is Shown by TV in Exploiting Teen-Agers," September 16, 1956. Copyright 1956 by The New York Times Company. Reprinted by permission.

p. 141: From "Television Mailbag: Mr. Presley," September 23, 1956. Copyright 1956 by The New York Times Company. Reprinted by permission.

p. 143: From George Marek, "It Isn't All Junk." Copyright © 1956, reprinted from *Good Housekeeping*. Used by permission.

p. 145: From "The War of the Generations," by John Sharnik. *House and Garden*, October 1956. Courtesy *House & Garden*. Copyright 1956 (renewed 1984) by The Conde Nast Publications, Inc.

p. 148: From Milton Bracker, "Experts Propose Study of 'Craze'," February 23, 1957. Copyright 1957 by The New York Times Company. Reprinted by permission.

p. 150: From Dorothy Barclay, "British Expert Unrocked by Current Music Trend," March 1, 1957. Copyright 1957 by The New York Times Company. Reprinted by permission.

p. 151: From Gertrude Samuels, "Why They Rock 'n' Roll—And Should They?" January 12, 1958. Copyright 1958 by The New York Times Company. Reprinted by permission.

p. 156: From "Editorially Speaking," *Music Journal*, February 1958, p. 3. Reprinted by permission of the publisher.

p. 158: From "Rock 'n' Roll Stabbing." Reprinted with permission of United Press International, Copyright 1958.

p. 159: From "Rock 'n' Riot," Copyright 1958 Time Inc. All rights reserved. Reprinted by permission from *TIME*.

p. 160: From "Your Kids Dig That Crazy Music, Too?" Reprinted with permission from *Changing Times* Magazine, © 1959 Kiplinger Washington Editors, Inc., February 1959. This reprint is not to be altered in any way, except with permission from *Changing Times*.

p. 163: From "R & R Still Beams Plenty of Life," *Billboard* (January 18, 1960), pp. 6, 18. Reprinted by permission of the publisher.

p. 164: From "Rock 'n' Roll's Global Wane," *Variety* (March 2, 1960). pp. 55, 57. Reprinted by permission of the publisher.

p. 170: From Robin L. Bartlett, Charles Poulton-Callahan, and Patricia Somers, "What's Holding Women Back?" *Management World* (November 1982). Reprinted by permission of the publisher.

p. 175: From Alice G. Sargent, "Women and Men Working Together: Toward Androgyny," Copyright 1983, *Training and Development Journal*, American Society for Training and Development. Reprinted with permission. All rights reserved.

p. 180: From Michael Evan Gold, "The Case for Comparable Worth." This article first appeared in *The Humanist* issue of May/June 1986 and is reprinted by permission.

p. 187: From Matina Horner, "A Bright Woman is Caught in a Double Bind," reprinted with permission from *Psychology Today* Magazine. Copyright © 1969 American Psychological Association.

p. 193: From Suzanne Gordon, "The New Corporate Feminism," *Nation* 236 (February 5, 1983), p. 129. Copyright 1983 by The Nation Company, Inc. Reprinted by permission of the publisher.

p. 202: From Robert Ardrey, *African Genesis*. Copyright © 1961 Literat S.A. Reprinted with the permission of Atheneum Publishers.

p. 205: From Desmond Morris, *The Naked Ape*. Copyright © 1967 by McGraw-Hill Book Company. Reprinted by permission of the publisher.

p. 211: From Ashley Montagu, *Man and Aggression*, Second Edition. Copyright © 1968, 1973 by Ashley Montagu. Reprinted by permission of Oxford University Press, Inc.

p. 214: Adapted from Richard E. Leakey and Roger Lewin, *Origins*. Copyright © 1977 by Richard E. Leakey and Roger Lewin. Reprinted by permission of the publisher, E. P. Dutton, a division of NAL Penguin, Inc.

p. 221: From Nancy Tanner, *On Becoming Human*. Copyright 1981 Cambridge University Press. Reprinted by permission of the publisher.

p. 223: From Glynn Isaac, "The Food-Sharing Behavior of Protohuman Hominids," Copyright © 1978 by *Scientific American*, Inc. All rights reserved. Reprinted by permission.

p. 237: From James Rachels, "Do Animals Have a Right To Life?" in *Ethics and Animals*, ed. Harlan B. Miller and William H. Williams. Reprinted by permission of Humana Press and the author.

p. 241: From Michael Fox, "'Animal Liberation': A Critique," *Ethics* 88 (1978), pp. 111–13, 118. Copyright © 1978 by The University of Chicago Press. Reprinted by permission of The University of Chicago Press and the author.

p. 244: From Thomas L. Benson, "The Clouded Mirror: Animal Stereotypes and Human Cruelty," *Ethics and Animals*, ed. Harlan B. Miller and William H. Williams. Reprinted by permission of Humana Press and the author.

p. 255: From Tom Regan, *The Case for Animal Rights*, pp. 364–69. © 1983 The Regents of the University of California. Used by permission of the publisher, University of California Press.

p. 259: From Michael E. Levin, "Philosophical Vegetarianism: Con and Pro." This article first appeared in *The Humanist* issue of July/August 1977 and is reprinted by permission.

p. 266: From Paula Fass, *The Damned and the Beautiful: American Youth in the 1920's*. Copyright © 1977 by Oxford University Press, Inc. Reprinted by permission.

p. 273: From Irwin Ross, "What They Really Think, And Why," Copyright © 1941 by *Harper's* Magazine. All rights reserved. Reprinted from the January issue by special permission.

p. 278: From Reuel Denney, "American Youth Today: A Bigger Cast, A Wider Screen," in "Youth: Change and Challenge," *Daedalus*, Vol. 91, No. 1, winter 1962, pp. 124–144. Reprinted by permission of *Daedalus*, Journal of the American Academy of Arts and Sciences.

p. 286: From Tad Szulc, "Youth in America," in *Innocents At Home: America in the 1970's*. Copyright © 1974 by Tad Szulc. Reprinted by permission of Viking Penguin, Inc.

p. 289: From Rolf A. Weil, "College Youth Attitudes Today," reprinted from *School & Society*, April 1971. Copyright 1971 by the Society for the Advancement of Education.

p. 293: From "Now, the Self-Centered Generation," Copyright 1974 Time, Inc. All rights reserved. Reprinted by permission from *TIME*.

p. 296: From David Wank, "Who Are We? A Self-Portrait of College Students Today," *Ms.*, October, 1984, pp. 62–66. Reprinted by permission of the author.

p. 306: From *I Can Sell You Anything* by Carl P. Wrighter. Copyright © 1972 by Ballantine Books, Inc. Reprinted by permission of Ballantine Books, a Division of Random House, Inc.

p. 315: "It's Natural! It's Organic! Or Is It?," Copyright © 1980 by Consumers Union of the United States Incorporated, Mt. Vernon NY 10550. Reprinted by permission from *Consumer Reports*, June 1980.

p. 320: From Maurine Christopher, "When TV Ads Become Disreputable." Reprinted with permission from *Advertising Age*, November 5, 1984. Copyright Crain Communications, Inc. All rights reserved.

p. 323: From Frank McConnell, "Ads & Addictions: Booze on the Tube," *Commonweal*, 110 (December 16, 1983), pp. 689–92. Reprinted by permission of the publisher.

p. 327: From *The Image Makers* by William Meyers. Reprinted by permission of Times Books, a Division of Random House, Inc.

p. 333: From "Advertising Says, 'Let Us Feel Good About Ourselves'," reprinted from *U.S. News & World Report* issue of January 28, 1985. Copyright 1985 U.S. News & World Report.

p. 338: "A Rose for Emily," Copyright 1930 and renewed 1958 by William Faulkner. Reprinted from *Collected Stories of William Faulkner* by permission of Random House, Inc.

p. 345: From "An Interpretation of 'A Rose for Emily'," in *Understanding Fiction*, Third Edition, pp. 227–231. © 1979. Reprinted by permission of Prentice Hall, Inc., Englewood Cliffs, New Jersey.

p. 355: From Jack Scherting, "Emily Grierson's Oedipus Complex: Motif, Motive, and Meaning in Faulkner's 'A Rose for Emily'," in *Studies in Short Fiction*, 1980, pp. 397–405. Reprinted by permission.

p. 362: From Judith Fetterly, *The Resisting Reader*, pp. 34–45. Copyright © 1978. Reprinted by permission of Indiana University Press.

p. 369: From T. J. Stafford, "Tobe's Significance in 'A Rose for Emily'," in *Modern Fiction Studies*. Copyright © 1968 by Purdue Research Foundation, West Lafayette IN 47907. Reprinted with permission.

p. 381: From Robert Crossman, "How Readers Make Meaning," in *College Literature 9*, (1982), pp. 207–214. Reprinted by permission of *College Literature* and the author.

p. 456: From Laurie Wheeler, "DDT Banning: The Result of Silent Spring," reprinted by permission of the author.

Index of Authors, Titles, and Terms

A

Acknowledging sources. *See* Documentation of sources
"Ads & Addictions: Booze on the Tube" (McConnell), 323–327
"Advertising Says, 'Let Us Feel Good About Ourselves'" (Schudson), 333–335
"All Animals Are Equal" (Singer), 56–61
America: History and Life, 405
"American Youth Today: A Bigger Cast, A Wider Screen" (Denney), 278–286
"Animal Rights Evaluated" (Levin), 259–263
"Animals Do Not Have Moral Rights" (Fox), 241–244
Annotation of sources, 18–23. *See also* Marking significant details
APA documentation. *See* Documentation of sources
Ardrey, Robert, 202–205
"Atmosphere and Theme in Faulkner's 'A Rose for Emily'" (West), 349–354
Attribution of sources, 37, 50, 130–134, 433–435
Audience, consideration of, 5
 in individual projects, 5, 38, 54, 76–77, 103, 123
Author background in previewing strategy, 7–8

B

Barclay, Dorothy, 150–151
Bartlett, Robin L., 170–175
Benson, Thomas L., 244–245
Bibliographies, library research and, 396–417
Bibliography cards, 407–408, 422
"Boob Rubes: The New Ruralism in Advertising" (Greenfield), 105–107
Book review indexes, 406
Books:
 footnote or endnote entries for, 444–446, 452–453
 indexes to, 399–401, 405–406
 in lists of sources, 409–413, 416
"Boston, New Haven Ban 'Rock' Shows" (*New York Times*), 158–159

Bracker, Milton, 148–149
Brackets, 71–72, 437
"Bright Woman Is Caught in a Double Bind, A" (Horner), 187–193
"British Expert Unrocked by Current Music Trend" (Barclay), 150–151
Brooks, Cleanth, 345–348

C

"Cain's Children" (Ardrey), 202–205
Card catalog, 399–401
"Case for Comparable Worth, The" (Gold), 180–183
"Change and Stability: Youth in the 1920's" (Fass), 266–273
Christopher, Maurine, 320–323
"Clouded Mirror, The: Animal Stereotypes and Human Cruelty" (Benson), 244–255
"College Youth Attitudes Today" (Weil), 289–292
"Comparable Worth: Unfair to Men and Women" (Schlafly), 183–187
Comparison, 75–101
 closing, 99–100
 defined, 75–76
 devising a thesis, 93–94
 finding similarities and differences, 90–93
 opening, 98–99
 structure for, 94–98
Conclusions. *See* Endings
Critical reading, 64–66
Critique, 53–74
 analyzing assumptions, 72
 clarifying a complex idea, 72–73
 defined, 53
 evaluating a source, 62–72
 exemplifying ideas in a source, 73
 explaining practical implications of a source, 73
Crosman, Robert, 381–389

D

Dart, Raymond, 39–41
Denney, Reuel N., 278–286

Disagreeing with a source, 108–110
"Do Animals Have a Right to Life?" (Rachels), 237–241
Documentation of sources, 132–134, 438–448
   APA format for
      internal documentation, 442–443
      list of references, 416–417
   MLA format for
      internal documentation, 439–442
      list of works cited, 409–416
      notes, 443–448, 452–453
      sample list of works cited, 469
Drafting techniques:
   building on a source, 115–120
   comparison, 94–100
   critique, 69–73
   research paper, 432–454
   simple synthesis, 46–50
   summary, 25–31
   using sources as evidence, 130–134

E

"Editorially Speaking" (*Music Journal*), 156–158
Ellipsis in quotations, 436–437
"Elvis Presley: Lack of Responsibility Is Shown by TV in Exploiting Teen-Agers" (Gould), 139–141
"Emily Grierson's Oedipus Complex: Motif, Motive, and Meaning in Faulkner's 'A Rose for Emily'" (Scherting), 355–362
"Emily's Rose of Love: Thematic Implications of Point of View in Faulkner's 'A Rose for Emily'" (Nebeker), 371–381
Endings of papers, 99–100
Endnotes, supplementary, 452, 468
Evaluation, writing an, 62–72
   defined, 62–63
Exemplifying an idea, 112–115
"Experts Propose Study of 'Craze'" (Bracker), 148–149
Expository prose, 4
Extending an idea, 110–112

F

Fass, Paula S., 266–273
Faulkner, William, 338–345
Fetterley, Judith, 362–368
"Food Sharing Behavior of Protohuman Hominids, The" (Isaac), 223–229
Footnotes (endnotes), 443–448, 452–453
Fox, Michael, 241–244

G

Gold, Michael Evan, 180–183
Gordon, Suzanne, 193–198
Gould, Jack, 139–141
"Government in the Lead" (Moscow), 11–14
Greenfield, Jeff, 105–107

H

"History in 'A Rose for Emily'" (O'Conner), 354–355
Horner, Matina, 187–193
"How Readers Make Meaning" (Crosman), 381–389
Humanities Index, 405

I

Illustrations in research papers, 451–452
"Interpretation of 'A Rose for Emily,' An" (Brooks and Warren), 345–348
Introductions. *See* Openings of papers
Investigative questions in a research paper, 395–396
Irony, 108
Isaac, Glynn, 223–229
"Is It Our Culture, Not Our Genes, That Makes Us Killers?" (Leakey and Lewin), 214–220
"It Isn't All Junk" (Marek), 143–145
"It's Natural! It's Organic! Or Is It?" (*Consumer Reports*), 315–320

K

Key ideas, finding in a source, 15–18, 43, 62, 89, 108

L

Leakey, Richard E., 214–220
Length of papers, 30–31, 69–70
Levin, Michael E., 259–263
Lewin, Roger, 214–220
Library facilities, use of in research, 393–406
Library of Congress Subject Heading Catalog, 397–398
"Logic of the Larder, The" (Salt), 232–235

M

McConnell, Frank, 323–327
"Man as Predator" (Dart), 39–41
Marek, George, 143–145
Marking significant details, 18–23, 43–44
Meyers, William, 327–333
MLA documentation. *See* Documentation of sources
Montague, M. F. Ashley, 211–214
Morris, Desmond, 205–211
Moskow, Michael H., 11–14

N

"Naked Ape, The" (Morris), 205–211
Nebeker, Helen, 371–381
"New Corporate Feminism, The" (Gordon), 193–198
"New Litany of 'Innate Depravity,' The" (Montague), 211–214
New York Times Index, 403–404
Nineteenth Century Readers' Guide, 405

Notes from sources, taking, 23–25, 44–45, 68–69, 130, 417–427
"Now, The Self-Centered Generation" (*Time*), 293–296

O

O'Conner, William Van, 354–355
"Of the So-Called Rights of Animals" (Rickaby), 236–237
"On Becoming Human" (Tanner), 220–223
Openings of papers, 26, 49–50, 70, 98–99, 110, 114
Organization of papers. *See* Structure of a paper
Outlines, preparing and using, 68, 418–419, 429–431, 457–459

P

Paragraphs:
    coherence, 117–119
    development, 119–120
    unity, 116–117
Paraphrasing, 47, 423–425
"Passing Fad" (*Musical America*), 149–150
Periodicals:
    footnote or endnote entries for, 446–447, 452–453
    indexes to, 401–406
    in lists of sources, 413–415, 417
Perspective, 28–29, 435
Plagiarism, 23, 47–49, 438–439
Poole's Index to Periodical Literature, 405
Poulton-Callahan, Charles, 170–175
Prewriting techniques:
    building on a source, 105–115
    comparison, 79–94
    critique, 56–69
    research paper, 392–431
    simple synthesis, 39–46
    summary, 7–25
    using sources as evidence, 126–130
"Psychographics: Advertising Discovers the World According to VALS" (Meyers), 327–333
Public Affairs Information Service Index (P.A.I.S.), 405

Q

"Question of Questionable Meanings, A" (*Life*), 136–137
Quotations, 45, 47, 71–72, 421–422, 425–427, 435–438
    additions to, 71–72, 437
    block, 437–438
    omissions from, 436–437
    reasons for using, 45, 47, 421–422, 425

R

Rachels, James, 237–241
"R & R Still Beams Plenty of Life" (*Billboard*), 163–164
Readers. *See* Audience, consideration of
Readers' Guide to Periodical Literature, 394, 401–403
Regan, Tom, 255–259
Research papers, 391–469
    bibliographic forms, 409–417
    bibliography cards, 407–408
    documenting sources in, 438–448
    drafting, 432–448
    format of, 448–454
    integrating sources into, 432–438
    investigative questions, 395–396
    library resources for, 396–406
    notes for, 417–428
    outlines for, 418–419, 429–431
    plagiarism, 47–49, 438–439
    sample, 455–469
    subject for, selecting and limiting, 392–395
    thesis of, 418–419, 428–429
Revision techniques:
    building on a source, 120–121
    comparison, 100–101
    critique, 73–74
    simple synthesis, 50–52
    summary, 31–34
    using sources as evidence, 134–135
Rickaby, Joseph, 236–237
"Rock and Roll Called 'Communicable Disease'" (*New York Times*), 137
"Rock 'N' Riot" (*Time*), 159
"Rock 'N' Roll: A Frenzied Teen-Age Music Craze Kicks Up a Big Fuss" (*Life*), 137
"Rock 'N' Roll Opponents Are Due for a Big Break" (*New York Times*), 156
"Rock 'N' Roll's Global Wane" (*Variety*), 164–165
"Rock 'N' Roll Stabbing" (*New York Times*), 158
"Rose for 'A Rose for Emily,' A" (Fetterley), 362–368
"Rose for Emily, A" (Faulkner), 338–345
Ross, Irwin, 273–277

S

Salt, Henry S., 232–235
Samuels, Gertrude, 151–156
Sargent, Alice G., 175–180
Scherting, Jack, 355–362
Schlafly, Phyllis, 183–187
Schudson, Michael, 333–335
"Segregationists Would Ban All Rock, Roll Hits" (*Billboard*), 138
Sentence outline, 17, 68, 418–419, 429–431, 449, 457–459
Sharnik, John, 145–148
Singer, Peter, 56–61
Social Sciences Index, 405
Somers, Patricia, 170–175
Stafford, T. J., 369–371
Stevens, Paul, 306–314

Structure of a paper, 26–29, 36–37, 49, 67–68, 94–98, 129–130, 427–431
Subheadings in sources, 16–17, 88–90
Summary:
 defined, 4
 use of in writing, 38, 46–47, 69–70, 104, 128, 417, 427
 writing a, 3–34
Synthesis of sources, 35–52
Szulc, Tad, 286–289

T

Tables (charts and illustrations) in research papers, 451–452
Tanner, Nancy, 221–223
"Television Mailbag: Mr. Presley" (*New York Times*), 141–143
Thesis of a paper, devising and stating, 45–46, 67–68, 93–94, 108–115, 128–129, 418–419, 428–429
 by disagreeing with a source, 108–109
 by exemplifying a source, 112–115
 by extending a source, 110–112
Thesis of a source:
 discovering and stating, 7–15, 39–43, 56–62, 79, 88–89, 107
 explicit, 8–10
 implicit, 10–15
"Tobe's Significance in 'A Rose for Emily'" (Stafford), 369–371
Tone of a source, 47
Topic outline, 449–450
Transitions, 28, 50, 118–119

U

"Use of Animals in Educational Settings, The" (Regan), 255–259

W

Wank, David, 296–303
"War of the Generations, The" (Sharnik), 145–148
Warren, Robert Penn, 345–348
"Weasel Words" (Stevens), 306–314
Weil, Rolf A., 289–292
West, Ray B., Jr., 349–354
"What's Holding Women Back?" (Bartlett, Poulton-Callahan, Somers), 170–175
"What They Really Think, And Why" (Ross), 273–277
"When TV Ads Become Most Disreputable" (Christopher), 320–323
"White Council Vs. Rock and Roll" (*Newsweek*), 138–139
"Who Are We? A Self-Portrait of College Students Today" (Wank), 296–303
"Why They Rock 'N' Roll—And Should They?" (Samuels), 151–156
"Women and Men Working Together: Toward Androgyny" (Sargent), 175–180
Writing suggestions, 5, 37, 54, 72–73, 76–77, 103, 108–115, 123, 198–199, 229–230, 263–264, 303, 335, 389

Y

"Younger Generation, The" (*Time*), 79–88
"Your Kids Dig That Crazy Music, Too?" (*Changing Times*), 161–163
"Youth in America" (Szulc), 286–289